Wills of the County of Suffolk

INDEX OF WILLS OF THE ARCHDEACONRY
OF SUDBURY

INDEX OF WILLS FROM THE REGISTER 'BALDWYNE'
1439–1474

Suffolk Record Office (Bury St Edmunds)
IC500/2/10

INDEX OF WILLS OF
THE ARCHDEACONRY OF SUDBURY

1439–1474

WILLS FROM THE REGISTER 'BALDWYNE'

Compiled by
† PETER NORTHEAST and HEATHER FALVEY

The Boydell Press

Suffolk Records Society

A Suffolk Records Society publication
First published 2010
The Boydell Press, Woodbridge

ISBN 978–1–84383–593–6

The Boydell Press is an imprint of Boydell & Brewer Ltd
PO Box 9, Woodbridge, Suffolk IP12 3DF, UK
and of Boydell & Brewer Inc.
668 Mt Hope Avenue, Rochester, NY 14620, USA
website: www.boydellandbrewer.com

A catalogue record for this book is available
from the British Library

This publication is printed on acid-free paper

Printed in Great Britain by
CPI Antony Rowe, Chippenham and Eastbourne

Contents

Preface   vii

INDEX OF WILLS OF THE ARCHDEACONRY OF SUDBURY

Wills from the Register 'Baldwyne', Part I, 1439–1461

    Index of People and Places   1

    Index of Subjects   91

Wills from the Register 'Baldwyne', Part II, 1461–1474

    Index of People and Places   127

    Index of Subjects   203

Preface

Peter Northeast completed his work on Part I of the Baldwyne Register (Suffolk Records Society, volume 44) in 2000, and in the following year introduced the volume at the Society's AGM at St Mary's Church, Bury St Edmunds. This was probably the last opportunity we had of hearing Peter speak in public. He spent the next two years compiling a detailed index for Part I, which on completion was made available via our website. Unfortunately his editing of the rest of the Register was cut short in 2007 by increasingly serious illness but, much to his satisfaction before he died in 2009, he saw Part II (SRS 53) fully and admirably completed by Dr Heather Falvey and indexed along the lines which he had previously established. This supplementary volume presents Peter's index for Part I together with Heather's for Part II, thus covering the whole of the Baldwyne Register.

The Records Society is grateful to all the individuals, notably the Bowden-Smith family trust, who have contributed towards the costs of this volume, and especially to Clive and Christine Paine who generously offered to cover any financial shortfall in the printing costs, in recognition of their personal and professional debt to a remarkable local historian.

The Officers of the Suffolk Records Society
April 2010

Wills of the Archdeaconry of Suffolk
The Register 'Baldwyne' Part I
(Suffolk Records Society volume 44)

Index of People and Places

All references are to item numbers, not pages, except the italicised Roman numerals which refer to pages of the Introduction. References in **bold** indicate which persons were testators, while ***italic bold*** shows that the item is a probate-sentence only, containing no will or testament.

Major place-names have been capitalized and given their modern form; minor place-names appear under the relevant parishes and are spelt as in the original register. For places not in Suffolk counties have been indicated, apart from well-known cities. As it was usual for testators to mention churches and land in their own parishes, these have not been separately indexed unless further specific details are given.

Modern forms of Christian names have been used but the original spelling of surnames has been retained and chief variants given. Where there are no means of differentiation, references may relate to two or more individuals bearing the same name. An asterisk * after a reference indicates that more than one person of that name occurs in that item; an 'n' following a reference indicates that the subject is to be found in a footnote to that item. The phrase '& family' signifies the mention of members of the family who are incompletely named (e.g. daughters) and cannot be indexed by surname.

Abbreviations: BVM = Blessed Virgin Mary; Berks = Berkshire; Cambs = Cambridgeshire; Esx = Essex; Glos = Gloucestershire; Herts = Hertfordshire; Hunts = Huntingdonshire; Leics = Leicestershire; Lincs = Lincolnshire; Mdx = Middlesex; Northants = Northamptonshire; Nfk = Norfolk; Staffs = Staffordshire; Surr = Surrey; Yorks = Yorkshire; unspec. = unspecified.

Abell, Anne, of Thurston, 1437
  Helen, of Pakenham, 514
  John, of Thurston, 1437*
  Richard, 288; of Stowmarket, 410
  Thomas, 1001, 1199
  William, of Elmswell, *1199*; of Pakenham, *514*
Abbot, John, 1328
  Margaret, 1328
  Ralph, of Thorpe, **1328**
Ab(e)thorp, Ralph, of Troston, 583
  see also Clare *alias* Abthorp
Abraham, John, servant, 1240
ACTON, church, 91, 1280
    curate of, 1181
    vestments for, 1384, 1385
    vicar of, *see* Nicholas Hacon
  gilds in, 289
  inhabitants of, 289, 404, 813, 1312

places in, 'Aylovyslond', 259
  'Tye, le', 289
  poor of, 91
  testators of, **259, 404, 813, 1312, 1384, 1385**
  wills proved at, 758, 833, 837, 1167
Adam, Walter, 380
Adgor, Alison, of Old Newton, 340
  Isabel, of Combs, 609
  John, 609, 952; of Combs, 145; the elder, of Combs, **609**; of Old Newton, **340**
  Richard, 609, 660; of Combs, 145
  see also Edgor
Agas (Agace), Isabel, of Barningham, 889
  John, 159, 889; of Barningham, **159**
  Katherine, of Barningham, 159
  Robert, 121, 159; of Barningham, **889**, 1225; of Thurston, 552
  Roger, the elder, of Thurston, 1451

Agnyseye, Hugh, of Chippenham (Cambs), 588
Akrys, John, of Sudbury college, 91
Albred, Christian, of Fornham, 1099; of Fornham
    St Martin, 1152
  John, of Fornham, *1099*; of Fornham St Martin,
    1152
ALBY (Nfk), rector of, *see* Thomas Tyler
Alco(c)k, Edmund, of Badley, 1169n
  Robert, 330
ALDEBURGH, use of 'cottage' in, 969n
Aldeby, *see* Breuster *alias* Aldeby
ALDHAM, church, 162
  'Huntes' (barn) in, 1416
Aldham, Robert, 24
  Simon, 949
Aldhous (Aldhows), John the elder, of
    Mendlesham, 932
  Thomas, 1035
Aleyn, Agnes, 246
  Alice, of Sudbury, 717
  Joan, of Bildeston, *1141*; of Groton, 1388
  John, 316; of Barrow 290; of Boxford, 257; of
    Boxted, 1387; of Groton, **1388**
  Robert, 1141
  William, of Sudbury, **717**
Alfey, John, of Cavendish, **83**
Alger, Alice, of Stoke by Clare, 1185
  John, 1185
  Robert, of Lavenham, *1114*
  William, of Stoke by Clare, *1185*
Algood, John the elder, 1093; the younger,
    1093
Allote, John, of Occold, *250*
Almen, Joan, 758
Almere, Joan, of Silverley (Cambs), 1029
  William, of Silverley (Cambs), *1029*
Almot, William, 536
Alnwyk, William, bishop of Norwich and Lincoln,
    210n
Alot, William, of Kersey, 342
ALPHETON, church, 1091
  inhabitants of, 454n, 773n
  places in, Bridge Street, 88n
    'Mellers' (tenement), 507
  testator of, *1106*
Alsey, John, 1142
Alston, Isabel, 539
  John, 994
  Richard, of Fornham All Saints, *994*
Alun, Thomas, 757
Alunday, John, 1094
  Katherine, of Kedington, 1094
  Thomas, 1094
  William, of Kedington, **1094**
Alyngton, Robert, 165n
Ambrous, Richard, 719, 1228
Amener, Thomas, 429
Amerows, Richard, 1245

Amey (Ammory), William, rector of Chelsworth,
    516, 516n
Amgot, *see* Amyot
Ammory, *see* Amey
AMPTON, church, 180
    ornaments of, 1400
  inhabitants of, 180, 305, 749, 1260, 1400n
  testator of, **1400**
Amyot (Amgot, Amyat), John the elder, of Long
    Melford, 1387
  Simon, of Long Melford, 195, 201
Andrew (Andru, Andrw), Alice, of Eye, 58
  Henry, 721
  John, 58, 1203; chaplain, of Burwell (Cambs),
    682; the elder, of Eye, **58**; chandler, of
    Lavenham, 329
  Margaret, of Brockford, 721
  Matilda, of Hawkedon, 1203
  Richard, 1203; of Bures, *1335*; of Hawkedon,
    1203
  Simon, of Brockford, **721**
  William, 721
Angold, Agnes, of Hengrave, 61
  William, of Hengrave, & family, **61**
Aniys, *see* Annes
Anjou, Robert of, 588n
Annes (Aniys), Joan, of Wetheringsett, 345
  John, 248
  Richard, of Wetheringsett, *xlvi*, **345**
  William, of Brockford, 248, 1417
Annewre, Robert, 925
Anows *alias* Smyth, John, 442; of Botesdale, *442*
Ansty, John, 114
Antyngham, Katherine, 1048
  Walter, 1048
Anyell, Robert, of Eye, 58, 492, 623, 624, 1293
Appekyn, Agnes, 1262
Appylthorp, Isabel, of Troston, *1019*
  John, 1019
Apylt(h)weyt, Henry, of Stoke Ash, *223*, **285**
  Isabel, of Stoke Ash, 223, 285
  Margaret, 285
  William, 223, 285
Apylton, John, of Little Waldingfield, 593
Archer, Agnes, 446; of Lavenham, 446
  Isabel, of Lavenham, 446
  John, 292, 661n; of Lavenham, 416, **446**, **661**;
    of Thorpe Morieux, & family, 446
  Margaret, of Lavenham, 446
  Matilda, 661; of Lavenham, 446
  Robert, of Lavenham, 446
Arford, Alice, 100
  Mary, of Hawstead, *100*
Arlond, *see* Arnold
Arnere, Alice, 894
  John, 894
Arnold (Arlond), John, of Dalham, 450; chaplain,
    of Eye, 1293

Thomas, of Old Newton, **1419**
Artur, Ellis, 1346
  Geoffrey, of Wattisham, & family, **1346**
  Rose, of Wattisham, 1346
  Thomas, 1346
ASHFIELD, GREAT, church,
  bell for, 1033n, 1249, 1258
  tower of, *xlvii*, 1033, 1033n, 1495
  gild in, 1249
  inhabitants of, 828, 1249
  lands in, 1001
  places in, 'Awbryswykes', 231
    'Flaxeyerd, le', 1258
    'Goryslond', 1258
    'Greneyerd, le', 1258
    'Nomannyscroft', 1258
    'Pollardes' (close), 1495
    'Whiteooke' (land), 1001
  poor of, 231
  testators of, *136*, *218*, **1249**, **1258**
Ashfield (Asshfeld), family, of Stowlangtoft,
  patrons of Stanton All Saints, 457n
  Robert, of Stowlangtoft, 457
ASHIL (Nfk), land in, 877
Ashle (Asshle), Thomas, 381, 822, 1473
ASHLEY (Cambs), church, 247n, 822, 1473
  rector of, *see* Richard Smyth
  vestment for, 247
  inhabitants of, 381, 822, 1082, 1473
  poor of, 270
  roads in, 822
  'Sloo, le' in, 247, 247n
  testators of, **247**, **381**
  will proved at, 1145
Aspy (Aspi), Agnes, 940
  Joan, 853
  William, 853
Asselot, *see* Astlot
Asshfeld, *see* Ashfield
Asshle, *see* Ashle
ASSINGTON, church, 108, 573
  inhabitants of, 941, 1057
  land in, 586
  testators of, **176**, **215**, **1057**
Assy, William, of Cockfield, 615, 1367
Astlot (Aslote, Asselot), Alice, of Sudbury, 127,
  1365
  John, of Sudbury, 1365; of Sudbury, & family,
    127
  Richard, 127
  Stephen, 127, 1267
Aston, John, the younger, 865
Asty, Peter, of Market Weston, **295**
  Robert, 295; vicar of Gazeley, 295, 295n
  William, 295
atte Fen, William, of Glemsford, *644*, 1068n
  see also Fen
Atherne, Isabel, of Bardwell, 858

William, of Bardwell, **858**
  at Medwe, Richard of Wakes Colne (Esx), 301
  see also Medwe
atte Mere (at the Mere), Isabel widow, of Sudbury,
  539
  Margaret, of Cavenham, 387
  William, of Cavenham, **387**
  see also Mere
Atsan, William, of Kentford, 762
Attewoode, Adam, of Great Waldingfield, **186**
  Isabel, of Great Waldingfield, 186
  Hugh, 186
  Richard, 186
Aubre (Aubry), Walter, 941
  William, of Woolpit, 469
Aubyn, John, of Edwardstone, 308
Austyn, Isabel, of Fornham St Martin, 849, 1152
  John, of Fornham St Martin, 45, **849**, **1152**
  Lucy, 849, 1152
  Margaret, of Fornham St Martin, 849, 1152
  Margery, of Thorney, 408
  Richard, 849, 1152
  Robert, 408
  Thomas, 408
  William, 852; of Thorney, **408**
Avelyn, Emma, of Thrandeston, 973
  Katherine, 492
  Robert, of Thrandeston, *973*
Avenant, Alice, 677
  Marion, of Thrandeston, 1317
  Thomas, of Thrandeston, *1317*
Avys, Geoffrey, 1285
  William, 692
Awnselme, Henry, of Wyverstone, *1408*; of
  Wyverstone, & family **1402**
Awty, John, 1035
Ayl(l)of (Ayloth), John, 127, 1246
  Simon, 1280
Aylmer(e), Ed., 1158
  Margaret, 1158
  Nicholas, dyer, 1361; of Bury St Edmunds,
    1361n
  Simon, of Barningham, 124
  William, 997
Aylnoth, John, of Burwell (Cambs), 1265; of
  Burwell (Cambs), & family, **237**
  Margaret, of Burwell (Cambs), 237
  Thomas, 237
Aywern, Thomas, 37

Baa, Margaret, 940
Baas, Isabel, 311
  Nicholas, 311
BABWELL, house of Franciscan friars (Minors),
  xlix, 5, 17, 18, 21, 33, 34, 41, 44, 46, 52, 55,
  56, 90, 96, 97, 98, 124, 126, 132, 133, 137,
  158, 159, 164, 180, 185, 187, 213, 222, 228,
  249, 252, 261, 263, 269, 270, 271, 286, 287,

3

289, 290, 294, 297, 303, 305, 311, 321, 347,
350, 351, 352, 353, 357, 362, 370, 373, 377,
381, 385, 387, 388, 393, 409, 438 449, 457,
471, 474, 497, 507, 517, 549, 552, 583, 599,
616, 619, 663, 676, 684, 692, 693, 708, 713,
726, 735, 749, 760, 775, 776, 779, 782, 787,
790, 799, 806, 821, 822, 823, 836, 849, 854,
867, 879, 889, 890, 899, 933, 939, 940, 945,
965, 969, 971, 977, 981, 1002, 1031, 1033,
1035, 1036, 1054, 1063, 1075, 1076, 1079,
1082, 1083, 1097, 1104, 1123, 1129, 1156,
1158, 1164, 1170, 1172, 1183, 1186, 1191,
1200, 1210, 1217, 1221, 1225, 1231, 1233,
1240, 1244, 1246, 1255, 1258, 1262, 1265,
1268, 1272, 1276, 1280, 1289, 1291, 1312,
1313, 1337, 1344, 1356, 1363, 1368, 1369,
1371, 1390, 1395, 1397, 1409, 1410, 1418,
1424, 1437, 1439, 1441, 1451, 1465, 1466,
1467, 1468, 1469, 1478, 1495, 1497
  church of, burial in, 1279
    leading of, 1279
    memorial service in, 1246
  friars of, 359, 474, 494, 1191
Babynton, Henry, chaplain, of Lavenham, 374;
  rector of Lawshall, 374n
Badey, [*unnamed*], *635*
BADLEY, inhabitant of, 1169n
  manor of, 1169n
BADLINGHAM, *see* CHIPPENHAM (Cambs)
Bachbrook, John, of Sudbury, 175
  Nicholas, 175
Bacon (Bacown), Alan, 232
  Edmund, 232
  Hawise, of Haughley, 1406
  John, 232, 1240; the elder, of Haughley, *1406*
  Margery, 1240; of Hessett, 232
  Nicholas, knight, lord keeper, 1240n
  Stephen, of Hessett, **232**
  William, 320
Bacot, Ed., of Sudbury, *593*
  see also Bakhot
Bacown, *see* Bacon
BACTON, church, 497, 1097, 1402
  land in, 497, 795n
Baculer, John, of Thorndon, *242*
BADDOW (Esx), church, 1050
BADWELL ASH, church,
    antiphoner for, 1399
    chancel of, 339n
    land of, 96
    light before image of Our Lady of Pity, 674
  gilds in, 1397
  inhabitants of, 96, 798, 798n, 842, 944, 1039,
    1397, 1399
  places in, 'Blakelond', 96
    'Brende, le' (field), 96
    'Detthys' (close), 1039
    'Drakes' (tenement), 674

'Gentylmannys' (tenement), 1039
'Hawkeris' (tenement), 1399
'Holpet, le', 96
'Joynyoures' (tenement), 674
'Leferysgap', 96
'Longstubbyng' (field), 96
'Mellefeld, le', 96
'Mellepath, le', 96
'Meys Close', 1399
'Queyntes' ('place'), 674
'Regweye, le', 96
'Schepgateweye', 96
'Scortfen, le' (meadow), 96
'Scortstubbyng' (field), 96
'Segravys', in Badwell Street, 674
'Smethysgate, le', 96
  testators of, **96**, *339*, **674**, **842**, **944**, **1039**,
    1342, **1397**, **1399**, *1491*
  wills proved at, 1039, 1491
  wood in, 96
Baff, Margery, 1186
  Michael, 1271
  Nicholas, 1186
  Stephen, of Thelnetham, **1186**
Bagot, John, 1259
  see also Bakhot
Bailsham, Thomas, of Bury St Edmunds, 28
Baker(e), Agnes, 1295
  Alice, widow, of Elmswell, & family, **397**
  Andrew, of Eye, 367
  Emma, 339
  Geoffrey, of Stradishall, **571**
  Joan, 1218
  John, 33, 42, 339; servant, 375; the elder, 385;
    the younger, 385; the elder, of Badwell Ash,
    339; of Gislingham, 385; of Lavenham, 661
  Katherine, of Stradishall, 571
  Nicholas, of Finningham, 385
  Richard, 397, 385
  Thomas, 385, 851, 1294
  William, the elder, 1295; of Clare, *149*; of
    Elmsett, 1427
  see also Wareyn *alias* Baker
Bakhot, family, of Mildenhall, 1403n
  Joan, of Mildenhall, 1481
  John, of Mildenhall, 1156, 1156n, 1403
  Margaret, 749
  Richard, 749; of Mildenhall, 311n, 894n
  Robert, 749
  Simon, rector of Worlington, 311, 311n, 1119
  Thomas, mercer, 749
  William, mercer, of Mildenhall, **1481**
  see also Bacot, Bagot
Bakke, John, of Combs, 877
  Margaret, of Combs, & family, **877**
Bald(e)wyn, John, 71, 1033; of Thrandeston, *71*,
  199
  Margaret, of Thrandeston, 199

Stephen, chaplain, 831
William, 274
Baldry (Baldre), Agnes, of Thornham Parva, 811
    Cecily, of Creeting All Saints, 309
    Clarissa, of Barningham, 1225
    Geoffrey, of Barningham, 59, 121, 807; of
        Barningham, & family, **1225**
    John, 309; the elder, 1225; the younger, 1225;
        of Thorney, 410, **444**
    Margaret, of Thorney, 444
    Richard, 309; of Thorney, 444
    Robert, 1225
    Roger, 811
    Thomas, 1225; knight, lord mayor of London,
        444n
    William, 1225; & family, *230*; of Creeting All
        Saints, **309**; of Thornham Parva, *811*
Ballard, Henry, of Kettlebaston, 1300
    John, 607
Ballard *alias* Canown, John, of Wickhambrook,
    1450
Balle, John, & family, 1398
BALLINGDON (Esx), *see* SUDBURY
Bally, Thomas, of Brettenham, 761
Balsham, Thomas, of Little Thurlow, *1490*
Baly(e), Agatha, 385
    see also Rede *alias* Baly *and* Tredegold *alias*
        Baly
Banham, John, 492
    Richard, 492
    Robert, of Wattisfield, 1409
Banyard, John, 335, 1046
    William, of Great Barton, 335
Barbour (Barbere, Barbore), Agnes, of Ixworth,
    1072
    Alan, of Lavenham, *73*, 126
    Joan, of Lavenham, 73
    John, of Hengrave, 41; of Sudbury, 632
    Lucy, widow, of Fornham St Genevieve, 729
    Margaret, of Boxford, 144
    Margery, 103
    Nicholas, 90
    Richard, of Clare, 832
    Robert, 1404; of Lavenham, 126
    Stephen, of Sudbury, 758, 1365
    Walter, 152, 152n; of Boxford, **144**
    William, 111; of Sudbury, 144
    see also Smyth *alias* Barbour
BARDFIELD, LITTLE (Esx), rector of, *see* John
    Moore
BARDWELL, church, 69
    porch, 1231, 1231n
    sepulchre light, 1368
    vicar of, *see* Robert Doke
    work on, 78, 858
    gild in, 78
    inhabitants of, 55, 78, 97, 212, 372, 451, 583,
        838n, 858, 1231, 1368

manor in, 838n
places in, Bardwell Heath, 78
    'Bobebek' ('street'), 97
    Bowbeck, 78
    'Bulbrookheth', 78, 78n
    'Burcroft', 1368
    'Berecruch' (cross), 1231
    'Chyrchepath, le', 97
    'Crowdesland' (field), 97
    'Dolys', 1231
    'Gorys' (messuage), 1275
    'Holleweye, le', 97
    'Hundrydmere' (footpath/boundary), 858,
        858n
    'Northcroft', 97
    'Prestysbusk', 97
    'Purchasweye', 1231
    'Salterysweye' (leading to Woolpit), 97
    testators of, **55**, **78**, **97**, *212*, *451*, *433*, *519*,
        583, *858*, *1230*, **1231**, *1232*, *1275*, **1368**
    will dated at, 41
    wills proved at, 583, 872, 974, 975, 1395
Bardwell (Berdwell), family, 1333n
    Elizabeth, widow, 41, 838n
    John, monk of Bromholm (Nfk), 97
    Robert, esquire, of Tostock, 836, 836n
    William, esquire, 41, 41n, 97, 836n, 838n;
        knight, of Bardwell, 41n, 1231n
Barel(l), Isabel, 849
    John, 158
Baret(t), Alan, 465
    Agnes, of Fornham All Saints, & family, 222
    Amy, 1152
    Nicholas, of Fornham All Saints, **222**
    Ralph, of Little Fakenham, 920
    Robert, of Harston (Cambs), 222
    William, 1035
Barfoot, Margaret, 1001
Barker(e) (Barkar(e)), Agnes, 164, 354, 1424; of
        Clare, 43; widow, of Clare, *64*
    Beatrice, of Long Melford, 1064, *1208*
    Gilbert, 1208, 1424
    Henry, of Clare, 832, 1010
    Joan, 1424; of Thelnetham, 1262
    John, 105, 167, 354, 408, 610, 1001, 1424,
        1456; the younger, 1208; of Brent Eleigh,
        375; of Clare, **43**, 64; of Long Melford, 82;
        the elder, fuller, of Long Melford, lii, **1064**;
        of Thelnetham, 349, **1262**
    Margaret, of Little Horringer, 422
    Marion, of Suddon hamlet, Eye, 105
    Richard, 422, 434; of Wetherden, 33
    Robert, 105, 1262; of Suddon hamlet, Eye,
        105, 367; of Hepworth, 1494
    Rose, of Lavenham, **570**
    Thomas, 43, 64; of Hundon, 967, 1083; of
        Little Horringer, **422**, 1291n; of Little
        Thurlow, 1432; of Sudbury, 1489

Walter, of Bildeston, *592*
William, rector of Rushbrook, 1262, 1262n
[*unnamed*], 1353
see also Michill *alias* Barker
Barleston, Alice, 1400
John, of Hepworth, & family, **353**
Margaret, of Hepworth, 353
Barnard, Henry, 1151
John, *1151*
see also Bernard
BARNARDISTON, inhabitants of, 85, 549, 654,
1488
testators of, *39*, *84*, 85, 249, *536*, **654**, **1229**,
1488
will proved at, 84
Barnardiston (Bernston), Roger, esquire, of
Kedington, 1213, 1216n
Thomas, of Kedington, 1216n; the younger,
1213
William, esquire, of Kedington, 1216, 1216n
BARNHAM, church (unspec.), bells of, 1139
church of St Gregory, 281, 281n, 377
church of St Martin, 281, 281n, 377, 854
bell for, 1078
inhabitants of, 281, 377, 983, 1007n, 1139,
1171n, 1206, 1268, 1303, 1362
places in, 'Balrames' (tenement), 983
'Blethowe', 534
'Magotshall' ('Magotysplase'), 281
testators of, **281**, **377**, **534**, *885*, *974*, **983**,
1007, **1078**, **1139**, *1171*, **1206**, *1235*, **1268**,
1302, *1303*, *1362*
BARNHAM BROOM (Nfk), chaplain of Sudbury
born at, 128n
BARNINGHAM, church, books for, 889, 1225,
1248
land of, 889, 1248
mortuary payment to, *xlvi*
ornaments in, 889
tabernacle of BVM in chancel of, 807n
tower of, *xlvii*n, 59, 59n, 124, 159
churchyard, chapel of St Margaret in, 807,
807n
inhabitants of, 59n, 121, 124, 807, 889, 954,
955n, 1225, 1226n, 1247, 1278
land in, 1307n
manor, land of, 1225
places in, 'Agas' (messuage), 1248
'Aldebrege' ('Alebreche'), 124, 889
'Alferismer', 124
'Baldryes' (tenement), 1225
'Baldryes Halfakre' (furlong), 124
'Bandlond', 954
'Bellond' (field), 124
'Blolond, le', (close), 1278
'Buchysacre', 889
'Bukkys' (tenement), 807
'Cecylyis' (close), 1248

'Coldhamys' (tenement), 807
'Dale, le', 889
'Daleclos', 1247
'Dermannys' (land), 807
'Estfeld', 1225
'Ferthynges' (close), 889
'Flotemerys' (close), 1248
'Frebodyis' (messuage), 1248
'Frerys, le', 889
'Fustymer', 124
'Fylyowrysclos', 1225
'Fystenerod' (furlong), 1248
'Haldenys' (tenement), 954
'Happe, le', 889
'Hols' (field), 954
'Honypot' ('Honypet'), (land), 889
'Howeweye', 1248
'Ingham' (close), 124
'Langlond', 889
'Langmer', 954
'Litlefeld' (furlong), 889
'Longehege' ('Longhegg'), 124, 889
'Medewys, le', (land), 1225
'Munnysyerd', 889
'Nedyrbelcroft', 1225
'Nethyryerde, le', 889
'Norsselond', 1247
'Petakre', 124
'Robynes' (tenement), 124
'Roselond', 889
'Rowmere', 954
'Rowys' (tenement), 1225
'Rychemanys' (tenement), 954
'Ryngaldys' (land), 807
'Sevenackres, le', 124
'Smethemere' ('Smythmere'), 124, 889
'Southcroft', 124
'Southfeld', 124
'Stantonweye', 124, 807
'Stanygate', 1225
'Stypathmere' (way), 1225
'Swetesmanlond', 1247
'Vymteres' ('Vynteres), 889
'Waggels' (land), 889
'Waynemere', 889
'Welleclos', 124
'Westfeld', 1225
'Woleskeherne', (land), 1247
'Wolsike', 124
'Wrangland' (furlong), 1225
'Wynscrofte', 889
poor of, 954, 1278
rector of, *xlin*
rectory (house) of, 124
roads in, 889, 1225
tax (fifteenths) of, 954
testators of, **59**, *121*, **124**, **159**, **807**, **889**, **954**,
955, **1225**, *1226*, **1247**, **1248**, **1278**, *1359*

Baron, *see* Baro(u)n
Barough, Edmund, 583
  Henry, 583
  John, 583; gentleman, of Bardwell, & family, **583**
  Marion, of Bardwell, 583
  Richard, 583
  Robert, 583
  Thomas, 583
  William, 583
Baro(u)n, (Barow), Alice, 90
  Joan, of Hitcham, 820, 1013, 1461n
  John, 90, 820; of Bildeston, 162, **744**; tailor, of Bildeston, 273; of Hitcham, 1461
  Margaret, of Newmarket, 28
  Richard, 820
  Rose, 820
  Thomas, of Hitcham, 699, **820**, **1013**, 1461n
  William, 820; of Little Maplestead (Esx), 258; of Newmarket, & family, **28**
BARROW, church, altar cloth for, 495
  basin for 488
  light on candlebeam in, 57
  processional cross for, 290
  rector of, arrears due to, 290
  rectors of, *see* George Hawys, Robert Westyngton
  rectory (benefice) of, farmers of, 471
  torch for, 488
  community of, 471
  gildhall in, 471
  inhabitants of, 25, 57, 77, 187, 290, 291, 471, 693, 890, 1191
  manor in, 46n
  parish priest of, 471
  places in, 'Barwe Grene, le', 291
    'Belys' (tenement), 471
    'Brondeslond' 290
    'Denam Lane', 290
    Green yard, house in, 471
    'Ingelesdene', 290
    'Lylye Croft', 290
    'Mille Hull, le', 290
    'Revis, le', 290
    'Stonbregge' (bridge), in Barrow field, 57
    'Vernon Crofte', 290
    'Whilesam' (wood), 290
    'Wyotyscroft', 291
  testators of, *23*, *25*, **57**, **187**, **290**, **291**, **471**, **488**, **494**, **495**, **693**, **890**, **1191**
  wills proved at, 57, 290, 291
Barry, Adam, friar of Clare, 149
  William, servant, 722
BARTON, GREAT, church, 116
  altar of St Mary in, 294
  tower, 180, 180n, 430, 430n, 1240n
  vicar of, *see* Robert Crull
  gild in, 430

  inhabitants of, 180, 335, 1236, 1240
  land in, 1195, 1240
  places in, Conyers Green, 294n
    Necton Hall, 294n
  testators of, **40**, **294**, **1236**
BARTON MILLS (BARTON TOGRIND), church, 708, 1403
  inhabitants of, 131, 311, 1389, 1403, 1407, 1441
  poor of, 708
  testators of, **46**, **131**, **1037**
  will proved at, 980
BARTON TOGRIND, *see* BARTON MILLS
BARWAY, *see* SOHAM (Cambs)
Basely, Robert, of Hinderclay, 1198
Basham, John, clerk, 1433
Bass, Richard, 393
Bateler, John, vicar of Stowmarket, 288, 288n
Bat(e)man, Agnes, 696
  John, 696; rector of Burrough Green (Cambs), 193, 193n, 368n, 499
  Roger, friar, of Clare, 416
  Thomas, 696
Batoun, John, 744
BATTISFORD, church, 1180
  preceptory/hospital of Knights Hospitallers, chapel of, 1180
    master of, 1180
Batyngore, John, servant, of Little Cornard, 356
Bawle, Henry, 177
  Marion, 177
Bax(s)ter(e), Agnes, 385
  Alice, of Wickham Skeith, 1419
  John, 622, 908, 972; of Eye, 320, 479, *972*; of Wickham Skeith, 1419
  Juliana, of Eye, 479, 972
  Katherine, 5
  Thomas, chaplain, 866
Bayle, John, 664
  Richard, of Combs, 660
  Thomas, 917
Baynard, John, 821
BAYTHORN END, *see* BIRDBROOK (Esx)
Beamis (Beamys, Demis), Robert, of Belchamp St Paul (Esx), 1132
  William, 1446
Beauchere, John, 1033
Beche, Henry, 691; of Soham (Cambs), 691n
  Joan, of Soham (Cambs), 691
  John, the elder, 691; the younger, 691; of Soham (Cambs), **691**
  William, 691, 1199
Beche *alias* Wrotham, Robert, of Worlington, 311
BEDFORDSHIRE, mortuary payments in, *xlvi*n
Bedford (Bedforth), Nicholas, 567, 1093, 1196, 1197, 1413, 1488, 1490
Bedingfield, family, of Oxburgh (Nfk), 489n
  Edmund, knight, 489n

7

Beene, *see* Bene
Beerd, *see* Berd
Beeton, William, 202
Bekysby, *see* Byxby
Belamy, Isabel, of Tuddenham St Mary, 1460
　Robert, of Boxted, 109, **1005**
　William, of Tuddenham St Mary, *1460*
Belcham (Belsham), Clarissa, of Kersey, 1212
　Gregory, 1212
　John, 1212; of Kersey, & family, **1212**
　Thomas, 39
BELCHAMP OTTON (Esx), curate of, 1181
BELCHAMP ST PAUL (Esx), inhabitant of, 1132
BELCHAMP WALTER (Esx), curate of, 1181
Belcher, John, of Rickinghall, *989*
Bele, John, 27
Belham, John, 514
Bell(e), John, 1295; of Haughley, 174
　Roger, 795, 795n, 862, 966; of Haughley, 174,
　　497, 1411
　Thomas, of Haughley, **174**
Belman, Isabel, of Hitcham, *791*
Belsham, *see* Belcham
BELSTEAD, inhabitant of, 1346
Bemays, Katherine, of Combs, 145
　William, of Combs, 47, **145**
Bemis, *see* Beamis
Bemond, John, of Norwich, 460
Bene (Beene), Edmund, chaplain (later rector) of
　　Stanton All Saints, 457, 457n, 1275, 1299
　John, the elder, 308; the younger, 308
Beneffaunte, *see* Bonef(f)aunte
Beneshef(e) (Benecheff), Thomas, 1255; of
　　Thurston, 222, 552
Benet (Beneyt, Beny(e)t(t), Benyth), Agnes, 90
　Christopher, of Debenham, 1466n
　Joan, of Thornham Magna, 1
　John, 79, 1417; of Mickfield, 15, 248; of
　　Semer, 143; of Thornham Magna, *xlviii*, **1**,
　　338
　Robert, 93
　Walter, friar, of Clare, 1375
Benne, Joan, 694
　John, of Troston, *694*
　Richard, 694
Bens, John, friar, of Clare, 149
Bensele, [*unnamed*], *486*
Berd (Beerd), Henry, servant, of Little Saxham, 41
　John, 867, 1348; the younger, 850; of Dalham,
　　850
　Katherine, 185
　see also Bird(e), Bryde, Byrd
Berdwell, *see* Bardwell
Bere, Isabel, of Norton, 441, **1313**
　John, 161, 402, 570
　Thomas, 179; of Norton, & family, **438, 441**,
　　1313
Berehors, Richard, of Fordham (Cambs), *94*

Bereve (Berewe), Adam, of Thurston, 232, 287,
　552
Bergham (Brigham), William, rector of
　　Kilverstone (Nfk), 56
　see also Bregham
Bermeer, *see* Berne(e)r
BERMONDSEY (Surrey), Cluniac abbey, monk
　of, 1424
Bernard, John, knight, of Thetford, 281
　see also Barnard
Berne, Beatrice, of Felsham, 613
　John, 470, 613
　Thomas, of Felsham, **613**
Berne(e)r (Bermeer), Isabel, of Long Melford,
　1160
　John, the elder, 1160; the younger, 1160; of
　　Long Melford, **1160**; the elder, of Stoke by
　　Nayland, **992**
　Matilda, of Stoke by Nayland, 992
　Thomas, 992
Bernereve (Bernerewe), William, of Chevington,
　411, 417
Bernewell, Thomas, of Long Melford, 1369
Bernham, John, 955
　Nicholas, 955
Bernston, *see* Barnardiston
Berry (Bery), John, 865; friar, of Clare, 149
　William, friar, of Sudbury, 816
　see also Bury
Berte, John, 1369
Bertlot, Isabel, of Wickham Skeith, 24
　John, 24; of Wickham Skeith, & family, **24**
　Simon, 24
Berton, John, 202; rector of Santon Downham, 99
　[*unnamed*], friar, of Babwell, 1191
　see also Knyth *alias* Berton
Berton *alias* Kyng, William, friar, of Babwell,
　1156
Berweham, Adam, 1247
　Agnes, of Barningham, 1226n, **1247**
　Geoffrey, 1247
　John, 1226, 1247; of Barningham, *1226*, 1247;
　　servant, of Barningham, 1278
　William, 1247
Bery, *see* Berry
Beterych, John, 552
　Thomas, 208; of Barway in Soham (Cambs),
　　1319
Bet(t)e (Bettis, Bet(t)ys), Agnes, 1242
　Amice, of Pakenham, *956*
　Anne, of Pakenham, 821
　Edward, of Ipswich, *xlviin*
　John, 464, 497, 862, 1137, 1137n; of Elmswell,
　　787; of Harleston, **497**, 862n; of Haughley,
　　787; of Sapiston, *464*
　Margaret, of Burgate, 787; of Sapiston, 464,
　　1137
　Marion, of Harleston, *862*

Mariota, of Harleston, 497
Nicholas, 1041
Richard, 787
Robert, of Burgate, & family, **787**
Thomas, 464, 497, 787
William, 497, 787; of Pakenham, **821**
Bevereche (Beverych), Annabel, of Sudbury, 805
John, 188; of Sudbury, & family, **805**
BEVERLEY (Yorks), pilgrimage to, 489
Beyheld, Robert, 395
BEYTON, gild in, 52
inhabitant of, 1394
'Mayhows' (tenement) in, 52
testators of, **52**, **1394**
BILDESTON, bailiff of, 566
church, 1115
basins for, 415
books for, 1125, 1486
rector of, *see* Richard Swettok
thurible for, 1125n
cloth in, *li*
funeral at, *xlvi*
inhabitants of, 151, 162, 273, 415, 680, 895,
1103, 1125, 1141, 1194n, 1459, 1486
market place, 520
cross in, 1459n
'Newberystrete' in, 895, 1125
testators of, **415**, **520**, *592*, **680**, **744**, **895**, **982**,
1103, **1125**, *1141*, **1486**
wills proved at, 130, 265, 273, 365, 380, 390,
512, 516, 650, 744, 819, 895, 917, 921, 978,
982, 990, 1071, 1103, 1116, 1120, 1125,
1141, 1234, 1458, 1459, 1486
BIRDBROOK (Esx), Baythorn End in, 1423n
Bird(e), John, of Burwell (Cambs), 1162
William, 1265
see also Be(e)rd, Bryde, Byrd
Bischop (Byschop), John, 533, 1494
see also Byssop
Blackbourn, river, 920
Blacot, Nicholas, Master, 581
Blak, Joan, of Fornham St Martin, 45
Robert, 924; of Fornham St Martin, & family,
45
Blakeman, Alice, 725
BLAKENHAM, LITTLE, rector of, *see* William
Fuller
Blakgroom, John, of Sudbury, *26*
Margaret, 26
Blaksale, Alan, of Bures, *477*
Joan, of Naughton, 745
John, of Naughton, *745*
Matilda, of Bures, 477
Blakwell, John, 701
Blanchard, William, 197
Blodgett, family, 1276n
see also Blogat
Bloffeld, John, of Littleport (Cambs), 903

Blogat, John, the elder, 1307
see also Blodgett
Blok, *see* Blook
Blome, Joan, of Rattlesden, 747
Nicholas, 1114
Peter, 179
Richard, of Rattlesden, *747*
William, 307
BLO NORTON (Nfk), church, 1164
inhabitant of, 1307
land in, 1307n
Blook (Blok), Margaret, servant, of Buxhall, 1065
Thomas, of Bildeston, 1125
Blowbolle, John, of Hadleigh, 516
Blumvyle, Ed., 912
Blunte, Alexander, of Wiston, & family, *685*
Isabel, of Wiston, 685
Blyawnt, Simon, of Thornham Magna, 3, **1169**
BLYTHBURGH, inhabitant of, 97, 97n
Blythe, Alexander, of Stowmarket, *999*
Margaret, of Stowmarket, 999
Boc, *see* Buk(ke)
Bochard, John, of Barnardiston, *536*
Bocher, Agnes, 146
Helen, of Chelsworth, 559
Joan, of Stansfield, *835*; *afterwards* Hecham,
741
John, 1405; of Haughley, **741**
Margaret, of Haughley, 741
Margery, 57
Roger, 741
Stephen, 741, 741n
Thomas, 57
William, 1327; of Chelsworth, 516, *559*
see also Hecham *and* Hecham *alias* Bocher
Bocher *alias* Grondysborgh, Joan, of Stansfield,
507
Thomas, of Stansfield, **507**
BOCKING (Esx), deanery, *xxxix*
Bode, Isabel, of Tostock, 836
John, 469; of Bury St Edmunds, 836; of
Tostock, **836**
Katherine, 469
Margaret, 836
Ralph, 469; of Woolpit, 469, 836
Walter, 836
William, of Tostock, 836
Bogays (Bogeys), Agnes, of Edwardstone, 1455n
John, of Boxford, 612
Thomas, of Edwardstone, 196, *1455*
William, 1455
Bokelond, Joan, 831
John, 831
Margery, 831
Bokely (Bokele), John, 1001
Bokenham, Alice, widow, of Hawstead, **493**
Hugh, esquire, of Thelnetham & Great
Livermere, 41

John, 1422; of Fornham All Saints, *950*;
     gentleman, of Hawstead, 493
Philip, 1183, 1236
Thomas, chaplain, 333
Bokett, Katherine, of Boxford, 529
Bokyll, Alice, of Elmswell, 1338
     John, of Elmswell, *1338*
Boldyroo, Christian, of Rougham, 584
     Ed., of Rougham, 364, *584*
     Edmund, 1113
     Joan, of Hessett, *364*
Boleman, Joan, of Rattlesden, & family, **146**
Bolesham, Thomas, gentleman, of Bury St
     Edmunds, 574
Bole (Bolle, Boole), Agnes, of Little Livermere,
     304
     Alice, nun, of Redlingfield, 749
     Ed., of Great Livermere, 827, 828
     Henry, of Little Livermere, **304**
     Isabel, of Little Livermere, 684; of Wetherden,
     394
     Joan, of Timworth, 594
     John, 305, 394, 594, 601, 1136, 1427; of
     Hartest, 456; of Little Livermere, **684**; of
     Timworth, 749, 1288; of Wetherden, 394,
     394
     Margaret, of Timworth, 305; widow, of
     Timworth, **749**
     Richard, 594n; of Timworth, 749, **305**
     Robert, 250, 537, 852; of Combs, 601, 753,
     852n
     Roger, of Little Livermere, 684
     Simon, 601
     Stephen, of Combs, & family, **601**
     Thomas, 394, 601
     William, 305, 601, 1109; of Timworth, **594**
Bolount, John, 320
Bolton, John, 298; of Lavenham, & family, **298**
     Thomas, 298
     William, 298
Bolyngton, Joan, of Glemsford, 319
     William, of Glemsford, **319**
Bond(e), Cecily, of Fornham St Martin, 359
     James, 359
     John, 359; of Fornham St Martin, & family,
     359
     Marion, 1258
     Simon, of Walsham le Willows, *1042*
     Thomas, 497; of Stanton, 457
Bonef(f)aunte (Beneffaunte, Bonyffaunte,
     Donyfaunte), John, 389
     Marion, 389; of Burwell (Cambs), 1133
     Thomas, 389; of Burwell (Cambs), 67, 1133n;
     the elder, of Burwell (Cambs), & family, **389**
Boner, John, 131, 521
     Margery, 131, 521
Boner *alias* Jerweys, Alice, of Barton Mills, 131
     Ed., 131

Ralph, of Barton Mills, & family, **131**
see also Jerveys (Jerweys)
Boosk, Walter, 641
Bootre, Isabel, *262*
Borelt, John, of Stanstead, 137
Borle, Agnes, 493
     Eleanor, of Sudbury, 800
     John, 310, 800; of Sudbury, 277n; of Sudbury,
     & family, **800**
     Richard, gentleman, 493
     Seyva, of Sudbury, 800
BORLEY (Esx), church, 1489
     cope for, 1489
     curate of, 1181
     rector of, *see* Thomas Fen
     land in, 800
     meadow in, 1489
Borman, Thomas, 317
Boryball, John, 1188
     Thomas, 384
BOSTON (Lincs), gild in, 1216, 1216n
Boston, Richard, of Hadleigh, 639
Boswell, [*unnamed*], friar, of Ipswich, 1392
BOSWORTH (Leics), battle of, 1194n
Boteld, John, of Sudbury, & family, **667**
     Robert, 667
Boteler, James, earl of Wiltshire, 1246
     John, 1197
     Matilda, 863
     Nicholas, of Eye, 367
Botell (Rotyll), John, 1315
Boter, John, of Newmarket, 1470
     William, of Tuddenham St Mary, *1470*
BOTESDALE, *see* REDGRAVE
Boton (Botoon), Alice, 1262
     John, 582
     Margaret, of Little Waldingfield, 582
     William, of Little Waldingfield, & family, **582**
BOTTISHAM (Cambs), inhabitant of, 1398
     testator of, **1398**
Boudere, Isabel, 421
Boues, John, of Long Melford, 890
Boule, *see* Bowle
Bounde, *see* Bownde
Bovell, Anne, 1419
     Ralph, 1419
Bowde, John, 1231
Bowe, John, of Nayland, *909*
Bowle (Boule), Alice, 1234
     Henry, 110, 978; & family, 1234
     Katherine, 1234
     Margaret, 110
     Marion, 1234
     Richard, 1234
Bownde (Bounde), Ed., of Lavenham, 130
Edmund, 511
     John, 130*; of Lavenham, 350, **511**; of
     Lavenham, & family, 130

Katherine, of Lavenham, 130, 511
Robert, of Lavenham, 130
Bown(e), Katherine, widow, 1117
Margaret, widow, of Ixworth, *280*
Thomas, 1117, 1259; gentleman, 683; priest, 1258
William, of Gislingham, 280; of Ixworth, 280
Bownes, John, 932
Bowre, John, 1235
William, of Barnham, *1235*
Box, river, 308n
Box, Agnes, of Hitcham, 978
William, of Hitcham, *978*
BOXFORD, boundaries of, 296n
bridge in, 316
church, cross for, 144, 316
lamps in, 296
parsonage of (lease), 235n
porch of, 118, 316, 380, 458, 548, 1089
rector of, *see* Ralph Dorward
ship (for incense) for, 529
tower of, 458, 458n
inhabitants of, 118, 144, 155, 214, 257, 308, 316, 365, 375, 380, 458, 529, 586, 612, 1089, 1150, 1213, 1331, 1489
places in, Calais Street ('Caleys'), 118, 380n, 458
'Fennys' (Fennes) (croft), 529; (tenement), 235, 529
'Hogownnys' (garden), 155
'Holywade' (street), *see* Olywade Street
'Kerverys' (tenement), 308
'Leftleys in the Fen', 308
'Longcroft', 458
'Maryscrof', 296
Olywade Street ('Holywade'), 155, 155n, 1150n
'Pundrys' (tenement), 308
'Simonis at Moore', 586
'Sowthfeld', 458
Stone Street, 155n, 296, 296n, 1150n
'Thorncroft', 1089
'Wodekekstrete' ('Wodekestret'), 144, 144n, 316
'Wrygthys in the Fen', 308
'Wyllefeeld', 586
poor of, 1388
river in, 308n, 1150
road in, 930
tenters in, *li*
testators of, **118, 144, 155, 208, 214, 235, 257, 296, 308, 316,** *378*, **380,** *403*, **414, 458, 547, 548, 586, 612, 1089**
weaving looms in, *li*
wills proved at, 51, 118, 142, 143, 144, 208, 384, 573, 586, 755, 816, 843, 930, 931, 1038, 1089, 1115, 1150, 1335, 1336, 1479, 1496

BOXTED, church, altar of BVM in, 205
tower of, 109, 158, 205, 1006
churchyard, burial in, 789
inhabitants of, 109, 1387
lands in, 109
testators of, **205, 1005**
Boxsted, Cecily, of Sudbury, 62
John, of Sudbury, **62**
Boyes (Boys), John, 282, **602**
Boyhe (Bouhe), Edmund, 538
Isabel, 538
Boyhoo, Ed., 152
Boys, *see* Boyes
Bradfeld, Roger, of Great Barton, 1240, 1240n
William, of Great Barton, 1407
BRADFIELD (unspec.), inhabitant of, 1394
BRADFIELD COMBUST, church, 868
rector of, 899, 1367
see also John Smyth
inhabitants of, 407, 1367
land in, 531
places in, 'Berardes Gardyn', 412
testators of, **407, 412, 1367**
BRADFIELD ST CLARE, inhabitants of, 848, 1045
testators of, **848, 867, 1045**
BRADFIELD ST GEORGE, church, 185, 867, 1240
antiphoner for, 611, 662
inhabitants of, 611, 867
land in, 232
road in, 611
testators of, *466*, **611, 662**
BRADLEY, GREAT, church
rector of, *see* Peter Derman
inhabitants of, 368, 568, 736
places in, 'Jelyanys', 368
'Smethys', 368
testators of, **193, 368,** *568*, **736,** *1196*
BRADLEY, LITTLE, church, land of rector of, 876
tower of, 876
inhabitant of, 664
places in, 'Croundenfeld', 876
'Mapylgate', 876
'Overden, le', 876
'Sotherham', 876
poor of, 368
testators of, *664*, **876,** *1430*
Braham, John, esquire, of ?Brantham, 42
Brakstrete, Henry, 1200
John, of Wickham Skeith, **1273**
Margery, of Wickham Skeith, 1273
Robert, 1200, 1273
Simon, 1273
Thomas, 1273
see also Brastrete

Brame, John, 716, 962; the elder, 918; of
    Wickham Skeith, 87, 705, 706, 771
    Richard, 1033
    William, 1238
Brampton, William, 1351
BRANDON, church, 708
    altar cloth for, 1008
    antiphoner for, 1008
    surplice for, 1008
    inhabitants of, 928, 1433
    poor of, 708
    testators of, *99*, *141*, *884*, *928*, **1008**, **1433**
    will proved at, 1008
BRANDON PARVA (Nfk), confusion with
    Brandon, 99n
BRANTHAM, Braham Hall in, 42n
    inhabitant of, 42
Brastrete, William, 103
    see also Brakstrete
Brawe, Augustine, friar, 756
Brawnche, Margaret, 1422
Bray, Agnes, of Badwell Ash, 842
    Joan, 626; of Rougham, 1345
    John, of Rougham, & family, **1345**; of Sudbury,
        758; of Walsham le Willows, 767
    Roger, the elder, 1345; of Little Livermere,
        180, 304, 684
Braybrook, Hugh, 1190
    Margaret, of Poslingford, 1190
    Thomas, 1190
    William, of Poslingford, & family, **1190**; the
        younger, of Poslingford, 173, 332
Breche, Richard, vicar of Kirtling (Cambs), 881
BRECKLAND, 1309n
Bredge (Bregge), Agnes, of Bottisham (Cambs),
    & family, **1398**
    Joan, of Stoke by Clare, 1382
    William, of Stoke by Clare, 1382
Bregeman, William, of Snailwell (Cambs), 240,
    724, 793
Bregge, *see* Bredge
Bregham, Simon, 663
    see also Bergham
Bremsham, John, & family, 50
    William, 50
Brend(e), John, 445
    Simon, of Felsham, *1452*
Brendwod(e), John, of Thorndon, **962**, 1102
    Katherine, of Thorndon, 962
    Robert, 962
    Thomas, 962
BRENT ELEIGH, church, 130
    aisle of, 375
    bells in, 165, 360
    chancel of, 375
    rectory (living) of, 375n
    vicar of, 130
    manor, farm of, 165

    lady of, 165, 165n
    places in, 'Cowperis Croft', 375
        'Ferthyngis Croft', 375
        'Gerveys medue', 375
        'Goodyngys Croftes', 375
        'Lanelond', 375
        'Longlivis' (tenement), 375
        'Stevenys atte Wode', 375
    testators of, *167*, **375**
    wills proved at, 31, 165, 374, 454, 455, 529,
        592, 593, 1193, 1194, 1244, 1312
Breon, Alice, of Sudbury, 398
    Benedict, 1183
    John, the elder, 398; the younger, 398; the
        elder, of Sudbury, **398**
    Seikman, of Sudbury, 398
BRESSINGHAM (Nfk), land in, 595
Bret (Brette), Amy, of Stanningfield, 531
    John, 531; of Preston, *1124*
    Richard, of Stanningfield, **531**
    Robert, 1249, 1258
    William, 531
Breton (Bretan), Helen, of Rickinghall Inferior,
    900
    John, the younger, 900
    Richard, of Rickinghall Inferior, 213n, **900**
    Thomas, 349; the younger, 900; rector of
        Thelnetham, 213, 900, 1186
    William, rector of Euston, 213n, 900, 969,
        969n
Brette, *see* Bret
BRETTENHAM, church, 921
    rector of, 1466
        see also John Musket
    window for, 632n
    gild in, 634
    inhabitants of, 90n, 761, 840, 917, 1036, 1436
    testators of, *840*, *917*, **1036**, *1324*, **1466**
    Willisham's manor in, 90n
    wills proved at, 559, 560, 815
Breuster *alias* Aldeby, James, 1006
    see also Browster
Bridbek, *see* Brydbek
BRIDLINGTON (Yorks), pilgrimage to, 489
Brigham, *see* Bergham, Bregham
Brightewell, Christine, of Gazeley, 303
    John, 303
    Richard, 303; of Gazeley, & family, **303**
    William, 303
    see also Bryghwelle
Brock, John, of Walsham le Willows, **169**
    Isabel, of Walsham le Willows, 169
    see also Brok(e)
BROCKFORD, *see* WETHERINGSETT
BROCKLEY, church, bell for, 1390
    land of rectory of, 160
    inhabitants of, 472, 1390
    land in, 417

testators of, **191**, **472**, **1390**
Brodhed, Richard, 548
Brodok, Joan, of Ousden, 449
  Stephen, of Ousden, **449**
Brogate, Richard, 966
Brok(e), John, of Langham, 8
  Margaret, of Langham, & family, **8**
  Simon, of Thorpe Morieux, 1466
  see also Brook, Obroke
Brokhole, Thomas, of Long Melford, 122
Brokley, John, of Shimpling, 184
BROME, church, chancel stalls in, 1158n
  rector of, *see* Richard Pye
  inhabitants of, 920, 1158
  land in, 949
  manor of Ling Hall in, 920n
  testators of, **920**, **1158**
  will proved at, 920
BROMEHILL (Nfk), priory of Augustinian
  canons, 180
Bromend (Broomend), John, 552, 584
BROMHOLME (Nfk), priory of Cluniac monks,
  97
  monk of, 97
Brond, *see* Broond
Bronwyn (Broneweyn, Brounewyn, Brownwyn)
  Agnes, 1289
  Alice, 1289
  Joan, of Wetheringsett, 1023
  John, 1023; the younger, 1023
  Margaret, of Wetheringsett, 1023
  Robert, 1023
  Roger, 1023
  Simon, 1289
  Thomas, 1023; of Wetheringsett, 721, 764,
    1023
  William, 1023
Brook, Alice, 1180; of Sudbury, 1168
  John, the elder, 1168; the younger, 1168; of
    Sudbury, 420, 539; the elder, weaver, of
    Sudbury, **1168**
  Robert, 1168
Broomend, *see* Bromend
Broond (Brond), John, 528
  Margery, 528
  Nicholas, 228; of Gislingham, 178
  Richard, 681; of Kedington, *528*
  Sabina, of Sudbury, 818
  Thomas, of Kedington, 528
  William, of Boxford, 1150; of Higham, 548
Broun, *see* Brown
Brounewyn, *see* Bronwyn
Brouster, *see* Browster
Brouston, Isabel, of Stanton, *1130*
  John, 1130
Browden, John, 103
Brown (Broun), Agnes, 120
  Alice, of Hopton, 723

Christian, 120
Isabel, of Pakenham, 1378
Joan, of Palgrave, 1350; of Sudbury, 1132
John, 120, 622, 862, 955, 1026, 1026n, 1378;
  the younger, 426; 863; of the Chamber,
  863n; of Hopton, 723, **723**; of Pakenham,
  1378; the elder, gentleman, of Stradishall,
  863; of Sudbury, *xlvi*n; carpenter, of
  Sudbury, **1132**; rector of Thornham Magna,
  1169, 1169n
Marion, of Hopton, 723, **1026**
Robert, 734, 1132; friar, 1409
Stephen, apprentice, 1186; of Wickham Skeith,
  1169
Thomas, of Palgrave, *1350*
William, 146, 1132
[*unnamed*], friar, of Babwell, 494, 1191
see also Brunne
Brownwyn, *see* Bronwyn
Browster (Brouster), James, 109
  John, 109, 329, 744; of Bildeston, 1125, 1140;
    of Somerton, & family, **216**
  Margaret, of Lavenham, 329
  Margery, of Somerton, 216
  Peter, 18
  Robert, of Lavenham, & family, **329**
  Thomas, 216, 329; of Stoke by Clare, 1382
  see also Breuster
BRUISYARD, abbey of Franciscan nuns
  (Minoresses), 20
Brumpton, John, rector of Woolpit, 60n
BRUNDISH, master of chantry, 489n
Brundych, William, 1031; of Felsham, 1031n
Brunne, Thomas, 791
Brush (Brussh), John, of Badwell Ash, 96
  Robert, of Badwell Ash, 96
Bryan (Bryon), Benedict, 1345
  John, of Long Melford, *668*; chaplain, of
    Mildenhall, 46, 219, 311, 489, 569, 683,
    727, 938, 1009
  Richard, of Preston, *761*
  Sayene, 539
  William, chaplain, of Lavenham, 161
Bryce, Lawrence, tailor, 229
  Margaret, servant, 790
Brycete (Brysete), John, 1291; of Great
  Horringer, 422, 436
Bryche, Geoffrey, of Haughley, & family, **1307**
  Margaret, of Haughley, 1307
  Robert, 1307
Bryd, *see* Byrd
Brydbek (Bridbek), Alice, 420
  Dennis, 420
  John, 420
Brygh, Agnes, 500
  [*unnamed*], 500
Bryght, Robert, 540
  William, 466

Bryghwelle, John, of Mildenhall, 1156
 William, 1156
 see also Brightwell
Brygman, Richard, of Snailwell (Cambs), *505*
Brynkle(y) (Brynkely), Margery, of Kedington,
 681
 Richard, 915
 Thomas, husbandman, of Kedington, **681**
Bryon, see Bryan
Brysete, see Brycete
Brystow(e), Audrey, 57, 494
 Joan, of Exning, 995
 Margaret, 995
 Thomas, of Exning, 435, 590, **995**
Bryth, John, 1106
 Richard, 1329
 Robert, of Alpheton, *1106*
Bug(g)(e), Andrew, 1256, 1325
 Joan, of Soham (Cambs), 1325
 John, of Soham (Cambs), 478, 902, 1483,
  1483n
 Petronilla, 1325
 Robert, 902
 Thomas, of Soham (Cambs), & family, **1325**
 William, of Soham (Cambs), 1483, 1483n
 see also Bygge
Buk(ke) (Boc), John, of Bury St Edmunds, 1153;
 of Wetheringsett, **641**
 Matilda, of Wetheringsett, 641
Bukkele, John, 725
Bull, John, 925
Bulleson, Thomas, of Bury St Edmunds, 729
Bullok (Bulloc), Adam, 757
 Alice, of Risby, 1210
 James, 1210
 John, 98, 1210*; of Boxford, 155; of Risby,
  963, **1210**; of Woolpit, 107, **757**
 Margery, of Woolpit, 757
 Rose, 619
 Sabina, of Woolpit, & family, 757
 Thomas, 155, 1210, 1437; of Thurston, 1210,
  1451
 William, 1300; chaplain, of Boxford, 144;
  rector of Groton, 529, 942
Bullington (Bullyngton), Henry, 1353
 Isabel, of Long Melford, 1051
 John, of Long Melford, *1051*
Bullyng, Anne, 877
BULMER (Esx), church, 1077
 curate of, 1181
 'Grove, le', by the Tye, 421
 Smeeton Hall in, 1246
 wood in, 740
Bulney, Roger, of Long Melford, **195**
Bunch, Richard, chaplain, 186
 Roger, clerk, 1469
Bunne, Alice, of Elmsett, 1427
 Godfrey, 525

Isabel, of Little Whelnetham, **525**
John, of Little Whelnetham, 525
Richard, 1427
Thomas, 1427
William, of Elmsett, & family, **1427**
Buntyng, John, of Tostock, & family, **133**
 Richard, 133, 552, 836; of Pakenham, 335
 William, of Bury St Edmunds, 407
BURES ST MARY, church, dedication of, *xlv*,
 317n
 inhabitants of, 317n, 356n, 403, 1135, 1188,
  1335
 'Sowerys' (tenement) in, 317
 testators of, *274*, *275*, *317*, *384*, *477*, *657*,
  1135, *1188*, *1335*
 will proved at, 172
BURES HAMLET (Esx), in parish of Bures St
 Mary, *xl*
BURGATE, church, 369, 723
 rector of, see John Gentylman
 gild in, 406, 787
 inhabitants of, 369, 406, 726, 787, 976n
 land in, 1097
 places in, 'Malownd', 787
  'Overlownd', 787
 testators of, **406**, **787**, *976*, *1477*
Burgeys, Agnes, of Bury St Edmunds, 1263
 John, of Rickinghall Inferior, 900
 Robert, of Bury St Edmunds, 1263
Burgh, Bartholomew, & family, 1371
 Robert, 1189
 Roger, 1305
Burghward, William, of Exning, 435
Burgon, Simon, rector of Elveden, master of
 hospital of St Nicholas, Bury, *xxxix*
?BURNAM, inhabitant of, 1346
Burne, Roger, 942
BURROUGH GREEN (Cambs), church, chantry
 in, 193n
 rector of, 368
  see also John Bateman
 inhabitant of, 499
Burteyn, George, 1298
 John, 1298*
 Margaret, of Soham (Cambs), 1298
 Richard, of Soham (Cambs), **1298**, 1319
 William, 1298
Burton (Burtun), John, friar of Sudbury, 122, 421,
 474
 Roger, 453
BURWELL (Cambs), church of St Andrew, 150n,
 284, 313
 image of St Christopher in, 313
 church of St Mary, *xlvii*, 150n, 682n, 927,
  927n, 1265
 aisle of, 682, 1162, 1162n
 bells in, 927n
 chancel of, 682n, 927n

tower of, 911n, 1133n
vestment for, 278
vicar of, *see* John Heigham
windows in, 1265
gilds in, 1052, 1052n, 1265
inhabitants of, 67, 79, 278, 389, 682, 697, 911,
    927, 1052, 1133, 1162, 1475
places in, 'Belysfeld', 1475
    'Bradwey, le', 1475
    'Breche, le', 1475
    'Bunt ..., le', 1475
    'Castelmartyn', 1475
    'Dichefeld', 1475
    'Dullynghames', 1475
    'Estfeld', 1052, 1475
    'Fyshstrete, le', 1265
    'Heybredge' (bridge), 682
    high town, 911
    'Hyllyngeworth', 1265
    'Lytylholm', 1475
    'Mellewey, le', 1475
    'Northfeld', 1475
    'Northstrete', 1162
    'Swyniles' (tenement), 682
    'Wakelyns' (tenement), 682
    'Westfeld', 1265
    'Wyndmellefeld', 1265
testators of, *66*, *67*, **150**, **237**, *244*, **284**, **313**,
    389, *482*, *555*, **556**, **682**, *697*, **911**, **927**,
    1030, **1052**, **1133**, **1162**, **1265**, **1357**, **1475**
wills proved at, 313, 1162, 1265
Burwell, John, of Kirtling (Cambs), **881**
Bury, Anne, of Kersey, 1184
    John, friar, 929; of Kersey, *1184*
    Nicholas, friar, 777
    Thomas, of Icklingham, 1309
    William, of Ingham, 227
BURY ST EDMUNDS, archdeacon of, *xxxix*,
    279n
abbey of Benedictine monks, abbot of, 160n,
    180
    cellarer of, 180
    cross of St Thomas in churchyard of, *xlii*
    dissolution of, *xxxix*
    gilds in, 1216n
    land of, 160, 343, 713, 1200
    lord of Pakenham Hall manor, 335
    mill belonging to, 924
    monks of, 180, 1240
    patron of Stanton All Saints, 457n
    prior of, 180, 1240
    sacrist of, 180, 279n, 574n, 1240; as
        archdeacon, *xxxix*
    sacrist's court, *xxxix*, 279n
    shrine of St Edmund, 1207n; pilgrimage
        to, 1207
    tower of, *xlviii*n, 180, 180n, 271, 1240, 1495
    woods of, 457

benefactors of, *xli*, *xlii*
chapel of St Mary (Risbygate) in, 1279n
church of St James in, 279, 279n
    altar of St Lawrence in, 1279n
church of St Mary in, 279n, 574
college of priests in, *xli*
ecclesiastical peculiar of, *xxxix*
Guildhall, Feoffment of, *xli*n
hospital, by Risby gate (of St Peter), 130, 187
    of St Nicholas, *xxxix*n, *xlii*n
    of St Saviour, 891
inhabitants of, 4, 10, 28, 55, 100, 180, 226,
    246, 394n, 407, 421, 430, 439, 443, 462,
    468, 477,542, 552, 574, 611, 616, 653, 729,
    749, 777, 807, 836, 859n, 1123, 1153, 1158,
    1220, 1255, 1263, 1279, 1356, 1441
inhabitants' wills proved elsewhere, *xxxix*,
    *xxxix*n
inhabitants' wills 'selectively registered',
    *xxxix*n
land in, 574, 574n
places in, Babwell (house of friars, actually in
    Fornham All Saints), *see* BABWELL
    'Brakelond, le' (street), 417
    'Longbrakelond', 1279
    Risby gate, 1279n
    'Rysbygatestrete', 187
    'Tolcote, le', 97
    'Toretyerd, le' (pightle), 1279
    'Whytyngstrete', 1279
poor of, *xlvi*, 415
prisoners in, 61, 130, 187
probate jurisdiction in, *xxxviii-xl*
testament dated at, 1493
testator of, **279**
testators' occupations in wills of, *xliv*
will dated at, 530
wills proved at, 377, 477, 838, 883, 1302, 1321
woollen cloth at, 1313
Busk, Peter, 912
Bussh, Geoffrey, of Mendlesham, 1315, 1482
    Richard, of Mendlesham, 1035, *1482*
Bust, John, 398
BUTLEY, priory of Augustinian canons, 497
Butt, William, 1025
BUXHALL, church, advowson of, 90n
    rector of, 538
        see also William Copenger, John Haward
gilds in, 90, 1393
inhabitants of, 1065, 1366, 1393
land in, 348, 1343
manor of Buxhall Hall in, 90n
places in, 'Copyngerys' (tenement), 90n
    'Fauncebrounys' (tenement), 90, 90n
    'Pie Hatch', 439n
    'Smythes' (tenement), 90
poor of, 231
rent called 'Welyshamrente' in, 90

testators of, **90**, *465*, **1065**, *1366*, **1393**
  will proved at, 288
Byewode, John, 186
Bygge, John, of Mildenhall, **569**
Bynd, John, of Little Thurlow, *567*
  Matilda, of Little Thurlow, 567
Byng, Hugh, of Wickham Skeith, 228
Byrch, Geoffrey, 18
Byrd (Bryd), Alice, of Fordham (Cambs), 626
  Emma, of Sudbury, 356
  John, the elder, of Lavenham, 446, 510; of
    Sudbury, 48
  Stephen, 48; of Sudbury, 356, 539
  Thomas, 662
  see also Berd, Bird(e)
Byschop, *see* Bischop
Bysse, Christian, of Assington, 176
  John, 176
  Walter, of Assington, & family, **176**
  William, 176
Byssop, Geoffrey, of Nayland, *666*
  Margaret, of Nayland, 666
Byxby (Bekysby), Margery, of Thorpe Morieux,
  1244
  Nicholas, 1244
  Robert, 1244
  Walter, of Thorpe Morieux, & family, **1244**

C[*damaged*], Thomas, of Eye, 367
Caas (Kaas), John, vicar of Wickhambrook, 696
Cabaw (Cabaugh, Cabow), Alice, 146
  John, 823, 1300; of Woolpit, 619, **823**
  Margaret, of Hitcham, 110, 177, **1234**; of
    Woolpit, *508*
  Margery, 619; of Woolpit, 823
  Ralph, 1066; of Kettlebaston, 1300
  Thomas, 979; of Hitcham, 1234n; of Hitcham,
    & family, **110, 177**
  William, 823
Cach, Richard, 332
Cade, Agnes, of Stuston, *1163*
Cage, Agnes, of Whepstead, 160
  John, 1465; of Rickinghall Superior, & family,
    1334
  Margaret, of Rickinghall Superior, 1334
  Margery, servant, 160
  Peter, of Wattisfield, *1377*
  Robert, 160
  Thomas, 160; of Rattlesden, 1032
  William, of Rattlesden, 558; of Whepstead, **160**
Cagor (Cager), Henry, 1419
  Joan, 1419
  William, 1033
Caister, Richard, vicar of St Stephen's, Norwich,
  tomb of, 1207n
Cake, Agnes, housekeeper, 346; of Mendlesham,
  1315
  Joan, of Mildenhall, 1009

John, 346, 1315; of Mendlesham, & family,
  1315
Margaret, of Mildenhall, & family, 1009
Marion, 346
Robert, 1155; draper, 346; of Mendlesham,
  1315
Thomas, chaplain, 346; of Mildenhall, **1009**
Cakestrete, John, of Poslingford, *524*
Calabyr, John, the younger, 1287; of Pakenham,
  1287
Margery, of Pakenham, 1287
Caldewell (Caldwell), Isabel, 1009
  John, 311, 1009; vicar of Exning, 435; of
    Hopton, 1494n
  Thomas, of Thelnetham, 1186
Calewe, *see* Calwe
Calfawe, Alice, 51
  John, 1079
Calf(f), Edmund, 5; of Stanton, 802
  Joan, & family, 802
  John, of Badwell Ash, 96; of Boxford, 1489
  Katherine, 802
  Robert, 1033
  see also Calve
Calle, James, & family, 380
  Robert, 1280
  Simon, of Little Waldingfield, 1193
Calt, Robert, of Barrow, 290
Calve, Joan, of Little Waldingfield, 92
  John, of Little Waldingfield, & family, **92**
Calvesbane (Calvisbane, Calvysbane), John, the
  elder, 1357, 1475
  Ralph, 1475
  see also Galvysbane
Calwe (Calewe), John, 187
  Roger, 187
  William, 187; of Barrow, **187**, 290
Caly, Brythreve, of Kersey, 1227
  John, 1465; of Great Ashfield, **1249**; of Kersey,
    1227; of Norton, & family, **1465**
  Marion, 671, 1258; of Norton, 1465
  Matilda, of Great Ashfield, 1249
  Roger, 1191
  William, 1249, 1258
  see also Galy
Cambrege, Thomas, monk, of Bury, 180
CAMBRIDGE, friars in, unspec., 1123, 1418
  Augustinian, 270, 381, 499, 553, 683, 822,
    903, 1041, 1325, 1468
  Carmelite, *xlix*, 132, 137, 158, 353, 381,
    491, 499, 507, 549, 682, 776, 790, 822,
    903, 939, 1041, 1083, 1246, 1289, 1325,
    1390, 1468
  Dominican (Preachers), 381, 499, 682, 822,
    903, 1041, 1325, 1467, 1468
  Franciscan (Minors), 381 499, 682, 903,
    1041, 1325, 1467, 1468
  King's college in, 1133n

St Radegund's priory (Benedictine nuns) in, 180, 180n
university, annual to be celebrated at, 929
Campe, Robert, 1031
Camplyon, John, the elder, 711; of Stowmarket, & family, **711**
Richard, the younger, 711; of Stowmarket, 711
Campyon, William, priest, 603; of Icklingham, & family, **603**
Candeler, Joan, of Botesdale, 971
Robert, of Botesdale, 325, **971**, 971n
see also Chaundlere
Canon, Agnes, 90
Canoham, Katherine, 624n
Canown, *see* Ballard *alias* Canown
Cansoham, John, of Cheveley (Cambs), *625*
Thomas, 625
CANTERBURY, archbishop of, *xxxix*
Christ Church Cathedral priory in, *xxxviii*
pilgrimage to shrine of St Thomas in, 346, 489
prerogative court of, *xxxviii*
Canvas, John, 1259; of Mildenhall, 1117, 1404
Capell, Agnes, of Brockford, & family, **764**
Ed., of Brockford, 764
Joan, 365; of Stoke by Nayland, 365*
John, the elder, 365; of Stoke by Nayland, **365**
Thomas, the younger, 365
William, 365
Capon, Alice, 1079
John, 1079
Cappe, Thomas, of Eye, *1316*
Carles, John, 941
see also Karles
Carman, Agnes, 1116
John, the elder, of Thrandeston, 1062
Thomas, clerk, 1276
CARROW (Nfk), priory of Benedictine nuns, 347
Carter(e) (Carteer), Alice, 158; of Long Melford, 202
Benedicta, 326
Henry, of Sudbury, *l*, **326**
Isabel, of Hitcham, *1066*
Joan, of Mellis, 1097
John, 326; of Mellis, **1097**; servant, 1168
Matilda, of Sudbury, 326
William, of Long Melford, *202*
see also Kartere
Carver (Kerver), Edmund, 757
Casse, John, of Great Bradley, 736; *1196*; the younger, of Great Bradley, *736*
Cassin, Joan, 680
Castell, John, of Barton Mills, 311
CASTLE HEDINGHAM (Esx), priory of Benedictine nuns, 421
Cat(e), John, 156
Roger, 156
Thomas, priest, of Woolpit, 713
Walter, of Stuston, *156*

William, 93
Catel(e)yn (Catelene, Cattelyng), Alice, of Burwell, (Cambs), 1133; of Ixworth, 1133n
John, 523, 927n; chaplain, 284; of Burwell (Cambs), & family, **1133**; of Haverhill, 490
Matilda, of Burwell (Cambs), 284
Richard, 1052
Thomas, 389, 1133; of Burwell (Cambs), 1133, 1475, **284**; chaplain, of Burwell (Cambs), 682
William, 1052
see also Katelyn
Catour, John, 1474, 1474n
William, of Lidgate, 1474
Catour *alias* Neve, Anne, of Ixworth, & family, **321**
see also Neve
Catton (Cotton), Joan, of Mildenhall, 119
John, 'skepmaker', of Mildenhall, **119**
see also Cotton
Caugh, John, chaplain, 90
see also Cawe
CAVENDISH, gild in, 776
inhabitant of, 776
land in, 205, 735
'Mothyll, le', 1375
testators of, **80**, **83**, **776**, *946*, **1375**
wills proved at, 946, 1375
Cavendych, Peter, 1301
CAVENHAM, gild in, 387
inhabitants of, 387, 1145
testators of, **95**, **387**, *987*, *1145*
wills proved at, 387, 1155, 1156
Cavenham, Henry, of Westley, *4*
Isabel, of Acton, 1312
John, 153, 813, 1267; of Sudbury, *1267*
Philip, of Fordham (Cambs), 550
William, of Acton, & family, **1312**
Cawe, John, 186
see also Caugh
Cayfen, Adam, 59
Cayle, Gregory, rector of Somerton, 234, 234n
Cayw(e)yn, Adam, 124; of Barningham, 889
Robert, 1078
Chaas, Andrew, of Withersfield, *396*
Chalener (Chavenere), William, 537
Chamber (Chambyr, Cha(w)mbre), John, of Nayland, *32*; del, 549; esquire, of Stratford (Mdx), **863**
Margaret, of Nayland, 32
Robert, friar, 612
Chamberleyn (Cha(w)mbyrleyn, Chambyrlayn, Schamberleyn), Agnes, 1411
Alice, of Poslingford, **113**
Denise, 725
John, 756
Thomas, 1014; of Thornham Magna, 1445
[*unnamed*], of Redlingfield, **756**

Chapel(l)eyn (Chapyllayn), Richard, of
    Poslingford, 113
    Robert, 1301
    William, 339, 339n, 1093, 1337; clerk, 674,
        842, 944
Chapman (Schapman), Adam, 471, 488, 940; of
    Barrow, 290
    Agnes, of Mildenhall, 1155
    Alice, of Coney Weston, 957
    Christian, widow, of Rattlesden, *123*
    Euphemia, of Hopton (near Harling), **331**
    Geoffrey, of Haughley, 18, **775**
    Joan, of Haughley, 775; of Livermere, *483*; of
        Thorndon, *1102*
    John, 331, 471, 815, 860, 1155, 1181; chaplain,
        1477; clerk, 488; of Burgate, *1477*; of
        Needham (in Gazeley), 881; of Oakley,
        1476; of Rattlesden, 123
    Katherine, servant, 180
    Margaret, 406
    Nicholas, of Coney Weston, 1278n, **957**
    Richard, 1155; of Mildenhall, **1155**; of
        Rickinghall Inferior, & family, **393**
    Robert, 1005; chaplain, 957; clerk, 1278; rector
        of Thorpe Morieux, 773
    Roger, 683, 1221, 1476; of Mildenhall, 1155
    Stephen, 957
    Thomas, 193, 331; of Little Thurlow, *866*; of
        Livermere, *656*
    William, 1009; the younger, 676; of
        Mildenhall, 683
Chaterle(e) (Chatterlay), Robert, chaplain, 268
    Thomas, of Hinderclay, *268*
    William, of Ixworth, 268
Chatisle, William, 829
CHATTERIS (Cambs), abbey of Benedictine
    nuns, 1115
Chaucer, Alice, duchess of Suffolk, 1076n
Chaunceler, Richard, of Great Saxham, 77
Chaundlere (Chaundeler), John, 365
    Margaret, 1454
    Robert, 1454
    Simon, of Semer, *1454*
    see also Candeler
Chavenere, see Chalener
Chawmberleyn, see Chamberleyn
Chawmbre, see Chamber
CHEDBURGH, church, 960
    land in, 314, 279
    places in, 'Baydines', 279
        'Pompyslond, 1410
        'Pumpyes', 279
        'Webbys', 279
Chelmyssey, Robert, of Kersey, 719
CHELSWORTH, church, canopy over high altar
    in, 1279n
    rector of, 347n
        see also William Amey, Thomas Moryell

inhabitants of, 143, 1194, 1279, 1459
    land in, 42
    testators of, **204**, **516**, *559*, **629**, **1194**, *1428*,
        1458
    wills proved at, 151, 167, 221, 292, 570, 745,
        763, 1427, 1428, 1429
Chenery, Alan, 1260
    Helen, of Cockfield, 1260
    John, the elder, 1260; the elder, of Cockfield, &
        family, **1260**
Cheny, Roger, 107
Cheperon, Nicholas, 87, 705, 706
Chepperd, see Shepperd
Cherche, see Chyrche
Cheryaunt, see Seriaunt
Chesewrygh, Andrew, chaplain, of Fordham
    (Cambs), 1131
Chesteyn, Margaret, 1333
Chestre, Richard, 1489
Chetelerth, Adam, of Drinkstone, *115*
    Clemence, of Drinkstone, 115
    Thomas, 115
Cheveler, Roger, 492
CHEVELEY (Cambs), church, 247, 381, 1473
    chapel of St Nicholas in, 676, 676n
    Easter sepulchre in, 1082
    rector of, see John Dryle
    gilds in, 1082
    inhabitants of, 822, 1081, 1082
    land in, 28
    poor of, 270
    roads in, highway to lord's hall, 1082
        '... geslane', 1082
    testators of, *625*, **676**, *739*, **792**, **822**, *1081*,
        1082, *1426*
    wills proved at, 284, 428, 553, 738, 739
CHEVINGTON, church, 449
    bells for, 314n
    image of salutation of BVM in, 589
    rector of, see Henry Purlond
    tower, 314, 314n
    gild in, 589
    inhabitants of, 168, 314, 314n, 411, 417, 589,
        1410
    land in, 41, 279
    places in, 'Belyslond', 1410
        'Durentes' (tenement), 1410
        'Goerlond', 1410
        'Maystris' (tenement), 1410
        'Palmerescroft', 314
        'Wycombys' (tenement), 1410
    testators of, **314**, **589**, **1410**
Child, see Chyld
Childer(i)ston, see Chylder(e)ston
Chilston, John, 821
    see also Chylder(e)ston
CHILTON (by Sudbury), land in, 541
CHIPLEY, land in, 507

CHIPPENHAM (Cambs), BADLINGHAM in,
    inhabitants of, 440
    testator of, **440**
    church, holy-water carrier of, 1100n
    cottage in, 440
    inhabitants of, 588, 1100
    preceptory of Knights Hospitallers, master of,
        114
    testators of, *93*, *1100*
    wills proved at, 95, 440, 499, 724, 793, 1358,
        1480
Chirche, *see* Chyrche
Christemasse (Crystemesse), Helen, 1162
    John, of Stoke by Nayland, **36**
    Margaret, 1162; of Stoke by Nayland, 36
Christian, *see* Cristian
Churchman, William, rector of Combs, 609
    see also Chyrcheman
Chyld (Child), Isabel, of Badwell Ash, 96
    John, 96; of Badwell Ash, **96**; of Higham (in
        Gazeley), **1439**
    Margaret, of Higham (in Gazeley), 1439
    Richard, 96
    Robert, 96
    William, 96, 1438
Chylder(e)ston (Childer(i)ston, Chyld(y)r(i)ston,
        Chylder(y)ston), Alice, of Mildenhall, 727
    Christian, of Mildenhall, 1156
    Emmot, 530
    John, 1084, 1156, 1286; of Eriswell, 166; of
        Mildenhall, 498, **865**, **870**
    Margaret, of Mildenhall, 865
    Matilda, of Mildenhall, 1084
    Richard, of Mildenhall, **1084**
    Robert, 1117; of Mildenhall, 220, 727
    Simon, of Mildenhall, 865, 865n, **1156**
    Thomas, 119, 683
    William, 1084, 1156; of Mildenhall, 727
    see also Chilston
Chylle, John, 101
    Thomas, 101
Chylton, Marion, 1346
Chyrche (Cherche, Chirche), Elizabeth, widow, of
        Barnham, 1007n, **1206**
    Geoffrey, 1178
    John, 1007 1206; of Barnham, *1007*, 1206; of
        Hopton, *1178*
    Katherine, 704
    Margaret, of Herringswell, *704*
Chyrcheclerk, Margaret, 278
Chyrcheman, Joan, of Icklingham, 1129
    John, 1129
    Ralph, 1145
    Richard, of Icklingham, **1129**
Clak, John, 399
Clapman, Richard, 86
CLARE, blind persons of, 149
    Chilton in, gild in, 1216

church, altar of St Mary in, 112
    benches in, 642
    burial in, 149
    clerestory window in, 1218
    roodloft in, 642
    vicars of, 1218n
        see also William Hall, Richard Pumpy
        alias Tylney
house of Augustinian friars in, *xlix*, 1448n, 21,
    43, 44, 49, 50, 60, 112, 118, 122, 125, 126,
    130, 132, 137, 149, 158, 164, 180, 185, 188,
    195, 249, 261, 263, 270, 287, 289, 303, 308,
    310, 317, 329, 350, 351, 362, 380, 420, 474,
    507, 511, 539, 548, 613, 619, 632, 643, 713,
    735, 776, 790, 812, 818, 823, 832, 860, 939,
    1036, 1058, 1079, 1083, 1123, 1168, 1172,
    1216, 1244, 1246, 1280, 1343, 1363, 1369,
    1382, 1418, 1462. 1469
    Friar Roger Bateman of, 416
    Friar Walter Benyth of, 1375
    Friar Gilbert Kyrton of, 112
    Friar Robert Lyster of, 1094
    Friar Dr Slowle of, 1142
    Friar Robert Yekesworth of, 833
    gild held in, 1216
inhabitants of, 112, 113, 593, 642, 670, 730n,
    832, 915, 948, 1010, 1375, 1448, 1471
market stalls in, 62
'moneqy, le', in, 1448
roads in, 1218
testators of, *64*, **43**, **112**, **149**, **260**, *642*, *646*,
    670, **832**, **833**, *915*, *948*, **1010**, *1127*, **1218**,
    1448
wills proved at, 70, 260, 522, 523, 524, 580,
    776, 781, 832, 915, 939, 948, 988, 1127,
    1185, 1189, 1190, 1216, 1490
Clare *alias* Abthorp, Isabel, of Troston, 599
    Richard, of Troston, **599**
Clavyere, Robert, 852
Claydon, Alice, of Haverhill, 50
    Joan, of Haverhill, 106, 210
    John, 50, of Haverhill, **106**, **210**
    William, 50; of Haverhill, & family, **50**
Clement, Joan, 1132
    John, & family, 1249; of Stowlangtoft, 777; of
        Sudbury, 602, 1364
Clerk, Agnes, of Great Ashfield, 136; of Sudbury,
        554
    Alice, 368, 1231; of Clare, 1448; of Ixworth,
        372; of Whepstead, 417
    Basse, 1478
    Ed., chaplain, 942
    Edmund, of Lavenham, **130**, 511n
    Henry, 170, 372
    Hervey, & family, 1231
    James, of Ixworth, *372*, 1231n
    Joan, of Lavenham, 130
    John, 358*, 457, 554, 1012, 1148, 1313, 1320

19

1415, 1448; & family, 438, 683; the elder, 1313; the younger, 1313; of Boxford, *403*; of Bures, 403; of Chelsworth, & family, **629**; of Clare, 670; the elder, of Clare **1448**; of Great Ashfield, *136*; of Hartest, 1075; of Occold, 537, 659; of Thorndon, 22
Margaret, 1231, 1313, of Stanton, 457
Matilda, of Wetheringsett, 1438
Nicholas, of Freckenham, 135
Richard, 113, 524, 1375; rector of Little Whelnetham, 824n
Robert, 22; 238, 828, 1148, 1378; rector of mediety of Stanton All Saints, 457; of Wetheringsett, & family, **1438**
Roger, of Stuston, *170*; of Wetheringsett, 741
Sarah, 1415
Simon, of Stanton, *1*, **457**
Thomas, 1415; & family, 457; servant, 683; of Great Ashfield, 828; of Lakenheath, 708
Walter, 193
William, of Great Ashfield, *218*; of Sudbury, **554**
Clerkek, Thomas, 1384, 1385
Cletyr, Margery, of Hundon, 448
Richard, of Hundon, 448
Clopton, John, esquire, of Long Melford, 201, 201n, 375, 493n, 640, 929, 1064, 1246, 1280
Katherine, of Woolpit, 107
Stephen, of Woolpit, *107*
Clovyere, John, of Hadleigh, 48
Clubber, Robert, 723
COATES, GREAT (Lincs), will made at, 1213n
Cobayn, Isabel, 193
Cobb(e), Alice, 1031; of Glemsford, 1353
Joan, 871, 877; of Long Melford, 88; of Soham (Cambs), 254
John, 88, 270, 538, 871, 894, 1280, 1446; of Edwardstone, **1446**; of Glemsford, & family, **1353**; of Soham (Cambs), **254**
Katherine, of Edwardstone, 1446
Margaret, 538
Margery, of Shelland, 977
Robert, 977
Thomas, 977, 1446; the elder, 376; of Lavenham, 130; of Shelland, **977**
Walter, of Long Melford, **88**
William, 1353
Cob(b)old (Coberld), Agnes, 618
Henry, of Preston, *1111*
John, 102; of Lavenham, 126, **618**
Thomas, of Lavenham, 1243
COCKFIELD, church, 17, 263
rectory of (house), 1260
tabernacle of St Peter in, 1260n
inhabitants of, 470, 607, 675, 899, 901, 1108, 1260, 1367
testators of, *9*, *179*, *470*, *607*, *615*, *675*, **899**, *1108*, *1175*, **1260**

wills proved at, 102, 204, 308
Codenham, Ed., 856
Codman, Elizabeth, of Cockfield, 179
John, of Cockfield, **179**
Coggeshal(l) (Coggesale, Cogsale), John the elder, of Hundon, **1216**
Katherine, of Hundon, 1216
Robert, 1216
Thomas, 1216
William, 833, 939; of Clare, 593; of Hundon, 1216n
see also Coksale
Cogman, Joan, of Lavenham, *510*
Cogsale, *see* Coggeshal(l)
Cokat, *see* Coket
Cok(e) (Cokke), Agnes, of Norton, 1381
Alice, of Chevington, 1410
Henry, 1406, 1410; of Saffron Walden (Esx), 1410n
John, 1080, 1410; of Chevington, **1410**; of Withersfield, 1092
Katherine, of Haverhill, 633
Margaret, of Stoke by Clare, *437*
Nicholas, 1410
Robert, 390; canon, 1410
Roger, ?cordwainer, 566
Thomas, 476, 633, 1410; of Norton, & family, **1381**; of Withersfield, 1107
Walter, of Haverhill, & family, **633**
William, 633
Cokefeld, Alice, 288
Cokerell, Robert, of Badwell Ash, 96
Coket (Cokat), Agnes, of Stoke by Clare, 1187
Alice, 1400
Henry, of Westhorpe, *206*
John, chaplain, 1280; the younger, 1187; of Ampton, 594, 749, 1260; the elder, of Ampton, 180, 1400n; the younger, of Ampton, 305, 305n; of Bury St Edmunds, 468, 749*, 1441; of Hitcham, *273*; of Stoke by Clare, *1187*; of Timworth, 1201, 1441; of Woolpit, 806
Margaret, widow, of Ampton, **1400**; of Bury St Edmunds, 749; of Ingham, 227n, 1441
Thomas, 96, 255, 674
Walter, 1152, 1441; woolman, of Ingham, **1441**
William, 1187
Cokke, *see* Cok(e)
Cokkow, Isabel, of Little Wratting, 1146
John, of Little Wratting, *1146*
Coksale, John, 1246
William, 1246
Coksegge, Baldwin, of Felsham, 1255
Denise, of Felsham, 1255
Cokwold, Henry, 723
Cokyn, John, 36
Colberd, John, of Wickhambrook, **846**
Thomas, 846

Walter, 846

Colby, Richard, friar, 359

COLCHESTER (Esx), abbey of Benedictine
  monks (St John's), 899n
  Carmelite [sic] friars in, 548
  house of Franciscan friars (Minors), 108, 118,
    130, 301, 308, 317, 350, 380, 463, 548n,
    554, 643, 717, 860, 930, 941, 1080, 1104,
    1469
  inhabitants of, 126, 275, 836
  priory of Augustinian canons (St Botolph's),
    899n
  prisoners in, 130
  russet cloth of, 474, 474n

Colchestre, Ralph, friar, 288

Coldhakeld, Joan, 408

Coldham, John, 1248; of Barningham, 807, **807**,
  955n
  Margaret, of Barningham, 807, *955*

Coldhope, Alice, 1319
  Peter, 1319

Coldyng, Cecily, of Woolpit, 713

Cole, Alice, 1009
  Anne, 893
  William, 1009

Colet(t), Joan, 247
  John, of Ashley (Cambs), 381, 1473
  Robert, of Long Melford, 201

Colewen, Thomas, 816

Colman, Agnes, of Little Waldingfield, 1024
  Alice, 1169
  Edmund, 1403
  Henry, 1366
  John, 1267; of Sudbury, 593
  Nicholas, of Stowmarket, **1126**
  Richard, 171; & family, 1126; of Little
    Waldingfield, 92, **1024**; of Mildenhall, **1403**
  Stephen, 1024
  Thomas, of Thorndon, 1090; of Wortham, **1076**
  William, 898; of Wortham, 595, 873, 1076,
    1224

Colne, William, friar, 308

Colray, John, of Little Livermere, 1003

Colyn, John, the younger, 429

Comayn, William, of Rattlesden, 747

Comber(e), John, 1142; the elder, 1142; the
  younger, 1142
  Margaret, of Stradishall, 1142
  Thomas, 1142
  William, of Stradishall, **1142**

Combes, Thomas, of Wyverston, *841*

COMBS, church, 20, 1180
  aisle of, 609, 660
  rector of, *see* William Churchman
  window in, 609
  inhabitants of, 145, 497, 601, 609, 743, 753,
    795n, 852n, 877, 952, 1392
  land in, 348, 810

places in, 'Awbryis', 609
  'Bakkys', 609
  'Ballelond, le' (close), 609, 609n
  'Bonnetyslond', 1392
  Combs Ford, 660
  Edgar's Farmhouse, 609n
  'Hangeris', 609
  'Mellefeld', 609
  'Raneldes and Reves' (tenements), 47
  'Webberes', 609
  testators of, **47**, **145**, **410**, **601**, **609**, **660**, *743*,
    753, **877**, *952*, **1392**
  wills proved at, 47, 952

COMPOSTELLA (SANTIAGO de
  COMPOSTELLA) (Spain), shrine of St
  James, 17, 345, 346, 367, 1035, 1432

CONEY WESTON, church, 271, 286, 1279
  'Dotteme, le' (field) in, 1497
  inhabitants of, 17, 271, 535, 854, 954, 957,
    1278n
  land in, 286
  testators of, **330, 957, 1497**

Conyn, Geoffrey, of Buxhall, **1065**
  Isabel, of Buxhall, 1065
  John, 1065

Coo, Helen, 278
  James, of Boxford, 375
  Joan, servant, 1489
  John, barber, of Boxford, 308, **548**
  William, & family, 389; of Burwell (Cambs),
    556

Cook(e), Alice, of Nayland, 192
  John, 192, 623, 998; of Badwell Ash, 96; of
    Badwell Ash, & family, 96; of Bury St
    Edmunds, 443; of Clare, 112; of Combs,
    410; of Creeting St Peter, *998*
  Katherine, 982
  Lawrence, 888
  Matilda, of Occold, 104
  Robert, 104, 415, 923, 923n
  Thomas, 91, 409, 541; of Cotton, 400; of Great
    Livermere, 827, 828; of Lavenham, 130
  Walter, butcher, of Nayland, **192**
  William, 415, 592, 998, 1125, 1294, 1458; of
    Occold, *104*
  see also Coke *and* Fermere *alias* Cook

Cook *alias* Parker, John, of Lavenham, & family,
  454
  Katherine, of Lavenham, 454
  Lawrence, 773n; of Alpheton, 454n
  Thomas, 454

Coole, John, of Snailwell (Cambs), *239*
  Margaret, of Snailwell (Cambs), 239

Coote, William, 380; co-founder of the college,
  Bury St Edmunds, rector of Barningham and
  Fornham All Saints, *xli*

Cootes, William, of Mildenhall, 1117, 1117n

Copcy, Agnes, of Brockley, 1390

Roger, of Brockley, **1390**
Sybil, of Brockley, 1390
Copenger (Copynger), Alice, of Buxhall, 90
Helen, of Rattlesden, 1144
John, 231; of Buxhall, & family, **90**
Margaret, nun, of Thetford, 90, 231
Richard, of Rattlesden, *1144*
Robert, of Woolpit, 806
Walter, 90, 806; & family, 231
William, 90; rector of Buxhall, 90, 231
Cop(p)yng, Isabel, 56
John, 1295, 1390; of Hartest, & family, 456
Richard, of Hartest, 1390
Robert, 1295
Roger, 1390
Thomas, 456; of Brockley, 1390; of West Stow, 56
William, 56, 1251
Corbet, John, esquire, 529
Corbow, John, 1476
Thomas, 1005
Corby, John, 376; bailiff of Lavenham, 416
William, 416
Cordy (Corde), Eleanor, 877
John, the younger, 1262
William, 1186
CORNARD (unspec.), inhabitant of, 1177
testators of, *1027, 1177*
CORNARD, GREAT, church, 188
curate of, 1181
portasse for, 941
vicar of, *see* Thomas Wombe
inhabitants of, 800, 941, 1149, 1365
places in, Abbas Hall, 941n
'Camberis Croft', 49
'Kentyscroft', 941
'Mellebush', 941
Melle Tye, 941
'Sharneforde Medewe', 941
testators of, **630, 941, 1149, 1365**
CORNARD, LITTLE, church, bells in, 356n
tower of, 356, 356n
inhabitant of, 356
testators of, **356, *565***
Cornewaleys, Thomas, esquire, of Brome, 920
Corneys, John, 1165
Corray, Alice, of Little Livermere, 138
John, of Little Livermere, **138**
Richard, 138
William, 138
Corrowr, Robert, 736
Costyn, Clarice, 1471
Isabel, 1009
John, 683, 1009
Robert, 945
Cosyn, Agnes, of Cavenham, 95
John, 95; the younger, of Cavenham, *987*
Robert, of Stowmarket, 600

Thomas, of Cavenham, & family, **95**
William, 95, 987; of Cavenham, 1145
Cote, Thomas, of Boxford, 1331
William, of Boxford, 155
Coteler, John, of Palgrave, 1350
Roger, 1023, 1034
Coteras, Agnes, of Long Melford, 272; of Sudbury, 651
Joan, of Long Melford, 1387
John, 1387, 1424
Nicholas, of Sudbury, *651*
Robert, 1424; of Long Melford, & family, **1387**
Roger, 1387
Seman, of Long Melford, *272*, 1424
[*unnamed*], monk of Bermondsey, 1424
COTTON, church, chalice for, 400
inhabitants of, 400, 409, 764, 807n
lands in, 497, 764, 1169n
testators of, **400, 409**
wills proved at, 87, 206, 706
Cotton, John, of Glemsford, 1246
Walter, clerk, 319; the younger, 137
William, esquire, of Landwade (Cambs) & Exning, 489n
see also Catton
Cotyngham, Robert, 1419
Coullum, John, 1102
Counter, Henry, priest, 744
Coupere, *see* Cowper(e)
Cove, Thomas, 3
Covell, William, 345
Cowe, Alice, of Wickham Skeith, 22
John, of Wickham Skeith, & family, **22**
Cowelle, Agnes, of Sudbury, 1364
John, of Sudbury, **1364**
COWLINGE, church, 247, 897
porch of, 1386, 1386n
sepulchre light in, 1386
torches in, 896, 1386
inhabitants of, 730, 896
land in, 1390
places in, 'Botelerysfeld', 1387
'Cokerell & Struttonys', 863
'Deyyes' (tenement), 549
'Homondes Croftes', 897
'Symundes' (tenement), 1386
testators of, **549, *561*, *730*, 896, 897, 1386**
woods in, 863
Cowper(e) (Coupere), Agnes, 308; of Bradfield St George, 611; of Stowmarket, 53
Alice, 308; of Bardwell, 97; of Boxford, 547
Cecily, of Walsham le Willows, 672
Joan, 85; of Badwell Ash, **944**; of Boxford, 458; of Long Melford, 1167
John, 458, 548, 1231; the elder, 308, 458; the elder, clerk, 208; the younger, 308, 458, 529, 780; of Badwell Ash, 944; of Bardwell, & family, **97**; of Boxford, 144, **316**, 612; clerk,

of Boxford, 118; the elder, of Boxford, 380; the younger, of Boxford, 586; of Bradfield St George, **611**; of Diss, 492, 492n; of Walsham le Willows, & family, **672**

Margaret, servant, 1489

Marion, 148

Matilda, of Boxford, 316

Nicholas, of Knettishall, *1321*

Richard, of Gipping, 1291

Roger, of Long Melford, *1167*; servant, of Long Melford, 790

Stephen, of Stowmarket, **53**

Thomas, 168, 611, 1321; the elder, 458; the younger, 458; of Boxford, **458**; of Bury St Edmunds, 97; of Lawshall, 1241; of Old Newton, 908

Walter, 316, 547

William, 97, 308; of Boxford, 458, **547**; barker, of Boxford, 144; of Bradfield St George, 611

Crane, Adam, of Redgrave, 341, *1015*

Agnes, of Redgrave, 341

Anne, of Wortham, 6

Ed., of Palgrave, *997*

Isabel, of Botesdale, 1373

George, 6; of Redgrave, **341**

John, 341; of Botesdale, **1373**; of Wortham, **6**

Margaret, of Redgrave, 1015

Nicholas, priest, 1459; priest, of Thrandeston, 1459n

Richard, 1372; of Botesdale, 1373

Robert, 71, 199

Thomas, the younger, 873, 1239; of Wortham, 1372; the younger, of Wortham, 733, 1164

Walter, 341; of Wortham, **1372**

William, 6; of Thrandeston, 369

Cranewys(e) (Crenevys), John, vicar of Stoke by Nayland, 1088

Thomas, chaplain, 692

Crask, John, of Euston, 1250

Matilda, of Market Weston, **1250**

Robert, rector of Euston, 1250

Roger, 1250

CREETING (unspec.), inhabitants of, 851, 1161

testators of, *1161, 1294*

will proved at, 224

CREETING ALL SAINTS, rector of, *see* Thomas Dunch

land in, 348

testators of, *283*, **309**

will proved at, 309

CREETING ST PETER, church, 882n

inhabitants of, 665, 882, 1049

'Knyghtys' (tenement) in, 665

land in, 348

testators of, **20, 209, 665**, *998*, **1049**

Crek(e), Robert, barker, 874

William, 337; of Kirtling (Cambs), 1467

Creketot, *see* Cryketot

Creme, Alice, 842

Henry, of Rougham, 584, 611

Thomas, 552

Crenche, Alice, of Kedington, 572

John, of Kedington, **572**

Thomas, of Kedington, 572

Crenevys, *see* Cranewys(e)

Cressent, Edward, 1306

John, of Harleston, **1306**

Matilda, 1306

Richard, 1306

Rose, of Harleston, 1306

CRESSINGHAM (Nfk), land in, 877

Cristian, Katherine, of Ixworth Thorpe, 1396

Robert, of Ixworth Thorpe, *1396*

Crochon, William, of Sudbury, 800

Croft(y)s (Crofftes), Joan, 1400

John, archdeacon's official, of Bury St Edmunds, *xli, xlii*, 180, 180n, 1495, 1495n

Cros(se) (Croos), John, 557, 576, 1343; friar, 1132; the elder, 1246, 1448

Robert, 3

Thomas, 799, 1177

William, 1246

[*unnamed*], of Bury St Edmunds, 807

Crote, William, 781

Crouch (Crowche), Agnes, of Fornham St Genevieve, 443, 729

Geoffrey, of Fornham St Genevieve, & family, **443**

John, of Fornham St Genevieve, **729**

Crowe, Cecily, of Hitcham, 1116

Margaret, 1379

Matilda, of Soham (Cambs), 903

Thomas, of Hitcham, 1116; of Soham (Cambs), *xlix*, **903**

Crudde, Katherine, 91, 1077, 1168

Cruggeman, John, 453

Crull, Robert, vicar of Great Barton, 294, 294n, 430

Cryketot (Creketot), Ed., 1393

Joan, of Buxhall, 1393

John, 90; of Buxhall, & family, **1393**

Roger, 1393

Walter, 1393

Crymbyl(l), Joan, of Worlington, 1119

John, 1119; of Worlington, & family, **1119**

Cryspyn(g), John, of Gislingham, *970*

Margaret, of Gislingham, 970

William, 567

Crystemesse, *see* Christemasse

Crytot(t), Roger, of Lavenham, 618, 1243; clothier, of Lavenham, 1048

Cukhoo, *see* Wrottyng *alias* Cukhoo

Cukkokes, Thomas, 1369

CULFORD, rector of, *see* John Leder(e)

inhabitant of, 315

manor of, 315
  places in, 'Sheld' (land), 729
    'Syffrawastes', 489n
    'Sykysende', 315
    'Wykthornhill', 315
  testators of, **315**, *1464*
Cullum, family, 742n
  Isabel, of Thorndon, 785
  John, of Thorndon, 785
  Robert, 742, 785
  William, of Thorndon, **785**
  see also Coullum
Cullyng (Culling), John, of Eye, 320, 479
  Margaret, 320
  Richard, 320; of Eye, 972n; of Eye, & family,
    479
  Robert, 320
  Rose, 320
  Thomas, 479
  Walter, 479
Cumplyn, Joan, 1356
Curby, John, 769; of Lavenham, 126
  Margaret, of Lavenham, 768
  William, of Lavenham, 73, 102, *766*, **768**
Curray, John, 1083; of Little Livermere, 1074
  Richard, 1361
Curteys (Curtes), Agnes, of Westhorpe, 385
  Alice, of Wetherden, 557
  Emma, of Mildenhall, 219, 598, 598n, **1117**
  Helen, of Mildenhall, 1117
  Joan, of Brockford, 1417
  John, 219; servant, 375; the younger, 1117; of
    Brockford, **1417**; of Mildenhall, 1117; of
    Snailwell (Cambs), *703*
  Katherine, 703
  Thomas, of Wetherden, *557*
  William, the elder, 1117; the younger, 219; of
    Mildenhall, 598n; the elder, of Mildenhall,
    217, 1117; smith, of Pakenham, 343
Cusset, Katherine, of Newmarket, 732
  William, of Newmarket, **732**
Cutt, John, 1279
Cuttmay, Thomas, 951
Cuttyng, Thomas, 737

Dacrys, Reginald, of Woolpit, **655**
  Rose, of Woolpit, 655
Dade, John, 105
Dag, Katherine, of Acton, **1384**
DAGWORTH, *see* OLD NEWTON
Dak(k)e, William, rector of Palgrave &
  Sudbourne, 894
Daldeyn, John, Master, 362
Dale, Agnes, 828
  Alice, of Wickham Skeith, 879
  Edward, 879, 880, 1200
  Henry, 379, 399
  John, 581; of Ixworth Thorpe, 827

  Simon, of Wickham Skeith, 658, 801, **879**
  Thomas, the younger, 101
DALHAM, church, 247, 381, 1473
    tabernacle of Ascension of BVM in, 1285n
    tower of, 850
  'Dunstall' in, 1285, 1285n
  inhabitants of, 269, 450, 553, 1204, 1285, 1473
  land in, 269
  manor of, 553n
  poor of, 270
  testators of, *450*, **850**, *1204*
  wills proved at, 163, 190
Dalham, Joan, of Cowlinge, 730
  John, of Bottisham (Cambs), 1398
  Stephen, of Cowlinge, *730*
Dallyng, John, of Lavenham, 863
  Katherine, 863
  Margaret, 863
Dalton, John, vicar of Little Waldingfield, 1193
Damok, Agnes, of Elveden, 1211
  Thomas, of Elveden, *1211*
Damport, Alice, of Eye, 367
  Roger, of Eye, & family, **367**
Daniell, *see* Danyell
Danown, Agnes, of Sudbury, 1058
  Simon, of Sudbury, **1058**
  William, of Sudbury, 1058
Danyell (Daniell), Alice, 1346
  Geoffrey, 1346
  John, the elder, 1346
  Katherine, 1371
Darry, John, of Sudbury, 49
  Margaret, nun, of Malling (Kent), 49, 539
  Richard, 539n; of Sudbury, & family, **49**
  Sarah, of Sudbury, 49
Dassh, John, of Botesdale, rector of North Cove,
    596, 596n
  Peter, of Redgrave, 596
  Walter, of Botesdale, *596*
Daunham, Simon, of Sudbury, 276
Davy, Alice, 400; of Sudbury, 165
  John, 165, 409, 783; of Honington, 690*
  Margery, of Wratting, 919
  Michael, of Honington, **690**, **783**
  Richard, 409
  Thomas, of Sudbury, **165**; of Wratting, *919*
Dawe(s), John, of Ashley (Cambs), 381; the elder,
    of Ashley (Cambs), 822
  Robert, 529
de Gippewic, de Gypewic, *see* Yepisswich
de Leycestria, *see* Leycestria
de Mundeford, *see* Mundeford
de Newestrete, *see* Newestrete
de Thelton, *see* Thelton
DEBENHAM, gild in, 756
  inhabitants of, 1453, 1466n
Debenham (Debynham), Emme, of Stradishall,
    426

John, 2, 1070; of Shimpling, **184**; of Stoke by
Nayland, 638
Katherine, of Shimpling, 184
Richard, of Stoke by Nayland, 365
Robert, 426
Stephen, of Rickinghall, & family, *1070*
Thomas, of Stradishall, & family, **426**
William, the elder, 365; the younger, 365
Debyn, Thomas, 1123
Deeke (Deke), Thomas, 580
William, 435, 984, 1480
Deen, Henry, warden of house of friars, Ludgate,
London, 489
Deere (Dere), John, of Exning, **435**
Margaret, of Exning, 435
Richard, 429, 435
Thomas, 435, & family, 429; of Exning, **429**
William, 1437
Deersle, *see* Derisle
Dego, John, 799
Margaret, 711
Thomas, of Thorney, 386
Deke, *see* Deeke
Dekys (Dyxys), Edmund, 824
Geoffrey, 824
Joan, of ?Little Whelnetham, **824**
Thomas, 1195
Dele, Beatrice, 1005
John, 1005
Robert, 1005; of Oakley, 1005
Stephen, of Oakley, & family, **1005**
Deneys (Denys, Denyse, Denise, Deynys), Anne,
619
John, 1000; of Debenham, & family, 1453; of
Woolpit, 619, 757, 806
Rose, of Haughley, & family, **795**
Thomas, 795, 1453
see also Deynes, Denysy
DENHAM (by Barrow), inhabitants of, 269,
1110n
land in, 693
manor of, 41
testator of, **269**
Denham, Alice, of Ousden, 926
John, of Ousden, *926*
Thomas, 926
Densi, Margaret, 213
DENSTON, inhabitants of, 507, 696, 731
testators of, *715, 731*
Denston, Clement, archdeacon of Sudbury, *xli,
xlii, liv*n, *lv*, 231
John, esquire, 1142, 1246; esquire, of Denston,
507; of Rickinghall Superior, 900; of
Stansfield, 776
William, esquire, of Denston, 507n
Denton, Katherine, 515
[*unnamed*], *515*
Denysy, John, of Ixworth Thorpe, *1323*

see also Deneys
DEPDEN, church, 1218, 1418
tower of, 472
gild in, 125
inhabitants of, 472, 1218
land in, 279, 1410
places in, 'Beelyslond', 1410
testator of, **125**
wills proved at, 125, 205
Depden, Thomas, 1463
Derby, Joan, of Sudbury, 803
John, of Sudbury, 127, 276; mercer, of
Sudbury, **803**; of Thrandeston, *1304*
Derham, John, 91
Dere, *see* Deere
Derisle (Deersle), Richard, of Kirtling (Cambs),
379, 1468
Walter, of Kirtling (Cambs), 379
Derman, Peter, parson of Great Bradley, 193, 876
Deve, Agnes, of Burwell (Cambs), *555*
Dewe, Robert, of Redgrave, 671
Dexster, Anne, of Wetherden, 1215
John, 1215; of Wetherden, *1215*
Dey(e), Agnes, 794
Alice, 794
Avice, 146
Isabel, of Creeting, 1161
John, 517, 794, 1051, 1161, 1266, 1369; the
younger, clerk, 1174; of Creeting, **1161**;
of Hawstead, **411**, 417; of Lackford, 1361;
cordwainer, of Long Melford, 1369; the
elder, cordwainer, of Long Melford, &
family, *xlvi*n, **517**
Katherine, of Hawstead, 411
Margery, 794*
Nicholas, 231
Ralph, of West Stow, **1361**
Richard, 1259, 1370
Robert, 224
Stephen, 794
Sybil, of Eye, *886*
Thomas, 1161
William, of Mildenhall, 1259
[*unnamed*], *224*
Deynes, Alice, of Sudbury, 740
Joan, 421; of Sudbury, 740
John, 421n, 740
Matilda, 421, 740*
Robert, of Sudbury, & family, 421; dyer, of
Sudbury, **740**
Roger, 740; & family, 421
Rose, 740
William, 740
see also Deneys
DIDLINGTON (Nfk), warrener of, 489
DISS (Nfk), inhabitants of, 241, 241n, 242, 492,
1470
Dister, *see* Dyster

DITTON VALENS, *see* WOODDITTON (Cambs)
Dobbe, Melanie, of Sudbury, 1364
    Robert, tailor, 221
Dobbys, Thomas, of Sudbury, **188**
Dobyll, John, of Layham, 639
    Margery, of Layham, 639
Dobyn, John, 1117, 1259, 1404
Doffouus (Doffows), John, of Bardwell, **212**
Dogat, John, 343
Doke (Dooke), Robert, vicar of Bardwell, 97, 583
    Thomas, 1198
Doket, Richard, 42
Dole, Simon, 24
Dolet, John, of Westhorpe, 206
    Richard, 340
Doll, Robert, chaplain, 1419
Dolyngham, John, of Exning, 995, 995n
    Thomas, 1121
    see also Dulyngham
Donek, John, 1210
    Margery, 1210
Donewych, Anne, of Rushbrook, 1205
    John, of Rushbrook, *1205*
Donkon, Thomas, 932
Donyfaunte, *see* Bonef(f)aunte
Doo, Richard, 858
Dooke, *see* Doke
Doraunt (Dorawnt), John, of Dalham, *450*; of
    Nayland, *1222*
    Richard, 1234, 1324; of Brettenham, *1324*
    William, 1, 1222; of Thornham Magna, 1096
Dore, John, of Little Cornard, 356
Dormour (Dormowr), Joan, of Wickham Skeith,
    87, 705, 706
    John, 87, 706
    William, of Wickham Skeith, & family, **87,
    705, 706**
Dorward, Ralph, rector of Boxford, 1213, 1213n
Dow(e), Annabel, of Barnham, 281
    Gilbert, of Lakenheath, **388**
    Isabel, of Long Melford, 1424
    Joan, servant, 1473
    John, of Barnardiston, 85; of Barnham, **281**; of
      Kirtling (Cambs), **1348**; of Long Melford,
      1387; tailor, of Long Melford, 195, **1424**
    Katherine, of Haverhill, 1383
    Margaret, of Lakenheath, 388
    Matilda, of Kirtling (Cambs), 1348
    Peter, 281
    Thomas, of Ashley (Cambs), 1081, 1082; of
      Haverhill, **1383**
    William, 281
Dowres, Isabel, of Combs, 952
    Robert, of Combs, **952**
Drake, John, 188
Draper, Bartholomew, of Thetford, 59, 124
    John, of Great Wratting, *447*
    Robert, vicar of Woodditton (Cambs), 553n

Draweton, Richard, 1109
Drawswerd, Alice, widow, of Finningham, **385**
Drayton, John, of Drinkstone, 439
Drew, James, & family, 1371; of Mellis, 1163; the
    elder, of Mellis, & family, **1371**
    Matilda, of Mellis, & family, 1371
DRINKSTONE, church, 777
    light of BVM in, 1054, 1079
    inhabitants of, 370, 423, 439, 497, 777, 778,
      1054, 1056, 1253, 1339, 1459n
    places in, 'Berevys', 1054
      'Bowr, the' (land), 1253
      'Brantone medewe', 439
      'Calerwellefeld', 439
      'Cherchefeld, le', 439
      'Couperespyghtle', 439
      'Croftstretefeld', 439
      'Crostrete', 439n, 1253, 1253n
      'Jekesrowesende', 439
      'Lydgate Meadow', 1253
      'Lye, the' (land), 1253
      'Monewode, le', 439
      'Olde Monewode, le', 439
      'Pooles', 439
      'Poustrete, le', 439
      'Stubbynge', 439
    poor of, 1253
    roads in, 1253
    testators of, *115*, **423**, **439**, *778*, *922*, **1054,
      1056, **1079**, **1253**, *1339***
    wills proved at, 423, 439
Drinston, William, of Botesdale, 1368
Drury, Constance, of Troston, 1174, 1174n
    Joan, of Hessett, 231
    John, 231
    Matthew, 744
    Nicholas, the elder, esquire, of Bury St
      Edmunds, 552; esquire, of Thurston, 1246n
    Roger, esquire, of Hawstead, 1246, 1390;
      knight, of Rougham, 231, 552n
    Thomas, 231; esquire, 1240; esquire, of
      Hessett, 90, **231**; esquire, of Rougham, 827,
      827n, 828; of Troston, 1174, 1174n
    Walter, 231
    William, 231; of Bury St Edmunds, *l*; knight,
      231; knight, of Rougham, 827n
Dryle, John, rector of Cheveley (Cambs), 676,
    676n
Dryver(e), Ed., of Combs, & family, **660**
    Helen, of Combs, 660
    Hugh, 964
    John, 24, 880, 1376
    Nicholas, 1376
Duffeld, William, archdeacon's official, *xlii*
Duke, John, of Westley, 692
Dulyngham, John, 813
    see also Dolyngham
Dun, Gilbert, of Finningham, *75*, **178**

Sarah, *476*
William, servant, 69
Dunch, John, 13, 716; of Kennett (Cambs), *13*;
     stainer, of Mendlesham, 932; of Thornham,
     771; of Wordwell, 1060
   Robert, the elder, 1035; of Mendlesham, 3,
     333, 1159; the elder, of Mendlesham, 932
   Thomas, rector of Creeting All Saints, 3
   see also Knyth *alias* Dunch
Dunham, John, of Stanton, 1395
   Nicholas, friar, 90
   Thomas, 1395
Dunkon (Duncon), Augustine, of Stoke by
     Nayland, 192
   John, 333
   Katherine, of Mendlesham, 333
   Robert, of Mendlesham, & family, **333**
Dunton, Augustine, 153, 529
DUNWICH, friars (unspec.), 345
   house of Dominican friars (Preachers), 920,
     1371, 1402
Dyer, Nicholas, 1288
   see also Turnour *alias* Dyer
Dymbyll, Robert, of Groton, *1157*
   Rose, of Groton, 1157
Dymerssh, Robert, of Sudbury, *1311*
Dymmoke, John, 193
Dynglowe, John, of Walsham le Willows, 767
Dysney, Nicholas, 1072
Dyster (Dister, Dyxster), Agnes, 1104
   Alan, clothier, of Lavenham, 300n
   Isabel, of Long Melford, 1104
   Joan, of Long Melford, **181**
   Margaret, of Boxford, 296
   Robert, painter, of Boxford, & family, **296**,
     414; of Long Melford, & family, **1104**
   Thomas, 1104
   William, 1104
   see also Lorkyn *alias* Dyster
Dyt(t)on (Ditton), Robert, 454, 1048, 1114; of
     Lavenham, 446, 1446
Dyx, Thomas, 1400
Dyxster, *see* Dyster
Dyxys, *see* Dekys

EAGLE (Lincs), pilgrimage to, 489
EARL STONHAM, *see* STONHAM, EARL
EAST BRADENHAM (Nfk), land in, 877
EASTON BAVENTS, chapel of St Margaret in,
     1090n
Edelen, John, of Woodditton (Cambs), 28n
Ederych, Henry, 887
   see also Ederyk, Ordrych
Ederyk, Thomas, rector of Kettlebaston, 1300
Edgor, Edward, 53, 117, 714, 1050, 1126, 1134
   John, 117
   Robert, of Thorndon, **117**
   William, 117

Edo(w)n, Richard, 575, 604
   Thomas, 1364
Edward, Alice, 1233; of Fornham All Saints, 297
   Helen, of Fornham St Martin, 1233
   John, 826, 1233, 1379; of Fornham St Martin,
     849, 1152, **1233**; of Great Horringer, *826*; of
     Haverhill, *1147*
   Margaret, of Great Horringer, 826
   Thomas, 950; & family, 271; of Fornham All
     Saints, **297**
   Walter, 297
   William, 1033; of Great Horringer, 1233,
     1233n
Edward(e)s, Marion, 1255
   William, 141
EDWARDSTONE, boundaries of, 296n
   church, 548, 1388
     celebration on roodloft in, 931n
     vicar of, *see* John Framlyngham
   inhabitants of, 196, 196n, 234, 308, 931, 1209,
     1223, 1281, 1388, 1446, 1455n, 1496
   places in, 'Bolys' (tenement), 1209
     'Clowyeres' (tenement), 1209
     'Cocharys' (tenement), 1223
     'Hersentes' (tenement), 1223
     'Howmays Croft', 1209
     'Lyndoldys' (land), 1496
     'Lynys' (tenement), 1446
     'Schytborowstret', 308
     'Slonys' (tenement), 529
   testators of, *76*, **196**, **234**, **931**, **1209**, **1223**,
     1281, **1446**, *1455*, **1496**
Edwyn, Isabel, of Occold, 74
   Philip, 74
   William, 1486; of Bildeston, 520; of Occold,
     74
Egel(e)yn (Eglyn), Isabel, of Rickinghall Superior,
     1271
   John, 1271; of Rickinghall Superior, **1271**
   Richard, 206; of Gislingham, 726
   Roger, 1334
   Thomas, 1271; of Redgrave, & family, **726**
Egelot, John, of Clare, *646*
Egmere, John, 18
Elezs, *see* Elys *and* Talyour *alias* Elezs
ELMSETT, church, bells in, 1427
   gild in, 1427
   inhabitant of, 1427
   testator of, **1427**
ELMSWELL, church, legend for, 1495
   rector of, *see* Robert Hamelyn
   rood in, 397, 397n
   community of, 469
   inhabitants of, 397, 445, 563, 700, 725, 777n,
     787, 1001, 1112, 1337, 1338, 1495
   land in, 231, 713
   places in, 'Armournys', 1001
     'Apecrofte', 1001

'Barownys' (tenement), 1495
'Blakefen', 713
'Byll *alias* Calfawys' (land), 1001
'Cokkystrete', 1001
'Cressemedew', 1001
'Heggeforthebregge', 469
'Kebotyscroft' (close), 1495
'Langelonde', 1001
'Slederaker' (land), 1001
'Stapelys' (meadow), 713
'Westfeld', 1001
rye grown in, li
testators of, *397*, *445*, *496*, *700*, **725**, *855*,
    1112, *1199*, *1337*, *1338*, **1495**
will proved at, 107
Elmyswell, Amice, of Thwaite, 658
    John, of Thwaite, **658**
    Simon, 658
Elot, Thomas, clerk, 1461
Elsegood, John, of Elmswell, 496
Elsyng, Robert, of Hundon, *1189*
    Thomas, 1189
ELVEDEN, church, 1433
    rectors of, *see* Simon Burgon, John
        Heygham
    inhabitants of, 377, 891, 1211
    testators of, **111**, *780*, **891**, **1001**, *1211*
ELY (Cambs), cathedral priory, pilgrimage to,
        1207, 1466
    shrine of St Audrey in, 1207n
    diocese of, *xxxviii*n
    inhabitants of, 1319, 1471
    prisoners in, 256
Elyne, Agnes, of Hitcham, *265*
    Alice, 877
    Joan, of Haughley, *746*
Elyot, Nicholas, of Wangford (nr Brandon), *1266*
    Robert, 1266
Elys (Elezs, Helys, Helyis), Agnes, widow, of
        Lavenham, **172**
    John, of Lavenham, 172; of Stanton, 457, 677
    see also Elezs, *see* Talyour *alias* Elezs
Enderby (Endyrby), John, esquire, 41, 41n
    Robert, 1193
Engesthorp, William, 91
Erill, Margaret, servant, 1181
ERISWELL, birthplace of Sir Thomas
        Tuddenham, 489n
    churches, 352
    church/chapel of St Lawrence, 708, 352
    church of St Peter, 352
    rector of, 1484n
        see also William Starlyng
    inhabitants of, 166, 352, 751, 1101, 1484
    places in, 'Bullokes', 352
        'Butterys' (tenement), 352
        'Coclesworth', 352n
        'Dendyes' (cottage), 352

'Gossynes', 352
poor of, 708
testators of, *166*, *352*, *751*, *1101*
will proved at, 1121
Erl(e) (Erll), John, 823
    Thomas, of Haughley, 174, 795, *966*
    William, 18
    see also Erill
ESSEX, land in, 106
    'Coppydbussh' in, 800
    'Grenestret ende' ?in, 106, 210
        'Westfeld' in, 106, 210
    'Gromysland' in, 740
Eston, Richard, of Stowmarket, 288
Eton, Anne, of Haughley, 18
    John, of Haughley, & family, **18**
EUSTON, bridge, 535
    church, image of BVM in, 900n
        rectors of, *see* William Breton, Robert Crask
    consolidated with Little Fakenham, 920n
    inhabitants of, 535, 969n, 985
    testators of, *30*, **985**
    will proved at, 1206
Everard, John, 381; the younger, & family, 631;
        the elder, of Stoke by Clare, & family, **631**
    Margaret, of Stoke by Clare, 631
    Richard, 631
    Robert, 320
    William, of Lawshall, & family, **293**
Evisson, Thomas, of Needham (in Gazeley), 1110
Evrond, Alexander, of Wortham, 595
EXNING, church, 399, 499
    mortuary payment to, 440
    roodloft light in, 429
    sepulchre light in, 1480
    vestment for, 278
    vicar of, *see* John Caldwell
    gilds in, 278, 429, 435
    inhabitants of, 435, 590, 984, 995, 1265, 1480
    land in, 1265, 1463, 1475
    Newmarket originally partly in, 28n
    places in, 'Blakdenfeld', 278
        'Caldewell', 278
        'Cukkys Lane', 429
        'Estfeld', 278
        'Hallegate', 278
        'Herbesfeld', 278
        'Herberwfeld', 556
        'Hotyllery', 278
        'Ixnyngfeld', 1475
        'Lytylmoryfeld', 278
        'Partrychegate', 278
        'Westfeld', 1265
        'Wymyllefeld', 278
    sheriff's aid in, 995
    testators of, **278**, **429**, **435**, *590*, **984**, **995**,
        1128, *1308*, **1480**
    wills proved at, 337, 870, 1133

Exsale, James, friar, 1006
EYE, borough of, 354, 367, 623
    castle, 367
    church, 1276
        burial in tower of, 58n
        tower, building of, 886n, 1076, 1076n,
            1158n, 1276n
        vicar of, *see* Thomas Hervy
    gilds in, 492, 624
    hospital of Mary Magdalene in, 1293
    inhabitants of, 58, 320, 354, 367, 425, 432,
        433, 460, 492, 623, 707, 886, 906n, 972,
        1276, 1293, 1318, 1359n
    land in, 785
    manor of Netherhall in, 920n
    market-place, 367, 623
        stalls, 58n, 1023
    places in, 'Cokyngle' hamlet, 425, 479
        'Derneslowghwyeye', 479
        '?Goyses' (tenement)
        'Jekelys', 367
        Lambseth bridge, 624, 624n
        Langton, 623, 623n
        'Paradysch' (tenement), 367
        'Suddon' hamlet, 105, 367
    poor of, 369
    priory of Benedictine monks, 105
        church of, 1276n
        monks of, 479
    road, market-place to castle, 367
    testators of, **58**, **105**, **320**, **354**, **367**, *425*, **433**,
        460, *479*, *480*, **481**, **623**, **624**, **707**, *752*, *808*,
        886, *972*, **1293**, *1316*, *1318*
    wills proved at, 2, 15, 16, 58, 104, 105, 170,
        199, 241, 242, 345, 354, 409, 424, 425, 432,
        433, 460, 479, 480, 481, 509, 537, 595, 623,
        624, 707, 808, 886, 970, 972, 973, 981,
        1062, 1097, 1163, 1164, 1293, 1317, 1318,
        1334, 1340, 1341, 1438, 1476
Ey(e)re, Edith, of Glemsford, 251, *1087*
    Henry, 1492
    John, 251, 1087; of Lavenham, 161
    William, 251; of Glemsford, **251**, 1087n
Eyres, Christian, of Sudbury, 718
    John, the elder, of Sudbury, **718**

Fabbe, Elizabeth, of Burwell (Cambs), 1265
    John, 1357, 1475, 1480; the elder, 1265; the
        younger, & family, 1265; the elder, of
        Burwell (Cambs), **1265**
    Margaret, 1265
    Richard, of Burwell (Cambs), 1265
    Thomas, 1265
    William, of Burwell (Cambs), 1265
Fabyan (Fabyon), Isabel, of Exning, 1480
    John, 429; the elder, 435; the younger, 429,
        1480; of Exning, **1480**
Faco(u)n (Facown, Fakon), Alice, of Groton, 843

Joan, of Nayland, 860; widow, of Nayland,
    1080
John, 860, 1080, 1314; of Boxford, 308;
    the elder, of Boxford, **380**, 458; fuller, of
    Boxford, 118; of Nayland, 1080; the elder,
    of Nayland, **860**
Matilda, 380, 548; & family, 308; of Boxford,
    118
Regnold, of Groton, **843**
Thomas, 529
William, of Cavenham, *1145*
see also Nelyngge *alias* Facon
FAKENHAM, GREAT, church, 17
    testator of, **69**
    village of, 920n
FAKENHAM, LITTLE, church, 69, 920, 920n
    thatching of, 920n
    consolidated with Euston, 920n
    inhabitant of, 920n
    land in, 464
Fale, John, 33
Fannere, John, the elder, 707
Fareman, Roger, 221
Far(e)well, Alice, of Ashley (Cambs), 381; of
    Silverley, & family, **1473**
    Margery, of Newmarket, 54
    Ralph, 247; of Ashley (Cambs), **381**, 1472n
    Simon, rector of Ousden, 247, 247n
    Thomas, 896
    William, of Newmarket, & family, **54**, 381
Farowr, John, 523
Felaw(e), Katherine, 57
    Richard, merchant, of Ipswich, 1194
FELSHAM, 'cherchehous, le', in, 613
    church, 1244
        image of St Peter in, 611
        paving of, 901
        rector of, *see* John Munnyng
        tabernacle of St Katherine in, 613
        tower of, *xlvii*n
    inhabitants of, 613, 867, 1031n, 1255
    road to Gedding in, 901
    testators of, **185**, **613**, **901**, *1452*
    will proved at, 867
FELTWELL (Nfk), church of St Mary, 1008n
    cloth for altar of, 1008
    church of St Nicholas, 1008n
        tower of, 1008n
    inhabitant of, 1008
    land in, 1008
Feltwell, John, of Santon Downham, *371*
    Margery, of Santon Downham, 371, *1069*
    [unnamed], *418*
Felyp(p), John, 113, 368, 1213
    Margaret, 113
    William, 113
Femnale, John, the elder, 247; the younger, 247

Fen(n) (Fenne), Alice, of Kersey, 720; of
  Withersfield, 1456
  Isabel, of Boxford, 235
  Joan, the elder, 529
  John, 235, 529, 728, 953; the elder, 529; the
    younger, 529; the elder, of Boxford, &
    family, **235**; baker, of Boxford, 214; of
    Semer, **728**; of Soham (Cambs) *953*
  Katherine, 158; of Glemsford, & family, **1068**
  Margaret, 529; the younger, 529; of Groton,
    529
  Richard, 265, 728, 820; of Hitcham, 520, 1013,
    1416, 1459, 1461, 1461n; of Kersey, *720*
  Robert, of Withersfield, *1456*
  Stephen, 920; of Hopton, 975
  Thomas, 235, 953; of Groton, & family, **529**;
    chaplain, of Sudbury, rector of Borley (Esx),
    398, 421, 632, 740, 803, 937, 1181, 1469n,
    1489
  William, 158
  see also atte Fen
Fenforth, Joan, of Cheveley (Cambs), 739
  John, of Cheveley (Cambs), *739*
Fenkele, John, of Gipping, 346
  Marion, of Gipping, *xlivn*; & family, of
    Gipping, **346**
Fermer(e), Geoffrey, 73; of Lavenham, 102, 446
  Isabel, 944
Fermere *alias* Cook, Richard, of Badwell Ash,
  1397
  see also Cook
Ferour (Ferowr), Robert, vicar of Stowmarket St
  Mary, 90, 538, 1462n
Ferthyng, Ed., 177
  Edmund, 110
FINBOROUGH, GREAT, church, image of
    St Andrew in, 538
  palm cross at, 538
  inhabitants of, 129, 348, 810, 1343
  manor of 'Boytonhalle' in, 348
  places in, 'Baronys' (messuage), 90n
    'Cordes' (tenement), 90n
    'Davyes', 129
    'Helyouns', 538
  testators of, **129, 538, 810, 1343**
FINBOROUGH, LITTLE, church, 877
  places in, 'Cokerell by les Quens' (tenement),
    129
    'Cokerell by Davyes' (tenement), 129
  testator of, **1180**
FINNINGHAM, church, 87, 705, 706
    image of BVM in, 385
    sheet for high altar of, 385
    table-cloth and towel for, 385
  gild in, 385
  inhabitants of, 178, 347, 385, 879
  testators of, *75*, **178, 385**
  wills proved at, 24, 117, 344, 385, 406, 484,

    485, 486, 579, 658, 659, 746, 756, 764, 786,
    787, 788, 798, 906, 907, 932, 958, 962, 964,
    971, 1014, 1015, 1034, 1035, 1238, 1239,
    1315, 1316, 1349, 1350, 1445, 1453, 1482
FINCHAM (Nfk), inhabitant of, 1400
Firmage, Ed., 1403
  Joan, 1403
  John, the elder, of Barton Mills, 1403
  William, 1403
Fitzjon, *see* Fytzjon
Flawner, John, of Isleham (Cambs), 1041
Flegge, John, of Sudbury, 1181n
Fletcher(e) (Fleccher), Agnes, of Stradishall, 669
  Alice, of Botesdale, 325
  John, 1424; the younger, 82
  Robert, 1402; of Botesdale, **325**
  Thomas, of Stradishall, *669*
FLEMPTON, road from Fornham to, 61
Flemyng(e), Joan, of Wortham, 1239
  John, 928; of Wortham, 1239
Flete, Nicholas, 1304
Floure (Fowre), Clement, 1375
  John, the younger, 1375; the elder, of Clare,
    1375
  Meliora, of Cavendish, 1375
  Robert, of Cavendish, & family, **1375**
Flynthard, John, 599n
  Robert, of Troston, 599
Folkys, Ed., & family, 222
  Herry, of Kedington, & family, **1213**
Folour, John, of Sudbury, 234
  see also Fotour
Foot, Alice, 90
  John, of Long Melford, *1301*
Foorth (Forth), Alice, of Cockfield, 675
  Ed., of Cockfield, 1108
  Elizabeth, 899
  John, 899, 1108; of Cockfield, *1108*
  Robert, clerk, 1260, 1260n
  Simon, of Cockfield, *675*
  Thomas, of Cockfield, 675, 773, 773n
FORDHAM (Cambs), church, altar-cloth for,
    1131
  bells in, 1351n
  chantry chaplain of, 1131n
  porch of, 550
  roodloft painting in, 1351n
  inhabitants of, 240, 626, 839, 986, 1131, 1351
  places in, 'Burwellhalys', 1131
    'Cartestrete', 1277
    'Chypsalefeld', 1131
    'Fryth, le', 1131
    'Lytelhalys' (field), 1131
    'Morestrete Croftes, le', 1131
  poor of, 1277
  road in, to Soham (Cambs), 1131
  testators of, *94*, *550*, *551*, *839*, **986, 1131**,
    1277, *1351*, *1442*

wills proved at, 550, 551, 555, 556, 627, 683, 839, 986, 987, 1277, 1414, 1415

FORDHAM, deanery of, *xxxix*, *xxxix*n

Fordham (Foreham), Benedict, 662
George, of Bradfield St George, & family, **662**
John, chaplain, 1088; rector of Eriswell, 1484, 1484n
see also Fortham

FORNHAM (unspec.), inhabitant of, 1099
road to Flempton from, 61
testator of, *1099*

FORNHAM ALL SAINTS, church, books for, 271
churchyard wall of, 271
rectors of, *see* William Coote, Thomas Schercroft, John Smyth, William Woode
house of Franciscan friars in (Babwell), *see* BABWELL
inhabitants of, 12, 41, 180, 271, 1279
land in, 41, 443n, 683
poor of, 271
testators of, **12**, **222**, **229**, **271**, **297**, *950*, *994*, **1279**

FORNHAM ST GENEVIEVE, abbey mill in, 924
church, bells in, 729n, 924
books in, 1153
desks in chancel of, 1153
tower of, 729, 729n
inhabitants of, 271n, 443, 729, 924, 1153
land in, 315, 1279
places in, 'Mentill, la', 315
poor of, 271
testators of, **443**, **729**, **924**, **1153**

FORNHAM ST MARTIN, church, chalice for, 1152
cloths of altar in, 1356
panel on altar in, 1356
rector of, *see* John Nicoll
walls of, 849
gilds in, 1152
inhabitants of, 45, 849, 1152, 1233, 1356
places in, 'Cherchegrene, le', 1233
'Cowperesgrene, le', 1233
poor of, 271
testators of, **45**, **359**, **849**, **1152**, **1233**, **1356**

wills proved at, 4, 10, 11, 17, 23, 25, 30, 34, 35, 40, 44, 45, 56, 60, 61, 77, 90, 97, 98, 99, 100, 101, 103, 108, 109, 115, 116, 123, 138, 139, 150, 162, 164, 180, 181, 185, 187, 191, 194, 200, 230, 232, 233, 268, 269, 287, 293, 294, 297, 298, 300, 302, 303, 304, 306, 314, 315, 334, 340, 341, 343, 347, 350, 351, 363, 364, 370, 388, 393, 395, 411, 412, 422, 427, 430, 431, 436, 438, 441, 443, 445, 446, 450, 465, 466, 467, 468, 469, 470, 472, 473, 483, 488, 493, 495, 500, 501, 514, 525, 530, 531, 533, 534, 535, 536, 540, 542, 554, 558, 563, 576, 582, 584, 585, 588, 589, 594, 603, 606,

607, 611, 612, 614, 615, 616, 617, 619, 620, 633, 640, 644, 645, 653, 655, 656, 661, 663, 673, 675, 677, 684, 690, 692, 693, 694, 695, 698, 700, 709, 713, 722, 723, 740, 747, 749, 759, 760, 762, 777, 779, 780, 782, 783, 784, 796, 807, 821, 823, 824, 825, 826, 287, 828, 830, 831, 836, 848, 853, 855, 856, 861, 863, 868, 869, 874, 877, 884, 885, 887, 888, 890, 891, 892, 898, 899, 922, 924, 925, 928, 933, 954, 955, 957, 959, 960, 963, 965, 983, 994, 1002, 1003, 1004, 1006, 1007, 1017, 1018, 1019, 1020, 1021, 1025, 1036, 1041, 1046, 1054, 1055, 1060, 1069, 1075, 1076, 1078, 1079, 1086, 1098, 1099, 1108, 1109, 1110, 1113, 1117, 1122, 1129, 1131, 1137, 1139, 1152, 1153, 1160, 1171, 1172, 1180, 1183, 1191, 1195, 1201, 1205, 1210, 1211, 1217, 1219, 12120, 1233, 1236, 1240, 1246, 1251, 1254, 1256, 1260, 1261, 1263, 1264, 1266, 1268, 1279, 1287, 1288, 1289, 1291, 1297, 1298, 1299, 1301, 1303, 1345, 1346, 1353, 1356, 1361, 1362, 1363, 1367, 1368, 1369, 1378, 1386, 1387, 1390, 1391, 1394, 1400, 1401, 1402, 1403, 1404, 1407, 1410, 1433, 1436, 1437, 1441, 1450, 1463, 1465, 1471, 1472, 1474, 1478, 1481

Fornham, Robert, friar, 297

Forst, Margaret, 925

Forster, Nicholas, canon, of ?Kersey, 390

Forth, *see* Foorth

Fortham, Florence, of Kirtling (Cambs), 203
John, of Kirtling (Cambs), & family, **203**
Thomas, 203
see also Fordham

Foster, Alice, of Sudbury, 157
Peter, of Sudbury, & family, **157**
Richard, esquire, of Stoke by Nayland, **42**
William, 157*

Foster *alias* Geldere, Alice, of Glemsford, 109
Robert, of Glemsford, **109**

Fotour (Fotowr), John, 1086
Katherine, 1340
Thomas, 61
William, 1340; of Rickinghall Inferior, 101
see also Folour

Fowler, Geoffrey, 271
John, 271

Fowre, *see* Floure

FOXEARTH (Esx), church tower of, 362
land in, 800
meadow in, 578
wood in, 1246

Framlyngham, John, vicar of Edwardstone, 931, 931n

Fraunceys (Francceys), Alice, of Ixworth, 357, 366
John, of Long Melford, 1237
Katherine, 1370

Robert, of Ixworth, 78, 357, **366**
Stephen, 1186
Thomas, 1030, 1265
Walter, 366; of Long Melford, 1064
William, 1275
Freat, *see* Fryot(e)
Frebern, Helen, of Soham (Cambs), 1443
   John, of Soham (Cambs), *1443*
FRECKENHAM, inhabitants of, 135, 311
   peculiar of, *xxxix*
Freman, John, 335*, 1270; of Dalham, 1473; of
   Ixworth, **335**; of Redgrave, *1270*; of Stoke
   by Nayland, **1088**
   Margaret, of Ixworth, 335
   Richard, of Sudbury, 1364
Frend, John, 1159
Freng', John, 166
   see also Frynge
Freot(e), *see* Fryot(e)
Frere, Alice, of Mildenhall, 683
   Ed., rector of Hawkedon, 1369, 1387; chaplain,
     of Long Melford
   John, & family, 180; of Fordham (Cambs), *551*;
     of Mildenhall, li, **683**
   Margaret, 180; of Mildenhall, 683
   Robert, 683
   Thomas, 87, 180, 706
Fresswater (Freschwater), John, of Wetherden,
   1182, 1295
   Thomas, 231
Freton, Carole, 1306
   John, 21; the elder, 1306
   Lettice, servant, 1479
   Thomas, 1479
Frost, Agnes, of Wickhambrook, 302
   Joan, of Ousden, 1285
   John, 302*; of Hartest, 456; of Ousden, **1285**;
     of Wickhambrook, **302**
   see also Forst
Froyle, Richard, 774
Fryate, *see* Fryot(e)
Frynge, John, of Eriswell, *1101*
   Margery, of Eriswell, 1101
   see also Freng'
Fryot(e) (Freat, Freot(e), Fryate, Fryotthe), Agnes,
   758
   Alice, of Glemsford, 362
   Henry, 1123
   John, 322; of Glemsford, 1246; mercer, of
     Sudbury, **758**
   Katherine, **831**
   Margaret, 831
   Mariota, 362
   Peter, 758
   Robert, of Glemsford, 362
   Thomas, & family, 831; of Barrow, 494; of
     Glemsford, & family, **362**; of Sudbury, 157
FULBOURN (Cambs), Scargill family of, 446n

Fulcher, William, 1276; of Palgrave, 432
Fuller(e) (Fulere), Agnes, 1160
   Alice, of Barnham, **1362**
   Andrew, of Hawstead, 640
   Helen, of Walsham le Willows, 1040
   Isabel, 1259
   Joan, & family, 381; of Colchester (Esx), 126;
     of Mildenhall, 1259
   John, 719, 869, 1259, 1471; & family, 1473;
     chaplain, 803; 864; yeoman, 1123; of
     Barnham, 1303, 1362; of Hawstead, 640;
     of Little Saxham, 34, 245, 499, 1044; of
     Mildenhall, **1259**; of Sudbury, 864; mercer,
     of Sudbury, & family, **864**; of Walsham le
     Willows, *1040*
   Margaret, 944, 1174
   Margery, of Hawstead, 640
   Mary, of Hawstead, 640
   Robert, 1259
   Simon, of Mildenhall, 1259
   Thomas, 722, 864; collar-maker, of Bury St
     Edmunds, 616; of Colchester (Esx), 126; of
     Great Horringer, 297; of Mildenhall, 1259,
     1259n; of Soham (Cambs), 253
   William, 654, 1042, 1259, 1409; of Dalham,
     & family, 1473; rector of Little Blakenham,
     831, 831n
Furceney, John, of Bury St Edmunds, 729
Fyches, Robert, 1077
Fynch(e), John, 605; of Tostock, 133, 836
   Richard, of Tostock, *605*
Fyngham, William, 37
Fyn(n), Cecily, 406
   Richard, 1458
   Rose, 699
   Stephen, of Knettishall, 957
   William, 1458; of Rattlesden, *699*
Fyrmin (Fyrmyn), Agnes, of Boxted, 205
   John, 205, 1251
   Richard, 158, 205
   Robert, 205
   Thomas, 205
   William, of Boxted, 109, **205**
Fysch, Isabel, widow, of Worlington, **311**
   William, of Worlington, 311
Fyshyve (Fysyve), John, of Stoke by Nayland,
   1283
Fyss(c)her(e) (Fysher), Alice, of Redgrave, 1238
   Ed., 994
   Edmund, of Fornham All Saints, 12, 41
   John, 1238; of Redgrave, **1238**
   Margaret, of Hepworth, 17
   Nicholas, rector of Hengrave, 41
   Peter, of Hepworth, **17**

   Ralph, 69
   Richard, 17
   Robert, of Hengrave, 41

William, 17
Fysshhake, William, 740
Fyston(e), Alice, of Pakenham, 1046*
  Richard, & family, 749
  Thomas, of Pakenham, 343, *1017*, **1046**
  William, 1017
Fysyve, *see* Fyshyve
Fitzjo(h)n, John, 564, 595
Fytzkeys, John, the younger, of Lynn (Nfk), 1008
  Olive, 1008
  Petronilla, 1008
  Robert, 1008; of Brandon, **1008**
  Thomas, of Lynn (Nfk), 1008
  William, of Lynn (Nfk), 1008
Fyzstevene, Joan, of Hitcham, 51
  Roger, of Hitcham, **51**

Gale, William, 1446
Galey, Agnes, 1327
  John, of Soham (Cambs), 1319n, **1327**
  Margery, 1327
  Nicholas, 1319n, 1327
  Richard, 1319, 1327
  see also Gale, Caly
Galfawe, Agnes, of Woolpit, 1172
  John, 1172
  Roger, 1172
  William, of Woolpit, & family, **1172**
Galion, *see* Galyon
Galvysbane, John, 1052
  Thomas, 1052
  see also Calvesbane
Galy, William, 1258
Galyon (Galion, Gelyon), Isabel, of Fornham All
    Saints, 229; dame, of Mildenhall, 489, 489n,
    865
  John, the younger, 229
  Thomas, of Fornham All Saints, **229**; of
    Thetford, *xl*
  William, esquire, of Mildenhall, 489n
Gambo(w)n, Isabel, of Pakenham, 343
  John, 343, 1442
  Robert, 343
  William, of Pakenham, **343**
Game, Thomas, 97
Gamelyng, William, of Glemsford, 362
Gamon, Amy, 722
  see also Gamyn
Gamsay, Lawrence, 1061
Gamyn, Isabel, 146
  see also Gamon
Gant, Thomas, 1331
GARBOLDISHAM (Nfk), church of St John, 954
  church of All Saints, 954
  lands in, 954
  places in, 'Candelland-acre', 954
    'Goldpet', 954
    'Longfurlong', 954

'Mellemer', 954
'Stonhyll', 954
West Field, 954
'Wythtcrowche', 954
Gardener(e) (Gard(e)yner), Agnes, of Lidgate, 190
  Alice, of Beyton, 1394
  Eleanor, of Haverhill, 834
  Joan, 1369
  John, 190, 1394; the elder, of Beyton, **1394**; of
    Lidgate, & family, **190**
  Margery, of Stanton, **802**
  Nicholas, 1037
  Robert, 190
  Stephen, of Cotton, 764
  Thomas, 677, 1037; of Barton Mills, 46; of
    Haverhill, *834*
  William, of Combs, 743, 753; of Stanton, **677**
  see also Smyth *alias* Gardyner
Gareyn, John, servant, 254
Garland, William, 1270
Garre, Alice, 626
Garsun, Florence, 626
GASTHORPE (Nfk), rector of, *see* Thomas Hunt
Gatle (Gatteley), Alice, of Great Livermere, 180;
    widow, of Great Livermere, **116**
  Henry, & family, 180
  Robert, 180
  Thomas, 180, 1240; of Great Livermere, 116,
    180, 271, 1279n
Gaton, John, 522
Gawge (Gauge), Margaret, 1375
  Richard, 437, 1457
GAZELEY, church, 381, 1156
  burial in, 759
  vicar of, *see* Robert Asty
  window in, 303
  Heygham family of, 682n
  HIGHAM in, inhabitants of, 41n, 1439
    land in, 270, 270n, 693
    poor of, 270
    testator of, **1439**
  inhabitants of, 693, 759, 1439
  land in, 894, 894n
  lord of manor of, 682
  NEEDHAM in, inhabitants of, 881, 1110
    land in, 270, 270n, 894, 894n, 1439
    poor of, 270
    will dated at, 759
  places in, 'Oldebrightewell' (tenement), 303
    'Sparkes' (tenement), 303
  poor of, 270
  testators of, **303**, **759**, **1344**
  wills proved at, 193, 850, 926
Gebon, Richard, of Feltwell (Nfk), 1008
  William, of Euston, & family, *30*
GEDDING, land in, 413
  road to Felsham church, 901
Geddeney, William, & family, 278

Geddyng, Thomas, esquire, 853, 876; esquire, of
    Lackford & West Stow, 41
Geffrey, Peter, 1268
Gegenere, John, 1389
    Margery, of Worlington, 1389
    Robert, of Worlington, **1389**
    Simon, 1389
Gegge, John, 1328
Geldere, *see* Foster *alias* Geldere
Gelham (Jelham), Isabel, of Mildenhall, 1117,
    1404
    William, of Mildenhall, 1117, **1404**
Gell(e), John, 556; of Burwell (Cambs), **556**
    Katherine, 556
    Robert, 278, 556*, 995
Gelyon, *see* Galyon
Gen, John, of Kentford, 1110
Genistas, John, 1448
    see also Genytas
Genot, John, 492, 1053
    Thomas, 492
Gent, Alice, 1369
    John, of Euston, **535**
    Margaret, of Euston, 535
    Thomas, 1497; of Coney Weston, 535
    see also Jent
Gentylman, John, chaplain, 929; rector of
    Burgate, 438n; of Norton, 438
Genytas, Nicholas, 83
    Robert, 83
    see also Genistas
Gerard(e), Isabel, of Botesdale, 1354
    John, 1174, 1354
    Robert, 744, 1354
    Walter, rector of Hepworth, 17, 347, 353,
        802
    William, of Botesdale, & family, **1354**; of
        Needham in Gazeley, 759
Gerlyng, Margaret, 798
    William, of Stradbroke, 798
Gernays, John, of Long Melford, *201*
Gernoun (Gernown), Matilda, 897
    Thomas, of Haverhill, 312
Gerold, Thomas, of Glemsford, 1246
Gest, [*unnamed*], friar, 308
Gesyer, Petronilla, of Redgrave, 1016
    William, of Redgrave, *1016*
Gey. . .[*damaged*], Edmund, of Kedington, 266
Geyton, Nicholas, of Fincham (Nfk), & family,
    1400
Gibbesone, William, 756
Gilly, John, of Bradfield, 1394
Ginnote, Alexander, 816
    Clare, 816
Gippewic, *see* Yepisswich
GIPPING, chapel of St Nicholas in, *xlivn*, 346,
    1315
        painting of St Christopher in, 346

chapelry of, in Thorney, 19n, 20n
    inhabitants of, *xlivn*, 346, 1291
    places in, 'Cobelotis' cross, 346
        'Donkonys' (land), 1296
        'Trendlysheg' (meadow), 1296
    poor of, 20, 346
    testator of, **346**
GISLINGHAM, gild in, 958
    inhabitants of, 178, 280, 385, 726, 958, 970
    places in, 'Aldewestrete', 958
        'Caketon' (tenement), 958
        'Faverallstrete', 958
        'Maryonnys' (tenement), 958
        'Mekylcroft', 958
    testators of, **958**, *970*
    will proved at, 1140
Gladewyn, John, of Exning, 1265
Glanvyle, Margaret, 877
Glaswrygh, William, of Pakenham, *887*
GLEMSFORD, barn of the bishop of Ely in,
    1246
    church, meadow of rectory of, 1246
        silver cross for 1246
        tabernacle in, 158
        windows in, 362, 838
    gildhall in, 991n
    inhabitants of, 362, 391, 576, 805, 991, 1021,
        1246, 1353
    land in, 205
    places in, 'Alferymere', 1247
        'Brokestrete', 319
        'Cherchestrete', 391
        'Cobislane', 1246
        'Crekstrete', 137
        'Farenhell', 137
        'Ipscyes' (tenement), 1246
        'Jackes tenement', 391
        'Lally *alias* Peyes' (pasture), 205
        'Octedone' (field), 251
        'Pepelond', 1247
        'Peryerd, le' (tenement), 1246
        'Potylstrete', 362
        'Quatso' bridge, 158
        'Randispasture', 1246
        'Rithe, le' (close), 1246
        'Rodelowe' (pasture), 1246
        'Tylneyisweye', 137
        'Tylyeplace', 391
    poor of, 1068
    testators of, **109**, **137**, **158**, **251**, **319**, **362**, **391**,
        576, **644**, **688**, **838**, *991*, *1021*, **1068**, *1087*,
        1246, **1353**
    wills proved at, 122, 137, 587, 687, 1237
Glemsford, Agnes, 626
    Margery, of Somerton, 789
    Robert, of Somerton, **789**
Glover(e) (Glowere), Alice, 354; of Kersey,
    1067

John, of Kersey, & family, **1067**
Nicholas, 1067
Stephen, of Clare, & family, **833**
Thomas, 354; of Stanton, 457
William, & family, 833
Goche, *see* Gooche
Godale, Katherine, 944
Goday, Alice, servant, 1168
Rose, of Sudbury, 310
Thomas, carpenter, of Sudbury, & family, **310**
God(d)ard, Alice, 471
Geoffrey, servant, 346
Joan, 146; of Bradfield Combust, 1367
John, 868, 1119; the elder, 412; the younger, 412; of Rattlesden, **868**
Margaret, of Bradfield Combust, 412; of Fornham St Genevieve, 924
Nicholas, 412
Robert, 868, 1200; of Bradfield Combust, **1367**
Thomas, of Bradfield Combust, **412**
William, 412; the elder, 412
Godewyn(e) (Godwene), Agnes, 143, 1369
Beatrice, of Thornham Magna, 1096
John, 591, 1035, 1369
Richard, of Thornham Magna, **1096**
Thomas, 256, 1035
Godf(e)rey, Alan, of Little Whelnetham, & family, **533**
George, of Hessett, **933**
Isabel, of Little Whelnetham, 533
Joan, of Hessett, 933
Peter, 1078
Robert, 933
Godman, Joan, 1221
Margaret, servant, 865
Robert, of Cockfield, 901
Godwene, *see* Godewyn(e)
Godyng(e), Emma, of Groton, 816
Richard, 816
Thomas, 1419; of Groton, & family, **816**
William, 1242; of Pakenham, *10*
Gojon, Margaret, of Lakenheath, 1018
Robert, clerk, 69, 1018
Thomas, of Lakenheath, *1018*
Gold, Margaret, 90
Thomas, 90
see also Goolde
Goldfynche (Goldfinche, Golfynch), Thomas, of Botesdale, 1374n
William, 1238; of Botesdale, 1374
Goldston (Golston, Gorldston), Alice, of Old Newton, 1411
Richard, 1411
Thomas, of Old Newton, 340, **1411**
Goldyng, Audrey, of Preston, 814
John, 80, 946, 1246; the elder, 1375; of Cavendish, **80**; of Sudbury, 740
Richard, 740

Thomas, of Preston, *814*
William, of Eye, 886
Golfynch, *see* Goldfynche
Golofre, Isabel, of Eye, 354
Thomas, of Little Thurlow, *1197*
William, of Eye, **354**
Golston, *see* Goldston
Gonevyn, Agnes, of Kirtling (Cambs), 1432
Henry, of Kirtling (Cambs), **1432**
Gooch(e) (Goche), Amfrith, 48
Geoffrey, of West Stow, 1022
John, 336, 373, 1379; of Norton, 1313; saddler, of Sudbury, 632
Lawrence, of Elveden, 891
Nicholas, of Sudbury, **48**
Robert, 48
Thomas, 48
Walter, 373
Goode, Amice, 6
Goodreve, John, chaplain, 180
Goodynche, Agnes, 1133
Googh, John, of Wickhambrook
see also Reede *alias* Googh
Goolde, John, 1001
see also Gold
Goore (Gore), Alice, of Bardwell, 55, *1275*; of Barnham, 1303
John, of Bardwell, **55**, 1275n; of Barnham, *1303*; the elder, of Barnham, **377**
Katherine, of Barnham, 1302
Lucy, of Barnham, 377
Margaret, of Elveden, 891
Robert, of Bury St Edmunds, 55
Thomas, 377; of Barnham, **1302**
William, of Elveden, 377, **891**
see also Sampson *alias* Goore
Goos, Margaret, 488
William, 488
Gore, *see* Goore
Goslyn(g) (Gos(s)elyn), John, 5; friar, of Babwell, 474
Thomas, chaplain, of Hartest, 158, 158n, 687
William, 241; commissary, 365; Master, of Ipswich, 158n; rector of Ipswich St Matthew, 365n
Gosse, Agnes, of Fordham (Cambs), 986, **1131**
Henry, of Fordham (Cambs), **986**
John, 986, 1131
Thomas, of Hawkedon, *1251*
Gosselyn, *see* Goslyn(g)
Goule, Alice, 799
John, 799; of Mendlesham, **799**
see also Gowle
Goundre, Rose, 795
Gowin, John, 1289
Gowle, John, chaplain, 1462; of Stowmarket, 882, **1462**
Margery, of Stowmarket, 1462

Richard, 1462
Thomas, 1462
see also Goule
Graunt(e) (Grounte), Agnes, 278
John, 278
Grave, John, 1478
Gregory (Gregori), John, rector of Worlington,
    865, 870, 1009, 1156
Thomas, of Thrandeston, *575*
Grene, Agnes, of Nayland, 318
Alice, 333, 893; of Lindsey, 1429; of Thurston,
    760
Andrew, of Fornham All Saints, & family,
    1279; of Risby, 271
Anne, of Creeting St Peter, 1049
Christian, 1497
Henry, of Thurston, 1451
Isabel, of Creeting St Peter, 20; of Fornham All
    Saints, 1279
James, 1429
Joan, of Thorney, 882
John, 131, 760, 893; esquire, 1181; the
    younger, of Bardwell, *453*; of Chelsworth,
    1428; of Lindsey, 1428; of Newmarket, **716**,
    724, **793**; of Rattlesden, *455*
Katherine, of Newmarket, 724, 793
Margaret, 271
Margery, of Withersfield, 893
Nicholas, of Thurston, **760**
Robert, 882; of Thorney, & family, **882**
Thomas, 724, 793; of Creeting St Peter, &
    family, **20**; of Thurston, 760
Walter, 20; of Withersfield, & family, **893**
William, 20, 1429; of Creeting St Peter, 882,
    1049; of Lindsey, **1429**; of Nayland, *318*
Greneg(r)es, Isabel, of Great Fakenham, 69
John, of Troston, 69
Ralph, 69; of Great Fakenham, **69**
Thomas, 1174
William, 69
Grenehale, Oliver, 390
Grenehyl, John, 639
Grey, Gilbert, friar, of Clare, 149
John, 58; of Clare, 730n; of Eye, 354, 479
Roger, 723
Greyve, Thomas, 334
Grom, *see* Groom
Grondysborgh, *see* Bocher *alias* Grondysborgh
Gronger, Alice, 1497; of Hitcham, 1047
Hugh, of Wickham Skeith, & family, **228**
Joan, of Hopton, 1179; of Wickham Skeith, 228
John, 1200; of Hitcham, *1047*; of Hopton, **1179**
Richard, 1179
William, 228
Groom (Grom), John, the elder, 300; of Long
    Melford, 790
Robert, of Lavenham, 1091
Rose, 1104

GROTON, boundaries of, 296n
church, 548
    ornament for, 816
    rector of, *see* William Bullok, Thomas
        Grygge
    silver cross for, 1150
    silver ship for, 529
inhabitants of, 812, 816, 942, 1150, 1157, 1388
land in, 42, 296, 458, 942
places in, 'Brom Pytyll', 1388
    'Casteleyns Brygge', 1280
    'Fawncys' (land), 1388
    'Foordes', 529
    'Ginnot' (tenement), 816
    'Holywad Brookes' (meadow), 1150
    'Ildyrbosse' (close), 812
    'Lysses Croft', 1388
    'Robynis', 296
    'Wodefynnys Smyth', 308
poor of, 1388
river at, 1150
road to church of, 529
testators of, **529**, **812**, **816**, **843**, **1150**, *1157*,
    1388
wills proved at, 42, 88, 195, 196, 383
Groundschawe, Richard, 1180
Grounte, *see* Graunt(e)
Growng(?), John, 24
Grubbe, Walter, of Thurston, 760
Grug(g)eman, Elizabeth, 1206
Emma, of Bury St Edmunds, & family, 859; of
    Ixworth, 859
Isabel, of Euston, 985
John, of Barnham, 1206n, **1078**; of Ixworth,
    859
Robert, of Euston, *985*
Gryce, Joan, of Stoke by Nayland, 154
John, of Stoke by Nayland, *154*; the younger, of
    Stoke by Nayland, 154
Gryffyn, Alice, 1098
Thomas, *1098*
Grygge, Agnes, of Lavenham, 350
Andrew, 350
John, of Lavenham, **350**; the elder, of
    Woodditton (Cambs), 135
Rose, of Lavenham, 350
Thomas, rector of Groton, 144
Grymprest, Walter, 623
Grymston, John, of Bury St Edmunds, 279
Grymsyk, John, 854; of Hepworth, **854**
Margaret, of Hepworth, 854
Gurcok, William, of Bury St Edmunds, 100
Gybb(e), Agnes, 342
John, 342; of Kersey, **342**
Margaret, of Kersey, 342
Simon, 390; & family, 342
see also Gyppe
Gygner, Thomas, 751

Gylberd, John, 80
Gylys, Ralph, of Wetheringsett, 641
    Reginald, 248; of Wetheringsett, 15
    Roger, of Nayland, 200
Gymer, Alice, of Bury St Edmunds, 462
Gypewic, *see* Yebyswych
Gyppe, William, of Kersey, 719
    see also Gybbe
Gyy(e), Alice, 676
    John, 676; clerk, 165

Hach(e), John, 571, 1331
    Rose, 57
Hachull, Robert, chaplain, 37
Hacon (Hakon), John, servant, 823
    Nicholas, vicar of Acton, 289, 289n, 1280
HADDENHAM (Cambs), church, 258
    poor of, 258
Haden(h)am, *see* Hadynham
HADLEIGH, gild in, 639, 1427
    inhabitants of, 48, 108, 197, 403, 516, 639,
        643, 942
    lands in, 942
    peculiar of, *xxxix*
    places in, 'Bryddys' (tenement), 1479
        'Tyleres Crofte', 334
HADLEIGH HAMLET, boundaries of, 29n
Hadley, John, 658
Hadynham (Haden(h)am, Hadnam), Agnes, of
        Kentford, 762
    John, the elder, 762; the younger, 762; of
        Kentford, 759, 894; the elder, of Kentford,
        762
    Thomas, 762
HAILES (Glos), abbey of Cistercian monks,
        1398n
    blood of, 1398
Hakon, *see* Hacon
Halff, Henry, servant, 150
Halke, Richard, 365
Hall(e) (Haule, Hawle), Elizabeth, of Semer, 990
    Joan, 680
    John, the elder, 680; the younger, 552, 680; of
        Semer, *990*; of Thurston, *1407*
    Peter, 680, 1407
    Robert, 680, 990
    Rose, of Withersfield, 914
    Thomas, 680; of Stradishall, 266; of
        Withersfield, *914*
    William, 128, 686; chaplain, 149; vicar of Clare,
        149n; of Hartest, 276; of Hopton, 969;
        rector of Newton (by Sudbury), 149n; rector
        of Redgrave, 1238
Halstede, John, of Mildenhall, 598
Hamelyn, Robert, rector of Elmswell & Redgrave,
        889, 889n
Hammyle (Hamvyll), Rose, of Little Bradley,
        1430

Thomas, of Little Bradley, **876**
    William, of Stradishall, 1430
Hamond (Hamaund), Emot, of Timworth, 1288
    Isabel, of Nayland, 142; of Tuddenham, 427
    Joan, of Lawshall, 140
    John, 1288; of Lawshall, *140*; of Thrandeston,
        543, *1062*; of Tuddenham, *427*
    Richard, 427, 488; of Barrow, 187, 471
    Thomas, of Lawshall, 140, 293
    William, 103; Master, 588; of Lawshall, 140; of
        Nayland, *xliii*n, **142**; of Timworth, **1288**; of
        Tostock, 1288
Hamond *alias* Pedder, Alice, of Ixworth, 1033
    Robert, of Ixworth, 961n, **1033**
Hamvyll, *see* Hammyle
Hamylden (Hamulden), Joan, 1077
    Richard, 740
Hancok (Hankok), Joan, of Newmarket, 379
    John, 379; of Freckenham, 311
    Ralph, the younger, 399; of Newmarket, **379**,
        379n; the elder, of Newmarket, **399**
    Richard, 379
    Thomas, of Mildenhall, 311
    Walter, 379
    William, 379
Hanyngfeld, William, esquire, 293n
Hanyngton, William, 1321
Harald (Harold), Roger, 734, 875, 1165; of Mellis,
        1371
    Thomas, 1276
    William, 1371
Hard, Robert, 1157
Hard(e)hed (Harded, Hardherd), Alice, 674; of
        Bury St Edmunds, 394n
    John, chaplain, of Bury St Edmunds, 394n
    Margaret, 674
    Robert, of Buxhall, 394; of Rattlesden, 1031
    Thomas, of Hitcham, *979*
    Walter, & family, 674; of Rattlesden, 394,
        394n, 1032
HARDINGHAM (Nfk), rectory (living) of, *xlii*n
Hardman, Henry, chaplain, 772
HARDWICK (extra-parochial), road in, 640
Hardy (Haydy), Alice, of Rattlesden, 1032
    Matthew, of Rattlesden, 1032
Hardyng, Joan, 367
Hare, William, 869; of Pakenham, 887, 1017
HARGRAVE, church, 271, 449
    land in, 449, 1410
    places in, 'Clayacre', 1410
        'Weerden', 1410
        'Weerden Mede', 1410
    poor of, 271
Harie(?), William, of Bardwell, 78
HARKSTEAD, manor of Netherhall in, 90n
Harlegrey, Agnes, of Mildenhall, 1219
    Henry, of Mildenhall, li, **1219**
    John, 1219

William, 1219
HARLESTON, church, manual for, 497
  'Geggys Croft' in, 1306
  inhabitant of, 1306
  lands in, 977
  testators of, **497, 1306**
  will proved at, 394
Harleston (Harlstone), Elizabeth, 838n
  John, 1021; esquire, 838
  Margery, 838n
HARLING, WEST (Nfk), church, 534
  hall in, 836n
Harlstone, *see* Harleston
Harlyng(e), Alice, of Hopton, 68
  John, 622
  Katherine, 723
  Nicholas, of Hopton, 323, 622
  Richard, 68; of Hopton, & family, **622**
  Stephen, 622
  Thomas, of Hopton, *68*, 622*, 723, 1178
Harold, *see* Harald
Harp(e)ley, Alice, dame, of Great Barton, 180n,
  294n
  John, knight, 294n
HARSTON (Cambs), inhabitant of, 222
HARTEST, chapel of St Mary, 158n
  church, 1390
    roodloft in, 456
  inhabitants of, 158, 276, 456, 687, 1075, 1356,
    1390
  places in, 'Hervyis', 456
    'Smythys' (land), 456
  testators of, **456, 687, 1075,** *1136*
  wills proved at, 1087, 1136
HARTISMERE, deanery of, *xxxviii*n, *xxxix*
Harward, Hugh, friar, 1386
Harwell, Joan, of Barrow, 290
Harwham, *see* Horowham
Hasylwode, Katherine, of Haverhill, 781
  Thomas, of Haverhill, *781*
HATFIELD BROAD OAK (Esx), priory of
  Benedictine monks, 1473n
HAUGHLEY, church, 497, 1134, 1462
    candlesticks for, 741
    chapel of BVM in, 741
  inhabitants of, 18, 174, 710, 741, 775, 795,
    977, 1252, 1307, 1406, 1411
  land in, 497
  places in, 'Bell Lane', 174
    'Morebys' (tenement), 461
    New Street, 1295n
    'Okyes' (tenement), 795
  testators of, **18, 174, 461,** *710*, **741,** *746*, **775,**
    795, *966*, **1307,** *1406*
  wills proved at, 18, 174, 410, 461, 795, 862,
    1306, 1307, 1392, 1393
Haule, *see* Hall(e)
Havell, John, of Bildeston, 1459

Robert, 1459
Havelyn, Margery, 341
HAVERHILL, churches, 50n
  lower church of St Mary (market chapel),
    50, 50n, 306, 633
    'daybelle' and 'curfewe' in, 633
    roodloft 'vice' in, 50
  upper church of St Mary ('Button', 'St
    Botulph'), 50n, 490, 491, 1092
  gilds in, 491, 1383
  Hamlet (formerly Esx), *xl*
  inhabitants of, 210, 211, 306, 312, 633, 708,
    781, 834, 968, 1011, 1012, 1092, 1383, 1457
  places in, 'Angnyestrete', 490
    'Bradcroft' (field), 50
    'Clobbesgardyn', 490
    'Dedemanyslane', 1457
    'Dounhel Croft', 490
    'Frithecroft', 50
    'Fychettys', 211
    'Harpelond', 633
    'Jonet Webbesland', 50
    'Kennyfeld', 490
    'Mechylfeld', 490
    'Romelane' (?Esx), 106, 210
    'Segreynys, le', 490
    'Stall, le', 633
  testators of, **50, 106, 210, 211, 306,** *312*, **490,**
    491, **633,** *781*, *834*, **968,** *1011*, *1012*, **1092,**
    1147, *1148*, **1383, 1457**
  wills proved at, 149, 236, 312, 491, 646, 834,
    876, 967, 968, 1068, 1092, 1093, 1094,
    1146, 1148, 1229, 1383, 1456
Haward (Howard), John, 664; esquire, 1194;
  rector of Buxhall, 90, 877
Hawe, Nicholas, of Cavendish, *946*
  William, 946
HAWKEDON, church, 109
  new bells for, 735
  parishioners owe money to, 735
  rector of, *see* Ed. Frere
  cloth in, *li*
  inhabitants of, 735, 1203
  testators of, **735, 1203,** *1251*
  Thurston End in, 735, 735n
Hawkedon (Hawketon), John, chaplain, 1458,
  1486
Hawker, William, 551
Hawle, *see* Hall(e)
HAWSTEAD, church, tower of, 411, 411n
  Cullum family of, 742n
  inhabitants of, 351n, 411, 417, 640, 1246, 1390
  land in, 417
  testators of, *100*, **411, 493, 640**
Hawys, George, chaplain, 169, 1272; rector of
  Barrow, 169n
  Stephen, of Market Weston, 17
Hay, William, of Barnardiston, **85**

Hayde, Thomas, 455
  see also Hardy
Haydyff, Alice, of Rattlesden, 1143
  Thomas, of Rattlesden, *1143*
Hebyll, John, 1251
Hecham, Joan, 475; *formerly* Bocher, 741
  [*unnamed*], *475*
Hecham *alias* Bocher, Stephen, of Haughley, 741n
Hedge (Hedgh), *see* Hegge
Hedgeman, Elizabeth, of Glemsford, 1246
  Joan, of Glemsford, 1246
  John, 1246; the elder, of Glemsford, & family,
    1246
  Ralph, 1246
  Robert, 1246
  Thomas, 1246
Hedirsete, Edmund, knight, patron of Buxhall,
    90n
  Isabel, widow, 90n
Heed, Thomas, of Long Melford, 1363
Heerne, *see* Herne
Hegelyn, John, 952
Hegge (Hedge, Hedgh), Alice, 963
  Andrew, 585
  John, 585, 1269; servant, 1001; of Ingham, &
    family, **227**, 963n, 1074n
  Margaret, of Icklingham, 585; of Ingham, 227;
    widow, of Ingham, & family, **963**
  Ralph, of Icklingham, **585**
  Thomas, & family, 963; of Timworth, 963n
  William, 227, 856, 963; of Ingham, 1074
Heggesete, Thomas, 33
  see also Hesset(e)
Heigham (Heygham, Hygham), John, vicar of
    Burwell (Cambs) St Mary, 682, 682n, 927n,
    1162, 1265
  Thomas, 236; of Denham (by Barrow), 1110;
    of Higham in Gazeley, 41
Hekedon, John, of Timworth, *225*; of Tuddenham,
    363
  see also Hykedon
Hel(l), Alice, of Stowmarket, *386*
  Joan, of Polstead, 529
  John, 529; of Elmswell, 563
  Thomas, 158
Helm, John, of Barrow, 57
Helpston (Helpyston), Isabel, 1240
  John, 1240
  Nicholas, 783
Helys (Helyis), *see* Elys
Hemgrave, Joan, dame, of Hengrave, 41
  Thomas, knight, of Hengrave, 41, 41n
Hempston, Nicholas, 690
Hempyngham, Ralph, 69
Hemysby, Geoffrey, friar, 429
HENGRAVE, church, burial in, 41
  rector of, *see* Nicholas Fyssher
  inhabitants of, 41, 924

land in, 1279
manor of, 41
testators of, **41, 61**
will proved at, 41
Henman, John, of Occold, *659*
  Margaret, of Occold, 659
HENNY, GREAT (Esx), curate of, 1181
HEPWORTH, church, 802
  alabaster 'table' for, 1257n
  rector of, *see* Walter Gerard
  community of, 802
  inhabitants of, 854, 1063; 1494
  land in, 802, 1186
  places in, 'Agas's' (tenement), 353
    'Brounescroft', 353
    'Burchardes' (tenement), 854
    'Feldwey', 802
    'William Smethys' (tenement), 854
    'Wrothelond', 353
  testators of, **17**, **353**, **854**, **1257**
  wills proved at, 393, 672, 807, 951
Herberd (Herbert), Alice, 1276
  Anne, 1276
  Cecily, 1276
  Joan, 1276; widow, of Yaxley, **1276**
  John, 1276; of Yaxley, 1276
  Katherine, 1276
  Richard, 492, 1276
  Robert, 1276
  Rose, 1276
  Thomas, 1276; of Long Melford, 1064
Herd(e), John, butcher, 322; the elder, 993
  see also Hirde
Herfrey, Peter, 575
Hergiswell, Ed., of Westley, *542*
Heris, John, 1298
Herman, Avice, of Rickinghall Superior, 194
  Henry, 194
  William, of Rickinghall Superior, **194**
Hermer, Alice, of Little Horringer, 1291
  John, of Great Saxham, 57, 77; of Great
    Saxham, & family, **77**
  Margaret, of Great Saxham, 77
  Richard, 77; of Little Horringer, 422; of Little
    Horringer, & family, **1291**
  Robert, 77, 1291; of Lavenham, 77
  Thomas, 77
Herne (Heerne), John, 1319; of Soham (Cambs),
    478
  Margaret, of Soham (Cambs), 1483
  William, of Bardwell, 97
  [*unnamed*], of Soham (Cambs), **1483**
Hernyngiseerth, John, 340
HERRINGSWELL, church, 1481
  rector of, *see* John Wagge
  land in, 894n
  poor of, 270
  testator of, *704*

wills proved at, 14, 1030
Herry, Agnes, of Fornham All Saints, 1279
  Andrew, 1279
  Geoffrey, 1279*; of Fornham All Saints, 180;
    of Fornham All Saints, & family, **271**
  John, of Fornham All Saints, 1279
  Marion, 1279
  Mariota, of Fornham All Saints, 271
  Robert, 744, 1279; of Bildeston, 520
  Thomas, 1279
  William, 1279
Hersent, Cecily, of Edwardstone, 1223, 1281
  Stephen, of Edwardstone, & family, **1223, 1281**
  Thomas, 458, 816, 1223, 1281
Herset(e), Isabel, of Long Melford, *217*; of
    Sudbury, 31
  John, 31; of Sudbury, 217n, *31*
  Robert, 31, 1175
Hert(e), Agnes, 1495
  Alice, of Worlington, 89
  Henry, of Wetheringsett, 641; of Wetheringsett,
    & family, 345
  Isabel, of Wetheringsett, 345
  Joan, 777; of Elmswell, 397; of Haverhill, 306
  John, 580, 897, 777; of Bardwell, 97, *1232*;
    cordwainer, of Bardwell, 1231; of Cowlinge,
    897; of Elmswell, 397; of Haverhill, **306**; of
    Worlington, **89**
  Margery, of Elmswell, 1495n
  Nicholas, clerk, 89
  Robert, 397
  Thomas, 448; of Wixoe, **580**
  William, 580, 777; of Elmswell, 445, 1001,
    1338, 1495
HERTFORD (Herts), gild of, 1216, 1216n
  hospital in, 1216n
Herv(e)y (Hervye), Alice, of Wortham, 595
  Amice, 595
  Anne, of Barnardiston, 1488
  Helen, of Layham, 1336
  Joan, 146
  John, 161, 595, 663, 1488; of Lavenham, 376;
    of Layham, *1336*; chaplain, of Sudbury
    college, 91
  Katherine, 161
  Nicholas, 595
  Richard, 568; & family, 876; of Barnardiston,
    249, 549, *1488*
  Robert, parish chaplain, of Lavenham, 263,
    446, 1002, 1048
  Thomas, 552, 1340; vicar of Eye, 886, 1293; of
    Thorney, 711; the younger, of Wortham, **595**
Herward, Agnes, 988
  Alice, of Sudbury, 1077*; widow, of Sudbury,
    993
  Isabel, 1077
  Joan, of Sudbury, 1077

John, 889, 1077*, 1226, 1230, 1247; of
    Bardwell, 212; of Sudbury, *606, 645*, 740
  Matilda, of Sudbury, 606, 645
  Margery, of Sudbury, 947
  Richard, 740, 947, 988, 993, 1077, 1364
  Thomas, of Sudbury, *947*, 1077
  William, 956, 1077; of Sudbury, 740, 947n; the
    elder, of Sudbury, 993, **1077**
Heryot, Thomas, of Bures, *384, 657*
Hesset(e), Agnes, 1295; of Wetherden, 1182
  John, the elder, 33; of Wetherden, 519, 1182
  Thomas, of Wetherden, **1182**
  Walter, of Glemsford, 1246
  see also Heggesete
HESSETT, church, 1240
  altar of St Mary in, 1113
  rector of, *see* William Chapelleyn
  inhabitants of, 90, 232, 370, 933
  land in, 1410
  places in, 'Mellefeld, le', 232
    'Mundyslane', 857, 1113
    'Stonhames' (land), 583
  poor of, 231, 933
  road in, 933
  testators of, **231**, **232**, *364*, *370*, *825*, *857*, *933*,
    1113
Hethe, family, 305n
  Anne, of Hengrave, 41
  Joan, of Long Melford, 221
  John, of Long Melford, **221**
  Robert de, of Little Saxham, 41n
  Thomas, 409; esquire, of Hengrave, **41**
Hetheman, Alice, 274
  John, of Bures, *274*
Hewet, Richard, of Edwardstone, 1388
Hewloth, John, webster, of Barnham, 281
Hewy, Thomas, 703
Heyford, Edmund, 69
Heygham, *see* Heigham
Heylok, Alice, 249
  John, 249; of Barnardiston, **249**
  Richard, 249, 1146
  William, 249
Heyn, Robert, 1492
Heyward, John, 1346; of Barnardiston, *84*; of
    Hessett, 825
  Marg', *852*
  Thomas, the younger, 193
  William, 81, 1227, 1228
  [*unnamed*], *503*
Heywode, Agnes, of Woodditton (Cambs), 553
  John, of Woodditton (Cambs), 135, 678, **553**
HIGHAM (in Gazeley), *see* GAZELEY
HIGHAM (by Stratford St Mary), inhabitants of,
    154, 458
  lord of manor of, 682n
HILBOROUGH (Nfk), warreners of, 489
Hill, *see* Hyll

HINDERCLAY, church, 726, 1164
  inhabitant of, 1198
  land in, 1186
  testators of, *268*, *1198*
Hirde, Joan, 909
  see also Herd(e)
HITCHAM, church, light of St Christopher in, 820
  community hall in, 772
  'Crokys' in, 151
  gilds in, 772
  inhabitants of, 51, 151, 520, 699, 712, 772, 820, 921, 978, 1013, 1047, 1066, 1116, 1234n, 1416, 1459, 1461
  manor of, 820
  poor of, 712
  testators of, *27*, **51**, **150**, **177**, *265*, *273*, **487**, *560*, **712**, **772**, *791*, **820**, **921**, *978*, *979*, *1013*, *1047*, *1066*, **1234**, **1459**, **1461**
Hobberd (Hoberd, Hobert), Adam, of Wattisfield, 1409
  Alice, 389
  Joan, 1475; of Oakley, 16
  John, 16, 67, 204, 878, 1070, 1334; wheelwright, 1238; of Oakley, *16*
  Katherine, of Burwell (Cambs), *67*
  Margaret, 150
  Richard, 636; of Thrandeston, & family, **543**
  Thomas, 167
  William, 1282
  see also Huberd
Hobbys, Alice, of Timworth, **1201**
  John, 693
Hoberd (Hobert), *see* Hobberd
HOCKWOLD (Nfk), inhabitant of, 46
Hod (Hoode), John, 334
  Thomas, 901; of Felsham, **901**
Hog(ge) (Hougge), James, of Clare, 915
  John, 1183; of Market Weston, 506
  Margaret, widow, of Clare, *915*
  Thomas, 828, 1383; of Bury St Edmunds, 1356
Hogger, Joan, of Old Newton, 340
  John, of Old Newton, 908
  William, of Old Newton, 340
Hoggysson, John, of Woolpit, 713
Hogo(o)n (Hugon), Henry, 929; of Preston, 761, 1111, 1111n, 1124
  John, of Preston, 102
Hoker (Hokyr), Alice, of Edwardstone, 1209
  John, of Edwardstone, **1209**; the younger, of Edwardstone, **931**
  Lettice, of Edwardstone, 931
  William, 1209
Hoket, Agnes, of Long Melford, 122
  John, 122; the elder, of Long Melford, **122**
  Richard, 122
Holbek, Margery, 1422
HOLBROOK, inhabitant of, 1216n

Holbro(o)k, John, of Hadleigh, 942
  Thomas, 342, 639
Holderness (Hordernes), Ralph, rector of Little Saxham, 1044, 1123
Holde(y)n, John, tailor, 1087; of Glemsford, 362
Holm(e), Agnes, of Long Melford, 540
  Alice, of Brent Eleigh, *167*
  John, 562; of Barrow, & family, **290**; the younger, of Barton Mills, 1403; of Kersey, 1067n; of Long Melford, *540*; the younger, of Long Melford, 540
  Margaret, of Barton Mills, 1403
  Margery, of Barrow, 290
  Nicholas, glover, 1067
  Richard, glover, 1067
  Thomas, of Cotton, **400**; of Layham, 334
HOLME HALE (Nfk), land in, 877
Holond, Agnes, of Icklingham, **853**
Homelyn, Rose, 404
Homfrey, Thomas, of Great Livermere, 1195
  see also Humfrey, Omfrey, Umfrey
HONINGTON, 'Blodhewepath' in, 1269
  church, font-cover of, 690n
    porch windows of, 690n
    rector of, 1269
  inhabitant of, 690
  testators of, **530**, **690**, **783**, *959*, **1269**
  will proved at, 802
Hony, Cecily, of Buxhall, 465
  John, 465
  Richard, servant, 1169; of Buxhall, *465*
Hoode, *see* Hod
HOPTON (near Harling), bridge in, 723
  church, 975
    aisle, 622, 723n
    porch, 723, 723n
    rector of, *see* John Worlych
  gilds in, 723, 1026
  inhabitants of, 230, 331, 347, 369, 622, 723, 794, 954n, 969, 975, 1178, 1179, 1292, 1494n
  land in, 1186, 1494
  places in, 'above the Portweye' (furlong), 794
    'Boyboys, le' (tenement), 723
    'Brymbyllond' (furlong), 794
    'Fowlaker', 347
    'Hogetlong' (furlong), 794
    'Hougys, le' (tenement), 723
    'Northgatestrete', 1026
    'Perkynnys Busch' (furlong), 794
    'Stamgate', 213
    'Thorn, le' (furlong), 723
    'Westonfeld', 794
  testators of, *68*, **286**, *323*, **331**, *347*, *621*, **622**, **723**, **794**, **1026**, *1178*, **1179**, *1214*, **1292**, **1332**
  wills proved at, 286, 331, 622, 1178, 1179
Hordernes, *see* Holderness

HORKESLEY (Esx), inhabitant of, 108
Horn, Agnes, of Cheveley (Cambs), 822
 Joan, of Snailwell (Cambs), 183
 John, of Cheveley (Cambs), 381, **792, 822**; of
  Soham (Cambs), 903
 Robert, 183, 822
 Thomas, of Snailwell (Cambs), **183**
Horner, Lawrence, of Fordham (Cambs), 94, 240
Horol(l)d, Agnes, of Lakenheath, 861
 John, 149, 642, 1289; of Lakenheath, & family,
  861
 Ralph, 861
 Robert, 1392
Horowham (Harwham), Robert, 1404, 1404n; of
 Mildenhall, 1117
HORRINGER, GREAT, church, 297, 1220, 1233
 roodloft in, 1233
 inhabitants of, 422, 436, 722, 826, 1233
 land in, 41, 41n
 places in, 'Hopley' (field), 1233
  'Manyscroft, le', 1233
 testators of, *436, 722, 826*
HORRINGER, LITTLE, church, 41n
 inhabitant of, 422
 land in, 41, 41n, 1279
 places in, 'Chevyngtonveyfeld', 1291
 testators of, 422, 1291
HORSEHEATH (Cambs), inhabitant of, 396
Horspet, Richard, of Horkesley (Esx), 108
Hose, Alice, of Botesdale, 981
 Peter, 981
 Robert, of Botesdale, & family, **981**
 Thomas, 981
Hosle, John, of Hadleigh, 197
Hotty, Thomas, chaplain, of Rattlesden, 439
Hougge, *see* Hog(ge)
HOUGHTON ON THE HILL (Nfk), land in,
 877
Hounte, *see* Hunt(e)
Houteyn, Alice, 1337
Hovyl(e) (Hovell, Howell), Alice, 549
 John, 549; of Brockley, 472
 Margaret, 549
 Richard, of Cowlinge, **549**
 Thomas, 549
Howard, *see* Haward
Howardyn, John, 566, 719
Howat, John, fuller, 638
Howchon (Howchyn, Huchon), Cecily, of Ixworth
  Thorpe, 827, **828**
 Ed., 827, 828, 1086
 John, the younger, 827, 828; of Great
  Livermere, 827, 828; the elder, of Great
  Livermere, 827, 827n, 828; of Ixworth
  Thorpe, **827**, 828
 Marion, of Livermere, *1086*
Howe, John, 494
Howell, *see* Hovyl(e)

Howlot(e), Agnes, of Barnham, 1139
 Elizabeth, 1206
 John, 895; of Barnham, 1268; the elder, of
  Barnham, & family, **1139**; of Mendlesham,
  2; of Thelnetham, 969
 Olive, of Mendlesham, 2
 Peter, 1139
 Thomas, 2
Howton, John, of Great Livermere, *405*
 Mariota, of Great Livermere, 405
Howyger, John, of Bildeston, 1125
Howys, John, the younger, of Fornham St
  Genevieve, 443
 Katherine, of Market Weston, *935*
 Matilda, of Fornham St Genevieve, 443
 William, of Market Weston, 935
Hoy, Alexander, 603
Huberd (Hubert), William, of Eye, 354
Huchon, *see* Howchon
Hucton, Agnes, of Hawkedon, 735
 John the younger, of Hawkedon, & family, **735**
 Robert, 735*; of Stansfield, 507
Hugon, *see* Hogo(o)n
Hukton, Agnes, of Clare, 642, 642n
 John, of Clare, *642*
 Richard, 642
Humfrey, John, the younger, 387
 see also Homfrey, Omfrey, Umfrey
HUNDON, church, fire at, 967n
  lady chapel in, 1216n
  vestry of, 967
  vicar of, *see* John Wrygh
 gild in, 1216
 inhabitants of, 448, 561n, 730, 939, 967, 1083,
  1216
 places in, 'Brokhole', 967
  'Cherche Strete', 939
 poor of, 654
 testators of, ?327, *689, 847,* **939, 967,** *1083,
  1189,* **1216**
 wills proved at, 173, 835, 847, 1081, 1083,
  1488
Hune, Thomas, of Bury St Edmunds, 477
Hungyr (Hunger), Elizabeth, of Thwaite, 996
 John, chaplain, of ?Diss (Nfk), 241, 241n, 242;
  of Thwaite, *996*
 Rose, widow, of Mellis, **798**
Hunne, Robert, 57
HUNSTON, church, 583
  chalice for, 1322n
  missal for, 1322n
 gild in, 583
 inhabitants of, 1255, 1322, 1397
 land in, 674
 places in, 'Nicolys', 41, 41n
  'Pollardes' (close), 1495
 testator of, **1217**
Hunt(e) (Hounte), Agnes, of Hopton, 1332

Alice, 794
John, 193, 740; clerk, 437; rector of
    Riddlesworth (Nfk), 1332; of Stowlangtoft,
    373; of Whatfield, **162**
Margery, of Barrow, 1191
Robert, 942; of Lindsey, 162
Roger, of Barrow, 25, 291, 693, **1191**
Stephen, 622, 1332
Thomas, 794; rector of Gasthorpe (Nfk), 1332
Walter, 373
William, 396, 794*; of Hopton, **1332**
Hurlebate, Thomas, 1180
Hurry, Margaret, 939
Hurt, Joan, of ?Fordham (Cambs), 550
    William, of ?Fordham (Cambs), **550**
Hurton, Agnes, of Icklingham, 1221
John, 1221; of Icklingham, & family, **1221**
Thomas, 1221
Huscher, Margaret, nun of 'Nonnysham', 777
Hyde, John, 666
Hygham, *see* Heigham
Hygne, Denise, of Mildenhall, 980
    Robert, of Mildenhall, *980*
Hykedon, William, 987
    see also Hekedon
Hyldersham, John, 237
    William, 237
Hyll (Hill(e), at(te) Hyll, at Hill), Agnes, of Little
    Saxham, **1044**, 1123
Joan, of Long Melford, *1004*; of Whepstead,
    965
John, 248, 313, 434, 700, 725, 965; the
    younger, 1123; of Elmswell, **1337**; of
    Glemsford, 1246; of Little Saxham, 44,
    1044n, **1123**; of Rickinghall, *878*; the elder,
    of Whepstead, **965**
Henry, of Cockfield, 607, *615*; the elder, of
    Cockfield, 615
Margaret, 248
Margery, 1462
Matilda, of Elmswell, 1337
Nicholas, 313
Thomas, 94, 1004, 1208; chaplain, 1462;
    Master, 1462n; rector of Semer, 90, 273,
    273n
William, 816, 1337
Hyllys, William, 812
Hyndebeste, Adam, of Thurston, **1440**
Hyne, Agnes, of Bury St Edmunds, 421
John, 421, 740; dyer, of Sudbury, 398
Margaret, 740
Matilda, *formerly* Deynes, 740; widow, of
    Sudbury, **421**
Robert, 740; of Sudbury, 421
Thomas, 188, 421; of Bury St Edmunds, 421
    see also Hyve
Hyntelesham, Robert, 1180
Hynton, John, of Great Bradley, 368

Katherine, of Great Bradley, & family, **368**
Hyon, Godwin, of Occold, **537**
    Joan, of Occold, 537
Hyppr', John, chaplain, 871
Hyrland, Thomas, 325
Hyve, Cecily, of Lakenheath, 1289
    Thomas, of Lakenheath, **1289**
    see also Hyne

Iccham, Margaret, 172
ICKLETON (Cambs), priory of Benedictine nuns,
    1279
ICKBURGH (Nfk), chapel of Newbridge in, 489n
ICKLINGHAM, churches in, 166n
    church of All Saints, 1219
        rector of, *see* Richard Seynour
    church of St James, 1219
    inhabitants of, 585, 1129, 1221, 1309
    places in, 'Astoneslane', 1221
        'Buttes, le', 1221
        'Crospathwey', 1221
        'Lakynghethweye', 1221
    poor of, 940
    tenters in, *li*
    testators of, *581*, **585**, **603**, **853**, **940**, **1129**,
        1221, **1472**
    wills proved at, 166, 311, 984, 1221, 1286
ICKWORTH, land in, 41, 314, 422
    testator of, **139**
Ide, Agnes, of Glemsford, & family, **137**
Thomas, 158, 1300
Walter, 1300
Ildryard, Walter, of Bury St Edmunds, 468
Ilger, Robert, 1123
Illey (Ilye), Margaret, 1116
    Thomas, 820
Illyon, Alice, of Finningham, 879
    John, 879
Ingayn, Thomas, esquire, 41
INGHAM, church, 138, 180, 182
    rector of, *see* William Throwley
    tower of, 227, 227n, 963
    inhabitants of, 182, 227, 227n, 1074, 1201,
        1441
    land in, 315
    testators of, **227**, **963**, **1441**
Ingham, Margaret, of Newmarket, 574
    Robert, of Newmarket, **574**
Inglond (Inglong), Henry, 1231
    John, 951; chaplain, 211; of Market Weston,
        854
    Robert, 1231
    William, of Bardwell, 372, **1231**
Ingold, Ed., 455
    Rose, of Brandon, 928
    Thomas, of Brandon, *928*
    [*unnamed*], *485*
Instans, John, 1436

Robert, of Rattlesden, *1436*
IPSWICH, administrative centre of archdeaconry
  of Suffolk, *xxxviii*
  church of St Matthew
    rector of, *see* William Goslyng
  friars (unspec.) in, 285, 1244
  grammar school, 1194n
  house of Carmelite friars, *xlix*, 20, 21, 47, 58,
    60, 63, 105, 117, 129, 180, 261, 287, 288,
    345, 350, 380, 393, 413, 444, 457, 497, 600,
    619, 713, 775, 797, 823, 921, 1036, 1126,
    1134, 1272, 1462
  house of Dominican friars, 20, 47, 63, 288,
    345, 444, 600, 797, 977, 1126, 1134, 1194n,
    1427, 1462
  house of Franciscan friars, 20, 47, 63, 103, 288,
    345, 390, 444, 600, 797, 1126, 1134, 1462
  inhabitants of, 108, 158n, 469, 1194n, 1392
  priory of Austin canons (St Peter & St Paul),
    gild at, 1216n
  will proved at, 1209
Irby, Henry, chaplain, of Tostock, 782, 782n, 1313
  Nicholas, rector of Norton, 441, 441n, 782n,
    1255, 1381
Isaak, William, 741
ISLEHAM (Cambs), church, 281, 708
  inhabitant of, 1041
  peculiar of, *xxxix*
  poor of, 708
Ive (Yve), Henry, of Little Waldingfield, *1487*
  John, 348, 1487; the elder, of Great
    Finborough, **348**
  Margaret, 348
  Richard, 632
  Robert, 348
  see also Yvys
IXWORTH, archdeacon's official at, 1323n
  church, 519n, 1078
    book in, 321
    chancel of, 961, 961n, 1033
    Easter sepulchre in, 321
    light of BVM in, 1033
    surplice for, 1033
    torches in, 321
    tower of, 905n
  gilds in, 321, 335, 357, 827
  gildhall of, 1396n
  inhabitants of, 78, 268, 357, 366, 372, 452,
    702, 829, 859, 905, 961, 1033, 1133n, 1176,
    1231n, 1242, 1323
  places in, 'Barboures' (tenement), 1033
    'Bell' inn, 1033
    'Rogeres' (tenement), 1033
    'Shermannys' (messuage), 1176
    'Sumptones' (tenement), 1033
  poor of, 1033
  priory of Austin canons in, 180, 321, 339n,
    674, 961n, 1033, 1242n

canons of, 321, 827
land of, 96, 101, 1225
prior of, 827
road in, 357
testators of, *280*, **321**, **335**, **366**, *372*, *452*, *628*,
  829, *859*, **961**, **1033**, *1072*, **1176**, *1405*
wills proved at, 7, 55, 59, 78, 96, 124, 307, 321,
  330, 335, 353, 357, 366, 397, 451, 452, 453,
  508, 562, 591, 671, 859, 905, 944, 945, 961,
  985, 1033, 1040, 1042, 1043, 1059, 1072,
  1176, 1186, 1225, 1226, 1230, 1231, 1232,
  1247, 1248, 1249, 1257, 1258, 1269, 1272,
  1274, 1278, 1313, 1322, 1332, 1337, 1338,
  1359, 1397, 1399, 1409, 1495, 1497
IXWORTH THORPE, church, 321
  burial in nave of, 1396n
  ornaments of, 827
  tower of, 828
  gilds in, 101
  inhabitants of, 101, 827, 1072n, 1396
  manor of, 101, 838n
  places in, 'Braderassh', 101
    'Longeakyr', 101
    'Saxwelle', 101
  testators of, **101**, **827**, **828**, *1323*, *1396*

Jacob, Agnes, of Sudbury, 578
  Joan, 578
  Margaret, of Stowmarket, 1420
  Thomas, of Stowmarket, *1420*
  William, of Lavenham, 766, 768; of Sudbury,
    667, 768, 1311; the elder, of Sudbury, **578**;
    the younger, of Sudbury, 578
Jaffrey, Marion, of Barnham, 534
  Peter, of Barnham, 534
  William, of Barnham, **534**
  see also Jeffrey
Jakeman, John, of Ousden, *883*
  Margery, of Ousden, 883
  see also Jekman
Jakys (Jakkes), Isabel, of Depden, 125
  John, 695, 1246
  Lawrence, of Depden, **125**
  see also Jekkys
Jamys, Cecily, of Milden, 81
  William, of Milden, **81**
  see also Jemys
Janyn, John, 33
Jay, Isabel, of Burwell (Cambs), 66
  John, of Burwell (Cambs), *66*
  William, 66
Jeffrey, John, 1057
  Marion, of Barnham, *974*
  Peter, 974
Jekell (Jekyll), John, 548, 612; of Boxford, 529
Jeken, Thomas, the younger, 1289
Jekkys, Thomas, of Sapiston, 464
  see also Jakys

Jekman, [*uunamed*], of Mildenhall, 1404
    see also Jakeman
Jekyll, *see* Jekell
Jelham, *see* Gelham
Jemys, Katherine, 1032
    see also Jamys
Jen(n)ew(e)s, Agnes, of Eye, 624
    John, of Eye, 623, **624**
    Walter, of Waldringfield, 624
Jenney, William, 497
Jenowr, Joan, of Old Newton, 908
    John, of Old Newton, **908**
Jent, Walter, of Whepstead, 160
    see also Gent
Jentyll, Richard, 1222
Jerveys (Jerweys), Joan, of Bildeston, **982**, 1194n
    John, 1246; the elder, 982; of Bildeston, 982;
        the elder, of Bildeston, 1194
    Thomas, of Barton Mills, 46
    see also Boner *alias* Jerweys
Joly, family, of Lavenham, 446n
    Robert, butcher, of Lavenham, 446
    Simon, of Lavenham, 661
Jolyf(f), Katherine, 1073
    Robert, weaver, of Lavenham, 1243
Jonessone (Jonsone), Matilda, of Mildenhall, 1155
    William, 1155; of Gazeley, 1439
Jonyour, John, of Bury St Edmunds, 1279
Jorge, Agnes, 90
    John, of Exning, *590*
    Margaret, of Exning, 590
    Richard, 90
Josep, John, of Nayland, 318
Josse, Joan, 1116
Journey, John, servant, 1437
Jowde, John, the younger, 1011
    see also Judy
Jowell, John, 529
Joye, Cecily, servant, of Pakenham, 335
Judy (Jude), Agnes, 828; of Badwell Ash, 798
    Bartholomew, chaplain, 1342
    John, 944, 1039
    Robert, of Badwell Ash, 798, **1342**
    Walter, 1342; of Walsham le Willows, 1193n
    see also Jowde
Julian, Florence, of Wickham St Paul (Esx), 175
    Margaret, of Bardwell, 1368
    William, of Bardwell, **1368**

Kaas, *see* Caas
Karles, William, 1446
    see also Carles
Kartere, Katherine, of Acton, **1385**
    see also Carter(e)
Katelyn (Kattelyng), Joan, of Snailwell (Cambs),
    702
    John, the elder, of Haverhill, *523*
    Robert, of Snailwell (Cambs) **702**

Thomas, of Ixworth, 702
    see also Catel(e)yn
Keb(b)yll (Kebell), John, 1421; the elder, 797; the
    younger, 797; the younger, of Stowmarket
    Margaret, 799
    Peter, 983
    Richard, 799; the younger, 797; the elder, of
        Stowmarket, 346, **797**
    Thomas, 797
    William, 797; of Old Newton, 908
KEDINGTON, church, land of rectory of, 681
    inhabitants of, 266, 572, 681, 1094, 1213
    land in, 1083
    manor of, 1213, 1216n
    places in, 'Chapelfeld, le', 1094
        'Maystrys', 236
        'Stantunne chapel', 1094n
        'Sutton', 681
    poor of, 654
    road to, 1423n
    testators of, *38*, *236*, *528*, *572*, *681*, **1094**, **1213**
    wills proved at, 526, 527, 528, 572, 896, 897,
        1107
Kedyngton, John, of Chippenham (Cambs), *1100*
    William, 1100
Keg(g)yll (Kegill), Agnes, of Bildeston, 520
    John, 744; the elder, 520; of Bildeston, 415,
        520, 1486
Kelyng, John, 106; of Haverhill, 210, 306, 491,
    1457; of Haverhill, & family, **968**
    Margaret, of Haverhill, 968
    Robert, 1119; of Worlington, 1241
Kembold (Kembell, Kymbold), Agnes, of
    Hitcham, 560, 712
    John, 487, 560; of Hitcham, 1066; the younger,
        of Hitcham, 1047
    Robert, 334
    Thomas, of Hitcham, *560*; the elder, of
        Hitcham, & family, **712**
Kemp(e) (Kenpe), Agnes, 1133
    John, 703; chaplain of St Mary in Stowmarket
        St Peter, 288
Kendale, Alice, of Stansfield, 382
    Simon, of Chelsworth, 629
    William, of Stansfield, *382*
Kene, Henry, 278
    William, 203, 1147
Kengeth, Joan, of Nayland, 763
    John, of Nayland, *763*
KENNETT (Cambs), poor of, 270
    testator of, *13*
    wills proved at, 93, 702, 703, 704, 1204
Kenpe, *see* Kemp(e)
Kent(e), Agnes, of Burwell (Cambs), 313
    Alice, of Stowmarket, 288
    Joan, of Withersfield, 709
    John, the elder, 313; the younger, 313;

apprentice, 1181; of Burwell (Cambs), & family, 313; of Long Melford, 1424
Robert, of Stowmarket, 797; of Stowmarket & family, **288**
Thomas, of Withersfield, 312, 396, *709*
KENTFORD, bridge in, 894
  church, parish priest of, 762
    sepulchre light in, 894
  dovecote in, 1110
  gilds in, 762, 894, 894n
  inhabitants of, 44, 708,, 759, 762, 894, 1110
  places in, 'Baldokysacre', 1110
    'Cock' inn, 894
    'Grauntes', 270
    'Hadynhamys' (tenement), 762
    'Hulkysacre', 1110
    'Kentyll' 1110
    'Mellefeld, le', 1110
    'Mounpleres' 270
    'Stag's Head', 270
  testators of, **44**, **270**, **762**, **894**, *1020*, **1110**
  wills proved at, 278, 1439
Kepenham, Thomas, of Wortham, 1164
Keppyng, Isabel, of Ixworth, 829
  William, of Ixworth, *829*
KERSEY, church, 162
  bells of, 342, 342n, 390, 392
  chapel in, 566n
  legend for, 342
  psalter for, 342n
  tower of, *xlvii*, 342, 342n
  gilds in, 342
  inhabitants of, 342, 392, 719, 720, 923, 1067, 1115, 1184, 1212, 1227, 1228, 1245
  manor of, 90n, 1115n
  places in, 'Berlys' (tenement), 342
    'Dreyes' (croft), 521
    market-place, 719
    Sampson's Hall (manor), 90n
    'Wodekestret' (Wicker Street), 144, 144n
  poor of, 1115
  priory of Austin canons, 390n
    canon of, 390
  roads in, 'Bylston' lane, 566
    from church to bridge, 342
    from 'Prentys' door to priory gate, 566
  testators of, **390**, **392**, **521**, **566**, **719**, *720*, **923**, **1067**, **1115**, *1184*, **1212**, **1227**, **1228**, **1245**
  wills proved at, 257, 544, 546, 719, 728, 772, 923, 1067, 1173, 1184, 1227, 1228, 1331
  workshop in, 719
Kertleng, Thomas, 1044
Kerver, *see* Carver
KETTLEBASTON, church, 929
  rector of, *see* Thomas Ederyk
  inhabitants of, 929n, 1066n, 1300
  will proved at, 814
Ketyll, Alison, of Preston, 929

George, of Preston, 929
John, 606; of Preston, 929
Katherine, of Preston, 929
William, of Preston, **929**
Keverell, John, singleman, 207
KILVERSTONE (Nfk), rector of, *see* William Bergham (Brigham)
King, *see* Kyng
KIRTLING (Cambs), church, 247, 381
  bell in, 1467
  vicar of, *see* Richard Breche
  gilds in, 203
  inhabitants of, 379, 1348, 1432, 1467, 1468
  places in, 'Colynys Yerd', 1468
    'Genotes' (land), 1468
    'Mellaneysende', 1468
    'Smalbrookfeld, le', 337
    'Thunderlees', 1467
    'Towneyfeld', 1468
    'Upeyeme' (Upend), 1467, 1467n
    'Vaylondes' 1468
  poor of, 270
  'Saxton lane', leading to, 1463
  testators of, **203**, **337**, **881**, **1348**, **1432**, **1467**, **1468**
  wills proved at, 625, 676, 1426
Knappyng, John, 967
KNETTISHALL, church, 920
  tower of, 975, 723, 723n
  inhabitant of, 957
  testators of, **975**, *1321*
Knot, John, 280
  Thomas, chaplain, 1216
Knot(t)yng, Margaret, 869
  William, of Stowmarket, **103**
Knyght (Knygt, Knyth), Nicholas, 1359; of Eye, 1359n
  Simon, servant, 1110; of Barningham, *1359*
  Thomas, of Brockford, 1453
Knyth *alias* Berton, William, friar, 708
Knyth *alias* Dunch, William, of Creeting, *1294*
Koo, Geoffrey, 1104
  Margaret, the younger, 308
  Margery, widow, of Woolpit, **619**
  Richard, 619
Kooc, Joan, servant, 317
Ky, Isabel, of Thorney, 264
  John, of Thorney, **264**
  Simon, of Stowmarket, 264
Kylle, William, 589
Kymbold, *see* Kembold
Kymys, William, of Combs, *743*
Kyng, Agnes, of Soham (Cambs), *904*; of Thorney, 600
  Andrew, 350
  Elizabeth, of Wetheringsett, 248
  Joan, 350, 944; of Mendlesham, & family, 3
  John, 90, 248, 600*, 737; the younger,

of Brockford, 248; of Hessett, *825*;
of Mendlesham, *361*, *786*, 1035; of
Stowmarket, **1134**; of Swaffham (Cambs),
183; the elder, of Wetheringsett, & family,
248
Margaret, of Wetheringsett, 15
Marion, of Stowmarket, 1134
Nicholas, of Brettenham, & family, **1036**; of
Worlington, 1389
Olive, of Mendlesham, 786; widow, of
Mendlesham, **1035**
Peter, of Sapiston, 464
Richard, of Wetheringsett, **15**
Robert, of Nayland, 763; of Wickhambrook,
737
Sabina, of Brettenham, 1036
Thomas, 904, 1085, 1497; & family, 1036; of
Mendlesham, **3**; of Wattisfield, *936*
William, 1134; of Thorney, **600**
see also Berton *alias* Kyng
Kyngesbery, Marion, of Cornard, 1177
Thomas, of Cornard, *1177*
Kynget, John, of Nayland, 32
Kyrkeby (Kyrbeby), Henry, 381, 822
John, 381
Kyrre, Peter, of Ipswich, & family, 53
Kyrtelynge, *see* Tew *alias* Kyrtelynge
Kyrton, Gilbert, friar of Clare, 112

LACKFORD, church, 377, 1129
inhabitants of, 41n, 1361
Lacy (Laci), Christine, 5
John, shepherd, 1289
Katherine, 1419
Margaret, 1289
Richard, 5; of Westhorpe, 347n
Thomas, 841
William, 1289
Lady(s)man, John, the elder, 129; the younger,
129; the elder, of Great Finborough, **129**
Thomas, of Little Whelnetham, 525; of Little
Whelnetham & family, 533
Lagdyn, Joan, 1398
Laggard, Joan, of Lavenham, 86
John, 1369; of Lavenham, & family, **86**
Robert, 86
LAKENHEATH, church, 352, 708, 1471
antiphoner for, 1289
bell for, 861
'stooling' of, 1289n
vicar of, *see* Reginald Troys
gilds in, 1289
inhabitants of, 352, 388, 708, 779, 861, 1018,
1289
places in, 'Budys' (tenement), 1289
'Legates' (curtilage), 861
'Northolme', 779
path in middle of town, 388

'Snypes' (barn), 1289
poor of, 708
testators of, **388**, **779**, **861**, *1018*, **1289**
will proved at, 1101
Laker, James, chaplain, 1448
Lambe, William, of Haughley, 795
Lamberd (Lambert), John, 417; of college,
Sudbury, 91
Richard, of Lavenham, 402, *769*
Robert, of Whepstead, 160; of Whepstead, &
family, **417**
William, 769, 1386
Lamme, John, of Thwaite, 869
Lana, John, 282
Lanam, Joan, of Ely (Cambs), 1319
Lancastre, John, 850
Lande, Margaret, 549
LANDWADE (Cambs), inhabitant of, 489n
road leading to, 1475
testator of, *627*
Lane, Agnes, of Nayland, 815
Isabel, of West Stow, & family, **56**
James, 282, 564
John, 491; of Ixworth, & family, **101**; of
Nayland, 318, *815*
Katherine, of Woolpit, 836
Margery, 383
Peter, of Nayland, *383*
LANGHAM, church, altar of BVM in, 7
vestments to, 457n
gild in, 842
inhabitants of, 8
testators of, **7**, **8**
will proved at, 218
Langham, Alice, of Snailwell (Cambs), & family,
588
Margaret, of Bury St Edmunds, 749
Richard, chaplain, 114
[*unnamed*], friar, 806
Langlond, Isabel, of Eye, *707*
John, of Eye, 623, 707, **1293**
Large, Margaret, 1395
Largeaunt (Largeawnt), Alan, 1361
John, of Elveden, **111**
Larke, John, of Stanton, 457, 1258
Katherine, 1258
Matilda, of Stanton, 1261
Peter, 1261
Ralph, of Stanton, *1261*
Rose, 1258
Launce, Elizabeth, 1206
Laurens (Lauerauns), Margaret, of Eye, *752*
William, 623, 752
LAVENHAM, bailiff of, 416
bedeman of, *xlvii*, 126, 350
borough of, 161, 446, 661, 1073, 1485
church, altar of St Katherine in, 511
chantry in, 454n, 773n

47

cloth for high altar, 1048
cruets for high altar, 172
font-cover for, 376
organs in, 446
parish chaplain receiving tithes, *xlv*
rector of, *see* John Sad
tower of, 1048n
gilds in, 289, 415, 416, 618n, 768
gildhall of, 415n
inhabitants of, 73, 77, 86, 102, 126, 130, 161,
164, 172, 211, 263, 300n, 305, 329, 350,
355, 374, 376, 402, 416, 446, 454, 462, 618,
661, 766, 768, 790, 805, 816, 820, 863,
1002, 1013, 1048, 1073, 1091, 1243, 1260,
1280, 1446, 1461, 1485
land in, 674
looms in, *li*
market cross, 768n
stalls, 62, 329
places in, barn of John Hervy, 376
'Boltonstrete', 102, 402
'Branstons', 298
'Brontys' (tenement), 126
'Cherchestrete, le', 86
'Crystemesse lane, le', 86
'Downe, le', 298
'Dounestrete', 446
'Garl Grove', 1073
'Halle lane, le', 1073
'Heyerownnys', 164
'Heystrete, le' [*etc*], 161, 263, 446, 462,
1073, 1485
'Maystyrjonstrete', 102
'Nell' (tenement), 126
'Parych' (tenement), 446
'Prentyestrete' [*etc*], 102, 164
'Presthows', 102
'Rookes' (tenement), 1073
'Sarbys Grene', 161
'Tenwynter strete', 462
poor of, 511, 768
road, to Bury St Edmunds, 102
testators of, *73*, **86**, **102**, **126**, **130**, **161**, **164**,
172, **263**, 298, 299, **329**, **350**, **355**, **376**, **402**,
416, **446**, **454**, **462**, *510*, **511**, 570, **618**, **661**,
766, **768**, *769*, *804*, **1002**, **1048**, **1073**, *1114*,
1243, **1485**
will dated at, 863
wills proved at, 86, 211, 214, 263, 299, 316,
318, 329, 375, 376, 392, 402, 416, 510, 511,
547, 548, 618, 667, 680, 761, 769, 820, 860,
1013, 1024, 1047, 1048, 1066, 1073, 1091,
1104, 1114, 1124, 1135, 1212, 1243, 1267,
1311, 1360, 1388, 1446, 1454, 1455, 1469,
1484, 1485
Lavenham, Alice, 1274
Joan, of Sudbury, 1274
John, 1274

Katherine, 1364
Matilda, of Sudbury, 1274
Thomas, 1364; of Sudbury, 818; cutler, of
Sudbury, *xlvii*n, **1274**
William, 1274
Laverok, Joan, of Cockfield, **1175**
LAWSHALL, church, new, 293
rector of, *see* Henry Babynton
inhabitants of, 140, 293, 488, 587, 1241
testators of, *140*, **293**, *587*, *701*,
wills proved at, 168, 362
Lay, John, of Bures, *1188*
Margaret, of Bures, 1188
LAYHAM, church, painting candlebeam in, 197
churchyard chapel, 197, 197n, 334, 639
inhabitants of, 334, 639, 1336
places in, 'Bathemans', 334
'Costemes' (cottage), 639
'Crownell', 334
'Raymoundes', 334
'Waterhows', 334
road, to 'Bally', 639
testators of, **197**, **334**, **639**, *1071*, *1336*
Leche, Agnes, of Botesdale, 344
Alice, of Stoke by Nayland, 324
Lawrence, barker, of Stoke by Nayland, **324**
Robert, 971, 1354; of Stowmarket, 1134n, 1296
Walter, of Botesdale, 1374n, **344**
Leder(e), John, rector of Culford, 11, 12, 41, 315
Lee, Eleanor, 490, 491
Margaret at, 1220
Thomas, 491
William, & family, 491
Leff, John, of Woodditton (Cambs), *135*
Lefflet, Robert, 1102
Leg, Thomas, 1300
Legat(e), Alan, 351
Alice, 146
John, rector of Tuddenham, 1061
Robert, 146, 148
Leman, John, of Wetheringsett, 721, *1202*
Simon, 721
Lemys, *see* Lenys
Lenad (Lenas), William, *349*
Lene, John, of Norton, 441
Leng(g)e (Lyenge, Lynge), Agnes, 287
Ed., 287
George, fuller, of Bury St Edmunds, 4, 226,
430
John, 20, 552, 665; chaplain, 1049; of
Thurston, & family, **287**
Katherine, 287
Margery, 722
Roger, 287
Stephen, 287*
Thomas, 287
William, of Thorney, 711
[*unnamed*], *617*

Lennard, John, the elder, 193
Lenys (Lemys), John, 614
   Matilda, 467; of Tostock, *614*
   Nicholas, *467*
   William, 614
Lerlyng, William, 936, 1214; of Hopton, *1214*
Lery, Emma, 227
Lethenard, John, 601
Leton, William, 283
Levald, John, the elder, of Norton, 964
Leve, John, 836
Levenethorp, John, of Snailwell (Cambs), *240*
   Margaret, of Snailwell (Cambs), 240
Leverich (Leverych), Isabel, of Felsham, 185
   John, of Felsham, **185**, 867
Levos, Margery, 1174
Levote, Ralph, of Little Saxham, *501*
Levyngton, John, & family, 91
Levyssey, John, servant, 91
Leycestria *alias* Wethringsette, Richard de, rector
   of Wetheringsett, chancellor of Cambridge
   University, 15n, 345
Leyr, John, bailiff, 1298
LIDGATE, church, 247, 1418
   altar of St Anne in, 1474n
   inhabitants of, 1028, 1474
   testators of, **114**, **190**, *1028*, **1474**
   will proved at, 396
LINCOLN, bishop of, 106, 210, 210n
LINDSEY, church, candlebeam in, 1429
   crucifix in, 1429
   inhabitants of, 162, 586, 942, 1428, 1429
   land in, 42
   testators of, *292*, **942**, **1429**
   Tye, 1429
   will proved at, 566
Linton, John, of Lindsey, 586
LISTON (Esx), manors in, 1246n
LITTLEPORT (Cambs), inhabitant of, 903
LIVERMERE (unspec.), testators of, *483*, *656*,
   1086
LIVERMERE, GREAT, church, 864
   alabaster panel for, 116
   land of, 827, 828
   ornaments in, 827
   rectory (house) of, 1195
   vestment for, 1195
   inhabitants of, 41, 180, 271, 405, 827, 828,
     1195, 1279n, 1441
   land in, 828
   manor of, 180, 827, 828
   places in, 'Bro(o)mhall', 827, 828
     'Clynt', 1003
     'Lampet Went', 827, 828
     'Medueweye, le', 827, 828
     'Overpeselond' (furlong), 827, 828
     'Pesland Acyr', 1003
     'Stubbydcrowche' (land), 827, 828

   poor of, 231
   testators of, *35*, **116**, **180**, **182**, *405*, **1003**, **1195**
LIVERMERE, LITTLE, inhabitants of, 180, 304,
   684, 1003, 1074
   testators of, **138**, **304**, **684**
   will proved at, 858
Lodekyn, John, of Burgate, 369
Lokton, Thomas, esquire, 911
Lokwode, Joan, widow, of Sudbury, *898*
   John, of Sudbury, 898
Lombe, William, 775
Lomkyn, *see* Lumkyn
LONDON, hospital of St Anthony, 1478
   hospital of St Thomas of Acon, *l*, 1478, 1478n
   house of Friars Preachers, Ludgate, 489
   lord mayor of, 444n
   priory of Carthusian monks, Charterhouse, 90
     burial in cloister of, 90n
     payment due to, 90n
   priory of Knights Hospitallers, Clerkenwell,
     1478
   testator's goods at, 90
London, *see* Loudon
LONG MELFORD, bailiff of, 122
   chapel of St James, 1329, 1363
   church, bells of, 300, 474, 790, 1091, 1104,
     1237, 1369
     choir copes for, 1091
     Jesus mass in, 916, 1365, 1369
     Lady Chapel of, 88, 88n, 181, 221, 474,
       517, 790, 837, 1091, 1237, 1329, 1363,
       1369, 1424
     light of St Mary in, 837
     missal for, 916
     necessaries for, 916
     rector of, *see* John Mildewelle
     silver thurible for, 790
     tabernacle over pyx at high altar, 916
     tower of, 1329, 1329n
   gilds in, 474, 474n, 916n, 1329, 1363, 1365,
     1369, 1424
   inhabitants of, 31n, 82, 88, 122, 195, 201, 375,
     421, 474, 640, 790, 837, 890, 916, 929,
     1051, 1064, 1075, 1091, 1104, 1105, 1160,
     1167, 1237, 1241, 1246, 1329, 1363, 1369,
     1387, 1424
   looms in, *li*
   places in, Chapel Green, 1329n
     'Coleynsscroft', 1104
     cross on green, 1237
     Cuckoo Tye, 195
     'Fottysforth', 837
     'Gerneys' (pasture), 790
     'Glemsford Brygge', 1237, 1237n
     Kentwell Hall, 201n
     Lower Green, 1237n
     'Prowds' (tenement), 1329n
     'Prowdysbregge', 1329

'Shankes' (tenement), 1369
'Smale, le' (pasture), 790
Thurgors Tye, 195
poor of, 916
rental of, 1237n
roads in, 'Brygestrete', 88, 88n
  Bull Lane, 195n
  'Fotysfordstreet', 195, 195n
  'Hallestrete', 1064
  'Lakforthestrete', 195n
  way at three crosses, 181
testators of, **82**, **88**, **122**, **181**, **195**, *201*, *202*,
  217, **221**, *272*, **300**, **474**, **517**, *532*, *540*, *545*,
  668, **790**, **837**, **916**, *1004*, *1051*, **1064**, **1091**,
  1104, *1105*, **1160**, *1167*, **1208**, **1237**, *1301*,
  1329, **1363**, **1369**, **1387**, **1424**, *1425*
wills proved at, 456, 476, 545, 701, 766, 768,
  916, 929, 1051, 1064, 1105, 1106, 1181,
  1208, 1424, 1425, 1447
Longe, Agnes, of Acton, 404
  John, 259*; the elder, of Acton, **259**; smith, of
    Acton, & family, **404**
  Margaret, of Acton, 259
  Margery, of Wickham Skeith, *880*
Lopere, Alice, 612
LOPHAM, NORTH (Nfk), church, 726
LOPHAM, SOUTH (Nfk), church, 1262
Lord, Agnes, of Cockfield, 899
  John, 899
  Walter, of Cockfield, **899**
Lore, John, of Kentford, 894
Lorkyn, John, chaplain, of Clare, 149
Lorkyn *alias* Dyster, Alice, of Long Melford, 300
  John, the elder, 300; the younger, 300; weaver,
    of Long Melford, & family, **300**
Lote, Alice, 876
  Margery, 1463
  Ralph, 1463
Lotkyn *alias* Roper, Richard, 980
Loudon (Louden, London, Lundon), Alice, of
  Thorndon, 742, **1090**
  John, 229, 742, 950
  Peter, 742; of Thorndon, 1090
  William, of Thorndon, 241, 1090, **742**
Love, Christine, 779
  Joan, 779
  John, 779*, 1116
Lovelych, John, 1193
  Robert, servant, 1193
Lovetop, John, 292; chaplain, 719; chaplain, of
  Kersey, 521, 923, 1227, 1228
  Thomas, 292
  William, 1227; of Kersey, 342, 390, 719
LOWESTOFT, chapel of Holy Rood, 1207n
  pilgrimage to, 1207
Lowyn, Margery, of Wicken (Cambs), 1121
  Thomas, of Wicken (Cambs), **1121**
Ludbrooke, Richard, 1094

Lumkyn (Lomkyn), John, 1098; of Stanningfield,
  431, 1098n
Lundeneys, John, 1277
  Rose, 1277
  William, 1277
Lundon, *see* Loudon
Lunt, Helen, of Stoke by Nayland, 638
  Joan, of Stoke by Nayland, 638
  John, of Stoke by Nayland, 638
  Robert, **1088**, 1412; of Holbrook, 638; of Stoke
    by Nayland, 638
Lutkyn, John, 406
Luton, John, of Lindsey, & family, **942**
  Marion, of Lindsey, 942
Lye, Robert de, 1358
Lyenge, *see* Leng(g)e
Lyhert, Walter, bishop of Norwich, 428n
Lylye, Audrey, 23
  John, 23; of Barrow, *23*
  William, 1062
Lymnour *alias* Lynne, Thomas, 611n
Lynch, Agnes, of Great Cornard, 1149
  John, of Great Cornard, **1149**
Lyndyshey (Lyndyssey), *see* Lynsey
Lynge, *see* Leng(g)e
LYNN (Nfk), inhabitant of, 1008
Lyn(n)e, Isabel, of Burwell (Cambs), 482
  John, 522
  Richard, of Poslingford, *70*
  Robert, of Burwell (Cambs), *482*
  Thomas, canon, 611n; limner, 933; of Bury St
    Edmunds, 611, 611n
  see also Lymnour *alias* Lynne
Lynsey (Lyndyshey, Lyndyssey), Isabel, 1077
  John, 1077
  Richard, 1077
  Robert, 1077
  Thomas, 1077; of Stoke by Nayland, 189, 301
  William, 1077
Lynton, Robert, rector of Woolpit, 60n
Lys (Lysse), Joan, 1193
  Katherine, of Edwardstone, 76, *196*
  Robert, 76; of Groton, 942
  Walter, of Edwardstone, *76*, 196n
Lyster, John, the younger, hawker, of Hunston, 1255
  Robert, friar, of Clare, 1094
Lythman, Margaret, of Long Melford, 837
  Thomas, of Long Melford, & family, **837**
Lytyll, Isabel, of Stowmarket, 1050
  Margaret, of Bures St Mary, 317
  Richard, the younger, butcher, of Bures St
    Mary, & family, **317**; of Stowmarket, **1050**
  [*unnamed*], *502*

Machon (Macham), Margery, of Preston, 1173n
  Thomas, of Preston, 1173, 1173n
Macro (Makeroo), John, 493
  William, of Soham (Cambs), 254

Madle, Audrey, 1398
Maes, John, 1088
   Margery, 1088
Magges, Joan, 520
Makell, John, of Long Melford, & family, 929
Makemere, John, of ?Rattlesden, *148*
Makeroo, *see* Macro
Makkworth, John, the elder, 903
Malcher (Malcer), Agnes, of Great Waldingfield,
   1280
   Joan, of Great Waldingfield, 1280
   Margaret, 1280
   Thomas, 1280; of Great Waldingfield, 204,
   1280
Maldon, John, of Sudbury, 1058
Malkyn, Henry, of 'Dunstall', in Dalham, 1285
MALLING (Kent), abbey of Benedictine nuns
   abbess of, 941n
   nun of, 539
Maltiward, John, 1054
Man(ne), Clement, 784
   Isabel, of Brettenham, 917; widow, of
      Brettenham, **1466**
   Joan, of Clare, 948; of Rattlesden, *784*
   James, 521; chaplain, 200, 521; chaplain, of
      Nayland, 192
   John, 738, 913, 917, 1023, 1202, 1466; the
      elder, 521; of Brettenham, *917*; the elder, of
      Hunston, 1322; the elder, of Kersey, 521; of
      Lakenheath, 388; of Stowlangtoft, 1322
   Katherine, of Kersey, & family, **521**
   Margaret, servant, 346
   Robert, 521
   Stephen, of Stowlangtoft, *1322*; of Troston, *255*
   Thomas, 255, 521; of Stanton, 457
   William, 521; of Clare, *948*; of Wetheringsett,
      913
MANNINGTREE (Esx), chapel of, 1115
   land in 192
Mannok, Alice, of Stoke by Nayland, 546
   Katherine, of Stoke by Nayland, 546
   Marion, of Stoke by Nayland, 546
   William, tawer, of Stoke by Nayland, *xlviii*, **546**
Mannyng, Anne, 373
   Christine, of Norton, 671
   Helen, of Badwell Ash, 1039; of Bardwell,
      1230
   Joan, 1039; of Bradfield Combust, 407; of
      Norton, 373
   John, of Badwell Ash, & family, **1039**; of
      Norton, **671**; the younger, of Norton, 373
   Margaret, 823
   Walter, 373; priest, 671, 1465; of Norton, *373*
   William, 1230, 1232; & family, 373; of
      Bradfield Combust, **407**; of Hunston, 1397
Mansell, John, the younger, 1044
   Thomas, of Nettlestead, 1044
Manser, Alice, 231

MANSTON (Dorset), maiden of (image), 1466n
   pilgrimage to, 1466, 1466n
Manton, Henry, vicar of Great Thurlow, 134
Manwode, Isabel, of Shimpling, & family, **1154**;
   widow, of Shimpling, & family, **830**
   Robert, 1154; of Shimpling, 701, 830*, 1154
   Thomas, 380, 830, 1154
   William, 830, 1154
MAPLESTEAD, LITTLE (Esx), inhabitant of,
   258
Marant, Margaret, of Stowmarket, & family, 754
   Robert, of Stowmarket, *754*
Marbyll, Thomas, clerk, 367
Marcaunt, *see* Markaunt
Marchall, John, esquire, of Great Thurlow, 193
   Matilda, of Stoke by Nayland, *153*
   Richard, 709
   Thomas, 278
Marcha(u)nt (Marchaunth, Marchawnth)
   Alexander, bailiff, of Bildeston, 520, 566, 744
   Henry, of Bradfield St Clare, 1045
   Robert, of Bradfield St Clare, **1045**
   see also Markaunt
Marcyon, Stephen, 981; of Botesdale, 1170
Mardon, Helen, of Fordham (Cambs), 1277
   William, of Fordham (Cambs), **1277**
MARHAM (Nfk), abbey of Cistercian nuns,
   abbess of, 894n
Marham, Agnes, 498
   [*unnamed*], *498*
Mariot (Maryat), William, 247, 381
Markaunt (Marcaunt), Alice, of Badwell Ash, **674,**
   1176
   Elizabeth, 674
   John, 674, 1039, 1176; of Ixworth, **1176**
   Margaret, of Ixworth, 1176
   Thomas, of Stanton, 457
   William, 674
   see also Marcha(u)nt
Markeday, William, of Thornham Magna, 228
MARKET WESTON, church, 945
   candlebeam in, 1250
   rector of, *see* Thomas Moryell
   cross between town and Hopton, 794
   inhabitants of, 17, 506, 854, 935, 951
   tenement in (?), 489
   testators of, **295**, *935*, *951*, **1250**
   will proved at, 794
Markys, Alice, of Old Newton, 1192
   John, 1296; the elder, 1296; the younger, 1296;
      of Old Newton, **1296**
   Margaret, of Old Newton, 1296
   Marion, of Old Newton, 1296
   Richard, 1296; of Old Newton, **1192**
   Robert, 1192
   Thomas, 1192; the elder, 1296; the younger,
      1296

Marler, Clement, of 'Burnam', 1346
  Helen, & family, 172
Marleton, Margaret, of Wetherden, & family, **1295**
  Rose, of Bardwell, *519*
  Stephen, of Wetherden, 1295
Marram, [*unnamed*], 254
Martelysham, Robert, of Wattisham, 1346
Martyn (Martin), Agnes, 1253; of Drinkstone,
    778, **1253**
  Alice, 1253
  Augustine, of Semer, **143**
  Cecily, 1253
  Helen, 1009
  John, 283, 778, 959, 1009, 1253, 1300; of
    Soham (Cambs), **207**; of Sudbury, *322*; of
    Troston, *1401*
  Lawrence, 195
  Margaret, 193, 959; of Troston, 1401
  Roger, 1409; of Drinkstone, *778*
  Rose, 1253
  Thomas, 778, 1401; of Drinkstone, 1253;
    parish chaplain, Mildenhall, 489, 569, 708,
    865n, 1009, 1117, 1156, 1259
  William, 341, 545
Maryat, *see* Mariot
Masanger (Massanger), John, of Bury St
    Edmunds, 421
  Rose, of Bury St Edmunds, 421
Mascall, John, of Naughton, 162
Mason, Henry, of Exning, 995
  John, 433
  Margaret, of Eye, 433
  Richard, of Eye, *480*
  Robert, of Eye, & family, **433**
  Thomas, of Hartest, *1136*; of Littlebury (Esx),
    550
Massanger, *see* Masanger
Massham, Robert, chaplain, 1049
Mast, Nicholas, of Hadleigh, 108
Mathew, Christian, of Mildenhall, 1434
  Robert, of Mildenhall, *1434*
Maunger, John, 2
Mavesyn, Alice, of Thrandeston, 509
  John, of Thrandeston, *509*
  Thomas, chaplain, 509
Mawdyon, *see* Mawedyon
Mawe, Robert, chaplain, 1245; rector of Little
    Whelnetham, 1245n
Mawedyon (Mawdyon), Margaret, of Boxford,
    612
  William, of Boxford, 296, 380, 612n
May, John, poor man, 144
  Richard, of Stowmarket, 497
  see also Mey
Maydego(o)de, John, of Great Bradley, **193**, 368
  Katherine, of Great Bradley, 193
Maygod, John, of Tuddenham, 1470
Mayh(e)w, Cecily, 722

John, 52; of Boxford, **208**; of Rede, 125
Margery, 52
Rose, of Boxford, 208
Thomas, 881
Mayner, Roger, 498
Mayster, Joan, of Kedington, 236
  John, 1386
  Peter, of Kedington, & family, **236**
  Richard, 231
  Thomas, 633, 1008
  William, 876
Meche, William, 1158
Medfrey, Agnes, of Sudbury, 1364
Medwe (Medowe, Medue), Joan, 158
  John, 1088
  Thomas, of Great Livermere, & family, 1441
  Walter, of Sudbury, 717
  see also at Medwe
Medylton (My(l)dylton), Agnes, & family, 897
Meire, *see* Meyr
Mekelfeld, John, 1274
Mekylwo(o)de, John, 103, 1402
Melkesop (Mylsehopp), Agnes, of Stoke by Clare,
    1423
  John, of Stoke by Clare, 1423, 1423n; of Stoke
    by Clare, & family, **1423**
  Thomas, 1423
Mell(e), Joan, 930
  William, 384; of Stoke by Nayland, 992
Meller(e), Agnes, 164; of Hinderclay, 1198
  John, 56, 77, 936, 945, 1246, 1248; the
    elder, of Barningham, & family, **1248**; of
    Lakenheath, 388
  Robert, 1248; of Barningham, 59n; of
    Hinderclay, *1198*
  Thomas, of Barningham, 124
  see also Millere, Moeller *and* Mondessone
    alias Meller
MELLIS, church, Easter sepulchre in, 1371
  torch in, 1371
  gilds in, 369, 798, 1165, 1371
  inhabitants of, 798, 1097, 1163, 1371
  land in, 406, 1165
  places in, 'Damfeld', 1371
    'Haverlond' (tenement), 1371
  testators of, **369**, *484*, *734*, *798*, *875*, **1097**,
    1371
  wills proved at, 996, 997, 1273, 1304
Melo(w)n, Agnes, of Stradishall, 776
  John, 1386; of Stradishall, 1386n, 1450; tailor,
    of Stradishall, 1142
  Rose, 1127
  Thomas, of Stradishall, 776
Melton, Emote, 845
  John, 254, *845*; of Soham (Cambs), 871
  William, of Soham (Cambs), **1256**
MENDHAM, inhabitant of, 58
MENDLESHAM, church, 775, 1169, 1200, 1462

footpath to, 1315
panel on high altar of, 799, 1315
tithes paid to former vicar of, *xlv*
vicar of, *see* William Starlyng
gild in, 775, 932, 1035, 1315
inhabitants of, 3, 333, 413, 786, 799, 932,
1035, 1159, 1315, 1482
land in, 348, 775, 801
places in, 'Crowyscroft' ('Crowistoft'), 1035
'Dunkonys', 333
'Elete & Gernonis', 1169
'Holmedewe',1169
'Palentys' (close), 775
'Reves' (tenement), 799
'Rowyscroft', 799
'Sothyrton', 775
'Stonefeld', 1169
roads in, in market place, 1035
'le rode', 333
testators of, **2**, **3**, **29**, **333**, *361*, **413**, *786*, **799**,
932, **1035**, *1159*, **1315**, *1482*
wills proved at, 634, 635, 636, 1330
Mere, Joan, servant, of Combs, 47
see also atte Mere
Mergeri, William, 1042
Meriell, *see* Meryell
Merk, John, 991
Mer(s)che (Mersh), Ed., 278
Isabel, of Creeting All Saints, *283*
Robert, & family, 544
William, 544
Meryell (Meriell), John, dyer, of Sudbury, 1181
Katherine, of Long Melford, 1091
Richard, of Long Melford, 88, **1091**
William, of Barton Mills, 1389
see also Muriell
Metessharpp, Roger, of Mendlesham, **932**
METHWOLD (Nfk), warrener of, 489
Mettewynd, John, of Wattisfield, **945**
Katherine, of Wattisfield, 945
METTINGHAM, college of priests, master of,
489n
Mey, Agnes, of Lavenham, 263
Alice, 254
John, 63, 263*; the elder, of Bury St Edmunds,
263; of Lavenham, **263**; the elder, of
Thornham Magna, & family, **63**; rector of
Timworth, 225
Matilda, of Thornham Magna, 63
Richard, 63
Thomas, 63
William, 63, 1358
see also May
Meyn, Edmund, 39
John, of Barnardiston, *39*
Matilda, of Barnardiston, 39
Meyr(e) (Meire), Alice, 321, 633
John, the elder, 1284

Thomas, servant, 1033
Walter, 896
MICKFIELD, church, 345, 1417
inhabitants of, 15, 345
MILDEN, church, 1280
MILDENHALL, Bakhot family of, 749n
church, 489, 816
basin & cruets for altar, 1481
bell for, 1152
burial in, 1156n
cloths for altars, 119
cope for, 1009
image of St Leonard in, 1117n
light of Easter sepulchre, 81
light of St Mary in, 865
parish chaplain of, 1156
tower of, 120, 120n, 1404
vestment for 1156
vicar of, *see* Thomas Oldbury
gilds in, 120, 569, 683, 708, 1156, 1403
inhabitants of, 46, 220, 245, 311, 569, 598,
683, 708, 727, 750, 865, 894n, 938, 980,
1009, 1084, 1117, 1155, 1156, 1219, 1259,
1263, 1286, 1361n, 1403, 1404, 1434, 1471,
1481
manor of, 1403
open-field land in, *liii*
places in, 'Bargatewaye', 727
'Bekfeld', 683
Beck Row, 683
'Blomesyerd' (meadow), 683
'Breeche, le', 1117
'Calcallane', 865
'Clerkesmedewe', 1259
'Estfennys, le', 1403
'Frydaystrete', 1084
'Glemesfordes' (land), 683
'Holmereseye', 683
Holywell Row, 683n, 865
'Lampettes', 1403
'Lytleye', 683
market place, 865, 870, 1009, 1259
'Nycollesyerde' (meadow), 1117
'Prallys' (meadow), 683
'Reedrond, le' (marsh), 727
'Rowys, le', 683n, 870
'Sadeleris' (tenement), 1403
'Sedmanesholig', 683
'Stok, le', 683
'Styestrete, in Halywelle', 1259
'Terreirs' (land), 81
'Thevyslond', 1403
'Westfeld, le', 1403
West Row, 683n
'Wyldemeresende, 1117
poor of, 708, 1009, 1263
processional way, 569
roads in, 1009, 1117

sheep in, *li*

stots in, *li*

testators of, **65**, **81**, **119**, **219**, *220*, *512*, **569**, **598**, **683**, **708**, **727**, *750*, **865**, **870**, **938**, *980*, **1009**, **1084**, **1117**, **1155**, **1156**, **1219**, **1259**, **1263**, *1286*, **1403**, **1404**, **1404**, *1434*, *1435*, **1471**, **1481**

wills proved at, 119, 120, 239, 240, 381, 429, 489, 498, 569, 598, 708, 727, 750, 751, 865, 938, 940, 995, 1009, 1061, 1084, 1319, 1320, 1348, 1351, 1434

Mildewelle, John, rector of Long Melford, 916, 916n

MILE END (Esx), inhabitant of, 843

Millere, *see* Myller(e)

MISTLEY (Esx), land in, 192

Manningtree, a chapelry of, 1115n

MOATENDEN (Kent), priory of Trinitarian friars, 1216n

Mody, Agnes, 877

Joan, of Great Finborough, 810

John, 810*

Richard, of Newton (by Sudbury), 91, 277

Robert, of Great Finborough, **810**

Moeller, Thomas, of Kersey, 342

see also Meller(e)

Molows, Almeric, of Wattisfield, *xlvi*n, **1409**

John, 1409; smith, 945, 1409

Monde, *see* Munde

Mondessone *alias* Meller, Agnes, of Long Melford, 1105

Thomas, of Long Melford, *1105*

see also Meller

Mone, Joan, 271, 271n

John, of Fornham St Genevieve, 271n; the elder, miller, of Fornham St Genevieve, & family, **924**; the younger, of Fornham St Genevieve, 443

Margaret, of Fornham St Genevieve, 924

Money, *see* Mony(e)ye

Monk, John, of Thetford, 69, 69n

MONKS ELEIGH, church, 1280

ornaments of, 1280

rector of, *see* Walter Stapul

inhabitants of, 375, 392, 1455

land in, 42

manor (site) of, 1280

peculiar of, *xxxix*

places in, 'Higgeles' (tenement), 1280

'Reyneris' (tenement), 1280

'Wynne' (tenement), 86

roads in, 1280

Monnyng, Henry, 366

see also Munnyng

Mon(y)eye, Matilda, 725

Robert, 725

Rose, 876

Moore (More), Cecily, 586

Joan, of Fornham St Martin, 1356; of Stanstead, 132

John, 132*, 630, 1246; chaplain, 144, 942; the younger, 132; the elder, 586; of Hartest, 1356; of Haughley, *710*; rector of Little Bardfield (Esx), 942n; of Stanstead, **132**; of Whepstead, 549

Margaret, of Boxford, 586

Marion, of Haughley, 710

Richard, 132

Robert, 516, 559, 586

Simon, 529; of Boxford, & family, **586**

Thomas, 1152; of Fornham St Martin, **1356**; of Timworth, 849

Walter, of Stowmarket, *1305*

William, 132, 710

Moothows, John, 393

Morall (Morell), Richard, friar of Babwell, 1246, 1390

see also Muriell

Morchall, William, friar, 818

More, *see* Moore

Moriell, *see* Muriell

Morle, Henry, of Mildenhall, *220*

John, of Mildenhall, 727

[*unnamed*], of Mildenhall, 220

Mors, John, of the college, Sudbury, 91

William, 683

Mors *alias* Mos, Nicholas, of Bury St Edmunds, *xxxix*n

Mortemer, Alice, of Haverhill, 1011

John, of Haverhill, *1011*

Morwhyll, Thomas, 1315

see also Muriell

Moryell, *see* Muriell

Mos, *see* Mors *alias* Mos

Motte, John, of Wickhambrook, 1431

MOULTON, church, 247, 708

inhabitants of, 44, 450

land in, 759, 894

peculiar of, *xxxix*

poor of, 270, 708

Mous (Mows), Simon, 1458

Thomas, 1458*

William, 1458; of Chelsworth, **1458**

Mowe, Margaret, 227

Margery, of Bradfield St Clare, 848

Richard, of Bradfield St Clare, **848**

Mows, *see* Mous

Multon, John, of Little Thurlow, *1093*

Munde (Monde), John, 200

Thomas, 278

see also Mundys

Mundeford, John, 648; of Rishangles, **648**

Margaret, of Rishangles, 648

Osbert de, of Hockwold (Nfk), 46

Mundys, Robert, 346

see also Munde

Munnyng, Henry, rector of Wyverstone, 487, 487n
  Isabel, of Badwell Ash, 842
  Joan, of Badwell Ash, 842
  John, rector of Felsham, 185
  Richard, of Badwell Ash, **842**
  see also Monnyng
Muriell (Muryell, Moriell, Moryell), Agnes, of
    Hopton, 347
  Clarissa, of Barrow, 471; widow, of Barrow,
    488
  Isabell, 295
  Joan, of Burwell (Cambs), *1030*
  John, 740; chaplain, 1352; the younger, 295; of
    Barrow, **471**, 488; of Hopton, **347**
  Katherine, of Stanton, 1352
  Margaret, 421
  Margery, widow, of Hawstead, **640**
  Matilda, of Sudbury, 421
  Nicholas, mercer, of Stanton, **1352**
  Robert, 295; of Finningham, 347; the younger,
    of Sudbury, 421
  Roger, of Long Melford, 421; the elder, of
    Long Melford, 790
  Simon, of Lavenham, 1073
  Stephen, 295
  Thomas, of Belstead, 1346; rector of
    Chelsworth, 516n, 1279; rector of Market
    Weston, 935n; rector of Westhorpe, 347
  William, 295, 347, 673
  see also Meryell, Morall, Morwhyll
Muskett (Muschat), Agnes, of Drinkstone, 1079;
    of Sudbury, 632
  Henry, of Haughley, 977
  Isabel, of Sudbury, 632
  John, rector of Brettenham, 632, 632n, 1036,
    1466; of Drinkstone, & family, **1079**
  Marion, 1134
  Thomas, 922, 1079
  William, 632, 1079; of Sudbury, & family,
    632
Mussell, Katherine, of Bures St Mary, 317n
Mustler, John, 308, 375
Mychell, John, 1251; of Horseheath (Cambs), 396
Mychill *alias* Barker, John, *910*
  Margaret, 910
Mydylton, *see* Medylton
Myggys, Agnes, 807
  William, 807
Mylde, Thomas, of Clare, 149
Myldylton, *see* Medylton
Mylis, *see* Myllys
Myller(e) (Millere), Alice, 696; of Chedburgh,
    279
  Joan, of Lakenheath, 779
  John, 603, 893, 964; the younger, 779; of
    Lakenheath, 352; the elder, of Lakenheath,
    779; of Wattisfield, 591
  Katherine, 779; of Mildenhall, 1286

  Richard, 247
  Roger, of the college, Sudbury, 91
  Thomas, 514; of Chedburgh, 279; of
    Mildenhall, *1286*
  William, 580, 893
Myllys (Mylys, Mylis), John, chaplain, 798
  Robert, 1000, 1050, 1126, 1134, 1305, 1421
Mylsehopp, *see* Melkesop
Mylys, *see* Myllys
Mynton, Joan, of Mendlesham, 413
  John, of Mendlesham, **413**
  Thomas, 413
Myte, Alice, 1295

Narbour (Norbowr), Richard, of Thriplow
    (Cambs), 780
  William, of Elveden, *780*
NAUGHTON, church, 143, 162, 1416
  inhabitants of, 162, 745
  testator of, *745*
NAYLAND, church, 610
  antiphoner in, 108
  bell for, 142n
  burial in porch, 108
  chaplain of, 108
  churchyard, 1080n
  paving of, 142
  porch, making of, 108
  'St Mary priest' in, 573
  'St Mary service' in, 108, 108n, 860, 1080
  gilds in, 108, 142, 860, 1080, 1479
  inhabitants of, *xlivn*, 32, 108, 142, 192, 200,
    318, 573, 666, 755, 763, 815, 860, 909, 930,
    1080, 1290, 1479
  places in, 'Cruddes' (tenement), 192
    'Lallefordstrete', 192
  road, from Stoke by Nayland, 930
  testators of, *32*, **108**, **142**, **192**, *200*, *318*, *383*,
    573, *666*, *755*, *763*, *815*, **860**, *874*, *909*,
    1080, *1222*, *1290*, *1314*, **1479**
  wills proved at, 32, 1222
NEDGING, church, 162
  places in, 'Abbotes' (tenement), 1346
NEEDHAM (in Gazeley), *see* GAZELEY
NEEDHAM MARKET, poor of, 20
Neell, Dennis, of Landwade (Cambs), *627*
  Isabel, 545
  Richard, of Lavenham, 86
  Robert, of Coney Weston, 17
  Roger, of Long Melford, *545*
  Thomas, 627; of Haverhill, *312*
Nelyngge *alias* Facon, Joan, of Boxford, 257
  John, of Boxford, **257**
NETTLESTEAD, inhabitant of, 1044
Neuhawe, *see* Newhawe
Neuhous, William, & family, 507
Neve, Joan, 835
  John, 833, 869

Marion, 152
Thomas, 835; tailor, of Great Finborough, 538
  see also Catour alias Neve
Newborg, William, rector of Wordwell, 1060
NEWBRIDGE, see ICKBURGH (Nfk)
Newelond, Alice, of Bildeston, 1103
  John, of Bildeston, *1103*
Newestrete, Robert de, 1295
Newhawe (Neuhawe), John, of Great Horringer,
  722, 826
  Thomas, 1291
Newman, Alice, of Sudbury, 818
  John, 790; the younger, 164, 511, 1073; of
    Lavenham, 350; the elder, of Lavenham,
    164, 1073; baker, of Sudbury, 26, **818**
  Robert, of Lavenham, & family, 790
  Roger, 818
  Thomas, 818
NEWMARKET, chapels/churches of, 28n
  church/chapel of All Saints, *xxxix*n, 28, 28n,
    54, 379, 381, 399, 574, 724, 1029, 1100,
    1357, 1463
    chaplain of, 1463
    light in, 1463
    roodloft in, 28, 28n
  church/chapel of BVM, 28, 28n, 381, 399, 499,
    724, 793, 1463
    chapel of St Theobald in, 708, 708n
  'Gryffyn, le' (messuage) in, 28
  inhabitants of, 724, 732, 793, 1463, 1470
  (market) stall in, 50
  poor of, 270, 708
  testators of, **28, 54, 379, 399, 499, 574, 716,**
    724, *732,* **793, 1358, 1463**
  wills proved at, 28, 46, 54, 203, 219, 243, 244,
    389, 435, 505, 697, 732, 822, 909, 911,
    1029, 1037, 1100, 1119, 1308, 1357, 1463,
    1467, 1468, 1468
Newporte, Thomas, of Kedington, 1094n
NEWTON (in Thornham), see THORNHAM
  MAGNA
NEWTON (by Sudbury), church, bells in, 463
  rector of, see William Hall
  inhabitants of, 91, 257, 463
  testator of, **463**
  will proved at, 813
Newton, William, 1080
Nicholson, William, 907
Nicoll, John, chaplain, 351; rector of Fornham St
  Martin, 351n
Nicole, Henry, 589
  Joan, of Chevington, 589
  John, the elder, clerk, 589; the younger, 589
  Roger, of Chevington, **589**
Nobyl(l) (Nob(e)le), Adam, of Westley, **1220**
  Agnes, of Westley, 1220
  Alice, of Bury St Edmunds, 1220
  Henry, of Little Saxham, 1220

John, of Bury St Edmunds, 1220; of Great
  Horringer, *436*; of Yoxford, 346n
  Margaret, 232
  Robert, 1291; of Great Horringer, 1220
  Walter, of Great Horringer, 436; of Little
    Saxham, & family, 1220
Noche, Peter, of Lavenham, 86
Nog, William, clerk, of Sudbury, 157
Noke, see Nook(e)
Nonne, see Nunne
'NONNYSHAM', see SWAFFHAM BULBECK
  (Cambs)
Nook(e) (Noke), Robert, 923, 1227; of Kersey,
  1115
Norbert, John, 1426
Norbowr, see Narbour
Noreys, John, 1453
  William, of Brockford, 1453
Norfold, Joan, 146
  see also Norfolk
Norfolk, John Howard, duke of, 1194n
Norfolk (Norfokk, ?Noff'), Christian, 1118
  William, 1118; chaplain, 958
  [unnamed], *1118*
  see also Northfolk
Norman, Alice, widow, of Barrow, & family, **890**
  Isabel, 291; of Badlingham, in Chippenham
    (Cambs), 440
  Joan, of Barrow, 291
  John, 291, 1180; the elder, of Barrow,
    291; mercer, of Barrow, **693**; of Little
    Finborough, **1180**
  Margaret, of Barrow, 693
  Margery, 187
  Richard, 1127; of Clare, 832, 1010
  Robert, of Gazeley, 693
  Simon, of Barrow, 187
  Thomas, of Badlingham, in Chippenham
    (Cambs), 440, of Badlingham (Cambs) &
    family, **440**; of Chippenham (Cambs), *93*
  William, 187, 440, 693; of Barrow, 890; of
    Great Thurlow, *134*
Nors, Robert, 1099
North, Joan, of Bardwell, 78
  John, 78; of Bardwell, **78**
Northery, John, 676
  Robert, 676
Northfolk, William, 517
  see also Norfolk
NORTON, church, 726
  altar of St Mary in, 438
  bells in, 373
  light of BVM in, 438, 671, 782, 1313,
    1333, 1379, 1465
  rector of, 1249, 1465
    see also John Dassh, Nicholas Irby
  gilds in, 373, 1249, 1249n, 1333, 1379, 1381

inhabitants of, 373, 438, 441, 671, 964, 1255, 1313, 1333, 1379
land in, 725, 760, 1437
manors of, 552, 836, 836n, 838n, 1333, 1333n
places in, 'Chyrchfeld', 441, 1379
  'Dalme' (field), 441
  'Frawnceys' (wood), 441
  'Hassockemere', 441
  'Litlehaughe' (Little Haugh, manor), 552, 836, 836n
  Norton Hall (manor), 552, 1333, 1333n
  'Pykes' (tenement), 1465
  'Pykes Cloos', 1465
  'Rogynys' (tenement) 441
  'Shayngar' (land), 1333
  'Tunstret' ('Townestrete'), 1249n, 1333, 1381, 1464
  'Upstrete', 1249
  'Weswell', 441
  'Wysham' (land), 1333
poor of, 782, 1313
testators of, *307*, *336*, *373*, **438**, **441**, **671**, **782**, **1313**, **1379**, *1380*, **1381**, **1465**
wills proved at, 146, 336, 1379, 1380, 1381
Norton, Roger, priest, 671
  Thomas, friar, 488
NORWICH (Nfk), archdeaconry of, *xl*
  cathedral, 882, 1096, 1200, 1419, 1462
    image of Holy Trinity in, 1207n
  church of St Stephen, 1207n
    pilgrimage to, 1207n
    vicar of, *see* Richard Caister
  college of St Mary in the fields, *xliin*
  deanery of, 1493
  diocese of, *xxxviii*
    bishop of, 106, 210, 210n
    consistory court of, *xxxix*, *xl*n, 939, 939n, 954n, 1008n
  hospital of St Giles, *xliin*
  house of Austin friars, 1276
  house of Carmelite friars, *xlix*,17, 398, 723, 1026, 1076, 1372, 1497
    friar of, 539
  house of Friars Preachers, 1276
    inhabitant of, 460
    pilgrimage to, 1207
  priory of Bendictine nuns, Carrow, 347
  will proved at, 1493
Norwold, Matilda, of Icklingham, **940**
  Peter, 65
  Robert, of Eriswell, 352
  Thomas, of Norton, 441
Note, Alice, of Langham, 7
  John, 7, 358*, 552; of Norton, *307*; of Thurston, & family, **358**
  Margaret, of Norton, 307
  Thomas, of Thurston, & family, 358
  William, 358; of Langham, **7**; of Thurston, 552

see also Nott(e)
Nott(e) (Not, Noot), Alice, of Groton, 812
  John, 308, 812, 1193, 1388; barber, of Boxford, 308; of West Stow, *1022*
  Margaret, of West Stow, *1022*
  Richard, 316
  Robert, of Groton, 1388; of Groton, & family, **812**
  Simon, 812
  see also Note
Notyng, Margaret, 1034
NOWTON, church, 116
Nunne (Nonne), Agnes, of Felsham, 185
  George, of Bradfield St George, 867; of Felsham, 185
  Isabel, of Rougham, 124
  Joan, of Rougham, 1297
  John, 825, 1244, 1297; of Hessett, 370; of Rougham, 59; of Rougham, & family, 124; the elder, of Rougham, 1297; the younger, of Rougham, & family, **1297**
  Nicholas, of Hessett, & family, **370**
  Thomas, 1297
  Walter, 1113; of Hessett, 232
  William, 1297
Nydyll, Isabel, of Lavenham, 299
  John, of Lavenham, **299**
Nyghtynghale, Andrew, 521

OAKLEY, church of St Andrew, 16n
  church of St Nicholas, 16n
  inhabitants of, 636, 949, 1005, 1166
  places in 'Lambcote Weye', 1005
    'Pecolyscroft'in, 636
  testators of, *16*, **636**, **949**, **1005**, *1166*, *1476*
OAKLEY MAGNA, testator of, *1166*, 1166n
Obchester, David, chaplain, of Newmarket, 1463
Obroke, Alice, 1466
  Isabel, 1466
  Margaret, 1466
  see also Brok(e) *and* Brook
OCCOLD, inhabitant of, 659
  land in, 785
  mortuary paid in, *xlvin*
  testators of, *74*, *104*, *250*, **537**, *659*, **1165**
  will proved at, 1165
Ode, Alice, of Barway in Soham (Cambs), 1319
  John, of Barway in Soham (Cambs), **1319**
Od(e)ham, Margaret, benefactor of Bury St Edmunds, *xli–xlii*
  John, 98
  William, 1246
Odlyn, Ed., of Wortham, & family, *733*
Ofwode, Alice, 90
  John, the elder, 90; the younger, 90
Oky, John, of Mellis, *734*
Olavyur, Thomas, servant, 1255

Oldale, Anne, of Sudbury, *1447*
  Walter, of Sudbury, 1447
Oldbury (Oldburgh), Thomas, vicar of Mildenhall,
  865, 865n, 1117, 1117n
OLD NEWTON, church, 346, 775
    altar of St John in, 908
    altar of St Mary of Pity in, 908
    candlebeam painting, 908
    celures over altars in, 908
    furnishings of, 908
    light of St John in, 908, 908n
    land for bell-ropes in, 908
    reredos for rood in, 908
    roof painting, 908
    tower, 908n, 1192, 1192n
  DAGWORTH in, 20n, 1192
    chapel of, 20n
  gildhall in, 1419
  inhabitants of, 340, 346, 908, 1097, 1097n,
    1192, 1296, 1411
  land in, 497, 775, 1169n, 1296
  origins of parish of, 20n
  places in, 'Aptheweytys' (tenement), 1192
    'Morys' (land), 1296
  testators of, **340**, **908**, **1192**, **1296**, **1411**, **1419**
  will proved at, 348
Olyve, Alice, of Cavendish, 776
  Joan, of Haughley, 461
  John, 29, 1375; of Haughley, & family, **461**; of
    Mendlesham, **29**
  Margaret, of Mendlesham, 29
  Thomas, 776
  William, 776; the elder, of Cavendish, **776**
Omfrey (Owmfrey), John, the elder, of Combs,
  1392
  Margaret, of Combs, 1392
  Roger, 1392
  Thomas, of Lavenham, 164
  see also Homfrey, Humfrey, Umfrey
ONEHOUSE, church, 497, 775, 977
    panel on high altar in, 1306
Onge, Adam, of Barningham, **59**, **124**
  Margaret, of Barningham, 59, 124
  William, 124
Ordrych, William, of Hitcham, 1047
ORFORD, house of Austin friars, 345, 908, 1035,
  1276, 1453
Orger, Thomas, of Mendlesham, *1159*
Ormond, James le Botiller, earl of, 1246n
Osbern(e), Geoffrey, of Stowmarket, *1000*
  John, 1333; friar, 1216; the elder, of
    Rickinghall Inferior, 900
  [*unnamed*], friar, 421, 740
Osmo(u)nd, Stephen, 547
  Thomas, 91, 816
Osteler, Adam, 21; of Drinkstone, 497
  Joan, of Shelland, 21
  Roger, of Shelland, & family, **21**

Ot(t)ley (Ottele), Agnes, of Little Saxham, 34, 246
  Joan, 671
  John, 34; of Little Saxham, & family, **246**
  Robert, 34
  William, 246; of Little Saxham, & family, **34**
OUSDEN, church, 247, 1191, 1418
    porch of, 1285, 1285n
    rector of, *see* Simon Farwell
  inhabitants of, 449, 883, 926, 1285
  roads in, 1285
  testators of, *163*, **449**, *883*, *926*, **1285**
Outtyng, Isabel, nun of Malling (Kent), 539
Overall, John, of Haverhill, 633
Overey, Thomas, of Ingham, 182
Oversouth, Katherine, & family, 1044
  Margaret, of Westley, 226
  Margery, 1123
  Richard, of Little Saxham, 226, 616
  Thomas, 1044
  William, of Westley, 4; of Westley, & family,
    226
Owmfrey, *see* Omfrey
OXBOROUGH (Nfk), Oxburgh (house) in, 489n
  testator of, **489**

Paas, John, 1008
Padyll (Padle), John, of Haughley, 795; of
    Snailwell (Cambs), 902
Page, Agnes, of Ickworth, 139; of Ixworth, 452
  Emma, of Mildenhall, 219
  John, 139, 337; chaplain, 1422; of Ingham,
    1201; of Ixworth, *452*; of Stanstead, 132
  Ralph, of Mildenhall, 219
  Roger, of Risby, 1279
  Thomas, 139; servant, 611
  Walter, of Ickworth, & family, **139**
Paier, William, 556
PAKENHAM, church, light of BVM in chancel
    of, 343, 1255, 1287
  gilds in, 335, 343, 1255, 1287, 1451
  inhabitants of, 191, 335, 343, 821, 887, 1017,
    1046, 1287, 1378, 1449
  land in, 335, 760, 1240n, 1437
  manor of Pakenham Hall, 335
  places in, 'Breggestrete', 1255
    'Dereburgh' (land), 1033
    'Dopes & Waternays' (land), 1255
    'Fyssheryswanch', 343
    'Galfhowe', 343
    'Grymston' (street), 1255
    'Litleburghhyll', 343
    'Peperes' (tenement), 1033
    'Redcastell' (land), 1255
    'Woodeclos, le', 1437
  road in, to Pakenham church, 821
  testators of, *10*, **343**, *514*, **821**, *887*, *956*, *1017*,
    1046, **1255**, *1378*, *1449*

Pakenham, Andrew, of North Pickenham (Nfk), 877, 877n
John, 814, 1111, 1124, 1282; of Cockfield, *607*
Robert, esquire, of North Pickenham (Nfk), 877n
Pakke, Marion, of Eye, 1318
William, of Eye, *1318*
Paleyser, John, of Culford, **315**
Margery, of Culford, 315
Reginald, 315
PALGRAVE, church, 492, 1076
burial in, 1330n
burial in chancel of, 1418n
rector of, *see* William Dakke
stools in, 1418n
gild in, 492
inhabitants of, 432, 1330, 1349, 1350, 1418
land in, 22, 1492
testators of, *432, 997, 1330, 1349, 1350*
wills proved at, 369, 543, 875, 989, 1151, 1417, 1418
Palgrave, Joan, of Newmarket, 499
John, 499
Katherine, of Wetheringsett, 1034
William, of Newmarket, **499**
Palmer(e), Christian, of Elmswell, 445
Henry, of Elmswell, *445*
Joan, 449
John, 449, 478, 807, 846; of Soham (Cambs), & family, **478**
Margaret, of Soham (Cambs), 478
Richard, 173, 524
Robert, 1001
Simon, 90
Thomas, 626; of Layham, & family, **197**; of Soham (Cambs), 903
William, 696; of Wordwell, *1060*
Paman, Robert, of Chevington, 314n, 589
Panell, William, 1246; of Glemsford, 805
Pap', Walter, of Glemsford, *576*
Parker, Augustine, 1067, 1416
Ed., 845
Henry, of Semer, & family, **1416**
Joan, 791
John, 415, 536, 1147, 1416; chaplain, 52; chaplain, of Thorndon, 962; rector of Timworth, 892, 962; rector of Great Wratting, 536n
Katherine, of Lidgate, 114; servant, 1315
Lawrence, 773; of Alpheton, 773n
Margaret, of Semer, 1416
Richard, 1416; of Colchester (Esx), 275
Robert, of Lidgate, & family, **114**
Thomas, of Thorpe Morieux, *773*
see also Pek' (Parker) *and* Cook *alias* Parker
Parkyn, Joan, of Barningham, 1278
John, 1464; the younger, 807; of Barningham,

1226n; the elder, of Barningham, **1278**; of Ingham, 182; of Great Livermere, **182**
Katherine, of Great Livermere, 182
Margaret, of Culford, *1464*
Simon, 794
Thomas, 794
William, 1464
Parle, Alice, of Bildeston, 1125
John, of Bildeston, **1125**; barker, of Lavenham, **402**
Rose, of Lavenham, 402
Parman, John, of Stradishall, 1081, 1082
Parmenter, Alice, 714
Beatrice, of Hitcham, 27
John, 714
William, of Hitcham, *27*
Parson, *see* Person
Part, Clarissa, 1248
John, 1248
Partrych, John, 757
see also Peretrych
Parys(h), John, of Soham (Cambs), 903
Richard, canon of Spinney (Cambs), 254
Paternoster, Roger, 543
Patt(e)le, *see* Patyll
Patter, John, 196
Patye, Mary, 749
Walter, butcher, 749
Patyll (Patt(e)le), John, 775, 842, 1491
Marion, 152
William, of Badwell Ash, 842n, *1491*
Paule (Powle), John, chaplain, 732; rector of Great Waldingfield, 732n
Thomas, 417, 888
Walter, 1291
Paxman, Alice, of Burwell (Cambs), 911
Edmund, of Burwell (Cambs), 67, 389, 911, 1133, 1265
John, & family, 911
Margaret, 1265
Matilda, of Burwell (Cambs), 682
Thomas, 911*; of Burwell (Cambs), **911**
William, 682, 1265; of Burwell (Cambs), 1133, **682**
Payche, Thomas, of Soham (Cambs), 238n
Payn(e), Agnes, of Sudbury, 1492, 1493; of Thelnetham, 1494
Cecily, of Thelnetham, 1494
Ed., 1494
Geoffrey, of Wortham, **873**
Hugh, Master, 863
Joan, of Sudbury, 1466n
John, 816, 1457; of Haverhill, 211; of Stoke by Nayland, 546; of Sudbury, 1492; of Wortham, *424*, 1140n
Margaret, widow, of Haverhill, **211**; of Thelnetham, 1494; of Wortham, 424, 873, *1140*

Richard, 424, 1140
Robert, 1492, 1494; of Sudbury, **1492**; of
 Thelnetham, 506, **1494**
Stephen, of Roydon (Nfk), 1140
William, of Lavenham, 211; of Sudbury, **1493**
Paynet, John, 1263
Payntour, Agnes, of Burwell (Cambs), 150
 John, 150; the elder, husbandman, of Burwell
 (Cambs), & family, **150**
Pec, John, 341
 see also Peek
Pecok (Pekok), Joan, 676
 John, 676
 Margaret, of Great Barton, 180
Pedder, *see* Hamond *alias* Pedder
Peek (Peke), Agnes, of Lawshall, 587
 Thomas, of Lawshall, *587*
 William, of Higham (by Stratford St Mary)
 see also Pec
Peg . . .[*damaged*], Geoffrey, 238
Pegas, Christian, of Brandon, *141*
Pek' (Parker), Edmund, 19
 John, 19; of Chilton in Stowmarket, **19**
 Margaret, of Chilton in Stowmarket, 19
 William, 19
 see also Parker
Peke, *see* Peek
Pekerel(l) (Pekrell, Pekyrrell, Pykerell), Agnes, of
 Thurston, 1451
 Isabel, of Thurston, 358n, 782, 1437
 Joan, of Rickinghall Superior, 1207
 John, 1437; chaplain, 358, 552, 782, 1437;
 of Thurston, 358n, 782, **1437**; the elder, of
 Thurston, 552; rector of Westhorpe, 358n,
 1451; of Wetherden, **33**
 Robert, of Norton, 358n, **782**
 Roger, of Thurston, 347n, **1451**
 Thomas, 33, 1437, 1451*; of Lavenham, 130;
 of Rickinghall Superior, **1207**
Pekok, *see* Pecok
Pellycan (Pellican), James, 277, 800
 John, 404, 277, 813; of Sudbury, 800n, **277**
 Seyve, of Sudbury, 277, 800n
 Thomas, 277, 800
 William, 277, 800
Penteneye, Ralph, 961
Peper (Pepyr), Agnes, 1008
 Alice, 146, 1008
 John, 1008; & family, 320; of Eye, 432
 Richard, 1008
 Robert, 481; the elder, of Eye, **481**
 Rose, of Eye, 481
 Sarah, of Palgrave, *432*
Percyvale (Persivale, Persyvale), John, 894
 Margaret, 894
 Robert, of Newmarket, 724, 793
 Walter, of Sudbury, 1364
Pere, Agnes, 158

Peretrych (Pertrych), Gilbert, 289
 Katherine, of Acton, **289**, 823
 Margaret, 289
 William, 289
 see also Partrych
Perkham (Pykeham), William, vicar of Sudbury
 All Saints, 175, 175n
Perkyn, John, 889; of Barningham, 954, 957n; the
 elder, of Barningham, & family, **954**
 Simon, 954
 Thomas, of Coney Weston, 954, 957
 William, of Barningham, 954
Perle, Agnes, of Lavenham, 1073
 John, 1073; of Lavenham, **1073**
 Robert, 1073
Perpount (Perpontes), John, the elder, 715; the
 younger, of Denston, *715*
 Margaret, of Westhorpe, **5**
Perry, *see* Perye
Pers, Alice, 385
Persivale, Persyvale, *see* Percyvale
Person (Parson), John, of Lavenham, 102, 126;
 mercer, of Lavenham, 305
Pertrych, *see* Peretrych
Perye (Perry, Purey, Purye), Alice, of Kersey, 719
 Joan, of Nayland, 860
 John, 1115n; of Haverhill, *1148*; of Kersey, &
 family, **719**
 Meliora, of Kersey, 1115
 Robert, of Kersey, 342, 719, **1115**
 Thomas, of Bardwell, 97
 William, 594
Peryman, Peter, of Bures, 356n
Peteman, John, 361, 786
 Richard, 932, 1035, 1482
'Peterthorp', *see* THORPE ST PETER
Pethyrton, Henry, of Sudbury, **91**
Petite, John, 552
Petynggale, Agnes, 1218
Petywate (Petyvat(t)e), John, of Glemsford, 688,
 1353
 Margery, 1353
Pevsner, Sir Nikolaus, architectural historian,
 *xlvii*n
Peykot, John, of Withersfield, *504*
Peyntour, John, 927; chaplain, 537; of Burwell,
 927n
Peyton, Alice, 146
 Thomas, priest, 142
Philip (Philyp, Phylyp), John, 193; of Long
 Melford, 375
 Rose, 375
 William, 375
Picher (Pycher), Meliora, widow, of Kentford,
 1020
 Robert, 1020
PICKENHAM, NORTH (Nfk), Cotes (hamlet)
 in, 877

inhabitant of, 877
land in, 877
manor of 'Virlyes' in, 877
PICKENHAM, SOUTH (Nfk), land in, 877
Place, Andrew, 938; of Mildenhall, 938
Eleanor, of Lavenham, 126
John, 938; of Lavenham, 102, *126*, 161
Rose, widow, of Mildenhall, & family, **120**
Thomas, of Mildenhall, **938**
William, 311, 938; chaplain, 938, 938n; of
Mildenhall, 311
Plandon, Edmund, 1190
Richard, of Long Melford, 1091
Plante, Joan, of Great Finborough, 538
John, of Great Finborough, **538**
Plasshe, William, of Sudbury, 632
Playford, John, 1117, 1286, 1404; of Mildenhall,
120, 683
Margaret, of Mildenhall, 683
William, of Mildenhall, 683
Plesawns, Geoffrey, 57
Pole, William de la, duke of Suffolk, 1076n
Poley (Polay), John, 1169
Margaret, 1169n
Margery, 1169n
Richard, of Stoke Ash, 1169n
Simon, 1169
Poleyn, William, 1173
see also Pollyng
Polle, Adam, of Barnham, **1268**
William, 1268
see also Poole
Pollyng, John, clerk, 1027
see also Poleyn
POLSTEAD, alms-deeds to be done in, 257
boundaries of, 296n
inhabitants of, 529, 650, 1484
land in, 586, 1347
places in, 'Normanys' (tenement), 1484
'Warwell' (tenement), 1484
testators of, *650*, **1484**
will proved at, 188
Polsted, William, of Kersey, 342
Polych, Agatha, of Oakley, 1166
Thomas, 1166
William, of Oakley, **1166**
Ponder (Pondyr), John, of Waldingfield, & family,
1469
Katherine, 725
Lucy, 174
Margaret, of Waldingfield, 1469
Robert, of Great Waldingfield, 758
Thomas, 1280
William, 174
Ponge (Pure), Agnes, of Poslingford, *332*
see also Punge
Pood, John, of Stoke by Nayland, 192
Poole, John, of Fordham (Cambs), 1351

William, of Fordham (Cambs), *1351*
see also Pole *and* Polle
Pope, Alice, of Mellis, 369
Henry, of Mellis, & family, **369**
John, of Burgate, 726; of Wattisfield, *591*; of
Yaxley, 369, 798
Richard, 1276; of Knettishall, **975**
Robert, of Redgrave, 649
Walter, of Thrandeston, *649*
William, priest, 369, 798, 1371
Poperyk(e) (Poperync), John, of Chippenham
(Cambs), 1100
Margaret, of Chippenham (Cambs), 1100
[*unnamed*], 1265
see also Poperyng
Poperyng, Joan, of Colchester (Esx), 836
Richard, of Colchester (Esx), 836
see also Poperyk(e)
Port, John, 1225; of Barningham, *121*
Porter, John, 399, 1194; of Chelsworth, **1194**
Katherine, 399; of Chelsworth, 1194
Portewey, William, of Ipswich, 108
Portrose, John, of Sudbury, 277
POSLINGFORD, inhabitants of, 112, 113, 332,
1190
land in, 507
testators of, *70*, **113**, **173**, *524*, *988*, **1190**
Potager (Potenger), John, chaplain, 1274, 1493
William, chaplain, of Walsham le Willows, 457,
562, 672, 1042, 1272
Poteer, Agnes, of Bures, 1135
William, of Bures, *1135*
see also Potter(e)
Potenger, *see* Potager
Potter(e), Agnes, 474
Beatrice, 1218
John, 1218*; of Mendham, 58
Marion, of Clare, **1218**
Richard, 1218
Robert, 1218
Rose, 1218
Simon, 529
Power, Henry, of ?Great Barton, *1236*
Margaret, of ?Great Barton, 1236n
Nicholas, of Rougham, 1345, 1345n
Powle, *see* Paule
Powlyn, John, of Timworth, **892**, 1109n
Katherine, of Timworth, 892, *1109*
Poye, Margaret, of Walsham le Willows, 518
Peter, of Walsham le Willows, *518*
Prat, John, 381
Prath, Geoffrey, chaplain, 247
John, the elder, 247
Richard, of Ashley (Cambs), & family, **247**
Rose, of Ashley (Cambs), 247
Thomas, 247
Pratyman, William, 24
Pravy, Stephen, of Great Livermere, 827, 828

Precor, John, 586
Prentys (Preyntese, Prentyzys), Agnes, of Clare, 1010
   Alexander, 420
   Alice, 566
   George, of Sudbury, 1364
   Joan, 1364
   John, 997; of Clare, **1010**; of Kersey, **566**
   Katherine, of Sudbury, & family, **420**
PRESTON, church, 374
   light of image of Our Lady in, 929
   cloth in, *li*
   inhabitants of, 102, 761, 814, 929, 1111, 1111n, 1124, 1173
   land in, 102, 374, 773n
   places in, 'Hyestret', 1111n
      Preston Hall, 1111
      'Treves' (tenement), 929
   testators of, *761, 814, 929, 1111, 1124, 1173, 1282*
   will proved at, 391
Preston, John, friar, 47
   Ralph, of Stoke by Nayland, 544
   William, 544
Preyntese, *see* Prentys
Priest, Robert, 421
Prime, John, of Thrandeston, 649
Prince, Margaret, of Sudbury, 1364
Priowur, *see* Pryo(u)r
Profete, Richard, of Newton (by Sudbury), 257
Prom, John, 801; of Brockford, **801**
   Olive, 801
   William, 801
Pryce, Robert, 660
Pryk (Prylke, Prykke, Prykes), Eden, 640
   Isabel, of Lavenham, 462
   John, 1162
   Katherine, poor woman, 640
   Roger, chaplain, 90, 265
   William, 57, 693
Pryme, James, of Thrandeston, *604*
   John, 604
   Margery, of Thrandeston, 604
Prynchet, Agnes, of Chelsworth, 204
   Joan, of Chelsworth, 204
   John, of Chelsworth, **204**
   Simon, 204
Pryo(u)r (Priowur), Isabel, of Great Cornard, 941
   John, the younger, 1255
   William, 630; of Great Cornard, **941**
Pryt, John, of Creeting St Peter, 1049
Puget, John, 683
Pulham, Richard, 875
   Robert, chaplain, of Old Newton, 908n
Pulkoo, Henry, 355; of Lavenham, 355
   John, of Lavenham, 462, **355**
   Lettice, of Lavenham, 355
   Thomas, 355

Pultere, John, of Badwell Ash, 674
Pumpy *alias* Tylney, Richard, vicar of Clare, 43
Pundre, *see* Pundyr
Pundye, Ralph, clerk, 674
Pundyr (Pundre), John, 136
   Katherine, 1337
Punge, Richard, of Poslingford, **173**
   see also Ponge
Punte, Agnes, of Palgrave, 1349
   John, the elder, 1165; the younger, 1165; of Palgrave, *1349*
   Thomas, of Occold, **1165**
Pure, *see* Ponge
Purey, *see* Perye
Purlond, Henry, clerk, 168; rector of Chevington, 168n, 314, 438, 441, 589, 615; rector of Stanningfield, 168n
Purpyll (Purpylt), Henry, of Denham (by Bury), & family, **269**
   John, 269, 1396
   Margaret, of Denham (by Bury), 269
   William, 269
Purser(e), Christine, of Stoke by Nayland, 610
   John, 610; of Stoke by Nayland, & family, **610**
   Thomas, 610; chaplain, of Boxford, 308, 316, 365, 380, 529, 586, 1089; parish priest of Boxford, 612
   William, 610; of Stoke by Nayland, 610, 610n
Purye, *see* Perye
Pusk, James, of Kersey, 342, **392**; of Woolpit, 713
   John, of Kersey, 392, 1245
   Katherine, 392
Pycher, *see* Picher
Pye, Alice, of Assington, 215, 1057
   Edmund, 215, **1057**
   Joan, of Assington, 1057
   John, of Assington, 1057
   Lettice, of Assington, 1057
   Richard, the elder, of Assington, 1057; the younger, of Assington, 1057; rector of Brome, 1158
   Thomas, of Assington, **215**; 1057*
Pykchese, Walter, 1473, 1473n
Pyk(e), Agnes, of Stanton, 634
   John, of Stanton, & family, **634**; chaplain, 438, 634
Pykeham, *see* Perkham
Pykerell, *see* Pekerel(l)
Pylcrek, Walter, 181
Pymbyll, Robert, 750
Pynne, Margaret, of Walberswick, 1090n
Pyper, Geoffrey, 131
   Joan, servant, 474
   Thomas, of Hawstead, 640
   William, of Lavenham, 446, 661
Pyrty, Christian, of Thorndon, 817
   Thomas, of Thorndon, 809, **817**
Pytman, Richard, of Mendlesham, 1482n

Pyt(t), John, the elder, of Wattisfield, **964**
    Robert, 591, 964

Quarry (Qwarre, Qwarry), Christine, 1364
    Geoffrey, 795, 1459; of Drinkstone, 1459n
    Henry, of Hitcham, **1459**
    John, dyer, 874
    Katherine, of Hitcham, 1459
    Thomas, of Drinkstone, 777
Quenyve, William, vicar of Stoke by Nayland, *lii*,
    610, 610n
    see also Wynyeve
Qwakefen, Geoffrey, chaplain, 1302
Qwarre, Qwarry, *see* Quarry
Qwedewelle, John, 317
Qweler, *see* Wheler
Qwethereld (Qwedereld), Robert, 250, 537
    see also Whedereld
Quintyn, *see* Qwyntyn
Qwych, William, 931
Qwyk, Alice, of Edwardstone, 1496
    Henry, 1496
    John, 1496
    Walter, 1496*; of Edwardstone, **1496**
Qwyn, Marion, of Thrandeston, 808, *906*
    Thomas, of Eye, *808*, 906n
Qwyntyn (Quintyn, Qwyntyn), Margery, 91, 1077,
    1168
Qwypp, Amicia, 1422
Qwy(y)thand, Ralph, 581
    Sarah, of Icklingham, *581*
Qwytlok, John, 725
    see also Whytlok
Qwytop, Agnes, 982
    see also Whytop
Qwytynge, Margaret, 1471
    see also Whytyng

Rampoly (Rampo(y)le), Clarice, of Rickinghall
    Superior, 679
    Isabel, of Rickinghall Superior, 679
    John, of Rickinghall Superior, **679**, 1376n
    Margaret, of Rickinghall, 1376
    Matilda, of Rickinghall Superior, 679
    Thomas, 1409; of Rickinghall, 679, *1376*; of
    Walsham le Willows, 767
RAMSEY (Hunts), abbey of Benedictine monks,
    1052, 1052n, 1475
Ramsey, John, archdeacon's official, rector of
    Thelnetham, *xlii*, *xlii*n
Rand(e) (Raunde), Joan, 513; of Sporle (Nfk),
    1400; of Little Wratting, *266*
    John, of Sporle (Nfk), 1400, 1400n; of Great
    Waldingfield, *513*
    Richard, 1400, 1400n
    Thomas, of Bardwell, 55
Randolff (Randolf(e), Randolphe), Joan, 1398
    John, 1197; chaplain, 9; the younger, 1398; the

    middle, of Great Thurlow, 1398; of Little
    Thurlow, 1398; the elder, of Thurlow, 1398
    William, 1489
RATTLESDEN, church, 1075
    image of BVM in, 1031
    fire at (20th century), 1310n
    gild in, 1031
    Hardhead family of, 674n
    inhabitants of, 439, 439n, 699, 747, 1031,
    1032, 1075, 1143, 1144, 1310
    Man family of, 784n
    places in, 'Buttes Croft', 1310
    'Butts', 1310n
    'Cherchestrete, le', 1031
    Poy Street, 439n
    'Wodecroft', 90
    testators of, *123*, **146**, ?*148*, *455*, *558*, *699*,
    747, *765*, **784**, **868**, **1031**, *1143*, *1144*, **1310**,
    1436
    wills proved at, 699, 765, 942, 1031, 1143,
    1144
Ratlesden, Thomas, monk, 160
Raunde, *see* Rand(e)
Rawlyn, Lawrence, of Denham (by Bury), 269
Ray, Agnes, 289
    Anne, of Newmarket, 1463
    John, 696, 1320; of Newmarket, & family,
    1463; of Wickhambrook, & family, **696**; of
    Woodditton (Cambs), *1320*
    Robert, of Denston, 696
    William, monk, of Thetford, 1463
RAYLEIGH (Esx), land in, 489
Rayner (Raynor), Alice, of Soham (Cambs), 1041
    Andrew, of Soham (Cambs), **1041**, 1326n
    Elizabeth, 1041
    John, 1041
Reche, Augustine, 1089
    John, the younger, 1089
    Margaret, widow, of Boxford, **1089**
    Thomas, 1089
Recheford, Margery, of Worlington, *1053*
REDE, inhabitants of, 125, 960
    land in, 279
    pigs in, *li*
    testator of, **960**
Rede, *see* Reede
Rede *alias* Baly, John, 1196
Redelysworth, John, 1399
    Robert, 1399
    Rose, of Badwell Ash, 1399
    William, of Badwell Ash, & family, **1399**
Reder, *see* Reeder
REDGRAVE, BOTESDALE in, chapel of St
    Botolph, 252, 252n, 325, 344, 889n, 900,
    971, 981, 1005, 1170, 1170n
    inhabitants of, 252, 344, 401, 726, 971,
    981, 1015, 1170, 1341, 1354, 1368,
    1371, 1373, 1374

land in, 1170
testators of, **252**, **325**, **344**, *442*, *596*, *925*,
971, **981**, *1015*, *1016*, **1341**, **1354**, **1373**,
1374
wills proved at, 492, 873, 442, 596, 604,
726, 878, 879, 880, 900, 976, 1005,
1070, 1170, 1224, 1270, 1271, 1354,
1371, 1372, 1373, 1376, 1477
church, 981, 1076, 1373
Botesdale parish clerk in, 252
rector of, *see* William Halle, Robert
Hamelyn
vestments for, 1354
Fen Street ('Fenstrete') in, 341, 341n
inhabitants of, 341, 596, 649, 671, 1016, 1238
land in, 406, 787
testators of, **341**, **726**, **1238**, *1270*
Redgrave, Clement, of Great Livermere, *35*
REDLINGFIELD, priory of Benedictine nuns, 20,
479, 749, 1276, 1315
nun of, 305n
testator of, **756**
Rednale, Alice, of Rattlesden, 1075
Thomas, 1143; of Rattlesden, 1075
Rednesse, Nicholas, of Kedington, 1213
Redstone, Vincent Borough, Suffolk historian, *x*/n
Redy, William, of Lavenham, 126
Ree, Simon at, of Chevington, 314
Reede (Rede), Henry, of Old Newton, 1097
John, 1218, 1445; of Thornham, *1445*
Marion, 1218
Thomas, of Hawstead, 493, 493n
Reede *alias* Googh, John, of Wickhambrook, *473*
see also Rede *alias* Baly
Reeder (Reder), Alice, 180; of Timworth, 856
John, & family, 180; of Timworth, *856*
Thomas, 180
William, 697
Reefham, John, 682; of Burwell (Cambs), 1475
see also Reyffham
Regewyn, Christine, of Sudbury, 258
John, of Sudbury, **258**
Regham, Thomas, 186
Regnold, Alice, of Sudbury, 632
Sabina, 1206
Rekedon, John, of Gazeley, 759
Margery, widow, of Gazeley, **759**
Reson, Robert, 571
Ress(c)hebrook, Alice, 47; of Combs, 47
John, 47; of Combs, 145; the elder, of Combs,
47
Robert, 47
see also Rosshbrook, Russhbrook
Reve (Rewe), Agnes, of Thelnetham, 1063
Henry, 1165
Isabel, of Thelnetham, 1063; of Wickham
Skeith, 1252, *1264*
Joan, of Cowlinge, 896

John, 1063, 1252; of Cowlinge, **896**; of
Hepworth, 1063; of Santon Downham, 371,
1069; of Weeting (Nfk), 359; of Whepstead,
& family, **351**; of Wickham Skeith, 1264n;
the elder, of Wickham Skeith, 24, **1252**
Margaret, 179
Margery, of Whepstead, 351
Matilda, 1165
Robert, 1252
Thomas, 903, 1213
William, 1252, 1264, 1426; of Thelnetham, &
family, **1063**
Revell, William, 968
Revet, William, chaplain, 807, 954
Revys (Rewys), William, 931
Rewe, *see* Reve
REYDON, church, 958n
Reyffham, Margaret, of Fordham (Cambs), 839
William, the elder, of Fordham (Cambs), *839*
see also Reefham
Reygham, Thomas, of Waldingfield, *647*
Reymes, Roger, of Higham (by Stratford St
Mary), 41
Reynold (Reynod), John, 794
Margery, 794
Matilda, of Thetford, 101
Richard, 563, 823; of Woolpit, 619, 1172
Thomas, of Hopton (near Harling), 323, 369,
794
William, of Woolpit, *563*
Reynoldysson, Edward, of Great Thurlow, *527*
RICKINGHALL (unspec.), inhabitants of, 726n,
1376
testators of, *878*, *989*, *1070*, *1376*
wills proved at, 333, 597
RICKINGHALL INFERIOR, church, 1334, 1340
rector of, *see* Edmund Spark
tower of, 1170, 1170n
inhabitants of, 101, 900, 1354
land in, 1334, 1340
places in, 'Busk, le', 393
'Northfeld', 393
'Saryslane', 1170
'Westrete', 900
'Wodelynges' (land), 900
road in, 1170
testators of, **393**, **900**, **1170**
will proved at, 68
RICKINGHALL SUPERIOR, church, 406, 1371
candlebeam in, 679
dedication (sanctification) of, 194, 194n
land of rectory of, 679
rector of, *see* Robert Sheep
cottage in, 900
inhabitants of, 679, 900, 1207, 1271, 1334,
1494n
land in, 406, 1170
places in, 'Bauglys', 679

'Bergh, le, 679
'Boyschys' (pightle), 1271
'Hevedstech' (land), 194
'Pateloteweye', 194
testators of, **194**, *579*, **679**, **1207**, **1271**, **1334**,
  1340
wills proved at, 156, 679
RIDDLESWORTH (Nfk), rector of, *see* John
  Hunt
RIDGEWELL (Esx), church, 1457
RINGSHALL, church, 1180
RISBY, church, image of BVM in, 1210
inhabitants of, 271, 963, 1210, 1279
land in, 41
testator of, **1210**
RISHANGLES, inhabitant of, 648
testator of, **648**
Roberd, Alan, of Sudbury, **128**
Alice, of Sudbury, 128, *686*
Cecily, of Sudbury, *770*
Walter, of Stanstead, 132
Robho(o)d, Joan, of Walsham le Willows,
  1272
John, 767*, 1272; the elder, 944; of Walsham le
  Willows, 672, 1272
Robert, **767**
Thomas, 1272
Robyn, Agnes, of Exning, 984
William, of Exning, & family, **984**
ROCHESTER (Kent), bishop of, *xxxix*
Rodelond (Rodeland), Alice, of Great
  Waldingfield, 643
Christine, 1469
Joan, of Ipswich, 469; of Kersey, 1245; widow,
  of Kersey, **1228**
John, 643, 1228, 1245, 1469*; of Kersey, 923,
  1228; the elder, of Kersey, **1245**
Richard, 941
Thomas, 643; of Ipswich, 469
William, 643; of Great Waldingfield, **643**
see also Rotelond, Rudlond
Rodyng, Adam, of Great Horringer, 1233
Roger(e), John, of Barrow, & family, **495**
Thomas, of Snailwell (Cambs), *1414*
Rogere *alias* Wever, Agnes, of Eye, 460
Andrew, of Eye, & family, **460**
Rogyll (Rogill), Thomas, of Glemsford, 1246
William, 362, 688, 1068
Rogyn, Agnes, of Rattlesden, 1031
John, 1031; of Rattlesden, **1031**
Robert, 1031
Rokeby, William, of Fordham (Cambs), *1442*
Rokell, Alice, of Lavenham, 376
Emma, of Lavenham, 805
John, of Lavenham, 376, *804*; of Long Melford,
  1237
Nicholas, of Long Melford, 790
Richard, 376

Robert, 339, 944
Thomas, of Lavenham, 355, **376**, 804n
William, 668; of Long Melford, 1237n
Roketh, Geoffrey, 1139
Role (Roole), Alice, 1475
John, 1475; & family, 1357
William, & family, 389
Rolf(f), Alice, 1162; of Burwell (Cambs), 927; of
  Snailwell (Cambs), 243
Elizabeth, 1162
Ellen, 150
Joan, 1162
John, 744, 1162*; the elder, 927; the younger,
  927; of Burwell (Cambs), 927n, **1162**
Margaret, 1162; of Burwell (Cambs), 1162
Nicholas, 927
Robert, 979
Thomas, 927, 1162; the elder, 1133; of Burwell
  (Cambs), *xlvii*, 150, **927**, 1162
William, of Snailwell (Cambs), *243*
Rollecros(s), Beatrice, of Stanton, 796
John, rector of Stanton All Saints, 457n, 796,
  796n
Margaret, of Stanton, 796, 1395
Margery, of Stanton, 796
Roger, 1130, 1299, 1395; of Stanton, 796
Thomas, of Stanton, 457, **796**, 1299n
Walter, of Stanton, 796, **1395**
ROME, Bury abbey subject only to, *xxxix*
church of, 708
pilgrimage to, *l*
pilgrim to go to, 124, 194, 677, 971, 1278
priest to go to, 20, 144, 180, 212, 288, 346,
  393, 775, 889, 908, 1209, 1269, 1459
Scala Celi chapel in, 180, 194, 387, 775
mass at, 1209
stations of, 1209, 1269
Rongnyng, Margaret, of Little Bradley, 664
William, of Little Bradley, *664*
Ronton, Thomas, 1143
Roole, *see* Role
Roos, John, of Nayland, & family, **1479**; the
  younger, of Nayland, 108
Sabina, of Nayland, 1479
Thomas, 1479
Roote, *see* Rote
Roper(e), Alice, of Hopton (near Harling), 794
Henry, 878
John, of Nayland, *1290*
Katherine, of Nayland, 1290
Thomas, of Hopton (near Harling), **794**
see also Lotkyn *alias* Roper
Ropkyn, Andrew, 492
Isabel, of Thrandeston, 492
John, 492; of Diss (Nfk), & family, 492
Nicholas, 1163; of Thrandeston, 156, 492
Robert, of Scole (Nfk), & family, 492; vicar of
  Sutton, 492

Roger, of Thrandeston, & family, **492**
Thomas, 492
Rose, Agnes, 552
   Edmund, 552
   John, 1240; the elder, 552; the elder, of
      Thurston, 358; the younger, of Thurston, &
      family, **552**
   Richard, 1254
   Thomas, 351, 552, 960; of Whepstead, 293
Roskyn, William, 57
Rosshbrook, John, 917
   see also Ress(c)hebrook, Russhbrook
Rote (Roote), Christine, of Glemsford, **391**
   Joan, 391
   John, of Glemsford, 391, **838**, *1021*
   Margery, of Glemsford, 838, 1021
   Matilda, of Glemsford, *688*
   Richard, 391
   Robert, 391*
Rotelond, John, 1298
   see also Rodelond, Rudlond
Rotyll, *see* Botell
ROUGHAM, burial at, 231
   church, book for, 231
      tower of, 59n, 1240, 1240n, 1297, 1345,
         1345n, 1478
      inhabitants of, 59, 116, 124, 231, 364, 552n,
         584, 611, 827n, 1183, 1240, 1297, 1345,
         1441n, 1478
      land in, 232
      places in, 'Betes Sloo', 1240
         'Cherchfeld', 1240
         'Dokelyingys' (close), 1240
         'Hemnynggys' (tenement), 1240
         'Parsoneslane', 1240
         Rougham Hall (manor), 552
         'Tyllotes' (tenement), 1240
      poor of, 231
      sheep in, *li*
      testators of, *584*, **1183**, **1240**, **1297**, **1345**,
         1478
Rougton (Rougeton, Roungtun), John, 191
   Matilda, of Troston, & family, **1174**
   Rose, of Rattlesden, 1032
   Thomas, of Rattlesden, 1032
   see also Ronton
Rous (Rows), Agnes, of Long Melford, 1363
   Elizabeth, of Brockley, 191
   John, of Brockley, **191**; of Pakenham, 191,
      1255
   William, of Long Melford, & family, **1363**
Rowe, William, 836
Rowhed, Alice, of Thorndon, 907
   William, of Thorndon, *907*
Rowland, Joan, widow, of Bury St Edmunds,
      *xxxix*n
Rows, *see* Rous
Rowt (Rownt), John, 13

William, 592
ROYDON (Nfk), inhabitant of, 1140
Rudlond, James, of Waldingfield, 463
   Phyllis, of Great Barton, 40
   Richard, 463
   William, of Great Barton, **40**
   see also Rodelond, Rotelond
Rukke, John, of Wetheringsett, **1034**
Rumbold, Margaret, 1008
Rumbylowe, John, 1344; of Gazeley, **1344**
   Richard, 1344
   Robert, 1344
   Walter, 1344
   William, 1344
   see also Rummylowe
Rummylowe, Richard, of Kentford, 762
   see also Rumbylowe
Runneye, William, of Preston, *1282*
Rusch, *see* Russch
RUSHBROOK, church, 1240
      rector of, *see* William Barker
      inhabitant of, 1205
      testator of, *1205*
Russch (Rusch), John, of Wetherden, & family,
      608
   Roger, 608
   Thomas, 608
Russell, Elizabeth, of Burwell (Cambs), 1162
   John, of Barrow, 290; of Barway in Soham
      (Cambs), 253
   Robert, of Barway in Soham (Cambs), 253
   Thomas, of Burwell (Cambs), 1162
Russhbrook (Russ(c)h(e)brook), Joan, 982
   John, 1324; of Combs, 497
   see also Ress(c)hebrook, Rosshbrook
Russ(h)ford, Amicia, 1461
   Joan, of Hitcham, **1461**
   Richard, of Hitcham, 1461
Rykynghale, Richard, of Bury St Edmunds, 1279
Ryngbell(e), Margaret, 854
   Robert, of Coney Weston, 854
   William, of Nayland, 142
Rynger, Hugh, of Westhorpe, 194
Ryngesel, Simon, 1360
Rynglage, Joan, of Fornham St Genevieve, 1153
   John, of Fornham St Genevieve, 443, **1153**
Ryngram, Rose, 1398
Rysby, Alice, servant, 90
Ryschey, John, 1188
Rysyng, William, 1133; of Mellis, *875*

Saby, John, 1489
Saccvyle, Thomas, 114
Sad, John, rector of Lavenham, 126, 130, 161
   Matilda, of Clare, *1127*
SAFRON WALDEN (Esx), inhabitant of, 1410n
Saham, Agnes, 869
   Richard, 1202

Robert, 721, 869, 912, 913, 1417, 1453
Thomas, 869
St Edmund, liberty of, *xxxviii–ix*n
ST EDMUNDSBURY & Ipswich, diocese of,
*xxxix*n
ST OSYTH (Esx), abbey of Augustinian canons,
375n
saints: for individual saints, *see* Subject Index,
sub advower; church & chapel (dedication);
church equipment (image; light; side-altar
dedication); cross; devotion; feast-day; gild-
patron (dedication); pilgrimage
Salman, John, of Stanton, 457
Salter, John, 1152; of Bury St Edmunds, 443,
729
Salysbery (Salysbure, Salysbury), Isabel, of
Soham (Cambs), 871
Joan, of Soham (Cambs), *819*, 871
John, 871
Richard, of Soham (Cambs), 238, 819, **871**
Sampson (Samson, Samston, Sawmpson), John, of
Harkstead, 90n
Katherine, of Harkstead, 90, 90n
Richard, 1410; of Stansfield, 695, 735, 1410n
Thomas, of Bardwell, 1231; of Stansfield, *695*
William, of Boxford, 316, 316n
see also Sawnsum
Sampson *alias* Goore, Thomas, 1275, 1275n
SANTIAGO de COMPOSTELLA *see*
COMPOSTELLA (Spain)
Santon, Agnes, of Wangford (by Brandon), 1254
William, of Wangford (by Brandon), *1254*
SANTON DOWNHAM, church, 1481
tower, 1069n
rector of, *see* John Berton, John Walter
gild in, 419
inhabitants of, 371, 419, 1069
testators of, *371*, **419**, *1069*
SAPISTON, church, 17, 69
inhabitants of, 69, 464, 872, 1059
places in, 'Awtlond', 464
'Cawtyestoft', 464
'Elmcroft', 464
'Letys' (messuage), 464
'Levyslond', 464
'Postweye', 464
'Pytellacre', 464
'Sir Robertys Akyr', 464
testators of, **464**, *872*, *1059*, *1137*, **1242**
Sare, John, 1001; of Withersfield, *1107*
Robert, 1448
Thomas, 1107
Saresson, *see* Wygenhale *alias* Saresson
Satre, John, 158
Saverey, Richard, 529
Sawer, *see* Sawyer
Sawge, John, 1180
Sawmpson, *see* Sampson

Sawnsum, Lawrence, of Great Cornard, & family,
630
William, 630
Sawyer (Sawer), John, 461, 969; & family, *434*; of
Lavenham, **462**
Matilda, of Thelnetham, 969
Richard, 1265
Robert, 461, 969; of Lavenham, 618, 1073,
1260
Thomas, of Thelnetham, & family, **969**
SAXHAM (unspec.), inhabitant of, 77
land in, 77
SAXHAM, GREAT, church, 474, 1279
nave of, 57
rector of, *see* William Place
tower of, 77, 77n
croft, formerly John Meller's, in, 77
inhabitant of, 57
land in, 41
testator of, **77**
SAXHAM, LITTLE, church, 41
canopy in, 1123
rector of, *see* Ralph Holderness
tower of, 34
walls of, 246, 1044
yard, fencing of, 1123
cross by way to church, 1044
inhabitants of, 34, 41, 41n, 44, 226, 245, 499,
616, 1044, 1123
land in, 41, 77
manor of, 41
places in, 'Bayardysbrege' ('Bayardebrege'),
34, 246
'Mondesford Cros', 246
'Wodwallestrete' ('Wodewallstrete'), 34,
246
testators of, **34**, **245**, **246**, *501*, **1044**, **1123**
SAXHAM STREET, *see* THORNEY in
STOWMARKET
SAXON STREET, *see* WOODDITTON (Cambs)
Saxsy (Saxi, Saxy, Saxsi, Saxti), Agnes, of Eye,
623
Alice, of Stanningfield, 233
Clement, of Eye, **623, 625**
John, 233, 425, 623; of Eye, *425*; of
Stanningfield, **233**; monk, 233
Robert, 425, 623
Sayken (Saykyn), William, 1437; of Thurston,
185, 185n
Scalder (Skaldere), Margaret, 308
William, 632, 740, 818; of Sudbury, 717
Scateron (Scatoron, Skateron), Joan, of Elmswell,
1001
John, 1001; of Elmswell, 397, 855, **1001**
Robert, 1001
William, 1001
Scargill (Scargayle), family, 446n
Thomas, esquire, 446

Scarp, John, 1391; of Fornham All Saints, 271
Schafftyng (Schaftlyng), Henry, 1300; of Thorpe
    Morieux, 402
Schamberleyn, *see* Chamberleyn
Schapman, *see* Chapman
Schappe, Robert, 895
Schardlowe, John, of Saxham, 77
Scheldrake, *see* Sheldrake
Schelton, *see* Shelton
Schelyng, John, 863
Schep, *see* Sheep
Schepperd, *see* Shepperd
Schercroft (Sherecroft), Thomas, rector of
    Fornham All Saints and Icklingham, 1472
Scherde, Thomas, of Mildenhall, 1403
Scherman, Cecily, 857
    Ed., 1113
Scherwynd (Scerwynd, Sherwyn), John, 1289,
    1449
    Robert, 'corvoser', of Bury St Edmunds, 10
    Thomas, 1449
Schokforth, *see* Schucford
Schomer, John, of Layham, **334**
    Katherine, of Layham, 334, *1071*
Schoppe, William, of Monks Eleigh, 1455
Schorthose, Margaret, of Sudbury, 1181
    Thomas, weaver, of Sudbury, **1181**
Schotesham (Schotlysham), John, Carmelite friar,
    of Norwich (Nfk), 398, 539
Schouthar, Geoffrey, of Mellis, *484*
    John, 484
Schucford (Schokforth), Agnes, 506; of
    Thelnetham, 506
    John, 506
    Robert, 213, 506; of Thelnetham, & family, **506**
    Thomas, 213
Schyrlok, John, 738
    [*unnamed*], *738*
Sclawe (Slawe), John, 401; of Botesdale, **252**
    Matilda, of Botesdale, 401, *925*
    Robert, 983, 1171, 1235, 1302
    Walter, of Botesdale, 252, 401, 925n
Sclygh, John, 569
    Simon, 569
SCOLE (Nfk), church, 949
    inhabitant of, 492
    land in, 949
Scot (Scoot, Skot), Andrew, of Stretham (Cambs),
    & family, 626
    Cecily, of Hopton (near Harling), 1292
    John, of Hopton (near Harling), **1292**
    Katherine, of Stretham (Cambs), 626
    Margaret, of Hopton (near Harling), 1292
    Nicholas, chaplain, 1292
    Robert, 278
    William, of Mildenhall, 1471
Scoyle (Skoyle), John, of Brockley, *472*
    Thomas, 570, 610

William, 610
Screvener(e) (Skrev(e)yner), John, clerk, of
    Palgrave, 1418; of Wickhambrook, 1055,
    1418
    Roger, of Bildeston, 680
    Thomas, 1450; of Stradishall, 1418, 1450n
Scrope, [*unnamed*], lord, of Nayland, 1080n
Scut (Skut(t), Sckut), Ellen, of Soham (Cambs),
    238
    John, 321, 366, 985, 1033
    Thomas, of Soham (Cambs), & family, **238**
Sef(f)rey, John, 457; of Bardwell, 97, 212
Segbroke, John, of Stowmarket, 746
Selot(t) (Selote), John, of Bardwell, 97;
    archdeacon of Sudbury, *xlii*, *liv*n, 180n, 1493
Selwode, Richard, 1156
Sely, Richard, 735
    Robert, 735
    Thomas, 735
Selyf, Richard, friar, of Sudbury, 474
Seman, Alice, of Thelnetham, 213
    John, chaplain, 207
    Margaret, servant, 588
    Robert, 213
    Thomas, 213; of Thelnetham, **213**
    William, of Little Cornard, **356**
SEMER, bridge, in Ash Street, 1416
    church, 162, 1115
        bell for 1416
        image of St Christopher in, 1416
        rector of, *see* Thomas Hyll
        torches in, 1416
    inhabitants of, 143, 990, 1416, 1454
    land in, 1429
    places in, Ash Street, 1416
        'Caketon', 1416
        'Fennys' (tenement), 1416
        'Huntes' (tenement), 1416
        'Westfeld', 1416
    testators of, **143**, **728**, *990*, **1416**, *1454*
    wills proved at, 415, 520, 521, 1412, 1416
Senclow, Ed., 45
Sengylton, Agnes, widow, of Stowmarket, 1305,
    1305n
    Ed., 920
    Thomas, of Stowmarket, 1305n
Sephar, Alice, of Brandon, & family, *885*
Sergeaunt, John, 949
    Richard, 128
    see also Seriaunt
Seriaunt (Cheryaunt, Serjawnt), Agnes, 1258
    Joan, of Sudbury, 276
    John, 136, 1249, 1258; the elder, 189
    Richard, of Sudbury, **276**
    Robert, 189
    William, 276; of Stoke by Nayland, **189**
    see also Sergeaunt
Serle, Agnes, of Hundon, 967

Amice, of Stanton, 663
Joan, of Combs, 660
John, of Great Wratting, *1284*; of Hundon, **967**; of Stanton, **663**
Margery, of Great Wratting, 1284
Sevelose, John, 1366
Sewale (Sewall), John, of Stowmarket, 53, 264, 346, 797; cordwainer, of Stowmarket, *1138*
Sext(e)yn, Alan, of Lavenham, 454, 1048
John, servant, of Ixworth, 357
Rose, 1048
Seymour, John, the elder, 431; the younger, 431; the elder, of Stanningfield, **431**
Margery, of Stanningfield, 431
Seynour, Richard, rector of Icklingham All Saints, 603, 603n, 1472n
Shakesper, Agnes, of Snailwell (Cambs), 588
William, pauper, of Snailwell (Cambs), 588
Shedde, William, of Lavenham, 172
SHEEN (Surr), priory of Carthusian monks, *l*, 865, 870
Sheep (Schep, Shepp), John, 11, 1001; of Woolpit, **11**
Margaret, of Woolpit, 11
Robert, rector of Rickinghall Superior, 878, 1340, 1340n, 1494n
see also Schappe
Sheldrake (Scheldrake), Joan, of Little Waldingfield, 1193
John, lettered man, of Little Waldingfield, **1193**
Margaret, 1088; of Little Waldingfield, 171; of Waldingfield, *1360*
Stephen, 1360
Thomas, 930
William, & family, 643; of Little Waldingfield, & family, **171**, 1360n
SHELLAND, church, 497
cloth in, *li*
'Duces Clos' in, 497
inhabitant of, 977
testators of, **21**, **977**
Shelton (Schelton), John, of Brent Eleigh, 165n
Margaret, widow, lady of Brent Eleigh Hall manor, 165n
Richard, 18, 90, 231, 713, 714, 977; of Great Finborough, 538
Shepperd (Chepperd, Schepperd, Sheperde), John, 248, 1341; of Glemsford, 1246; clerk, of Lavenham, 102; of Mickfield, 248
Katherine, of Botesdale, 1341
Peter, of Waldingfield, 1469
Thomas, of Botesdale, & family, **1341**
Sheryff (Shreve), William, of Palgrave, 1330, 1330n
Sherwyn, *see* Scherwynd
SHIMPLING, church, 1241
inhabitants of, 184, 701, 1154
testators of, *168*, **184**, **1154**

Shomere, *see* Schomer
Shreve, *see* Sheryff
Shylle, Thomas, 1072
Sibton, Margery, 128n
Thomas, chaplain, of Sudbury college, 128, 128n
William, 128n
SICILY, Robert, king of, 588
Sideler, Richard, of Lawshall, 488
SILVERLEY (Cambs), church, 247, 247n, 381, 822
paving of, 1473
vestment for, 1473
inhabitants of, 1029, 1473
testator of, *1029*
wills proved at, 1052, 1053
Simond, *see* Symond
Sire, John, smith, 1405
Skaldere, *see* Scalder
Skarlet (Skorlet), Eudo, 884, 928
William, 1279
Skateron, *see* Scateron
Skeet (Skeyt, Skeyth), Geoffrey, of Santon Downham, 1069n
John, the elder, 342
Robert, chaplain, of Kersey, 342
Thomas, of Stanton, 457
Skelfyn, John, 1319
Skepper, Thomas, 278
Skeyt(h), *see* Skeet
Skorlet, *see* Skarlet
Skot, *see* Sco(o)t
Skouthare, John, of Thornham Parva, 1014n
Skoyle, *see* Scoyl
Skrev(e)yner, *see* Screvener
Skut, *see* Scut
Skylman, John, of Preston, 929
Skynner(e), Adam, 1170
Agnes, 1170; of Stoke by Nayland, 1347
Henry, 639
Joan, 146
John, of Stoke by Nayland, 1347, **1347**
Margaret, 1170
Richard, of Moulton, 450
Thomas, 527; of Stoke by Nayland, 1347
Walter, of Rickinghall Inferior, **1170**
William, of Kedington, *38*
Skyppe, Agnes, 488
Skyppyng, Anne, of Haverhill, 1012
Robert, of Haverhill, 491, *1012*
Slade, Ed., of Stoke by Nayland, **1331**
Margery, of Stoke by Nayland, 1331
Slawe, *see* Sclawe
Slawter, Thomas, 1458
Sley, *see* Sly(e)
Slowle, John, doctor, friar of Clare, 1142, 1142n
Sly(e) (Sley), John, vicar of Soham (Cambs), 691n, 865, 870, 1298

Smert, John, 876
Smethe, John, 681
  Matilda, of Cowlinge, 561
  Thomas, 561
  William, of Cowlinge, *561*
  see also Smyth
Smyth, Agnes, of Badmondesfield, in
    Wickhambrook, 459; of Badwell Ash, 1397;
    of Thurston, 1437
  Alice, 626; of Badwell Ash, 1397; of
    Rattlesden, 1310
  Anne, of Beyton, 52; of Hadleigh, & family,
    197
  Cecily, of Burwell (Cambs), *79*
  Denise, of Eriswell, *166*
  Ed., of Bury St Edmunds, 653
  Elizabeth, of Badwell Ash, 1397; of Great
    Livermere, 1003
  Emma, of Badwell Ash, 1397
  Geoffrey, 698, 837
  George, chaplain, 1370; rector of West Stow,
    1370n
  Gillian, of Stoke by Nayland, 1120
  Helen, of Eriswell, 352
  Henry, 1003, 1067, 1468; of Great Livermere,
    1003, 1195; of Rattlesden, & family,
    1310; of West Stow, *698*; servant,
    192
  Isabel, 1008; of Kirtling (Cambs), 1468; of
    Tuddenham St Mary, 14
  James, 262, 352; of Eriswell, & family, **352**; of
    Sudbury college, 91
  Joan, of Clare, 832; of Polstead, 650; of
    Worlington, 1241
  John, 52, 72, 352, 520, 544, 799, 923, 1008,
    1019, 1241, 1310, 1370; chaplain, 707;
    & family, 1229; fuller, 559; priest, 363;
    the elder, 1170; of Badmondisfield in
    Wickhambrook, **459**; limeburner, of
    Ballingdon, & family, *147*; the elder, of
    Barnardiston, & family, **1229**; of Beyton,
    52; rector of Bradfield Combust, 407, 1367;
    (Jankyn), benefactor of Bury St Edmunds,
    xli-xlii, 439, 1123; of Diss (Nfk), 1470; of
    Exning, *1308*; rector of Fornham All Saints,
    427, 427n; of Hopton (near Harling), 230;
    of Hundon, *847*; of Kersey, *923*; of Kirtling
    (Cambs), & family, **1468**; of Lavenham,
    130; of Lindsey, *292*; of Little Livermere,
    1003; of Mellis, 798; shoemaker, of
    Mildenhall, 865, 865n; of Polstead, *650*; of
    Soham (Cambs)1319; of Stoke by Nayland,
    & family, **1120**; of Stratford St Mary, 1120;
    weaver, of Sudbury, 1132; of Thurston,
    1437; of Wickhambrook, *653*; of Yeldham
    (Esx), 632
  Katherine, 292; of Walsham le Willows, 1370;
    of Wyverstone, 72

Margaret, 554; of Badwell Ash, 1397; of
    Barnardiston, 654; widow, of Boxford, **308**;
  Margery, 1229; of Mildenhall, 245
  Matilda, of West Stow, 698
  Meliora, of Kersey, 923
  Nicholas, 723; of Walsham le Willows, &
    family, **1370**; 'carwan', of Thetford, 56
  Olive, 799
  Peter, 1310; of Badwell Ash, 1397
  Ralph, 978, 1116
  Richard, 98, 109, 367; rector, of Ashley, 114;
    of Badwell Ash, 1397; of Horkesley (Esx),
    544; of Great Livermere & family, **1003**; of
    Shimpling, *168*; of Stoke by Clare, 1382; of
    Stowmarket, 152; of Tuddenham St Mary, *14*
  Robert, 192, 923, 1151; of Palgrave, 1151n; of
    Thurston, 1437; of Wyverstone, *72*
  Roger, of Barnardiston, & family, **654**;
    carpenter, 1132
  Rose, of Walsham le Willows, 1370
  Simon, 168; of Worlington, **1241**
  Stephen, 1450; chaplain, of Blo Norton (Nfk),
    1307n; of Stradishall, 1450n
  Thomas, 549, 847, 939, 1310, 1468, 1490;
    servant, 298; of Eye, 367; of Hadleigh,
    403; of Hessett, **857**, **1113**; of Honington,
    530; of Long Melford, 1241; of Mildenhall,
    245; barker, of Sudbury, 1168; of Thurston,
    52, 287, 358; webster, of Thurston, 552; of
    Walsham le Willows, 1397; of Westley, **98**
  William, 167, 754; of Badwell Ash, 1397; the
    elder, of Clare, **832**; of Palgrave, 1330; of
    Thetford, 253
  see also Smethe, Anows *alias* Smyth *and*
    Watlok *alias* Smyth
Smyth *alias* Barbour, Marion, of Stowmarket, &
    family, **152**
Smyth *alias* Gardyner, Richard, 1006
Smyth *alias* Tostok, Margaret, of Blo Norton
    (Nfk), 1307n
SNAILWELL (Cambs), church, 822
  gild in, 183, 183n, 702
  inhabitants of, 240, 505, 588, 702, 724, 793,
    902
  testators of, **183**, *239*, *240*, *243*, **588**, **702**, *703*,
    1414
  wills proved at, 482, 590, 626
Snawe, John, of Nayland, *874*
Snode, Joan, of Westley, 616
  Richard, of Westley, *360*, 616n, **692**
  Robert, of Westley, **616**, 692
SOHAM (Cambs), BARWAY in, chapel in, 253,
    253n, 256
  inhabitants of, 253, 1319
  testators of, **253**, **256**, **1319**
  chapel of Our Lady in, 238, 238n, 626
  church, burial in porch of, 691n

John, parish chaplain of, 1256
vicar of, *see* John Slye
cross (new) in, 1041
gilds in, 256, 903, 1319, 1327
inhabitants of, 183, 238n, 253, 254, 625n, 819,
    871, 902, 903, 1041, 1298, 1319, 1325,
    1326, 1327, 1443, 1444, 1483
mortuary paid in, *xlvi*
nuns of [*sic*], ?*recte* Swaffham Bulbeck, *q.v.*
places in, 'Bangroft', 'Bankecroft', 626, 1319
    'Bradmede', 1325
    'Brecham', 'Bercham', 1256, 1319
    'Brookstrete', 254, 478, 478n
    'Burwellmere', 1325
    'Cobb' (messuage), 871
    'Cotys', 871
    'Down, le', 1256
    'Dychende', 626
    'Estfeld', 1325
    'Gerweysend' (field), 1325
    'Hallestrete, le', 902, 902n, 903
    'Lytylham Hale', 626
    'Mardell', 626
    'Nowdych', 'Nawdych', 1256, 1319
    'Sandestrete', 478, 478n, 1041
    'Saweslake', 1319
    Soham field, 253
    Soham marsh, 253
    'Turnours' (messuage), 1041
    'Wethiam', 1041
poor of, 903
roads in, 903, 1131
testators of, **207**, **238**, **254**, **478**, **626**, **691**, *819*,
    871, **902**, **903**, *904*, *953*, **1041**, *1085*, **1256**,
    1298, *1326*, **1327**, *1443*, *1444*, **1483**
wills proved at, 207, 237, 238, 253, 254, 256,
    478, 691, 902, 903, 904, 927, 953, 1085,
    1325, 1326, 1327, 1443, 1444, 1483
Soham, Robert, 1023
SOMERTON, church, 109, 362
    bell for, 1390
    rector of, *see* Gregory Cayle
    inhabitant of, 789
    land in, 205
    testators of, **216**, **789**
Somerton, Isabel, of Chevington, 314
    John, 314
    Robert, of Chevington, **314**
Soot (Sot), Margery, 178
    Thomas, 178
Sopere, Elizabeth, of Barton Mills, 46
    John, 46
    Robert, of Barton Mills, **46**
    William, 46
Sorell, John, of Chelsworth, **516**
    Juliana, of Chelsworth, 516
    William, 516
Sot, *see* Soot

SOUTHWOLD, chapel of St Margaret in [*sic*],
    1090n
    church, 958n
    inhabitant of, 958n
Sown, George, & family, 429
Sowter, William, 466
Spaldyng, Andrew, 1224
    Elizabeth, of Wortham, 1224
    John, 222; of Wortham, **1224**
    Katherine, of Wortham, 1224
    Margaret, of Wortham, 1224*
    Walter, 222
Spark(e), Edmund, rector of Rickinghall Inferior,
    1494, 1494n
    John, 246; of Hawstead, 640; of Wetheringsett,
    918
    Simon, 495, 831; of Barrow, 1191
Sparman (Sperman), Margaret, of Groton, 1150
    Philip, of Groton, **1150**
    Ralph, 910
Sparwe, John, 316, 378; of Bury St Edmunds, &
    family, *279*; of Chedburgh, 279
    Margaret, of Bury St Edmunds, 279
    Simon, of Sudbury, 1365
    Walter, of Boxford, & family, *378*
Speed (Sped), Adam, chaplain, 757
    Agnes, of Little Saxham, 245
    Anne, 1395
    John, 245
    Richard, of Mildenhall, 245
    Thomas, 245
    William, of Little Saxham, **245**
Speling, Henry, holy water carrier, of Boxford,
    308
Spencer(e) (Spenser), John, 883; of Dalham, 163,
    1204
    Margaret, of Dalham, 1204
    Walter, of Ousden, *163*
    William, chaplain, of Burwell (Cambs), 79
Sperlyng, John, of Stoke by Nayland, 1283, *1283*;
    the elder, of Stoke by Nayland, 36
Sperman, *see* Sparman
Spetyl(l)man, Margaret, of Norton, 1333
    William, of Glemsford, **158**; of Norton, 1333
Spilman, *see* Spylman
Spink, Robert, servant, 421
SPINNEY, in WICKEN (Cambs), priory of
    Augustinian canons, 254, 702, 1121
Spiser, *see* Spycer(e)
Sponer(e), Isabel, of Sapiston, 872
    John, 655, 872; of Honington, 530
    Peter, of Sapiston, *872*
    [*unnamed*], *620*
Spore, Agnes, 207
    William, 207
SPORLE (Nfk), church, 1400
    burial in, 1400n
    inhabitant of, 1400n

land in, 877
   manor of East Hall, Palgrave, in, 1400n
Spragge (Spraggy), George, friar, 877
   Lawrence, of Haughley, 795
Spring, *see* Spryng
Sprot, Joan, of Sudbury, 748
   John, of Sudbury, *748*
SPROWSTON (Nfk), land in, 406
Spryng(e), Agnes, of Lavenham, 102
   George, 902
   John, chaplain, 18; rector of Troston, 18n
   Katherine, of Soham (Cambs), 902
   Thomas, 18; ['I'], of Lavenham, & family, **102**;
     ['II'], of Lavenham, 102, 102n, 126
   William, 102; of Soham (Cambs), **902**
Spycer(e) (Spiser), Alice, of Bildeston, 895
   Joan, 619
   John, 342; of Bildeston, **895**
   Thomas, 895
   William, 529, 1099, 1152; of Fornham St
     Martin, 849
Spylman (Spilman), Robert, archdeacon's official,
     warden of Sudbury college, *xlii*, *liv*n, 1364,
     1365, 1403, 1473
Stacy (Stace), Anne, of Thurston, 430
   John, of Thurston, & family, **430**
   Roger, 476
STAFFORD (Staffs), archdeacon of, *xlii*n
Stale(y), Richard, of Thorndon, 1090
Stalo(u)n, Audrey, of Mildenhall, 708
   Christian, of Mildenhall, 708
   Joan, of Mildenhall, 708
   John, 306, 708; barker, of Haverhill, 708;
     of Kentford, 708; of Mildenhall, 120; the
     younger, of Mildenhall, & family, **708**
STAMBOURNE (Esx), church, 554
Stanbowe, Alice, of Great Livermere, 1195
   John, of Great Livermere, **1195**
Stannard, Joan, 799
   John, of Mickfield, 345
   William, 799
STANNINGFIELD, inhabitants of 431, 1098n
   places in, 'Gedyngys', 431
     'Multonys', 431
   spelling of place-name, 431n
   testators of, **233**, **431**, **531**
STANSFIELD, inhabitants of, 382, 695, 735, 776,
     1410n
   spelling of place-name, 431n
   rector of, *see* Thomas Westhorpe
   testator of, *382*, **507**, *835*
   will proved at, 319
STANSTEAD, church, land of rectory of, 391
     rector of, *see* John West
   inhabitants of, 132, 137
   land in, 137n
   places in, 'Benstres' 132
     'Bulkacre' (land), 132

'Tripperheg', 132
   testator of, **132**
STANTON, churches in, 59n
   church of All Saints, 59, 124, 1063
     altar of BVM in, 457
     image of St Petronilla in, 634, 634n
     mediety of, 457
     paving entrance of, 457
     rector of, *see* Edmund Bene, Robert Clerk,
       John Rollecros
     reeves of, 457
   church of St John the Baptist, 59, 124, 583,
     634, 677, 1214
     antiphoner for, 796
     land of, 457
     missal for, 677
     vestments for, 457n
   common pasture of, 457
   gild in, 1395
   inhabitants of, 634, 663, 796, 802, 1258, 1261,
     1299, 1352, 1395
   looms in, *li*
   mortuary paid in, *xlvi*n
   open-field land in, *liii*
   places in, 'Bekkystoft', 457
     'Brakyng', 457
     'Esegeriswood', 457
     'Estcroft', 457
     'Faukys' (tenements), 634
     'Forthhegh', 457
     'Galtre, le' (field), 796
     'Heygate', 1395
     'Heygateweye', 634
     'Holkecruche', 457
     'Hothweyte' (field), 457
     'Hothweythwell', 457
     'Huppethorp', 457
     'Huppethorpfeld', 457
     'Leteweve', 457
     'Lytilhawe', 457
     'Maydenyswey', 457
     'Mellemont', 457
     'Myddylfurlong', 457
     'Nyneacyrwey', 457
     'Oke', 457
     'Ovyrfodylhalle', 457
     'Ovyrfurlonge', 457
     'Sedylhawewey', 457
     'Slede', 457
     'Smaldole', 457
     'Snapecroft', 457
     'Sowthwode', 457
     'Stonys', 457
     'Sysmer, le' (footpath), 457
     '?Talthorpe', 457
     'Therhed', 634
     'Undale', 457
     'Wareyneshawe' (close), 457

'Williammysyerd', 457
'Wroyscroft', 457
testators of, **457**, **634**, **663**, **677**, **796**, **802**,
    1130, *1261*, **1352**, **1395**
wills proved at, 69, 212, 518, 628, 674, 1063,
    1198, 1199, 1214, 1292
Stanton, Alice, of Brome, 920
    Isabel, servant, 493
    James, of Brome, **920**
    John, of Clare, *670*; of Rougham, **1183**; of
        Westley, 542
    Mary, of Rougham, 1183
    Robert, 1183
    Roger, 1183
Stapilton (Stapylton), Brian, esquire, 41, 41n;
    knight, of Ingham (Nfk), 41, 41n
    Miles, esquire, 41, 41n
Stapul, Walter, rector of Monks Eleigh, 204
Stapynnel, John, apprentice, 157
Stapylton, *see* Stapilton
Starchant, Isabel, of Boxford, 155
    John, of Boxford, & family, **155**
Starlyng (Sterlyng), William, vicar of
    Mendlesham, rector of Eriswell, 413, 1121,
    1315
Staunford, Joan, of Rayleigh (Esx), 489
Stebbyng, John, 75; of Finningham, 178, 385
Stede, Thomas, warrener, of Hilborough (Nfk),
    489
Steer, John, 1237
Steff, John, 1255
    Robert, of Barrow, *25*
    Simon, 1255
Sterlond, Thomas, 1472
    William, of Icklingham, **1472**
Sterlyng, *see* Starlyng
Sterne, Thomas, of Great Barton, 180n
Sterre, Katherine, 311
    Richard, 552
    William, 311
Steward, John, 142
Stevenes, Joan, of Ixworth, 961
    John, of Ixworth, & family, **961**
Stevynesson, John, of Woolpit, **469**
Stewen, John, 9
Stiward, John, of Nayland, **573**
    Margaret, of Nayland, 573
STOKE ASH, church, 1169
    land of rector of, 1200
    inhabitants of, 785, 1169
    land in, 1169, 1169n
    testators of, *223*, **285**
STOKE by CLARE, chapel of St Mary in, 580,
    580n
    church of St Augustine
        light of BVM in, 1382
        roodloft in, 1423n
    college of St John the Baptist, 38n

inhabitants of, 1185, 1187, 1382, 1423
places in, 'Bauferne' [Baythorn] bridge, 1423,
    1423n
    'Boyton' [Boyton End], 1423, 1423n
    Chapel Street, 1423n, 580n
    'Chelchynforth' (meadow), 1423
    'Melkesoppis' (tenement), 1423
    'Millestrete', 1423
    'Neueton' (tenement), 631
    'Rogerouns' (tenement), 1423
    'Rogerouns Crofte', 1423
testators of, *437*, *522*, *526*, **631**, *1185*, *1187*,
    1382, **1423**
wills proved in, 38, 210, 437, 503, 504, 507,
    567, 568, 631, 844, 1423
STOKE by NAYLAND, church, 1484
    brass pot for, 992
    burials in churchyard of, 1080n
    porch of, 930, 930
    tower of, 36, 108, 365, 573, 610, 930
    vicar of, *lii*, 860
        see also John Cranewyk, William
            Quenyve (Whenyve)
    inhabitants of, *xliv*n, 36, 154, 189, 192, 301,
        365, 610, 638, 930, 992, 1120, 1194n, 1283,
        1314n, 1331, 1347, 1412, 1479
    places in, 'Bawchownys', 610
        'Birchlie Wode', 930
        'Cookys', 108
        'Longfeld', 1088
        'Marcolbrygge', 1120
        'Purseres' (tenement), 610
        'Thortonstret', 365
        'Wulfoot' (land), 992
    poor of, 1120
    road to Nayland, 930
    testators of, **36**, **42**, *153*, **154**, **189**, **301**, **324**,
        365, **544**, **546**, **610**, **638**, **930**, **992**, **1088**,
        1120, *1283*, **1331**, **1347**, *1412*
    wills proved at, 324, 378, 610, 1088, 1290
Stok(e) (Stokke), Thomas, 193, 571, 1142
Stonham, Agnes, 1008
    Helen, 1008
    Katherine, 1008
    Peter, 658
    Thomas, 1008; of Stoke Ash, 785
STONHAM ASPAL, inhabitant of, 1417n
STONHAM, EARL, church, 348
    'Fyliolys' in, 348
    poor of, 20
STONHAM PARVA, land in, 348
Stopperd, Thomas, of Sudbury college, 91
Stotevyle, Thomas, of Dalham, 553, 553n
Stoure (Stowr), Matilda, servant, 421, 740
Stovyn, John, 1382
STOW, deanery of, *xxxviii*n, *xxxix*
Stowe, William de, 159
STOWLANGTOFT, Ashfield family, 457n

church, 438
    rector of, *see* Nicholas Yepisswich
inhabitant of, 373
land in, 441
STOWMARKET, Chilton hamlet in, 19, 1134
    chapel of St Margaret in, 1134, 1134n,
    1296n
    churches in, 19n
    church of St Mary, 19n, 53, 346, 1462
        candlebeam in, 408n
        demolition of, 19n
        rebuilding of, 408n
        tower of, 408, 408n, 714
        vicar of, 1462n
            see also Robert Ferour, John Thorpe,
            Robert Wylde
    church of St Peter, *xliv*n, 19n, 53, 408, 882
        aisle of St John in, 346n
        aisle of St Mary in, 346, 346n
        books for, 444
        chapel of St John in, 600, 600n
        chapel of St Mary in, 47, 346n, 714, 882
        chaplain of St Mary in, 288
        image of St Peter in, 444
        mass of St Mary in, 711, 1126, 1134, 1462
        porch of, 288, 288n
        tabernacle of St Paul in, 1126
        vicar of, *see* John Bateler
        window in, 346
    church of St Peter and St Mary, 19n
    gild in, 444
        gildhall of, 1462
    inhabitants of, 288, 346, 444, 457, 497, 714,
        746, 754, 777, 797, 882, 934, 1050, 1134,
        1138, 1192, 1296, 1305, 1322, 1420, 1421,
        1462
    land in, 497
    places in, 'Alcokkes' (land), 19
        'Bellys lane', 1126
        'Bernardesyerd', 714
        'Breggester' (street), 714
        'Crowestrete', 714
        'Dowgates', 346
        'Fleggys' (land)
        'Gardownys', 288
        'Sereravyslond' (land), 19
    poor of, 20, 346, 714, 1126
    shop in, 346
    STOWUPLAND in, 19n, 20n
        see also THORNEY
    testators of, **19**, **53**, **103**, **152**, **288**, *386*, **711**,
        714, *754*, **797**, *934*, **943**, *999*, *1000*, **1050**,
        1126, **1134**, *1138*, *1305*, *1322*, *1420*, **1421**,
        1462
        see also THORNEY
    THORNEY in, 19n, 20n, 264, 882
        'Byll' (land) in, 711
        'Byllys' (house) in, 711

'Faryswe' (road) in, 797
'Govyes' in, 408
inhabitants of, 386, 410, 444, 600, 711, 882
land in, 288, 348
'Mangeres' in, 346
'Monestrete' in, 797
poor of, 346, 797
road in, 408, 346, 711
Saxham Street in, 348, 882, 1126
'Stubbyng' (close) in, 711
testators of, **264**, **408**, **444**, **577**, **600**, **882**
wills proved at, 3, 129, 145, 152, 209, 264,
    283, 444, 497 519, 538, 600, 601, 608, 609,
    660, 665, 711, 714, 753, 754, 775, 797, 799,
    810, 851, 852, 882, 908, 934, 966, 977, 998,
    1000, 1049, 1050, 1065, 1126, 1134, 1161,
    1192, 1215, 1294, 1295, 1296, 1305, 1343,
    1411, 1419, 1462
Stowr, *see* Stoure
STRADISHALL, church, 863
    bell for, 1142
    burial in porch of, 1418
    light of St Mary in, 571
    torches in, 1142
common way in, 1142
inhabitants of, 266, 426, 571, 669, 776, 798,
    863, 1082, 1142, 1386n, 1418, 1430, 1450n
land in, 776
places in, 'Cokerell & Struttonys', 863
    'Fowleres' (tenement), 1142
    'Northnowe', 1142
testators of, **426**, *669*, **1142**
wills proved at, 49, 50, 266, 327, 328, 332, 426,
    447, 448, 561, 571, 654, 681, 689, 730, 735,
    845, 846, 866, 881, 893, 919, 1010, 1011,
    1012, 1028, 1142, 1196, 1197, 1203, 1284,
    1398, 1413, 1430, 1431, 1432
woods in, 863
Strangman, John, 639
STRATFORD (Mdx), testator of, **863**
STRATFORD ST MARY, inhabitant of, 1120
STRETHAM (Cambs), church, 256
Stroude, Nicholas, of Stoke by Clare, 1423
Strut, Alice, of Bildeston, 1125
    Joan, of Acton, 813
    John, the elder, 813; the younger, 813
    Robert, of Acton, **813**
    William, the elder, 813; the younger, 813
Struth, Alice, of Hartest, 456
    Thomas, of Hartest, **456**
Studham, John, 33
Sturdy, John, the elder, of Kedington, 1213
Sturjon, John, 191
STURMER (Esx), highway in, 1457
Sturmyn, Christian, of Lavenham, 161, **1002**,
    1048
    Isabel, of Lavenham, 446
    John, 161, 1048; of London, 1002

Robert, 1048; of Lavenham, 1002
STUSTON, church, 492
    testators of, *156, 170, 1163*
    will proved at, 1166
Stuston, Margaret, of Oakley, 949
    Phyllis, of Oakley, 636
    Thomas, of Oakley, **636**
    William, 636; of Oakley, **949**
Stutvyle, Thomas, 1358
Subburn(e) (Sudburne), Agnes, 1340
    Ed., of Rickinghall Inferior, 1354
    Edmund, of Botesdale, 726, 971, 1371
    John, 1340
SUDBOURNE, rector of, *see* William Dakke
Sudburne, *see* Subburn(e)
SUDBURY, almshouses in, 740n
    archdeaconry of, *xxxviii*n
    archdeacon of, *xxxix*, 231, 711, 714, 715
        see also Clement Denston, John Selot, John
            Wygenhale *alias* Saresson
    archdeacon's court, 279n
    BALLINGDON in, 'le pondyerde' in, 740
        testator of, *147*
    chapel of St Sepulchre in, 1077, 1077n
    churches of, 48n
    church of All Saints, 421
        aisle (north) of, 740, 1181
        'le arche' in, 740n
        boardcloth for altar of, 175
        curate of, 1181
        martyrology for, 398n
        missal for, 740
        paving in, 1181n
        processional for, 740
        rebuilding of, 1181n
        stools in, 1181
        vicar of, 645
            see also William Hamond, William
            Perkham, John Spyrlyng, Thomas
            Tyler
    church of St Gregory, *xlii*, 49, 157, 188, 198,
        234, 258, 276, 326, 356
        image of St Gregory in, 420
        image on candlebeam in, 1077, 1077n
        light on candlebeam in, 91
        pyx for, 1077
        rood (painting) of, 1077, 1077n
        statue of Our Lady at, 1466n
    church/chapel of St Peter, 48, 48n, 49, 62,
        128, 157, 276, 277, 310, 398, 539, 632,
        1057, 1489, 1493
        bell for, 1365n
        copes for, 1058
        decoration of, 740n
        lectern for, 1365n
    cloth in, *li*
        dyeing, *li*
        looms, *li*

    college of St Gregory in, *xlii*n, 128n, 188, 539,
        632, 800, 1077, 1168
        chaplains of, 91
    cross in (at 'Wygaynende'), 188
    gilds in, 310, 1132
    grammar school in, *xlii*n
    house of Dominican friars (Preachers), *xlix*,
        49, 91, 108, 118, 125, 126, 128, 130, 132,
        137, 157, 158, 180, 185, 186, 188, 231,
        249, 258, 261, 263, 289, 300, 308, 310,
        317, 350, 356, 362, 380, 421, 474, 507,
        521, 539, 548, 619, 632, 643, 667, 713,
        740, 758, 776, 790, 800, 803, 805, 813,
        818, 823, 860, 939, 941, 1036, 1058, 1075,
        1077, 1079 1080, 1104, 1132, 1168, 1172,
        1181, 1237, 1240, 1244, 1246, 1280,
        1312, 1363, 1364, 1365, 1369, 1418,
        1466, 1469, 1469n, 1489
        burial at, 740n, 803n, 1365
        church of, 1274
        churchyard of, burial in, 1274
        cloister of, 1132
        friars of, 421, 474, 539, 790, 806, 816
        image of BVM in church of, 398n
        psalter for, 398n
    inhabitants of, 26, 48, 49, 91, 128, 144, 157,
        188, 214, 234, 276, 277, 310, 356, 398, 420,
        421, 578, 602, 632, 645, 651, 652, 667, 686,
        717, 718, 740, 748, 758, 768, 800, 803, 818,
        864, 898, 937, 941, 947, 993, 1058, 1077,
        1132, 1181, 1274, 1311, 1364, 1365, 1447,
        1466n, 1469n, 1489, 1492, 1493
    market, poultry, 632
        stalls, 62, 578
    pilgrimage to, 1466, 1466n
    places in, Ballingdon bridge, 740
        'Bertlylmewys', 188, 188n
        Borehamgate End, 49, 128, 740n, 1274
        'Bole, le' (messuage), 128
        'Cherchestret', 717
        'Coppedbussh', 326
        'Coppydchoppe' (shop), 49
        'Crowyscroft, le', 864
        'Dokepetlane', 1058
        'Freristrete', 1492
        Friars Preachers, street of, 1364
        'Holgate', 326
        'Maldoneslane', 1058
        'Northmedue', 188
        Northstreet, 127
        'Rakhous', 805
        School Street, 1181n
        'Stonhalle, le', 1181
        Stour Street, 1181n
        'Stywardes Medew', 864
        'Wygaynende' (Wiggen End), 127, 127n,
            188, 758
    poor of, 800

roads, 188, 768
  testators of, *26*, *31*, **48**, **49**, **62**, **91**, **127**, **128**,
    157, **165**, **175**, **188**, **198**, **258**, **276**, **267**, **310**,
    322, **326**, **374**, **398**, **420**, **421**, **539**, **554**, **578**,
    593, *602*, *606*, **632**, *645*, *651*, *652*, **667**, *686*,
    717, **718**, **740**, *748*, **758**, *770*, **800**, **803**, **805**,
    818, **864**, *898*, **937**, *947*, **993**, **1058**, **1077**,
    1132, **1168**, **1181**, *1267*, **1274**, *1311*, **1364**,
    1447, **1489**, **1492**, **1493**
  well, common, 1077
  wills proved at, 48, 62, 81, 82, 83, 92, 127,
    128, 147, 171, 198, 215, 216, 217, 258, 259,
    274, 275, 277, 289, 301, 310, 326, 355, 356,
    398, 403, 404, 458, 462, 474, 502, 517, 539,
    541, 578, 602, 630, 637, 638, 639, 643, 647,
    651, 652, 717, 718, 740, 748, 770, 773, 774,
    790, 791, 800, 803, 804, 805, 818, 864, 909,
    937, 947, 992, 993, 1027, 1057, 1058, 1080,
    1111, 1118, 1132, 1149, 1168, 1177, 1188,
    1274, 1281, 1282, 1283, 1314, 1347, 1365,
    1461, 1487, 1489
  windmill in, 188
Sudbury, Thomas de, 62
  William, of Kettlebaston, 1300
SUFFOLK, county of, *xxxviii*
SUFFOLK, EAST, county (abolished 1974),
  xxxviii
SUFFOLK, WEST, county (formed 1889,
  abolished 1974), *xxxviii*, *xxxviiin*, *xxxix*
Suffolk, Alice (Chaucer), duchess of, 1076n
  William (de la Pole), duke of, 1076n
Sugge, Annabel, widow, of Edwardstone, **234**
  Richard, servant, of Sudbury, 234
  Seman, of Edwardstone, 234
Sulyard, John, 920
Susan, Alice, of Cockfield, *9*
  John, 9; chaplain, 362
SUTTON, vicar of, *see* Robert Ropkyn
Sutton, Alice, 185
  Christine, 185
  Clemencia, of Bradfield St Clare, & family,
    867
  John, 1174
  Margaret, of Tuddenham St Mary, *1061*
  Richard, of Oxborough (Nfk), **489**
  William, 489; yeoman of the crown, 489, 489n
SWAFFHAM (Cambs) (unspec.), inhabitant of,
  183
SWAFFHAM (Nfk), land in, 877
SWAFFHAM BULBECK (Cambs), priory of
  Benedictine nuns in, 180 ('Soham'), 180n
  church of ('Nonnysham'), 777
  nuns of ('Nonnysham'), 588, 777
Swalwe, Christian, of Thorney, 711
  Joan, of Chelsworth, 1459
  John, the younger, of Chelsworth, 1459
Swan, Alice, of Creeting St Peter, **1049**
  Margery, of Thorndon, 241

Richard, of Brandon, 1433
  Thomas, chaplain, of Lavenham, 350, 1073; of
    Thorndon, *241*
  see also Swayn
Swanton, Phyllis, of Denston, 731
  William, of Denston, *731*
Swayn (Sweyn), Alice, of Creeting St Peter, 665
  James, of Glemsford, 576
  Joan, of Rattlesden, 558
  John, sexton, 576; of Assington, 941; of
    Creeting St Peter, **665**, 1049n; of Lavenham,
    402; of Lavenham, & family, **164**; the
    younger, of Lavenham, 164; of Rattlesden,
    558
  Katherine, of Creeting St Peter, 665
  Margaret, of Lavenham, 164
  Thomas, of Creeting St Peter, 665
  William, of Harleston, 1306
Swettok(e) (Swettott), Richard, rector of
  Bildeston, 415n, 744, 1486
  Thomas, 415
Swyft(e), Agnes, of Long Melford, 1237
  John, 1237, 1425; of Walsham le Willows, 562,
    672, 767
  Thomas, of Long Melford, & family, **1237**
Sybbys, Agnes, 1497
  Alice, of Coney Weston, **1497**
Sybeton (Sybton, Sypton), Thomas, chaplain, of
  Sudbury, 188, 277, 310, 398, 539, 632, 686,
    758, 818
Sybly (Sylby), John, of Cheveley (Cambs), *1081*,
    1082; of Wattisham, 1346
  Margaret, of Cheveley (Cambs), 1081, 1082
Sybry, John, of Kersey, 342
Sybton, *see* Sybeton
Sydey, Alexander, 541
  Alice, of Long Melford, 541
  Joan, of Long Melford, 541
  John, 541; of Pebmarsh (Esx), 541; weaver, of
    Great Waldingfield, **541**
  Katherine, 541
  Richard, 541; of Alphamstone (Esx), 541
Syger, Matilda, of Burwell (Cambs), 1133
  William, of Burwell (Cambs), 284n, 1133
Sygo(o), Agnes, 245
  Matilda, of Mildenhall, 65
  Robert, 65, 119, 245; of Mildenhall, **65**
  William, 65
Sylby, *see* Sybly
Syllote, John, & family, 1231
  William, 1231
Symond (Simond), Agnes, 1478; of Botesdale,
  1374
  Elizabeth, of Thelnetham, 1355
  Isabel, of Rougham, 1478
  John, 1426, 1435, 1478; chaplain, 784; of
    Botesdale, 344, *1374*; of Cheveley (Cambs),
    822

Nicholas, 1478
Roger, 1478
Thomas, 1355; of Cheveley (Cambs), *1426*; of
  Rougham, **1478**; of Thelnetham, & family,
  1355
William, 1355, 1478; of Mildenhall, *1435*
Synton(e), William, of Sudbury, 310, 1274
Synys, Agnes, 958
  John, 958
  Margaret, 958
Sypton, *see* Sybeton
Syre, Richard, of Ixworth Thorpe, 101
Syrych, Isabel, of Nayland, 755
  John, 755; of Nayland, *755*
Sytewell, Katherine, 681
Sythyng, Henry, archdeacon's official, rector of
  Wortham, warden of Sudbury college, *xli-*
  xlii, *lv*n
Syward, John, 892
  Thomas, of Stoke by Nayland, 301
  William, of Stoke by Nayland, 546

Tabbard, Alice, of West Stow, 1309
  John, of West Stow, **1309**
  Walter, of West Stow, 1309n
  William, 1309
Tabham, Alice, 180
Taillour, *see* Taylour
Talbon, Robert, of Long Melford, 1064
Talbot, Ed., servant, 760
Talmage, John, of Great Finborough, 129
Talworth, John, 844, *844*
  Margaret, 844
Talyour, *see* Taylour
Talyour *alias* Elezs, Thomas, 1104
Tame, John, 803
Tavell, Margaret, of Lavenham, 462
Taylour (Taillour, Talyour, Tayler, Taylor(e),
  Taylouur, Taylowr), Alice, 1104, 1357; of
  Sudbury, 198
  Anne, 335
  Cecily, of Buxhall, 1366; of ?Hundon, *327*
  Henry, 1285, 1357; of Brockford, & family,
    1453; of Dalham, 269; of Lavenham, 1073
  Joan, of Eriswell, 751; of Old Newton, 346; of
    Thorndon, 809
  John, 193, 198, 533, 921, 809, 1210, 1345,
    1453; of Bradfield St George, *466*;
    of Buxhall, *1366*; of Stanton, 802; of
    Thorndon, 817; the younger, of Thorndon, &
    family, **809**
  Katherine, of Lavenham, 416
  Margaret, 1210; of Hitcham, 921
  Margery, 195
  Richard, 892, 921, 989; of Lavenham, **416**
  Roger, 195
  Simon, 260
  Thomas, 809, 1104, 1285; of Hitcham, **921**

  William, 195; of Eriswell, *751*; of Preston,
    1173; of Sudbury, **198**
  see also Talyour *alias* Elezs
Taylour *alias* Wyllyamsone, Anne, of Mildenhall,
    1263
  John, of Mildenhall, **1263**
Tebaude (Tebawd), Andrew, 94
  John, of Fordham (Cambs), 1277
Tendryng, Elizabeth, of Holbrook, 1216n
Tenwynter, John, of Lavenham, 820, 1013, 1461,
    1461n
Terell (Teroll), Edward, esquire, 106, 210
  William, 1340
Terlyng (Therlyng), Agnes, of Little Thurlow,
    1413
  William, of Little Thurlow, *1413*
Teroll, *see* Terell
Teryngton (Theryngton), Peter, of Rayleigh (Esx),
    489
  Robert, of Mendlesham, 1035
  Thomas, 486
Testwoode, John, 233
Tew *alias* Kyrtelynge, John, of Stoke by Clare,
    522
Thacher, Edmund, of Bardwell, 97
THELNETHAM, church, 1164
    rectors of, *see* Thomas Breton, John Ramsey
    ?second beam in, 1186
    sepulchre light in 506, 1186
  gilds in, 1063, 1262
  inhabitants of, 41, 969, 1063, 1186, 1262,
    1355, 1494
  places in, 'Crofftes, le', 969
    'Drenkstonys' (tenement), 1494
    'Dunnis' (tenement), 1494
    'Fyscherys' (pightle), 506
    'Grenewye', 1355
    'Haweboschakyr', 506
    'Hawe Closse', 1355
    'Hegge Lane', 1186
    'Howhywys' (cottage), 969
    'Lentonhege', 506
    'Paynys Lane', 1186
    'Pekookesacre', 1355
    'Rakestrawys', 506
    'Ratonys Lane', 1355
    'Snape' (acre), 1355
    'Websters' (cottage), 969
    'Websteres' (croft), 969
    'Wrythys' (close), 969
    'Wylmere, le' 969
    testators of, *213*, *349*, **506**, **969**, **1063**, **1186**,
      1262, **1355**, **1494**
  wills proved at, 405, 1355
Thelton, Matilda de, 406
Therlyng, *see* Terlyng
Theryngton, *see* Teryngton

THETFORD (Nfk and Sfk), burgess of, 281n
   chapel of St Mary in (Bailey End), 17, 321, 491
   church of St Cuthbert in, 281
   friars (unspec.) in, 357, 1039, 1123
   gilds in, 489, 491
   house of Austin friars in ('the New House'), 17,
      41, 55, 56, 69, 96, 97, 97n, 101, 124, 180,
      213, 252, 271, 286, 305, 347, 377, 388, 393,
      457, 530, 599, 726, 787, 821, 889, 891, 945,
      964, 1063, 1170, 1186, 1225, 1255, 1258,
      1262, 1272, 1279, 1302, 1368, 1371, 1395,
      1397, 1409, 1465, 1497
   friar of, 530
   house of Dominican friars in ('the Old House'),
      17, 46, 55, 96, 97, 97n, 124, 138, 180, 182,
      213, 252, 271, 286, 287, 294, 304, 305, 373,
      377, 388, 393, 438, 456, 457, 552, 599, 663,
      672, 679, 684, 723, 726, 749, 760, 779, 782,
      794, 821, 836, 889, 842, 945, 964, 1033,
      1063, 1129, 1155, 1170, 1186, 1191, 1210,
      1221, 1225, 1255, 1258, 1262, 1272, 1279,
      1289, 1302, 1313, 1333, 1334, 1337, 1371,
      1395, 1397, 1409, 1437, 1439, 1441, 1451,
      1465, 1495, 1497
   inhabitants of, 56, 59, 69, 101, 124, 253, 281,
      1069, 1164
   land in, 281
   parish of St Mary the Less in, *xl*
   partly in Suffolk, *xl*
   priory of Austin canons in, 69, 180, 303, 1399
   priory of Benedictine nuns in, *xlix*, 17, 56, 59,
      69, 90, 124, 180, 231, 271, 286, 305, 347,
      377, 393, 457, 530, 599, 749, 849, 983,
      1225, 1240, 1268, 1272, 1279, 1302, 1441
   nun of, 90
   priory of Cluniac monks in, 1463, 1463n
Thirlowe, John, 893
Thodenham, *see* Tuddenham
Thoffay, John, of Great Livermere, 1195
Thomas, John, 1448
Thomson (Tomson), Alexander, 99; of Brandon,
   884
   Alice, widow, of Haverhill, **1457**
   Margaret, 1256
   William, 683, 884, 1256
Thorn, Emma, 1343
THORNDON, church, 648
   light of BVM in, 809
   sepulchre light in, 817, 962
   gild in, 648, 742, 817
   inhabitants of, 22, 241, 597, 658, 742, 785,
      809, 817, 907, 962, 1090, 1102
   land in, 648
   mortuary paid in, *xlvi*
   places in, 'Blakelond', 742
   testators of, **117**, *241*, *242*, *597*, **742**, **785**, **809**,
      817, *907*, **962**, **1090**, *1102*
   wills proved at, 785, 817

THORNEY, *see* STOWMARKET
THORNHAM (unspec.), inhabitant of, 771
   land in, 1165
   testators of, *1095*, *1445*
   wills proved at, 223, 285, 949
THORNHAM MAGNA, church, altar in, painting
      of, 1169
   rectors of, *see* John Broun, Robert West
   stools in, 1
   tower of, *xlvii*n, 63, 63n
   vestment for, 1169
   inhabitants of, 228, 771, 788, 1095, 1096, 1445
   land in, 1014, 1273
   mortuary paid in, *xlvi*n
   places in, 'Byllyngfordes' (tenement), 63
      'Mellefeld', 63
      Newton (manor), 1169, 1169n
      'Oxlund' (field), 228
      'Stabilmedewe', 1
      'Watyrsalwdych, le', 228
      'Wylwenner' (land), 228
   testators of, **1**, **63**, **771**, **788**, **1096**, **1169**
   wills proved at, 475, 648, 742, 1169
THORNHAM PARVA, church, 1169
   dedication of, *xlv*
   wall-paintings in, 1014n
   inhabitants of, 811, 1014
   testators of, *811*, **1014**
   will proved at, 811
Thornton, Geoffrey, 1041
THORPE (unspec.), testator of, **1328**
Thorpe, John, 232; of Stowmarket, 497; vicar of
   St Mary, Stowmarket, 19n
THORPE MORIEUX, inhabitants of, 402, 446,
      773, 1122, 1244, 1466
   rector of, 1260
   testators of, *773*, *774*, *1122*, **1244**
   will proved at, 901
THORPE ST PETER, pilgrimage to
      ('Peterthorp'), 1207, 1207n
THRANDESTON, church, 369
   aisle of, 1459n
   leading of, 1459n
   legend for, 808n
   tower of, 492, 492n
   window in, 492
   inhabitants of, 156, 369, 649, 808, 906, 973,
      1062, 1317, 1459n
   places in, 'Croweslane', 543
      'Drewys' (tenement), 543
      'Smalforthe', 1371
   testators of, **71**, **199**, **492**, **509**, **543**, *575*, *604*,
      649, **906**, *973*, *1062*, *1304*, *1317*
   wills proved at, 400, 641, 809, 1422
Threchere, John, of Clare, **260**
   Marion, of Clare, 260
   see also Throssher
THRIPLOW (Cambs), inhabitant of, 780

Throssher, John, of Hitcham, 921
  see also Threchere
Thrower, William, 808; rector of Ingham, 227,
  227n
Thrustayn, Richard, of Mile End, by Colchester
  (Esx), 843
Thruston, *see* Thurston
THUNDERSLEY (Esx), land in, 489
Thurgo(u)r, John, of Waldingfield, *1038*
  Robert, 1038; of Acton, 404
  William, of Great Waldingfield, 1039, 1039n
THURLOW (unspec.), will proved at, 1382
THURLOW, GREAT, vicar of, *see* Henry Manton
  inhabitants of, 134, 193, 395, 1398
  poor of, 368, 654
  testators of, *134, 395, 527*
  wills proved at, 249, 914
THURLOW, LITTLE, chapel of St Petronilla in,
  1398
  church, 1398
    rector of, 1398
  inhabitants of, 567, 1398, 1413, 1432
  poor of, 368, 654
  testators of, *567, 866, 1093, 1197, 1413, 1490*
Thurmo(o)d, Ed., 1122
  Eleanor, of Thorpe Morieux, 1122
  John, 774, 1486; of Bildeston, 520, **1486**; of
    Thorpe Morieux, *774*
  Richard, of Thorpe Morieux, *1122*
  Robert, 1486
  William, of Bildeston, 1486
THURSTON, church, 21, 782, 821, 1240
  land of, 552
  light of BVM in, 287, 358, 552, 1437, 1451
  vicar of, 760
    see also William Chapelleyn
  church-house in churchyard, 1437
  gilds in, 287, 1451
  inhabitants of, 52, 222, 232, 287, 347n, 358,
    430, 760, 782, 1210, 1246n, 1437, 1440,
    1451
  land in, 1240n, 1255
  places in, 'Altonemedewe', 552
    'Amablysaker', 552
    'Balley', 1437
    'Balleyfeld', 287
    'Botinehyll', 287
    'Brayesweye', 287
    'Brokys' (tenement), 1451
    'Brookonowey', 552
    'Calfhooslade', 552
    'Calkebron', 358
    'Chyrchgate, north', 552
    'Chyrchegate, west', 552
    'Chyrchewey, le', 552
    Common, the, 552
    'Eldecroft', 358
    'Eldhalle' (field), 552

'Eryslond', 552
'Fedehalfaker', 552
'Fuookyslond', 552
'Fyrseclos, le', 552
'Fyrsez, le', 552
'Goodyscroft', 552
'Gorydlond', 552
'Grenewey, le', 552
'Grymysakre', 552
'Havedys, le' (land), 552
'Hethende', 287
'Jonyslegge', 287
'Keches', 760
'Knellefeld', 552
'Kyngyscrouch', 552
'Ladyesheg', 552
'Langelond *et* Chyrchegovyll', 358
'Langelond' (furlong), 552
'Litleheth', 552
'Longeaker', 552
'Longestrete *alias* Hethende', 552
'Longgeacres, le', 552
'Litilbussh', 552
'Makkenysmere', 552
'Malleys' (close), 552
'Millers' (tenement), 1451
'Nethyrknellefeld', 552
'Nethyrstrete', 552
'Overknelfeld', 552
'Potteresweye', 552
'Pytellond', 287
'Ramesys', 552
'Rodehalfaker', 552
'Rychardyshalle' (manor), 552
'Scochys, le', 552
'Skyrpyslond', 287
'Snapys', 358
'Sondpeth', 552
'Stokehoofeld', 552
'Stretysende', 552
Thurston field, 1437
'Tweyneacrys', 552
'Watyrrennelys, le', 552
'Weykcs' (tenement), 1437
'Whetecroft', 552
'Whylughmere', 552
'Whytstetchys', 552
'Wodeende', 552
'Wythyesrow', 552
sheep in, *li*
testators of, **287, 358, 430, 552, 760,** *1407,*
  1437, 1451
Thurston (Thruston), Agnes, 1469
  John, 1246; of Bury St Edmunds, 1279
  Robert, 541, 1280, 1469
  see also Thrustayn
THWAITE, church, 87, 285, 705, 706, 1097, 1200
  inhabitants of, 658, 869, 996

land in, 1200
poor of, 775
testators of, **658**, *996*
Thweyt, Margaret, 492; of Wetheringsett, 869
   Matthew, of Wetheringsett, 345, *869*
   Thomas, 361
   William, 869
Thweytes, family, of Hardingham (Nfk), *xlii*n
   William, notary & registrar, of Bury St
     Edmunds, *xli-xlii*; the younger, *xlii*
Thyknesse, Eleanor, of Newmarket, 1358
   John, of Newmarket, **1358**
TIBENHAM (Nfk), pilgrimage to, 1090
Tibetot, *see* Toptoft
Tilbrook, John, 337
   Peter, of Kirtling (Cambs), & family, **337**
   Thomas, 337
Tiler, *see* Tyler
Tille, *see* Tylle
TIMWORTH, church, 180
    bells of, 1074
    rectors of, *see* John Mey, John Parker
   gilds in, 749, 1074
   inhabitants of, 849, 856, 892, 963n, 1074,
    1109n, 1201, 1288, 1441
   land in, 1441
   places in, 'Hethys' (manor), 305, 305n
    'Rasshys', 305
    'Reymers', 305
   testators of, *225*, **305**, **468**, **594**, **749**, *856*, **892**,
    1074, *1109*, **1201**, **1288**
Toby, Thomas, of Bury St Edmunds, 246
Toffeld, *see* Tuffeld
Toke, Isabel, servant, 335
Toly, Margaret, of Barnham, 983, *1171*
   Walter, 1304
   William, 983, 1171; of Barnham, **983**, 1171n
Tomson, *see* Thomson
Tone, Isabel, of Little Whelnetham, 1025
   John, of Little Whelnetham, *1025*
Toptoft (or Tibetot), John, earl of Worcester, 1162,
   1162n
Torald (Torold), Joan, of Thornham, *1095*
   John, 1095, 1096
TOSTOCK, church, 1054
   rectors of, *see* Henry Irby, Robert
    Wol(e)man (Wulleman)
   closes in, *liii*
   inhabitants of, 133, 467, 782n, 836, 1288
   land in, 287, 1465
   places in, 'Beggeres Wong', 836
    Berdwells (manor), 836n
    'Gerecroft', 836
    Green, the, 836
    'Pondyerd', 836
    'Schepherdes' (messuage), 836
    'Suppelane', 836
    Tostock Hall (manor), 836n

'Trakes' (messuage), 836
'Trakescroft', 836
'Tuft, le' (close), 836
road in, 836
testators of, **133**, *605*, *614*, **836**
will proved at, 605
Tostok, Stephen, chaplain, of Blo Norton (Nfk),
   1307
Totay, Robert, of Bury St Edmunds, 542
Tought, John, chaplain, of Stonham Aspal, 1417
TOWTON (Yorks), battle of, 1246n
Traford, John, 1425
Trapet, Ralph, 1257*
   Thomas, of Hepworth, 1257n; of Hepworth, &
    family, **1257**
   William, of Hepworth, 1257; of Thelnetham,
    969
Travac(?), John, servant, 90
Tredegold *alias* Baly, Henry, of Exning, *1128*
Trool, Margery, of Wickhambrook, 1055
   Stephen, of Wickhambrook, **1055**
TROSTON, church, 231
    candlebeam in, 1174
    lamps in, 1174
    light of BVM in, 1174
    parishioners of, food and drink for, 599
    rector of, *see* John Spryng
   inhabitants of, 69, 583, 1174
   land in, 231
   testators of, *255*, **599**, *694*, *1019*, **1174**, *1401*
   wills proved at, 506, 599
Trowman, William, 1007
Troys, Reginald, vicar of Lakenheath, 1121
Trumpour, Margaret, 693
Trybolle, William, 90
Tyker, William, 743
Tryp, Alice, 1217
   Joan, of Wickham Skeith, 1200, 1200n
   John, 1200
   William, of Wickham Skeith, 1200, 1200n
Tubby, Richard, of Bury St Edmunds, 1279
   William, of Wortham, & family, **1164**
TUDDENHAM ST MARY, church, 708
    rector of, *see* John Legate
   inhabitants of, 427, 1061, 1460
   poor of, 708
   testators of, *14*, *363*, *427*, *1061*, *1460*, *1470*
Tuddenham (Thodenham), Thomas, knight, of
   Oxburgh (Nfk), 489, 489n
Tuffeld (Toffeld), Alice, of Whepstead, *267*
   John, 267
Tukke, William, of Bury St Edmunds, 806
Turno(u)r (Turnowr), Adam, 806
   Agnes, 624
   Alice, of Woolpit, 60
   Beatrice, of Woolpit, **806**
   Henry, 668, 740, 770; of Haverhill, 491, 633;
    gentleman, of Haverhill, 968

Isabel, of Sudbury, & family, **175**
James, of Drinkstone, **439**
Joan, of Haverhill, 633n
John, *328*, 806, 1253; of Dalham, 553; of
    Depden, 472; of Drinkstone, 439; the elder,
    of Kirtling (Cambs), 1467; of Lavenham,
    374; of Norton, *1380*; of Sudbury, 717; of
    Whepstead, 417, *888*; of Woolpit, **60**
Margaret, of Drinkstone, 439; of Haverhill,
    633n
Richard, 337, 1380
Robert, 623, 624, 806*
Thomas, 60, 439; warrener, of Hilborough
    (Nfk), 489; of Sudbury, *374*
William, 37; of Bury St Edmunds, & family,
    806; of Sudbury, 175
Turnour *alias* Dyer, Christine, 1369
Henry, of Long Melford, 668n, *1369*
Rose, of Long Melford, 1369
Tyd, Alice, of Mildenhall, 727
Henry, 727
Isabel, 1117; of Mildenhall, 598
John, of Mildenhall, **727**
Reginald, 727
Robert, 1117; of Mildenhall, & family, **598**
Theodora, 727
Thomas, 727; of Mildenhall, 598
Tye, Joan, of Lavenham, 1243
John, of Poslingford, *988*
Robert, of Lavenham, **1243**
Thomas, 1243
Tyell, Cecily, 526
William, of Boyton End, Stoke by Clare, *526*
Tyler(e) (Tiler), Alice, of Wetheringsett, *912*
Hawise, of Westley, 1391
John, 209, 848; the younger, 209; of Monks
    Eleigh, 375; of Sudbury, 128
Margaret, of Creeting St Peter, 209
Thomas, 209; of Fornham St Genevieve, 729;
    of Monks Eleigh, 392; vicar of Sudbury All
    Saints & rector of Alby (Nfk), 1181, 1489;
    of Westley, *1391*
William, of Creeting St Peter, **209**
Tylie, *see* Tylye
Tylle (Tille), Alice, of Sudbury, 1489
John, weaver, 803; of Boxford, *214*, 1489; of
    Rattlesden, *765*; of Sudbury, 748, 800; dyer,
    of Sudbury, & family, **1489**; the elder, of
    Sudbury, 214
Rose, of Boxford, 214
Thomas, 765
Tyllot(e) (Tylott), Edmund, 1240, 1345
Isabell, 1240
John, 294, 1240, 1478; of Great Barton, 1441
Katherine, of Rougham, 1240
Margaret, of Great Barton, *294*
Margery, 1240
Robert, 1240*

Roger, of Rougham, li, 116, **1240**, 1441n
Thomas, 850, 1240; husbandman, 124n
Tylney, *see* Pumpy *alias* Tylney
Tylott, *see* Tyllot(e)
Tylye (Tylie), John, of Tostock, 133, 467, 836
Reginald, of Hessett, 364
Tymtewell, *see* Tyntwell
Tymton, *see* Tynton
Tynker, Margaret, 1034
Robert, of Woodditton (Cambs), 135
Tynton (Tymton), John, 129; of Finborough, 1343;
    the elder, of Great Finborough, *lii*, **1343**
Katherine, 129
Thomas, 129, 1343
Tyntwell(e) (Tymtewelle), Joan, of Stowmarket,
    288, 1421
William, of Stowmarket, 288, **1421**
Tymworth, John, of Timworth, & family, **468**
Margaret, of Timworth, 468
Tyso, Agnes, of Drinkstone, 1054
George, 1054
John, 1054*; of Drinkstone, 370
Margaret, of Drinkstone, *922*, 1056
Thomas, 1079; of Drinkstone, 922n, **1054**,
    1056

Ufford, Agnes, of Hundon, 1083
Robert, of Hundon, & family, **1083**
Ulott, John, 257
Umfrey, Isabel, of Sapiston, **1242**
John, 243
Thomas, & family, 1398
see also Humfrey, Homfrey, Omfrey
Underwode, John, 1057
Robert, 1461
Unkyll, Anne, 1419
William, 1419

Vale, Alice, of Long Melford, 82
John, 1410; of Long Melford, **82**
Valentyn(e) (Walentyn), John, 249, 527; of Great
    Thurlow, 134
Velle, John, 1435
Veneve, *see* Wynyeve
Venour, George, of Cornard, *1027*
John, 1027
William, esquire, 1246
Verions, John, 394
William, 394
Vesey, John, 1104; the younger, 1104
Margaret, 1104
Veston, *see* Weston
Vyell (Vyal, Wyell), John, 905, 961; of Ixworth,
    1242
Thomas, of Ixworth, 905, 905n
Vyncent, Agnes, of Ixworth Thorpe, 101
Vyne (Wyne), John, 578, 717, 770, 993, 1077,
    1168

Wace, John, 659
Wade, Alice, of Woolpit, 564
　Helen, of Creeting, 851
　James, of Woolpit, **564**, 655, 655n
　John, 890; of Creeting, *851*
　Katherine, of Woolpit, 564
　Margaret, of Woolpit, 564
　Rose, of Woolpit, 564
　Thomas, 564
　William, 564
Wagecok, Robert, 1008
Waggard, Alice, of Sapiston, 1059
　Davy, of Sapiston, *1059*
　William, 1059
Wagge, Alice, of Haverhill, 1092
　John, 1092; of Haverhill, **1092**; rector of
　　Herringswell, 894
　William, 1092
Wagon, Agnes, of Timworth, 1074
　John, 1074; of Timworth, **1074**
　William, 1074
Wakeryng, Thomas, 847
WAKES COLNE (Esx), inhabitant of, 301
WALBERSWICK, inhabitant of, 1090n
Walcard, William, the elder, of Risby, 1210
Walcote, Joan, 583
WALDINGFIELD (unspec.), inhabitants of, 463,
　624, 1469
　places in, 'Chyltoncroft', 1469
　　'Colmannys & Rawlynes' (tenement), 1469
　　'Crokes' (cottage), 1469
　　'Crokes' (tenement), 1469
　　'Shypcroft', 1469
　　'Stonylond', 1469
　testators of, **647**, *1038*, *1360*, **1469**
　will proved at, 1324
WALDINGFIELD, GREAT, church, 548
　altar cloth for, 186
　new building at, 1280
　ornaments of, 1280
　rector of, *see* John Powle
　rectory (house) of, 1280
　inhabitants of, 204, 643, 758, 1039, 1280, 1469
　land in, 1446
　places in, 'Baberheth', 1280
　　Brookstreet, 643
　　'Calwecroft', 1280
　　'Dermannys Croft', 1280
　　'Dunstall', 1280
　　'Feeld, le', 1280
　　'Lanelond', 643
　　'Mathewys' (messuage), 186
　　'Morynys', 643
　　'Paton Croft', 643
　　'Peend, le' (grove), 643
　　'Pondfeld, le', 1280
　　'Poweres' (tenement), 1280

　　'Rokedews' (tenement), 186
　　'Webbes' (tenement), 1280
　　'Wode, le', 1280
　poor of, 1280
　roads in, 1280
　testators of, **186**; *513*, **541**, **643**, **1280**
　wills proved at, 36, 37, 685, 1329
WALDINGFIELD, LITTLE, church, 1280
　new building at, 171
　roodloft painting 1193
　seating in, 1024, 1024n
　vicar of, *see* John Dalton
　inhabitants of, 92, 582, 593, 1024, 1193, 1280,
　　1360n
　testators of, **92**, **171**, **582**, **1024**, **1193**, *1487*
Waldyngfeld, Thomas, canon, 1242
Waldyngfeldhall, William, 476
Wale, Alice, of Thornham Magna, 788
　Henry, 1014
　Isabel, of Thornham Parva, 1014
　John, 1014n; the elder, of Thornham Magna,
　　& family, **788**; of Thornham Parva, 788; of
　　Thornham Parva, & family, **1014**
　Simon, 788
　Thomas, the younger, 788
Walenger, Nicholas, of Nayland, *200*
Walentyn, *see* Valentyn(e)
Waleys, Alice, of Soham (Cambs), *1085*
　Edony, of Thorndon, 597
　John, 689; of Hundon, *689*
　Margaret, of Hundon, 689
　Thomas, 278
　Walter, of Thorndon, *597*
Walkard, John, of Culford, 315
Walkford (Walkefar), Richard, of Hitcham, 51; of
　　Hitcham, & family, **487**
Wall(e), Edmund, 612
　John, 612, 1228, 1285; the elder, 612; of
　　Boxford, & family, **612**
　Richard, 612
　Thomas, 719; of Kersey, 612
Waller, Robert, 1335
Wallock, *see* Watlock
Walour (Walowr), Beatrice, of Market Weston,
　　951
　Nicholas, of Market Weston, *951*
Walpoll, Ed., 1174; of Ixworth, 1323
WALSHAM le WILLOWS, church, beam in, 169,
　　672
　carpentry work in, 562n, 767n
　chapel of St Katherine in, 457n
　clerestory windows of, 562n, 767n
　stone-work in, 1272
　vestments for, 457n
　gilds in, 357, 1370
　inhabitants of, 672, 767, 1040, 1042, 1043,
　　1193n, 1370, 1397
　places in, 'Howchownis Close, le', 1370

road in, 169
testators of, **169**, **518**, *562*, **672**, 767, *1040*,
  1042, *1043*, **1272**, **1370**
wills proved at, 854, 889, 1001, 1112, 1342,
  1370
Walsham (Walsom), Joan, of Woolpit, 282
  John, 1349; 1465; of Norton, 1255; of Woolpit,
    282
WALSINGHAM (Nfk), pilgrimage to shrine
  of Our Lady at, 175, 345, 346, 489, 1090,
  1090n, 1207, 1207n, 1466
Walsom, *see* Walsham
Walter(e), Agnes, of Hopton (near Harling), 286
  Edmund, of Elmswell, 1495, 1495n
  Geoffrey, 286; of Coney Weston, 957
  John, 286; the elder, 586; the elder, of Hopton
    (near Harling), **286**, *323*; rector of Santon
    Downham, 419n
  Lettice, of Hopton (near Harling), 323
  Richard, 286*, 723
  Robert, the younger, 286
Waltham, Edmund, friar, 172
WANGFORD (by Brandon), inhabitant of, 1254
  land in, 1289
  testators of, *1254*, *1266*
Wanton, Margery, of Stanton, 1299
  Robert, of Stanton, **1299**
Warde, Agnes, 594
  Alice, 1008; of Fornham All Saints, **12**
  Clarissa, 488
  Edith, of Walsham le Willows, 1043
  Helen, of Saxon Street, Woodditton (Cambs),
    428
  John, of Saxon Street, Woodditton (Cambs),
    428
  Katherine, servant, 180
  Ralph, 428
  Robert, 1246; of Walsham le Willows, *1043*
WARE (Herts), bequest to, 692n
Ware, James, of Hadleigh, 643
  Robert, rector of Westley, 692
Wareyn (Waren, Waryn), Agnes, of Bildeston,
  415; of Kirtling (Cambs), 1467*
  Alice, 406; of Long Melford, 790, 916
  Amflote, of Long Melford, & family, 474
  Geoffrey, 406
  Helen, of Stoke by Nayland, 301
  Henry, of Combs, *753*
  Joan, of Great Ashfield, 1258; of Kirtling
    (Cambs), 1467
  John, 390, 474, 1071, 1245, 1258, 1467;
    mason, 1387; of Bildeston, *xlvi*, **415**;
    of Brettenham, *840*; of Clare, 1471; of
    Hartest, 1075; of Kersey, 342, 1067; of
    Long Melford, 474, 1329n; the elder, fuller,
    of Long Melford, **474**; the younger, of
    Long Melford, 517, **790**, 916; the elder,
    of Mildenhall, **1471**; the younger, of

Mildenhall, 1471; barker, of Nayland, *xlivn*,
  108; fuller, of Stoke by Nayland, *xlivn*, **301**
  Laurentia, of Stoke by Nayland, 301
  Margaret, of Brettenham, 840; of Kirtling
    (Cambs), 1467; of Long Melford, 790, **916**
  Ralph, 840
  Richard, of Long Melford, 474, **1329**
  Robert, 1467; of Great Ashfield, **1258**; of
    Kirtling (Cambs), & family, **1467**
  Rose, of Kersey, & family, **390**
  Thomas, 474, 1329, 1467; of Long Melford,
    221
  William, 259; chaplain, 1335; of Ely (Cambs),
    1471
Wareyn *alias* Baker, John, of Clare, 1218
Warner, Alice, of Elmswell, *855*
  John, 57, 495, 871, 903, 1041; of Barrow, 77,
    494, of Great Livermere, 180; of Soham
    (Cambs), 183
  Katherine, 831; of Barrow, 494; of Great
    Livermere, 180
  Margaret, of Barrow, & family, **57**
  Robert, 25, 831
  Thomas, 290; vicar of Woodditton (Cambs),
    553, 553n
Warry, Thomas, of Boxford, 544
Warton, John, of Milden, *512*
Warwell, Joan, of Polstead, 1484
  John, 1484
  Robert, 1484
  William, of Polstead, & family, **1484**
Waryn, *see* Wareyn
Waschepoke, Eleanor, of Haverhill, 490, **491**
  William, of Haverhill, **490**, 491
Waspe, Thomas, 1057
Wasse, John, 537
Wasshman (Whasshman), Katherine, of
  Lavenham, **161**
Wastell, Richard, 207
Water, *see* Watter
Watlo(c)k (Wathelok), Agatha, of Clare, 112
  Hugh, 113
  Joan, 113; of Clare, 112; of Depden, 1218
  John, 113; of Clare, **112**, 113
  Margaret, 113
  Margery, 113
  Richard, 113
  Simon, of Poslingford, 112, 113
  Stephen, 112
Watlok *alias* Smyth, Elizabeth, of Rede, 960
  Henry, 960
  John, of Rede, **960**
  Nicholas, 960
Watter (Water), John, 378; the elder, of Layham,
  639
  Thomas, 1121; the younger, 1035
  William, 1288

Wattes, John, 893
WATTISFIELD, church, 945, 1409
    fifteenths of, 945
    funeral customs in, 1409n
    gild in, 945,1409
    inhabitants of, 945, 1409
    land in, 1446
    places in, 'Dawysatgrene', 945
        field of Wattisfield, 1409
        'Hall wateryng', 945
        'Molows' (close), 1409; (tenement), 1409
        'Robeys' (tenement), 1409
        'Upstrete', 1409
    testators of, *591*, *936*, **945**, **964**, *1377*,**1409**
    wills proved at, 767, 935, 936, 969, 1026, 1130, 1494
WATTISHAM, church, 1346
    bell for, 1346
    torch in, 1346
    inhabitants of, 1346
    testators of, **1346**
Watyrnas, Cecily, of Norton, 1379
    John, of Norton, & family, **1379**
Waynold, *see* Weyneld
Waytlove, George, 723
Webbe, Alice, 777
    Isabel, of Long Melford, 532
    John, 375, 395, 673, 1028; limeburner, 740;
        servant, 1001; of Little Waldingfield, 1280;
        the elder, of Palgrave, *1330*
    Katherine, of Great Thurlow, 395; of Lidgate, 1028
    Matilda, 193
    Robert, of Great Thurlow, *395*
    Thomas, 532, *673*; of Lidgate, *1028*
    William, 846; chaplain, 549, 561; of Long
        Melford, *532*
Webber, Thomas, 1211
Webster(e), Richard, 1165; of Ixworth, 335, *628*
Wechyngham, [*unnamed*], Austin friar of
        Thetford, 530
Weder, *see* Wethyr
Wedirhogge, John, 452
Wedyrdene, *see* Wethyrdene
Weder(e), *see* Wethyr
WEETING (Nfk), inhabitant of, 359
Wegeyn (Wegayn, Wygeyn), John, 546, 637, 637n
    William, of Bures, 477
Welde, Ada, of Woolpit, 261, **777**
    John, of Woolpit, *261*, 777
Weler, *see* Wheler
Well, *see* Wellys
Wellam, Joan, of Hitcham, 772
    John, of Hitcham, **772**
    Richard, 772
Welle(s), Wellis, *see* Wellys
Wellyng, Robert, esquire, of Lavenham, 1280

Wellyngham (Willyngham), John, of Glemsford, 991
Wellys (Well(e), Well(e)s, Wellis), James, 687
    Joan, of Stoke by Nayland, 1412
    John, 508, 713, 757, 1311, 1474
    Margaret, of Hartest, 687, **1075**; of Woolpit, 713
    Margery, of Newton (by Sudbury), 463
    Matilda, of Bardwell, *451*
    Richard, of Troston, 30
    Robert, 451; of Coney Weston, *330*; of Hartest,
        456, **687**, 1075; of Newton (by Sudbury),
        463
    Simon, of Woolpit, & family, **713**
    Thomas, of Long Melford, 1075; of Stoke by
        Nayland, *1412*; of Walsham le Willows, *562*
    William, 330, 464, 1137; of Bardwell, 451
WELNETHAM, *see* WHELNETHAM
Welton, Agnes, of Cheveley (Cambs), 676
    John, of Cheveley (Cambs), **676**
Wenden, Emma, of Bures, *275*, 1335n
    Robert, 275, 1290, 1335
Weneve, *see* Wynyeve
WENHASTON, church, 'doom' painting in, 908n
Wenheve, Wennif, *see* Wynyeve
Wepsted, *see* Whepsted
West, Eustace, of Barton Mills, 131
    John, of Moulton, 44; rector of Stanstead, 137
    Robert, rector of Thornham Magna, 63
    Thomas, esquire, of Sudbury, 740, 740n
WESTHORPE, inhabitants of, 194, 347n, 385,
        1437, 1451
    rector of, 1279n, 1437n, 1451
        see also Thomas Muryell, John Pekerell
    testators of, **5**, *206*
    wills proved at, 401, 704
Westhorpe, Thomas, rector of Stansfield, 382
Westle, Thomas, friar, 50
WESTLEY, churches, 226n
    church of St Thomas, 57
        lead roofing of, 692
        rector of, *see* Robert Ware
    inhabitants of, 4, 616, 692, 1220, 1391
    land in, 41, 57, 1279
    places in, 'Ludehalle' (Luce Hall), 41, 41n
        'Thomas Fadris lond', 692
    poor of, 692
    road in, 692
    testators of, *4*, **98**, **226**, **360**, *542*, **616**, **692**,
        1220, *1391*
WESTON, *see* MARKET WESTON
WESTON LONGVILLE (Nfk), tenement in (?), 489
Weston (Veston), William, 1174
WEST STOW, church, 17, 891
        rector of, *see* George Smyth
    inhabitants of, 41n, 56, 698, 1022, 1309
    land in, 315

testators of, **56**, *698*, *1022*, **1309**, **1361**
Westyngton, Robert, rector of Barrow, 290
Wedyr, *see* Wethyr
Wedyrdene, Mariola, of Bildeston, **680**
Wether, *see* Wethyr
Wetherard, (Wetherhard), Alice, 714
  Elizabeth, of Stowmarket, 934
  John, of Stowmarket, *934*, 1138; the elder, of
    Stowmarket, & family, **714**
  Margaret, of Stowmarket, 714, **943**
  Richard, 714
  Thomas, 714
  William, 714
WETHERDEN, church, 231, 497
  inhabitants of, 33, 394, 519, 1182, 1215,
    1295
  land in, 231, 497, 1001
  places in, 'Chirchstrete, le', 394
    'Goramys', 608
    'Okyes' (tenement), 795
  testators of, **33**, **394**, *557*, **608**, **1182**, *1215*,
    1295
  wills proved at, 408, 434, 557, 710, 1138, 1182,
    1366
WETHERINGSETT, BROCKFORD in, church,
    345n
  inhabitants of, 764, 1417, 1453
  lands in, 962, 1023
  parish clerk of, 345, 345n
  places in, 'Braunswode feld', 721
    'Goswaldes' (tenement), 1417
  road in, 1417
  testators of, **721**, **764**, **801**, **1417**, **1453**
  will proved in, 801
  church, 29, 285, 801, 1453
  candlesticks in, 1453
  chalice of, 15
  cope for, 1417
  images in: BVM, 15, 345
    Holy Trinity, 15, 248
    St John the Baptist, 345
    St Thomas the martyr, 345
  Lady Chapel in, 15n, 345
  lights in, 15, 345
  rector of, *see* Richard de Leycestria
  retable for, 248
  rood in, 345
  tomb of Master Richard in, 15, 15n, 345
  torches in, 345
  inhabitants of, 345, 641, 721, 741, 764, 869,
    1023, 1034, 1438
  land in, 785
  places in, 'Fentyng' (tenement), 1023
    'Simonys Clos', 641
    'Sowterys' (land), 1023
  stall in, 1023
  testators of, **15**, **248**, **345**, **641**, **869**, *912*, *913*,
    918, **1023**, **1034**, *1202*, **1438**

wills proved at, 248, 575, 721, 741, 912, 913,
    918, 1090, 1095, 1096, 1102, 1202
Wethringsette, *see* Leycestria *alias* Wethringsette
Wethyr(e) (Weder, Wedyre, Wether), Alice, of
    Elmswell, 1495
  Andrew, of Stanton, 457
  Ed., of Elmswell, *700*, 1495
  Isabel, of Elmswell, 725
  Joan, of Elmswell, 700, 1112
  John, 725; of Elmswell, 563, 700, 1001, 1112n,
    1495; the elder, of Elmswell, **725**
  Katherine, of Norton, 336
  Robert, of Elmswell, 725, *1112*; of Norton, *336*
  Thomas, 112
  William, 1495; of Stanton, 457
Wever, *see* Rogere *alias* Wever
Wevour, Margaret, of Little Cornard
  Richard, of Little Cornard, *565*
Weyneld (Waynold), Simon, of Chelsworth, 143,
    151, 629, 1459
Whasshman, *see* Wasshman
WHATFIELD, bridge in, 1416
  church, 143, 1115, 1416
    Romescot of, 1416
  'Gravenyng Medow' in, 1416
  testator of, **162**
Whedereld, William, 228
  see also Qwedereld
Wheler (Weler, Qweler), William, 448, 939
WHELNETHAM, GREAT, church, 17, 824n
  rector of, *see* Robert Forthe
WHELNETHAM, LITTLE, church, tower of,
    824, 824n
  rector of, *see* Richard Clerke, Robert Mawe
  Dekys family of, 824n
  inhabitants of, 1025
  testators of, *525*, **824**, *1025*
WHEPSTEAD, church, 411, 960
  candle before high altar in, 160
  chalice for, 351
  lamp before cross in, 160
  rector of, *see* John Wodeward
  gilds in, 351
  inhabitants of, 160, 293, 417, 549, 589n, 965
  land in, 314
  places in, 'Bradley' (field), 160
    'Cagewode', 160
    'Clareweye', 160
    'Mastonys lond', 160
    'Mellefeld', 160
  road in, 160
  testators of, **160**, *267*, **351**, **417**, *888*, **965**
Whepsted (Wepsted), Hugh, of Brettenham, 1036,
    1436
White, *see* Whyte
Whitt, John, 1041
  William, 1041
  see also Whyte

Whytbred, Agnes, of Eye, **320**
Whyte (White, Whyth), Agnes, 626
  John, of Kentford, 759, **894**
  Richard, 193; of Stoke by Clare, 1423
  Robert, servant, of Ixworth, 357
  see also Whitt
Whythede, Margaret, of Soham (Cambs), &
  family, **626**
Whytlok, John, 552
  see also Qwytlok
Whytop, William, 744
  see also Qwytop
Whytyng, George, 666
  John, & family, 816
  Margery, 816
  Thomas, 816
  see also Qwytynge
WICKEN (Cambs), church, vestment for, 1121
  inhabitants of, 1121
  Spinney priory in, *see* SPINNEY
  testator of, **1121**
WICKHAM ST PAUL (Esx), church, 1077
  inhabitant of, 175
WICKHAM SKEITH, church, 1169
  book for, 228
  porch of, 1273, 1273n
  gilds in, 879
  inhabitants of, 24, 87, 228, 705, 706, 771, 801,
    879, 1169, 1200, 1252, 1419
  land in, 385
  places in, 'Ballecroftesende' (land), 228
    'Berkelisbos', 228
    'Blakelond' (close), 1200
    'Buntynges' (tenement), 1252
    'Calfawe' (wood), 1200
    'Dormorrysyerde', 879
    'Elete & Gernonis', 1169
    'Goweysfeld', 1200
    'Hasenawe Feld', 879
    'Herewardystoft', 1200
    'Holm Medewe', 228, 879, 1169
    'Holmere' (land), 228
    'John Reve' (tenement), 1252
    'Jonesgate' (land), 228
    'Qwhytescroft' (land), 228
    'Ryngys' (close), 1200
    'Sarnsdon Hyll', 879
    'Stonefeld', 1169
    'Stublond' (land), 228
    'Thweyt Feld', 228
    'Tuftes, le', (land), 1252
    'Whytesfeld', 228
    'Wylwys, le', 879
  poor of, 775
  testators of, **22**, **24**, **87**, **228**, **705**, **706**, **879**,
    880, **1200**, **1252**, *1264*, *1273*
WICKHAMBROOK, church, burial in, 696n
  chalice for, 1418n

  chaplain of St Mary in, 459
  lectern for, 1418n
  light of BVM in, 696
  roodloft in, 696
  torches in, 1418
  vicar of, *see* John Caas
  window in 1418
  gilds in, 302, 696
  inhabitants of, 1055, 1431
  land in, 449
  places in, Ashfield, 1431
    Badmondisfield, 459
    'Derfold', 459
    'Heyfeld Croft', 459
    'Huntescroft', 459
  testators of, **302**, **459**, *473*, *653*, **696**, *737*, **846**,
    1055, **1418**, *1431*, *1450*
  wills proved at, 459, 549, 669, 670, 696, 1285
Wicks, *see* Wykes
Wigenhele, *see* Wygenhale
Willesham, *see* Wyllasham
Willymot, *see* Wyllymot(e)
Willyngham, *see* Wellyngham
Wilmot, John, 1489
  see also Wyllymot(e)
WILTON (Nfk), church, 1302
Wiltshire, earl of, *see* James Boteler
Windecoole, Alice, 375
WINDSOR (Berks), St George's chapel, secular
  college, in, 1478n
Wirilych, *see* Worlych
Wis(e)man, *see* Wyseman
WISTON (WISSINGTON), inhabitant of, 685
  testator of, *685*
WITHERSFIELD, 'Clanwoothlane' in, 893
  inhabitants of, 312, 396, 709, 914, 1092, 1107,
    1456
  testators of, *396*, *504*, *709*, *893*, *914*, *1107*,
    1456
WIXOE, church, 631
  'Colynys lane' in, 580
  testator of, **580**
Wode, *see* Wood
Wodecey, *see* Wodesey
Wodefen, Thomas, of Boxford, 308
Wodeman, Alice, of Sudbury, 937
  John, of Sudbury, & family, **937**
Woderoff, John, of Bardwell, 212
Woderys, Isabel, of Mildenhall, 750
  Robert, of Mildenhall, *750*
  Thomas, of Mildenhall, 1155
Wodesey (Wodecey), Matilda, of Stoke by
  Nayland, 930
  Stephen, of Nayland, 909, 930, *1314*
  Thomas, of Stoke by Nayland, 638, **930**, 1314n
  William, 930, 1314
Wodeward, John, 345; rector of Whepstead, 267,
    267n, 314, 314n, 351

Margaret, 146
Thomas, 1296; of Stowmarket, 1192
William, of Barningham, 124
Wolanty, John, 866
Woleman (Wolman, Wolleman, Wul(l)man,
    Wulleman), Edmund, 18
    Robert, 218; rector of Tostock, 280, 441, 469,
        614, 782n
Wollenger, John, 1232
Wolnoth (Wollenoth, Wulnoth), Matilda, 1242
    Ralph, of Sapiston, 69, 464
Wolvard, see Wulvard
Wombe, Alice, of Great Cornard, 1365
    Joan, of Great Cornard, 1365
    John, 941; of Great Cornard, & family, **1365**
    Thomas, vicar of Great Cornard, 800, 803n,
        941, 1365
Wood (Wo(o)de), Agnes, of Thornham Magna,
    771
    Cecily, of Drinkstone, 1339
    Helen, 1280
    Henry, 1369
    Isabel, 234
    Joan, of Elmswell, 496
    John, 234, 1369; notary, of Blythburgh, 97,
        97n; of Cowlinge, **1386**; of Elmswell, *496*
    Katherine, of Eye, 1276
    Margery, of Wickham Skeith, 879
    Matilda, of Ixworth, *1405*
    Nicholas, of Thornham Magna, **771**
    Richard, of Drinkstone, *1339*
    Roger, 234
    Thomas, 508, 1126, 1386
    Walter, friar, 833
    William, 1386; official of archdeacon of
        Sudbury, rector of Fornham All Saints, *xlii*
WOODDITTON (Cambs), church, image of Holy
    Trinity in, 553
    rectory (living) of, 1463n
    vicars of, see Robert Draper, Thomas
        Warner
    inhabitants of, 135, 428
    places in, 'Dermandeslane', 1463
    Ditton park, 1463
    Ditton Valens (manor), 28
    Newmarket, partly in, 28n
    'Saxton lane', 1463
    'Saxton' (Saxon) Street, 28, 399, 428, 553,
        678
    testators of, *135, 428, 1320*
Woodegate, Walter, 1474
WOOLPIT, church, 282
    ?doors of, 60
    porch of, 60, 60n, 261, 469, 619
    rectors of, see John, Brumpton, Robert
        Lynton
    tabernacle of BVM in, 469
    community of, 469

gilds in, 469, 619, 777
inhabitants of, 107, 282, 469, 564, 619, 655,
    713, 757, 777, 806, 823, 836, 1172
land in, 231, 439, 1001
pilgrimage to, *l*, 1090, 1466
places in, 'Bell, le', 713
    'Bradwater, le' (furlong), 757
    'Catourys garden', 713
    'Crostedewente', 469
    'Crostede' (field), 469
    'Heggeforthehegge', 469
    'Park', 'Parkes' (tenement), 149
    'Pekotes cross', 823
    'Rammysgran', 469
    'Sevenacres, le' (furlong), 757
poor of, 713, 757
testators of, **11**, **60**, *107*, **261**, **469**, *508*, *563*,
    564, **619**, **655**, **713**, **757**, **777**, **806**, **823**, **1172**
will proved at, 1056
Worcester, earl of, see John Tiptoft
WORDWELL, church, 17, 1309
    rector of, see William Newborg
    inhabitant of, 1060
    land in, 315
    testator of, *1060*
WORLINGTON, church, altar of Holy Trinity
    in, 311
    rectors of, see Simon Bakhot (Bagot), John
        Gregory (Gregori)
    sheets for altars in, 311
    inhabitants of, 311, 1119, 1241, 1389
    land in, 46
    testators of, **89**, **311**, *1053*, *1119*, **1241**, **1389**
Worlych (Wirilych), Joan, of Ixworth, 905
    John, 670; rector of Hopton, 622, 622n, 723n
    William, of Clare, 670
WORMINGFORD (Esx), church, 930
    cope for, 1076
    sepulchre light in, 1164
    rector of, *xlii*n
WORTHAM, gild in, 1372, 1422
    inhabitants of, 424, 595, 733, 873, 1076,
        1140n, 1164, 1224, 1239, 1422
    places in, 'Berhampigtell', 1224
        'Estgate', 1372
        'Furlong, le' (field), 1224
        'Lordes' (tenement), 1422
        'Morefeld, le', 1224
    testators of, **6**, *424*, **595**, *733*, *873*, **1076**, *1140*,
        1164, **1224**, **1372**, **1422**
    wills proved at, 5, 71, 325
Wortham, Robert, smith, 894
    Thomas, 1088
Wotegate, Walter, 561
Wrangyll (Wrangle), Henry, 423
    John, 423
    Katherine, widow, of Drinkstone, **423**
    William, of Drinkstone, 423

WRATTING (unspec.), inhabitant of, 919
  land in, 249
  Talworth family of, 844
  testator of, *919*
WRATTING, GREAT, inhabitant of, 1284
  poor of, 654
  rector of, *see* John Parker
  testators of, *447, 1284*
WRATTING, LITTLE, church, 681
  inhabitant of, 1146
  poor of, 654
  testators of, *266, 1146*
Wrenche, Walter, of Long Melford, *1425*
Wrenne, Mabel, 1276
Wrethe, Emma, of Soham (Cambs), 1444
  Thomas, of Soham (Cambs), *1444*
Wrinnyngham, [*unnamed*], 764
Wroo, Henry, of Rickinghall Superior, **1340**
  John, 1340
  Robert, 1340
Wrotham, John, of Mildenhall, 131
  Robert, smith, 762
  see also Beche *alias* Wrotham
Wrottyng *alias* Cukhoo, Thomas, chaplain, 116,
  180
Wrygh(e) (Wrygh, Wrygth, Wryth(e), Wryeth)
  Agnes, of Brome, **1158**
  Alice, 1258; servant, 350; of Barway in Soham
    (Cambs), 256; of Sudbury, 652; of Wickham
    Skeith, 1200
  Beatrice, widow, of Wortham, **1422**
  Edward, 1200
  Isabel, 1200
  Joan, 1459; of Barway, in Soham (Cambs),
    253; of Great Bradley, 568; the elder, 1276
  John, 253, 256, 424, 595, 1200, 1258, 1304,
    1422; chaplain, 48, 91, 409, 1090, 1274; of
    Barway in Soham (Cambs), & family, **253**;
    the younger, of Barway in Soham (Cambs),
    256; vicar of Hundon, 1083; chaplain, of
    Lavenham, 126, 130, 298, 350, 1058; of
    Mildenhall, 311; chaplain, of Sudbury, 758;
    of Wickham Skeith, 1200; the elder, of
    Wortham, 1422
  Katherine, of Hitcham, 151
  Margaret, 488, 494
  Matilda, of Cotton, 409
  Richard, 1422; of Brome, 1158; of Glemsford,
    991; of Hitcham, **151**
  Robert, 415, 744, 1459; of Bildeston, 151, 520,
    1125; of Sudbury, *652*; of Thrandeston, 808,
    906
  Simon, 253; of Cotton, **409**
  Thomas, 253, 1001, 1258; of Bury St
    Edmunds, 1158; of Soham (Cambs), 478,
    1041
  William, 47, 253, 1009, 1200, 1357; of Great
    Bradley, *568*

  see also Camplyon *alias* Wryght
Wulleman (Wul(l)man), *see* Wol(e)man
Wulnoth, *see* Wolnoth
Wulvard (Wulward, Wolvard), Hugh, 51
  John, 257
  William, 877
Wulvyrton, Thomas, friar, 379
Wybbyll, *see* Wymbyll
Wyburgh, Robert, 536
Wyell, *see* Vyell
Wyff, John, of Cockfield, *470*
  Margaret, of Cockfield, 470
Wygenhale (Wygenal(e)), Margaret, of Boxford,
  118
  Richard, 118, 308, 380, 458
  Roger, 118; of Boxford, **118**, 380n
Wygenhale (Wygenale) *alias* Saresson, John,
  archdeacon of Sudbury, *xlii, liv*n, 510, 511,
  512, 514, 516, 517, 595, 711, 714, 715, 772,
  773, 774, 775, 776, 781
Wygeyn, *see* Wegeyn
Wyggmour, Walter, 1174
Wykes (Wicks), John, of Great Barton, 1236; of
  Kentford, 894
  Peter, 833
  Thomas, of Great Barton, 1236n
Wykham, Joan, of Wickhambrook, 1431
  John, of Great Horringer, **722**; of
    Wickhambrook, *1431*
  Margery, of Great Horringer, 722
Wyllbye, Henry, friar, of Thetford, 1164
Wylchyn, Alice, 958
  John, & family, 958
  Matilda, of Gislingham, 958
  Thomas, clerk, of Southwold, 958, 958n
  William, 958; of Gislingham, **958**
  see also Wylkyn
Wylde, Robert, vicar of Stowmarket St Mary, 764,
  764n
Wylkyn, John, 1052; of Burwell (Cambs), *697*
  Margaret, of Burwell (Cambs), 1052
  Nicholas, 697, 1052
  Robert, of Burwell (Cambs), 697, **1052**
  Thomas, 1052; priest, 880
  see also Wylchyn
Wyllasham (Willesham), Roger, of Brettenham,
  90
Wyllyamsone, *see* Taylour *alias* Wyllyamsone
Wyllyham, Ame', 99
  Beatrice, of Brandon, *99*
Wyllymot(e) (Wyllymotte, Wylymot), Joan, of
  Lavenham, 1485
  John, 989; the elder, 1485; the younger, 1485;
    fuller, of Lavenham, 1485n
  Robert, 1485
  Thomas, of Lavenham, 126, 1048, 1073, **1485**
  see also Wilmot
Wyllyngton, John, 1008

Wymbyll (Wybbyll, Wymbell), Joan, of Hunston, **1217**
  Robert, 1217
Wymbych (Wymbush, Wymbysch, Wymbyssh)
  Henry, 270, 1110, 1123; of Kentford, 894, 894n
  James, 270; & family, 1110; of Kentford, 44
  Joan, 1044, 1110*, 1123
  John, 270; the elder, 1110n; the elder, & family, 1110; the elder, of Kentford,**270**
  Margaret, 1110
  Margery, 111; of Kentford, 44, 270; widow, of Kentford, & family, **1110**
  Robert, 1123; clerk, 270; priest, 1110
  William, of Kentford, **44**
Wymer(e), Davy, of Honington, 530n
  John, of Honington, 1269; of Honington, & family, **1269**
  Margaret, of Honington, & family, **530**
  Michael, of Honington, 1269
  Rose, of Honington, *959*
  William, chaplain, 406
Wynd, John, of Pakenham, 1449
  Margaret, widow, of Pakenham, *1449*
Wyne, *see* Vyne
Wyneld (Wynnold), Joan, 1276
  Margaret, 1276
  Robert, 1276; the younger, 1276
  William, servant, 1168
  see also Weyneld
Wynter (Wyntyr), Edward, of Cowlinge, 549
  John, the younger, 1012
  Nicholas, 960
  Richard, bailiff of Long Melford, 122
Wynton, John, 640
Wynyeve (Veneve, Wen(h)eve, Wennif, Wynyyeff)
  John, 1399; of Troston, 599, 694
  Robert, 371; of Thetford, 281, 1069
  Walter, 163
  see also Quenyve
Wyot, John, of Burwell (Cambs), *244*
  Margaret, of Burwell, (Cambs), 244
  Ralph, 389
  Robert, of Burwell (Cambs), 278, 555; of Exning, **278**
  Thomas, 555, 682, 911, 1475; the elder, 911; of Burwell (Cambs), 278
Wysbych(e), Andrew, 289
  Eudo, 1433
  John, of Brandon, & family, **1433**
  Katherine, of Brandon, 1433
  Margaret, 1433
  Robert, the elder, 1433; the younger, 1433
  Thomas, 1433
Wyse, Robert, of Dalham, 553
Wyseman (Wis(e)man, Wyisman, Wysman, Wysseman), Anne, 1169
  Clarissa, 823
  Eleanor, 1169

  Geoffrey, of Woolpit, 619, 757, 823
  George, 1169, 1169n
  John, 823; the elder, of Hengrave, 924
  Margery, 619, 823
  Nicholas, 1169, 1169n
  Simon, 1169, 1169n; of Rickinghall Superior, 900
  Thomas, of Stanton, 457
  William, 61, 1240
Wyskyn, Margery, of Hundon, 939
  Thomas, of Hundon, 561, 561n, 730, **939**
Wysman, Wysseman, *see* Wyseman
Wyth(e), John, 270, 1076
  Thomas, 1076n
Wytton, Thomas, of Thurston, 552
WYVERSTONE, 'Cotysham' in, 1402
  rector of, *see* Henry Munnyng
  testators of, *72*, *841*, **1402**, *1408*

Yakesley, Henry, 1326
  Richard, of Soham (Cambs), 1041, *1326*
  William, 1326
Yardley, John, 1474, **1474**
  Rose, of Lidgate, 1474
YAXLEY, church, 369, 1169
  porch of, 1276n
  tabernacle of Holy Trinity in, 1276n
  vicar of, 1276n
  inhabitants of, 369, 798, 1276
  places in, 'Blodegates' (tenement), 1276n
    Bulls Hall (manor) 1169, 1169n, 1276n
    'Maryes' (pightle), 1371
    'Nethergate' (tenement), 1276
  road to, 543
  testator of, **1276**
Yaxley, family, 1276n
  see also Yakesley
Ydeyne, Cecily, of Burwell (Cambs), **1357**, **1475**
  Thomas, 1475; chaplain, 1475
Yebyswych, *see* Yepisswich
Yekesworth, Robert, friar, of Clare, 833
YELDHAM (Esx), inhabitant of, 632
YELVERTOFT (Northants), tenement in, 1432
Yepisswich (Gippewic, Gypewic, Yebyswych, Yepyswych), Agnes de, of Burgate, 406
  John, 406, 976; of Burgate, 406, *976*; the younger, of Burgate, 787
  Margaret, of Burgate, 406
  Nicholas de, of Burgate, 406, **406**, 976n; rector of Stowlangtoft, 406n
  Thomas de, 406
  William de, 406
Yngeram, Margaret, of Stoke by Nayland, 544
  William, of Stoke by Nayland, & family, **544**
Yonge, *see* Young
Yongman (Yungman), Nicholas, of Hopton (near Harling), 331, *621*
You', John, of Lawshall, *701*

Young (Yonge), John, of Rickinghall Superior,
      579, 1271; of Santon Downham, & family,
      419
   Robert, of Barton Mills, *1037*
   Simon, of Rickinghall Superior, *579*
   Thomas, of Santon Downham, 419
   William, 419; baker, of Bury St Edmunds, 1153
YOXFORD, church, new tabernacle of BVM in,
      346n
   inhabitant of, 346n
Yungman, *see* Yongman
Yve, *see* Ive
Yvys, Rose, 1371

[*surname not given*]: Geoffrey, 37
   John, canon of Ixworth, 321
   Margaret, 37
   Richard, parish chaplain of Dalham, 850;
      hermit of Newbridge (Nfk), 489, 489n
   Walter, Sir, chaplain, of ?Cheveley (Cambs),
      822

Wills of the Archdeaconry of Suffolk
The Register 'Baldwyne' Part I
(Suffolk Records Society volume 44)

Index of Subjects

All references are to item numbers, not pages, except the italicised Roman numerals which refer to pages of the Introduction. An 'n' following a reference indicates that the subject is to be found in a footnote to that item; an asterisk * after a reference indicates that the subject occurs more than once in that item. **Bold** indicates that the reference is to a testator. Relationships mentioned are relationships to the testator (their brother, daughter, father, son, wife, etc.).

Abbreviations: BVM = the Blessed Virgin Mary; spec. = specified; unspec. = unspecified.

advower, *xliv*, 20n
  St Edmund the archbishop, 1014, 1014n
  St Margaret, 571
  St Nicholas, 213, 346, 636
  St Peter, 20, 20n
  St Peter and St Paul, 346, 481, 623
advowson, 90n*
age, of discretion, 1231
  full, 300
  of inheritance, 213, 296, 301, 352, 446*, 454, 589, 1057*
  legal, 77, 1231
agreement, bargain, 547, 578, 692, 771, 864, 873, 908, 1005, 1008, 1113, 1234n, 1264, 1269, 1397, 1467, 1495
  contract, 188, 221, 288, 550, 1023*, 1216, 1246, 1459
  concord, 228, 412, 957
  consent, 155, 280, 227, 343, 393, 600, 631, 696, 1110, 1245, 1249, 1280, 1475, 1495
  by licence of husband, 391, 1247
  willingness, 290, 899, 901, 1032
  see also contract; deed; disagreement; indenture
agricultural equipment and tools (gen.), *li*, 132, 254, 277, 556, 683, 692, 857, 911, 1094, 1325, 1394
  barrow, 857
  cart, *li*, 126, 131, 150, 245, 257, 277*, 289, 533, 556, 598, 682, 683, 708, 723, 727, 857, 911, 1001, 1052, 1094, 1113, 1200, 1240*, 1244, 1258, 1265*, 1306, 1325, 1394*
    shod (with iron), 277, 289, 533, 911, 1052, 1240*, 1258, 1265*, 1394

unshod cart, 1001
    see also tumbrel
  harness, 289, 598, 683, 692, 708, 727, 1113, 1240*, 1265*, 1394, 1475
    traces, 1200
  harrow, *li*, 857
  horse-mill, 799
  plough, *li*, 131, 257, 289, 598, 682, 683, 692, 708, 723, 727, 857, 1001, 1094, 1113, 1200, 1244, 1325, 1394, 1475
    coulter, 1200
    share, 1200
  sickle, 254, 556
  traces, *see* harness
  tumbrel, 126, 289, 823, 1001, 1200
agricultural work, carting, 249
  harvesting, 249, 1496
  ploughing, 211, 1001, 1306
  sowing, 351, 1001, 1327, 1496
  threshing, 249
  tilling, 1496
agriculture (gen.), *li*
  see also crops
alabaster, 116, 1045, 1257n
alb, *see* church equipment: vestment
alder carr (grove), *see* land
'alestonde', *see* household goods
alias (in name), **109**, **131**, **152**, 180, 205, **257**, **300**, 311, **321**, **442**, **454**, **460**, **473**, **599**, 611n, 668n, 741n, **910**, **960**, 980n, 1006*, **1033**, 1104, 1105, **1128**, 1156, 1196, 1218, **1263**, 1275n, **1294**, 1307n, **1369**, **1397**, **1450**
almsdeeds, *see* deeds of charity
almshouse, 613n, 740n

91

altar, altar-cloth, *see* church equipment
amber, 175, 397, 629, 1253, 1276
amice, *see* church equipment: vestment
andiron, *see* household goods
animals, farm (unspec.), *li*, 165, 254, 631, 641,
    939, 1371
  draught, 257, 682, 683*, 1001n
  as mortuary, 59, 95, 124, 150, 537, 549, 676,
    871, 1298, 1327
  see also livestock
anniversary, *see* church services
annual, *see* church services
annuity (pension), 180, 233*, 279, 589, 1169,
    1240*, 1245, 1248, 1259, 1260, 1296, 1310,
    1315, 1333, 1375
antiphon, *see* church services
antiphoner, *see* church equipment: book
anvil, *see* tools and equipment
apparels, *see* church equipment: vestment
apprentice, 157, 632*, 633, 1033, 1181, 1186
apprenticeship, 157, 1033
appropriator (of church), 375n
archdeacon (unspec.), *xxviii*
  of Norfolk, official of, *xl*
  of Stafford, *xliin*
  of Sudbury, *xxxix, xlii*, 279n, 1240
    see Clement Denston, John Selot, John
      Wygenhale
    official of, *xl–xli, xlii*, *xliii*n, *liv, liv*n, *lv*n,
      180n, 428, 1187n, 1240, 1240n, 1252,
      1364n, 1365, 1473, 1495n
      see John Crofftes, William Duffeld,
        John Ramsey, Robert Spylman, Henry
        Sythyng, William Woode
  of Suffolk, *xl*
    official of, *liii*, 158n, 365n
  proving will, *liv*, 231, 510, 511, 512, 514, 516,
    517, 595, 711, 714, 715, 772, 774, 775, 776,
    781, 1493
archdeaconry (unspec.), *xxxviii*
  of Bury St Edmunds, *xxxix*, 279n
  of Norwich, *xl*
  of Sudbury, *passim* in Introduction, 428, 863,
    863n
  of Suffolk, 20, 831n, 844n
archdeacon's court, *see* court
archdeacon's visitation, *see* visitation
ark, *see* furniture
arms, *see* weapons and armour
arms (heraldic), 863, 1231n, 1240n
arrows, *see* weapons and armour
ash (from wood), *see* wood-ash
avower, *see* advower
axe, *see* tools and equipment, weapons and
    armour

bailiff, 122, 416, 566, 1298, 1319
bank (ditch), 836

banker, *see* furniture and furnishings: cushion
banner-cloth, *see* church equipment: cloth
bargain, *see* agreement
bark, 164, 375
  bark-house, 1186
  bark vat, 164
  barkwose, 164
barley, *see* crops
barrow, *see* agricultural equipment
basilard, *see* weapons and armour
basin *see* church equipment *and* household goods
beads, 152n, 231, 308, 626, 1009, 1044
  amber, 175, 397, 626, 1253, 1276
  coral, 1295
  jet, 56, 175, 397, 457, 777, 1276, 1295, 1343
  paternosters ('gauds'), 175, 1276
  silver, 1276
beast, *see* cattle
bedeman, *see* parish officers
beds and bedding (unspec.), *l*, 46, 48, 54, 65, 90,
    97, 122, 126, 127*, 130, 131, 152*, 152n,
    157, 164, 176, 180, 186, 188, 194, 198, 215,
    216, 219, 221, 258, 269, 270, 286, 299, 300,
    310, 311, 335, 344, 352, 355, 358, 368, 376,
    394, 398, 412, 421*, 430, 469, 474, 517,
    541*, 546, 548, 594, 598, 603, 611, 612,
    618, 631, 632*, 640, 727, 740, 758, 768,
    779, 789, 803, 818, 830, 863, 864, 895, 929,
    937, 942, 960, 1032, 1033, 1044, 1064,
    1077, 1079, 1089, 1091, 1110*, 1115, 1121,
    1125, 1132, 1154, 1160, 1168, 1169, 1181,
    1231, 1237, 1243, 1258, 1274, 1280, 1341,
    1371, 1400*, 1409, 1433, 1462*, 1489*,
    1495
bed (specified), 91
  complete, 1400, 1433
  death-bed, 1169
  hanging, *l*
  new, 300
bed-cover, *see* coverlet *and* church equipment:
    cloth
bedstead, *l*
blanket, *l*, 146, 172, 278, 321*, 333*, 358,
    588*, 589, 757, 865, 1121, 1139, 1265,
    1279*, 1295, 1343, 1393, 1400, 1409
  furrour, 420
bolster (transom), *l*, 420, 863
canvas, 1279*
celure, *l*, 91, 1174
coverlet (bed-cover), *l*, 49, 91*, 113, 146, 172,
    278, 320, 321*, 331*, 333*, 358, 385*,
    397*, 399, 420*, 457, 517*, 539, 548, 588*,
    589, 603, 682, 757, 798*, 828, 865, 963*,
    1049, 1089*, 1139, 1165, 1255, 1258*,
    1265, 1279*, 1295, 1343, 1357*, 1393,
    1400, 1409, 1473*
curtains, *l*, 91, 1174
donge, *see* mattress

featherbed, 457, 612, 863, 1279
furrour, *see* blanket
mattress (donge), *l*, 49, 321*, 399, 588, 1258,
    1279*, 1295, 1409
pillow, 420, 863
quilt, 172, 1400
sheet, *l*, 49, 90, 120, 146, 172, 278, 311, 320,
    321*, 331*, 385*, 399, 420*, 457, 517, 539,
    588*, 589, 603, 612, 619*, 682, 757, 779,
    790, 861, 865, 929, 963*, 1039, 1049, 1121,
    1139, 1165, 1201, 1258*, 1265, 1276*,
    1279*, 1295, 1343, 1357, 1393, 1398*,
    1400, 1409*, 1462, 1474
    bearing-sheet, 1295
    burial sheet, 517
tester, *l*, 49, 91*, 321, 420, 548, 1201
transom, *see* bolster
undercloth, 682
beehive, *li*, 287, 385, 696*, 865*, 1210, 1463
beetle, *see* tools and equipment
behaviour (conversation, obedience), 124, 192,
    235*, 249, 287, 288*, 301, 348, 456, 460,
    492, 634, 691, 708, 857, 911, 1052, 1238,
    1489, 1492
bell, *see* church equipment
    bell-ringer, *see* parish officers
    bell-ringing, 1346
        at anniversary, 619
        at burial, *xlvi*, 126, 350, 415
        daybell and curfew, 633
belt (axe), *see* tools and equipment
    (girdle), *see* clothes
bench (in church), *see* church equipment: seating
blanket, *see* beds and bedding; (cloth), *see*
    material
blind (person), 149, 341, 479, 1331
boat, 256, 861, 1475
bolster, *see* beds and bedding
bona notabilia, *xxxviii*, 20
bond (agreement), *see* obligation
bond land, *see* land tenure
book (unspec.), 803n
    church records, *liv*
    of dates, *xliii–xliv*n
    Decameron, *l*, *l*n
    Domesday, 19n, 20n, 52n, 345n, 352n, 459n,
        1115n
    scrivener's, *lii*n
    will-register, covers of, *xli*
    see also church equipment
boot, *see* clothes
borough, 58n, 161, 263, 298, 354, 367*, 446*,
    623, 661, 1073*, 1485
bottle, *see* household goods
boundary, civil, *xxxvii*, *xl*
    county, *xxxviii*
    ecclesiastical, *xxxvii–xxxviii*, *xxxix*n, *xl*, 20n,
        252n

see also mere; metes
bow, *see* weapons and armour
bowl, *see* household goods
box, *see* furniture
brass, 269, 469, 474, 517, 1495
    basin, 1265
    candlestick, 1265
    cauldron, 430, 556, 612, 796, 1343
    chafer, 663
    ewer (laver), 938, 1265, 1398
    frying pan, 796
    jug, 691, 1154
    kettle, 399
    pan, 96, 120, 160, 229, 232, 293, 320, 326*,
        333, 391, 421, 546*, 548, 632, 671, 677,
        691, 708*, 727, 796*, 830, 861, 908, 982,
        1001, 1044, 1089, 1117, 1139*, 1154, 1181,
        1201, 1253, 1258, 1265, 1295, 1353, 1375,
        1400, 1453, 1489*
    pot, 49, 58, 122, 127, 133, 158, 160, 172, 175,
        232, 248, 277, 293, 298, 320, 321*, 326*,
        331*, 333, 342, 346, 358, 368, 369, 391,
        394*, 397, 399, 415, 417, 421, 430*, 458,
        464, 517, 533, 548, 556, 569*, 578, 589,
        601, 638, 663, 671*, 677, 682, 683*, 684,
        696, 708*, 723, 726, 727, 735, 741, 749,
        794, 795*, 796*, 798, 809, 830, 861, 908,
        911, 940, 963*, 982, 992, 1023, 1039, 1041,
        1044, 1058*, 1063, 1079, 1088, 1110, 1117,
        1139*, 1158, 1181, 1201, 1258, 1265*,
        1274, 1279, 1306, 1343, 1375, 1382, 1400*,
        1404, 1433, 1453, 1459*, 1478, 1489*
    vessel, 705, 1121, 1313
brass, monumental, 1218n
bridge, 342, 723, 1329, 1329n, 1416*
    building of, 57, 316*, 507, 1237, 1237n
    repair of, *xlix*, 34, 158, 180*, 246, 535, 624,
        624n, 682, 740, 740n, 894, 1120, 1280,
        1423, 1423n*
bridle, *see* harness
brother, brother-in-law, *see* relatives
bucket, *see* household goods
building (unspec.), *li*, *liii*, 77, 441, 456, 538, 541,
    586, 613n, 717, 807, 822, 1046, 1110, 1258,
    1297, 1364, 1403n, 1404
    failure to repair, 214
    repair of, to be kept up, 52, 77, 78, 126, 131,
        164, 214*, 221, 245, 296, 441, 456, 458,
        464, 538*, 541, 547, 586, 589, 632, 676,
        713*, 757, 758, 803, 813, 818, 822, 895,
        924, 1001, 1046, 1057*, 1058, 1181, 1209,
        1223, 1244, 1259, 1274, 1279*, 1297, 1354,
        1364, 1389
    materials for
        clay, tiles, 586
        'grounsell', 278
        roofing and clay, 458
        straw and clay, 456

timber, 1260

buildings (excluding churches and chapels) and
     rooms, *liii*
  bakehouse, 490, 818, 1252, 1258
  bark-house, 1186
  barn, 190, 211, 282, 334, 376, 544, 603, 639,
     818, 1073, 1110, 1168*, 1244, 1244n, 1246,
     1279*, 1289*, 1364*, 1383, 1416,
  chamber, 52, 90*, 97, 126, 229, 247, 282, 305,
     355, 367, 376, 402, 416, 546, 618, 632,
     713*, 740*, 790, 807, 818*, 830, 857, 864*,
     965, 1113, 1154, 1169, 1244*, 1252, 1265,
     1277, 1310, 1325, 1354, 1370*, 1448, 1495
     chapel-chamber, 90
     in hall, 52, 807
     lower chamber, 52, 97
     lower chamber called 'le spence', 53
     new chamber, 1325
     upper chamber, 965, 1448
  chapel (in house), 90
  chimney, *l*, 818*, 1495
  church-house, 613, 613n, 923n, 1088n, 1437
  cottage, 19, 278*, 346, 352*, 376, 440, 639,
     717, 900, 969*, 969n, 1064, 1246*, 1280,
     1310n, 1416, 1469
     'grounsell' for, 278
  gildhall, *see* gild
  granary, 556
  hall (separate building), 41n*, 42n, 90n*, 165,
     201n, 294n, 335, 552*, 682n, 827n, 836n*,
     920n, 941n, 945, 1082, 1111n, 1169n*,
     1246n, 1276n, 1333, 1400n
  hall (part of house), 52*, 229, 282, 305, 464n,
     807, 864, 965, 1354
     chamber in, 807
     lower part of, 52*, 464
     upper part of, 464, 965
  house (dwelling, place), *liii*, 3*, 48, 49, 57,
     90n, 97, 112, 113, 126, 188, 214, 263, 276*,
     281*, 277, 290*, 316, 329*, 337, 340*, 366,
     376, 377*, 435*, 441, 464*, 471, 474, 487,
     495, 534*, 541, 546, 549*, 596n, 633, 636,
     638, 674, 676, 680, 711, 719, 799, 805,
     846, 857, 873, 897*, 929, 949*, 960, 969,
     992, 1001, 1009, 1110, 1154, 1078, 1181n,
     1194n, 1209, 1244, 1257, 1260, 1315, 1345,
     1353, 1354, 1386, 1388*, 1404*, 1484
     entrance (door, gate) to, 864*, 1370*
     in 'le stall', 633
     new house, 97, 464, 923n, 1088n, 1260,
        1298, 1437
     poor, for, 376, 595n, 713*
     will made in, 112, 113
     see also cottage; messuage; renter; tenement
  kitchen, 90, 229, 305, 717, 1252, 1263, 1495
  messuage, 18, 19*, 28*, 48*, 77*, 96, 97*, 102,
     111, 127, 128*, 145*, 155, 161*, 186, 194,
     205*, 219*, 226*, 228, 237, 253*, 270*,

278, 288*, 296*, 301*, 308*, 313*, 333,
     342*, 346, 347*, 352*, 354*, 358, 359*,
     389*, 391, 392, 407, 408*, 422, 431*, 433,
     440, 457*, 463, 464*, 478, 497, 516, 538*,
     547, 552, 564*, 569, 578*, 585*, 600*,
     623*, 624, 626*, 632, 633*, 633*, 639, 641,
     660*, 679*, 683*, 684, 691, 692*, 702, 713,
     714*, 717*, 721, 727, 740*, 741, 760*, 790,
     801*, 818*, 830*, 836*, 848, 860, 861*,
     864*, 865, 867*, 870*, 871, 889, 891*, 899,
     900*, 902*, 927*, 939*, 940, 958, 981,
     1008, 1009, 1014, 1041*, 1052*, 1058*,
     1064, 1077, 1094, 1117, 1119*, 1121*,
     1129, 1132*, 1154, 1155*, 1162*, 1168*,
     1170*, 1176, 1181*, 1190*, 1195, 1213,
     1218, 1221, 1237, 1238*, 1241*, 1248*,
     1259, 1260*, 1268, 1274*, 1279*, 1298*,
     1307, 1319, 1352*, 1364, 1365*, 1375*,
     1386, 1392*, 1403*, 1432, 1433*, 1446*,
     1451, 1475, 1489
  pantry, 282
  parlour, 818, 1073, 1263
  renter, 49, 235, 660, 740*, 740n, 1489*
     new renter, 740
  shop, 2, 49*, 188, 190, 346, 492n, 632, 758*,
     960, 960n, 1073*, 1073n, 1160, 1160n,
     1181, 1341
     see also workshop
  smithy, 1110, 1370
  solar, 126, 464, 713, 818*, 864*, 965, 1073,
     1244, 1263
  spence, 52
  stable, 1073
  storeroom, 305, 1263
  tenement, *xxxix*n, *liii*, *passim*
  woolhouse, 464
  workshop, *li*, 511, 719, 960n, 1041, 1160,
     1160n, 1404
     see also smithy
bullimong, *see* crops
bullock, *see* cattle
'bure' (fur), *see* material: fur
burial (*inc.* funeral, obsequies), alms to the poor
     present at, *xlvi*, *xlvii*n, 15, 20, 28, 44, 90,
     108, 144, 301, 308, 342, 346, 348, 479, 499,
     529, 548, 640, 714, 797, 803, 1068, 1134,
     1194, 1216, 1255, 1473
     animal to precede body to, 59, 95, 124, 150,
        549, 676
     basin to be used at, 415, 415n
     bearers of body to, 174, 345, 1132
     bell-ringing at, *xlvi*, 415
     bier used at, *xlvi*, 1409
     coffin at, absence of, *xlvi*, *xlvi*n
     cost (expense) of, *lii*, 129, 248, 251, 415, 634,
        727, 744, 961, 962, 1032, 1033, 1123, 1181,
        1356, 1367, 1397, 1410, 1463
     customs at, 1409n

herse used at, *xlvi*, 113
lights at, *xlvi*, 15, 28, 113, 345, 415n, 1265
mass-pence at, *xlvi*, *xlix*, 78, 90, 101, 125, 302,
   335*, 343, 351*, 373, 387*, 696, 772*, 776,
   842, 940, 1249*, 1287, 1333, 1379, 1381,
   1393, 1395, 1397*, 1409, 1451, 1465
   mass-pence on bier, 1409
offering at, *xlvi*, *xlix*, 345, 1032
people present at, bedeman, 126
   chaplain (priest), 18, 28, 36, 50, 55, 91,
      108, 109, 120, 126, 130, 142, 144, 149,
      150, 155, 164, 189, 192, 193, 195, 208,
      210, 257, 263, 278, 284, 288, 296, 299,
      300, 301, 306, 308, 309, 316, 319, 320,
      321, 333, 342, 348, 350, 365, 376, 380,
      402, 415, 416, 460, 469, 479, 481, 497,
      499, 511, 529, 538, 546, 548, 618, 619,
      623, 682, 714, 759, 768, 790, 797, 843,
      896, 901, 903, 939, 942, 1002, 1033,
      1035, 1041, 1048, 1064, 1068, 1076,
      1077, 1080, 1091, 1092, 1126, 1134,
      1194, 1216, 1237, 1243, 1280, 1289,
      1293, 1298, 1315, 1319, 1331, 1357,
      1358, 1364, 1409, 1417, 1468, 1480
      parish chaplain, 402, 624
   choir, *xlvii*
      choir-boy, 55, 91, 149, 278, 903, 1077
   clerk, 18, 28, 36, 55, 91, 108, 109, 120,
      126, 130, 142, 144, 155, 164, 189, 192,
      193, 195, 207, 208, 210, 254, 257, 278,
      288, 296, 299, 300, 301, 306, 308, 309,
      316, 319, 320, 321, 333, 342, 348, 350,
      365, 376, 380, 402, 415, 416, 491, 497,
      499, 511, 529, 538, 546, 548, 618, 619,
      682, 714, 759, 768, 790, 797, 896, 901,
      903, 939, 943, 1002, 1033, 1035, 1041,
      1048, 1064, 1068, 1077, 1080, 1091,
      1092, 1126, 1134, 1194, 1216, 1237,
      1243, 1280, 1293, 1298, 1315, 1319,
      1331, 1357, 1358, 1364, 1409, 1417,
      1468, 1480
      parish clerk, 149
   gild-members, *xlix*
   monks, 1240
   rector, 126, 130, 164, 299
provision (food) at, *xlvi*, 15, 15n, 20, 44, 415,
   599, 640, 683, 1005, 1077, 1473
sheet, 517
torches at, *xlvi*, *xlvi*n, 28, 896, 1295, 1409
wax used at, 415
see also grave; gravestone
burial, place of, *xliv*
   in chancel, *xliv–xlv*, 43n, 90n, 126n, 294n,
      295n, 375, 406n, 603n, 632n, 633n, 900n,
      1014n, 1238, 1418n, 1472n
   in chapel, 1134n, 1216n
   in church, *xliv*, 41, 46, 50, 54, 90, 116, 142,
      149, 169, 180, 188, 210, 214, 313, 346, 347,

      398n, 406, 421, 439n, 479, 583, 618n, 696n,
      759, 797, 832, 1156n, 1330n, 1332n, 1396n,
      1400n
   in churchyard, *xliv–xlv*, *passim*
   before door, 112, 460
   before entrance to choir, 583
   next to font, 479
   at friars, 1132, 1274, 1279, 1365, 1423n
   in friars' cloister, 1132
   by grave of husband, 116, 346, 368, 397, 421,
      491, 1080
   before image, 313, 398n
   by parent(s), 69, 210
   in/by porch, *xliv*, 108, 348, 691, 1276n, 1418n
   by predecessor, 1472n
   in processional way, 569
   by sons, 211
   in tower, *xliv*, 58n, 352
   before tower door, 20
   by wife, 633n, 708, 832
burial-day, alms to poor on, 112, 149, 173, 183,
   261, 288, 314, 345, 415, 416, 497, 927,
   1001, 1076, 1169, 1459
   for alms to poor present at burial, *see* burial
burnet (cloth), *see* material
butts, 1221

calendar, Roman, use of, *xliv*
   regnal year in dates, *xliii*
calf, *see* cattle
candle, *see* church equipment: lights
candlestick, *see* household goods
canopy, *see* church equipment
cap, *see* clothes
card ('blewcard', cloth), *see* material
cart, *see* agricultural equipment
carting, *see* agricultural work
cart-load, *see* measurement
cattle (unspec.), 209, 858, 1001*, 1216, 1260,
   1410
   beast, 417, 641, 932, 969, 1036, 1247
   bullock, 34*, 133, 219, 344, 368, 394, 397,
      740, 861, 876*, 911*, 1131, 1172, 1203,
      1296, 1313, 1398, 1459, 1468, 1473, 1496
      female, 1496
      mother, 1473
      red, 1313
      white, 876
   calf, 186, 213, 231, 254, 281, 320, 358, 589,
      598*, 626, 691, 823, 1121, 1131, 1142,
      1395, 1404, 1423*, 1475
   cow, *li*, 20, 57, 59, 61, 90, 96*, 105, 120, 124,
      125, 129, 131*, 133, 145, 160, 162*, 186,
      191, 227*, 229*, 245, 246, 249, 254, 257,
      269, 278, 281, 289, 290, 302, 320, 326,
      335, 344*, 351, 358*, 368, 375, 385*, 394,
      397*, 417, 430, 433, 440, 441, 449, 478,
      479*, 492, 544, 549, 552, 553*, 556, 589*,

594, 598*, 611*, 638, 639, 643*, 665, 683,
684, 690, 711, 727, 735*, 779*, 783, 820,
822, 823, 831, 836, 837, 857, 861, 868, 869,
876, 890, 894, 900, 908, 911, 938, 960, 963,
965, 1001, 1008*, 1023, 1041, 1044, 1057,
1063*, 1079*, 1088, 1097, 1110, 1113,
1120*, 1121, 1131, 1164, 1172, 1183, 1193,
1200, 1210, 1225, 1233, 1240*, 1244, 1248,
1252, 1258, 1265*, 1269, 1276, 1289*,
1325*, 1333, 1343, 1346, 1352, 1375, 1393,
1394, 1395*, 1398, 1404, 1410, 1416*,
1423, 1433, 1453*, 1475*, 1489, 1495*,
1497
  black, 131, 358, 727, 779, 1265
  dun, 59, 124
  'garlyd howyd', 727
  'howyd', 727
  red, 1041, 1265, 1395, 1423
cow-calf, 213
heifer, 57, 96, 125*, 145, 150, 192, 254, 326,
  521, 552, 598, 691*, 711, 721, 809, 902,
  911*, 1212*, 1221, 1252, 1265, 1276,
  1319, 1325*, 1410*, 1495
  black, 125, 691, 1265, 1276
  red, 125, 691, 902, 911
heifer-cow, 1319
ox, *li*, 417, 1121, 1394
steer, 1404
cauldron, *see* household goods
celure, *see* beds and bedding *and* church
  equipment
censer, *see* church equipment
chair, *see* furniture
chaff, *see* crops
chafing-dish, *see* household goods
chalice, *see* church equipment
chantry, 108n, 193n, 773n
  certificate, 1216n
  chapels, masters of, 489n
  priest, 108n, 193n, 1131n
chapel, in church, 15n, 47, 88, 181, 221, 346n,
  474, 517, 600, 676, 708, 708n, 714, 790,
  837, 967n, 1090n, 1091, 1216n
  in churchyard, 197, 334, 639, 807, 1237, 1329,
  1363, 1369, 1424
  in hospital, 1180
  in house, 90, 90n
  separate building, 17, 20n, 28*, 38n, 238, 252,
  253*, 256, 321, 325, 344, 345, 346, 387,
  459n, 489n, 580, 626, 708, 724, 793, 900,
  958n, 971, 976, 981, 1005, 1029, 1077,
  1077n, 1080n, 1094n, 1115, 1134, 1170,
  1216n, 1296n, 1315, 1329, 1357, 1363,
  1398, 1489, 1493
chapel, burial in, *see* burial
chaplain, *see* parish clergy
charger (dish), *see* household goods
charges (on property), *see* dues

charitable giving, *xlix*
charity (mercy, piety), deeds of, *xlix*, 18, 19, 21,
  41, 77, 86, 91, 122, 139, 155*, 181, 222,
  231*, 232, 303, 314, 315, 359, 391*, 404,
  406, 422, 431, 454, 539, 541, 544, 578, 583,
  589, 599, 640*, 692, 713*, 725, 729*, 740,
  775, 800, 810*, 818, 833, 843, 865, 895,
  924, 957, 962, 1001*, 1036, 1074, 1077,
  1117, 1123, 1168*, 1190, 1219, 1241, 1245,
  1258, 1279*, 1280*, 1291, 1295, 1296,
  1297, 1337, 1388*, 1392*, 1403*, 1417,
  1437, 1469, 1492*, 1495
  at obit, 640
charter, 41, 254, 1052n, 1269, 1291
  see also deed; evidence; indenture
chasuble, *see* church equipment: vestment
chest, *see* furniture
chorister, *see* parish officers
children, at burial, 108
  not to cause trouble, 287
  poor, 529
  provision for, *passim*
  souls of, 41, 86, 97, 406, 1181
  widow to care for, in 'motherly manner', 1278
church, building, *xlvii*, 171, 293, 293n, 927, 1265,
  1272, 1280
  aisle, *xlvii*, 375, 622, 660, 682, 723n, 1162,
  1162n, 1181, 1459n
  'arche', 740n
  bell-chamber, 314n
  chancel, 682n, 961, 961n, 1033
  choir, 43n, 90n, 583, 1366n
  clerestory, 562n, 1218
  door, 60
  lady chapel, 346n
  nave, 57*
  paving, 142, 352, 901, 1473
  porch, *xlvii*, 60, 60n, 118, 118n, 261, 288, 380,
  458, 469, 548, 550, 619, 690n, 723, 930,
  1089, 1231, 1273, 1285, 1386
  roof, *xlvii*, 692, 858, 908, 1279, 1459
  tower, *xlvii*, *xlviin*, 34, 36, 36n, 59, 59n, 63, 77,
  108, 109, 120, 124, 158, 159, 180*, 205,
  227, 271, 314, 342, 356, 362, 408, 365,
  411, 430, 458, 472, 492, 573, 610, 714, 723,
  723n, 729, 824, 824n, 828, 850, 876, 886n,
  905n, 908n, 911n, 930, 963, 975, 1006, 1033,
  1069n, 1076, 1133n, 1158n, 1170, 1192,
  1240, 1297, 1329, 1345, 1345n, 1404, 1478,
  1495*
  vestry, 967
  walls, 246, 271, 849, 1044
  window, 346, 362, 492, 562n, 609, 632n, 690n,
  838, 889n, 1218, 1265, 1418
church, burial in, *see* burial
church, dedication of (incl. chapel, aisle), *xlv*
  All Saints, 3, 12, 28, 28n, 37, 41, 46, 48n, 54,
  59, 59n, 69, 89, 96, 96n, 101, 124, 132, 151,

166n, 175, 203*, 214, 222, 229, 247n, 248, 249, 252, 271, 283, 286, 297, 309, 311, 317, 317n, 325, 337, 341, 344, 379, 381, 398n, 399, 421, 427n, 457, 457n, 463, 471, 487, 488, 499n, 554, 574, 603n, 634n, 645, 645n, 654, 667, 674, 690, 724, 726, 740, 740n, 783, 793, 796n, 802, 822, 827, 944, 954, 954n, 1029, 1100, 1129, 1132, 1181, 1181n, 1219, 1221, 1279, 1356n, 1357, 1364, 1367, 1373, 1417, 1458, 1463, 1463n, 1472, 1472n*, 1473, 1489

Blessed Virgin Mary (St Mary), 5, 7, 15n, 17, 19, 19n, 28, 28n, 36, 42, 46, 47*, 50, 50n, 53, 88, 88n, 96n, 103, 131, 150, 150n, 152, 158n, 181, 194, 197, 208, 210, 219, 221, 226n, 238, 238n, 247, 247n, 252n, 270, 278, 279n, 295, 308, 316, 317, 317n, 321*, 324, 333, 343, 345, 346*, 346n, 350, 352, 357, 365, 369, 381, 388, 389, 392, 393, 399, 406, 408, 408n, 474, 489, 489n, 491, 497, 499, 499n, 517, 549, 549n, 553n, 569, 574, 580, 586, 595, 612, 619, 626, 633, 660, 676, 679, 682, 682n*, 683, 708n, 714*, 724, 741, 762, 764n, 777, 787, 788, 790, 793, 822, 837, 911n, 927n, 932, 1008, 1008n, 1014n, 1035, 1052n, 1090n*, 1091, 1121, 1133, 1133n, 1162, 1169, 1170, 1172, 1216n, 1237, 1255, 1265, 1279, 1315, 1329, 1363, 1369, 1372, 1424, 1462, 1462n, 1463, 1481

Holy Rood, 1207n

Holy Trinity, 88, 122, 553, 609, 1076, 1216, 1216n, 1329, 1419, 1424

St Andrew, 16n, 22, 24, 59, 87, 111, 124, 150n, 191, 197, 228, 284, 313, 373, 400, 409, 468, 538n, 556, 594, 639, 691, 891, 1262, 1478, 1478n

St Audrey, see St Etheldreda

St Augustine, 38n, 631

St Bartholomew, 178, 188n, 227, 385,

St Botolph (Botulph), 50n, 325, 344, 899n, 900, 971, 976, 1005, 1170

St Edmund (king and martyr), 160, 180, 335, 343, 457, 1014n, 1240

St Ethelbert, 370

St George, 185, 611, 658, 662, 867, 1240, 1478n

St Gregory, 48, 48n, 49, 62, 91, 128n, 157, 188, 198, 234, 258, 276, 277, 281, 281n, 310, 326, 356, 377, 420, 534, 539*, 578, 632*, 717, 758, 800*, 805, 983, 1077, 1077n, 1078, 1078n, 1132, 1168*, 1302, 1364, 1466n

St James, 108, 132n, 142, 166n, 192, 279, 279n, 585, 853, 940, 1080, 1219, 1221, 1279n, 1329, 1363, 1432

St John the Baptist, 38n, 59, 59n, 124, 346n, 457, 457n, 583, 600, 600n, 634, 677, 796,

899n, 954, 954n, 1180, 1214, 1345n, 1352, 1395, 1478

St Katherine, 457n

St Lawrance, 352, 352n, 708

St Margaret, 440, 571n, 807, 1090, 1090n, 1134, 1134n, 1296n, 1409

St Martin, 4, 10, 11, 17, 23, 25, 30, 34, 35, 40, 44, 45, 56, 60, 77, 90, 97, 98, 99, 100, 101, 108, 109, 115, 116, 123, 138, 139, 162, 164, 180, 181, 185, 187, 191, 194, 200, 230, 232, 233, 268, 269, 278, 281, 281n, 287, 294, 297, 298, 300, 302, 303, 306, 314, 315, 334, 340, 341, 343, 347, 351n, 363, 370, 377, 393, 395, 411, 412, 413, 422, 427, 429, 430, 431, 435, 436, 438, 440, 441, 443, 445, 465, 467, 470, 472, 473, 499, 525, 530, 531, 534*, 535, 536, 542, 554, 576, 582, 584, 585, 588, 589, 594, 612, 633, 640, 644, 653, 673, 677, 684, 692, 721, 760, 762, 783, 806, 821, 827, 830, 848, 849, 854, 856, 868, 869, 874, 877, 884, 885, 890, 891, 892, 922, 925, 933, 957, 960, 963, 965, 994, 1002, 1004, 1019, 1054, 1060, 1069, 1076, 1078*, 1078*, 1078n, 1086, 1098, 1108, 1109, 1110, 1117, 1122, 1139, 1152, 1153, 1171, 1174, 1180, 1183, 1191, 1201, 1206, 1219, 1220, 1233, 1236, 1240, 1246, 1251, 1252, 1253, 1254, 1256, 1260, 1263, 1264, 1268, 1279, 1289, 1298, 1299, 1302, 1346, 1353, 1356, 1356n, 1362, 1363, 1378, 1386, 1465

St Mary Magdalene, 1293

St Mary (Our Lady), see Blessed Virgin Mary

St Nicholas, 16n, 146, 213n, 253n, 346, 506, 531, 636, 676, 676n, 726, 1008, 1008n, 1090, 1090n, 1315, 1346

St Paul, 1077

St Peter, 19n, 20, 41n, 47, 48, 48n, 49, 53, 62, 78, 81, 82, 83, 97, 103, 116, 127, 128, 129, 147, 152, 157, 171, 209, 264, 276, 277, 287, 288, 288n, 301, 310, 346, 352, 352n, 354, 358, 398, 408, 444, 458, 474, 539, 600, 600n, 632, 647, 652, 665, 681, 711n, 714, 714n, 740n, 758, 797, 800, 803, 805, 818, 864, 882, 937, 1049, 1057, 1058, 1126, 1126n, 1134, 1207, 1207n, 1274, 1365, 1462, 1489, 1493

St Peter and St Paul, 124, 260, 367, 433, 462, 583, 684, 1459, 1126n, 1216n

St Petronilla, 160n, 634n, 1398

St Thomas (martyr), 160, 160n, 226, 226n, 1478, 1478n

St Theobald, 708, 708n

see also altar; gild-patron

church, equipment and furnishings (unspec.), xlvii–xlix, 562n, 180n, 908

alb, see vestment

altar, and equipment, xlvii

high altar, *xlv, xlviii, passim*
  painting of, 1169
  side-altar, 7, 112, 119, 205, 294, 311, 438,
    457, 511, 600, 600n, 741, 882, 908*,
    1113, 1174, 1279n, 1474n
  dedication of, BVM, 7, 112, 205, 294, 438,
    457, 741, 882, 908, 1113
    Holy Trinity, 311
    St Anne, 1474n
    St John the Baptist, 600, 908, 908n
    St Katherine, 511
    St Lawrence, 1279n
    St Nicholas, 1113
  see also panel
amice, *see* vestment
antiphoner, *see* book
apparels, *see* vestment
banner-cloth, *see* cloth
basin, 488, 1481 (silver)
  for altar, 415
  on corpse, 415, 415n
bell, *xlvii*, 130, 142n, 165, 281n, 300, 314n,
  342, 342n*, 356n, 373, 390, 392, 463, 474,
  729n, 633n, 729n, 735, 790, 861, 924, 927n,
  1033n, 1074, 1078, 1091, 1104, 1139, 1142,
  1156, 1237, 1249, 1258, 1346*, 1351n,
  1365n, 1369, 1390*, 1416, 1427, 1467
  bell-ringing at death, 350
    at funeral, *xlvi*, 415
  bell-ropes, 114, 908, 1192n
bench, *see* seating
book (unspec.), *xlvii*, 101, 180, 228, 231, 271,
  321, 444, 583*, 680, 803n, 889, 894n, 1121,
  1153
  antiphoner, *xlviii*, 108, 113, 611, 662, 796,
    1008, 1050, 1225, 1248, 1289, 1399
  coucher, 889n
  gradual, *xlviii*, 603n, 1486
  legend, *xlviii*, 43n, 342, 603n, 808n, 1125,
    1495
  manual, 497
  martyrology, 398n
  missal, *xlviii*, 58, 677, 740, 916, 982, 1322n
  portasse, *xlviii*, 803n, 889n, 941
  primer, 1174
  processional, 740
  psalter, 342n, 398n, 982
  re-used for rents, 982n
candle, *see* lights
candlestick, on altar, 741
candlebeam, *see* roodloft
canopy (celure), over altar, 908, 1123, 1279n
censer, 1418n
chalice, 15, 351, 400, 438, 566, 982, 1152,
  1322n, 1418n*
chasuble, *see* vestment
cloth, for altar, 41*, 119, 175, 186, 311, 385,
  457, 495, 1008*, 1048, 1131, 1356*, 1356n

banner-cloth, 1063
  bed-cover, 113
  corporal, 1169
  cross-cloth, 290
  painted cloth, 1356
  table-cloth for altar, 175
cope, *see* vestment
corporal, *see* cloth
coucher, *see* book
cross, 144, 316, 1041, 1150, 1231, 1246
  churchyard, of St Thomas, *xliin*
  palm, 538
  processional, 290
cross-cloth, *see* cloth
cruet, 172, 511, 1481 (silver)
desk, *see* seating
Easter sepulchre, *xlviii*, 81, 113, 213, 302, 321,
  506, 817, 894, 962, 1082, 1082n, 1164,
  1186, 1368, 1371, 1386, 1480
font, burial by, *see* burial, place of
  position of, 479n
font-cover, 376, 690n
gradual, *see* book
image (statue) (unspec.), *xlvii*, 60
  BVM, 15, 111, 343, 345, 346n, 385, 398n,
    741, 837, 900n, 929, 1031, 1090n, 1210,
    1255, 1463, 1466n
    annunciation, 589
    of pity, 674
  Holy Trinity, 15, 248, 341, 341n, 553, 1207n
  maiden of Manston, 1466n
  St Andrew, 538
  St Christopher, 313n, 1416
  St Edith *recte* St Sitha, *q.v.*
  St Edmund, 22
  St Gregory, 420
  St James, 618n
  St John, 345, 1210
  St Leonard, 1117n
  St Margaret, 807
  St Paul, 1126, 1126n
  St Peter, 444, 611
  St Petronilla, 634, 634n
  St Sitha, 489n
  St Thomas, 345
lamp, *see* lights
lectern, 1365n, 1418n
legend, *see* book
lights (including candle, lamp, taper, torch),
  xlviii, 113, 296, 321, 345, 488, 516n, 566,
  742, 896, 908, 1035, 1142, 1174, 1343,
  1346, 1371, 1386, 1416, 1418
  before altar, *xlviii*, 15, 112, 160, 233, 345,
    516, 521
  in basin, 385, 415n
  of BVM, *xlviii*, 15, 111, 133, 151, 287,
    343*, 358, 419, 438, 552*, 571, 671,
    696, 742, 782, 809, 837, 865, 929, 1033,

1054, 1079, 1174*, 1287, 1313, 1333,
1379, 1381, 1382, 1437, 1451, 1463,
1465
funded by cows, *xlviii*, 57, 589
funded by land, *xlviii*
of gild, 1265, 1409
before image, *xlviii*, 15, 111, 343, 345*,
385, 553, 589, 674, 837, 908, 929, 1255,
1416, 1463
St Christopher, 820
St Katherine, 613
St Peter, 611
at mass, 81
before rood, *xlviii*, 160, 345
on roodloft, 57, 91, 429
of sepulchre, *xlviii*, 81, 113, 213, 302, 506,
817, 894, 962, 1082n, 1164, 1186, 1368,
1371, 1386, 1480
before tomb, 345
see also burial
maniple, *see* vestment
manual, *see* book
martyrology, *see* book
missal, *see* book
mural, *see* painting
oil (for lamps), 1174
organ, 446n
ornaments, 1, 101, 180, 289, 343, 393, 552,
583*, 599, 816, 827*, 889, 894n, 1280, 1400
painting, of altar, 1169
of cloth, 1356*
of image, 248, 346, 397, 589, 807, 900n,
1031, 1210*
of panel (retable), 1315
of rood, 345*, 397n, 1077, 1077n
of roodloft, 197, 908, 1193, 1351n
of roof, 908
wall-painting of St Christopher, 313n, 346
of St Edmund, 1014n
panel (retable, *tabula*), 116, 248, 799, 802,
1045, 1257n, 1306, 1315, 1356, 1459
of alabaster, 116, 1045, 1257n
parclose, 600
portasse, *see* book
primer, *see* book
processional, *see* book
psalter, *see* book
pyx, 916, 1077, 1418n
resin (for torches), 321
retable, *see* panel
rood, *xlviii*, 345n, 397, 397n, 908, 1077, 1077n,
1207n, 1429
roodloft (candlebeam), *xlvii*, 28, 28n, 50, 57,
169, 197, 408n, 456, 642, 672, 679, 696,
908, 931n, 1174, 1186, 1193, 1233, 1250,
1351n, 1429
see also light
roof, painting of, 908

seating (including bench, desk, stall, stool), 1,
642, 1024, 1024n, 1153, 1158n, 1181, 1289
ship (for incense), 529*
stall, *see* seating
statue, *see* image
stole, *see* vestment
stool, *see* seating
surplice, *see* vestment
tabernacle, for the host, 566, 916
tabernacle, for image, (unspec.), *xlvii*, 158,
566n, 1276n
of BVM, 346n*, 469, 807n, 1285n
of Holy Trinity, 1276n
of St John the Baptist, 1345n
of St Katherine, 613
of St Paul, 1126
of St Peter, 1260n
table-cloth, *see* cloth
taper, *see* lights
thurible, 1125n
torch, *see* lights
towel, 385
tunicle, *see* vestment
vestment (unspec.), 158n, 178, 180, 278*,
457n, 1001, 1121*, 1156, 1195n, 1384,
1385
alb, 247
amice, 247
apparels, 247
chasuble, 247
complete, 1473
cope, 247, 1009, 1058, 1076, 1169, 1417,
1473, 1489
choir-cope, 1091
deacon's 1473
subdeacon's, 1473
maniple, 247
principal, 1121
priest's, 41*, 247, 1169*, 1354, 1473
stole, 247
surplice, 126, 149, 376, 385, 768, 797,
1008, 1033, 1409
tunicle, 1169*
church, lost, 16n
church services and activities, anniversary (obit,
yearday), *xlvii*, 311, 430, 457, 469, 490,
539, 546, 573, 573n, 619, 640, 691, 693,
800, 803, 816, 903, 929, 935n*, 1032, 1041,
1041n, 1077, 1110*, 1181, 1256, 1298,
1397, 1463, 1486
alms to poor at, 619, 1032, 1077, 1110*
bell-ringing at, 619
deeds of charity at, 539, 640
obsequies at, 546, 1077
offering at, 430
payments at, 903, 1298
provision (food) at, 457
annual, 553, 816, 929

antiphon, 516, 566, 566n
benediction, 566n
certain (sangred), *xlviii*, 1, 5, 112, 113, 120,
    129, 276, 281, 402, 406, 416, 469, 492,
    539, 662, 723*, 742, 772, 785, 788, 809,
    833n, 871, 899, 1001, 1041n, 1045, 1075n,
    1078, 1173n, 1217, 1218, 1221, 1242, 1249,
    1250n, 1293, 1343n, 1344, 1397, 1409
churchale (drinking), 1088n
consecration (dedication), 194, 194n
Corpus Christi procession, 566, 566n
dedication, *see* consecration
dirige, *xlvi*, 305n, 546, 901, 1091, 1480
elevation of the host, torch to burn at, 521
gospel, reading of, 1365n
litany, 1313
    of the saints, 438
mass (divine service), *xlviii**, *xlix*, *passim*
    celebrated by, friar(s), *xlix*, 3, 47, 97, 172,
        208, 249, 301, 308, 356, 429, 816, 842,
        929, 1132, 1142, 1142n, 1156, 1164,
        1181, 1191, 1246*, 1343, 1390, 1424
        priest/chaplain, *passim*
    celebration of memorial at, 1246*
    celebration of priest's first, 1132
    celebration on roodloft, 931n
    mass of, BVM, 108, 288*, 459, 546, 573,
        711, 860, 1080, 1126, 1134, 1462
        five wounds, 1097, 1097n
        Holy Ghost, 546
        Jesus, 546, 916, 916n, 1365, 1369
        requiem mass, *xlvi*, *xlviii*, 50, 288, 308*,
            529*, 538, 546, 548, 682, 896, 901,
            1035, 1194, 1216, 1289, 1315, 1463
        of St Gregory, *see* trental
        Scala celi mass, 180, 194, 387, 775, 1209
        votive mass, *xlviii*, 108, 546*, 711, 916,
            916n, 1097, 1097n, 1126, 1134, 1365,
            1369, 1462
    mass-pence (at funeral), *see* burial
matins, *xlvi*, 1416
month-mind, *see* thirty-day
obit, *see* anniversary
obsequies, *see* burial
offering (at altar/shrine), 345, 346*, 640
offerings (defaulted), *xlvi*, *passim*
placebo, *xlvi*, 901
procession, 566, 566n
    cross for, 290
    processional (book), 740
    processional way, 569
requiem mass, *see* mass
sangred, *see* certain
Scala celi, *see* mass
service, of St Mary (Our Lady), 108, 108n,
    288, 459, 566, 566n, 573, 573n, 711, 860,
    1080, 1126, 1134, 1462
    memorial, 469, 816

seven-day, *xlvi*, 44, 90, 124, 311, 380, 416, 683,
    797, 903, 1237n, 1298, 1463
    food on, 44, 683
thirty-day (month-mind), *xlvi*, 311, 380, 416,
    683, 797, 903, 1237n, 1274, 1298, 1364*,
    1463
trental, *xlviii*, 29, 40, 52, 86, 97, 118, 120, 126,
    128, 130, 133, 161, 164, 186, 197, 228, 246,
    248, 261, 263*, 269, 270*, 288, 290, 310,
    321, 329, 351, 352*, 353, 355, 374, 379,
    380*, 381, 385, 409, 416, 456, 458, 463,
    499, 521*, 547, 570, 648, 663*, 676, 741,
    742, 756, 771, 794, 801, 806, 833, 842, 921,
    923, 924, 933, 961, 962, 965, 967, 969,
    977, 1026, 1033, 1039, 1041, 1049, 1063,
    1075, 1089, 1090, 1117, 1155, 1158, 1164,
    1172, 1183, 1186, 1192, 1217, 1224, 1227,
    1228, 1285, 1369, 1370, 1372, 1390*, 1393,
    1395*, 1397*, 1399, 1446, 1453, 1466*,
    1478, 1484, 1496
    celebrated by friar(s), 52, 118, 126*, 128,
        130*, 133, 164*, 186, 228, 261, 263*,
        269, 270, 288, 290, 310, 321, 329, 352*,
        353, 355, 379, 380*, 385, 409, 416, 456,
        463, 521, 663*, 676, 756, 794, 806, 833,
        842, 921, 933, 965, 969, 977, 1026,
        1033, 1039, 1041, 1063, 1075, 1155,
        1158, 1164, 1172, 1183, 1186, 1217,
        1369, 1372, 1390*, 1395*, 1397, 1453,
        1466*, 1478
    by priest/chaplain, 374, 381, 499
trental of St Gregory, *xlviii*, 2, 5, 18, 21, 22,
    24, 33, 34, 87, 88, 108, 112, 113, 114, 122*,
    124, 127, 129, 150, 180, 195, 258, 276, 284,
    300, 303, 345, 359, 373, 390, 394, 421, 479,
    497, 538, 609, 632*, 639, 658, 679, 705,
    706, 722*, 735, 758, 775, 788, 798, 842n,
    877, 890, 908, 981, 1005, 1006, 1010, 1031,
    1032, 1054, 1058, 1076, 1078, 1097, 1132,
    1213, 1216, 1218, 1243, 1265, 1272, 1292,
    1356, 1375, 1386, 1392, 1402, 1427, 1441*,
    1475
    celebrated, by friar(s), *xlviii*, 5, 18, 21, 33,
        34, 108, 112, 122, 124, 127, 129*, 195,
        258, 303, 359, 373, 390, 421, 497, 632*,
        679, 758, 775, 788, 877, 890, 908, 981,
        1006, 1031, 1054, 1097, 1216, 1265,
        1272, 1356, 1375, 1386, 1392, 1427,
        1441*
        master of preceptory, 114
        priest/chaplain, 180, 632, 722, 1001,
            1076, 1078, 1132, 1218
vespers, *xlvi*, 1416
yearday, *see* anniversary
churchale, 1088n
churchyard, burial in, *passim*
    not possessed by chapel, 1080n
    wall, etc., of, 271, 352, 681, 799, 1123

of abbey, cross in, *xlii*n
civil boundaries, *see* boundary
clergy, parish, *see* parish clergy
    superior, *see* archdeacon
clerk, registry, 146n, 313n, 338, 687n, 931n, 984n,
        1008n, 1117n, 1343n
    singing, *see* church officers
    writing, 97n
cloak, *see* clothes
'clostable', *see* furniture
close, *see* land
cloth, *see* material
    see also church equipment; cloth-making;
        cloths, household
    for poor, 421, 474, 735, 977
cloth-making, *li*
    cloth, 126, 454, 474, 740*, 790, 929, 1125,
        1125n, 1441n
    see also material: woollen cloth
    clothier, 1048n*, 717n
    dyer, equipment of, 1489
        'le maderyngled', 1421
    dyehouse, 1485
    fuller, 929, 1485n
        shears of, 865
    loom, 298*, 300, 458, 663, 1104, 1168
        broadloom, 1181, 1387n
        slay, 1181
        stoddles, 612
        trendle, 1181
    shearman, shears of, 1393
    spinning wheel, 321
    tenter, *li*, 458, 603, 717n
    weaver, 1181
        craft of, 1168
        equipment of, 667
    wood-ash, 740, 790
    wool, 126, 454, 638, 1364
    woolman, 1441
    yarn, 126, 1364
clothes (clothing), (gen.), *l–li*
    (recipients), brother, 180
        daughter, 139, 469
        daughter-in-law, 308
        father, 329, 572
        goddaughter, 640
        grandmother, 408
        mother, 228
        poor, 1277, 1293
        servant, 823
        son, 1001
        widow, 119, 194, 337, 408, 430, 1001, 1032,
            1096, 1113, 1248, 1273, 1296, 1331,
            1365, 1462
    belt, *see* girdle
    boots, 278
        see also shoes
    cap, 18, 626, 740, 1327

green, 18
    red-lined, 626
cloak, 17, 33*, 43, 56*, 103, 146, 172*, 175*,
        385, 419, 420, 421, 492*, 583*, 588, 626*,
        677, 721, 777, 903*, 963, 1041, 1067, 1295,
        1327
    blue, 583
    green, 33, 175, 903
    lined, 33, 146, 903
    russet, 33, 43, 146, 175, 492
    scarlet, 583
    violet, 903
coat, 146*, 346
    furred, 146
    green, 146
    russet, 146
collar-kercher, *see* kerchief
corse, *see* girdle
doublet, *li*, 18*, 90*, 492, 693, 740*, 863, 869,
        1451
    fustian, 18
    leather, 18
    red, 492
    velvet, 863
    violet, 1437
flocket, 863*
    black, 863
    blue, 863
footware, 194
frende, 588
fur, 588
garment as mortuary, 359
girdle (belt, corse), *li*, 91*, 126, 144, 152, 175,
        394, 397, 421*, 529, 548, 578, 612, 626,
        630, 640, 764*, 803, 877, 963, 982, 1041,
        1044, 1077, 1104, 1117, 1139, 1156, 1260n,
        1265, 1274, 1276, 1289, 1295, 1463
    black, 421
    gilt, 421*
    green, 421, 548, 578, 1117, 1289
    leather, 1104
    silk, 529*, 578, 877, 1139, 1260n, 1295,
        1463
    silver (silvered), 91*, 144, 152, 175, 394,
        421*, 529*, 548, 578, 612, 764*, 803,
        877, 963, 982, 1041, 1077, 1104, 1117,
        1139, 1156, 1260n, 1265, 1274, 1289,
        1295, 1463
gown, *l*, 5*, 8, 18*, 45, 56, 65, 90*, 103, 108,
        122*, 131*, 144*, 146, 152*, 159, 172*,
        175, 178, 189, 190*, 193*, 197, 237, 248*,
        254*, 278*, 289, 320*, 368, 385*, 389, 394,
        397, 399*, 400, 419, 420, 429, 440, 474*,
        493*, 516, 529, 541*, 548*, 556, 588*,
        603*, 612*, 626*, 636, 639, 671, 677, 691,
        714, 721*, 740*, 764, 790, 809, 810*, 857,
        863*, 869*, 876, 877*, 902*, 908, 945, 964,
        971, 982, 1005, 1009, 1039*, 1041*, 1044,

1052, 1058, 1067, 1077*, 1088, 1110*,
  1113, 1156*, 1174*, 1237, 1258, 1265*,
  1274, 1276, 1277, 1288*, 1295, 1298*,
  1319*, 1327*, 1344, 1346*, 1370*, 1379,
  1388, 1398, 1409, 1433, 1437, 1451*, 1453,
  1478, 1489*
  black, 193, 493*, 714, 863*, 869, 1156
  blue, 159, 385, 397, 419, 420, 516, 556,
    603, 721, 740, 863, 869, 902, 964, 1156,
    1237, 1258, 1265*, 1274, 1288, 1327,
    1379, 1478, 1489
  burnet, 740, 1489
  cloth for, 400, 541, 1174
  crimson, 863
  furred, 45, 56, 190, 368, 971, 1044, 1052,
    1174, 1274, 1276, 1319, 1489
  green, 172, 175, 254, 385, 399, 400, 493,
    548, 612, 691, 740, 809, 863, 869*,
    877, 902, 1005, 1077, 1174, 1265, 1288,
    1433, 1489
  Kendal, 493, 612
  lined, 90, 146, 863*
  livery, 193
  medley, 193, 278, 541, 740, 877, 1370
  musterdevillers, 18, 790, 1437, 1451
  parti-coloured, 1388
  russet, 131, 190, 248*, 278, 320, 474, 529,
    636, 721, 876, 945, 1265, 1370
  sanguine (blood-coloured), 18, 810
  scarlet, 394
  single, 90
  violet, 18, 368, 626, 1319, 1327, 1451
  white, 740
hat, 529
hood, l, 17, 18*, 90*, 108, 131, 146, 159, 172,
  175, 234, 237, 248*, 278, 321*, 368,
  399*, 474*, 529, 588, 603, 612*, 626*,
  740*, 764, 828, 848, 863, 869, 902, 903*,
  964, 1005, 1009, 1044, 1067*, 1077, 1079,
  1218, 1265*, 1276*, 1295, 1298*, 1327,
  1388, 1489
  black, 18, 131, 159, 588, 740, 1276
  burnet, 1489
  cloth for, 626*
  green, 146
  Kendal, 612
  lamb, 740
  parti-coloured, 902, 903
  ray, 234, 399
  red, 18, 321*, 368, 626, 764, 828, 903, 964,
    1218, 1276
  scarlet, 18, 172, 863, 1044, 1077
  striped, 248*, 254
  violet, 18, 175
hose, li, 18, 237, 254, 278, 321, 626, 740, 848,
  863*, 1005, 1451
  sanguine, 18
  white, 863

huke, li, 740, 877
  blue, 877
jacket, 764
kerchief (kercher), li, 146*, 320, 321, 493, 863,
  877*, 1206*, 1295*, 1466*
  collar-kercher, 863
  lawn, 493, 1295*
  thread, 1295
kirtle, li, 5, 146*, 346, 368*, 397, 777, 1044,
  1201, 1276, 1295, 1398*
  black, 1201
  blood-red, 1276
  cloth for, 1041
  green, 368
  'petikyrtyl', 90
  red, 146*, 368, 397
overcoat, 91*, 823, 1437
  blue, 823
  burnet, 91
  russet, 1437
'petikyrtyl', see kirtle
petticoat, li, 1295
shirt, 18
shoes, li, 254, 278, 321, 863
  see also boots; footware
smock, li, 146, 237, 254, 278*, 321, 626, 790,
  848, 1265, 1409, 1451
tabard, li, 90, 91, 146, 175, 207, 211, 278,
  321*, 368, 516, 539, 548, 588, 982, 1009,
  1044, 1052, 1089, 1218, 1276*, 1398
  black, 91, 1276
  blue, 146
  russet, 516
tunic, li, 8, 18, 56, 90*, 152, 207, 237, 254*,
  278*, 311*, 320, 321*, 337, 368*, 385, 420,
  421, 588, 626*, 714, 721*, 740, 764*, 848,
  869*, 877*, 1039, 1044, 1052, 1067*, 1201,
  1206, 1265*, 1276*, 1277, 1295*, 1313,
  1319, 1327, 1398*, 1409, 1466
  black, 1201
  blanket, 278
  blue, 311, 321, 385, 721, 877, 1201
  cloth for, 337, 626*, 1327
  furred, 56, 90, 207, 311, 368, 421, 764,
    877, 1295*
  green, 321, 1265
  medley, 1276
  murrey, 368
  russet, 311, 1265
  sanguine, 18
  violet, 321, 626
  white, 368
under-garment, 1023
  see also weapons and armour
clothier, see cloth-making
cloths, household (unspec.), 310, 344, 474
  bearing-sheet, 1295
  boardcloth, 175

cotton, 1295
'halling' (hanging), 474
linen, 112, 113, 194, 271, 320, 344, 760, 821,
    1174, 1216, 1231, 1313, 1375, 1465
napery, 180, 1115, 1174
painted cloth, 588
table-cloth, 269*, 385, 626, 828, 929
towel, 269, 321*, 385, 420, 588, 626, 929
woollen, 113, 180, 194, 234, 271, 344, 544,
    760, 779, 821, 1079, 1158, 1216, 1231,
    1313, 1375, 1465
see also material
coat, *see* clothes
coffer, *see* furniture
coffin, *see* burial
coin, as seal, 1080, 1080n
college, 38n, 91*, 128n, 180n, 188, 539, 632, 800,
    1077, 1077n, 1133n, 1168
commendation (of soul), *xliv, passim*
to BVM only, 802
commissary, *liv*, 142, 158n, 365, 889
court, *see* court of probate
community, *xliv*, 439, 469*, 471, 772n, 802
hall, 772, 1462
contract, 807n, 1244
see also agreement
consent, *see* agreement
conversation (manner of living), *see* behaviour
coomb (grain quantity), *see* measurement
copper, 1175
cross, 290
pan, 828, 1174
pot, 1174
copyhold, *see* land tenure
coral, 1295
corn, *see* crops
corporal, *see* church equipment: cloth
cotland, *see* land usage
cotton cloth, *see* material
coucher, *see* church equipment: book
coulter, *see* agricultural equipment: plough
county boundary, *see* boundary
court, ecclesiastical, *lii*
see also court of probate
court, manor, *see* manor
court of probate (gen.), Intro. *passim*, 249n, 421n,
    1240n
archdeacon's, Intro. *passim*, 279n, 1121, 1239,
    1252n
commissary's, (Bury), *xxxix, xl*n
    (London), 489n
consistory, (Norwich), *xxxviii–ix, xxxix*n, *xl*n,
    *xliii*n, 19n, 20, 90n, 142, 939, 939n
    (Rochester), *xxxix*n
Prerogative (archbishop's), *xxxviii–ix*, 192n,
    210n, 489n, 740n, 863n, 1432n, 1441, 1441n
sacrist's, *xxxix*, 279n, 574n
wills proved in more than one, *xxxix, xxxix*n

court of Rome, 20, 124*, 144, 288, 346*, 908,
    1209, 1459
courtyard, *see* land usage: yard
cousin, *see* relatives
coverlet, *see* beds and bedding
cow, *see* cattle
cradle, *see* furniture
craft (unspec.), 1023, 1031
    see also occupation
    equipment for, 48, 190, 219, 535, 717, 820,
        960, 1031
        see also tools
croft, *see* land usage
crops (unspec.), *li*, 165*, 188, 807, 846, 897n,
    1231, 1253, 1356
barley, *li*, 18*, 52, 56, 57*, 63*, 95, 96*, 101*,
    126, 131*, 133*, 150*, 183, 186, 203*,
    207*, 213*, 219, 222*, 232*, 238*, 246*,
    269, 278*, 282, 284, 285*, 287*, 310, 313,
    321, 335*, 337, 343*, 344, 353, 358*, 368,
    370, 373, 385, 389*, 394, 406*, 421*, 429*,
    433, 438*, 440*, 488, 492, 497*, 550*, 552,
    556, 583*, 598, 599*, 624, 626*, 648, 671*,
    682*, 683, 691*, 702*, 727, 740, 742, 749*,
    760*, 762*, 787, 817*, 823*, 828*, 836*,
    846, 876, 889, 903, 911, 960, 963, 969*,
    986*, 995*, 1001*, 1031, 1033, 1074*,
    1082, 1084, 1119, 1123, 1142, 1156, 1200*,
    1210*, 1220*, 1221, 1238, 1240, 1252*,
    1257, 1258*, 1259, 1265*, 1277, 1278,
    1289*, 1296, 1298*, 1306*, 1313, 1319,
    1325, 1327*, 1333*, 1343, 1357*, 1368*,
    1379*, 1388, 1410, 1427*, 1437, 1439*,
    1451*, 1465, 1474, 1480, 1483, 1495
bullimong, 269
chaff, 1289*
corn (unspec.), 65, 209, 229, 232, 245, 429,
    641, 857, 1091, 1200, 1280, 1319, 1375,
    1394, 1410
growing, 232, 429, 1200, 1319, 1394, 1410
fodder, 254
fruit, 90, 165*
grain (gen.), *li*, 846, 1001, 1495
    (unspec.), 126, 131, 132, 150, 180, 190,
        209, 219, 229, 249, 257, 259, 269, 358*,
        454, 464, 492, 544, 594, 598*, 631, 641,
        683*, 692, 708, 740, 799, 820, 842, 864,
        897, 1001*, 1039, 1113, 1200, 1216,
        1233, 1244*, 1260, 1265, 1269, 1280,
        1298, 1334, 1353, 1404, 1496
    growing, 126, 249, 269, 358, 464, 544, 631,
        740, 820, 864, 1039, 1200, 1216, 1244,
        1260, 1404, 1496
    harvested, 126, 150, 190, 219, 358, 464,
        492, 544, 631, 683*, 692, 799, 842, 897,
        1244*, 1244n, 1353
grass, 807, 864
haras, 186

hay, 683n, 1252
herbs, 90, 464, 864
maslin, 146, 186*, 254, 278*, 598, 823*, 1306, 1319
oats, *li*, 145, 351, 846, 1001, 1252, 1306
pasture, 441, 728, 960
peas, *li*, 18, 47, 51, 145, 146, 351, 441, 846, 960, 1001, 1306
rye, *li*, 57*, 544, 683, 1001, 1119, 1210, 1221, 1289, 1295*
straw, 254, 456, 1289*
wheat, *li*, 18, 44*, 47*, 57*, 59, 77*, 90*, 96*, 124, 126, 145, 150*, 169, 179*, 184, 185, 186, 193*, 237, 238, 246, 247*, 249*, 269, 278, 295*, 313*, 320*, 337*, 346, 351, 358, 368, 369, 373*, 385*, 389, 394, 406*, 474, 488*, 492, 494*, 544, 556, 598, 599, 682, 691, 693, 740, 742, 767, 787*, 799, 823, 828, 846, 908*, 927*, 960, 969*, 1001, 1052*, 1082*, 1119, 1162, 1200*, 1210, 1216, 1252*, 1258*, 1272, 1276, 1298*, 1306, 1313, 1319, 1325, 1333, 1357, 1371*, 1410, 1473
wood (timber), 90, 96, 158, 219, 264, 566, 820, 863, 923n, 1001, 1031*, 1041*, 1179, 1209, 1260, 1423
  'faget and talewode', 126
  firewood, 90, 126, 158, 194, 251, 385, 441, 474, 517, 566, 612, 683, 693*, 740, 818*, 1091, 1252, 1258, 1404*, 1495
  loppings, 1404
  oaks, 1423
  underwood, 96*, 900, 1397
cross, *see* church equipment
  market, 768n, 1459n
  roadside, 188, 246, 346, 690n, 794, 823, 1044, 1231, 1237, 1237n
cross-cloth, *see* church equipment: cloth
cross-roads, 181
cruet, *see* church equipment
cup, *see* household goods
cupboard, *see* furniture
curate, *see* parish clergy
curfew, 633, 633n
curtains, *see* beds and bedding
curtilage, *see* land usage
cushion, *see* furniture and furnishings
custom, 1200n, 1409, 1409n
  of England, 335
  of manor, 122*, 161, 205, 300, 408, 683
  of town, 957

dagger, *see* weapons and armour
date (of will, etc.), *xliii*
  regnal year in, *xliii*, *lii*
  Roman calendar in, *xliv*
daughter-in-law, step-daughter, *see* relatives
daybell, *see* church equipment: bell

deanery (unspec.), *xxxviii*, *liv*
  of Bocking (Essex), *xxxix*, *xxxix*n
  of Fordham, *xxxix*, *xxxix*n
  of Hartismere, *xxxviii*n, *xxxix*
  of Norwich, 1493
  of Stow, *xxxviii*n, *xxxix*
  of Thetford, *xl*n
debts, due to testator (unspec.), 1, 88, 90*, 90n, 91, 102, 128, 130, 164, 180, 256, 293, 333, 345*, 347*, 354, 398, 407, 421, 446, 454*, 456, 534, 566, 600*, 631, 660, 692, 729, 740, 768, 788, 790*, 797, 799, 802, 863, 932, 1050, 1068n, 1075, 1078, 1115, 1132, 1179, 1180, 1200, 1207, 1241, 1246, 1263, 1315, 1329, 1417, 1424, 1481, 1495
  (spec.), 538, 601
  schedule of, 1086, 1382
  owed by testator (unspec.), *xlv*, *lii*, *passim*
  (spec.), 1319
Decorated (style of architecture), *xlvii*n
dedication of church (patron), *see* church, dedication of
  (service), *see* church services: consecration
deed (legal document), 41, 49, 358, 406, 409, 497, 549, 682, 1162, 1169n, 1345, 1346, 1369, 1403*, 1409, 1495*
  tripartite deed, 41
  see also agreement; charter; evidence; indenture
deeds of charity, *see* charitable giving
  almsdeeds, 454
  deeds of mercy, 139, 231, 843, 1168
  deeds of piety (pity), 41, 77, 86, 155*, 303, 422, 544, 589. 599, 692, 729, 1117, 1168, 1279, 1291, 1388, 1417
degree (station in life), *see* status
desk, *see* church equipment
devotion, forms of, *xlviii*, 194, 546, 916, 916n, 1097, 1097n, 1365
diaper cloth, *see* material
dicker (of hides), *see* measurement
dike, 253*
diocese (gen.), *xxxviii*
  of Ely, *xxxvii*n, *xxxix*n
  of Norwich, *xxxviii*, *xlii*, 97*
    see also court of probate: consistory
  of St Edmundsbury and Ipswich, *xxxix*n
disagreement (discord between beneficiaries), 228, 412, 857, 957, 1032
  see also agreement
dish, *see* household goods
distraint (incl. re-entry), right of, 90*, 131, 683, 1152, 1259
ditch, 507, 836, 1001, 1246, 1260
Domesday book, *see* book: Domesday
doublet, *see* clothes
dovecote, 52, 270, 352n, 464*, 1110

dower, *liii*, 188, 333, 347, 409, 441*, 506*, 589, 671, 957, 969, 1410*
dozen (twelve), *see* measurement
drinking (churchale), 1088n
dropping-pan, *see* household goods
dues (charges, service, for house, etc.), 18, 28, 41, 46, 48*, 52, 77, 90, 96, 106, 160*, 205, 210*, 228*, 231, 245, 276, 314, 315, 343*, 348*, 441, 446, 497*, 531, 541, 547, 578*, 589, 595*, 632, 717, 724, 757, 758, 775, 793, 803, 822, 828, 895, 961, 1001*, 1058, 1088, 1097, 1181*, 1200, 1225*, 1246, 1259, 1279*, 1292, 1299, 1332, 1364*, 1382, 1403, 1465, 1492
dwelling (accommodation), 144
  for father, 329
  for grandmother, 408
  for mother, 228
  for son, 408, 1296
  for servant, 823
  for widow, 52, 112, 126, 144*, 194, 226, 408, 441, 464, 474, 490, 552, 631, 638,   648, 741, 818, 864, 921, 949, 965, 969, 1172, 1252, 1257, 1273, 1279, 1333, 1369, 1387
dyer, dyehouse, *see* cloth-making

earnest (of bequest), 889n
easement (access), 90, 529, 807, 921, 1113, 1172, 1279
  in bakehouse, 490, 818, 1252
  to fire, 90, 807, 1252
  in garden, 90, 247, 864
  to kitchen, 90, 1252
  to mill, 799
  to draw water, 90, 441, 818, 864, 1258
  in yard, 818, 864
Easter, 41, 90, 91, 609, 640, 894, 1032, 1246, 1259
  in date, 530, 1250, 1361
Easter sepulchre, *see* church equipment
ecclesiastical boundaries, *see* boundary
Ecclesiastical Commissioners, *xxxviii*
'Ecclesiastical Jurisdictions', *xxxviii*n, *xxxix*n
ecclesiastical parish, *see* parish
ekys (candles), 57
enfeoff, *see* feoffee
English, testament in, 282, 474, 495, 517, 1091, 1361, 1363
  will in, 340, 929, 1213, 1310, 1467
  words in, 456, 1073n
equipment, *see* agricultural equipment, church equipment, craft equipment, fishing equipment, household utensils, kitchen and table-ware
  see also tools
estate (property), 48n
  real estate, *l*, *liii*
estate (title to property), *liii*, 28, 42, 48, 77*, 97, 106, 122, 124, 127, 175, 180, 188, 269, 276,

282, 296, 300, 315, 342, 413, 457*, 538, 541, 569, 578, 583, 632, 722, 740, 758, 790, 800*, 803, 818*, 820, 864, 897, 937, 939, 941, 1058, 1064, 1088, 1094, 1104, 1123, 1132, 1153, 1168, 1169*, 1193*, 1200*, 1213, 1223, 1240, 1245, 1246, 1255, 1274, 1280, 1300, 1345, 1364, 1365, 1369, 1386, 1387, 1409, 1424, 1467*, 1478, 1489, 1492
evidence (legal document), 499, 1193, 1346*
ewer, *see* household goods
exchange (of land), 828, 1403
executor, *passim*
  accounts of, *lii*n, 48, 49, 720, 968, 968n
  appointment of, *li–lii*
  duties of, *lii*
  licence for religious to act as, 588
  payment of, 2, 45, 61, 92, 102, 108, 112, 113, 125, 126, 131, 164, 172, 180, 190, 204, 221, 222, 226, 229, 245, 246, 271, 281, 287, 288, 290, 293, 294, 296, 297, 314, 333, 342, 346, 351, 362, 365, 381, 397, 398, 399, 429, 472, 493, 520, 530, 533, 564, 566, 589, 594, 598, 611, 616, 619, 640, 641, 681, 692, 721, 722, 749, 758, 776, 800, 803, 806, 813, 820, 821, 822, 843, 849, 889, 903, 924, 930, 945, 967, 992, 995, 1006, 1008, 1009, 1023, 1039, 1044, 1046, 1064, 1067, 1077, 1080, 1123, 1155, 1181, 1183, 1200, 1210, 1219, 1233, 1253, 1255, 1263, 1279, 1291, 1298, 1300, 1346, 1353, 1356, 1358, 1361, 1364, 1371, 1375, 1388, 1390, 1394, 1400, 1404, 1417, 1441, 1453, 1459, 1469, 1473, 1475, 1480, 1489, 1493, 1495
  'power reserved' to, *liv*, *passim*
  renouncing administration, 10, 26, 60, 207, 238, 277, 278, 287, 343, 370, 434, 488, 509, 520, 589, 595, 632, 671, 698, 816, 863, 939, 951, 1239, 1365
  to be in agreement, 1280
  see also supervisor
eyes, having God before, 24, 806

family, dispersal of, 1471n
  executors drawn from, *li*
  extended family in messuage, 408
farm, leased property, 165*, 471, 471n, 521
  rent, 219, 288, 348*, 412*, 469*
  to let for rent, 546
farmer (agriculturist), *xlv*, 1330n
father, father-in-law, *see* relatives
feast-days and festivals, basin to be used on, 415
  celebration on, 1181
  light to burn on, 57, 385, 1416
  processions on, 290
  used in dating (gen.), *xiv-xv*, *xliii*
    All Saints, 20, 848, 1034, 1156
    BVM, annunciation, 5, 903, 1180, 1328
      assumption, 117, 353, 908

nativity of, 313, 641, 837, 1242, 1369, 1448
purification of, 103, 256, 461, 879, 1050, 1134, 1179
Christ, ascension of, 674
    nativity of, 850, 1478
Corpus Christi, 209, 429, 679
Easter, 530, 1250, 1361
Epiphany, 192, 1439
Holy Cross, exaltation of, 8, 449
    invention of, 261
Palm Sunday, 895, 1309
Pentecost, 151
St Agapitus, 2
St Alphege, 397, 566
St Ambrose, 801
St Andrew, 654, 929, 1357, 1475
St Augustine, 1125, 1256
St Barnabus, 248, 1126, 1458
St Bartholomew, 53, 345, 681, 1292
St Boniface, 317
St Cuthbert, 63
St Dunstan, 109, 347, 889
St Edmund, archbishop, 1346
St Edmund, king, 348, 1295
St Edward, king, 961, 1334
St Etheldreda (Audrey), 331
St George, 152, 164, 1045
St German, 471
St Gregory, 47, 391, 802, 821, 1036, 1194, 1203, 1342
St Hypolitus, 290
St James, 687, 900, 1296
St John the apostle, 246
St John the Baptist, 775, 836, 838
    decollation of, 186, 842, 858
    nativity of, 629, 1192
St Katherine, 182, 444
St Kenelm, 995
St Lambert, 69
St Lawrence, 456
St Leonard, 1033
St Leger, 1195
St Lucy, 426, 1427
St Luke, 538
St Margaret, 406
St Mark, 409
St Martin, 95, 1116, 1131
St Mary Magdalene, 19
St Matthew, 146, 399, 534, 609, 655
St Michael, 17, 51, 428, 672, 741, 1046, 1213
St Nicholas, 1389
St Paul, 1207
St Peter ad vincula, 309, 404, 881, 981
St Peter and St Paul, 511, 1217
St Petronilla, 1367
St Richard, 289

St Simon and St Jude, 213, 415
St Stephen, 61
St Sulpicius, 954
St Swithin, 259
St Thomas, apostle, 291, 377, 725
St Thomas, martyr, 55
St Valentine, 346, 435, 488
St Vincent, 1201
Seven Martyr Brothers, 788
feasts, liturgical, xlviii
    principal, 304, 429
    used in specifying time of year (for payments, etc.), xlv
        All Saints, 439, 683, 1246
        BVM, annunciation of, 446n, 457*
            ascension of, 446n
            assumption of, 446n, 1246
            conception of, 446n
            nativity of, 446n, 1246
            presentation of, 446n
            purification of, 446n
            visitation of, 446n
        Corpus Christi, 566, 566n
        Easter, 41, 90, 91, 609, 640, 894, 1032, 1246, 1259
        Maundy Thursday, 446
        Nativity (of Our Lord), 90, 278, 457*, 1032, 1246
        Pentecost, 1246
        St John the Baptist, 126, 457*,
            nativity of, 90, 683, 1032, 1219, 1244, 1246*
        St Michael (Michaelmas), 41, 90, 91, 126, 277, 385*, 428, 457*, 608, 609*, 713, 807, 818, 857, 944, 969, 980, 1032, 1057, 1113, 1244, 1244n, 1246, 1258, 1259, 1262, 1346, 1361, 1361n, 1429, 1437, 1458, 1473, 1496
        Seven Holy Sleepers, 1486
featherbed, see beds and bedding
fee, chief lord(s) of, liii, 28, 96, 150, 160*, 175, 214, 228*, 279*, 343*, 406, 441, 457, 494, 507, 531, 541, 679, 683, 717, 758, 775, 787, 803, 827*, 828*, 941, 1001*, 1181, 1221, 1225*, 1246*, 1287, 1364, 1382, 1403, 1437*, 1446*, 1451*
fee simple, 41, 314, 342*, 837, 1252
fee tail, 41*, 1280, 1291
fen, see land usage
fence, 507
feoffee (including enfeoff), xli–ii, liii*, liiin, 21, 28, 41*, 42*, 48, 49, 77*, 81, 96, 97, 106*, 109, 122, 124, 127, 131*, 145, 175, 180*, 188*, 191, 210, 228, 233, 234, 245, 269, 276, 282, 296*, 298, 300, 306, 314, 315*, 324*, 342, 343*, 348*, 352*, 359*, 366, 393, 404, 406*, 412, 413, 429, 441, 457, 494, 497, 538*, 541, 569, 578, 583*, 586, 589*, 595, 632*,

660, 679, 683*, 690, 692, 693*, 713*, 722, 729, 740, 757, 758, 759*, 775, 787, 788, 790, 797, 798, 800, 802, 803, 807*, 810, 818*, 820, 827, 828, 864, 894, 897, 937, 939, 941*, 957*, 961, 977, 1033, 1046, 1058, 1064, 1083, 1088, 1092, 1094, 1104, 1123*, 1132*, 1152*, 1153, 1168, 1169*, 1193, 1200*, 1213, 1223, 1245, 1246, 1255, 1274, 1280, 1285, 1291*, 1296*, 1300, 1337, 1345, 1364, 1365, 1369, 1386, 1387, 1399, 1409, 1411, 1424, 1467*, 1475*, 1489, 1492

feoffment, *xlin, liii*, 106, 210, 232, 342, 494, 589, 1257, 1345, 1364

festivals, *see* feast-days, feasts

field, *see* land usage

fifteenth(s), *see* tax

fire (conflagration), 967n

fire (domestic), access to, *see* easement

firepan, *see* household goods

firewood, *see* crops: wood

firing (sedges and turves), 598

fish (in pond), 90

  (in stock), 256

  for poor (herring), 342n

fishery, 253*

  fish-trap, 253*

fishing equipment, 1489

  net, 256, 1489

fish-kettle, *l*

fishing-lake, 1122

fishmonger, 489n

fodder, *see* crops

fold, liberty of, 1110, 1265

food (unspec.), at anniversary, *xlvii*

  at funeral, 1077, 1473

  at seven-day, *xlvi*

  for beneficiaries, 356, 1032

    for brother, 1001

    for daughter, 139

    for extended family, 408

    for father, 329, 572

    for grandmother, 408

    for mother, 228

    for ?relation, 1169

    for servant, 356, 823

    for son, 408, 1001

    for widow, 119, 155, 194, 337, 1032, 1096, 1113, 1273, 1331

    for workmen, 109

food and drink, for beneficiary, 1169

    for daughter, 517

    at funeral, *xlvi*, 20, 599, 640

    for servant, 1110

    at thirty-day, 1274

    for wife, 393*, 879, 911, 1001, 1310*

    see also food *above*

  ale, at funeral, *xlvi*, 15, 415, 683, 1005

bread, at funeral, *xlvi*, 15, 20, 44*, 415, 683, 1005

  at seven-day, 44, 683

  at thirty-day, 683

cheese, at anniversary, 457

  at funeral, *xlvi*, 15, 20, 415, 1005

  for wife, 1495

foot (length), *see* measurement

forcer, *see* furniture

form (seating), *see* furniture

fraternity (of religious house), *xlix*, 487

  letters of, 413, 444*

  prayers of, *xlix*

  see also gild

Friday, alms for poor on, 49, 118, 301, 832, 1479

  mass to be celebrated on, 1181

fruit, *see* crops

fryingpan, *see* household goods

fuller, *see* cloth-making

funeral, *see* burial

fur, *see* material

furlong, *see* land

'furnace', *see* household goods

furniture and furnishings, *l*

  ark, *see* chest

  box, 160

  chair, *l*, 457*, 612, 1044, 1139

    necessary-chair, 612

  chest (ark, coffer, forcer, hutch), *l*, 49, 90, 112, 120*, 126, 211, 321, 326*, 333, 342*, 365, 368, 397, 420, 429, 457, 474, 548, 556*, 578*, 588*, 626*, 632, 682, 696, 726, 863, 1023, 1041, 1044, 1110*, 1253, 1265, 1274, 1343, 1409*

    black, 120

    iron-bound, 49, 126, 457, 682

    painted, 112, 578, 696, 1041

    'pruys' chest, 342*

    small, 1409

    spruce, 90, 365, 457, 588, 863, 1265

    with two locks, 1409

  coffer, *see* chest

  cradle, 696

  cupboard, 1265

  cushion, 421, 474

    banker, 321, 421, 474

  forcer, *see* chest

  form (seating), *l*

  hutch, *see* chest

  stool, 321

  table, *l*, 112, 158, 326, 385, 420, 474, 1398

    'clostable', 612*

    trestle, 326, 420, 474

furrour, *see* beds and bedding

gallon, *see* measurement

garden, *see* land usage

garnish (of tableware), *see* household goods

gate, churchyard, 1023
  'postlegate', 1279
  tenement, 288, 368, 402, 439, 566, 818, 1117*, 1162, 1194n, 1279, 1370*, 1402, 1404n
  town, *xlix*, 130n
gauds (paternosters), *see* beads
gild, *xlix*, 17n, 52, 78, 90*, 101*, 108, 112*, 120, 125, 142, 183, 203*, 278, 287, 289*, 302, 310, 321*, 335*, 342*, 343*, 351*, 357*, 369, 373*, 385, 387*, 390, 406, 415, 416*, 419, 429*, 430, 435, 444, 469, 471, 474, 489, 491, 492*, 569, 583, 589, 618n, 619, 624, 634, 639, 648, 683*, 696, 702, 708*, 723, 742, 749*, 756, 762*, 768, 772*, 772n, 775, 776, 777, 787, 798*, 817, 827, 842, 860, 879, 879n, 894, 894n*, 903, 916n, 932, 945, 958, 1026, 1031, 1035, 1052, 1052n, 1063, 1074, 1080*, 1082*, 1088n, 1132, 1152*, 1156*, 1165, 1216*, 1216n*, 1249*, 1249n, 1255, 1262, 1265, 1287*, 1289*, 1315, 1319*, 1327*, 1329, 1333, 1363, 1369, 1370*, 1371*, 1372, 1379, 1381, 1383, 1393, 1395*, 1396n, 1397*, 1403, 1403n, 1409*, 1422, 1424, 1427*, 1451*, 1462n, 1465, 1479, 1485
  fraternal membership of, *xlix*, 413, 444, 489
  funeral attendance of members of, *xlix*
  gild-chaplain, 416, 1485
  gildhall, 415n, 471, 595n, 613n, 772, 879, 894, 991n, 1052n, 1396n, 1403, 1419, 1462
  gild-torch, 1409
  as prayer-provider, *xlix*
  statutes of, 373
gild-patron (dedication), All Saints, 101, 203, 491, 634
  BVM, 17n, 52, 112, 120, 125, 203, 310, 342, 387, 429, 444, 469, 474, 491, 492, 762, 776, 894, 903, 1052, 1052n, 1082, 1152, 1216, 1289, 1319, 1369, 1451
  Corpus Christi, 90, 335, 373, 415, 569, 708, 903, 1156, 1255, 1327, 1403, 1403n
  Holy Ghost, 289, 342
  Holy Trinity, 90, 108, 142, 183, 289, 302, 357, 406, 419, 435, 583, 618n, 619, 639, 648, 683, 702, 742, 756, 775, 777, 787, 798, 817, 860, 932, 1035, 1052n, 1080, 1165, 1216, 1265, 1315, 1371, 1372, 1383, 1397, 1422, 1427, 1479
  Jesus, 916n, 1329, 1363, 1365, 1395, 1424
  St Andrew, 373, 749, 1379
  St Augustine, 1216
  St Christopher, 278, 429
  St James, 321, 1132
  St John the Baptist, 90, 112, 256, 289, 321, 335, 343, 357, 387, 430, 589, 696, 708, 749, 762, 842, 879, 894, 958, 1074, 1082, 1216, 1216n, 1249, 1249n, 1262, 1289, 1319, 1333, 1370, 1381, 1397, 1465
  St Katherine, 683, 708, 1156, 1327, 1370
  St Margaret, 125, 287, 351, 945, 1031, 1249, 1409, 1451
  St Martin, 1152
  St Peter, 78, 287, 321, 335, 342, 343, 369, 385, 390, 492, 723, 879, 903, 1026, 1063, 1287, 1371, 1427, 1485
  St Peter and St Paul, 101, 416, 624, 798, 827
  St Thomas, 321, 351, 357, 1080
gilt (gilded), 175, 421*, 982, 1463
girdle (belt), *see* clothes
glebe terrier, 1094n
goblet, *see* household goods
godchild, 46, 49, 53, 56, 57, 59, 69*, 81, 95, 101, 110, 113, 124, 131, 133, 146, 150, 158, 159, 171, 175, 177, 183, 193, 204, 231, 238*, 247, 248*, 271*, 278, 286*, 288, 289, 302, 308*, 311, 316, 335, 342, 346*, 347, 362, 368, 369, 380, 390, 393, 421, 429*, 444*, 471*, 474, 488, 491, 492, 517*, 529*, 539, 552, 611, 624, 626, 633, 640*, 643*, 654, 682, 713, 723*, 779, 794*, 799, 812, 816, 818, 823*, 827, 889, 891, 894, 908, 927, 930, 958, 977, 995, 1001*, 1003, 1008, 1033, 1052, 1054*, 1076n, 1082, 1084, 1104*, 1110, 1123, 1155*, 1156, 1162, 1164, 1186, 1191, 1194, 1206*, 1216, 1217, 1231, 1237, 1238, 1240, 1244, 1248*, 1252, 1258*, 1262*, 1276, 1278, 1279, 1288, 1293, 1295, 1299, 1306, 1307, 1315, 1334, 1337, 1346*, 1357, 1358, 1364*, 1371, 1400*, 1409, 1418, 1419*, 1441*, 1458, 1459, 1469, 1471*, 1473, 1474, 1479, 1495
godparent, 302n, 444, 1186n
gold, cloth, 41*, 1048
  coin, 489
  chain, 583
  cross, 583
  (and silver) tabernacle, 566
good (real estate), 233, 282, 1153, 1213, 1423*
goods, insufficiency of, 48, 49, 688, 715, 810, 977, 991, 992, 1110, 1257, 1263, 1297
  only within jurisdiction, *xxxix*
  moneyworth of (value in), 129, 346, 611, 942, 1119
  residue of, *lii, passim*
  in shop, 2, 1404
  in testament, *xlii*
  time allowed for removal of, 818, 864, 1036, 1052, 1280
  widow's own, 55, 204, 671, 871, 969, 1258, 1298
  see also bona notabilia; inventory
gown, *see* clothes
gradual, *see* church equipment: book
grain, *see* crops
granary, *see* building
granddaughter, grandfather, grandmother, grandson, *see* relatives
grass, *see* crops

grave, *xlv, xlvii*, 174n 896
  burial near, *see* burial, place of
  making of, 350
  paving over, *xlvii*
gravestone, *xlvii*, 803, 803n, 863, 1218
  brass on, 1218n
green, *see* land
gridiron, *see* household goods
grove, *see* land

hammer, *see* tools and equipment
haras, *see* crops
harness, bridle, 1240
  saddle, 358, 1240
  see also agricultural equipment
harrow, *see* agricultural equipment
harvesting, *see* agricultural work
hat, *see* clothes
hauberk, *see* weapons and armour
hay, *see* crops
headland, *see* land usage
hearth equipment, *see* household goods
hedge, 836, 1001*, 1246, 1260
heifer, *see* cattle
heir, *passim*
  daughter as heir, sons living, 1057
  heirs general, 1110
  heirs male, 81*, 131*, 406*, 549, 1110*,
    1246*, 1259*, 1279*, 1237*
  right heirs, 41, 96, 131, 394, 406, 683, 764,
    876, 1240
herbs, *see* crops
heriot, *li*
'heyr', *see* tools and equipment
holy water carrier/clerk, *see* parish officers
hood, *see* clothes
horn, 91
horse, *li*, 20, 96, 98, 114, 125, 126, 131, 150,
  245, 249, 257, 277, 278, 281, 289, 344, 358,
  417, 429, 430, 533, 544, 598, 611, 683, 692,
  696*, 708, 727, 740, 831, 861, 868, 890, 903,
  911, 962, 1001, 1014, 1041, 1052, 1119, 1169,
  1200*, 1233, 1238, 1240*, 1244, 1265*, 1296,
  1319, 1325, 1394, 1395, 1402, 1404, 1416*,
  1433, 1475*, 1483, 1495
  cart-horse, 254, 257, 556
  colt, 1402
  foal, 254, 727*, 861, 1319, 1433
  mare, 683, 727*, 1319, 1404
  named horses, 1200
  stot, *li*, 683, 683n
horse-mill, *see* agricultural equipment
hose, *see* clothes
hospital: Battisford, St John the Baptist, 1180
  Bury, by Risby gate, 130n
    St Nicholas, *xxxix*n, *xlii*n
    St Saviour, 891
  Eye, St Mary Magdalene, 1293

Hertford, Holy Trinity, 1216n
London, St Anthony, 1478n
  St Thomas of Acon, *l*, 1478
Norwich, St Giles, *xlii*n
house, *see* buildings
household goods (stuff, utensils, ostilments),
    (unspec.), *l, passim*
  'alestonde', 1201
  andiron, *l*, 358, 1044, 1089, 1139, 1237
  basin, *l*, 49, 63, 91, 114*, 269, 321, 342, 415*,
    415n, 417, 420, 421, 570, 612*, 632, 638,
    671, 680, 758, 764, 908, 1023, 1041*, 1044,
    1089, 1174, 1181, 1265*, 1398
    barber's, 612
    hollow, 342, 612
  bottle, 277
  bowl, 126*, 172, 385, 638, 1279, 1400, 1489
    with foot, 1400
    see also silver
  bucket, 333
  candlestick, *l*, 321, 368, 548, 795, 1041*, 1201,
    1265, 1453
  cauldron, 321, 326, 333*, 358, 385, 430, 556,
    578, 612, 764, 796, 908, 1039, 1343, 1463
  chafing-dish (chafer), 321, 663
  charger, 45, 321, 638, 1041
  cup, 49, 112, 113, 152, 421*, 803
    see also silver
  dish, 321, 385, 1041*, 1044, 1201, 1422
  dropping-pan, 1044
  ewer (laver), *l*, 49, 63, 91, 112, 114*, 321, 417,
    420, 421, 492, 570, 612, 632, 638, 758,
    764, 938, 1023, 1041*, 1044*, 1089, 1181,
    1265*, 1398
    hanging laver, 112, 492, 612, 1044
  firepan, 421
  fryingpan, 548, 796
  'furnace', 458, 1209
  garnish (of tableware), 231, 982, 1400*
  goblet, 421, 1216
    see also silver
  gridiron, 358
  hearth equipment, *l*
    see andiron, gridiron, spit, trivet
  jug, 691, 940, 1044, 1049, 1131, 1154, 1201,
    1265
  kettle, *l*, 399, 908, 1201
  knife, 1274
  laver, *see* ewer
  lead (vessel), 130, 214, 417, 458, 723, 1209,
    1421
    brewing, 130
    hanging in furnace, 458
  mash-fat, 1110
  mazer, *l*, 91, 126, 375, 421*, 446, 474, 578,
    588, 638, 803, 1115, 1117, 1174, 1181,
    1218n, 1276*, 1289, 1463, 1489
    see also silver

mill (hand), 113, 214, 723, 1306
  see also quern
mortar, 421
pan, *l*, 58, 96, 112, 113, 120, 122, 127, 160,
  229, 232, 251, 293, 320, 321*, 326*, 333,
  358*, 385*, 391, 421, 462, 546*, 548, 578*,
  589, 603, 632, 671, 677, 683, 684, 691,
  708*, 727, 735, 757, 796*, 816, 828, 830,
  831, 861, 908, 911, 963, 982, 1001, 1041,
  1044, 1089*, 1117*, 1131, 1139*, 1154,
  1174, 1181, 1201*, 1216, 1253, 1258, 1265,
  1268, 1295, 1353, 1375*, 1400, 1453, 1475,
  1489*
  'stelyd' pan, 326, 1117, 1201
  'stert' pan, 358
  see also dropping-pan; firepan; fryingpan;
    and under brass
peel, 1258
pewter ware, *see* pewter
plate (fireback), 130, 211, 214, 612, 982
  'saunseplate' (?), 214
platter, 385, 638, 1041*, 1044, 1422
porringer, 638
posnet, 358, 385, 394, 397, 548, 779, 830
pot, *l**, 49, 58, 112, 113, 122, 127, 133, 158,
  160, 172, 175, 232, 248, 251*, 277, 293,
  298, 320, 321*, 326*, 331*, 333, 342, 345,
  346, 358, 368*, 369, 391, 394*, 397, 399,
  415, 417*, 421, 430*, 458, 462, 464, 492,
  517, 533, 548, 556, 569*, 578, 589, 601,
  603, 632, 638, 663, 671*, 677, 682, 683*,
  684, 696, 708*, 723, 726, 727, 735, 741,
  749, 757*, 779, 794, 795, 796*, 798, 809,
  816, 830, 861, 908, 911, 933, 940, 963*,
  982, 992, 1023, 1039, 1041, 1044, 1058*,
  1063, 1079, 1088, 1110, 1117, 1139*, 1158,
  1174, 1181, 1183*, 1201*, 1216, 1258*,
  1265*, 1268, 1274, 1279, 1306, 1333, 1343,
  1375*, 1382, 1398*, 1400*, 1404, 1424,
  1433, 1453, 1459*, 1475, 1478, 1489*
  cooking-pot, 417, 933, 1058, 1183*, 1201,
    1258*, 1265*, 1279
  pot with handle, 49
  see also under brass
powder box, 421
quern, 351, 458, 1201, 1306n
  see also mill (hand)
razor, 440, 612
'raselle', 1110
salt-cellar, 321, 368, 421, 583, 929, 1400
  see also silver
saucer, 321, 638, 1422
silverware, *see* silver
spit, *l*, 321, 358, 385, 394*, 421, 430, 830,
  1044, 1089, 1139, 1154, 1201, 1237, 1258,
  1279, 1306
spoon, *l*, 49, 90, 91, 112, 113, 126*, 375*,
  446*, 474*, 548, 578, 583, 588, 612*, 638,

683*, 740, 803, 929, 1041, 1058, 1077*,
  1104*, 1115, 1117, 1139, 1174, 1216,
  1265*, 1276, 1279*, 1289, 1295, 1400, 1469
stand (?), 1343
standard, *xlvi*, 612
tongs, 612
treen, *l*
trivet, *l*, 358, 385, 430, 1044, 1139
trough, 112
  salting-trough, 211, 1201
tub, 385, 1131
vessel(s), 90*, 180, 286, 462, 469, 612, 663,
  831, 1131, 1191, 1400*, 1421n, 1475
  brass, 269, 705, 1121, 1313
  cooking, *l*
householder, 1240
huke, *see* clothes
hundred (administrative unit), *xxxix*n, 858n*
  (quantity), *see* measurement
hutch, *see* furniture

image, *see* church equipment
implements, of agriculture, *see* agricultural
  equipment
  of trade, *li*, 190, 219, 301, 440, 511, 535, 667,
    790, 820, 960, 1168, 1489*
  see also tools
indenture (deed), 112, 406, 409, 417, 1032, 1152,
  1162
  tripartite indenture 1246
  see also agreement; charter; deed; evidence
indiction, 97
indulgence (pardon), *l*, 180n, 580n, 899, 1216n*
inheritance, right of, 358, 1057*, 1224, 1291,
  1345
inn, 28, 270, 894, 1033, 1110*
  inn-sign, 270, 894
inscription, 863, 905n, 1069n
insertion, scribal, 146
interest (on money), 231, 1397, 1495
inventory, 249, 249n, 644, 645, 720, 1240, 1240n
iron, 960, 1495
  andiron, 1044
  bands (bound), 49, 126, 457, 683
  frying pan, 548
  gridiron, 358
  hammer, 1119
  handle (bail), 49
  plate, 211, 214, 612
  'shoe' (of cart), 277, 533, 911, 1052, 1240*,
    1265*, 1394
  soldering iron, 612
  spit, 394*, 421, 430, 830, 1139, 1154, 1279,
    1306
  standard, 612
  trivet, 430
  work (for laver), 612

jacket, *see* clothes
'jakke', *see* weapons and armour
jet, *see* beads
jewel(s) (unspec.), 157, 165, 186, 188, 258, 277,
    299, 402, 541, 740*, 758, 803, 818, 1048,
    1115, 1181, 1243, 1246*, 1253, 1280, 1489
jewellery, beads, *see* beads
    brooch, 175, 231, 803
    crucifix, 175
    pearl(s), 1169, 1174
    ring, 175, 231*, 803, 1097n
        silver, 626, 1009, 1343
jug, *see* household goods

Kalends (in date), 341, 387, 539
Kendal (cloth), *see* material
kerchief (kercher), *see* clothes
kettle, *see* household goods
kin, kinsman, *see* relatives
king's tax, *xlix*, 714, 758, 954, 1033, 1278
kirtle, *see* clothes
knife, *see* household goods, tools and equipment
    knives for poor at thirty-day, *xlvii*n, 1274
knight, knight of shire, *see* status
Knights Hospitallers, *see* religious houses

lake, 626, 871, 1121, 1256
lambskin/wool, *see* material
lamp (in church), *see* church equipment: lights
land (and property), *xlv*
    claim by widow to, 188, 286, 347, 441, 589,
        671, 1410
    false acquisition of, 758
    given to church, 889
    given towards payment of tax, *xlix*, 1033
    paying for, 833
    profits of, 807, 945, 1001, 1033, 1132, 1168,
        1169*, 1467
    re-entry upon, 756
    surrender of, 122, 122n, 408, 683
    of 'three days ploughing', 211
    in will (real estate), *l*, *liii*
land tenure, form of, bond land, 24, 63, 228*,
    257, 288*, 335, 609, 672, 674*, 711, 722,
    836, 949, 957, 1096, 1200, 1306, 1333,
    1373, 1465
    charter land, 254, 1269
    copyhold, *liii*, 18, 150, 264, 1416
    free land, 18, 24, 63, 228*, 254, 264, 298, 335,
        393*, 494, 609, 672, 674*, 711, 722, 949,
        957, 1096, 1238, 1249, 1258, 1285, 1333,
        1373, 1392*, 1437*, 1465
    lands of inheritance, 358, 1058, 1291
    purchased lands, 37, 55, 101, 124*, 232, 270,
        367, 388, 489, 497*, 552, 580, 658, 785,
        797, 807, 810, 827, 828*, 1113, 1142, 1162,
        1200, 1240, 1246*, 1279*, 1280, 1309
land usage, alder carr (grove), 992*, 1256

close, 2, 77, 124, 228, 385, 457*, 469*, 497,
    541, 552*, 609, 609n, 634, 641, 679, 683,
    711, 729*, 775, 812, 836*, 889*, 958, 969,
    1001, 1003, 1039, 1046, 1195, 1200*,
    1224*, 1225, 1240, 1246*, 1247, 1248,
    1274*, 1277, 1278*, 1334, 1370*, 1379,
    1386, 1399*, 1409*, 1417*, 1437, 1465*,
    1483, 1484, 1495*
    camping close, 609n
cotland, 337
croft, 2*, 49*, 77*, 90, 97, 124*, 176*, 228*,
    251, 259, 278, 290, 291*, 301*, 313, 314,
    334*, 353, 358, 375*, 387, 457, 458, 459*,
    463, 464, 490, 506, 521*, 529, 549, 552*,
    626*, 636, 643*, 681*, 799*, 807, 836*,
    864, 871, 879, 889, 897, 911, 927*, 941,
    954, 958, 965, 969, 986, 1001, 1008, 1024,
    1035*, 1089, 1104, 1131, 1153, 1155,
    1162*, 1209*, 1221, 1224, 1225, 1233,
    1248, 1258, 1260, 1262*, 1265, 1280*,
    1306, 1310, 1319, 1364*, 1368, 1388,
    1392*, 1403*, 1409*, 1423, 1469*, 1475,
    1495, 1497
curtilage, 96, 186, 342*, 367*, 446, 818, 861,
    1058*, 1274*
fen, 308*, 308n, 341n, 683n, 713*, 1153, 1403,
    1404*
field, 45, 46, 50, 57, 63, 77, 96, 97*, 124*, 139,
    160*, 191, 213, 222, 228, 232, 247, 251,
    253, 269, 270, 278*, 287, 298, 335, 358*,
    370, 374, 389, 393, 399, 422, 435*, 439*,
    441, 457*, 458, 469, 492, 531, 552*, 634,
    639, 683, 760*, 796, 800, 822, 827, 828*,
    858, 894, 911, 954*, 1001*, 1033, 1046,
    1083, 1131*, 1162*, 1169, 1195, 1200,
    1221*, 1224, 1225*, 1233*, 1240, 1246,
    1255, 1265*, 1269*, 1279, 1280, 1285,
    1291, 1297, 1319, 1325,1332, 1333, 1356,
    1367, 1394, 1403, 1409*, 1429, 1437*,
    1451, 1463, 1465, 1468, 1475*, 1495, 1497
    infield, 1309, 1309n
    open field, *liii*, 374, 1309n
    outfield, 1309n
furlong, 124, 457*, 552*, 723, 757*, 794*,
    827, 828*, 889, 954*, 1224, 1225*, 1248,
    1355*
garden, 90, 96, 155, 247, 296, 301*, 324, 334,
    342, 385, 412, 441, 457, 464, 507, 612, 623,
    632*, 638*, 713, 758*, 800*, 818, 848, 864,
    879, 1115, 1160, 1253, 1274*, 1280
    herb-garden, 464
    see also easement
green, 20n, 291, 294n, 623n, 836, 1237, 1237n,
    1285n, 1329n*, 1431n
grove (grovet), 269, 290, 421, 552*, 643, 1073,
    1307
    alder grove, 1256
headland, 827, 828, 1475*

marsh, 253, 727
  see also fen
meadow, 1, 19, 46, 96*, 124, 131, 188*, 204,
    205, 212, 228, 269, 279, 290, 298, 308,
    319*, 324, 340, 348, 385*, 388, 391*, 439*,
    441*, 443, 444, 457, 469, 478, 490*, 497,
    507, 529, 552*, 578, 580, 626*, 641, 665,
    672*, 674, 681, 682, 683*, 690, 711, 713*,
    723, 729, 800*, 864*, 867, 879*, 900, 903,
    941*, 949, 1005, 1046, 1063, 1097, 1117*,
    1131, 1150, 1162, 1169*, 1186, 1200, 1225,
    1241, 1246*, 1249, 1253*, 1255, 1259,
    1265*, 1269, 1273*, 1276, 1279, 1280*,
    1292, 1296, 1299, 1332, 1334, 1346, 1352,
    1368, 1371, 1382, 1383, 1386, 1397, 1403,
    1410*, 1416*, 1423, 1427, 1437, 1446*,
    1467, 1469, 1489, 1492, 1494
orchard, 800
pasture, 19, 46, 124*, 126, 131, 204, 205*,
    269, 279, 298, 319, 324, 340, 348, 385, 388,
    439*, 441*, 443, 444, 469, 490, 507, 552*,
    639, 641, 665, 681, 683, 690, 711*, 713*,
    714, 723, 727, 729, 790*, 864, 867, 879,
    900, 929, 954, 960, 1005, 1033, 1046, 1063,
    1097, 1200*, 1241, 1246*, 1255, 1269,
    1276, 1279, 1280*, 1292, 1299, 1332, 1334,
    1337, 1346, 1352, 1382, 1383, 1397, 1410,
    1427, 1437, 1467, 1494*
  common pasture, 457
pightle, 160*, 288, 391*, 439, 464, 506, 674,
    889, 924, 1035, 1224, 1260, 1265, 1271,
    1279, 1280, 1371, 1388, 1469
summerland, 1306
toft, 288, 457, 464, 1035, 1200
warren, 489, 489n
wood, 96*, 160, 234, 269, 290, 340, 348, 421,
    439*, 441*, 457*, 552, 674, 679, 740, 863,
    900*, 929, 1001, 1024, 1200, 1246*, 1253,
    1280, 1386, 1397, 1467
yard, 471, 740, 818, 864*, 1041*, 1104, 1110,
    1131, 1263, 1429, 1468
  courtyard, 1244*
latten, 1495
  candlestick, 741, 1201
  counterfeit, 91
  cross, 290
  lectern, 1365n
laver, *see* household goods
law, 2, 3, 4, 335, 441*, 446n, 790, 1252
lawn (cloth), *see* material
'le', use of, 1073n
lead, for church, 692*, 858, 1279
  vessel, 130, 214, 417, 458, 723, 1209, 1421
lease (farm), 165, 219, 235n, 288, 348*, 412,
    469*, 471, 471n, 521, 546, 702, 717n, 863,
    894n, 1033, 1164, 1200, 1249
leather, 164
  belt, 1104

doublet, 18
  measurement of, 375
lectern, *see* church equipment
legacies, payment of, *lii*
legend, *see* church equipment: book
Lent, 1001, 1313
leper, 187
liberty, of fold, 131, 1110, 1265
  of St Edmund, *xxxviiin*
licence, of husband, 391, 1247
  of king, 1080n
  of lord, 335*
  of superior, 588
light (in church), *see* church equipment
linen, *see* household goods *and* material
livestock, 594, 1001*, 1216, 1280, 1334, 1459
lock (on chest), 1409
loom, *see* cloth-making
lord of the fee, *see* fee
  of the manor, *see* manor

madder, 1421n
  'maderyngled', *see* cloth-making: dyer
maid, 197, 929, 1337, 1473*
malt, 6, 47, 57*, 77*, 90*, 101, 146*, 151, 162,
    169, 179*, 184, 185, 193*, 197, 246, 247, 251,
    278, 288, 295, 320*, 335, 343, 346, 351, 358,
    369, 404, 406*, 429*, 433, 461, 471, 474, 488,
    492*, 494*, 497, 541*, 594*, 599, 603, 613,
    658, 691, 693*, 723*, 740, 767, 827*, 854,
    873, 876, 894, 902, 908, 911*, 927, 1001*,
    1052*, 1054*, 1063, 1079*, 1082*, 1091*,
    1110*, 1121, 1131, 1133*, 1155*, 1164*,
    1172*, 1174*, 1192, 1200*, 1216, 1237,
    1240*, 1244*, 1260, 1276*, 1295*, 1298*,
    1299, 1325, 1332, 1334, 1343, 1353, 1357,
    1422*, 1495*
  barley malt, 47, 1343
  malt-kiln, 1495n
maniple, *see* church equipment: vestments
manor, *xxxviii, xliin, li, liii*, 28n, 41*, 41n*,
    46n, 90n*, 101, 122, 122n, 161, 165*, 165n,
    180*, 204, 300, 305, 305n, 315, 335, 348*,
    408, 459n, 489n, 552*, 553n, 682n, 683,
    717n, 784n, 820, 827, 828, 836, 836n, 838n*,
    877*, 877n*, 920n*, 1080n, 1115n*, 1169*,
    1169n*,1213n, 1216n*, 1225, 1246n*,1280,
    1333n, 1400n, 1403, 1416
  custom of, 122, 161, 204, 300, 408, 683
  lord (lady) of, *xxxviii, xliin*, 19, 41n*, 42n, 46n,
    90n*, 165, 165n, 204, 305n, 408*, 489n,
    553n, 682n, 683*, 717n, 836n, 838n*, 877n,
    920n*, 1041, 1080n, 1082, 1110n, 1213n,
    1246n, 1400n
  manorial court, *liii*, 122n, 300, 1416
  manorial heriot, *li*
manual, *see* church equipment: book
'marblestone', 803, 863

market (function), 1023
    cross, 768n, 1459n
    place, 329, 367, 415n, 492n, 520, 578*, 623,
        632, 719, 865, 870, 1009, 1035*, 1259
    poultry-market, 632
    stall, 50, 58n, 62*, 188, 329, 578*, 758*, 1023
marriage, agreement, 1023, 1023n
    bequest at/for, 20, 50, 53, 92, 180, 216, 231*,
        235*, 317*, 342, 439, 444, 506, 541*, 564*,
        578, 595, 633, 638, 679, 740, 757, 796, 801,
        842, 849, 929, 1001, 1023, 1046, 1063,
        1077, 1168*, 1181, 1246*, 1252, 1262,
        1279, 1364*, 1369, 1383, 1390, 1397, 1467,
        1489*, 1494
    maintenance of children before, 28, 279, 1370
    remarriage, of widow, *liii*, 37, 45, 46, 52, 78,
        124, 152n, 165n, 208, 214, 249, 277n, 279,
        284n, 367, 411, 421n, 456, 495, 497, 506,
        541, 589, 626n, 680n, 712, 730n, 741, 741n,
        757, 772, 813, 822, 828n, 838n, 843, 861,
        867n, 942n, 957, 1001, 1050, 1133n, 1257,
        1262, 1269, 1296, 1297, 1346, 1354, 1400n,
        1404, 1433, 1451, 1495n
        alias in name the result of, 152n
        of widower, 626
    wife's possessions before, 55, 671, 969, 1276n
marsh, *see* land usage
martyr, 55, 61, 69, 152, 160, 164, 290, 317, 346,
    348, 370, 397, 444, 456, 788, 1014n, 1201,
    1427
martyrology, *see* church equipment: book
mash-fat, *see* household goods
maslin, *see* crops
mass-pence, *see* burial
material (cloth, fabric, fur, etc.)
    blanket, 278, 517, 823, 1110, 1131, 1237,
        1265
    burnet, 91, 740, 1489
    card ('blewcard'), 146*, 175
    cloth (unspec.), 146, 337, 400, 541, 626*,
        1041, 1174
        see also cloths, household
    cotton cloth, 1295
    diaper cloth 828, 1131
    fur (unspec.), 45, 56*, 90, 172, 190, 207, 311,
        368*, 583, 588, 764, 877, 971, 1052, 1174,
        1274, 1276, 1295*, 1319, 1489*
        'bure', 583
        grey, 421
        mink, 863
        otter, 740
        rabbitskin, 146, 1295
        'wild work', 1044, 1295
    gold cloth, 41, 1048
    'Kendal', 493, 612
    lambskin/wool, 740, 863
    lawn, 493, 1295*
    linen, 91, 112, 113, 194, 271, 320, 344, 457,

        760, 790, 821, 1008*, 1174, 1216, 1313,
        1356, 1375, 1465
    medley, 193, 278, 541, 740, 1276, 1370
    motley, 877, 1169
    musterdevillers, 18, 790, 1437, 1451
    painted cloth, 588, 1356
    ray, 234, 278, 399
    'Reynes', 929
    russet, 33, 43, 131, 146*, 175, 190, 248*, 278,
        311, 320*, 421, 492, 529, 626, 636, 721,
        876, 945, 1131, 1265*, 1327, 1370, 1437
        Colchester russet, 474, 474n
    silk, 41, 49, 175, 529*, 578, 877, 1139, 1260n,
        1295, 1463, 1489
    tapestry-work, 91, 321
    'thred', 1295
    velvet, 863, 1169*
    woollen cloth, 113, 126, 180, 194, 234, 271,
        344, 454, 474, 544, 735, 740*, 760, 779,
        790, 821, 929, 977, 1079, 1125, 1125n,
        1158, 1216, 1231, 1313*, 1375, 1465
    worsted, 1169
mazer, *see* household goods
meadow, *see* land
measurement, units of, *x*
    bushel, *passim*
    cart-load, 375*, 385, 517*, 693, 1252, 1404
    coomb, 56, 57, 213*, 232, 246*, 288, 321,
        335*, 440*, 461, 488*, 492*, 691*, 723,
        742*, 767, 902, 908*, 963, 969*, 1054*,
        1079*, 1210*, 1220*, 1240*, 1257, 1272,
        1289*, 1325*, 1327*, 1422*, 1483, 1495
    days of ploughing (land), 211, 211n
        value of, 1306
    dicker (of hides), 375*
    dozen, 90, 735, 977, 1274
    foot, 278
    gallon, 96, 120, 123, 133, 160*, 248, 277,
        320*, 358, 369, 385, 397, 399, 417*, 458,
        533, 548, 589*, 677*, 696, 723, 726, 727,
        757*, 796*, 809, 816*, 828, 861*, 911, 933,
        982*, 992, 1001, 1063, 1117*, 1139, 1174,
        1183*, 1201, 1268*, 1295, 1353, 1375*,
        1478
        de pruse, 1001, 1001n
    hundred, (marks), 180*
        (wood), 566, 1495
        long hundred, (chaplains), 1279
            (masses), 97, 124, 124n, 708, 1279*
            (sheep), 708
    mark (money), *passim*
    noble (money), 326, 641, 1003, 1014, 1179,
        1195*
    peck, 146*
    perch (length), 247
    quart, 397
    quarter (grain), 18*, 77*, 90*, 101, 126*, 131,
        145*, 151, 158, 185, 186*, 203*, 222, 238*,

251, 278*, 284, 285, 310, 313*, 337, 343, 344, 368*, 370, 394*, 406, 421*, 429*, 440*, 488, 492*, 497*, 541, 544*, 594*, 598, 589*, 671, 682, 683*, 702*, 723, 740, 827*, 894, 903, 927, 960*, 995, 1001*, 1033, 1052, 1079, 1091, 1133*, 1143, 1164*, 1172*, 1192, 1200*, 1210, 1221*, 1244, 1252*, 1258*, 1260, 1276*, 1278, 1292, 1306*, 1325, 1327, 1333*, 1343, 1357*, 1388, 1451, 1478
  (wood), 158, 158n
  (year), 131, 1181, 1292, 1390, 1493
rood (land), 97, 160, 194, 237, 278*, 358, 469, 490*, 626, 672, 794, 871, 908, 954*, 1131, 1133, 1224, 1256, 1265, 1475*
score (twenty), 20, 90, 1240
stone (wool), 321, 1174, 1361
yard (length), 180, 186, 234*, 320*, 474, 517, 544, 1110, 1131, 1158, 1313
mediety (of ecclesiastical living), 457, 457n*, 796n
medley (cloth), see material
merchandise, 454
mercy, deeds of, see charitable giving
mere (boundary), 1052, 858n
metal, see brass, copper, gold, iron, latten, lead, pewter, silver
metes and bounds, 1489*
Michaelmas (use of word), 1361n
mill, corn, 188, 708n, 924
  hand, 113, 214, 723, 1306, 1306n
  horse, 394, 799, 799n
  see also windmill
mink, see material: fur
missal, see church equipment: book
Monday, payment to poor on, 130
  hammer by name of, 1119
month-day (thirty-day), xlvi*, 311, 380, 416, 683, 797, 1237n, 1274, 1298, 1364*, 1463
mortgage, 1213
mortar, see household goods
mortuary (principal), xlv, xlvi, li, 59, 95, 117, 124, 150, 159, 359, 440, 537, 549, 676, 807, 871, 900, 962, 1036, 1041, 1169, 1225, 1247, 1248, 1278, 1298, 1327, 1352, 1483
  mortuary-roll, xlix
moryeve (dower), 333
mother, mother-in-law, see relatives
mother church, xlivn, 19n, 50n, 399n, 958n
  of diocese, i.e. Norwich cathedral, 882, 1096, 1200, 1419
motley (cloth), see material
mural, see church equipment: painting
musterdevillers (cloth), see material

name, Christian, three brothers sharing same, 1398
  three sisters sharing same, 235

names for animals, 779, 963, 1200, 1200n, 1247, 1289, 1375
religious name, 297n
surname, occupation used as, 343n, 550n, 611n, 960n, 1067n
necessary-chair, see furniture: chair
need (poverty), widow (etc.) being in, 53, 86, 122, 132, 155, 160, 180, 198, 259, 288, 324, 356, 391*, 408, 538, 547, 658, 681, 714, 810, 827, 828, 895, 967, 977, 992, 1089, 1190, 1227, 1263, 1281, 1331, 1346, 1379, 1462, 1492
  see also poor
  poverty of parish, 180
nephew, niece, see relatives
noble (money), see measurement
nonage, 929
notary, see occupation
notarial instrument, liii, 97
  notarial sign, xli, 97

oats, see crops
obedience, see behaviour
obit, see church services: anniversary
obligation (bond), 1032, 1494
occupation, xliv, li, 446n, 611n, 1067n, 1087n
  as aid to identification, xliv
    see also name
  baker, 26n, 214, 818, 1153
  barber, 308*, 440, 443n, 548, 729n
  barker, 108, 144, 324, 402, 708, 1168
  blacksmith, 1160n
    see also smith
  butcher, 119n, 192, 317, 322, 446n, 749, 1330n
  carpenter, li, 219, 310, 562n, 767n, 820n, 905n, 908, 927, 1031n, 1132, 1132, 1179
  chandler, 329
  clerk (writing), 97, 97n, 146n, 313n, 338, 687n, 931n, 984n, 1008n, 1117n, 1343
  clothier, 102n, 300n, 618n, 717n, 1048n, 1441n
  collarmaker, 616
  cordwainer, 10n ('corvoser'), 53n, (?)56n, 517, (?)566, 1138, 1231, 1369
    see also shoemaker
  cutler, 1274
  draper, 346
  dyer, li, 398, 740, 790, 874, 1181, 1361, 1489
  farrier, 1119n
  fuller, 4n, 118, 226, 301, 380n, 430, 474, 559, 638, 1064, 1319, 1485n
  glover, 1067*, 1067n
  hawker, 1255
  'hewerys and leggers', 109
  husbandman, 124n, 150, 681, 147
  'legger', see 'hewerys'
  limeburner, 740
  limner, 611n, 933
  mason, 550n, 1387

mercer, 102n, 305, **693**, **744**, 749, 749n, **758**,
   803, **864**, 1194, 1279n, **1352**, **1481**
miller, **924**
notary, 97
painter, **296**, **414**
plumber, 692
saddler, 632*
scrivener, *lii*
shepherd, 1289
shoemaker, 865, 865n
   see also cordwainer
skepmaker, **119**
smith, *li*, 343, 343n, **404**, 762, 894, 945, 1119n,
   1339, 1405, 1409
   see also blacksmith
tailor, 221, 229, 273, 538, 1087, 1142, **1424**
tanner, 164, 1186, 1279n
tawer, **546**
warrener, 489*
weaver, **300**, 355n, 443n, 511, 541, 667, 803,
   1132, **1168**, **1181**, 1243
   see also webster
webster, 281, 552
   see also weaver
wheelwright, 1031n, 1238
woolman, **1441**
offer, (give, at service, shrine, etc.), 345, 346*,
   430, 1032
   (willing to pay), 278, 942, 1365n, 1463
offerings (to church), *xlv*, *passim*
official, archdeacon's, *see* archdeacon
oil (for lamps), *see* church equipment
orchard, *see* land
orders, holy, intention of taking, 46, 63, 446n,
   827, 1092, 1168
ordinary (ecclesiastical official), 346
organ, *see* church equipment
ornaments (of the body), *see* jewels
   (of a church), *see* church equipment
osmond (type of iron), 960
ostilments, *see* household goods
ox, *see* cattle

painted chest, *see* furniture
painted cloth, *see* material
painting (in church), *see* church equipment
pan, *see* household goods
panel (retable), *see* church equipment
parclose, *see* church equipment
pardon, *see* indulgence
parent(s) (living), 5, 18, 152, 158, 216, 228, 246,
   256, 280, 329, 368, 415, 446, 430, 495, 516,
   546, 564, 572, 595, 605, 611, 612, 631, 632,
   632, 661, 719, 735, 782, 810, 873, 916,
   1039, 1057, 1079, 1094, 1119, 1133, 1142,
   1165, 1200, 1302, 1306, 1327
   grandparent(s) (living), 408, 735
   (named), 5, 18, 47, 77, 152, 228, 231, 256, 280,

   287, 291, 358, 368, 394, 406, 421, 516, 546,
   595, 605, 611, 612, 631, 632, 661, 690, 719,
   735, 740, 741, 764, 782, 810, 827, 828, 849,
   916, 1003, 1039, 1133, 1142, 1152, 1170,
   1200, 1280, 1281, 1306, 1327, 1492
parish, civil, 20n, 252n
   ecclesiastical, *xl**, 20n, 252n
parish clergy, (general), bequests to, for prayers,
   xlviii
   as execs and supervisors, *lii*
   chaplain (unnamed), *passim*
   (named), 9, 18, 46, 48, 49, 79, 90*, 91, 114,
   126, 130, 137, 144, 145, 149*, 161, 169,
   180, 186, 192, 200, 211, 219, 241, 242, 248,
   263, 268, 284, 288, 298, 308, 310, 311, 316,
   333, 342, 346, 350*, 358, 362, 374, 380,
   398, 406, 421, 435, 439, 457, 489, 521,
   529, 537, 538, 539, 549, 561, 562, 569*,
   596, 632, 634, 672, 674, 682*, 683, 686,
   687, 692, 707, 719, 727, 732, 740, 757, 758,
   764, 773, 782*, 784, 803, 818, 822, 831,
   850, 864, 866, 871, 923, 929, 937, 938*,
   942, 954, 957, 958, 962, 1002, 1009, 1042,
   1088, 1089, 1090, 1117, 1156, 1181, 1216,
   1227, 1259, 1262, 1272, 1274*, 1275, 1280,
   1293*, 1299, 1313, 1335, 1352*, 1369,
   1370, 1371, 1387, 1417, 1419, 1422, 1448,
   1458, 1462*, 1463, 1475, 1477, 1484, 1486,
   1489, 1493
   chantry, 1131n
   employed to say masses, *xlviii*
   clerk (in holy orders) (named), 11, 12, 41*,
   69, 89, 90*, 102, 116, 118, 144, 157, 165,
   168, 185, 188, 193*, 208, 231, 270, 277,
   295, 314*, 315, 319, 365, 367, 409, 413,
   415, 430, 437, 438, 457, 469, 488, 489, 499,
   529, 586, 589*, 614, 632, 671, 674*, 692,
   708, 796, 807, 828, 842, 870, 876, 877, 878,
   941, 942, 944, 958, 1009, 1018, 1027, 1044,
   1060, 1119, 1123, 1174, 1255, 1260, 1265,
   1272, 1276, 1278, 1279, 1280, 1298, 1332*,
   1418, 1433, 1437, 1461, 1472
   curate, 288, 1181*, 1193
   deacon (at mass), 1473
   subdeacon (at mass), 1473
   parish chaplain, *xlv*, *xlvii*, 44, 108, 184, 190,
   248, 263, 271, 308n, 319, 325, 342, 345,
   402*, 446, 446n, 491, 499, 624, 767, 768,
   850, 865, 903, 962, 984, 1002, 1225, 1248,
   1256, 1278, 1319
   secondary, 345
   see also prayers
parson, 161, 193*, 193n, 347*, 368n, 1352
priest, (unnamed), *passim*
   (named), 142, 369, 471, 552, 671*, 1459,
   1459n
   celebrating masses for souls, *xlix*
   chantry, 108n, 193n

hired to celebrate, *xlviii*

parish, *xlvii*, 207, 254, 308, 308n, 316, 469, 471, 762, 894*, 944, 1077n, 1249, 1285

soul, 282

see also burial, prayers

rector (unnamed), *xxxix*n, *xlin*, *xlii*n*, 1, 3, 5, 11n, 15n, 17n, 18, 41n, 56, 59n, 60n*, 63n, 90n*, 99n, 114, 116n, 125, 126*, 126n*, 130*, 133, 137n, 144n*, 149n, 164, 168*, 169n, 185n, 203, 204, 204n, 213, 225, 225n, 227, 227n, 234, 234n, 213, 225, 225n, 227, 227n, 234, 234n, 247, 247n, 267n, 273, 290*, 290n, 299, 311, 311n, 314n, 339n, 347n, 351n, 353, 358n, 365n, 368, 369, 373, 382, 382n, 398n, 407, 413n, 415*, 415n, 419, 419n, 423, 427n, 438, 438n, 439n, 441n*, 457, 457n, 463, 471, 471n*, 487n, 492*, 507, 516, 529, 530, 536n, 538, 538n, 596n, 601, 603n*, 609, 609n, 615, 622, 622n, 632n, 676, 676n, 681, 682n, 690, 692, 692n, 723n, 732n, 745, 773n, 782n*, 783, 796n, 803, 807, 809, 824n, 831, 831n, 865, 876, 889n*, 892, 892n, 894n*, 895, 899*, 900n, 916, 916n, 929, 935n, 938n, 942n, 962n, 969, 969n, 1005, 1009n, 1033n, 1036, 1044, 1044n, 1049, 1060n, 1061, 1061n, 1078, 1119n, 1121, 1156n, 1158, 1158n, 1169, 1169n, 1181n, 1186, 1200, 1201, 1213n, 1220, 1221, 1238n, 1245n, 1249, 1250n, 1255, 1260*, 1260n, 1262n, 1269, 1279n*, 1285, 1300, 1300n, 1332*, 1332n*, 1333, 1340n, 1356, 1367, 1370n, 1379, 1381, 1387n, 1398, 1409*, 1437n, 1451, 1463n, 1465, 1466, 1472n*, 1484n, 1494n*

(named), *xxxix*n, *xlin*, *xlii*n*, 3, 11n, 15n, 17, 17n, 18n, 41n, 56, 60n*, 63n, 90n*, 99n, 114, 116n, 126, 126n, 130, 137n, 144n*, 149n, 168n, 169n, 185n, 204, 213, 225, 227, 234, 234n, 247, 267n, 273n, 290, 311, 311n, 314n, 339n, 347n, 351n, 353, 358n, 365n, 368n, 382, 398n, 407, 413n, 415, 419n, 427n, 438, 438n, 441n, 457, 457n*, 487n, 516, 529, 536n, 596n, 603n, 609, 609n, 615, 622, 622n, 632n, 676n, 682n, 692, 723n, 732n, 745, 773n, 782n*, 796n, 803, 824n, 831, 831n, 865, 878n, 889n, 892, 892n, 894n, 895, 900n, 916, 935n, 938n, 942n, 962n, 969n, 1009n, 1033n, 1036, 1044n, 1060n, 1061n, 1119n, 1121, 1156n, 1158, 1169, 1213n, 1238n, 1245n, 1250n, 1255, 1260n, 1262n, 1279n, 1300, 1332*, 1340n, 1367, 1370n, 1381, 1387n, 1437n, 1451, 1463n, 1466, 1472n*, 1484n, 1494n*

lay rector, 375n, 471n

see also prayers

vicar (unnamed), *xlv*, *lii*, *lii*n, 19n, 43, 43n,

50, 55, 90n, 97, 97n, 112, 113, 129, 130, 134n, 149n, 174, 175, 175n, 288, 288n, 289, 289n, 294, 294n, 295n, 306, 333, 339n, 387, 435*, 435n, 492n, 553*, 583, 610, 633, 645, 645n, 682n, 691, 691n, 696, 696n, 760, 764n, 800, 800n, 803n, 860, 865*, 865n, 881n, 886, 886n, 927n, 929, 931n, 941, 1083*, 1083n, 1088, 1088n, 1117, 1117n, 1121, 1121n, 1173n, 1181, 1181n, 1193n, 1207n, 1218*, 1218n, 1276n, 1280n, 1293, 1298, 1315, 1319, 1343, 1365n, 1384, 1385, 1451, 1462n, 1489

(named), *lii*, 19n, 43, 43n, 90n, 97, 134n, 149n, 175, 175n, 288, 289, 294, 294n, 295n, 339n, 413n, 435, 492n, 553, 610, 645n, 682n, 691n, 696, 764n, 800, 803n, 865, 865n, 881n, 886, 927n, 931n, 941, 1083, 1088, 1117, 1121, 1181, 1193n, 1207n, 1276n, 1280n, 1315, 1365n, 1462n, 1489

see also prayers

parish (church) officers, bedeman, *xlvii*, 126, 350

bell-ringer, 126, 350, 406, 415, 619, 633

chorister, 91

clerk (singing), 18, 28, 36, 55, 91, 108*, 109, 122*, 126, 130, 142, 144, 155, 164, 189, 192, 193, 195*, 207, 208, 210, 212, 254, 257, 278, 288*, 296*, 299, 300, 301, 306, 308, 309, 316, 319*, 320, 321, 333, 342, 348, 350, 365*, 376, 380*, 402, 415, 416*, 491, 497, 499, 511*, 529*, 538, 546, 548, 618, 619*, 682, 714*, 759, 768*, 790*, 797, 896, 901, 903, 939, 942, 1033, 1035, 1041*, 1048, 1064, 1068, 1077, 1080, 1091, 1092, 1126, 1134, 1194, 1216, 1237, 1243, 1280, 1293, 1298, 1315, 1319, 1331, 1357, 1243, 1280, 1293, 1298, 1315, 1319, 1331, 1357, 1388, 1364, 1409, 1417, 1468, 1480

holy water carrier/clerk, *xlvii*, 12, 108, 144, 308, 435, 469, 1100n

parish clerk, *xlvii*, 14, 50, 55, 56, 59, 60, 78, 96, 101, 108*, 124, 126, 144, 149, 169, 171, 174, 207, 226, 252, 271, 282, 294, 306, 343, 345*, 347, 353, 370, 393, 406, 421, 438, 457, 460, 479, 481, 491, 552, 583, 589, 599, 619, 623, 624, 674, 677, 679, 682, 713, 725, 740, 744, 777, 794, 796, 823, 827*, 828, 944, 964, 1002, 1039, 1054, 1113, 1172, 1248, 1255, 1272, 1278, 1289, 1332, 1334, 1395, 1409, 1468

reeve (warden), 415, 457*, 589, 991n, 1246, 1277, 1483

sacrist, *xlvii*, 12, 55, 60, 78, 126, 173, 174, 287, 294, 350, 370, 406, 491, 552, 690, 713, 744, 775, 783, 1039, 1054

sexton, *xlvii*, 576

warden, *see* reeve

parishes, consolidation of, 16n

parson, *see* parish clergy
parsonage, lease of, 235n
pasture, *see* crops, land
paternosters, *see* beads
patron saints, *see* advower; church dedication
payment, for or out of, property
  allowance (reduction) of, 57, 132, 144, 227,
    247, 326, 329, 354, 365, 391*, 547, 585,
    632, 641, 679, 691, 735, 842, 889, 1110,
    1240, 1252, 1256, 1262, 1281, 1295, 1346,
    1388, 1463, 1483, 1485
  arrears of, 90, 290, 409, 1259
  defaulted, and re-entry, 683, 760, 1152, 1259
  instalments of, 48, 91, 126, 969n, 1240, 1240n
  for soul, not to be hurried, 57
  see also land; purchase; rent
peas, *see* crops
peck (of grain), *see* measurement
peculiar (ecclesiastical), *xxxviii*, *xxxix**, 279n
peel, *see* household goods
pension, *see* annuity
perch (length), *see* measurement
petticoat, *see* clothes
pewter ware (pewter vessels), *l*, 45, 90, 231, 269,
  321, 358, 469, 474, 517, 612, 638, 828, 982,
  1115, 1175, 1265, 1400*, 1422, 1495
  charger, 45, 638
  dish, 1422
  platter, 638, 1422
  porringer, 638
  saucer, 638, 1422
piety, deeds of, *see* charitable giving
pig, *li*, 145, 254, 331, 351, 368, 375, 417, 430,
  544, 960*, 1131, 1200, 1306, 1495
pightle, *see* land
pilgrimage, *l*, 17, 20, 124*, 144, 175, 180, 212,
  288, 345*, 346*, 367, 393, 489, 552n, 677,
  708n, 889, 908, 971n, 1035, 1090*, 1090n,
  1207, 1207n*, 1209, 1259n, 1269, 1278, 1346,
  1364n, 1398n, 1432, 1459, 1466
  Beverley (Yorks.), St John, 489
  Bridlington (Yorks.), St John, 489
  Bury St Edmunds, St Edmund, 1207, 1207n
  Canterbury, St Thomas, 346, 489
  Compostella, St James, 17, 345, 346, 367,
    1035, 1432
  Eagle (Lincs.), St Edith (?*recte* Sitha), 489
  Ely, St Etheldreda, 1207, 1207n, 1466
  Hailes (Glos.), Holy Blood, 1398n
  Lowestoft, Holy Rood, 1207, 1207n
  Manston (Dorset), Maid of, 1466
  Norwich, Holy Trinity/Richard Caister, 1207,
    1207n
  Rome, 212, 393, 677, 889, 1269, 1278
    curia of St Peter and St Paul, 20, 124*,
      144, 288, 346, 908, 1209, 1459
    Scala Celi, 180, 1209

Southwold (Easton Bavents), St Margaret,
  1090, 1090n
Sudbury, 1466
Thorpe St Peter, 1207, 1207n
Tibenham (Nfk), St Nicholas, 1090, 1090n
Walsingham (Nfk), Our Lady, 175, 345, 346,
  489, 1090, 1090n, 1207, 1207n, 1466
Woolpit, Our Lady, 1090, 1090n, 1466
pillow, *see* beds and bedding
plate, iron, (fireback), *see* household goods
platter, *see* household goods
pledge (guarantor), 1041
plough, *see* agricultural equipment
ploughing, *see* agricultural work
  days of ploughing, *see* measurement
pond, 90, 247, 247n, 740, 836, 864, 1280
poor, bequests to, (of goods), of clothing, 144,
  271, 421, 474n, 714, 735, 790, 977, 1293,
  1313, 1409
  of firewood, 251, 1404
  of food, *xlvi–vii*, 15, 44, 47, 51, 151, 179,
    186, 207, 251, 254, 259, 278, 342n, 404,
    429, 461, 471, 640, 1079, 1274, 1343,
    1473
  of knives, *xlvii*n, 1274
  of livestock, 782
  of money (unspec. and unconditional),
    *xlix**, 3, 20, 41, 42, 61, 91, 131, 139,
    180*, 195, 208, 219, 254, 270*, 285,
    289, 290, 296, 306*, 311, 346, 367*,
    368, 369, 388*, 406, 415, 446, 448,
    462, 553, 619, 654, 676, 680, 692, 708*,
    712, 757, 775*, 800, 803, 831, 833, 877,
    903, 933, 940, 1009, 1032, 1097, 1097n,
    1110, 1117, 1120, 1126, 1134, 1156,
    1191, 1194, 1253, 1259, 1263, 1277,
    1279, 1280, 1348, 1382, 1388, 1417,
    1469
  bequests to, payable at anniversary, 573, 619,
    1110, 1032
  on burial day, 44, 90, 112, 149, 173, 183,
    260, 288, 314, 345, 365, 380, 416, 497,
    640, 714, 927, 1001, 1068, 1076, 1169,
    1459, 1473
  on seven-day, *xlvi-vii*, 44, 90, 380, 797
  on thirty-day, *xlvi-vii*, 380, 797, 1274
  weekly, 126, 402, 454, 768, 1115, 1280
    on Monday 130
    on Wednesday, 102, 570
    on Friday, 49, 118, 301, 832, 1479
    on Saturday, 511
  annually, in Lent, 1313
    on Maundy Thursday, 446
  in perpetuity, 231, 1110
  through gilds, 768
  bequests to, (status, situation), attending friary,
    270*

bearing torches, *xlvi*n, 1409
being blind, 479, 479n,
children, 529
being crippled, 258, 479, 479n, 714
in hospital, 1293
man (named), 1174
present at burial, *xlvi**, 20, 28, 108, 144,
301, 308, 342, 346, 348, 415, 479, 499,
529, 548, 797, 1216, 1255
woman (named), 640
women, 446, 1313
debts of, to testator, excused, 103
dwelling for, 376, 595n, 713
see also almshouse
tax on, relief towards, 1, 954, 1033, 1278
tithe-payments of, *xlv*
portasse, *see* church equipment: book
porringer, *see* household goods
posnet, *see* household goods
possession (seisin), 41, 77, 97, 188*, 269, 342,
343, 412, 457*, 520, 552, 586, 692, 740, 758,
802, 807, 818, 827, 894, 939, 941, 1035, 1036,
1083, 1213, 1223, 1255, 1274, 1300, 1399,
1409, 1475, 1492*
see also estate
'postlegate', 1279
pot, *see* household goods
poultry, 186
poultry-market, 633
poverty, *see* need
poverty of parish, 180*
powder-box, *see* household goods
prayers for souls, *xlv, xlvi*, *xlviii–ix**
'high altar payment' including, 210, 661, 1075,
1092, 1457
beneficiary to pray, 857, 1113, 1229
chaplain to pray, 47, 358, 362, 393, 1225, 1256,
1265, 1313, 1463, 1489
exhortation to pray, 1240n
friar(s) to pray, *xlix*, 50, 125*, 222, 347, 398,
406, 420, 421, 429, 444*, 672, 713, 740,
803, 806, 818, 879, 908, 939, 977, 1076,
1094, 1132*, 1168, 1200, 1468, 1489
mourners to pray, 1005
nuns to pray, 421, 1115
poor to pray, 1216, 1404
priest to pray, 58n, 90, 211, 398, 438, 517,
691n, 889, 1168, 1344, 1365, 1416
rector to pray, 415, 807, 1078, 1381, 1466
testator 'bound to pray', *xli*n, *xlii*n, *passim*
vicar to pray, 50, 633, 800
widow to pray, 19
price (spec.), of bed, 300, 421, 1433
cloth, 474
cow, 1001
gravestone, 803
horse, 1001
lands and tenements, 1240, 1295

malt, 1079
pan, 321
pewter, 321
plough, 1001
pot, 321
sheep, 1001
silver salt, 929
spinning(?) wheel, 321
spit, 321
torch, 1371, 1409
wool, 321
priest, *see* parish clergy
primer, *see* church equipment: book
principal, *see* mortuary
prisoners, relief of, *xlix*, 61, 130*, 187, 256, 1469
probate, *passim*
bona notabilia, xxxviii, 20
costs of probate, 1033, 1240n, 1410
inventory, *l* , 249, 249n, 644, 645, 720, 1240,
1240n
irregular probate, 645
jurisdiction, *xxxvii-xl*
peculiars, *xxxix*
Principal Probate Registry, *xxxvii*
Probate Act (1857), *xxxvii*n
probate sentence, *xlii, liv*
sede vacante, xxxviii
see also court of probate
procession, Corpus Christi, 566, 566n
processional, *see* church equipment: book
processional way, 569
burial in, *see* burial
promise, son's to father, 929
property, *see* land, purchase
psalter, *see* church equipment: book
purchase, preference in, of property, 188, 227,
247, 354, 391*, 641, 1110, 1155, 1240, 1252,
1281, 1388, 1429, 1463
see also payment
purgatory, *xlv–vi, xlviii, l*
'Pye' road, 439n
pyx, *see* church equipment

quart (capacity), *see* measurement
quarter (quantity), *see* measurement
quern, *see* household goods
quilt, *see* beds and bedding

rabbit, 489
'raselle', *see* household goods
ray (cloth), *see* material
razor, *see* household goods, tools and equipment
reckoning, 831
rector, *see* parish clergy
rectory (benefice), 160, 368n, 375n, 391, 471,
679, 796n, 878n, 894n, 1246, 1463n
(building), 124, 1195, 1260, 1280
re-entry, *see* distraint

reeve (churchwarden), *see* parish officers
register, will, *xl–xlv*
  binding errors in, *liv-lv*, 547n
relatives, brother, 9, 19n, 66, 77, 90, 157, 159,
    180, 186, 198, 228, 231, 246, 253*, 259,
    284, 295, 301, 315, 346, 355, 368, 385, 412,
    420*, 429, 438, 441, 458, 489, 497, 499,
    529, 541*, 549, 556, 566, 583, 610*, 610n,
    611, 612, 623*, 623n, 624, 631, 632, 649,
    696, 702, 714, 721, 735, 740, 767, 772,
    776*, 782, 810, 822, 823, 846, 865n, 902,
    930, 938, 947n, 960, 992, 1001, 1054, 1063,
    1079, 1088, 1119, 1156*, 1165, 1200, 1215,
    1257*, 1262, 1296, 1298*, 1310, 1327,
    1343, 1356, 1365, 1388, 1395n, 1402, 1451,
    1458, 1486, 1489
  brothers with same Christian name, 1398
  brother-in-law, 65, 610n
  cousin (incl. kinsman), 157, 180, 219, 271,
    311, 346*, 421, 446*, 600, 601, 683, 708,
    727, 735, 740, 995, 1183, 1418
  daughter, *passim*
    daughter-in-law, 723, 911, 1276, 1325
    stepdaughter, 164, 213, 222, 321, 334, 474,
      487, 683*, 754, 758, 1009, 1116*, 1364,
      1371, 1375, 1459, 1495
  father, 1*, 77, 90*, 92, 127, 192, 210, 231,
    254, 256, 280, 282, 287*, 291, 329, 358,
    376, 394, 406, 421, 429, 441, 497, 507, 516,
    564, 595*, 605, 611, 612, 631*, 661*, 690,
    719, 735*, 764, 788, 790, 810, 827, 849,
    863*, 916, 1003, 1008, 1039, 1057*, 1079*,
    1097, 1119, 1142, 1152, 1162, 1165*, 1170,
    1200*, 1213, 1216, 1246*, 1256, 1269,
    1280, 1302, 1327, 1433, 1451, 1465, 1474,
    1492*, 1493
    grave of, 69, 210
    father-in-law, 41n, 776n, 828*
  granddaughter, 130, 175, 321, 358, 375, 381,
    391, 397, 421, 433, 474*, 674, 726, 833*,
    893, 897*, 911, 958, 963*, 969, 1036*,
    1078, 1155, 1162*, 1210, 1229*, 1276*,
    1277, 1279, 1325, 1424, 1459, 1495
  grandfather, 735*, 1256
  grandmother, 408, 735, 1246
  grandson, 130, 132, 160, 180*, 213, 333, 358,
    375, 381, 391, 406*, 406n, 421*, 430, 433,
    438n, 469, 517, 534, 549, 674, 726, 833*,
    854, 897, 911, 958, 963*, 969, 1036*,
    1077*, 1089, 1162*, 1229, 1248, 1265,
    1276, 1277, 1347, 1403, 1410
  husband, 8, 64n, 113n, 116, 120, 123, 152*,
    152n, 172, 175, 196n, 211, 217n, 234, 280,
    289n, 311, 346*, 368*, 391*, 397, 423, 488,
    488n, 491, 493, 521*, 530n, 619, 626, 640,
    749, 759, 764, 777, 828*, 830, 835n, 862n,
    877, 898, 906n, 915, 922n, 925n, 944, 955n,
    963, 963n, 993, 1026n, 1032, 1035, 1044n,

    1049n, 1068n, 1075, 1087n, 1109n, 1110,
    1117*, 1137n, 1140n, 1154, 1158, 1171n,
    1206, 1218, 1228, 1234n, 1247, 1253n,
    1264n, 1275n, 1276, 1276n, 1295*, 1313,
    1360n, 1398, 1400n, 1422, 1449, 1461*,
    1466*, 1473, 1473n
  mother, 5, 18, 127, 158, 192, 228, 231, 246,
    254, 282, 291, 368, 406, 415, 441, 495, 507,
    546, 631, 661, 740*, 740n, 741, 741n, 782,
    788, 802, 849, 863*, 873, 903, 916, 1008,
    1039*, 1057*, 1079, 1094, 1097, 1119,
    1133, 1152, 1165, 1170, 1200, 1246*, 1280,
    1302, 1306, 1327, 1393, 1402, 1433, 1451
    agreement with wife, 228
    grave of, 69, 210
    mother-in-law, 152, 430, 632, 776n
    stepmother, 394n
  nephew, 159, 271, 347, 368, 385, 469, 556,
    612, 632, 690, 696, 783, 806, 823, 830, 960,
    1154, 1200, 1298, 1333, 1373, 1458, 1486
  niece, 133, 231, 271, 347, 566, 631, 719, 740
  sister, 180*, 185, 246*, 271, 288*, 321, 368,
    438, 471, 491, 492, 546, 583, 586, 608, 619,
    631, 711, 719, 735, 777, 782, 863, 864, 876,
    916*, 1039, 1125, 1133*, 1231
    sisters with same Christian name, 235
    sister-in-law, 152, 489, 556
  son, *passim*
    grave of, 211
    son-in-law, 131n, 178, 288, 340*, 393, 441,
      495n, 517, 574n, 1046, 1069n, 1117,
      1158n, 1169n, 1174n, 1211, 1313*
    step-son, 3, 45, 321, 334, 470, 624, 800*,
      942, 1319, 1459
  stepchild, 1459*
  uncle, 1492
  wife, *passim*
    pregnant, 18, 41, 87, 246, 276, 583, 706,
      735, 741, 757, 938, 1023, 1079, 1125, 1133,
      1200, 1224, 1379
release, of property, rights, etc., 41, 578, 589, 671,
    1410
religious (persons), abbess, 894n, 941n
  abbot, 160n, 180, 180n, 335, 713, 924, 1052,
    1200, 1475
  canon, 69, 180*, 254, 254n, 303, 321*, 321n,
    390, 390n, 497, 611n, 674, 702n, 827, 1033,
    1216n, 1225, 1225n, 1242, 1242n, 1399,
    1410
  cellarer, 180
  friar priest, 356
  friar (gen.), *xlix*
    (unspec.), 3, 18, 20, 47*, 50, 90, 122, 137,
      149*, 172, 247, 249, 285, 288*, 297,
      308*, 345, 355, 356, 379, 388, 406, 421,
      487, 488, 492, 499, 507, 599, 612, 619,
      682, 687, 708, 740, 756, 776, 777, 788,
      818, 833, 877, 903, 929, 1006, 1041,

119

1123, 1126, 1132, 1134, 1164, 1216,
1244, 1315, 1325, 1333, 1386, 1390,
1392, 1409, 1418, 1462, 1468, 1497
Augustinian (Austin), 17, 21, 41, 43, 44,
49, 50, 55, 56, 60, 69, 96, 97, 97n, 101,
112*, 118, 122, 124, 125, 126, 130, 132,
137, 149, 158, 164, 180*, 185, 188, 213,
249, 252, 261, 263, 270*, 271, 286, 287,
289, 303, 305, 308, 310, 317, 329, 345,
347, 351, 362, 377, 381, 388, 393, 416,
420, 457, 474, 511, 530, 537, 539, 548,
553, 599, 613, 619, 632, 643, 713, 726,
735, 776, 787, 790, 812, 818, 821, 822,
823, 832, 833, 860, 889, 891, 908, 939,
945, 964, 1035, 1036, 1058, 1063, 1079,
1083, 1091, 1094, 1123, 1142n, 1168,
1170, 1172, 1186, 1216, 1225, 1244,
1246, 1255, 1258, 1262, 1272, 1276*,
1279, 1280, 1302, 1343, 1363, 1368,
1371, 1375, 1382, 1395, 1397*, 1409,
1418, 1453, 1462, 1465, 1469, 1497
Carmelite (White), 17, 21, 47, 58, 60, 63,
105, 117, 129, 132, 158, 180, 261, 287,
350n, 352, 381, 393, 398, 413, 444, 457,
491, 497, 537, 539, 548, 548n, 549, 713,
723, 775, 790, 798, 822, 823, 921, 921n,
939, 1026, 1036, 1076, 1083, 1246,
1272, 1289, 1372, 1390, 1497
Carthusian (*recte* monk), 90
Dominican (Preachers), 5, 17, 46*, 49, 55,
63, 91, 96, 97, 97n, 108, 118, 124, 125,
126, 127, 128, 130, 132, 133, 137, 138,
157, 158, 180*, 182, 185, 186, 188, 208,
213, 231, 249, 252, 258, 261, 263, 271,
286, 287, 287n, 289, 294, 300, 304,
305, 308, 310, 317, 350, 356, 357, 362,
373*, 377, 381, 388, 393, 398n, 421*,
429, 438, 444, 456, 457, 474*, 489n,
521, 537, 539*, 548, 552, 599, 619, 632,
643, 663, 667, 672, 679, 684, 713, 723,
726, 740, 749, 758, 760, 776, 779, 782,
790*, 794, 798, 800, 803, 805, 806, 813,
816, 818, 821, 822, 823, 836, 842*, 860,
889, 920, 939, 941, 945, 964, 977, 1033,
1036, 1039, 1058, 1063, 1075, 1078,
1079, 1080, 1091, 1104, 1123, 1129,
1132, 1155, 1168, 1170, 1172, 1181,
1186, 1210, 1221, 1225, 1237, 1240,
1244, 1246, 1255, 1258, 1262, 1272*,
1274, 1276, 1279, 1280, 1289, 1302,
1312, 1314, 1333, 1334, 1337, 1363,
1364*, 1365, 1371*, 1395, 1397, 1402,
1409, 1418, 1427, 1437, 1439, 1441,
1451, 1465, 1466, 1467, 1469, 1489,
1495, 1497
Franciscan (Minors), 5, 17, 33, 34, 41, 44,
46, 52, 55, 56, 63, 90, 96, 97, 97n, 98,
103, 108, 118, 124, 126, 129, 130, 132,

133, 137, 158, 159, 164, 180, 185, 187,
213, 222, 228, 249, 252, 261, 263, 269,
270, 271, 286, 287, 289, 290, 294, 297,
301, 303, 305, 308, 311, 317, 321, 347,
350, 351, 352, 353, 357, 359, 362, 370,
373, 377, 381*, 385, 387, 388, 390, 393,
409, 438, 444, 449, 457, 463, 471, 474*,
494, 497, 537, 549, 552, 554, 583, 599,
616, 619, 643, 663, 676, 684, 692, 693,
708, 713, 717, 726, 735, 749, 760, 775,
776, 779, 782, 787, 790, 798, 806, 821,
823, 836, 854, 860, 867, 889, 890, 899,
930, 939, 940, 941, 945, 965, 969, 971,
977, 981, 1003, 1031, 1033, 1035, 1036,
1054, 1063, 1075, 1076, 1079, 1080,
1082, 1083, 1091, 1097, 1104*, 1123,
1129, 1156, 1158, 1164, 1170, 1172,
1183, 1186, 1191*, 1200, 1210, 1217,
1221, 1225, 1231, 1233, 1244, 1246*,
1255, 1258, 1265, 1268, 1272, 1276,
1279*, 1280, 1289, 1291, 1312, 1314,
1337, 1344, 1356, 1363, 1368, 1371,
1390, 1395, 1397*, 1409*, 1410, 1418,
1424, 1437, 1439, 1441, 1451, 1465,
1466, 1467, 1468, 1469*, 1495, 1497
Trinitarian, 1216n
hospitaller, 114, 1180
monk, *xlviii*, 90, 97, 160, 180*, 233, 297n, 479,
870n, 1240, 1424, 1424n, 1463, 1495
nun, *xlviii–xlix*, 17, 20, 49, 49n, 56, 59, 69,
90*, 90n, 124, 180*, 180n, 231*, 271, 286,
305, 305n, 347*, 377, 393, 421, 457, 479,
530, 539*, 588*, 599, 749*, 777*, 849,
894n, 983, 1115, 1115n, 1225, 1240, 1268,
1272, 1276, 1279*, 1302, 1315, 1441
pope, *l*, 180n, 580n, 1216n
(in date), 47, 97, 317, 391
St Gregory, 124
prior, 101, 180, 322, 352, 479, 489n, 674, 702,
827, 1033, 1181*, 1240
sub-prior, 674
prioress, 90n, 286, 421, 588
sacrist (monastic), *xxxix*, *xxxix*n*, 180, 279n,
574n, 1240
religious houses, *xlviii*
for individual houses *see* Index of People and
Places, *sub*:
BABWELL, house of Franciscan friars
BATTISFORD, preceptory/hospital of Knights
Hospitallers
BERMONDSEY (Surr), abbey of Cluniac
monks
BROMEHILL (Nfk), priory of Augustinian
canons
BROMHOLME (Nfk), priory of Cluniac
monks
BRUISYARD, abbey of Franciscan nuns

BURY ST EDMUNDS, abbey of Benedictine
    monks
    college of priests
    hospital by Risby gate (St Peter)
    hospital of St Nicholas
    hospital of St Saviour
BUTLEY, priory of Augustinian canons
CAMBRIDGE, house of Augustinian friars
    house of Carmelite friars
    house of Dominican friars
    house of Franciscan friars
    St Radegund's priory of Benedictine nuns
CASTLE HEDINGHAM (Esx), priory of
    Benedictine nuns
CHATTERIS (Cambs), abbey of Benedictine
    nuns
CHIPPENHAM (Cambs), preceptory of
    Knights Hospitallers
CLARE, house of Augustinian friars
COLCHESTER, abbey of Benedictine monks
    (St John's)
    house of Franciscan friars
    priory of Augustinian canons (St Botolph's)
DUNWICH, house of Dominican friars
ELY, cathedral priory
EYE, hospital of St Mary Magdalene
    priory of Benedictine monks
HATFIELD BROADOAK (Esx), priory of
    Benedictine monks
HERTFORD (Herts), hospital
ICKLETON (Cambs), priory of Benedictine
    nuns
IPSWICH, house of Carmelite friars
    house of Dominican friars
    house of Franciscan friars
    priory of Austin canons
IXWORTH, priory of Austin canons
KERSEY, priory of Austin canons
LONDON, hospital of St Anthony
    hospital of St Thomas of Acon
    house of Friars Preachers, Ludgate
    priory of Carthusian monks, Charterhouse
    priory of Knights Hospitallers, Clerkenwell
MALLING (Kent), abbey of Benedictine nuns
MARHAM (Nfk), abbey of Cistercian nuns
METTINGHAM, college of priests
MOATENDEN (Kent), priory of Trinitarian
    friars
NORWICH, college of St Mary in the fields
    hospital of St Giles
    house of Austin friars
    house of Carmelite friars
    house of Friars Preachers
    priory of Benedictine nuns, Carrow
ORFORD, house of Austin friars
RAMSEY (Hunts), abbey of Benedictine
    monks
REDLINGFIELD, priory of Benedictine nuns

ST OSYTH (Esx), abbey of Austin canons
SHEEN (Surr). priory of Carthusian monks
SPINNEY (in WICKEN, Cambs), priory of
    Augustinian canons
STOKE by CLARE, college of St John the
    Baptist
SUDBURY, college of St Gregory
    house of Dominican friars
    priory cell (Benedictine) of St Bartholomew
SWAFFHAM BULBECK, (Cambs)
    (?'Soham'), priory of Benedictine nuns
THETFORD, house of Austin friars
    house of Dominican friars
    priory of Austin canons
    priory of Benedictine nuns
    priory of Cluniac monks
WINDSOR (Berks), St George's chapel
remarriage of widow/widower, *see* marriage
rent (income from property), 41, 52, 90, 90n, 131,
    290, 314, 693, 717, 717n, 857, 1033, 1164,
    1249, 1259, 1260, 1404, 1469, 1496*
    (in firewood), 693
    (written down), 982
rental, 1237
repair (house, etc.), *see* buildings
    (road, etc.,) *see* road
resin, *see* church equipment
retable, *see* church equipment: panel
reversion (of right to property), 18, 41*, 41n,
    90n*, 245, 408, 538, 702, 818, 830, 864, 1168,
    1181, 1280*, 1492
'Reynes' (cloth), *see* material
river, 1150
road (*incl.* lane, path, street, way), 97*, 155, 160,
    188, 194, 238n, 247, 333, 334, 342, 367*,
    439n, 441, 457*, 529, 552*, 623, 682, 836*,
    858, 911, 1044, 1131*, 1218, 1221, 1225,
    1403, 1417n, 1423n*, 1475*, 1489
    processional way, 569
    repairs to, *xlix*, 34, 61, 88, 102, 137, 151, 161,
        169, 174, 180*, 181, 195, 222, 246, 287,
        290, 296, 306, 311, 320, 346, 357, 362, 367,
        368, 370, 388, 408, 429, 471, 479, 488, 507,
        543*, 566*, 580, 611, 639, 640*, 692, 711,
        723, 727, 768, 797, 807, 821, 822, 823,
        857, 858, 865, 870, 889, 893, 894, 901,
        903, 930*, 933, 945, 967, 992, 1001, 1009,
        1035,1036, 1082*, 1084, 1113, 1117*, 1126,
        1131, 1134, 1142, 1170, 1186*, 1218, 1225,
        1231, 1233, 1240*, 1253, 1255*, 1280*,
        1285, 1315, 1329, 1348, 1372, 1375, 1397,
        1402, 1404*, 1417, 1418, 1457*, 1463*,
        1469, 1485
    work with tumbrel on, 823
Roman road, 439n
Roman site, 1255n
Romescot, *see* tax
rood, roodloft, *see* church equipment

rood (land measure), *see* measurement
russet (cloth), *see* material
rye, *see* crops

sacrist (of church), *see* parish officers
   (of monastery), *xxxix*, 101n*, 574n, 1240
saddle, *see* harness
saints, *see* advower, church dedication, feast-
   days, feasts, gild-patron, image, pilgrimage,
   tabernacle
   litany of, 438
salary (stipend), of chaplain/priest, 20*, 45, 53,
   61, 63, 85, 102, 126, 130, 161, 164, 192, 221,
   264, 288, 314, 342, 346, 348, 350, 354, 358,
   374, 376, 388, 393, 400, 402, 416*, 444, 446,
   454, 457*, 489, 511, 546, 573, 632, 661, 677,
   708, 727, 740, 803, 805, 818, 865, 1002, 1009,
   1033, 1034, 1084, 1110, 1115, 1116, 1155,
   1186, 1216, 1262, 1265, 1274, 1296*, 1298,
   1313, 1334, 1340, 1359, 1369, 1370, 1395,
   1397, 1400, 1417, 1421, 1441, 1453, 1458,
   1459, 1462, 1463, 1473, 1494
   of pilgrim, 677
sallet, *see* weapons and armour
salt-cellar, *see* household goods
sand, 823
Saturday, alms to the poor on, 511
saucer, *see* household goods
Scala Celi, see ROME, *also* church services: mass
schedule, of debts, 1382
   of souls, 1424
   of will, etc., 97
school, schooling, 46, 446n, 682, 1194n, 1265
score (twenty), *see* measurement
seal, *xln*
   coin used as, *lii*, 1080, 1080n
   of dean, 1493
   official seal, 44, 47, 69, 145, 180, 193, 232,
     283, 284, 289, 313, 315, 324, thereafter
     passim till 428, 474, 553, 632, 671, 676,
     795, 807, 816, 863, 957, 1181, 1252, 1298,
     1365, 1367, 1403, 1417, 1489
   seal-tag, *xln*, *lii*, 40n, 402n, 868n
seating (in church), *see* church equipment
sedge, 598
sepulchre, *see* church equipment: Easter sepulchre
service(s) (for house, etc.), *see* dues
service(s), customary, 96, 160, 279, 343, 803, 828,
   1001, 1181, 1246, 1382
seven(th) day (after death/burial), *see* church
   services
sexton, *see* parish officers
shears, *see* cloth-making: fuller
shearman, *see* tools and equipment
sheep, *li*, 56*, 59, 61, 69, 95, 96*, 105, 124*,
   150*, 159, 180, 187*, 192, 227*, 237, 247*,
   251, 278, 281*, 287, 289, 290, 295*, 302,
   311*, 320, 331, 335, 344, 354, 358*, 369,

389, 394, 397, 399*, 417, 419, 430*, 438,
440, 464*, 471, 478*, 491, 492, 521, 530,
533*, 544*, 552, 556, 598, 626*, 633*, 639,
640*, 654, 665, 676, 682, 683, 691*, 696,
708*, 735, 742, 760, 779*, 782*, 807, 809*,
816*, 822, 823*, 831*, 865*, 889, 890, 891,
902, 903, 963, 969, 977, 984*, 1001, 1003,
1008*, 1044, 1054*, 1079, 1088, 1110*,
1121, 1162*, 1174, 1203, 1210*, 1219*,
1221, 1233, 1238*, 1240*, 1244, 1258,
1259*, 1277, 1278, 1288, 1289*, 1298,
1313, 1315, 1337, 1356, 1390*, 1398, 1404,
1433*, 1437*, 1459, 1475, 1478*, 1479,
1480*, 1497
   ewe, 59, 61, 69, 96*, 105, 124*, 150*, 159,
     187*, 227*, 254, 278*, 287, 311*, 335*,
     358, 389, 417, 419*, 430*, 478*, 491*, 530,
     552*, 654, 682, 691*, 696, 708*, 735, 760,
     779*, 823*, 865*, 891, 902, 903, 963*,
     984*, 1001*, 1003, 1044*, 1054*, 1088,
     1162*, 1174*, 1210*, 1238*, 1240*, 1244,
     1259*, 1337, 1390, 1433, 1437*, 1473, 1497
   hogg, hogget, 311*, 1313
   lamb, 56*, 105, 150*, 251*, 254, 287, 295,
     302, 335*, 369, 417, 419*, 438, 491*, 492,
     556, 598, 633*, 681, 691*, 823*, 865, 903,
     984*, 1008*, 1044, 1054*, 1162*, 1174,
     1258*, 1298, 1337, 1404, 1459, 1496
   wether, 61, 397, 696, 708*, 1240*, 1278, 1433,
     1478*
sheep-fold, 1289
   see also liberty of fold
sheet, *see* beds and bedding
ship (for incense), *see* church equipment
shoe, *see* clothes
shop, workshop, *see* buildings
shrine, *see* pilgrimage
shroud, *xlvi*
sickle, *see* agricultural implements
sickness, 1, 22, 24, 36, 41, 44, 54, 55, 63, 108,
   116, 118, 169, 186, 195, 231, 235, 258, 284,
   285, 286, 300, 301, 313, 320, 324, 374, 393,
   398, 415, 417, 438, 459, 469, 478, 489, 569,
   626, 806, 818, 832, 900, 929, 984, 1023, 1033,
   1033n, 1054, 1077, 1077n, 1089, 1092, 1181,
   1193, 1364, 1365, 1372, 1409, 1458, 1473
sign, inn, *see* inn
   notarial, *see* notary
silk, *see* material
silver, silverware, *l*, 49*, 90, 91, 126*, 152, 172,
   375*, 421*, 421n, 446*, 474*, 491n, 548, 578,
   583, 588, 612, 633n, 638, 683*, 740, 803, 929,
   1041, 1058, 1077, 1104*, 1115, 1117, 1139,
   1174, 1218n, 1265, 1276, 1279, 1289, 1295,
   1400, 1469, 1489
   bowl, 126, 172, 1279, 1489
   basin, *see* church equipment
   beads, *see* beads

cover, 421*, 583*, 588, 1400*
cross, 144, 1150
   stem, 290
cruet, *see* church equipment
cup, 49, 152, 421*, 803
   goblet, 421
   mazer, *l*, 638, 803, 1115
   piece, 474*, 583, 588, 929
   powder box, 421
ring, *see* jewellery
salt, 421, 583, 929, 1400
spoon, *l*, 49, 90, 91, 126*, 375*, 446*, 474*,
   548, 578, 583, 588, 612*, 638, 683*, 740,
   803, 929, 1041, 1058, 1077*, 1104*, 1115,
   1117, 1139, 1174, 1265*, 1276, 1279*,
   1289, 1295, 1400, 1469
   studs, 1139
silver-bound, mazer, 1463
silver-gilt, mazer-foot, 1218
silvered (harnessed, etc.), 91*, 144*, 152, 175*,
   394*, 421*, 529*, 548, 578, 583, 612, 764*,
   963, 982, 1041*, 1058, 1077, 1104, 1117*,
   1139, 1156, 1260n, 1265, 1274*, 1289, 1295,
   1364, 1437, 1463
sister, sister-in-law, *see* relatives
slay (in loom), *see* cloth-making: loom
slough, 1280
smock, *see* clothes
soldering-iron, *see* tools and equipment
son-in-law, stepson, *see* relatives
soul, health of, *xlv*
sowing, *see* agricultural work
spade, *see* tools and equipment
spinning wheel, *see* furniture
spit, *see* household goods
spoon, *see* household goods
spring, of water, 945
spruce (chest, etc.), 90, 365, 588, 863, 1001n,
   1265
stall, *see* market
   (not in market), 633, 1023*
stall, in church, *see* church equipment: seating
stand, standard, *see* household goods
statue, *see* church equipment: image
status (degree), *xlv-xlvi*, 180, 194, 228, 393, 415,
   1193, 1248, 1371
   abbot, *see* religious (persons)
   abbess, *see* religious (persons)
   apprentice, 157, 632*, 1033, 1181, 1186
   bailiff, 122, 416, 566, 1298, 1319
   bishop, 106, 210*, 210n, 428, 939, 1246,
   1246n
   burgess, 281n, 439
   canon, *see* religious (persons)
   chaplain, *see* parish clergy
   clerk (in holy orders), *see* parish clergy
   coroner, 69n
   curate, *see* parish clergy

dame (title), 180n, 294n, 489, 865
dean, 1493
doctor, 1142
esquire, *xliv*, **41**, 41*, **42**, 42, 46, 90, 97, 106,
   193, 201, 210, **231**, 293n, 375, 446, 489n*,
   491n, 493n, 507, 507n, 529, 552, 633n, 640,
   740, 776, 827, 828, 836, 838, 853, **863**, 876,
   877n, 911, 920, 1064, 1142, 1181, 1194,
   1213, 1216, 1240, 1246*, 1246n, 1280*,
   1390
friar, *see* religious (persons)
gentleman (gent.), *xliv*, 493*, 574, **583**, 683,
   729n, 863, 968, 1123, 1255
housekeeper, 346
knight, *xxxviii*, 41*, 41n, 90n, 231*, 281*,
   294n, 489*
   knight of shire, 920
lettered man, **1193**, 1193n
lord, keeper, 1240n
   mayor, 444n
   of the fee, *see* fee
   of the manor, *see* manor
Master (title), *xliin*, 15, 15n, 102n, 149, 158n,
   231, 280, 345, 362, 363, 413, 427, 441*,
   441n, 493n, 553n, 581, 588, 603, 682, 682n,
   692, 782n, 863, 865n, 889, 894, 900, 916,
   929*, 935n, 942, 942n, 1064, 1088, 1110,
   1117, 1121, 1142, 1162, 1181, 1186, 1216,
   1238, 1255, 1265, 1315, 1364, 1365, 1403,
   1462n, 1473, 1493, 1495
   (of hospital, etc.), *xxxixn*, *xliin*, 114, 489n*,
   800, 1180, 1216n
mayor, 69n, 214n, 800
   lord mayor, 444n
merchant (mercer), *see* occupations: mercer
monk, *see* religious (persons)
notary, 97, 97n
nun, *see* religious (persons)
official, archdeacon's, *see* archdeacon
   see also seal
parish chaplain, *see* parish clergy: chaplain
parish clerk, *see* parish officers
parish priest, *see* parish clergy: priest
parson, *see* parish clergy
poor man/woman (pauper), 144, 588, 640, 1174
priest, *see* parish clergy
prior, prioress, *see* religious (persons)
rector, *see* parish clergy
sacrist (monastic), *see* religious (persons)
   (parochial), *see* parish officers
servant, 41, 47, 69, 90, 91*, 95*, 133*, 150,
   157*, 160, 175, 180*, 192, 197, 203, 219,
   234, 254, 298, 300, 310, 317, 321, 335*,
   346*, 350, 352, 356, 357*, 362, 375*, 421*,
   429*, 440*, 474, 492, 493, 533, 583, 588,
   611, 683, 722, 740, 760, 790*, 823, 865,
   929*, 942, 969*, 1001*, 1023, 1033, 1064,
   1065, 1110*, 1133, 1168*, 1169, 1181,

1193, 1226n, 1238, 1240, 1255, 1278, 1315, 1398, 1400, 1453, 1473*, 1479, 1489*, 1496, 1437, 1438n
sexton, *see* parish officers
singleman, 207
vicar, *see* parish clergy
widow, *xxxix*n, *xliv*, *liii*, 41n, **64**, 64n, 90n, **116**, **120**, **123**, 165n, **172**, **175**, 196n, **211**, 217n, 219n, 227n, **234**, 271, **280**, **308**, **311**, **385**, **397**, **421**, **423**, 435n, **488**, 489, 489n*, **493**, 530n, **539**, **570**, **619**, **640**, 642n, 645n, 655n, 683n, 687n, 706n, 729n, **749**, **759**, **777**, **798**, **830**, **831**, 835n, 862n, **890**, **898**, 906n, **915**, 922n, 925n, 955n, **963**, 963n, **993**, 1007n, **1020**, 1026n, **1032**, **1035**, 1044n, **1049**, 1049n, 1068n, 1075n, **1080**, 1087n, **1089**, 1100n, 1109n, **1110**, 1110n, **1117**, 1117n, 1133n, 1137n, 1140n, **1154**, 1171n, **1206**, **1228**, 1231n, 1234n, 1236n*, 1244n, 1246, 1253n, 1264n, 1275n, **1276**, 1305n, 1360n, **1400**, 1400n, **1422**, **1449**, 1455n, **1457**, **1461**, **1466**, 1466n, 1473n, 1495n
yeoman, *xlv*, 1123, 1123n
of the crown, 489
steer, *see* cattle
stepchild, stepmother, *see* relatives
stipend, *see* salary
stock (animals), 1001*
(crops), 188, 245, 351, 1280, 1459
(money), 444
(possessions), 1280, 1334, 1459
see also livestock
stoddles, *see* clothmaking: loom
stole, *see* church equipment: vestment
stone (quantity of wool), *see* measurement
stot, *see* horse
stool (in church), *see* church equipment: seating
(in house), *see* furniture
'story' on painted cloth, 588
straw, *see* crops
Sunday, bede-roll on, *xlviii*, 1343
light to burn on, 233, 553, 1416
mass celebrated on, 1181
obit on, 640
supervisor (of executors), *passim*
appointment of, *li-lii*
duties of, *liin*, 968n
payment of, 180, 185, 204, 347, 381, 390, 469, 520, 693, 800, 822, 903, 968, 1035, 1200, 1255, 1298, 1356, 1358, 1367, 1469, 1473
surety (security), 77, 188, 359, 589, 683, 865, 1152, 1210, 1260
surname, *see* name
surplice, *see* church equipment: vestment
surrender (of copyhold), 122, 122n, 408, 683
sword, *see* weapons and armour

tabard, *see* clothes

tabernacle, *see* church equipment
table, *see* furniture
table-cloth, *see* church equipment: cloth; cloths, household
taper, *see* church equipment: lights
tapestry-work, *see* material
tax, including fifteenth(s), 1, 108n, 713, 945, 954, 995, 1033, 1278
land given towards tax, *xliv*, 194
Romescot, 1416
sheriff's aid, 995, 995n
tenant-in-chief, *liii*
tenter, *see* clothmaking
tester, *see* beds and bedding
thatch, 683, 683n
of buildings, 586
of church, 692n, 920n
thirty-day, *see* church services
'thred', *see* material
threshing, *see* agricultural work
thurible, *see* church equipment
Thursday, Maundy, alms to poor on, 446
tiles, *see* building
timber, *see* crops: wood
tithes, *xlv*, *passim*
to parish chaplain, *xlv*, 1002
toft, *see* land
tomb, 15, 15n, 345, 1207n
tongs, *see* household goods
tools and equipment, of craft, anvil, 1160
axe, 326, 385
beetle, 1119
belt (axe), 358
hammer, 326, 1119*, 1160
'heyr', 1253
knife, 440
razor, 440, 612
shears, 865
soldering-iron, 612
spade, 556
vat (tanner's), 164, 1186
of craftsman, barber's, 440
carpenter's, *li*, 219, 905n, 927, 1179
saddler's, 632
smith's, *li*
tanner's, 164, 375, 1186
weaver's, 667
see also agricultural equipment; cloth-making
torch, *see* church equipment: lights
towel (in church), *see* church equipment
town (used of village and small settlement), *passim*
traces, *see* agricultural equipment
transom, *see* beds and bedding
travis, 1160
treen, *see* household goods
trendle (in loom), *see* cloth-making: loom
trental, *see* church services

trestle, *see* furniture
trivet, *see* household goods
trough, *see* household goods
tub, *see* household goods
tumbrel, *see* agricultural equipment
tunic, *see* clothes
tunicle, *see* church equipment: vestment
turves, 598

uncle, *see* relatives
undercloth, *see* beds and bedding
underwood, *see* crops: wood
university of Cambridge, 15n, 929, 1133n
utensils (ostilments), *see* household goods

vat (tanner's), *see* tools and equipment
veghtam, 1325
velvet, *see* material
vessel(s), *see* household goods
vestment, *see* church equipment
vicar, *see* parish clergy
visitation, archdeacon's, *liv*, 605
    bishop's, 428

wages, of servants, 1278, 1473
    of workmen, 109, 692
    see also salary
wall, church, *see* church, building
    churchyard, *see* churchyard
    roadside, 247
    of tenement, 247
warden, church, *see* parish officers: reeve
warren, *see* land usage
waste, committing of, 77, 81, 124, 126, 164, 232,
    314, 406, 626, 639, 660, 1110, 1209, 1259,
    1279, 1297, 1389, 1410, 1467
    impeachment of, 314, 713, 1001
water, access to, 90, 441, 818, 864, 945, 1077,
    1258
    expanse of, 490, 1162
    watering, 945
    see also well
wax, for general church use, 321, 566*, 1343
    before altar, 516
    at burial, *xlvi*, 15, 345, 415
    before image, 385, 1174
    before sacrament, 233
    about Easter sepulchre, 81
    at shrine, 346
    for gild use, 619
    on seal-tag, 868n
weapons and armour, arrows, 18, 1240*
    axe, 91
    basilard, 91, 144, 529, 583, 803, 1058, 1274,
    1364*
    bow, 18*, 1240
    dagger, 394, 440, 1041, 1437
    defensive arms, 1489

hauberk, 91
'jakke' (defensive jacket), 529, 1265, 1453
knife, 1274
sallet, 529, 1240, 1453
sword, 91, 394, 1453
weaver, weaving, *see* cloth-making
Wednesday, mass to be celebrated on, 1181
    distribution to the poor on, 102, 570
well, 818, 864, 1263
    common well, 1077
    holy well, 1090n
wheat, *see* crops
widow, *see* status
    disputing will, 282
    remarriage of, *see* marriage
wild-work (fur), *see* material: fur
will, *passim*
    brought to court late, 1252, 1252n
    burial directions in, *xliv*
    commendation of soul in, *xliv*
    dating error in, 313n
    disputed, 706n
    in English, *see* English
    entered in later register, 827
    form of, *xlii-xliii*
    invocation in, *xliii*
    land (real estate) in, *xlii-xliii*
    made in open field, 374
    obstruction of, 1110, 1255
    'original', *xl*, *xl*n
    original with seal-tag, *see* seal
    preamble (notable) to, 421, 492, 571
    in print, *xxxvii*
    proved by archdeacon, *liv*
    read in house, 97
    testament within, *xlii-lii*, *liv*
    testament proved separately from, 1252
will, nuncupative, *xliv*, 8, 41, 42, 85, 98, 137, 236,
    300, 331, 423, 448, 449, 461, 464, 521, 572,
    622, 629, 640, 655, 662, 672, 687, 719, 720,
    767, 795, 838, 850, 853, 881, 892, 923, 929,
    931, 944, 967, 975, 1026, 1034, 1045, 1049,
    1055, 1057, 1065, 1067, 1088, 1090, 1120,
    1123, 1128, 1129, 1158, 1165, 1179, 1201,
    1203, 1206, 1207, 1217, 1223, 1227, 1228,
    1242, 1245, 1250, 1281, 1288, 1300, 1328,
    1344, 1384, 1385, 1389, 1398, 1448, 1461,
    1472, 1474
will 'proper', *xlii-xliii*, *lii-liv*, 2, 41, 77, 78, 90,
    91, 96, 106, 109, 114, 124, 128, 132, 137, 145,
    180, 188, 210, 228, 231, 232, 245, 248, 249,
    251, 295, 287, 289, 296, 301, 306, 308, 315,
    342, 346, 358, 366, 367, 391, 406, 408, 421,
    426, 435, 439, 441, 469, 490, 492, 497, 541,
    552, 572, 595, 671, 679, 690, 692, 693, 712,
    723, 725, 740, 757, 771, 772, 787, 800, 807,
    810, 818, 833, 836, 857, 861, 867, 895, 924,
    929, 941, 942, 957, 961, 1001, 1008, 1033,

1041, 1046, 1057, 1092, 1110, 1152, 1160, 1193, 1200, 1213, 1240, 1246, 1252, 1255, 1256, 1263, 1276, 1279, 1280, 1291, 1295, 1298, 1310, 1333, 1345, 1347, 1409, 1410, 1423, 1427, 1465, 1467, 1469, 1475, 1484, 1492
will registers, *xxxix–xl*
  assembling of, *liv*
  commendation and burial directions omitted in, *xlv*
  irregularities in binding of, *lv*, 342n, 692n, 716n, 786n
  references of, *xl*, *xl*n
windmill, 188
witness(es) (to will), *lii*, 3, 24, 41, 46, 69, 97, 109, 126, 144, 164, 247, 248, 253, 257, 270, 277, 308, 311, 311n, 316, 337, 340, 342, 350, 362, 365, 380, 381, 390, 398, 409, 415, 417, 423, 435, 448, 458, 464, 489, 489n, 516, 521, 529, 537, 541, 552, 569, 571, 580, 586, 622, 623, 632, 639, 655, 672, 674, 676, 683, 687, 719, 725, 727, 740, 744, 757, 758, 767, 795, 799, 803, 816, 818, 820, 822, 831, 833, 836, 850, 865, 865n, 892, 894, 894n, 923, 929, 931, 932, 941, 942, 1034, 1035, 1048, 1057, 1067, 1083, 1088, 1090, 1111n, 1117, 1123, 1151n, 1156, 1158, 1165, 1181, 1193n, 1201, 1213, 1217,

1227, 1228, 1238, 1242, 1245, 1246, 1252, 1259, 1274, 1276, 1285, 1288, 1300, 1315, 1331, 1353, 1369, 1375, 1386, 1387, 1417, 1441n, 1446, 1453, 1458, 1459, 1461, 1474, 1489, 1492
  omitted in register, *lii*
  to will 'proper', *liii*, 342, 740, 818
woad, 740*, 790
wood (area of), *see* land usage
  (timber), *see* crops
  wood-ash, *see* cloth-making
wool (unwoven), 126, 321, 454, 517, 638, 1174, 1361, 1364, 1441n
  cogware wool, 517
  fleeces, 626
  see also cloth-making; yarn
woolhouse, 464
woollen cloth, *see* cloth-making
woolman, *see* cloth-making
workshop, *see* buildings
worsted, *see* material

yard (ground), *see* land
  (length), *see* measurement
yarn, 126, 1364
yearday, *see* church services

Wills of the Archdeaconry of Suffolk
The Register 'Baldwyne' Part II
(Suffolk Records Society volume 53)

Index of People and Places

Italicised Roman numerals refer to pages of the introduction, but all other references are to item numbers, not pages. References in **bold** indicate which persons were testators, while *italic bold* shows that the item is a probate-sentence only, containing no will or testament.

Major place-names have been capitalized and given their modern form. Minor place-names appear under the relevant parishes and are spelt as in the original register. The counties of places not in Suffolk have been indicated, apart from well-known cities.

Modern forms of Christian names have been used but the original spelling of surnames has been retained and chief variants given. Where there are no means of differentiation, references may relate to two or more individuals bearing the same name. An asterisk * after the reference indicates that more than one person of that name occurs in that item; an 'n' following the reference indicates that the subject is to be found in a footnote to that item. The phrase '& family' signifies the mention of members of the family who are not named but simply described as 'daughter of', 'son of', 'wife of', etc. For named daughters, if they were married and their married name is given, they are so indexed and their maiden name indicated in brackets (née Abc); if they were (probably) married but no married surname is given, they are indexed under their birth surname followed by (née).

Abbreviations: BVM = Blessed Virgin Mary; Cambs = Cambridgeshire; Esx = Essex; Herts = Hertfordshire; Hunts = Huntingdonshire; Mdx = Middlesex; Nfk = Norfolk; unspec. = unspecified.

Abbott, John, 267
　Nicholas, of Chelsworth, **267**
　Thomas, 267
Abell, Alice, 548
　Anne, 548n
　John, 103, 615; of Thurston, **548**
　Margaret, 103
　Richard, of Stowmarket, *lxxii*n, **103**
　Thomas, 570
Abry, Thomas, 512
Ace, John, 331
　Petronilla, (née Mawdyon), 331
ACTON, church, 20, 83, 261, 311, 518, 651
　vicar of, *see* Thomas Webbe
　inhabitants of, 311, 431n, 651, 651n
　lands in, 651
　places in, 'Chaundelere' (tenement), 20
　poor of, 20, 311
　testators of, **20**, **261**, **518**, **651**
　way in, 261

Adam, Alice, 420
　Eleanor, (née), 420
　Giles, 191
　John, of Haverhill, **14**
　William, of Withersfield, **420**
Adgor, Edward, 103
Agace (Agas), Adam, 414
　Isabel, 338
　Joan, (née), 414
　John, 364
　Robert, 364, 364n; of Thurston, *lxiv*, *lxiv*n, **414**, 797n
　Roger, 74; of Bardwell, **364**, 414n
Akworth, John, 638
Albon, John, of Soham (Cambs), *749*
ALBY (Nfk), 166n
ALDHAM, church, 406
Aldhous (Aldows), Joan, the elder, 32
　Thomas, 89
Aleyn, Joan, of Bildeston, 359n

Richard, 'kerver', of Bury St Edmunds, 347
Simon, 545, 766
Thomas, clerk, 89
Algere, John, 637, 803
Alisandyr, *see* Alysaundre
Allington (Alyngton), William, esquire, of
    Bottisham, & family, 650, 650n
Alpe, Roger, 402
ALPHAMSTONE (Esx), church, 460
ALPHETON, church, 154
    inhabitants of, 151, 350
Alsey, John, 490
    William, 333
Alston, Isabel, 290
    John, & family, 290
    Thomas, of Sudbury, *lv*n, *lxii*, 189n, **290**
    William, 290
Alysaundre (Alisandyr, Alyesawndre), John, of
    Rushbrooke, **558**
    Richard, 30
    Robert, 558
    Thomas, 759; of Little Livermere, 684
Ameot, *see* Amyot
Amerowce, Richard, of Kersey, 283
AMPTON, church, 515, 538
    gild in, *lxii*n, 515, 538, 538n
    inhabitants of, 61, 66, 69, 114, 437n, 538n
    lands in, 515
    parson of, 538
    testators of, *lxii*n, *114*, **515**, **538**
Amyot (Ameot), John, 464; the elder, 446; the
    elder, of Melford, 733
Anable, John, 297
    Rose, 297
    Thomas, of Hargrave, **297**
Andrew(e), Geoffrey, 299
    Joan, 780
    John, 581; of Baylham, 89; chaplain of St
        Mary's Burwell (Cambs), 551n; of Bury
        St Edmunds, 61; of Hawkedon, **780**; of
        Hessett, 113; of Ousden, **696**
    Margaret, (née), 780
    Richard, 780
    Thomas, 780
    William, 780
Angold, Agnes, 58
    John, of Fornham All Saints, & family, **58**
    Lucy, 93
    Thomas, 58
Annes (Anneys, Aniys), Richard, of
    Wetheringsett, 778n
    William, of Wetheringsett, 64, 559
Annour, Robert, 467
Anty?, John, 374
Anyell, Robert, of Eye, 126
Appylby, John, of Bury St Edmunds, 66
Apylthorp, John, esquire, 789, 789n
Apylton, John, the elder, 83

Archer, John, of Lavenham, 552n
Arlond, Nicholas, & family, 572
Armesby, Joan, 142
Arnewey, Alice, 375
Artur, Geoffrey, of Wattisham, 111n
Aschele, Edward, 80
    Thomas, 80
ASHEN (Esx), places in, 'Stonyland', 46
ASHFIELD (unspec.), church, 639
    steeple of, 579
    lands in, 334, 639
    places in, 'Berardes' (tenement), 639
    testators of, **639**,
ASHFIELD, GREAT, church, 192, 362, 390, 415,
    667, 667n
    bell of, 390, 667
    candle before image of BVM in, 667
    inhabitants of, 743n
    lands in, 192
    testators of, **192**, **390**, **415**
ASHFIELD, LITTLE, church, 667, 667n
    testators of, **667**
    see also BADWELL ASH
Ashfield (Asshfeld), Florentia, 174n
    John, 338, 435; esquire, of Stowlangtoft, 174,
        174n
    Robert, 174n
ASHLEY (Cambs), church, 80
    inhabitants of, 623
    lands in, 80
    places in, cross, 80
        'Goystones' (tenement), 80
        rectory, 80
        'Roundell Pytell', 80
        'Volwencroft', 'Wolvencroft' (field), 80
    testators of, *lxxii*, **80**
    ways in, 80
        'Chevele Path', 80
ASPALL, inhabitants of, 280
Aspy, Alexander, 479
    [*unnamed*], of [*place not given*], **730**
Asshfeld, *see* Ashfield
ASSINGTON, church, 247, 370, 407, 458, 459,
    658
    chalice for, 459
    vicar of, *see* Robert Cutte
    inhabitants of, 311, 459
    lands in, 407, 459
    places in, 'Cogmans', 459
        'Levenheyheth', 370
        'Sowdens' (tenement), 407
    testators of, *li*n, *lii*, **370**, **407**, **458**, **459**
    ways in, highway from Leavenheath to
        Wissington, 459
Assy, Joan, 129
    William, 115, 488
Aston, John, 580
    Katherine, 580

Thomas, of Woodditton (Cambs), **580**

Asty, Thomas, vicar of Clare, 46, 276, 276n

atte Fen, William, of Glemsford, *lxxiv*n
  see also Fen

att Herne, Agnes, 72
  Andrew, 'bocher', of Icklingham, *li*n, **72**, **403**
  Isolde, 72, 403
  Katherine, 72
  Margaret, 72

at Ho(o), Isabel, 464, 464n; of Long Melford, 290, 290n
  John, the younger, 464
  Robert, 464
  Roger, 464
  Thomas, of Melford, 290n, **464**
  see also Hoo

at (the) Hyll(e), John, 233
  Matilda, wife of Thomas, of Glemsford, 662
  Nicholas, 550, 550n
  Thomas, 643
  see also Hyll

at Lee *alias* Hurlebate, Agnes, 370
  John, 370
  William, of Assington, *li*n, **370**
  see also Lee

at the Mere, William, of Cavenham, 77n

at the Tye, Walter, 131
  see also Tye

Attemore, John, 137

Aubry (Awbry), William, 579, 579n, 704, 786, 786n
  [*unnamed*], of Woolpit, **786**

Auncell, Thomas, the elder, 614; the younger, of Stanstead, **614**

Aunger, Robert, 372

Austyn, John, 107

Avbre, John, of Woodditton (Cambs), *lxi*n, **630**

Avenant, John, 241

Aves, Cecily, (née), 428
  Robert, of Exning, **428**, 450n
  [*unnamed*], Augustinian friar of Cambridge, 428

Awbyn, John, 247
  Margaret, 247

Awnselme, Henry, of Wyverstone, 140n

Awty, John, 568

Aylmer (Aylemere), Agnes, 248, 437
  Joan, 437
  John, of Thelnetham, **437**

Ayloth, William, of Hundon, 677

Aynoth, Alice, (née), 160
  John, 160; of Hundon, **160**
  Richard, 160
  William, 160

Ayschdon, Isabel, 676

Aysshfeld, *see* Ashfield

Baas, John, chaplain, 596

Robert, 218

BABWELL, house of Franciscan friars (Minors), *lx*, 1, 1n, 10, 11, 35, 37, 38, 39, 50, 65, 68, 72, 74, 78, 79, 80, 81, 83, 85, 87, 88, 93, 95, 101, 107, 109, 112, 115, 119, 120, 121, 125, 127, 128, 131, 133, 134, 135, 136, 138, 145, 149, 152, 154, 157, 159, 160, 168, 179, 180, 184, 191, 202, 205, 207, 209, 210, 219, 223, 227, 228, 238, 239, 240, 241, 243, 246, 253, 258, 260, 265, 266, 268, 281, 291, 294, 300, 302, 313, 317, 321, 322, 323, 324, 333, 334, 339, 348, 350, 361, 362, 365, 366, 367, 378, 379, 381, 388, 391, 392, 399, 404, 410, 415, 432, 436, 448, 451, 453, 454, 461, 467, 470, 477, 482, 485, 486, 490, 494, 502, 507, 508, 515, 519, 528, 529, 536, 538, 540, 567, 568, 569, 570, 573, 579, 588, 590, 591, 599, 604, 606, 609, 613, 615, 624, 625, 628, 634, 636, 647, 654, 655, 657, 665, 666, 668, 672, 681, 682, 700, 705, 706, 709, 712, 719, 723, 725, 733, 734, 738, 751, 754, 760, 770, 772, 773, 775, 779, 785, 786, 789, 792, 797, 812, 816, 817, 820, 821, 822
  burial at, 470
  burial ground of, 295
  church of, 651
  confraternity of, 751
  Friar Robert Brown of, 741, 741n
  Friar John Habyngton of, 760
  [*unnamed*], friar of, 109, 372, 381

Bacon (Bacun, Bako(u)n), Agnes, (née Turnour), of Drinkstone, 495
  Alice, 300
  Joan, 300*
  John, 231, 272; the elder, 113; 'smyth', of Brent Eleigh, *li*n, *lvii*, **300**; of Drinkstone, 495, 495n; of Hessett, 184
  Thomas, salter, of London, *lxxvi*n

Bacott, *see* Bakhot

BACTON, church, 495, 700
  inhabitants of, 700
  lands in, 495, 621, 694, 700
  places in, 'Denseys medowe', 700
  'Pynfold, le', 700
  ways in, lane to Cotton church 700
    way on north side of 'le Pynfold', 700

Badewyn, *see* Baldwyn

BADLEY, church, 89
  lands in, 344

BADLINGHAM, *see* CHIPPENHAM (Cambs)

BADWELL ASH, church, 527, 644, 644n
  inhabitants of, 207n, 527
  lands in, 644
  places in, 'Jestys' (close), 644
  testators of, *lxxv*, **527**, **644**
  wills proved at, 415, 625, 644, 777
  see also ASHFIELD, LITTLE

Badwyk, Richard, *lxxii*, 80

Baghot, Bagoote, *see* Bakhot
Baker(e), Agnes, (née), 822
    Alice, 751, 660n, (née), 224, 822
    Christian, (née), 751
    Helen, (née), 822
    Henry 687
    Isabel, (née), 822; widow, of Market Weston,
      822
    James, chaplain, 46
    Joan, 201, 739
    John, *li*n, 728, 728n, 729, 739, 822; the
      middle, 224; the younger, 224, 729; of
      Cavendish, **224**; of Glemsford, *lxi*n, **751**;
      of Stowmarket St Peter, *201*; of Wetherden,
      451n, **573**; & family, of Woodditton
      (Cambs), 630, 630n
    Katherine, 224
    Margaret, 148, (née), 822
    Margery, 573, (née), 739
    Ralph, 666
    Robert, servant, 89; Master, of Cambridge,
      822; of Stanton, **739**
    Thomas, 331, 480
    William, of Clare, 148n
    see also Shyllyng *alias* Bakere
Bakhot (Bacott, Baghot, Bagoote), Alice, 683
    John, 683; & family, 229; of Mildenhall, 107n,
      229, 230n, **287**
    Margaret, 229
    Richard, 229; of Mildenhall, 612n
    Robert, 119; of Icklingham, **683**; Master, of
      Mildenhall, 650, 650n
    Simon, rector of Worlington, 612, 612n
    William, mercer, of Mildenhall, 229n
Bakke, John, the elder, 344
Bako(u)n, *see* Bacon
Baldere, Ralph, 372
    Thomas, 372
Baldewyn, *see* Baldwyn
Baldre(e) (Baldry), John, 673; the elder, 661,
      673; the younger, 673; of Barningham, 771;
      of Thorney in Stowmarket, 673, 673n
    Margaret, 673
    Richard, of Thorney in Stowmarket, **673**
    Robert, 673
    Thomas, the elder, 673; the younger, 673
    William, 89, 673
Baldwyn (Baldevyn, Badewyn), Alice, 219
    John, 407, 458
    Katherine, 669
    Mariota, widow, of Assington, *lii*, **458**
    Robert, of Assington, 459
    Roger, of Rickmansworth (Herts), *lxvii*n
    Stephen, clerk, 152, 152n; 136, 136n
    Thomas, 786; of Woolpit, 704
    William, 219; of Moulton, 696
    [*unnamed*], missing from eponymous register,
      xlvi, lxxvii

Balery, Isabel, (née Chapman), wife of John, of
    Knettishall, 522
    John, of Knettishall, 522
Ballard, Henry, of Kettlebaston, **455**
    Joan, 455
    Margaret, the younger, 455
    Richard, 519
Ballard *alias* Canown, John, of Wickhambrook,
    787n
Balle, John, 692, 761; of Exning, 427; of
    Hitcham, *444*
    Katherine, 444
    Margaret, 211
    Richard, of Freckenham, 485
Balley (Bally), Katherine, 130
    Simon, of Little Whelnetham, 93n, **130**, 413n
    Thomas, 130
BALLINGDON, inhabitants of, 259
Balston, John, 503
Baly, Ann, 692
    Thomas, of Hanchet End in Withersfield, **692**
    William, 692
    see also Bayle
Bangatt, Sir Alan, 284
Banham, Robert, 240; of Wattisfield, 273
Bankes, Christopher, Master, notary public, 459n
Bantofth, Robert, 806
Banyard, Agnes, of Stoke by Nayland, 38
    Henry, of Bury, *lxxi*, 128
    Richard, 576
Barbore (Barbour), Alice, servant, 698
    Christian, 46, 662
    Christine, 456
    Emme, (née), 418
    John, 408, 738; the elder, 354; of Redgrave,
      418; of Sudbury, 505
    Petronilla, 408
    Richard, of Clare, *liv, lvii, lxn*, **46**, 276n
    Stephen, of Sudbury, **408**
    see also Rosshey *alias* Barbour
BARDWELL, church, 16, 159, 168, 241, 364,
    489, 526, 604, 738
    meadow of, 738
    sepulchre light in, 738
    vicar of, 526
    inhabitants of, 220, 241, 364, 414n, 489n,
      770n
    lands in, *lxxvi*n, 16, 159, 526, 604, 738
    manor of, 69n
    places in, 'Bowrys, le', 604
      'Brake ...' [*damaged*], 16
      'Caldwellemedewe', 738
      'Campsones', 16
      'Croftes, le', 604
      'Dolys', 738
      gates, 604
      'Gorys' (messuage), 738, 738n
      'Grenehowe' (furlong), 16

'Gunneldeys' (tenement), 738
'Lottes' (tenement), 544
mill-mounds, 159
'Netherfonton' street, 738
'Sondeweywent', 16
'Welhowsyerd' (croft), 604
testators of, 16, 159, 168, 364, 526, 604, 738
ways in, common way, 738
Barell, Avice, wife of George, 463
George, 463
Henry, 463
Robert, servant, 540; of Long Melford, 436n
Thomas, 463
Baret(t), John, of Bury St Edmunds, 444n
Lora (*Lore*), 466
William, 203, 554
Barker(e) (Barkar), Agnes, 820; servant, 698
Alice, *lxxiii*, 138, 490
Edmund, 490
Emma, 207, 227
Henry, of Clare, 46, 148
Joan, 301, 490
John, *lxxiii*, 138, 420, 490, 708, 761; the elder,
346; & family, 820, 820n; of Cowlinge,
lxvii, *lxviii*, **490**; of Culford, **227**; of Great
Thurlow, 490; of Thelnetham, 186n, 392n,
820n; of Withersfield, 356
Katherine, 490, 591
Margaret, 138
Nicholas, 138; of Ickworth, *lxxiii*, **138**
Richard, 142, 820, 821; of Wetherden, 573
Robert, 490, 573; & family, 820, 820n
Thomas, *lxxiii*, 138; of Hundon, 276, **301**; of
Thelnetham, **820**
William, 687; chaplain, 820, 820n; rector of
Rushbrooke, 191, 191n
see also Smyth *alias* Barkere, Wareyn *alias*
Barkere,
Barkere *alias* Judy, *see* Judy
BARKING (Esx), inhabitants of, 454
Barnard, Henry, 636
BARNARDISTON, church, 598, 655, 677
mortuary given to, *livn*, 598, 655
rector of, *see* Richard Simpson
inhabitants of, *lxxiv*n, 490, 598n, 655n
lands in, 655
testators of, *lin*, *livn*, **598**, **655**, **677**
Barnardiston (Bernardeston), Agnes, 447
Edward, 447
family, of Keddington, 447n
Henry, of Kedington, **447**
Isabel, 447
William, 447
BARNHAM, church of St Gregory, 282, 282n,
493, 578, 684, 699
rector of, *see* John Twychyn
church of St Martin (now lost), 282, 282n,
299, 493, 578, 699

chapel of BVM in, 699
image of BVM in, 699
rector of, 299
inhabitants of, 493n, 684n
lands in, 292, 293, 493, 578, 684, 699
places in, 'Palmers Brygge', 282
testators of, *ln*, *lxn*, *lxxvn*, **73**, **282**, **292**, **293**,
299, **493**, **578**, **684**, **699**
ways in, high street, 684
'Holgate' way, 282
BARNINGHAM, church, 16, 338, 411, 452, 555,
738
'Candlybem' in, 452
rector of, *see* William Coote
tabernacle of BVM in, 338
inhabitants of, 338n, 452, 555n, 771
lands in, 338, 411, 452
manor in, 411
places in, 'Alderbreche', 338
'Alfatysmer', 452
'Bastardeshill', 338
'Beltcrofte', 452
'Coldhamys' (tenement), 338n
'Daleclos', 452
'Delacrys', 452
'Ferthynges', 338
'Fystemer', 452
'Ryngoldysheflond', 338, 338n
'Stonhyll', 452
testators of, *lxxiv*, **63**, **338**, **411**, **452**
ways in, 'Stanton Weye', 338, 338n
'Westrete', 338, 338n
Baron (Barown), John, of Reach, 747
Richard, 351
Barough, John, of Bardwell, 770n
BARROW, church, 62, 136, 152, 502, 530, 531,
600
rector of, *see* George Hawys
inhabitants of, 62, 126n, 136, 152, 276n, 507,
530, 531, 600n
lands in, 62, 502, 530, 534, 600
manor of Denham near, 243n
places in, 'Aleyns' (messuage), 152
'Barghgrene', the green, 502, 600
'Harwellys', 600
'Holmys', 600
'Ketelys' (messuage), 152
'Molond', 502
'Py Rowe', 600
'Stevys', 600
poor of, 136, 152, 600
testators of, **62**, **136**, **152**, **502**, **530**, **531**, **600**
ways in, 'Burthorp' street, 502
BARTON MILLS, *alias* 'Berton Toryng', 243
church, 377, 379, 717
rector of, *see* Robert Lute
inhabitants of, 107n, 230n, 246, 379, 379n,
650, 754

lands in, 717
places in, common way, 228
private water way, 717
testators of, **379**, **717**
BARTON (unspec), inhabitants of, 705
BARTON, GREAT, church, 266, 736
    banner-cloth for cross in, 736
    vicar of, *see* William Bushy
    steeple of, *lvi*, 266
    inhabitants of, 266, 584, 736
    lands in, 266, 736
    testators of, **266**, **584**, **736**
Bas(s)e, Agnes, 367
    Nicholas, 416; of Rickinghall Inferior, **367**
BASSINGBOURN (Cambs), churchwardens'
    book, 626n
Batayle, Richard, gentleman, 295
Batell, Thomas, 782
Batman (Bateman), Agnes, wife of John, 808
    Joan, 377
    John, 297, 808
BATTISFORD, house of Hospitallers of St John
    of Jerusalem, 449n
    lands in, 275, 344
Baude [*or*, Bande], John, 704
Bax(s)tere, Joan, 42
    John, of Knettishall, 661
    Katherine, 42
    Margaret, wife of John, of Knettishall, 661
    Margery, 666
    Matilda, 661
    Peter, of Hundon, **42**
    William, of Hundon, 198; of Stanton, **666**
Bay, Alice, 385
    John, 385
Bayle (Bayly), Alice, 357
    Cecily, 377
    Henry, 673
    Joan, 196,
    John, 357, 357n; the elder, 692; & family, 655;
        of Hanchet End in Haverhill, **357**
    Rose, of Dover (?Kent), 196
    Thomas, 357, 357n
    see also Baly
BAYLHAM, inhabitants of, 89
Bedford, Nicholas, 23; of Little Thurlow, 91
BEDFORDSHIRE, mortuaries paid in, *livn*
    places in, 174n
BEDINGFIELD, lands in, 809
Bedwell, Alice, 827
    Hugh, of Mildenhall, **827**
    John, 827
Bedyngfeld, John, 764
Beere, Agnes, 237
    Alice, 237
    Denise, 237
    Joan, the younger, 237
    Katherine, the younger, 237

Margaret, of Lavenham, 190n, **237**
    Matilda, 237
Bek(ke), Agnes, 173
    Robert, 173
Bekon, William, 579
Bekysby, Robert, of Thorp Morieux, 613
Belamy, Robert, of Boxted, 133n, 803n
BELCHAMP (unspec) (Esx), inhabitants of, 163
BELCHAMP OTTEN (Esx), church, 290
BELCHAMP ST PAUL (Esx), lands in, 148
    places in, 'Wylwenhegge' (wood), 148
Bell(e), John, 334, 570, 571
    Roger, 324, 511
Belton, William, 126
Bemys, John, 587
Bend, John, of Great Whelnetham, 66
Bene (Been), Edmund, rector of All Saints',
    Stanton, 333, 333n, 566, 666, 680
Beneyt, John, of Thornham Magna, 193
Benhale, John, 331
Bensty, John, of Denston, 485
    Richard, 485
    William, of Herringswell, & family, **485**
Benttysle, Joan, 374
Benygth, Walter, friar, 276
?BERANS, testator of, *144*
Berard, John, 394
    Matilda, 394
    William, of Knettishall, *394*
Bercher(e), John, 365
    Robert, 37
Berd, John, 482
    Thomas, of Cotton, 788
Berd(e)well, Robert, 207, 644; esquire, 69
    William, Sir, knight, 372, 372n
?Bere, John, 350
Bereve, Roger, 205
Berhors, William, 602
Bernard, *Dido* [*or, Dide*], 606
    Margaret, (née), 606
    Richard, 606
    Robert, rector of Rattlesden, 57
    William, of Thurston, **606**
Bernardeston, *see* Barnardiston
Berne, John, 371
    Thomas, 371
Berner(e), Ellen, 197
    Isabel, 197
    John, of Stoke by Nayland, **197**; the elder, of
        Stoke by Nayland, 197n, 491n
Bernryve, Thomas, the younger, 517
Bertlott (Bertlote, Bretlote), Simon, 210, 498
Berton, Henry, 768
    John, 387
    Robert, 671
    see also Burton
Berweham, Adam, of Barningham, 338n, **452**
    Agnes, (née), 452; of Barningham, 452n

Geoffrey, of Ixworth, 452
Isabel, (née), 452
John, of Barningham, 452n
Margaret, 452
Bery, Joan, 534
John, Master, friar of Clare, 779
Beryle, Thomas, the elder, 552
Bete (Bette), John, 706; of Sapiston, 16
Thomas, subdeacon, 342
Betrich (Betryche), Robert, 331, 440
Bettes (Betys), Alice, of Badwell Ash, **527**
Edward, of Ipswich, *lvn*
John, 240, 313, 519; of Sapiston, 544n
Thomas, 451,
Beylham, William, of Stowlangtoft, 445
BEYTON, church, 74, 205, 821
inhabitants of, 560
testators of, **572**
BILDESTON, church, 284, 285, 303, 359, 360,
431, 484, 720, 721, 799
books in, 359
housling towel for, 360
ornaments in, 799
rector of, 303
see also Richard Swettock
thurible for, 303
torches in, 359,799
inhabitants of, 284, 303, 359n, 360, 431n, 613,
713, 720
lands in, 181, 284, 285, 484, 720, 799
places in, 'Bretoneslond', 721
'Calstok', 'Calst...', 720, 721
'Frelond', 'Frelonde', 720, 721
'Lokyn croft', 'Loke crofte', 720, 721
market, *lxxi*n, 359
'Parker(e)s' (tenement), 720, 721
shop in the market, *lxxi*n, 359
testators of, *lxxii*, *lxxii*n, 284, 285, 303, 359,
360, 431, 484, 720, 721, 799
ways in, 'Newberystrete', 285
wills proved at, 33, 43, 92, 96, 97, 104, 111,
153, 154, 181, 190, 274, 283, 284, 285,
298, 300, 303, 431, 433, 483, 484, 674,
712, 713, 720, 721, 799
Bird, see Byrd
BISHOP'S LYNN (Nfk), gilds in, 229
Bisshop(p), John, 183
William, 337
Blak(e), Joan, 717, (née), 717
John, 700, 717
Margaret, (née), 717
Thomas, of Barton Mills, 107n, 230n, **717**
William, 717; chaplain, 189
Blakpayn, John, 761
Blaunteyn, Isabel, 630
BLO' NORTON (Nfk), church, 522
Blogate (Blowgate), John, 180, 253, 313, 511
Blome (Bloome), Agnes, 540

Cecily, 173
Marion, 173
Peter, 540
Richard, of Ixworth, **174**; of Rattlesden, 536n
Robert, 173
Stephen, of Cockfield, *lxii*n, **540**
Blomevyle, Gilbert, of Little Stonham, 805
Blowere, John, 285
Rose, *lxxii*, 285
Thomas, 285; of Bildeston, *lxxii*, **285**
Blythe, John, 668
Bocher(e), John, 232; of Haughley, 180n
Robert, of Thorpe Morieux, 713
William, 332
see also Hecham *alias* Bochere
Bocher *alias* Grondysborgh, Thomas, of
Stansfield, 213n
BOCKING (Esx), deanery of, *xlv*, *xlv*n
Bockyng (Bokkyng), Joan, 332*
John, 332
Margaret, 332
Thomas, 332; the elder, of Boxford, **332**
William, 332
Bogays (Bogeys), Agnes, (née Cowpere), 247;
widow, of Edwardstone, 247n, **352**
John, 331; of Boxford, 352
Thomas, 352, 352n
William, 96; of Edwardstone, 247, 247n, 352,
352n,
Bokenham, John, 254; of Pakefield, 449n
Philip, 184, 584
[*unnamed*], friar of Dunwich, 799
Bokyll, John, of Elmswell, 519n
Boldiroo (Boldyro), Joan, 113
John, 113
Margaret, 113*
Margery, 113
Richard, of Hessett, **113**,
Thomas, 634,
Bole (Bolle), Joan, (née Orderych), wife of John,
587
John, 587, 721; of Garboldisham (Nfk), 561;
of Little Livermere, 129n
Rose, of Hartest, 183
see also Boole
Boleman, Joan, of Rattlesden, 90n
Bolowre, John, of Thwaite, **218**
Margery, 218
Bolton, Edmund, 89
Bolyngton, Herry, 262
Bond(e), Agnes, 562
Joan, of Tostock, **435**
John, 385; of Walsham, **562**
Robert, 435
Thomas, of Walsham, 16
Bonewell, Master John, monk (later, prior), of
Norwich, 790, 790n
Bonnell, Ralph, 576

Bonsergeaunt (Boneseriaunt), Adam, of
  Pakenham, *167*
  Margaret, 167
  Robert, 372
Bonyfaunte, Marion, daughter of Margaret Rolfe,
  732
  Matilda, daughter of Margaret Rolfe, 732,
  Thomas, 289,
Bonyng, William, of Little Horkesley (Esx), 141
Boole, Edmund, of Great Livermere, **134**
  Isabel, of Little Livermere, *lx*n, **129**
  John, of Garboldisham (Nfk), 132
  Margery, 129
  Roger, 129, 129n
  Sarah, 134
  William, Sir, 118
  see also Bole
Boorman, Henry, clerk of All Saints', Sudbury,
  259
Boourne, Stephen, 247
Boowstere, John, 285
Borgayn(e) (Burgeyn), John, *li*n, 677
BORLEY (Esx), inhabitants of, 59
Borugh, Roger, 381
Borwe, *see* Burwe
Boryball, Thomas, 67
Bosard, Thomas, 73
Boteler(e), Agnes, 221
  John, of Meppershall (Beds), 174n; of
  Palgrave, **221**
  Margaret, 221
BOTESDALE, *see* REDGRAVE
Bothe, Agnes, 697
  Alice, (née), 697
  Henry, of Shelland, *lix*, *lxvii*, **697**
  Joan, (née), 697
  John, 697
  Katherine, (née), 697
  Robert, 697
  [*unnamed*], Master, 786
Botildes, John, of Eye, 457
BOTTISHAM, inhabitants of, 650
Bottysham (Botilssham), Richard, chaplain of
  Barrow, 276, 276n, 531, 531n
Botwright (Botwryght), Ellen, 399
  John, of Lakenheath, *liv*, *lxix*n, **384**, **399**
Bouchier (Bourgchier), Henry, earl of Essex, 67n
  Thomas, archbishop of Canterbury, *xliv*n
Boule (Bowle), Henry, 43, 806, 806n
  Marion, (née Cabow), wife of Henry, 806n
Bover, Margaret, servant, 32
Bowes, Thomas, of Ware (?Herts), 530
Bowne, Katherine, relict of Thomas, of
  Mildenhall, 754n, 766n, **768**
  Margaret, *15*
  Thomas, 768; of Mildenhall, 768
Bowyere, John, *249*; of Bury St Edmunds, 816
BOXFORD, church, 70, 117, 247, 331, 332, 440

aisle in, 331, 440,
'clokbelle' of, 247
crucifix in, lamp burning before, 331
image of BVM in, 440
image of BVM on north side of, 247, 331
mitre and crozier for feast of St Nicholas
  in, 247
officials of, *lvi*n, 247
ornament for, 440
pinnacle or lantern on, 247
porch of, *lvi*n, 331, 332, 440
porch on south side of, 247
psalter for, *lviii*, 247
rector of, 247
tower of, 247
gilds in, 247, 247n, 331, 331n
inhabitants of, 247, 331n, 352, 698
lands in, 70, 117, 247, 331, 440
places in, 'Brounes, le' (tenement), 117
  'Byrchfeld', 247
  'Cotys' (tenement), 440
  'Coye' (tenement), 247
  'Dorys' (tenement), 440
  'Loverownys Wente', 331
  'Sowthfeld', 247, 331
  stone, the, 247
testators of, *lvi*n*, *lviii*, **70**, **247**, **331**, **332**, **440**
ways in, 'Cokkystrete', 247
  highway between Lavenham and, 339
  'Olywade' Street, 'Alywade' Street, now
    Stone Street, 117, 247, 247n, 332, 440,
    440n
  'Whigtstrete', 'Whytstrett', 331, 440
wills proved at, 54, 55, 247, 352, 353, 359,
  360, 460, 491, 556
BOXTED, inhabitants of, 133n, 332, 803n
  Mores manor in, 181n
Boys, Agnes, 243
  Joan, 243
  John, the younger, 243
  Robert, 243
  William, of Tuddenham, **243**
Braby, John, the elder, 71; the younger, 71
  Margaret, of Elmsett, *71*
Bradbrook, William, of Stradishall, *lxiii*, 785,
  785n
Bradfeld, William, 736
BRADFIELD COMBUST, church, 710
  lands in, 710
  places in, 'Wysys' (tenement), 710
  testators of, **710**
BRADFIELD ST CLARE, church, 66
  rector of, *see* Edmund Tylney
  lands in, 772
BRADFIELD ST GEORGE, church, 61, 270,
  583, 663, 672, 772
  light of BVM in, 672
  ornaments of, 61

rector of, *see* Walter Tylere
inhabitants of, 61, 270, 583, 772
lands in, 61, 583, 663, 772, 825
places in, 'Bakonnys croft', 583
  'Ballysdenhill', 583
  'Gylden Acre', 583
  'Harne(y)ssys', (tenement), 583
  'Magna Rawhawfeld', 583
  'Newecroft Morepytyll', 583
  'Smallwood Green', 583n
  'Templeres', 'Templerys' (tenement), 583
testators of, *lii, lxx*, **61**, **270**, **583**, **663**, **672**, **772**
BRADLEY, GREAT, church, 23, 56, 461, 642
  antiphoner for, 642
inhabitants of, 56, 457n
lands in, 56, 461, 482, 642
places in, 'Cowpers', 482
  'Pycotes' (croft), 56
testators of, *lxiii*, **56**, **642**
ways in, 'Mellestrete', *lxiii*, 457n, 642, 642n
  'Pycotes Lane', 56
wills proved at, 56
BRADLEY, LITTLE, church, 23
inhabitants of, 91
Bradstret(e), Joan, 523; of Little Whelnetham, **523**, 825, 825n
John, 523
Roger, 523, 523n, 825, 825n
William, of Little Whelnetham, 523n, **825**
Bradwater, Marion, 669
Richard, 669
Braham, Geoffrey, 796
John, the elder, 796
Brakstret, William, 468
Brame, John, 38; esquire, 409, 409n
BRANDON (FERRY), church, 377, 466, 776, 792
  altar of BVM in, 776
  image of St Michael for, 466
  latten candlesticks for, 776
  ornament for, 776
  painting of (image of) St Paul, 466, 466n, 776
gilds in, 466, 466n
lands in, 377, 776
places in, 'Archeres' (house), 776
  'Bolterys' (house), 776
  'Ferowres Yard', 776
testators of, **377**, **466**, **776**, **792**
wills proved at, 120
Brastret(e) (Braxstrete), Henry, 210
Robert, 210, 745
Simon, son of Robert, 745
Thomas, 745
William, 745
Bray, Agnes, 82
Alice, relict of John, of Barnham, **699**,

Joan, 82
John, 226, 699; of Gazeley, **82**; of Nayland, **761**; of Needham, 82
Katherine, 82, 385
Margaret, 82
Thomas, 82
William, 82, 699
Braybeff, Agnes, (née Browster), 359
Ellen, 359
John, 359
Robert, 359
William, of Naughton, 483
Bredstret, *see* Bradstret
Bregeman, *see* Bryggeman
Bregge (Brygge), Alice, 693
Robert, of Withersfield, 693
William, 249; of Hanchet End in Haverhill, **693**
Brende, Joan, wife of John, 519
John, 519
BRENT ELEIGH, church, 83, 122, 300
  window in, *lvii*, 300
lands in, 300
places in, 'Musteleres', 300
  'Parkfeld' (close), 300
  '?Priestowe' (meadow), 300
  'Wrenne Parke' (grove), 300
testators of, *lin, lvii*, **300**
wills proved at, 196, 197, 536, 716
Breon, Henry, 500
John, 83n; 'bocher', of Little Waldingfield, *lin*, **349**
Katherine, 500
Margery, 349
Thomas, 349
Bretlote, *see* Bertlott
Breto(u)n (Bretown), Richard, of Rickinghall Inferior, 820n
Robert, 544
Thomas, rector of Thelnetham, 820, 820n
William, of Dullingham, 646; rector of Euston, 820, 820n
Bret(t), Agnes, 784
Christian, 784
Richard, 784
Robert, 784; of Hunston, 415
William, of Nayland, **784**
BRETTENHAM (Nfk), church, 522
BRETTENHAM (Sfk), church, 298, 322
  bachelors' tapers in, *lxii*, 298
  chalice for, 322
  cope for, 298
inhabitants of, 298
lands in, 181, 322
places in, 'Goodales', 322
  'Rowlye', 322,
testators of, *lxii*, **298**, **322**
Breustre, *see* Browster

Brewer(e), John, 783
    Isabel, 783
Brig(g)eman, *see* Bryggeman
BRINKLEY (Cambs), church, 23
Brithwelle, John, 260
BROCKLEY, church, 35, 76, 125, 252, 682
    rector of, *see* John Taylore
    inhabitants of, 53, 76, 125n, 473n
    lands in, 76, 125, 473, 682
    places in, 'Heyfeld' (field), 76
        'Millars Crofte', 682
        'Stolis' (messuage), 53
    testators of, *lii*, **35**, **76**, **473**
    ways in, 76
    to Bury St Edmunds, 125
Broke, Agnes, 253
    Reginald, of Rickinghall Superior, **253**
Brokho(o)le, Agnes, 45
    John, of Long Melford, *lvi*, 45n, **363**
    Rose, 363
    Thomas, of Long Melford, **45**, 363n
Brome, Thomas, 587
BROMEHILL (Nfk), canons of, 429, 429n, 776
BROMHOLME (Nfk), priory of Clunaic monks,
    159, 159n
Bron, George, of Felsham, 705
    Joan, 705
    Robert, of Felsham, 705
    Thomas, of Barton, 705
    William, of Fornham St Martin, **705**
Brond(e), Alice, 247
    Joan, 117; wife of William, of Boxford, the
        younger, & family, 440
    John, of Boxford, 117, 247; the elder, of
        Groton, **117**, 247n; & family, of 'Olywade'
        Street, 247
    Matilda, 117
    Nicholas, 395,
    Robert, of Gislingham, 222, 581,
    Rose, (née Cowpere), 247,
Brondyssh, Thomas, 17, 369
    William, of Felsham, **369**
Brone, Robert, 557
Bronewyn, *see* Brunwyn
Brook(e), Agnes, 435
    Alice, of Sudbury, widow, **596**
    John, the elder, 408, 434; & family, 596, 596n;
        of Sudbury, 702; of Sudbury, weaver, 596,
        596n; the younger, & family, 596, 596n
    Richard, of Pakenham, 101
    Robert, 596, 596n
Broom, William, 471
Broun, *see* Brown
Brounewyn, *see* Brunwyn
Browdyere, Joan, 260,
Browgton (Broughton), John, esquire, 785, 785n
Brown (Broun), Elizabeth, & family, 170
    Geoffrey, 141, 170; & family, 439

John, 170, 189n 640; Sir, 38; of Cockfield, *lxx*,
    350; of Denston, 785; of ?Deopham (Nfk),
    34; of Hopton, 661n; rector of Hopton, 36n,
    186, 393, 555; of Wortham, **170**
    Marion, of Hopton, 661n
    Robert, friar, 240, 240n; of Babwell, 741,
        741n
    Thomas, 30; of Palgrave, 688n
    Walter, 170; of Bradfield St George, 61
    William, 119, 170
Brownyng, Alice, 678
    Margaret, 678
    Richard, of Haverhill, **678**
Browster (Breustre), Agnes, of Bildeston, *lix*,
    359, 359n, **360**
    James, 528
    John, of Bildeston, *lxxii*n, **359**, 360
BRUISYARD, abbey of Franciscan nuns
    (Minoresses), *lx*n, 89n
BRUNDISH, church, 348
Brundysche, *see* Brondyssh
Brunwyn (Bro(u)newyn, Brwnwyn), Joan, 788
    John, 788; the elder, 'mercer', 788, 788n,
    Margaret, 788
    Robert, 788; of Mendlesham, 559n, 568n, **788**;
        of Wetheringsett, **559**, 788n
    Thomas, of Wetheringsett, 559n, 788n
    William, 788n
Brustall, Rose, 667
Bryan (Bryon), Henry, of Troston, 760
    John, 549, 716; of Acton, 651
    Matilda, 549
    Richard, 549
    Roger, of Pakenham, 219
    Stephen, 549
    Thomas, of Nayland, **549**
    William, 416
Bryce, John, 504
Brycet(e) (Bryset(t)), John, 88; the elder, of
        Horringer, 10; the younger, 654
    Thomas, 432
Brygge, *see* Bregge
Bryg(g)eman (Bregeman, Brigeman, Brygman),
        John, of Burwell (Cambs), **551**
    Margaret, 551
    Richard, 9, 214, 551, 824; of Snailwell, 551n
    William, 9, 824; the elder, 214
Bryght (Brygth), Elizabeth, 52
    Joan, (née Othoo), 772
    John, 52; servant, 634; of Long Melford, **52**;
        of Thurston, 74
    Margaret, 52
    Robert, 52
    Rose, 52
    William, 663, 772
Brygthyew, Simon, of Lawshall, 541
Brykeman, John, of Hadleigh, 150
Brymmyng (Brynnyng), Thomas, 138

Brynglofe, Edward, 350
Bryon, *see* Bryan
Bryset, *see* Bricet
Brystowe, Thomas, of Exning, 450n
Bug(g)e, Alice, 823
 Andrew, 397, 397n
 Joan, 659
 John, 659; John, of Hall Street, Soham
  (Cambs), **659**, 823, 823n
 Richard, 823
 Robert, 659
 Thomas, 659
 William, of Soham (Cambs), 659n, **823**
Bugge *alias* Gronge, John, 498
Bukden, Agnes, 398
 Joan, 398
 John, 398
 Margaret, (née Wymbyssh), 398
 Robert, 398,
Buke, John, of Sudbury, 505
Bukkenam (Buknam), Thomas, 108
Bull, Stephen, 63
Bullebrook, Edith, of Whepstead, *lxvii*, **135**
 John, 135
 William, 135
Bullok, Joan, 211
 Thomas, 331, 548; of Thurston, 321, 364
Bullyngton, Henry, 728
 John, *lin*, 728, 728n
Bulsmyth, Thomas, 641
Bunne, Agnes, 93
 Alice, 93
 Isabel, 93; of Little Whelnetham, 93n, 413n
 Joan, 93
 John, 93, 413n; of Little Whelnetham, **93**, 130,
  130n
 Matilda, 93
Buntyng, Joan, 821
 John, of Tostock, 821n
 Richard, of Tostock, *lxn*, **821**
Burden, Roger, of Bardwell, 364
Burdews, Richard, 657
BURES, *xlvi*
BURES ST MARY, *xlvi*
 beadle of, *lvi*
 church, 51, 55, 67, 283, 309, 326, 354, 460,
  658, 781
  altar of St Peter in, 658
  bells of, 326
  candle for sepulchre in, 658
  light before image of Mother of Pity, in,
   460
  light before image of St Saviour in, 781
  panel for altar of St Peter in, 658
  vicar of, 283
  see also William Warner
 gilds in, 51, 55, 283, 283n, 326, 326n, 658,
  658n

 inhabitants of, 51, 55, 67, 354
 lands in, 283
 parishioners of, *liii*, 67
 places in, 'Bisshoppes', 67
  'Ferthynghoke, le', 354,
  'Heriotes' (tenement), 51
  'Tameres' (croft), 55
  'Tunmanholme' (meadow), 55
 testators of, *liii, lxix*, **51, 55, 67, 283**, 310,
  326, 354, 460, 658, 781
 wills proved at, 641, 658, 781
BURGATE, church, 170, 467, 522, 529, 718
 mortuary given to, *livn*, 718
 'Roode lofte' of, 718
 inhabitants of, 235, 416
 lands in, 170, 235
 testators of, *livn*, **715, 718**
 wills proved at, 323, 343
Burgeyn, *see* Borgayn(e)
Burgeys, Anne, servant, 89
 Robert, of Bury St Edmunds, 227; of Bury St
  Edmunds, 'barbour', 266
Burgon, Simon, rector of Elveden & master of St
  Nicholas's hospital, Bury, *xlvn*
Burgonye, John, 342
Burnell, Alice, 184
 Cecily, 711
Burton, John, friar of Sudbury, 32
Burwe (Borwe), Christine, 79*
 John, 79, 732
 Robert, of Hundon, *lxxii*, **79**, 380n
 Thomas, 79
 William, *lxxii*, 79
BURWELL (Cambs), church (unspec.), 234,
  234n, 509, 512, 514
 benches in, 514
 torches of, 512
 church of St Andrew, 215, 234n, 550, 626, 643
  bells of, *lvin*, 626
  missal of, 626
  parishioners of, *lvin*, 626
  wardens of, 626
 church of St Mary, 12, 215, 226, 233, 234n,
  551, 626, 631, 632, 732
  glazing of, *lvii*, 12
  rood-loft of, 12
 inhabitants of, 187n, 234, 289n, 512, 550n,
  626n, 631n, 732n, 732
 lands in, 215, 226, 233, 512, 514, 626, 631,
  632, 643
 places in, 'Belamyes Cornere', 626
  'Breche, le', 626
  'Dyschegate', 626
  'Dyschfeld', 626
  'Estbreche', 632
  'Estfeld', 'Estefeld', 626, 732
  'Larkedene', 626

'Northefeld', 'Northfeld', the North Field, 233, 632, 626, 732
'Northefenne', 632
'Rawlynesrode', 626
'Seint Tomers', 643
'Woodlaneshend', 626
testators of, *lvi*n, *lvii*, **12**, **215**, **226**, **233**, **234**, **289**, **509**, **512**, **514**, **550**, **551**, **626**, **631**, **632**, **643**, **732**
ways in, 'Foxleweye', 626
'Nessewey', 'Nesse Wey, le', 632, 643
'Newnham street, le', 12
'Northestret', 512
wills proved at, 226, 289, 631, 632,
BURY ST EDMUNDS, *xliv*
abbey of Benedictine monks, *xliv*n, *xlv*, 46, 68n, 128, 295, 432, 821n,
cellarer of, 821, 821n
church of, 291, 291n
churchyard of, *xlviii*n
hospitaller of, 128
lands of, in Icklingham, 492; in Rougham, 634
monks of, *lx*n, 88, 147, 636
new fabric of, 772
refectory, glazing of, *lvii*n, 519
sacrist of, *xlv*, *xlv*n, 826
tower of, 88, 88n
apprentice at, 803
archdeaconry of, *xlv*
church of St Mary, gild in, 88
college of priests in, *xlix*
Guildhall Feoffment of, *xlix*n
hospital in, 558n*
of St Nicholas, *xlviii*n
master of, *xlv*n
of St Peter (leper-hospital), *lxiii*, 126, 126n
of St Saviour, 128, 128n
inhabitants of, *xlv*, *xlv*n, *xlix*, *lxix*n, *lxxvi*n*, 61, 66, 68, 69, 114, 128, 134, 227, 266, 286, 347, 432, 444n, 539, 582, 586, 629, 629n, 738, 772, 816, 826
lands in, 181, 322
peculiar of, *xlv*
places in, Babwell (house of friars, actually in Fornham All Saints), *see* BABWELL
poor of, 311
ways in, 'Reyngatestrete', 181
road to, from Brockley, 125
'Rysbygatestrete', 126n
wills proved at, 334
Bury, Hugh, Sir, 69
Thomas, 471
William, friar, 670
Bushy, William, vicar of Great Barton, *lxxvi*n
Bussh(e) (Bussch(e)), Geoffrey, of Mendlesham, 6n, **202**
Isabel, 202

Margaret, 757
Richard, 202n, 229
Buste, John, 727
Thomas, 698
BUXHALL, church, 383, 398, 404, 591, 669, 786
gilds in, 404, 404n
inhabitants of, 180, 240n, 404n, 634n, 712
lands in, 275, 383, 398, 591, 786
places in, 'Aldewerk', *lxiv*, 383
'Banyardes', 404
'Combwall, le', 383
cross in 'Cherchestret', 591
'Hunteburugh', 1
'Hylles' (tenement), 398
'Jayes' (tenement), 398
'Paynys' tenement, 404
'Rysbyes' (tenement), 591
'Sohams', 398
'Terrent', 591
poor of, 90, 383
taxes of, *lxiv*, 240n, 383
testators of, *lxiv*, **383**, **398**, **404**, **591**
ways in, 'Bretonstrete', 383
'Cherchestret', 591
'Fenstrett', 591
wills proved at, 169, 478, 594
Byg(g)e, John, of Mildenhall, 230n
Thomas, 459n
Bygwood (Bygwode), Isabel, wife of Walter, 470, 470n
Walter, 470, 470n,
Bykby, Thomas, 557
Byll, John, 468
Byndere, Isabel, 761
Byrd(e) (Bird), Bryghtena, (née Marshall), 595
Isabel, 645*
Joan, 135, 645
John, 220, 645, 765; carpenter, 151, the elder, of Lavenham, **552**, 552n; the younger, 541
Katherine, 552
Margaret, 135
Robert, of Stowmarket, **645**
Rose, (née), 595
Stephen, of Kersey, husbandman, *lin*, **595**
Thomas, of Bradfield St George, 583,
William, 37
Byrlyngham, John, of Botesdale in Redgrave, **257***

Caase, Clement, 276
John, 276
Cabaw (Cabow(e)), Margaret, of Hitcham, 806n
Thomas, of Hitcham, **806**, 806n
Cag(g)e, Joan, 276
John, 362
Richard, of Cavendish, **574**
Robert, of Rattlesden, 797

Thomas, 623
William, 623
Cake, Elizabeth, (née Gavell) wife of Robert, of
    Stowmarket, *lin*, 648n, **689**
John, 818; of Mendlesham, 202n, 275n*,
    568n, **818**, 818n
Katherine, 818
Margaret, (née Neve), 275
Marion, (née), 648
Robert, *lin*, 202, 202n, 568, 689; & family,
    648; of Mendlesham, 275, 818, 818n
Thomas, of Mildenhall, 230n
William, 818
Cake *alias* Reve, Isabel, of Mildenhall, *lin*, **172**,
    177
John, 172
Margery, 172
Robert, 172
see also Reve
Caldenell (Kaldenell), Agnes, 19
Henry, 19
Cald(e)well, Agnes, 738, (née), daughter of
    Robert, 703
Ellen (*Elwyne*), (née Waysborn), 802
Isabel, (née), daughter of Robert, 703
John, 703*; of Thelnetham, 802; the elder,
    turner, of Thelnetham, *lin*, **703**
Katherine, 703
Margaret, (née), daughter of Robert, 703
Robert, of Thelnetham, 703
Thomas, of Thelnetham, & family, 703; son
    of John of Thelnetham, 802; son of Robert,
    703
William, son of Robert, 703
Calew, Roger, of Burwell (Cambs), **509**
Calfaw(e), John, 371, 570, 571
Calf(f)e, Agnes, 711, 775
Cecily, (née), 775
Isabel, (née), 775
John, 666
Richard, of Westhorpe, **775**
Stephen, 775,
Calle, John, 30
Simon, of Little Waldingfield, **30**
Calvysban(e), Agnes, 512, 632
Isabel, 234
John, of Burwell (Cambs), 512n, **632**
Thomas, 234, 234n, 512; of 'Northestret' in
    Burwell (Cambs), **512**, 632n
Calwe, William, of Barrow, 126n
Caly, John, of Great Ashfield, 743n
William, 667
Camayen, *see* Comayan
CAMBRIDGE, friars in, (unspec.), 79
Augustinian friars, 187, 187n, 204, 428, 461,
    482
Carmelite friars, *lx*, *lx*n, 42, 78, 80, 133, 136n,
    152, 160, 187, 191, 204, 246, 382, 436,

449n, 461, 482, 508, 528, 659, 733,
    751, 754, 779, 785
confraternity of, 751*
Dominican friars (Preachers), 80, 187, 204,
    281, 382, 427, 461, 482, 499, 732, 744
Franciscan friars (Minors), 187, 187n, 204,
    281, 427, 490, 732
friar chaplain of, 602, 602n
Friar Meryell of, 659
gild in, *lxin*, 427n
inhabitants of, 822
King's College in, 247n
CAMBRIDGESHIRE, gilds in, *lxi*, *lxin*
Campe, Robert, 439
Candelere, Thomas, 299; of Honington, 157
Canforth, Thomas, 732
Canown, *see* Ballard *alias* Canown
CANTERBURY, pilgrimage to St Thomas the
    Martyr, *lxiv*, *lxivn*, 437, 437n, 508, 640
Prerogative court of, *xliv*
priory of Christchurch, *xliv*, *xlivn*
Capell, John, 38
Cappe, Edith, wife of William, of Mildenhall,
    barber, 650
William, of Mildenhall, barber, 650
Careles, Agnes, 11
Carle, John, 199
Carleman (Carman), Agnes, 196, 196n
Carles, Avice, 212
John, of Sudbury, **212**,
Carleton, Lawrence, servant, 89
Carman, John, the elder, 765
Thomas, vicar of Yaxley, 790, 790n
see also Carleman
Carpenter, Joan, of Langham, 527
Carter(e) (Kartere), Agnes, 351,
Alice, 206,
Isabel, 259; of Hitcham, 674n,
Joan, 259; of Old Newton, **529**,
John, 213, 259, 351, 585; of Ballingdon, 259;
    of Mellis, 529n
Margaret, 259
Roger, of Long Melford, **206**
William, 799
Carwent, Joan, 395
John, of Eye, 2n, **395**
Caryngton, Henry, 529
CASTLE HEDINGHAM, inhabitants of, 276
Catelen (Catelyn), Eleanor, 691
John, son of Eleanor, 691; of Palgrave, 221
Thomas, chaplain of Burwell St Mary's, 551,
    551n, 631
William, servant, 239
Caton (Caten, Catton), Edmund, 493
Hugh, 441, 661, 661n, 707
Isabel, 661, 707
John, 282
Katherine, (née Fen), 661, 661n

Margery, 282
Robert, 661, 707
Catour, William, 482
Catour *alias* Neve, Anne, 69n, 219n
Catton, *see* Caton
CAVENDISH, church, 133, 423, 574
    aisle on south side of, 574
    chapel of St John the Baptist in, 133, 423,
      423n
      'tabell' in, 423
      cross in, 423
    churchyard, stone walls of, 574
    inhabitants of, 133, 276, 423n, 803n
    lands in, 133, 224, 243
    places in, 'Poleyns' (messuage), 133
      'Syotes' (tenement) 224
    poor of, 133
    testators of, **133, 224, 423, 574**
    ways in, highway to Clare, 423
      'Kemsynge' street, 133
    wills proved at, 133, 224,
CAVENHAM, church, 77, 243
    common light in, 77
    sepulchre light in, 77
    gilds in, 77
    inhabitants of, 77
    testator of, **77**
    will proved at, 664
Cavenham, Agnes, 60
    John, 60*; the elder, 60
    Margaret, 60
    Richard, 60; of Fordham (Cambs), **60**
    Thomas, 60
    William, 60; chaplain, 60
Caxstre(e)t, John, 255
    Robert, 255
Cayle, Gregory, rector of Somerton, 701, 701n
    John, 701
Cely, William, chaplain, 282
Chadenhalke, Joan, 107
    John, 107
    William, of Mildenhall, & family, 107
Chambere (Chambyr), John, 251; monk, *lx*n, 282
Chamberleyn (Chambyrleyn), Margaret, Dame,
    398, 398n
    Ralph, 398
    Roger, Sir, knight, of Gedding, 398, 398n
    Thomas, 193
Chapeleyn, Anne, 319
    Margery, (née), 319
    Petronilla, 591
    Robert, of Wangford, **319**
Chapman, Adam, of Barrow, 136n, **152**
    Agnes, 152, 451, (née), daughter of Thomas,
      822; of Stanningfield, *lxiii*, 785, 785n
    Andrew, 725
    Anne, 522
    Ed., 522

Edmund, 401
Emma, 230
Geoffrey, of Haughley, 568n
Hugh, 806
Isabel, 401
John, 401, 503, 522, 725, 727; chaplain, 152,
    152n; the elder, of Rickinghall Inferior,
    522; of Shotley, 89, 417; of Tuddenham,
    340; parish chaplain of Wortham, 170
Margaret, (née), 152
Robert, rector of Thorp Morieux, 131, 131n,
    238, 613
Rose, 725
Thomas, 152, 725; of Gazeley, **725**
William, 152, 451; the elder, of Mildenhall,
    lxviii, **230**
see also Schapman
Chapmanys, Agnes, 232
Charite (Charyte), Roger, of Hitcham, *lxii*, 43n,
    75
Charles, He[nry], 1
Chaterys, Thomas, 503; of Stoke by Nayland,
    48
Chattysley (Chatysle), Agnes, 219
    Elizabeth, 219
    John, 219; of Ixworth, 219n, **575**
    Marion, 219
    Matilda, 219
    Robert, 219; Sir, 219, 575, 575n; of Bury St
      Edmunds, 219
    William, of Ixworth, *lvii*, **219**, 575n
Chauncerell, William, rector of Withersfield, 123
CHEDBURGH, church, 53, 400
    rector of, 682
    inhabitants of, 53, 366, 400
CHELSWORTH, church, 50, 154, 267
    rector of, *see* Thomas Muryell (Maryell)
    inhabitants of, 50, 284
    lands in, 50, 720
    places in, 'Barkeres Croft', 154
      'Bollyslond', 'Bollys lond', 720
      'Chellesworth Crofte' alias 'Skypps', 484
      'Edwardsely', 721
      'Edwardyshey', 720
      'Gangeys', 'Gawgys' (tenement), 720, 721
      'Hacchysfeld', 154
      'Haverynggale', 721
      'Sawyere', 721
    poor of, 50
    testators of, **50, 154, 267**
    wills proved at, 267
Chener(e)y (Cheneri), Alice, 713
    Ellen (Helen), of Cockfield, **115**
    Henry, 49
    John, 115; the elder, of Cockfield, 115n, 350n
    see also Chynery *and* Chynory
Cheppard, *see* Shepherd
Cherche, Thomas, 360

Cherecrofte, *see* Sherecroft
Cheryaunt, Richard, 782n
Chesewry(g)th (Cheswryte), Andrew, chaplain,
  60, 187, 602
  William, 602
Chester, Richard, 505
Chevelere, Nicholas, & family, 745
CHEVELEY (Cambs), church, 80, 182, 623, 649
  torches of, 623
  gilds in, *lxi*, *lxi*n, 623, 623n, 649
  inhabitants of, 623, 623n
  lands in, 182, 623
  places in, 'Broode Grene', 649
    'Chownescroft', 182
    'Cowthey' (pasture), 182
    'Dunnygges Appylton', 182
    little green, 'Lyttll Grene', 623, 649
    'Parkfeld', 182
  testators of, **182**, **623**, **649**
  ways in, 'Bredestrete lane', 182
    highway between 'Broode Grene' and
      'Lyttll Grene', 649
  wills proved at, 182, 199, 649
CHEVINGTON, church, 53
Childe, Luke, 199
Childerston (Chylderston, Schilderston,
    Schildyrston), Agnes, 239, 239n, (née), 629
  Alice, (née), 629; (née Tyd), 664, 664n
  Henry, 629
  Joan, (née), 629
  John, 239, 239n, 342, 664; son of William,
    629; the elder, of Mildenhall, *lxviii*, **629**,
    664n
  Margaret, 629, (née), 629
  Matilda, 230n, 239, 629, 664n; of Mildenhall,
    239, 629n
  Richard, 230n, 239, 664n; son of William,
    629; of Mildenhall, 239, 239n, 629n
  Robert, 664; the elder, of Mildenhall, *lxxiii*,
    664
  Simon, 664; son of William 629; of
    Mildenhall, 107n, 229n, 230n
  Thomas, 629, 664
  William, 629, 629n, 664, 819, 819n; & family,
    239, 239n; of Mildenhall, 230, 230n
CHILTON (unspec.), church, 311
  inhabitants of, 225
CHILTON, hamlet in CLARE, *see* CLARE
CHIPLEY, lands in, 785
CHIPPENHAM (Cambs), BADLINGHAM in
  inhabitants of, 199n, 438n
  testators of, *lxi*n, **108**, **438**
  church, 108, 199, 214, 438
    altar of BVM in, 438
    altar of the Holy Trinity in, 438
    vicar of, 438
      see also John Syngere
  gilds in, *lxi*, *lxi*n, 199, 199n, 438

inhabitants of, 107
lands in, 108, 199
testators of, *124*, *143*, **199**, *753*
will proved at, 438
Chirche, Robert, of Eye, *3*
  see also Chyrche
Chychele, Thomas, servant, 89
  William, of Creeting St Peter, 472
Chylderston, *see* Childerston
Chynery, Henry, 85
Chynory, Emma, 238
  John, 238
  see also Chener(e)y
Chyrche, John, vicar of Cratfield, 178
  Thomas, of Rushbrooke, 558
  see also Chirche
Chyrcheman, John, 449, 471, 479, 479n; of
    Icklingham, 469n, **471**, 479n
  Margaret, 471, 471n; widow, of Icklingham,
    479
  Ralph, 471
  Richard, 471*, 471n, 479, 479n
?Cirrirray, William, 40
  see also Curra(r)y
Clakston (Claxton), John, rector of Eriswell, 342,
    342n
Clampe, John, 783; of Nayland, 150
CLARE, CHILTON in, gilds in, 79, 380, 380n
  lands in, 380
  testators of, **380**
  church, 26, 46, 155, 276, 380, 456, 662, 687,
    815
    'Babylwyndowe, le' in, *lvii–lviii*, 46
    benches in, 276
    chapel of BVM in, 148
      altar in, 148
      image of BVM in, 148
      image of St Katherine in, 148
      image of St Peter in, 148
    roodloft in, 276
    table-cloth of 'diaperwerk' for, 276
    torches in, 46
    vicar of, *liv*, 276
      see also Thomas Asty, Robert
        Colyngham
    windows, attacked by Dowsing, *lviii*
  churchyard, stone cross in, 46
  house of Augustinian friars in, *lx*, *lxi*, 1, 11,
    21, 38, 42, 46, 50, 78, 79, 83, 87, 90, 96,
    121, 125, 131, 133, 152, 154, 160, 173,
    184, 189, 224, 238, 247, 290, 300, 311,
    317, 339, 404, 410, 420, 424, 436, 454,
    504, 508, 528, 537, 565, 570, 598, 628,
    634, 673, 682, 722, 729, 779, 785
    church of, 714
    confraternity of, *lxi*, 121
    John Bery, Master, friar of, 779
    Osbert Sparow, friar of, 779

[*unnamed*] friar of, 436
inhabitants of, 46, 148, 148n, 155, 276, 531n, 662
lands in, 46, 148, 276, 456, 662, 687
places in, 'Bay, le', 26
   'Cherchys' (messuage), 687
   footbridges of 'Chylton Cawse', 662
   market place, 26, 687
   'Nethyrgate, le', 687
   'Pesonbredge', 46
   'Tylkeulncroft', 687, 687n
poor of, 46
testators of, *lii, liv, lvn, lvii, lxn, lxvi,* **26, 46, 148, 155, 276, 456, 662, 687, 815**
ways in, 'Chylton Cawse', 662
   highway leading to Stoke, 687
wills proved at, 26, 42, 46, 99, 105, 106, 148, 155, 171, 242, 276, 380, 419, 420, 447, 456, 642, 655, 662, 687, 742, 780, 803, 808, 813, 814, 815
Clare, Richard de, earl of Gloucester, 1n
   William, clerk, 102; priest, 622
Clarew, Joan, 166
   John, 166
Clavery, Thomas, 377
Claveryng, Thomas, 776
Claxton, *see* Clakston
Clement, John, of Stowlangtoft, 295
Clere(s) (Clerys), Agnes, 653
   Edmund, 653; of Great Livermere, 759,
   John, 118, 118n; of Felsham, **137**; of Little Livermere, **653**
   Katherine, 137
   Thomas, 137, 653; of Little Livermere, **118**, 544n, 653n
   Walter, 137
Clerk(e), Agnes, 70, 274, 812,
   Alice, 70, 276; of Bardwell, **168**; of Drinkstone, **336**
   Christian, 60
   Ed., of Edwardstone, **274**
   Edmund, of Soham, 204
   Hervey, 168, 168n
   Isabel, 28, 70, 714
   James, of Ixworth, 168n
   Joan, 70; wife of Richard, of Preston, 613; wife of Robert, 779;
   John, 28, 70, 314, 336, 372, 646, 714, 812; servant, 636; of Cavendish, 276; of Chelsworth, 50n; of Nowton, **291, 296**; the elder, of Nowton, 291n, **812**; the elder, of Occold, **443**; of Preston, **716**; son of Richard of Preston, 336
   Margaret, 204
   Margery, 70, 714,
   Nicholas, 28
   Richard, 28, 46, 276, 336, 456, 528, 574, 662, 687, 751, 785, 803; of Preston, 336, 613

Robert, 70, 498, 779; of Little Waldingfield, 675; of Pakenham, 101
Roger, 70, of Edwardstone, **714**
Simon, 256n, 372
Thomas, 46, 155, 246, 470, 470n, 574, 726, 739; servant, 191, 191n; the elder, 264; of Boxford, **70**
Walter, 738
William, 10, 291, 334, 630, 710; of Bradfield St George, 772
see also Crek *and* Nicoll *alias* Clerk
Clerk *alias* Webbe, Isabel, 646
   John, of Woodditton (Cambs), *lin, lxin,* 630n, **646**
   Margaret, 646
   Robert, 646
   Thomas, 646
Cleypoll, Geoffrey, 307
Clopton, Alice, 779, 779n
   John, of Long Melford, esquire, 154, 154n, 181, 436, 436n, 733, 779
   William, 733
Clovere (Clovyer), Joan, 50
   John, of Cavendish, 276
   Margaret, 50
   Matilda, wife of John, 276
Clyffe, Henry, 754
Clynton, William, of Bury St Edmunds, 286
Cobbe (Cobe), Alice, 778
   Christian, 343
   Joan, 404
   John, 343, 404, 476n; of Gislingham, **343**, 800n
   Margaret, 343*
   Margery, 343
   Richard, 810
   Robert, & family, 404
   Thomas, 343, 778; of Shelland, 324n
   William, of Wetheringsett, *lxvi,* **778**
Cobberte, Simon, 580
Cobold, Anne, 205
   John, 205, 552
COCKFIELD, church, 85, 115, 350, 488, 540
   bells of, 350
   light before image of BVM in, 350
   'perch' candlebeam in, 488
   porch of, *lvin,* 350
   rector of, 350
     see also Robert Forthe
   surplices for, 540
   tabernacle of St Peter in, 115, 488
   gild in, *lxiin,* 540, 540n
   inhabitants of, 350n
   lands in, 350, 540
   places in, 'Anderwys' (tenement), 540
     'Croosgrene', 350
     'melhows, le', 350
     'Stowys Hyll', 350

poor of, 540
testators of, *lvi*n, *lxii*n, *lxx*, *49*, **85**, **115**, **350**, **488**, **540**
ways in, lane leading from 'Seven le Asshes' to church, 350
wills proved at, 49, 50, 85, 336, 488, 613, 614, 616, 761, 783, 784
Coddenham, Cecily, 135
Coggeshall, John, the elder, 79n
Cogman, Joan, of Lavenham, 552n
Cok(e), Agnes, 228; servant, 698
    Anne, 313
    Avice, 313
    Henry, 25, 706
    John, 139, 602; of Haughley, *lxvii*n, **313**; of Stowmarket, **139**; of Whelnetham, 572
    Marion, 313*
    Richard, of Kirtling (Cambs), 610
    Thomas, of Garboldisham (Nfk), 174; of Norton, 743n; of Withersfield, **419**
    William, 419
    see also Cook
Cokerell, Dame Katherine, 709, 709n
Coket(t), Henry, of Westhorpe, 361n
    Isabel, (née), 368
    Joan, & family, of Timworth, 368
    John, 650, 731; of Ampton, 61, 69, 437n, 538n
    Margaret, of Ingham, widow, **368**
    Simon, 570
    Walter, 368; of Ingham, 368, 368n; rector of Ingham, 368, 368n
    William, incumbent of Great Livermere, 241, 241n, 759,
Coksedge, Agnes, (née), 417
    Baldewin, of Felsham, gentleman, *li*n, *lii*, **417**, 613n
    Denise, 417, 417n
    Edmund, 417
    George, 417
    John, 417
    Katherine, nun of Redlingfield, 417
    Margaret, 417
    Margery, 417
    Robert, son of John, 417
COLCHESTER (Esx), house of Franciscan friars (Minors), 38, 48, 55, 67, 87, 89, 150, 247, 352, 424, 537, 595, 729
    inhabitants of, 67, 733
    lands in, 598
    parish of All Saints, 89
    parish of St Mary the Virgin, 598
    ways in, 'le Wyrestrete', 67
Colcy, Christian, 371
    Geoffrey, of Woolpit, **371**
    John, 371
Coldham, John, 338; of Barningham, *lxxiv*, **338**, 452n; the elder, of Barningham, 338n
    Katherine, 338

Margaret, 338
    Roger, 338
Cole, Anne, 522
    Henry, 313
    Margaret, widow of John, of Stoke by Nayland, *lxxiv**, **150**
Colet(t), John, of Ashley (Cambs), 623
    Robert, of Melford, 518,
Colman, Agnes, 349
    Henry, 587
    John, of Thorndon, 337; of Wortham, 34
    Juliana, 337
    Richard, 337
    Stephen, 349
    Thomas, 146; of Thorndon, *lix*n, 126n, **337**
    William, priest/chaplain, 436, 733, 779
?Colmore, Thomas, parish clerk of Rougham, 184
Colson, John, friar, 803
Colyere, John, of Bures St Mary, 55n, **283**
    Margery, 283
Colyn(g), Isabel, 630
    Joan, 630
    John, 826; of Colchester (Esx), 46
    Margaret, 630
    Walter, 630,
    see also Cowlynge
Colyngham, Robert, vicar of Clare, 380, 380n, 456, 687
Colyour, Henry, 383
Comayan (Comayen), Alice, 536
    Thomas, the younger, 536
    William, 536; of Rattlesden, **536**, 615n
Comber(e), Thomas, 213
    William, of Stradishall, 213n
COMBERTON (Cambs), manor of Burdeleys in, 213n
COMBS, church, 169, 344, 478, 594, 621, 669, 694
    aisle, south, *lvii*, 478, 594
    antiphoner for, 621
    candlebeam in, 344
    chalice for, 621, 694
    east window of 'south side' in, *lvii*, 478, 594
    image of St Thomas of Judea in, 621
    rector of, *see* William Smyth
    rood-stair in, *lvi*n, 478
    inhabitants of, 103n
    lands in, 169, 275, 344, 468, 594, 621
    places in, 'Combys, le', 621
    testators of, *l*, *lvi*n, *lvii**, **169**, *200*, **344**, **478**, **594**, **621**, **694**
    ways in, common way, 621
COMPOSTELLA, (Spain), St James of, pilgrimage to, *lxiv*, *lxv*, 89, 280, 294
    tomb of St James in, 89, 89n

CONEY WESTON, church, 294, 590
  churchyard, walls of, 294
  inhabitants of, 294n, 365, 555, 590
  lands in, 294
  places in, 'Reynoldys' (tenement), 590
    Walterys' (tenement), 590
  testators of, **294**, **590**
  ways in, way through middle of town, 590,
Coo, Agnes, of Stanton, **333**
  Isabel, 289
  John, 333
  William, of Burwell (Cambs), *289*
Cook(e), Agnes, (née Waysborn), 802
  Alexander, chaplain, *lxx*, 311
  Constance, 260
  Joan, (née Kendale), 607; of Badwell, 527
  John, 237, 765, 799; & family, 700; the elder,
    92; of Combs, 103n; of Cotton, 65; of
    Thrandeston, **765**
  Margaret, 700, 765
  Matilda, 700
  Richard, of Maldon, 398
  Robert, 89, 701, 802; the younger, 802
  Simon, & family, 799
  Thomas, 765; of Cotton, *lxx*, 6n, 421, **700**,
  Walter, canon, 125
  William, 260, 720, 721, 799; of Bildeston,
    613, 713; son of William of Creeting, 89
  see also Cok(e), *and* Salle *alias* Cook
Coole, John, 89, 824
  Margaret, (née), 824
  Richard, 766, 768, 768n
Coote, William, clerk, 338; rector of
    Barningham, *xlix*, *xlix*n, 338, 338n; rector
    of Fornham All Saints, *xlix*, *xlix*n
Copcy (Copsy), John, 91; of Cowlinge, **91**, 801n
  Roger, of Brockley, 22n, 125n
  [*unnamed*], 801, 801n
Copenger, John, of Buxhall, 404n
Coppyng(e), Agnes, daughter of Walter, 432
  John, 1, 704; the elder, 125; the younger, 125
  Katherine, 125
  Margaret, 125
  Richard, 125
  Roger, 125
  Thomas, 125
  Walter, 125; & family, 432
  William, clerk, 1; of Somerton, *lxxiii*, **125**
Copsy, *see* Copcy
Copyn(g), John, of Acton, 311, 311n, **518**
Cordy, John, of Thelnetham, *132*
  Margaret, 132
CORNARD, GREAT, church, 83, 87, 290, 465,
    607, 729
  inhabitants of, 212n, 408n
  lands in, 729
  places in, Abbas Hall, 212n
    'Smethes & Cracchedounhill', 212

  'Whyttes' (messuage), 516
  testators of, **729**
CORNARD, LITTLE, church, 87, 658, 729
  rector of, *see* John Frankeleyn
CORNWALL, inventories from, *lxxiv*
Costyn, Robert, 240, 240n
Cosyn, Agnes, 77
  Geoffrey, 750
  John, the elder, 77*; the elder, of Cavenham,
    77
  Marion, 750
  Robert, of Stowmarket, *liii*, **750**
  Thomas, 77, 750
Cote, Thomas, official of Boxford church, *lvin*,
    247
Coteler(e), John, of Barnham, *lxn*, *lxxv*, *lxxv*n,
    282
  William, 417, 532; of Felsham, 417
Cotelyn, John, 251, 688; of Palgrave, 618n, **688**
  Margaret, 688
  Margery, (née), 688
  Valentine, 688
Coteras, Alice, servant, 652
  Robert, 652, 780n
COTTON, carver and painter of, 338
  church, 6, 700
    roof of, 700
  inhabitants of, 6, 65, 421, 700, 700n
  lands in, 6, 700
  places in, 'Clarys close', 700
    'Garlekis', 'Garlekes', (close), 700
  testators of, *lxx*, **6**, **700**
  ways in, lane from Bacton to Cotton church,
    700
  wills proved at, 170, 554
Cotton, John, 313
Cotyngham, Margaret, daughter of Robert, 529
  Robert, the elder, 529
Coupere, *see* Cowper
Cove, Joan, (née), 568
  Katherine, 568
  Roger, of Mendlesham, **568**
Cowdon, Isabel, 28
  Richard, of Dalham, **28**
Cowell, Agnes, 60
  Thomas, 714; parish chaplain of Brandon, 776
Cowerde, Agnes, 182
  Amicia, 182
  John, 182; of Cheveley (Cambs), **182**
  Simon, 182
  Thomas, 182
  William, 182
Cowern, John, of Mildenhall, **611**, 635n, 638n
COWLINGE, church, 286, 340, 490
    torches in, 91
  inhabitants of, 340, 787n
  lands in, 272, 482, 490, 801
  places in, 'Cokkes', 801

'Copsyes', 801
'Cowlynge Brooke', 482
'Farwelles crofte', 'Farwelys crofte', 801
'Femot(t)es' (tenement), 490
'Hovelles' (tenement), 801
'Knappynges', 801
'Mellefeld', 801
'Potters' (messuage), 482
'Sclechys Crofte', 91
'Sowrall' (tenement), 490
'Wodgate' (messuage), 801
testators of, *lxvii, lxviii*, **91**, **490**, **801**
Cowlynge (Collyng), Agnes, 121
Margaret, 121
Thomas, 121
see also Colyn(g)
Cowper(e) (Coupere), Ada, 76
Alice, 247
Amye, 76
Cecily, 76
Edmund, 462
Elizabeth, 76
Joan, 166*; (née Blowere) of Boxford, 285
John, 57, 166*, 247, 247n, 331n, 440, 583;
the elder, 247, 380; at the Stone, Boxford,
*lvi*n, *lviii*, **247**, 352n; of Brockley, **76**,
473n
Katherine, 57; (née Abbott), 267; wife of John,
of Clare, 662
Margaret, 76*; the younger, 247
Marion, 57n
Matilda, 247
Richard, 169, 621, 694, 799
Robert, 440
Simon, 541
Thomas, 576; of Boxford, 247n; of Palgrave,
221
Walter, *lxix*n, 68, 76, 267, 440, 490, 801
William, 76, 159, 247; the elder, 247; of
'Olywade', 247
see also Hoy *alias* Cowpere
Cox, Thomas, chaplain, 798
Crakenell, Edmund, 559
Crakoll (Crakell), Richard, 716
Crane, Alice, 251
Elizabeth, nun of Bruisyard, 89
Isabel, of Redgrave, **308**
John, 251*; of Botesdale in Redgrave, 308n
Richard, 269, 269n, 327, 376; of Rickinghall
Inferior, 308
Thomas, of Wortham, **269**
Walter, 269; of Wortham, 269n, 323n
Cranevyle (Cranvyle), Isabel, wife of Thomas,
640
Thomas, 286, 640
Cranewys(e), John, vicar of Stoke by Nayland,
150, 150n, 236, 409, 556, 556n
Crask, Thomas, 822

Cratern, Margaret, of Icklingham, widow, **469**,
471n
William, 469
CRATFIELD, vicar of, *see* John Chyrche
Crayles, John, 688
CREETING ALL SAINTS, church, (now lost),
89
CREETING ST MARY, church, 89
CREETING ST OLAVE, church, (now lost) 89
rector of, 89
CREETING ST PETER, church, 89, 472
rector of, *see* Robert Masham
inhabitants of, 89, 472, 472n, 627
lands in, 472
places in, 'Cretyng Grene', 89
'Derboughtys' (tenement), 89
'Pulford', 89
testators of, *lxv*, **44**, **89**, **472**
ways in, 89
wills proved at, 591
Crek (Clerke *in margin*), Agnes, 456
Alice, 456,
James, 456,
Joan, 456,
Thomas, of Clare, **456**
William, 456
see also Clerke
Creme, Henry, 634
John, & family, 116
Nicholas, 362*, 821
Richard, 821; son of Nicholas, 821; son of
Richard, 821; son of Thomas, 821
Thomas, 821; of Thurston, 821
Cressenere, William, esquire, 181, 181n
Crispyn, *see* Cryspyn
Crocham, William, of Icklingham, 572
Croftys (Crofftes), John, official of archdeacon,
*xlviii, xlviii*n, *xlix*; rector of Elmswell, 318,
318n
Crople(y), John, 232, 232n, 734
Margaret, 734,
Thomas, of Dalham, **734**
Crosby, M' Mylys, drawing of, *lxxvi, lxxvi*n,
between 644 & 645
Cros(s) (Crose), Clemence, daughter of William,
529
Margaret, (née Smyth), 156; of Bury, 539
Thomas, 96; of Edwardstone, *liii*n, **96**
William, 96, 352, 529, 751; of Rougham, 535
Crowe (Krowe), Cecily, of Hitcham, **211**; widow,
of Hitcham, 196
Margaret, 196, 196n, 211
Thomas, of Hitcham, 196, 196n, 211n; of
Soham (Cambs), 204n; of Stonham Parva,
374
Crudde, Katherine, 698, 698n
Cryke, Thomas, son of John, 722
Cryketot(t), John, of Buxhall, 404n

Roger, 11
Cryott (Crytott), Roger, 681; of Lavenham, 339n
Crysale, Richard, parish chaplain of St Gregory's, Sudbury, 698
Cryspyn (Crispyn), Hugh, of Creeting, 627
    John, of Thorney in Stowmarket, **627**
    Richard, 627
Crystemess, William, 704
Crytott, *see* Cryott
Cukkoo, John, 598,
CULFORD, church, 207, 227, 368, 657
    inhabitants of, 657
    lands in, 227
    places in, 'Fystonys' (tenement), 227
    testators of, **208**, **227**
Cullyng(e), John, 451
    Thomas, 345
Cuntforth, William, 234
Curby, William, of Lavenham, 431n
Curpayle, John, of Haverhill, *250*
Curra(r)y, Isabel, 380
    John, the elder, of Ampton, *114*; the younger, of Ampton, 114; of Chilton hamlet in Clare, 79n, **380**
    Roger, 304
    see also ?Cirrirray
Curteys, Emma, of Mildenhall, 664n
    Margaret, 29
    Robert, 29
    William, 574; of Tostock, **29**
Custe, Alice, 88
    Simon, of Great Horringer, **88**
Cutte, Robert, vicar of Assington, 407, 407n

DAGWORTH, lands in, 576
Dale, Edward, 218, 498
    Simon, 193n
DALHAM, church, 28, 286, 734
    tower of, 28
    testators of, **28**, **734**
    wills proved at, 725, 734
Dalham, Simon, of Hundon, 99, 808
Dalton, John, vicar of Little Waldingfield, 349, 349n
Damecell, Thomas, 145
Danby, Alice, 625
    Isabel, 625
    Joan, 625
    John, 625
    Katherine, 625
    Margaret, 625
    Robert, 625
    Thomas, 625; of Market Weston, **625**
    William, the elder, 625
Danon, Agnes, 425n
    Isabel, 425
    John, of Horkesley (Esx), 783
    Simon, 425, 425n

    William, of Sudbury, **425**
Dantre, John, 599
Darle, Thomas, friar, 109
Davy, Thomas, & family, 655
Dawe, John, 428
de Foxherde, *see* Foxherde
de Hewell, *see* Hewell
de Pakenham, *see* Pakenham
de Rowgham, *see* Rowgham
de Walsham, *see* Walsham
DEBENHAM, lands in, 809
    manor of Bludhall in, 457n
    stall in, 818
Debenham, John, 822
Dec', William, 1
Deelyng, Thomas, 352
Dei, *see* Dey
Dekenys, Agnes, of Stoke by Clare, *813*
Den, Robert, of Newton by Sudbury, 398
Dene (?Deve), Robert, 516
    William, 512
Deneys (Deynes, Deynis Deynys), Agnes, 259
    Alice, & her mother Emma, 621
    Anne, (née), 621, 694
    Joan, widow, of Sudbury, *lxv*, *lxvi*, *lxvii*n, **259**, 608n
    John, 259, 259n, 579; of Woolpit, *lxv*, 570, 570n, 571, **579**, 786n
    Margaret, 259, 621, (née), 621, 694
    Phyllis, 251
    Robert, 251, 259; dyer, of Sudbury, 259, 259n
    Rose, of Haughley, 511n, 621n, 706n
    Thomas, 579, 621, 694; of Combs, *l*, **621**, 621n, **694**, 694n
    William, of Mildenhall, **260**
DENHAM, church, 83
    inhabitants of, 89
Denham, Anne, 263
    Isabel, 263
    John, 263
    Katherine, 263
    Margaret, 263
    Richard, 335
    Robert, of Wickhambrook, **263**
    William, 263
Dense, William, prior of Ixworth, 362n, 723n
DENSTON, church, 242, 286, 724, 785
    image of St Nicholas for, 785
    gild in, *lxii*n, 724, 724n, 785, 785n
    inhabitants of, *lxiii**, 213, 485, 724n, 785, 785n
    lands in, 286, 724, 785
    manor of, 785n
    poor of, 724
    needy poor man of, 785
    testators of, *lxii*n*, *lxiii*, **242**, **724**, **785**
    ways in, 'Cokestrete lane', 785
    wills proved at, 213

Denston, Clement, archdeacon, *xlviii, xlviii*n
John, esquire, 213, 213n
William, esquire, of Denston, 213n
[*unnamed*], Master, 785
Dentard, John, 213
Denton, John, 302, 319,
DEOPHAM (Nfk), 34
DEPDEN, church, 53, 286, 366, 400, 685
altar cloth for, 685
inhabitants of, 53
lands in, 53, 366
places in, 'Copeland's Hostelry' (tenement),
53
'Kentes' (tenement), 53
'Pylgrymys Croftes' (crofts), 53
'Suteres medewe' (meadow), 53
'Vaunces' (tenement), 53
testators of, *lii*n, **53, 366, 685**
Derby, Joan, (née), & family, 782
John, of Sudbury, **782**
Deresle, *see* Derysle
Derlyng, John, of Bury St Edmunds, 772; of
Snailwell (Cambs), **24**
Thomas, 24
Derman, John, 724; of Denston, *lxii*n, **724**, 785n
Matilda, 724,
Thomas, of Withersfield, 171
Derysle (Deresle, Derysley), Agnes, 461
Alice, 656, (née), 461, 482; late the wife of
Richard, of Kirtling (Cambs), 482, 482n,
656
Constance, 461
Flowr, 461
Joan, 461
John, 461, 482
Katherine, 461
Margaret, 461
Richard, 482; of Kirtling (Cambs), 281, 281n,
461, 461n, **482**, 577, 577n, 656
Thomas, 482, 656
Walter, 461*, 461n, 482, 609n, 610, 656,
656n; of Kirtling (Cambs), 281n, 482n,
461n, **577**
William, 461, 482, 577, 577n, 656, 656n; of
Kirtling (Cambs), *lxviii*, 281n, **461**, 482n
Dextere, Roger, of Mildenhall, 260
Dey(e) (Dei), Agnes, 149, 277
Alice, (née Cok), 313
Benedict, son of Margaret, of Stowlangtoft,
672
John, 313, 374, 498, 529; servant, 402
Margaret, of Stowlangtoft, 672
Richard, 475
Stephen, *lxix*n, 68
Sybil, of Eye, 2n
Thomas, of Stowlangtoft, 672
William, & family, 374
Deynes (Deynis, Deynys), *see* Deneys

Dil Hoo, Ed., of Stowmarket, **665**
Joan, 665
Ditton, Robert, 11, 339
DITTON VALENS, *see* WOODDITTON
(Cambs)
Dobbys (Dobbes), Robert, chaplain, of Old
Newton, 529, 529n
Dobyn, Edmund, 272
John, 172, 611
Dogott, John, of Groton, 309
Dokkyng(e), Joan, 635
Thomas, 776, 776n; son of William, 635; the
elder, of Mildenhall, 611n, **635**, 638n
William, 387; & family, 635
Dolet(t), Edward, 361
John, of Westhorpe, **361**
Donewych(e), Nicholas, Dominican friar of
Sudbury, 505
Robert, of Fornham All Saints, **798**
Doo, Rose, wife of Peter, 375
Dooke, Thomas, of Hinderclay, 795
Dookyll, Neville ('Newell'), 581
Dorant (Dorawnte), Beatrice, 193
William, of Thornham Magna, **193**
Dorcetre, Walter, of Bradfield St George, 772
Dorward, John, esquire, 51
Dounham, *see* Downham
DOVER (?Kent), inhabitants of, 196
Dowe, Agnes, 598
Alice, 598
Geoffrey, 468
Gilbert, of Lakenheath, 245n
John, 669; of Barnardiston, **598**
Katherine, wife of Geoffrey, 468
Lawrence, 363
Rose, 598
Thomas, 598
William, 299, 382; of Barnham St Martin, **299**
Dowes, Robert, Sir, chaplain, 133
Down, John, of Long Melford, 436n
DOWNHAM, inhabitants of, 731n
Downham (Dounham), George, 588; of
Rougham, 535
John, canon of Ixworth, 527; Sir, 777
Dowsing, William, destruction by, *lviii*
Draper(e), Edmund, 645
John, 200
Robert, vicar of Woodditton (Cambs), 630,
646, 646n
William, 89
Draw(e)swerd, Emmot, wife of Richard, 824
John, 243, 824*; of Snailwell (Cambs), **824**
Margaret, 824
Marion, wife of John, 824
Richard, 824*
Robert, 199
Thomas, 824
Draxes, [*unnamed*], 172

Drew(e), James, of Mellis, *lxxv*n, **391**; the elder, of Mellis, 391n
John, 517
Margaret, 391
DRINKSTONE, church, 18, 19, 95, 205, 336, 388, 821
  bells in, 19, 205
  painting of 'gawdes' before BVM in, 388
  tabernacle of BVM in, 19
  tabernacle of St Peter in, 18
  gilds in, 19, 19n, 95, 95n, 205, 205n
  inhabitants of, 19, 205n, 495
  lands in, 336, 375
  places in, 'Amyeshalfakyr', 205
    'Caldewellyerd' (close), 205
    'Halke, le', 205,
    'Halkmerch', 388
    'Hell' (messuage), 205
    'Langlond, le', 205
    'Myllehyll', 388
    'Nethirdale, le', 205
    'Overdale', 205
    'Prabell, le', 205
  poor of, 19, 90, 388
  testators of, **18**, **19**, **95**, **336**, **388**
  ways in, 19
  wills proved at, 19, 95, 746
Drory, Alice, wife of John, 693
Eleanor, wife of William, 693
John, 693
William, 693
Drowgth (Drowte), Alice, 329, (née), 647
Joan, 329, 329n; relict of Peter, of Felsham, **647**
Margaret, 329, (née), 647
Peter, of Felsham, **329**, 647, 647n
Drury, Elizabeth, 709n
Katherine, daughter of Roger of Hawstead, 417n
Nicholas, of Thurston, esquire, 125n
Roger, of Hawstead, 470; esquire, of Hawstead, 125, 125n; gentleman, of Hepworth, *li*n, 392n, **402**
Thomas, 402; of Rougham, 825, 825n; gentleman, of Troston, 789, 789n
William, 402
Drynkmelk, John, 667
Drynkston, William, 418
Dryvere, Hugh, of Wattisfield, 16
Simon, Sir, 240, 476, 476n
Ducheman, Alice, 13
John, of Haverhill, *13*
Duffeld, William, official of archdeacon, *xlviii*, *xlviii*n; commissary general, *lxxiv*, 804, 805
Duke, John, 373; husbandman, of Little Saxham, *li*n, **373**
Margaret, 373

Ralph, 373
Richard, 373
Robert, 373
Thomas, 373
DULLINGHAM (Cambs), gild of St James in, *lxi*n
  gildhall of, *lxii*n
  inhabitants of, 646
Dullyngham, Margaret, 314
Rose, daughter of William, 314
William, 314; of Wicken (Cambs), 747
Dun, Adam, of Yaxley, **790**
Joan, (née), 790,
Margaret, 790; wife of Richard, 790
Richard, 790
Robert, 790
Thomas, son of Richard, 790
Dunch(e), Alice, 657, (née), 374
Joan, 374
John, 374; of Mendlesham, 805, 805n; stainer, of Mendlesham, 374, 374n; of Thornham Magna, 374; of Wordwell, *liii*, **657**
Margery, *lxx*, 374
Robert, 218n; & family, of Ipswich, 374, 374n; the elder, of Mendlesham, *lxx*, **374**, 805n
Rose, servant, 89
Thomas, of Culford, 657
William, 89
Dunham, Joan, wife of William, 566
John, 566,
William, 566,
Dunkon, John, 581
DUNMOW (Esx), church, 470
Dunsteven, Arnold, gentleman, 67
DUNWICH, deanery of, *lvii*n
  friars of, (unspec.), 180
  Domincan friars of, 65
  Franciscan friars of, 65, 700
    Friar Bokenham of, 799
  inhabitants of, 765
Dunwyche, Thomas, 449
Dyer(e), Anne, of Rattlesden, 334
John, 517
Raymond, the elder, 782
Robert, of Botesdale in Redgrave, 522
see also Turnour *alias* Dyer
Dyke, Agnes, 803*; widow, of Stoke by Clare, *lv*, *lxvi*, *lxvii*, 133n, 637n, **803**
Alice, (née), & family, 803; wife of Thomas, 803
John, *lv*, 803*
Margaret, wife of Reginald, 803
Margery, wife of William, 803
Reginald, 803
Thomas, 803; son of John, apprentice at Bury St Edmunds, 803
William, & family, 803

Dykys (Dyx), Edmund, 413
  Geoffrey, of Ampton, 66
  Marjory, 423
  Richard, 423; of Cavendish, **423**
Dysneye, Nicholas, 174
Dysse, John, friar, 34
Dyster, Robert, of Boxford, painter, 331n
Dytton, Ed., 276
  Robert, 552; of Lavenham, 122
  Rose, wife of Ed., 276
Dyx, *see* Dykys

EARL STONHAM, *see* STONHAM, EARL
EARLS COLNE (Esx), inhabitants of, 779
EAST BERGHOLT, inhabitants of, 430
Ede, Joan, (née Smyth), wife of Thomas, 815
  Thomas, & family, 815; of Clare, 148
Edgore, Edward, 669
  John, of Stowmarket, 361
Edmund, John, apprentice, 219
Edon, Thomas, 660
Edryche, *see* Erdryche
Edward(e), John, of Fornham St Martin, 654n; of
    Great Horringer, 81n; of Norton, 362
  Robert, 1
  William, 654, 654n; the elder, 776; of Great
    Horringer, 88, 708, 708n, 709, 709n
EDWARDSTONE, church, 96, 247, 274, 352,
    353, 714
  aisle in, 96
  arch in, 274, 274n, 352
  image of cross in, 352
  parclose in, 96
  inhabitants of, *lxxii*, 247, 352, 714
  lands in, 96, 714
  places in, 'Howettes', *lxxii*, 353,
  poor of, 96
  testators of, *liii, lxxii, lxxv*n, **96**, **274**, *328*, **352**,
    353, 714
  ways in, 'Cheteburghstrete', 352
    footpath to church, 352
Edwyn, Elizabeth, 453
  John, 711
Eg(e)lyn, Joan, 711
  John, of Rickinghall Superior, 506n
Egmer, Geoffrey, 313
Eldhalle, James, 431
ELEIGH, BRENT, *see* BRENT ELEIGH
ELEIGH, MONKS, *see* MONKS ELEIGH
Elmham, John, friar, 46
ELMSETT, church, 406
  inhabitants of, 483, 563
  testators of, *71*
ELMSWELL, church, 116, 318, 519, 519n, 603,
    624, 660
  aisle of St John the Baptist in, 519
  chalice for, 603
  Easter sepulchre in, 519

light before image of BVM in, 519
  'selyng' in, 519
  rector of, *see* John Croftys
  tabernacle of BVM in, 519
  tower of, 519n
  inhabitants of, 88n, 318, 367, 430, 519n, 605,
    660n
  lands in, 116, 318, 519, 660
  places in, 'ad Leess, le' (tenement), 519
    'Blakfen', 519
    bridge, 519
    'Browness, le' (tenement), 660
    'Cressmedewe', 519
    'Dethes, le' (tenement), 660
    'Dotthorness, le', 519
    'Flaxlonde, le', 519
    'Gerveyss, le', 519
    'Gerveyss Crofte', 519
    'Halke, le', 519
    'Hardwyk, le', 519
    'Harwe, le', 519
    'Mabyl Cloos', 116
    'Maggescrofte, le', 519
    'Mundes of Halle', 519
    'Nunbregge closs', 519
    'Nunbregge Pytyll', 519
    'Owthren, le', 519
    rectory, 519
    tenement of rectory, 519
    'Terellecrofte, le', 519
    'Turtyll', 519
    'Wongefeld, le', 519
    'Wranggylyerd' (close), 660
  poor of, 116
  testators of, *lvii*n, *lx*n, **116**, **318**, **519**, **603**, **605**,
    660
  ways in, 'Becones lane', 519
  will proved at, 660
Elmyswell, John, of Thwaite, 764n
Elsegood, Joan, (née), 116
  John, 116; servant, 519; the elder, of Elmswell,
    116; the younger, 116
  Thomas, 116
  William, 519
Elsyng, Margaret, 301
ELVEDEN, church, 185, 731
  rector of, *see* Simon Burgon
  gilds in, 731, 731n, 826, 826n
  inhabitants of, 304n, 826n
  lands in, 185, 731, 826
  places in, 'Downynges', 185
  testators of, *xlv, lii*, **185, 731**
ELY (Cambs), cathedral, window in, *lviii*n
  diocese of, *xliv*n, *xlv*n
  inhabitant of, 638n
Elyis, *see* Elys
Elyne, Joan, of Haughley, 521n
Elyngham, John, 220, 776; of Sudbury, 652

Elyon, John, 622
Elyott, Reginald, 302, 319; Reginald, of
    Wangford, 120
Elys(e), (Elyis, Hellys, Hely(i)s), Agnes, 372;
    widow of John, of Lavenham, 339n
    Isabel, (née), 372
    John, 154, 547; of Stanton, **372**
    Margaret, (née), 372
    Robert, 372, 666
    Thomas, 372; of Long Melford, 463
Endrys, Agnes, 529
Englysche, John, the elder, 96
Erdryche (Edryche), Denise, 622
    Herry, of Finningham, **622**
    William, 622
ERISWELL, better sort of, *lxiii*
    church, 120, 342
    rector of, *see* John Clakston
    lady (of manor) of, 342
    lands in, 342
    places in, 'Bolnhowfeld', 342
        'Edryches' (tenement), 342
    testator of, *lxiii*, **342**
    ways in, 'le Wrogbrad Wey', 342
Erle, Katherine, (née Mansere), wife of William,
    476
    William, 476
Erlle *alias* Slaw, Robert, 282
Ernald, Agnes, 104
    Joan, 104
    John, of Polstead, **104**
Eryswell, Alice, 342
    John, parishioner, of Eriswell, *lxiii*, **342**
    Thomas, *lxiii*n, 342
Essex, John, 494; of Shimpling, **494**
    Margaret, 494
Estmore, John, 731
Eton, John, of Freckenham, 612
Eustas(se) (Eustac, Ewstasse), John, 810; of
    Rougham, **588**
    Ralph, 764
EUSTON, church, 522, 755
    rector of, *see* William Bretoun
    inhabitants of, 755n
    lands in, 755
    places in, 'Wyltonys' (tenement), 755
    testators of, **755**
Eve (Ive), Margaret, 83*
    William, 83; of Little Waldingfield, *lxix*, **83**,
    349n
Everard, John, 637
    Katherine, 278
    Thomas, of Soham (Cambs), 204n, **278**
    William, 151n
Ewstasse, *see* Eustas
Exale (Exsale), James, friar, 133, 133n, 803,
    803n
EXETER, inventory from, *lxxiv*

EXNING, church, 80, 428, 450
    roofing of, *lvi*n, 428, 428n, 450, 450n
    inhabitants of, 427, 450, 450n
    lands in, 160, 450
    places in, 'Wyndmel Feld', 450
    testators of, *lvi*n, **428**, **450**
Exsale, *see* Exale
EYE, borough of, 442
    castle, 251n
    church, 2, 83, 94, 178, 222, 252, 337, 395,
        396, 405, 442, 457, 726
    altar of BVM in, 94
    altar of St Thomas the Martyr in, 178
    image of BVM in, 252
    image of St Anne in, 252
    image of St John in, 252
    torch for, 252
    tower of, *lvi*, 2, 178, 222, 252, 395, 405
    vicar of, *see* Thomas Hervy
    gilds in, 2, 2n 94, 94n, 178n, 395, 405, 457
    hospital of St Mary Magdalene in, *lxiii*, 2, 2n,
        94, 126, 126n, 222, 222n, 457n
    poor men in, 222
    inhabitants of, 2, 126, 222, 405, 457
    lands in, 146, 178, 405, 442, 457
    places in, Lambseth bridge, 2, 94, 94n
    market, 405
    poor of, 94
    priory of Benedictine monks in, 178, 178n
    testators of, *lvi*, *lxiii*, **2**, *3*, **94**, *176*, **178**, **222**,
        252, **395**, **396**, **405**, **442**, **457**
    ways in, 'Kynggesstrete' way, *lxiii*, 457
        'Lamset' way, *lxiii*, 457,
        Priory way, *lxiii*, 457
        'Spetyll' way, *lxiii*, 457
    wills proved at, 2, 4, 5, 6, 34, 94, 210, 221,
        222, 235, 251, 252, 253, 308, 395, 396,
        405, 442, 457, 506, 617, 618, 765, 778, 791
Eylmyn, John, 814

Fabbe, John, 215, 631; the elder, of Burwell
    (Cambs), 215n
    Margaret, 215
    Richard, 215, 215n
    William, of Burwell (Cambs), **215**, 234n, 626,
        626n
Facon (Fakon), Alice, 310
    Joan, of Edwardstone, *lxxv*n, *328*; widow of
        John, of Nayland, 439n, 783n
    John, the elder, of Nayland, 439n
    Thomas, 354; of Bures St Mary, **310**
    William, 328
Fairwater, John, 629
FAKENHAM MAGNA, church, 590
    lands in, 590
    wills proved at, 555
Fakon, *see* Facon
Fanne, Elizabeth, 151

John, 151
Faryngton, Richard, rector of Rede, 35
?Faverell, Robert, 524
Fawkon, John, 331
Fayerware, Margery, 766
   Simon, of Mildenhall, **766**, 768n
Feen, John, 687
Feg(g)(e), William, clerk, parson of Whepstead,
   112, 112n, 135
FELSHAM, church, 137, 173, 329, 369, 417,
   532, 533, 557, 647
   chalice for, 137
   chancel of, 417
   font cover of, 369
   image of BVM in, 417
   light before image of Corpus Christi in,
      *lix*n, 557
   light before image of St Katherine in, *lix*n,
      557
   porch of, 533
   window and glass for, *lvii*, 533, 557
   rectors of, *see* John Munnyng, John Sterre
      and Robert Storur
   torches for, 173
   inhabitants of, 398, 417, 532, 613n, 647, 705,
      713
   lands in, 532, 557, 712
   manor of Felsham Hall, 417n
   places in, 'Beeryns', 417
      'Brookhallende', 'Brokhallende', 417
      'Coksedgys', 417
      'Coteleryscrofte', 417
      'Dychehows', 417
      'Lytyll Southfeld', 417
      'Mekyll Southfeld', 417
      'Meryeakyr', 417
      'Otecrofte', 417
      'Scottys', 417
      'Southwode', 417
      'Starlynges' (tenement), 329
      'Upwode Hall', 417
      'Walymerche', 417
   poor of, 369
   testators of, *lin*, *lii*, *lvii**, *lix*n, *lx*n, **137**, **173**,
      329, **369**, **417**, **532**, **533**, **557**, **647**
   will proved at, 329
Feltewell, John, 207
   Katherine, 207
   William, & family, 227; of Culford, **208**
FELTWELL (Nfk), church, (unspec.), 377
   of St Mary, 776
   of St Nicholas, 776
Felyp, Thomas, 540
Felix (Felyx), John, 503
Femnale, Agnes, 80
   John, 80; of Ashley (Cambs), *lxxii*, **80**
   Rose, (née) & family, 80
Fenkele, Marion, of Gipping, *lii*n

Fen(n), George, 624
   John, 661*, 707*; servant, 83
   Katherine, 707
   Matilda, wife of Stephen, of Hopton, 555,
      555n, 661, 707
   Richard, 27; of Hitcham, 75; of Kersey, *lxxiv*n
   Robert, & family, 661, 707
   Stephen, of Hopton, 555, 555n, **661**, **707**
   William, 661*, 707
   see also atte Fen
Fenrother(e), Richard, chaplain, 628, 628n, 742,
   742n
Ferdyng, Thomas, 195; of Rickinghall Inferior,
   365
Fermour, Robert, 338
Ferore (Ferour), Edmund, 621, 694
   Robert, vicar of St Mary's, Stowmarket, 38n,
      109, 109n, 669, 669n
Ferthyng, Margery, 298
FINBOROUGH (unspec.), inhabitants of, 142,
   634
FINBOROUGH, GREAT, church, 1, 142, 156,
   275, 358, 619, 669
   bell for, 275, 619
   lamp in chancel of, 156
   porch of, 1
   inhabitants of, 1, 156, 375, 383n
   lands in, 156, 275, 619
   places in, 'Cokerscote' (cottage), 142
      'Hunborugh', 1
      'Longlond' (croft), 1
      'Netherwent', 1
      'Schotelond' (croft), 1
      'Tyl(y)ers' (meadow), 1
   testators of, *lxvii*, **1**, **142**, **156**, **275**, **358**, **619**
   ways in, 'Churchestritte', 1
FINBOROUGH, LITTLE, church, 669
   lands in, 156, 275
   places in, 'Lesquens', 1
FINCHAM (Nfk), church, 377
FINCHINGFIELD (Esx), inhabitants of, 250
FINNINGHAM, church, 6, 65, 361, 622
   rector of, 65
   lands in, *lxxii*, 6, 65, 622
   testators of, **65**, **622**
   wills proved at, 146, 193, 194, 195, 217, 218,
      257, 391, 467, 476, 559, 622, 788, 800
Fleccher(e) (Flechere), Ada, 473
   Alice, 412
   Isabel, 412
   Joan, 412
   John, 473; needy poor man, of Denston, *lxiii*,
      785, 785n
   Margaret, 473
   Thomas, of Walsham le Willows, **412**
   William, 240; of Brockley, 76n, **473**
   see also Leve *alias* Fletcher, Worliche *alias*
      Flecchere

Flegge, Joan, 727
  John, 727; the elder, fuller, of Sudbury, *lin*,
    727
  Robert, 727
  William, 89, 727
FLEMPTON, inhabitants of, 539
Flemyng, Isabel, 731
  John, of Elveden, *lii*, **731**, 826n; of Wortham,
    269n
FLIXTON, priory of Austin nuns, 89, 89n
Flowre, Agnes, wife of Clement, 276
  Clement, of Cavendish, 276
  Margery, 815
Fodryngay, Cecily, 35
  Gerard, 35; of Brockley, *lii*, **35**
  Isabel, 35
  John, the elder, 35; the younger, 35
  Sybil, 35
Fole, John, 105
Folke(s), Christian, & family, 556
  Joan, (née), of Thrandeston, 252
  John, 322, 630; the elder, of Stoke by
    Nayland, **556**
  Margaret, of Eye, *lvi*, **252**
  Robert, 252
Folky(s), *Herry*, of Kedington, 105n
  William, 23
Foole, John, of Sturmer (Esx), 250
Foorth, *see* Forthe
Foot, Isabel, (née), 383
  Joan, 383*
  John, 383; of Buxhall, *lxiv*, 240n, **383**, 634n
  William, 383
Forde, Agnes, 407
  John, 407
FORDHAM (Cambs), chantry of Our Lady at, 60
  church, 60, 187, 187n, 602
    vicar of, Sir Robert [*no surname*], 187
  inhabitants of, 60
  lands in, 60, 602
  places in, 'Cherchefelde undyr downe', 60
    'Gosecrofte', 602
    'Halys, le', 602
    'Rogeres Walle', 60
    shop, *lxxii*, 80
    '?Toftetyestown-ende', 60
    'West fen', 602,
  poor of, 60, 204
  priory of Gilbertine canons in, 602n
  testators of, **60**, **187**, **602**
  ways in, 'Hygh Strete, le', 60
  wills proved at, 187, 239, 824,
FORDHAM, deanery of, *xlv*, *xlv*n
Fordham, Benedict, 61
  Thomas, 482
FORNHAM ALL SAINTS, church, 58, 798
    rector of, *see* William Coote, William
      Woode

house of Franciscan friars in (Babwell), *see*
  BABWELL
  inhabitants of, 798
  lands in, 58
  testators of, **58**, **798**
FORNHAM ST GENEVIEVE, church (now
    derelict), 110, 448
  testators of, **110**, **448**
FORNHAM ST MARTIN, inhabitants of, 654n
  lands in, 266, 497, 705
  rector of, *see* John Nicol
  testators of, **497**, **705**
  wills proved at, 9, 10, 16, 17, 27, 30, 35, 38,
    39, 48, 60, 61, 62, 63, 66, 73, 72, 75, 76,
    78, 81, 82, 87, 88, 90, 93, 100, 101, 108,
    110, 112, 113, 114, 115, 116, 118, 127,
    128, 129, 130, 135, 136, 137, 138, 145,
    147, 150, 151, 152, 157, 167, 173, 179,
    184, 186, 189, 191, 204, 205, 207, 209,
    211, 227, 228, 229, 230, 231, 241, 243,
    245, 256, 260, 261, 265, 266, 270, 275,
    288, 291, 292, 293, 294, 295, 296, 297,
    314, 318, 319, 320, 321, 327, 328, 333,
    335, 340, 342, 347, 364, 365, 368, 371,
    372, 373, 375, 376, 382, 386, 388, 389,
    392, 397, 399, 400, 401, 402, 404, 410,
    413, 414, 417, 430, 432, 435, 436, 454,
    455, 466, 470, 471, 473, 474, 479, 480,
    485, 486, 487, 489, 490, 493, 497, 499,
    500, 502, 507, 519, 523, 528, 530, 531,
    532, 533, 539, 548, 553, 557, 558, 560,
    567, 570, 571, 575, 577, 578, 579, 581,
    582, 583, 585, 586, 587, 588, 599, 600,
    606, 626, 627, 629, 634, 635, 639, 653,
    654, 657, 663, 670, 679, 682, 683, 684,
    685, 686, 695, 696, 697, 699, 701, 705,
    708, 709, 710, 711, 714, 731, 732, 736,
    743, 756, 757, 759, 771, 772, 773, 785,
    786, 789, 797, 798, 806, 807, 812, 816,
    819, 822, 823, 825, 826, 827
Fortham, John, of Kirtling (Cambs), 499n
Forthe, Agnes, (née), 350
  Joan, *lxx*, 350
  Katherine, 350
  Marion, 350
  Ralph, 350
  Richard, 350
  Robert, rector of Cockfield, 350, 350n
  Simon, of Cockfield, 350n,
  Thomas, *lxx*, 49, 85, 350; of Cockfield, *lvin*,
    lxx, **350**
  William, 115
Forwele, Joan, 11
Foster(e), Walter, parish chaplain of Mildenhall,
    260
  [*unnamed*], & wife, 211
Foster *alias* Geldere, Robert, 528n
Fotour, Katherine, (née Wroo), 365, 365n

Margaret, 365
    William, of Rickinghall Inferior, **365**, 376n
Fowlere, Agnes, 60
Fownghale, Robert, 248
FOXEARTH (Esx), Foxearth Hall, 31n
Foxherde, John de, 574
Fraas, John, 37
Franco, Richard, 628
Frankele(y)n, Ed., chaplain of Cowlinge, 490
    John, rector of Little Cornard, 729
    Richard, rector of Kirtling (Cambs), 281,
        281n, 610n
Fraunceys (Frawnce(y)s), Alice, 397
    Joan, 203
    John, 203, 481
    Margaret, 481
    Matilda, 446
    Robert, 7; of Ixworth, 219n, 258n
    Thomas, 643; of Long Melford, 436n, **446**; of
        Mendlesham, **203**; of Worlington, & family,
        481
    Walter, 446
Frawce, John, 701
Frawnceys, *see* Fraunceys
Frebarn, John, of Tuddenham, 243
Freborne, Thomas, 243
FRECKENHAM, inhabitants of, 485, 612
    lands in, 612
    peculiar of, *xlv*, *xlv*n
    road to, 60
Frede, Joan, wife of William, 662
    John, son of William, 662
    Margaret, daughter of William, 662
    Richard, 662
    William, 276, 662
Freman, Edmund, Sir, 92
    John, 219n
    Robert, of Gazeley, 82
Frend(e), Alice, (née Brett), 784
    John, clerk, 213
Freot, *see* Fryot
Frere, Agnes, 226*
    Ed., rector of Hawkedon, 780, 780n
    Henry, of Burwell (Cambs), **226**
    John, 226, 230n, 768; of Mildenhall, 107n
    Robert, 378
    Thomas, 82
    William, 226,
Fress(h)water, Agnes, 315
    John, 149, 149n; of Wetherden, *315*
Freyre, Margaret, (née Fotour), of Coney Weston,
    365
Frorre, William, 661
Frost(e), Helen, (née), 690
    Henry, 690
    Isabel, 690
    Joan, 807
    John, 297, 720, 807, 690; of Hartest,

690n, **807**; of Wicken (Cambs), *793*; of
    Wickhambrook, 586n
    Marion, 807
    Richard, 690; chaplain, 807; of Ousden, 335
    Thomas, 690
    William, 807; of Hartest, **690**, 807n
Fryot (Fryet, Freot), Agnes, (née), 600
    Herry[*sic*], 600
    Joan, (née), 600
    John, 600; of Barrow, 530; mercer, of Sudbury,
        408n
    Margaret, (née), 600
    Margery, 600
    Thomas, 62, 600; of Barrow, **600**
Fryotthe, Thomas, of Glemsford, 628n
Fryth(e), Agnes, 48
    John, of Nayland, **48**, **86**
    Peter, 549,
Fulcher(e), Robert, of Roydon (Nfk), 688
    Thomas, 251; of Palgrave, 688
    [*unnamed*], of Burgate, 416
Fuller(e), Alice, 553, 560; (née Caton), 493; of
    Barnham, 493n
    Anne, 38
    Elizabeth, 385
    Ellen (Helen), of Walsham le Willows, **385**
    Joan, 38
    John, 59, 770; of Barnham, **493**; of
        Glemsford, **262**; of Little Saxham, 320n,
        507; of Mildenhall, 553n; of Thurston, **560**;
        of Walsham le Willows, 385n
    Margaret, 507
    Marion, 770
    Robert, 1, 385; of Barningham, 452
    Roger, 59, 770
    Rose, 262
    Simon, of Mildenhall, *553*
    Thomas, 262
    Walter, 432
    William, 175, 262; of Hunston, **770**
Fulverston, William, 625
Funne, Thomas, 476
Furbusshere, John, 739
Fydyan, William, 687
Fyncham, Henry & family, 227
Fynn, Alice, 50
Fyppe, John, 681
Fyrmyn, John, of Hawkedon, 676
Fys(c)he (Fyssh), Ed'd, of Westhorpe, **102**
    Eleanor, 102
    Elizabeth, 102
    John, 8; of Stowlangtoft, 101
    Thomas, of Soham (Cambs), *8*
    Walter, 102
    William, 102; of Westhorpe, 4
Fyshyve, Isabel, 236
    John, of Stoke by Nayland, **236**
    Julian, 236

153

Fysk(e), John, 405
Fyssher, Richard, 549
Fyston, John, of Great Barton, 736
    Thomas, of Pakenham, 101n
Fytt(e), John [*or*, Anne], 522
    Thomas, 522
Fyzce, Adam, 711
    John, 711

Gadercold (Gadircolde), John, 243, 340
Gage, John, servant, 247
    Robert, 90
Galey, John, of Soham, 204n
Gallant, Walter, 463
    William, 463
Galte, John, 636
    Margaret, 426
    Simon, of Worlington, *l*, **426**
    William, of Brockley, 76
Galyot, John, 783
Gamelyn, John, of Polstead, **97**
    Matilda, 97
    Robert, 97
    Thomas, 780
    William, 163
GARBOLDISHAM (Nfk), church, 323, 555
    inhabitants of, 132, 174, 561
Gardener(e) (Gardyner), Agnes, 636
    Christine, 636
    John, 379, 455, 636; of Icklingham, **492**; of
        Whepstead, **314**
    Margaret, 379, 636
    Matilda, 492
    Nicholas, 636
    Richard, 317, 492
    Robert, 379, 636
    Simon, of Mildenhall, *lxiii, lxviii*, **636**
    Thomas, 636; of Barton, 379; the elder, of
        Barton Mills, **379**
    William, 492, 636; of Stanton, 372
    see also Smyth *alias* Gardynere
Garlond, Thomas, 67
Garlyng, Matilda, 396
    Robert, of Great Finborough, **358**
    Thomas, of Eye, **396**
Garnham, Nicholas, of Bacton, 700
Garsonne, John, 204n
Gasseleye, Richard, 1
GASTHORPE (Nfk), church, 522
    rector of, *see* Thomas Hunte
Gate, Daniel, 644
    Elizabeth, of Barningham, **411**
    Joan, (née), 411
Gateward, John, 649; of Cheveley (Cambs), *lxin*,
      623n, 642n, **649**
Gatle, Thomas, of Great Livermere, 599, 760n
Gauge, Alice, 440
    John, 440

Robert, of Groton, 440
Gavell, Robert, *li*n, 689
Gawge, Richard, 813
GAZELEY, church, 82, 428n, 725
    image of St Margaret in, 428n
    lands in, 82
    NEEDHAM in, gilds in, 428, 428n
    hamlet in, 428, 428n
    inhabitants of, 82
    lands in, 82
    places in, 'Sparkes Londys' (lands), 82
    'Sparkes' (tenement), 82
    testators of, **82**, **725**
Gebelon (Geb(e)lou), John, 51
    Richard, 306*, 306n
    William, the elder, 505; the elder, of Sudbury,
      702
    see also Gybelon
Gebo(w)n, Isabel, (née Buntyng), wife of John,
    821
    Joan, 821
    John, 821
    Katherine, 821
    Robert, 821
GEDDING, church, 398
    tower of, 398
    inhabitants of, 398n
    lands in, 532
    places in, 'Bregges Crofte', 532
Geddynge, John, 1
Gegge, Matilda, of Knettishall, *441*
Geldere, Alice, widow, of Glemsford, **528**
    see also Foster *alias* Geldere
Gelgett, Simon, 786
Gelle, John, of Burwell, 289n
    Robert, 450
Gelyon, Thomas, of Thetford St Mary, *xlvi*n
Gent(e), John, 115; of Euston, 755n; of
      Knettishall, 661
    Margaret, 755
    Richard, 473
    Thomas, 755
    William, the younger, of Euston, **755**
    see also Jentte
Gentilman (Gentylman, Jentilman), Agnes, 209
    John, 209; of Norton, **209**
    Marion, (née) & family, 209
    Robert, freeman, 417; & family, 209
    Thomas, & family, 209
Genytas, Roger, 733
Gerard(e) (Gerrad), Christian, (née Mansere),
    wife of John, 476
    John, 498
    Margaret, 578, (née), 578; servant, 457
    Nicholas, of Barnham, **578**
    Robert, son of Isabel Swanton, 546, 546n,
    William, 376, 376n, 546n,

Germayn (German), John, 733; of Stanstead,
494, 733
Robert, 728; of Melford, 733
Rose, 733
Thomas, of Melford, **733**
Walter, 733,
Gernoun, Nicholas, 89
Thomas, 692
Gerrad, *see* Gerarde
Gerrald, William, 508
Gerveys (Gerweys), Joan, 242
John, of the canons, 242; of Denston, **242**
Robert, 95, 336,
William, 380; Sir, 242
see also Jerveys
Gilbert, Elizabeth, of Troston, 386
GIPPING, chapel of St Nicholas, *liin*, 750, 750n
inhabitants of, 89
place in, 'Newtones' (tenement), 89
testators of, *liin*
GIPPING NEWTON, inhabitants of, 576
Gippys, *see* Gyppys
GISLINGHAM, church, 343, 467, 476, 800
gilds in, 343, 343n, 476, 800, 800n
inhabitants of, 222, 343n, 581
lands in, *lxxii*, 343, 395, 622, 800
places in, 'Wylchones', 395
testators of, **343, 476, 800**
ways in, way from 'Reedbregge', 343
way to church, 343
will proved at, 543
Glamvyle (Glaunvyle, Glaunvyll), Alice, 18; wife
of Thomas, 569
Cecily, 18
John, of Drinkstone, **18**; of Haughley, **569**
Peter, 569
Thomas, 569
Glaswryg(t)h, John, 675; the elder, of Great
Waldingfield, **675**
William, of Pakenham, 101n
GLEMSFORD, church, 21, 163, 164, 262, 316,
317, 504, 508, 528, 564, 628, 742, 751
churchwardens of, 317
crucifix in, 163
image of BVM in, 21
painting of rood of, 262
parclose in, 163
parish chaplain of, *see* Henry Rynggold
parson of, 262
sepulchre light in, 504
torches in, 316, 504
gilds in, *lxii*, 317, 317n, 508
inhabitants of, *lxxivn*, 21, 125, 163, 164, 213n,
463, 628n, 662, 742, 742n
lands in, 21, 164, 504, 508, 628, 742, 751, 752
places in, 'Bryces' (tenement) in 'Podelstret',
504
'Cattescrofte', 504

'Caustons' (tenement), 628
'Crowche Hows' (messuage), 508
'?Fedmelle', 262
'Jakes' (tenement), 508
'Longemedewe, le', 504
'Mondaylond' (pasture), 504
'Sloholes, lez', 751
'Tonpites' (croft), 742, 742n
'Turpyttis' (croft), 628, 628n
poor of, 21
testators of, *lxin*, *lxiin*, *lxivn*, *lxix*, **21, 100,
163, 164, 262, 316, 317, 504, 508, 528,
564, 628, 640, 742, 751, 752**
ways in, 'Egremanstret', 504
'Podelstret', 504
'Wodestrete', 164
wills proved at, 21, 22, 161, 162, 163, 164,
316, 317, 504, 564, 733, 751, 752
Glemyford, Ellen, 232
John, 232
Glinkford, Robert, 820
Glover(e) (Glovyere), Agnes, 133; widow, of
Woodditton (Cambs), *lxin*, 630n, **762**
Joan, 482
John, 133, 759; the younger, 762; of
Cavendish, **133**, 423n, 803n
Katherine, 218
Margaret, 133, 218; widow, of Stanton, **759**
see also Hawkedon *alias* Glovere
Gobett, Richard, 153
Goche, John, 589; 'smyth', of Norton, 743
Margery, 589,
Robert, 437n; & family, of Bacton, 700; of
Thelnetham, **589**
Thomas, 589,
Godard, John, the elder, 343, 476
Goday, Thomas, 189n; 'karpenter', of Sudbury,
31n
Goddrych (Goderyche), *see* Godrich
Godewyn(e), Richard, of Thornham Magna, 193
Robert, 593
Godfrey, Alan, of Little Whelnetham, 413n
John, 773
Margaret, 773
Thomas, 773
William, of Great Horringer, *lxiii*, **773**, 654n
Godhay, Henry, 708
Godlard, Alice, 498
John, of Thornham, 498
Margaret, (née), & family, 498
Simon, of Wickham Skeith, **498**
Godman, Elizabeth, (née), 351
Joan, 351
William, of Thorpe Morieux, *lxviii*, **351**
Godrich(e) (Goddrych, Goderyche Goodrych),
Alice, 417
John, 634; priest, 417; the younger, 557
Rose, of Felsham, widow, *lvii*, *lxn*, **533**

Roger, 804

Godyng, (Goodyng), Joan, 356
 John, of Withersfield, **356**
Goldbour (Goldsboro), Alice, 279, 382
 family, of Soham, 279n
 Joan, 279, 382
 Matilda, 279
 Thomas, of Soham (Cambs), **279**, 382n
 William, 279, 382; the elder, 382; the younger,
  of Soham (Cambs), 279n, **382**
Goldfynche, Alice, 467
 Thomas, of Botesdale in Redgrave, **467**
 William, 467, 467n
Golding, *see* Goldyng
Goldsboro, *see* Goldbour
Goldsmyth, John, clerk, 136
Goldston, Alice, 435
Goldyng (Golding), Agnes, 316
 family, of Eye, 2
 Joan, 316
 John, 504; & family, 316; barber, 224; of
  Glemsford, 564
 Katherine, 564
 Margery, (née), & family, 316
 Richard, chaplain, 440, 440n, 698, 698n
 Robert, of Glemsford, 316n, **564**
 Thomas, 505; & family, 316
 William, 178, 504; of Eye, **2**, 94n; of
  Glemsford, **316**, 564, 564n
Golofre, Agnes, 277
 John, of Soham (Cambs), **277**
 William, 277
Gooch(e), Adam, of Rushbrooke, **127**
 Agnes, 32
 Alice, 31, 127
 Joan, 32, 127
 John, 127; & family, 32
 Robert & family, 32
 Thomas & family, 32; of Sudbury, 31
 William, chaplain, 127
Goodale, John, servant, 823
Gooderyche, *see* Godrich
Goodewyn, Margaret, 12
 Olive, 12
 Thomas, 12
 William, of Burwell (Cambs), *lvii*, **12**, 550n
 see also Goodwyn
Goodhale, Robert, 511
Goodyng, *see* Godyng
Goodryche, *see* Godrich
Goodwyn, Alice, (née), 550
 Joan, 550
 John, 550
 Margaret, 550
 Thomas, 550
 William, of Burwell (Cambs), 12n, **550**
 see also Goodewyn
Goodyer, John, 490

Goold, Stephen, 707
Goole, Stephen, 661
Goore (Gore), Alice, 292, 293, 738n, 744
 Edmund, 292, 293,
 John, of Barnham, *In*, **292**, **293**, 493n
 Lucy, 292, 293
 Simon, 744
 Thomas, 525, 604; of Soham (Cambs), **744**
 William, 744
 see also Sampson *alias* Goore
Goose, Agnes, of Horringer, 786
 John, 773
Gore, *see* Goore
Gos(e)lyn, Robert, 729
 Thomas, Sir, of Hartest, 35
 William, 673; Master, 35n
Gosse, Agnes, 516
 John, 516; of Newton, **516**
 Richard, 516
 Robert, 516; of Assington, 311
Gotche, Laurence, 731, 826
 Thomas, 230
Gowle, John, of Stowmarket, 109, 669n
 Thomas, 645
Gowty, Thomas, 89
Greene (Grene), Anne, 89, 89n
 Isabel, of Creeting St Peter, 89n
 James, of Lindsey, 50
 Joan, 148
 John, esquire, 191, 191n; chaplain of
  Mildenhall, 611, 611n, 635, 635n, 638,
  638n
 Katherine, 136; of Great Livermere, 129
 Robert, 89; of Saxham Street, Thorney in
  Stowmarket, 89n
 Thomas, of Creeting St Peter, *lxvn*, 89n;
  gentleman, of Witham (Esx), 148
 William, 89n; of Creeting St Peter, *lxv*, **44**, **89**
Greneleff, Richard, 681
Grenhell, Alice, 54
 Joan, 54
 John, of Layham, **54**
 Margaret, 54
 Richard, 54
 Thomas, 54
Grey, Isabel, (née Lovell), 305
 John, 146; gentleman, of Nettlestead, 204n
 Peter, 814
 Thomas, 121
Greyve, John, of Hadleigh, 248
Gridge (Grigge, Griggys), *see* Grygges
Grocer, Joan, (née Turnour), of Walsham, 495
Grome, Isabel, wife of John, the elder, of
  Melford, *lin*, 436n, **728**
 John, the elder, *lin*, 728
 Marit', 722
 Thomas, son of Richard, 722
 William, 446, 728

Grondysborgh, *see* Bocher *alias* Grondysborgh
Gronge, *see* Bugge *alias* Gronge
Gronger(e), John, 210, 587n, 674n
Groos, Thomas, 11
GROTON, church, 117, 247, 309
   chalice for, 309
   rector of, *see* John Howse
   tabernacle of St Margaret in, 309
   inhabitants of, 247n, 309, 440
   lands in, 247
   places in, 'le forge', 247
   testators of, **117**, *254*, **309**
GRUNDISBURGH, church, 94
Grygges (Gridge, Grigge, Griggys, Grygge)
   Agnes, 11
   Alice, 11
   Andrew, of Lavenham, *lxiii*n, **11**, 87n
   Ellen, 422
   John, 11, 11n, 76, 76n, 314, 473, 473n, 690;
     the elder, 422; the younger, 422; of Hartest,
     422; of Lavenham, 87n
   Rose, 11n
Grymsyk, John, 338
Gunse, Thomas, gentleman, 508, 508n
Gybbe, John, 767n
Gybelo(u)n (Gybloue), Christine, 51
   Isabel, 84
   Joan, 84
   Margaret, 51; of Sudbury, 117
   Richard, 84, 84n; of Sudbury, **84**
   Thomas, of Bures St Mary, **51**
   William, 117
   see also Gebelon
Gylberd (Gylbert(t)), Agnes, 69
   John, 69
   Margaret, 69, 757
   Thomas, of Ixworth Thorpe, **69**
   William, of Troston, **757**
Gyles, Katherine, 301
Gylle, William, 695
Gylly, *see* Sawyer *alias* Gylly
Gylmyn, John, 815
Gynows, Alice, 805
   George, 805
   John, 805
   Thomas, of Mendlesham, **805**
   see also Jenews
Gyppys (Gippys), Andrew, of Bury St Edmunds,
   582

Habyngton, John, friar of Babwell, 760
Hac(c)he, Clemence, (née), 436, 779
   Joan, widow of John, of Long Melford, 436,
     779
   John, 264, 436; son of Joan, 779; of Long
     Melford, 436
   Katherine, 264, 480
   Marion, (née), 436, 779

Nicholas, 783; of Nayland, 439
   Robert, 436, 779
   William, of Stradishall, **264**
Hachet(t), John, 413, 583, 588
?Hacke, John, 232
Hactre, William, 620
Haddok, Agnes, servant, 150
Hadenam (Hadynham), John, the elder, 585n; of
   Kentford (Cambs), 585
Hadlay, John, 210
HADLEIGH, inhabitants of, 150, 248, 362, 440,
   713
   lands in, 11
   peculiar of, *xlv*
Hadleigh, John, 456
Hadynham, *see* Hadenam
Hagown, Thomas, 30
Hakon, Robert, 150
   Thomas, of Higham, 150
Hall (Hal(l)e), Agnes, 196
   Alice, 56
   Elizabeth, 430
   John, of East Bergholt, 430; of Great Bradley,
     56; of Woolpit, **430**, 519n
   Simon, 430
   Thomas, *lxxv*n, 56
   William, & family, 465; & wife, of Sudbury,
     607
Hallys, Andrew, of Acton, 311
Halse, John, 107
HALSTEAD (Esx), inhabitants of, 354
Halsted(e), John, 731, 819, 819n
Hamelyn, John, 36, 555
Hamond (Hamownd(e)), Agnes, 52, 62, 151
   Cecily, of Thorney in Stowmarket, 401n, **737**
   Isabel, 62
   Joan, 151n
   John, son of William, 151; of Lawshall, 151n
   Richard, of Barrow, **62**
   Thomas, of Lawshall, **151**
   William, 582, 799; & family, 151, 151n; of
     Nayland, 439n
Hamond *alias* Peddere, Robert, 37n, 228n
Hamyre, Alice, of Stanton, 415
Hancok, Ralph, 577n,
   Walter, 646
Hannyngton, William, 757
Harald, Henry, of Stuston, 165, 617
   Roger, of Mellis, 391n
   William, 391n
Hardeman, John & family, 1
   see also Herdman
Hard(e)grey (Harlegrey), Henry, of Mildenhall,
   600n
   John, 119, 600, 600n, 826n
Hardhed, Robert, of Buxhall, 712
   Thomas, 806n
HARDINGHAM (Nfk), incumbent of, *xlviii*n

Hardy, John, 169
   Thomas, of Thelnetham, 589
Hardyman, John, 639
Hardyng, Nicholas, 3; of Eye, 222
   Robert, of Eye, *lxiii*, 2n, 94n, **457**, 642n
   Thomas, 222
Hare, Margaret, 101
   William, of Pakenham, **101**
HARGRAVE, church, 53, 297
   testator of, **297**
Harlegrey, *see* Hardgrey
Harleston (Harlyston), Agnes, 183
   Elizabeth, 183
   Henry, of Stanton, **183**
   John, 183
   Thomas, 183
   William, esquire, of Debenham, 457, 457n; of
     Denham, 89
Harlewyn, John, 374
HARLING, EAST (Nfk), church, window in, *lviii*
Harlyng(e), Agnes, 393
   Matilda, (née), 393
   Nicholas, of Hopton, **393**
   Richard, of Hopton, 393n
   Thomas, 555; of Hopton, 393, 393n
Harlyston, *see* Harleston
Harpour (Harpowre), Elizabeth, 592
   John, of Glemsford, **752**
   Juliana, 752
Harrald, Thomas, 391, 391n
Harry, Elizabeth, 681
   Joan, 681
   John, 681; of Lavenham, 339n, **681**
   Olive, 681
   Thomas, 681
HARTEST, church, 422, 690, 807
   sepulchre in, 690
   inhabitants of, 183, 640, 807
   lands in, 422, 690
   places in, 'Gardeners' (tenement), 183
   testators of, **422, 690, 807**
HARTISMERE, deanery of, *xlivn, xlv*
Harvy, George, 784
   see also Hervy
Harwell, Robert gentleman, 297
Hasylwode, Alice, 331
HAUGHLEY, church, 25, 168, 180, 313, 324,
     511, 547, 569, 669, 700, 706
   chapel of BVM, window in, *lvii*, 180
   trunk of an oak for, *lviin*, 547
   vestment for, 706
   inhabitants of, 511, 521, 568n, 706
   lands in, 180, 313, 706
   places in, 'Fen, le' (pasture), 706
     'Haughle Grene', 25
     'Hawle markett', 669, 669n
   poor of, 706

   testators of, *lvii, lviin*, **25, 180, 313, 324, 511,
     547, 569, 706**
   ways in, way to 'Fliesgapp', 180
   way from market to 'Fysshpond', 706
   wills proved at, 315, 324, 383, 398, 547
Havell (Haveell), John, 154, 303
   Thomas, 455
HAVERHILL, *xlvi*
   chapel of 'Alwarton', 740, 740n
     land of, 740, 740n
   church, (unspec.), 13
   churches, 14n
     lower church of St Mary, 608, 678, 693,
       740
       sepulchre light in, 740
     upper church of St Mary, 14, 357, 678,
       691, 693
       image of crucifix in, 357
       lamp for Sundays & double festivals, 678
       light in, 357
       selure of holy cross in, 14
       incumbent of, *see* Nicholas Sylvester
       parish clerk, 14
   inhabitants of, 14, 107, 259, 608n
   manor of 'Alwarton', 740n
   lands in, 14, 357, 678, 691, 740
   places in, 'Belyngesbregge', 740
     'Closemedowe', 740
     'Dene, le' (field), 14
     'Hanchache', Hanchet End, 357, 693
     'Londoncroft', 678
     'Overeyfeld', 678
     'Sweynnesmede' (meadow), 678
   poor of, 691,
   testators of, *lxxvn*, *13*, **14**, *250*, *341*, *678*, **691,
     740**
     Hanchet End, **357**, 693, 693n
   wills proved at, 23, *249*, *250*, 330, 356, 357,
     676, 677, 678, 691, 692, 693, 740
Havet, Isabel, 172
   Robert, 172
Hawe, Elizabeth, daughter of Rose Goddrych,
     533
   John, 599
   Roger, 235
   William, 528
HAWKEDON, church, 125, 676, 780
   bell for, 780
   panel (of alabaster) on high altar of, 676,
     780
   rector of, *see* Ed. Frere
   rood of, 676, 676n
   torches & candles of, 676
   gilds in, 780
   inhabitants of, 676
   lands in, 125, 676, 780
   manor of Cresseners in, 181n
   places in, 'iiij Acres croft', 676

'Grene Yerd', 676
'Lytyll Medewe, le', 676
'Medylcrofte, le, 676
'Nedyr crofte, le', 676
testators of, *lxxii*, **676**, **780**
wills proved at, 366, 461, 462, 482, 609, 610
Hawk(e)don, Joan, 284
John, rector of Nedging, 284, 284n, 303, 406, 431, 720, 721
Margaret, 284
Rose, 284
Simon, 284
Thomas, the younger, 284
William, of Bildeston, 303
Hawkedon *alias* Glovere, William, of Bildeston, *li*n, **284**
Hawkere (Hawken), Agnes, of Elmswell, **605**
Ralph, 605
Hawkyn (Haukyn), Agnes, 410
John, 162; servant, 586; of Attleton in Wickhambrook, **410**
Robert, 162
see also Hawkere
Hawle, John, 319
HAWLEY, church, 529
wills proved at, 529
Hawngere, John, 752
HAWSTEAD, church, 39, 314
cross in churchyard, 314
missal for, 314
inhabitants of, 125n, 417n, 470
lands in, 39
testator of, **39**
will proved at, 125
Hawys(e), Alice, 294
George, rector of Barrow, 401, 401n, 502
James, 496; of Walsham, 65, 258, **475**
John, the younger, 294; of Walsham, 294
Margery, 475,
Hay, Ralph, 342
William, of Barnardiston, 598n
Hec(c)ham, Joan, 180
John, 180,
Matthew, 673, 673n
Roger, 180,
William & family, 180
Hecham *alias* Bochere, Stephen, of Haughley, *li*n, *lvii*, **180**, 180n
?Heche, Robert, 317
Hede, Richard, 101
Hedgeman (Heggeman), Joan, of Glemsford, **100**
John, 100*, 100n; the elder, of Glemsford, 22n, 125n, 164n, 213n
Thomas, 100
HEDINGHAM (Esx), priory/nunnery of, *lx*n, 698, 698n
Hedone, Ed., 243

Hegge, Thomas, 30
Heggeman, *see* Hedgeman
Heis(s)ham, William, rector of Wetheringsett, 778, 778n, 796
Hekedoun, Ed., 340
Heldhalle, [*unnamed*], & wife, 211
HELIONS BUMPSTEAD (Esx), church, 490
Hell(e), Henry, 488; of Cockfield, **488**
Joan, wife of William, of Clare, 662
John, of Chelsworth, 50; of Shelland, 109
Richard, 488
Hellys, Hely(i)s, *see* Elyis
Helperby, William, 471
Helpston, *see* Hepston
Helseden, William, 776
Hempman, Thomas, 467
Hendy, Agnes, 591
Joan, 654,
Hengessman (Hengestman), John, 380, 815
HENGRAVE, inhabitants of, 110n
Henn, Sir John, 555
Henry VI, readeption of, *li*, 426, 426n
Hepston (Helpston), Isabel, 816
John, of Rougham, **816**
Nicholas, 816
Roger, 816,
Thomas, 558, 816
HEPWORTH, church, 68, 240, 268, 392, 402, 522
light before sepulchre in, 392
rector of, *see* John Scole
inhabitants of, 268, 392, 392n, 590
lands in, *lxxv*in, 68, 268, 392
places in, 'Breche, le' (furlong), 68
'Buskesyerd' (close), 68
'Caldewellys Crosse', 268
'Carbredge', 268
'Collesyerde' (pightle), 68
'Crowys' (tenement), 392
'Hykkescrofftt', 68
'Longdyche' (close), 68
'Lugmannes' (close), 68
'Netherbreche at the Wylugg', 68
'Northgrene, le', 68
'Overheche' (furlong), 68
'Reveshale' hall, 68
'Slowgate', 268
testators of, *li*n, *lxviii*, *lxix*n, **68**, **392**, **402**
ways in, common way through, 402
'Rawneslane', 268
Herberd, Joan, of Yaxley, 790n
Thomas, of Long Melford, 436, 779
Herd(e), William, & family, 465; & family, of Sudbury, 607
Herdman (Hardman), Henry, Master, 444, 444n
Herevord, John, of Bardwell, 220
Herman, William, of Rickinghall Superior, 240n

Hermer(e), Geoffrey, 681
  Richard, 507, 534
Herne, *see* att Herne
Hernyng(e), Alice, (née), 777
  Isabel, 777
  John, the elder, 777; the younger, 777
  Thomas, of Santon Downham, **777**
Herri, Roger, chaplain, 23
HERRINGSWELL, church, 485, 719
  gilds in, 485, 485n
  lands in, 229, 719
  testators of, **485, 719**
  wills proved at, 481, 580, 611, 612, 753, 754
Herry, Thomas, 681
Herset(t) (Herstete), Margery, 451
  Robert, 363, 451
Hert(e), Elizabeth, (née), 519
  Joan, 660, 660n, (née), 519, 519n, 660
  John, Dom, 519; of Elmswell, 519, 519n, **660**
  Margery, 519, 519n, (née), 519
  Nicholas, 519,
  Robert, 519, 660, 660n,
  William, 116, 519; of Elmswell, *lvii*n, *lx*n,
    88n, 367, 367n, 430, **519**, 660n
Herverd, *see* Herward
Hervy (Hervey, Hervi), Alice, widow, of
    Rickinghall Inferior, **500**
  Elizabeth, of Stanton, 386
  Jane, Lady of Ickworth, 709, 709n
  Joan, 800
  John, 283, 333, 476n, 622, 739; friar, 171; of
    Gislingham, 343n, **800**; of Great Wratting,
    & family, 677
  Robert, parish chaplain of Lavenham, 552,
    552n, 681
  Thomas, 628; vicar of Eye, 2, 3, 222, 222n,
    395, 442, 457
Herward (Herverd), Margaret, of Wordwell, **539**
  John, of Sudbury, *lxxiv*n
Heryng, William, 72, 403
Hesset(e) (Hessett) Agnes, & family, 149
  John, of Wetherden, **149**
  Richard, 149, 149n
  Thomas, of Wetherden, 149n, 315n
HESSETT, church, 113, 746
    light of BVM in, 113
    light of Holy Trinity in, 113
  inhabitants of, 113, 184, 205n
  places in, 'Prentysys' (messuage), 113
  testators of, **113, 746**
Heth(e), Agnes, servant, 440
  Alice, daughter of John, 420
  George, 378
  John, 420
  Marion, of Rattlesden, *lii*n, **57**
  Thomas, *lii*n, 57
Hewell, Robert de, 6n
Hewet, *see* Howett

Heylok, John, of Barnardiston, *lxxiv*n
Heylott, Christian, 319
  Robert, 319
  Thomas, 319
Heynes, Eleanor, 17
  John, late of Thorpe Morieux, **17**
Heyvard (Heyward), Anne, 628
  Collette, 111
  Joan, servant, 50
  John, 111, 248, 598; friar, 574; of Hessett, **746**
  Katherine, 746
  Robert, of Wattisham, **111**
  Roger, 746
  William, the younger, 349
HIGHAM, church, 150
  inhabitants of, 150
Higham (Hygham), Thomas, esquire, 297;
    esquire, the elder, 243, 243n
Hill, *see* Hyll
HINDERCLAY, church, 323, 522, 795, 802
    book for, 802
  inhabitants of, 795, 802
  testators of, **795, 802**
HITCHAM, almshouse, *lxiii*, 587, 587n
  church, 43, 75, 181, 196, 211, 587, 720, 721,
    806
    cope, silk, of 'sateyn cremesyn' for, *lix*, 181
    image of crucifix in, 181
  gild in, 43
    gildhall of, *lxii*, 43n, 75
  inhabitants of, 43, 75, 154n, 806
  lands in, 181, 196, 211, 587, 720
  places in, house by gate of churchyard, 587
    small house next to manor, *lxiii*, 587
    'Wattys croft', 'Wattes crofte', 720, 721
  poor of, 196
  testators of, *lix, lxii, lxiii, lxiii*n, **43, 75, 181,
    196, 211, *444*, 587, *674*, 806**
  will proved at, 248
Hobbes, Agnes, 261
  Alice, 261
  Ellen, 261
  Joan, 261
  John, 261
  Margaret, 261
  Robert, 261
  William, of Acton, **261**
Hoberd, Adam, of Wattisfield, **273**
  Alice, 273
  Hugh, 273
  John, 273; glover, 376
  Margery, 273
  Robert, 273
  Roger, 273
  Thomas, 622
  William, 601
Hochown, John, 258
  William, 376

Hod, *see* Hoode
Hode, Anne, 488
   William, 488
Hog(g)e, Alice, 184
   John, 184, 634,
   Robert, of Rougham, **184**
Hogon, Eleanor, 145
Hoket, John, the elder of Long Melford, 32n, 45n
Holdeman, [*unnamed*], of Chippenham (Cambs),
   107
Holden, Agnes, 742; daughter of Thomas, of
   Icklingham, 683
   Alice, 628, (née), 742
   Anne, 628
   Edmund, 431
   Isabel, wife of Thomas, of Icklingham, 683
   Joan, (née), 431
   John, 431*, 431n, 628*; the elder, of
      Glemsford, **628**, 742n; the younger, 742,
      742n; the younger, of Glemsford, 628n, **742**
   Margaret, 628
   Richard, 628
   Rose, (née), & daughters, 431
   Thomas, 628; the elder, 628; of Icklingham,
      683
   William, 431
Holdernesse (Holdirnesse), Ralph, rector of Little
   Saxham, 320, 320n, 507, 507n
Holdeyn, John, tailor, 163
Hollond, Thomas, chaplain of Newton, 597
Holm(e), John, of Barrow, 152n
   Robert, 378
   Thomas, of Cotton, 700n
HOLY LAND, captives in, 636, 636n
Holy Trinity, friars of the order of, 634, 634n,
   636, 636n
Honge, Thomas, 822,
HONINGTON, church, 157, 474, 489
   mortuary given to, *liv*n, 157, 474
   inhabitants of, 157, 520
   lands in, 474
   testators of, *liv*n, **157**, **474**, *520*
   wills proved at, 299
Hoo, John, 746; of 'Foxherdhalle', 31
   see also at Ho(o)
Hood(e), Agnes, (née), 173
   George, 173
   Joan, 173
   Margery, 173
   Nicholas, 24
   Thomas, of Felsham, **173**, 173n
Hoog, John, of Rougham, 535
HOPTON, church, 36, 186, 393, 522, 555, 590,
   661, 707
   rector of, *see* John Brown *and* John
      Worlych
   thurible for, 186
   gilds in, 661, 661n, 707

inhabitants of, 392n, 393, 393n, 661n
lands in, 186, 393, 555, 661
places in, 'Fenfeld', 661
   'Lampettes Furlong', 661
   'Medilferlong', 661
   'Nethergate', 'Nethyrgate', 661, 661n, 707
   'Northegate', 661
   'Scottys' (tenement), 393
testators of, **36**, **186**, **393**, **555**, **661**, **707**
ways in, 'Northgatestrete', 661, 661n
   'Portwey', 661
wills proved at, 522, 542, 561, 562, 661, 739,
   811
Horarld, Horald, William, 782
HORKESLEY (Esx), inhabitants of, 783
HORKESLEY, LITTLE (Esx), inhabitants of,
   141
Horn(e), Henry, 661
   John, 182
Hornekek, Joan, (?née Yonge), 333
Horold, Clemence, 235
   John, 155; the younger, of Clare, 276, 276n;
      the elder, of Mellis, **235**
   Julian, 235
   Margaret, 235
   Roger, of Mellis, 235
   Thomas, 235; of Bildeston, 431
   William, 235
HORRINGER (unspec.), inhabitants of, 786
HORRINGER, GREAT, church, 10, 81, 88, 432,
   486, 654, 773
   image of St Leonard in, 432
   parson of, 654
   porch in, 88, 432, 654
   rector of, 432, 432n
   sepulchre in, 88
   gilds in, *lxii*n, 432, 654, 654n
   gildhall of, *lxii*, 432, 654, 654n
   inhabitants of, 10, 81, 88, 432n, 654n, 709,
      711n, 773n
   lands in, 10, 81, 432, 654, 773
   places in, 'Beryfeld', 773
      'Cowperisgrene', 432
      'Cundewyte, le', 773
      'Fynstoft', 773
      'Gooses' (pightle), 773
      'grendyll, le', 10
      'Hakferescroft', 773
      'Herdwyk' (wood), 10
      'Hopleyfeld', 773
      'Hurrelebattes Hetche', 10
      'Ikeworth Feelde', 654
      'Lytylmedewe', 773
      'Newplace, le' (tenement), 10
      'Penylond', 10
      'Potteris alfeacre', 10
      'Stubbyng feeld', 654
   poor of, 432

testators of, *lxii*, *lxii*n, *lxiii*, **10**, **81**, **88**, **432**,
    654, **773**
ways in, 'Clenewallstrete', *lxiii*, 773
    from 'Cowperisgrene' to church, 432
HORRINGER, LITTLE, church, sepulchre in, 88
    lands in, 128
Horsman, Emote, 280
    Robert, 280, 810
    William, of Wetheringsett, **280**
Hospitallers of St John of Jerusalem, Knights of
    Rhodes, house of, 449, 449n
Hotley, Robert, 318
Hotoft, William, 89; son of Thomas, 89
Hoton, Alice, 704
    Richard, 704
    William, of Woolpit, **704**
Hotott, Robert, 665
Hovell (Hovyle), Alice, (née More), 801, 801n
    Richard, of Cowlinge, 801n
    Thomas, of Cowlinge, **801**
    William, 801
Howard, Catherine, Lady, 38
    John, Sir, & family, 38; of Great Barton, **736**
    Margaret, 736; Lady, 38
    Thomas, 434
Howchon, John, 495
Howett (Hewet), John, *lxxii*, 353
    Richard, of Edwardstone, *lxxii*, **353**
    Thomas, *lxxii*, 353
Howlot(t), John, 154
    Thomas, 630
Howse (Hows, Howys), John, parish chaplain of
    Icklingham St James, 479, 479n, 471; rector
    of Groton, 714, 714n
    William, of Market Weston, 822
Howton, Isabel, 676
    Joan, 676
    John, the elder, 676; the younger, 676
    Margaret, *lxxii*, 676
    Thomas, of Hawkedon, *lxxii*, **676**
    Walter, 676
    William, 813
Howys, *see* Howes
HOXNE, prior of, 765, 765n
Hoxne (Hoxon), *see* Oxne
Hoy, John, 119; of Icklingham St James, **119**
    William, the elder, of Wormingford (Esx), 67
Hoy *alias* Cowpere, William, 119
Hub(b)erd (Hubert), Isabel, 416
    John, 65, 416, 416n; of Redgrave, *lvii*, **543**
    Margery, 543
    Matilda, 65
    Robert, 65, 543; of Finningham, **65**; of
    Redgrave, **416**, 543n
    Thomas, 65
    William, of Stow cum Quy (Cambs), 513
Huchon, John, 219n

Hucton (Hukton), Agnes, widow, of Clare, *lxvi**,
    276, 531n
    John, of Clare, 276, 276n
    Richard, 276
    Thomas, 780
Huite, Robert, 33
Hukton, *see* Hucton
Humfrey, Walter, 663; of Bradfield St George,
    270
Hum(m)ys, Britana, widow, of Kersey, *lii*, **701**
    Joan, (née), 701; daughter of John, 701
    John, 701
HUNDON, church, 78, 79, 160, 171, 301
    vicar of, 301
    gilds in, 79
    inhabitants of, 78, 99, 198, 276, 301n, 303n,
        380n, 677, 808
    lands in, 42, 79, 456
    places in, 'Barkeres Medewe', 456
        'Brokhoole', 160
        workshop, *lxxii*, 79
    poor of, 78, 79
    roads in, 78
    testators of, *lxxii*, **42**, **78**, **79**, **160**, **301**
    wills proved at, 79, 160, 198, 263, 264, 272,
        598, 724
Hundyrwod, Ellen, 667
    see also Underwoode
Hunger (Hungyre), Elizabeth, of Thwaite, **745**
    John, 745, 745n
    Rose, widow, of Mellis, 391n
HUNSTANTON (Nfk), church, 417n
HUNSTON, church, 362, 605, 770
    sepulchre light of, 605
    tower of, 770, 770n
    gilds in, 770n
    inhabitants of, 362, 415
    lands in, 770
    places in, common way, 770
    testators of, **770**
Hunte (Huntt), Agnes, 677
    Alice, 432; of Withersfield, *lviii*, *lix*n, **171**
    Ed., 171
    John, of Barnardiston, 677
    Katherine, of Rushbrooke, 125n, 191, 191n,
        470
    Margaret, (née), 171
    Margery, of Barrow, 152n, **136**; wife of John,
        of Barnardiston, *lin*, **677**
    Robert, 470, 470n; esquire, of Rushbrooke,
        lin, *liii*, **191**, 413n
    Roger, of Barrow, 136n
    Thomas, 171; rector of Gasthorpe, 555, 555n
    William, 171
Hurry, Matilda, of Wordwell, 539
Huske, Joan, 389, 708
    John, the elder, 389; the younger, 389

Thomas, 389, 708; the elder, 112; of Ickworth, **389**

Hurlebate, *see* At Lee *alias* Hurlebate

Huwet(t), John, 720, 721

Hyde, John, 48, 783; the elder, of Nayland, 439n, 783; the younger, of Nayland, 556

Hygge, John, 119

Hygham, *see* Higham

Hykedon, Richard, 60

Hyll(e) (Hill), Agnes, 40, 346

    Alice, of Stoke by Nayland, **38**, 109n

    Denise, lately wife of John, of Sudbury, 434, 434n, **505**

    Henry, 115

    John, 40, 507, 346; the younger, 346; of Sudbury, **434**, 505, 505n

    Julian, (née), 505

    Margaret, of Westhorpe, **4**

    Reynold, 38

    Robert, of London, grocer, 505, 505n

    Thomas, 38; clerk, 109, 673; Sir, 38; the elder, of Long Melford, **346**

    see also at (the) Hyll(e)

Hynard, John, 583

Hyncheman, John, 26

Hyndebest, Adam, of Thurston, **74**

    Alice, 74

    William, 74

Hynderwell, Robert, incumbent of All Saints', Sudbury, 670, 670n

Hyne, Matilda, of Sudbury, 32n

Hynge, Robert, of Mildenhall, 347n

Hyrby, *see* Irby

Hyve, Thomas, 399n

ICKLINGHAM, church of All Saints, 72, 403, 450, 469, 471, 479

    alabaster panel for, 469, 471

    cloth to hang before image of BVM in, 479

    rector of, *see* Thomas Sherecroft

    wills proved in, 492

    church of St James, 72, 403, 449, 450, 471, 479, 492, 683

    chalice for, 471

    ornaments of, 683

    painted cloth to hang before high altar of, 479

    parish chaplain of, *see* John Howys

    wills proved in, 545

    gilds in, 826, 826n

    inhabitants of, 469, 469n, 471n, 479n, 572, 683

    lands in, 72, 471, 492, 683

    places in, 'Byrissyerd', 471

    land of Bury St Edmunds abbey, 492

    'Masouns' (messuage), 72

    testators of, *l*in, 72, 119, 403, 449, 469, 471, 479, 492, 683

ways in, 'Birrwey', 683

wills proved at, 24, 119

ICKWORTH, church, 112, 138, 389, 695, 708, 709

    altar of BVM in, 112

    ornaments in, 112

    rector of, 708

    inhabitants of, 709

    lands in, 112, 138, 389, 695

    places in, 'Bayardbregge', 389

    'Bonyswode Ende', 112

    'Medyll tenewall, le', 112

    'Syre Robertes Crofte', 138

    testators of, *lxxiii*, **112**, **138**, **389**, **695**, **708**, **709**

Ilger, Margery, (née Fullere), wife of Robert, & family, 507

    Robert, 373, 507

Ingelond *see* Inglond

INGHAM, church, 368

    rector of, *see* Walter Coket

    tower of, 368

    inhabitants of, 368

    places in, 'Ingham Bussh', 544

    testators of, **368**

Inglond, Hervey, 168

    John, 392,

    William, or Henry, of Troston, **489**

    William, 168, 168n; of Bardwell, 489n

Ingold, William, 738n

INGRAVE (Esx), places in, 'Wymbyssh' (tenement), 398

Ingrham, John, of Langham (Esx), 197

IPSWICH, administrative centre of archdeaconry of Suffolk, *xliv*

    church of St Nicholas, 697

    friar of (unspec.), 484

    house of Austin Canons, 126, 126n,

    house of Carmelite friars, *lx*, 1, 50, 83, 87, 89, 90, 111, 126, 136n, 157, 205, 247, 381, 467, 576, 594, 665, 669, 673, 700, 706, 805

    house of Dominican friars (Preachers), 50, 87, 89, 109, 126, 381, 669, 673, 805

    house of Franciscan friars (Minors), 1, 11, 50, 54, 87, 89, 111, 126, 337, 381, 470, 665, 669, 673, 697, 701, 805

    house of friars (unspec.), 94

    house of friars of the BVM, 367, 367n

    inhabitants of, 374, 576

    leper-hospital in, *lxiii*, 126*

    of St Leonard, 126n

    of St Mary Magdalene & St James, 126n

    testator of, *lv*n

Irby (Hyrby), Henry, rector of Tostock, 295, 295n, 743

    Nicholas, rector of Norton, 29n

ISLEHAM, church, 450

    peculiar of, *xlv*, *xlv*n

Ive, *see* Eve
IXWORTH, church, 37, 69, 72, 168, 174, 219, 220, 228, 403, 575, 700, 723, 804
    altar of St James in, 219, 723
    light of BVM in, 219
    'stepyll' of, 723, 723n
    tower of, 575
    window of glass in, *lvii*, 219, 219n
    gilds in, 69, 69n, 219, 219n, 220, 723
      missals of gild of St John the Baptist, 69
    inhabitants of, 219, 228, 258n, 295, 452, 723, 738, 743, 804n
    lands in, 219, 220, 723
    places in, 'Grongeres' (messuage), 37
      Ixworth bridge, 219
      Ixworth field, 220
      'Purchas' (tenement), 219
    priory of Austin canons, 69, 220, 362, 527n, 723, 738, 777, 821
      canon(s) of, 220, 228, 398, 527, 723
      church of, 69, 228
      novices of, 723
      prior of, 69, 228, 362, 723, 777
      see also William Dense
      sub-prior of, 69, 723
    testators of, *lin*, *lvii*, *lxn*, *lxxvn*, **37**, **174**, **219**, **220**, **228**, **575**, **723**, **804**
    ways in, 'Heygstrete, le', 220
    wills proved at, 36, 37, 68, 69, 132, 159, 168, 174, 175, 207, 219, 220, 282, 338, 362, 452, 453, 603, 605, 615, 723, 817, 821
IXWORTH THORPE, church, 69, 228, 522
    inhabitants of, 365n, 661
    manor of, 69n
    testators of, **69**

Jacob, John, 259; of Sudbury, **98**
    Matilda, (née Deynys), 259, 259n
    William, 98, 517, 727; the elder, of Sudbury, 98n
Jaffrey (Jaferey), Isabel, 684
    Marion, of Barnham, 684n
    Peter, of Barnham, **684**
    William, of Barnham, 684n
Jakes, John, 751
    Robert, 752
James, William, gentleman, of the city of London, 204n
Jay(e), Cecily, 732
    John, 211; of Burwell (Cambs), 732n
    Margery, 409
    William, of Burwell (Cambs), **732**; of Stoke by Nayland, **409**, 556n
Jefferey, John, 407
Jegnere, Agnes, 246
    Christian, 246
    Robert, 246

    Thomas, of Lakenheath, 246; of Undley hamlet in Lakenheath, **246**
Jekeman, John, 600
Jenewe (Jenews), Agnes, 94; of Eye, 2n, **94**, 405, 405n
    Alice, (née) & family, 94
    Joan, 94
    John, 2n, 94, 94n, 405, 405n
    Robert, 94
    see also Gynows
Jenowr, John, of Old Newton, 576n
Jentilman, *see* Gentilman
Jentre, Agnes, 529
    John, 529
Jentte, John, of Preston, 145
    see also Gente
Jerold, William, clerk, 724
JERUSALEM, Hospitallers of St John of, house of, 449, 449n
Jerveys, Alice, daughter of Robert, 754
    Margaret, daughter of Thomas, 21
    Robert, of Barton Mills, 754; son of Robert, of Barton Mills, 754; son of Thomas of Pentlowe (Esx), 21
    see also Gerveys
Jobesson, Alice, (née Germayn), wife of Thomas, of Colchester, 733
    Thomas, 733; son of Thomas, 733
Joc', William, 53
Joli, William, of Lavenham, 552
Joly, Simon, 18
Jonson, Simon, 598
    William, 732
Jordan (Jordon), Robert, 516, 597
Joure, Alice, 344*
    Augustine, of Great Finborough, 156
    Isabel, 344,
    John, 344; of Combs, **344**
    Margaret, 344
Jude, John, of Badwell, 16
Judy, Katherine, 771
    Robert, barker, of Tostock, *lin*, *lxix*, **771** ('Barkere *alias* Judy' *in margin*)
    Thomas, of Thetford, 771
    Walter, of Walsham, 771
Julian, Alice, 385
Julyon, William, 738
Jurden (Jurdon), Henry, 671
    Isabel, 671
    John, 134, 348, 671
    Margaret, 671
    Margery, (née), 671
    Thomas, 348, 671
    William, of Newmarket, **671**
Justice, Agnes, 330
    Eleanor, 330
    John, 330
    William, of Withersfield, **330**

Kaldenell, *see* Caldenell
Karr(e), Robert, 439
   William, of Boxted, 332
Kartere *see* Carter
Kebenham (Kepenham), Richard, 323
   Thomas, of Wortham, **323**
Kebyll (Keeble) Anne, 576, (née), 576
   John, 576; the younger, 737; the younger,
     of Stowmarket, 576, 576n; the heir, of
     Thorney, 673, 673n
   Richard, 89, 576
   Robert, 576
   Thomas, of Gipping Newton, 576
   William, of Old Newton, **576**
Kechet, Ed., 372
KEDINGTON, church, 355, 447
   inhabitants of, 105n, 447
   manor of, 447n
   places in, Boyton Lane, 355
   testators of, *105*, **355**, **447**
   will proved at, 355
Kedlowe, David, 597
   Marion, 597
   Patrick, of Newton, *lii*, **597**
Keeble, *see* Kebyll
Kegyll, Anne, (née Smyth), wife of John, 815
   Thomas, 455
Kelyng, Robert, 426
Kembold, John, servant, 517
   Thomas, the elder, of Hitcham, 674n
Kempe, Alice, (née), 233, 234
   Cecily, 234
   John, 233, 772; servant, 634; sir, 778, 796,
     810; of Burwell (Cambs), 233, **234**, 512n;
     chaplain, of Wetheringsett, 559, 559n
   Katherine, of Burwell (Cambs), **233**, 234
   Margaret, 233
   Nicholas, 233
   Richard, of Cockfield, *49*, **85**
   Thomas, 85, 233
   William, 233, 643
Kendale, Agnes, 50
   Alice, 311
   Isabel, 726
   Joan, (née), 465
   John, 50; the younger, *lxx*, 698; the younger, &
     family, 465; friar, of Orford, 726; butcher,
     of Sudbury, & daughters, 607; the elder, of
     Sudbury, *lxiii*n, *lxvii*, **465**, **607**; the younger,
     of Sudbury, 311
   Margaret, wife of John the younger, 698
   Simon, of Chelsworth, **50**
   William, 126, 729; of Occold, 6n, **726**; friar,
     of Orford, 726
   [*unnamed*], sister of John, living in Acton, 311
Kenman, John, 63; of Barningham, *63*
KENNETT (Cambs), church, 302, 585
   gild in, *lxi*, *lxi*n, 585, 585n

lands in, 585
testators of, **585**
wills proved at, 143, 214
Kent(e), John, 719; of Burwell, 550n; the elder,
   of Herringswell, **719**
   Margaret, 719
   Robert, of Mildenhall, 719; of Stowmarket,
     421, 421n
KENTFORD (Cambs), church, 585, 624
   gilds in, 585, 585n
   lands in, 82
   wills proved at, 77, 429, 550, 551,
KERSEY, church, 92, 153, 595, 701, 767
   candlebeam in, 92
   chalice for, 767
   'Rochetes' for, 767
   gilds in, 767, 767n
   inhabitants of, *lxxiv*n, 92n, 247, 283
   lands in, 595
   places in, 'Bondyners' (tenement), 153
     'Dowys' (tenement), 595
     'Glovers' (messuage), 153
     'Levenhedge', 92
     'Sere Robertys Crofte', 92
     'Smertes' (tenement), 595
     'Wenysfeld', 92
   testator of, *lin*, *lii*, *lv*, **92**, **153**, **595**, **701**, **767**
   wills proved at, 440, 549, 563, 595
Kerver(e), John, 588
   Thomas, 184, 290
KETTLEBASTON, church, 455, 720, 721
   sepulchre light in, 455
   inhabitants of, 455n
   lands in, 455
   manor of, 11
   places in, 'Bellehowscroft', 455
   testators of, **455**
   town of, 11
Ketyll, Thomas, 743
   William, of Preston, 162n
KILVERSTONE (Nfk), church, 522
KIRBY CANE (Nfk), inhabitants of, 689,
KIRTLING (Cambs), church, 281, 461, 462, 482,
   499, 577, 609, 610, 656
   chapel of, lights of BVM in, *lix*n, 462, 609
   light before great cross in, 577
   light before image of St James in, 577
   light before image of St John the Baptist
     in, 577
   lights of BVM in, *lix*n, 462, 609
   rectors of, *see* John Mayn, Richard
     Frankeleyn
   sepulchre light in, 462
   vestment for, 461, 482
   gild in, *lxi*, *lxi*n, 499, 499n
   inhabitants of, 461n, 482n, 499n, 610, 610n
   lands in, 461, 482, 609
   places in, 'Aldercroft', 482

'Bakers' (tenement), 461
'Blakelonde', 482
'Cokes Felde', 482
'Cowlynge Brooke', 482
'Hogemans Croft', 482
'Kertelynge Hell', 482
'Lydgate Feld', 482
'Tuys' (tenement), 461
'Upheme', 'Uphem', Upend, 482, 482n,
    499, 610
'Vasys' (tenement), 461
poor of, 482, 577
testators of, *lix*n, *lxviii*, **281**, **461**, **462**, **482**,
    499, **577**, **609**, **610**, **656**
ways in, 'Tuftelane', 482
KNETTISHALL, church, 522
deed made at, 661
inhabitants of, 661
lands in, 661
places in, highway to Rushworth, 661
testators of, *394*, *441*
will proved at, 393
Knottes, John, 723
Knotyng, William, 140n
Knyght (Knygth), Elizabeth, 320
Margaret, 229
Robert, the younger, 320; the elder, of Little
    Saxham, **320**, 507n
Thomas, 320, 392, 562; of Brockford in
    Wetheringsett, 5; of Walsham, 393
Kobold, Robert, 95
Kok, Joan, & family, 463
Koo, Margery, widow, of Woolpit, 786n
Koone, Thomas, 339
Kreke, Thomas, 610
Krenche, Adam, 33
Joan, 33
Margaret, 33
Richard, of Polstead, **33**
Krowe, *see* Crowe
Kykeby, John, 80
Kykkele, John, 399
Kymbold, John, of Hitcham, *674*
Kyng(e), Agnes, 586, (née), 544; servant, 698
Alice, 763
Andrew, 11
Grace, (née), 710
Joan, 11
John, 354, 544, 746n, 782; the elder, 544;
    of Bradfield Combust, **710**; of Brockford
    in Wetheringsett, **763**; of Chilton in
    Stowmarket, 501n; of Nayland next Stoke,
    459; the elder, of Wetheringsett, **763**
Margaret, 544, 709, 710, 763, (née), 544
Margery, (née), 544
Olive, 763; widow of John, of Mendlesham,
    568n
Peter, of Sapiston, *lxx*, *lxxv*, 118, 118n, **544**

Robert, 292, 293, 586, 763
Thomas, 232, 294, 544, 695, 695n, 708, 708n;
    son of Thomas, 695, 695n; of Bury St
    Edmunds, 586; of Mendlesham, 374n
William, of Wickhambrook, **586**
Kynget, Thomas, & family, 439
Kyrkeby, John, of Icklingham, **449**
Maud, 449
Thomas, 632; Sir, 38
Kyrre, Thomas, 700
Ky(y), John, of Thorney hamlet in Stowmarket,
    468n
Marion, 468
Simon, of Stowmarket, **468**

L'Estrange, *see* Straunge
Lacy, William, *lxix*n, 246, 399
[*unnamed*], friar, 374
Ladde, Margaret, 466
Laderer, Richard, 555
Ladyman, Agnes, 413
Godfrey, 413
John, 413
Thomas, of Little Whelnetham, 93, 130, 130n,
    191, 191n, **413**
Lake, Thomas, 9
Lakenham, John, friar of Babwell, 372
LAKENHEATH, church, 245, 246, 399, 633
gilds in, 399, 399n
inhabitants of, 120, 245
lands in, 399, 633
neighbours in, 399
places in, 'Coppidmere', 399
    Undley hamlet, 246
poor of, 246, 399
testators of, *liv*, *lxix*n, **245**, **246**, **384**, **399**, **633**
Lakke, Agnes, 214
Henry, 214
John, the elder, 214; the younger, 214
Margaret, 214,
Thomas, of Snailwell (Cambs), **214**
Lakyngheth, Ed., chaplain, 23
Lalford, Alice, 32
Robert, 408
Lambard, Margaret, 135
Lambe, Joan, 754
Margaret, 706
Robert, & family, 706
William, of Haughley, **706**
Lamberd, William, of Cowlinge, 340
Lampytte, James, 764
Lane, James, 624, 786
John, 48; of Ixworth Thorpe, 365n; of
    Nayland, **503**
Katherine, 503; wife of John, 503
Nicholas, 503, 784; of Nayland, 439
Robert, 503
Thomas, 503

LANGHAM (Esx), inhabitants of, 197
LANGHAM (Sfk), church, 207, 604
   candlebeam in, 207
   vestments for, 175n
   gilds in, 207, 207n
   inhabitants of, 527
   lands in, 401
   places in, 'Botome, le', 207
      'Munnygges' (tenement), 207
   testator of, *lxxv*n, **207**
   wills proved at, 703, 769, 770
Langham, Thomas, friar, of Sudbury, 145, 145n,
   238, 670
LANGLEY (Nfk), Premonstratensian abbey,
   abbot and convent of, 555, 555n
Langle(y) (Langle(e)), Joan, 112*; widow, 709
   Katherine, 112
   Margaret, 112
   William, 138, 695; of Ickworth, **112**, 709,
      709n
Langlond, John, of Eye, 222n
Lapham, John, of Ixworth, 743
Lardynere, Joan, & family, 585
   William, of Kennett (Cambs), *lxi*n, **585**
Largaunt, John, of Tuddenham, 485
Large, John, of Stanton, **680**
Lathery, Richard, 555
LAVENHAM, almshouses in, *lxiii**, 11, 87, 339,
   339n
   bedeman of, *lvi*n
   borough/burgh of, 517, 552, 681
   church, 11, 87, 122, 223, 237, 339, 431, 454,
      517, 552, 681
      altar of BVM in, 11
      candlebeam in, 237
      cope for, 681
      lights before image of crucifix in, 339
      vestments for, 681
   gilds in, *lxiii*, 339, 339n, 431, 431n, 681,
      alderman of, 339
   inhabitants of, 11, 87, 122, 122n, 190, 223,
      303, 339, 431n, 552, 552n, 681
   lands in, 87, 223, 454, 517, 552, 681
   places in, 'Borythys croft', 681
      'Bramstonys croftes', 681
      market, 122
      'Parych' (tenement), 552n
      'Pereshows' (tenement), 87
      'Pykkys Pett', 517
      shop in the High Street, 87
      'Teyntour yerd, lee', 681
   poor of, *lxiii*, 11, 87, 122, 223, 339, 339n,
      431, 454, 517, 681
   testators of, *lvn*, *lxiii**, *lxiii*n, **11, 87, 122,
      223, 237, 339, 454, 517, 552, 681**
   ways in, 87
      highway between Boxford and, 339
      highway to Brent Eleigh, 681

      highway towards Sudbury, 122
      'Heighstrete', 'Heyestret(te)', 'Lyestrete',
         11, 454, 552n, 681
      Lady Street, 11n
      lane leading to the park, 681, 681n
      'Maisterjonestrete', 'Master John street, le',
         11, 681
      'Nethir street, le', 552
      'Prentystrett, le', Prentice Street, 517, 517n
   wills proved at, 11, 32, 70, 122, 131, 158, 223,
      238, 254, 311, 322, 339, 349, 350, 409,
      439, 517, 552, 607, 628, 681
Lavenham, Thomas, of Sudbury, 434, 596n;
   cutler, of Sudbury, 31n
LAWSHALL, church, 151, 541, 582
   bell for, 541
   chalice for, 582
   missal for, 541
   inhabitants of, 151, 541, 572, 686
   lands in, 541
   places in, 'Cherchestrete howse' (tenement),
      151
      'Gaytones' (tenement), 151
      'Kynges' (tenement), 151
      'Pelomes' (tenement), 151
   testators of, **151, 541, 582**, *616*
   wills proved at, 518, 540, 541
Lawshele (Lawshull), Richard, friar, 488
   Thomas, friar of Babwell, 109, 109n, 381,
      381n
Lay, Alice, 729
LAYHAM, church, 54, 97
   bells of, 54, 97
   testator of, **54**
Leche, Anne, 501
   John, 501
   Margaret, 501
   Robert, of Stowmarket, **501**
Ledgate, Margaret, servant, 665
Lee, Joan, 381
   John, 381; the elder, of Stowmarket, 109, **381**;
      son of William of Woodbridge, 381
   Margery, (née), 381
   Matilda, (née), 381; servant, 381
   William, of Woodbridge, 381
   see also at Lee *alias* Hurlebate
Le(e)m, Isabel, 776
   Joan, (née), 776
   Katherine, (née), 776
   Thomas, 776; the elder, of Brandon Ferry, **776**
   William, 776
Lefeld, Agnes, 740, (née), 740
   Thomas, 740; the elder, of Haverhill, **740**
   William, 740
Legat(t), Alan, 179; of Hawstead, **39**, 179, 179n
   Alice, 90*, 90n
   Joan, 90

John, 471; the elder, 39; the younger, chaplain,
39; rector of Tuddenham, 340, 340n
Robert, 57; of Rattlesden, **90**
Rose, 39
Legge, James, 572
Leigh (Lye), Hugh, rector of Wetherden, 451,
451n, 573
LEISTON, abbot of, *lxxvi*n
Lely, Robert, 540
William, 765
Leman, John, 174
Lem, *see* Leem
Lene, William, of Walsham le Willows, *lxxiv*n
Leneys [*or*, Leveys], John, 704
Lenge, John, 89n, 110, 448
see also Lynge
Lennard, John, 56
Lensere, John, fuller, 614
Lenys, John, 40
Richard, 40
Lerlyng, Margery, & family, 820
Lethenard, Joan, 665
Leve *alias* Fletcher, Robert, 4
LEVERINGTON (Cambs), chapel of BVM of
the Sea, 246, 246n
Leveson, William, of 'Hempeston', 223
Leveys, *see* Leneys
Levy, William, chaplain, 342
Levynge, William, friar, 665
Lewyn, Margaret, 617
Thomas, of Stuston, **617**
Leyr, John, 232
Leyston, John, of Barrow, 531
LIDGATE, church, 80, 188, 286
cross for, 656
lands in, 188, 482
testator of, **188**
will proved at, 188
LINDSEY, church, 50
LIVERMERE, GREAT, church, 134, 241, 599,
759, 760
incumbent of, *see* William Cokett
inhabitants of, 129, 241, 368n, 599n, 759, 760,
760n
lands in, 599
testators of, **134**, **241**, **599**, **760**
LIVERMERE, LITTLE, church, 129, 544, 653
rector of, 129
inhabitants of, 129, 544n, 653n, 684
lands in, 118, 653
places in, 'Bowyers' (messuage), 653
testators of, *lx*n, **118**, **129**, **653**
?Lode, John, rector of Snailwell (Cambs), 824
Lokton, Thomas, esquire, 187, 187n
Lokyere, Joan, servant, 31
Lombard, William, 490
Londe, William, 795, 811
Londen, (*or*, Louden), John, of Barrow, **530**

Margaret, 530
see also London *and* Loudon
LONDON, church of St Denis Backchurch, 213
Michael, Sir, parish chaplain of, 213
city of, 213
CLERKENWELL in, fraternity of the Knights
Hospitallers of St John, *lxiv*, 319, 319n
college of St Anthony in, 319, 319n
college (hospital) of St Thomas Acre in, *lxiv*,
319, 319n
Dominican friars (Preachers) of, 46
inhabitants of, *lxxvi*n*, 107, 204n, 398
London, Alice, daughter of William, 791n; of
Thorndon, 337n
Thomas, friar, 160
LONG MELFORD, chapel of BVM in
churchyard, 436, 436n, 722, 728, 733, 779
chapel of St James, 206, 206n, 436, 779
church, 45, 59, 162, 206, 346, 436, 446, 464,
722, 728, 733, 756, 779
bells of, 728
Mass of Jesu in, 45, 45n, 162, 206, 363,
722, 728
north clerestory of, 779, 779n
painting of image of St Leonard in, 722
rebuilding of, *lvi*, *lvi*n, 363, 436
tower of, 45, 206,
gilds in, 32, 436, 436n, 779
inhabitants of, 45, 52, 59, 154, 290, 363, 363n,
436, 436n, 463, 518, 698, 733, 779
lands in, 59, 206, 346, 464, 722, 728, 733,
756, 779
places in, Chapel Green, 206n
'Coppyinges', 'Coppynges', 779
cross, new, made by William Clopton, 733
'Crukkes Crofte', 733
'Duddescroftes', 464
'Hammundes Crycke', 290
Melford Tye, 59
'Steven(es) Hichen', (tenement), 733
'Waterhousyerde, le' (pasture), 464
poor of, 436, 779
testators of, *li*n, *lvi**, *lxvi*n, **45, 52, 59, 162,
206, 346, 363, 436, 446, 464, 722, 728,
733, 756, 779**
ways in, 'Fotysfordstrete', 52
'Hallestret', 'Halstrete', 'Hellestret', 206,
436, 779
'Heyghstret, le', 722
wills proved at, 45, 59, 236, 237, 262, 310,
346, 363, 446, 463, 464, 508, 516 690, 722,
782
Long(e), John, smith, of Acton, 20n; of Alpheton,
151
LOPHAM (Nfk), inhabitants of, 661
Lopham, John, gentleman, of Ixworth, 295
Lord(e), Christine, 269
John, chaplain, 23

Robert, 818
Roger, 23
Lorens, Thomas, 739
Lorkyn, John, 153
Lotkyn, John, of West Stow, 347
   see also Lutkyn
Lotkyn *alias* Roper, Alice, 347
   Richard, of Mildenhall, *li*n, **347**
Louden, *see* London
Loudon, William, of Thorndon, 126n, 337n
Love, John, 196, 196n, 211n
Lovell, Isabel, 305
   John, 305
Lovetop(p), Joan, 767
   William, 283; of Kersey, **767**
Lowke, John, 60
?Lows, John, of Hopton, 661
Lowyn, Joan, 232
Lucas, John, servant, 89
Lumkyn, John, carpenter, 151
Lunt(e), Robert, 409, 641; of Stoke by Nayland,
   236
Lute, Robert, rector of Barton Mills, 243, 243n
Lutkyn, Agnes, (née), & family, 445; daughter of
   Thomas, 445
   Alice, of Stowlangtoft, **445**
   Christine, daughter of Thomas, 445
   John, of West Stow, 445
   Thomas, 445,
Lye, Robert, 297
   see also Leigh
Lyly, Henry, 137
Lynch, William, 658
Lyncoln(e), Audrey, (née), 809
   Joan, (née), 809
   John, of Stonham Aspal, **809**
   Margaret, 809
   Marion, (née), 809
   Robert, the elder, 809; the younger, 809
   Thomas, 809; friar of order of Holy Cross,
   191, 191n
Lyndesell, *see* Lynsele
Lynge (Lenge), George, of Fornham St
   Genevieve, **448**
   John, 775; the elder, 560; of Hinderclay, 802;
   of Winston, 559
   Margery, 448
   see also Lenge
Lynke, John, 102
Lynkfeld, Robert, rector of Polstead, 248, 248n
Lynne, Dan. John, monk of Bury St Edmunds,
   *lx*n, 147
Lynsele (Lyndesell, Lynsell), John, son of Simon,
   470
   Simon, yeoman, 191, 191n; & family, 470,
   470n
Lynsey, Thomas, of Stoke by Nayland, 197
Lynton, Robert, rector of Woolpit, 624, 624n

Lyown, John, of Hadleigh, 50
Lyse, John, of Aspall, 280
Lyster(e), Margaret, servant, 669
   Nicholas, 372

Macho(u)n, Isabel, of Felsham, *lvii*, *lix*n, **557**
   John, 295
   Thomas, 145, 716
Madam, Edmund, 578
Maddy, Ellen, 513
   Simon, 513
   Thomas, of Wicken (Cambs), **513**, 747n
Makell, Clemence, 162, 162n
   John, 162; of Long Melford, **162**
Makemere, Emme, 57
   John, 57
Maket, Henry, 505
Makro, Agnes, 758
   Thomas, 758,
   William, of 'the Meere Strete' in Soham
   (Cambs), **758**
MALDON, inhabitants of, 398
MALLING (Kent), abbess of, 212, 212n
Maltywade (Maltyward(e)), Anne, of Bradfield St
   George, **270**
   John, 374; of Thurston, 270
   Thomas, 588
   William, of Felsham, 532
Malverne, Thomas, 467
Malveys, William, 39
Malyot, John, 783n
Man, Agnes, of Troston, 386
   Alice, 245, 713, 797
   [?Ed.], of Rattlesden, *lvii*, 414n, **797**
   Isabel, (née Trapet), 268
   Joan, of Rattlesden, 797n
   John, 245, 246, 581, 712*; the elder,
   of Lakenheath, **245**; the younger, of
   Lakenheath, 120; of Market Weston, 68,
   268; of Thorpe Morieux, *lxvii*, **712**; of
   Thurston, 606
   Margaret, *lxvii*, 712*
   Richard, of Hadleigh, 713
   Thomas, 245, 712
   William, vicar of college of Stoke by Clare,
   637, 637n; of Thorpe Morieux, **713**
Mannoke, John, gentleman, 480
Mannyng(e), Alice, 743
   Henry, 743
   John, of Little Whelnetham, 93; of Norton,
   743
   Richard, 743
   Walter, of Norton, 362n
   William, 604, 738; of Norton, **743**
Mansere, Henry, of Gislingham, 343n, **476**, 800n
   Joan, 476
   William, of Ipswich, 576
MANSTON (Dorset), pilgrimage to, 166, 166n

Manwod, Agnes, servant, 470
Marchall (Marshall), Joan, wife of John, 693
   John, 331, 595, 693
Mardon, Joan, of Shouldham (Nfk), 187, 187n
   William, of Fordham (Cambs), 187n
Margery (Margeri), John, 240, 385
Marham, Isabel, 387
   Robert, of Mildenhall, **387**
Markaunt(e) (Markawnt), Alice, 644; of Badwell
   Ash, *lxvii*, *lxxv*, **644**
   John, 644*
Markeday, Joan, 431
   John, 431; of Bildeston, 50, 720
   Margaret, 431
   Richard, 431
   Rose, wife of John, of Bildeston, 720, 721
MARKET WESTON, church, 240, 268, 522,
   555, 625, 822
     rector of, *see* Thomas Meryell (Muryell)
   inhabitants of, 68, 268, 822
   lands in, *lxxvi*n, 240, 625
   testators of, **268**, **625**, **822**
   will proved at, 240
Markys, John, draper, 381; of Old Newton, 501n
Marlere, John, 27
Marleton, Margaret, of Wetherden, 315n
   William, 334
Marshall, *see* Marchall
Marten, John, son of Roger, 380
   Robert, son of Roger, 380
   Roger, 380
MARTHAM (Nfk), inhabitants of, 661
Martham, Alice, 615
   Joan, (née), 615
   Peter, 615
   Thomas, of Rattlesden, 536n, **615**
Martyn, Agnes, of Little Ashfield, **667**
   Augustine, of Semer, 154n
   Isabel, 142
   John, 142, 327, 416, 467, 633, 820; of
     Lakenheath, **633**
   Katherine, 633
   Margaret, of Honington, **157**
   Richard, 206
   Robert, 299, 667
   Roger, 240, 273
   Thomas, chaplain, 107, 107n
   William, 271; of Sudbury, 189
Maryell, *see* Muryell
Maryott, John, 650
   Parnell, servant, 677
Maschall, John, of Naughton, 483
Masham, Isabel, 527
   John, 644, 644n
   Robert, rector of Creeting St Peter, 472, 472n
Mason, Adam, 733
   Edmund, the younger, of Rickinghall Inferior,
   194

Ellen, 194
Henry, 450; of Exning, *lvii*n, 428, 428n, **450**
Joan, 450
John, 824; the elder, 194; of Exning, 450
Ralph, 690
Robert, 450; the younger, 194
Thomas, 450
William, sir, 818
Massangere (Messangere), John, of Bures, 354
Mastyr, Thomas, of Little Bradley, 91
Mathelard, Clement, 111
Matsale, Thomas, 38
Matthew, Margaret, 435
Maunger, John, 554,
   Thomas, servant, 89
Mavsen, (Mavesen, Mavesyn), John, of
   Thrandeston, 765
   Thomas, chaplain, 765
Mawdyon, Isabel, 331
   Margaret, 331
   William, of Boxford, 247n, **331**, 440n
Mayhew(e) (Mayhow(e)), Agnes, the elder, 682;
   the younger, 682; wife of William the elder,
   785
   Edmund, of Cheveley (Cambs), 623; of Rede,
   682
   Henry, 682
   Isabel, 682
   John, 682, 726; chaplain, 785
   Katherine, 682
   Robert, 726
   Sibyl, 682
   Thomas, 9
   William, 682; the elder, 785
Mayn, John, former rector of Kirtling (Cambs),
   610, 610n
Mayner(e), Ed., of Great Thurlow, **601**
   Eleanor, 601
   Phyllis, 309
   Roger, 243
   Thomas, 601
   William, 601; of Groton, **309**
Mayowe, *see* Mayhew
Mayster, Adam, 680
   Margery, wife of Adam, 680
   Robert, the younger, 680
   Thomas, 678
Medew, (Medue, Medwe), Agnes, 368, 368n
   John, of Wetheringsett, 778
   Margaret, 368, 368n,
   Thomas, of Great Livermere, 368n
Mekylwoode, Isabel, 140
   John, *140*
Melche, Stephen, & family, 655
Melkesop, John, of Stoke by Clare, 637n
Melle, Alice, 161
   Joan, (née), 491
   John, 161

Margaret, 491
Matilda, 491
Robert, 161, 491
Thomas, 161, 491; of Polstead, **161**
William, 161; of Stoke by Nayland, **491**
Meller(e) (Millere, Myllere), Agnes, 112
Ellen, sister of Margaret, 803
Isabel, wife of Reginald, of Martham (?Nfk), 661
John, *lxix*n, 175, 399, 743, 751; chaplain, of Barningham, 338, 338n, 452; the elder, of Barningham, 338n; of Stanstead, *lv*, **463**; of Withersfield, 123
Katherine, 258; widow, 258
Margaret, 483:, (née), 563; servant, 803
Margery, 258, 483*, 563, (née), 563
Reginald, of Martham (?Nfk), 661
Robert, 338, 483, 563; of Naughton, **483**, **563**
Thomas, of Withersfield, **123**; of Woolpit, 375
William, 123, 727; of Barrow, 530, 531
MELLIS, church, 235, 391, 529
gilds in, 391, 391n
inhabitants of, 235, 391, 391n, 529n
lands in, 235, 391
places in, Mellis Green, 159n
testators of, *lxxv*n, **235**, **391**
Melon, Helen, 787
John, 155; of Stradishall, **787**
Thomas, 787
Mendham, John, 761
MENDLESHAM, church, 41, 202, 203, 210, 374, 421, 568, 700, 774, 788, 805, 818
lead roof for, 203
vestment for, 374
gilds in, 568, 568n, 774, 788
inhabitants of, 6, 41, 202, 275, 374, 559n, 568n, 805, 805n, 818
lands in, 41, 203, 374, 554, 568, 774, 788, 805, 818
places in, 'Bleantys' (tenement), 374
'Bramys' (tenement), 374
'churche style', 203
'Dentonys' (close), 818
'Legates' (tenement), 374
'Malyardes' (tenement), 202
'ston crosse', 203
'Whynnys', 554
poor of, 374
testators of, *lxx*, **41**, **202**, **203**, **374**, **554**, **568**, **774**, **788**, **805**, **818**
ways in, 'chirche wey', 203
wills proved at, 41, 202, 203, 374, 568, 620
MEPPERSHALL (Beds), inhabitants of, 174n
Merche, William, of 'Stroneton', 501
Mere, *see* at the Mere
Meriell, *see* Meryell
Merk, John, 21
Mersche, John, of the 'botery', 38

Mersheoner, Stephen, 327
Merv(e)yn, John, 399,
Meryell (Meriell), Agnes, of Barrow, 401n, **502**
John, 259*; of Glemsford, 463; of Stanstead, 463
Richard, chaplain, 727
Thomas, 111, 259, 502; rector (*also as* Muryell) of Market Weston, 154n, 822, 822n
William, 756
[*unnamed*], friar, of Cambridge, 659
see also Morall, Morehall, Moryell, Muryell
Messangere, *see* Massangere
Metessharpp, *see* Metscherpe
Metewyn (Mettewynd), Elizabeth, *lxix*, 240
John, 7; of Wattisfield, *lxiv*n, 7n, 240n
Katherine, of Wattisfield, 7
William, of Wattisfield, *lv*, *lxiv*, *lxvii*, *lxvii*n, *lxix**, **240**, 634n, 741n
METHWOLD (Nfk), church, 776
Metscherpe (Metessharpp), Isabel, 41
Margaret, 41
Olive, 41
Roger, of Mendlesham, 41n, 374n, 568n
Thomas, of Mendlesham, **41**
Mettewynd, *see* Metewyn
Mey, Agnes, of Lavenham, **122**
John, 122n; the elder, of Bury St Edmunds, 122; of Lavenham, 122n
Robert, the elder, 754
Thomas, 754
Meyner, Edmund, 490
Eleanor, 490
William, 490
Meyr, Alice, 228; the elder, 228
John, 228
Marion, 228
Michell (Mychell), John, 490
William, of Exning, 450
MICKFIELD, church, 374, 805
antiphoner for, 805
MIDDLETON (Esx), church, 189
lands in, 727
places in, 'Apton', 727
'Hydes', 727
'Peke, le', 727
MILDEN, church, 83, 122, 261
lands in, 30
Mildenhale, Brother Thomas, of Bromehill (Nfk), 429, 429n
MILDENHALL, charnel of Ralph de Walsham, 378, 378n
church, 107, 147, 172, 216, 229, 230, 239, 260, 312, 345, 347, 387, 378, 545, 611, 629, 635, 636, 638, 650, 664, 668, 735, 754, 766, 768, 819, 827
great bell of, 230
ornament for, 754

parish chaplain of, *see* Walter Fostere
south aisle of, 229
tower of, 230
gilds in, 107, 107n, 229, 229n, 230, 230n, 378,
   378n, 717, 717n, 754, 819
inhabitants of, *lxxvi*n, 107, 229, 230, 260, 342,
   347, 378n, 545n, 553n, 600n, 638, 650,
   664n, 717, 719, 766n, 768, 768n, 819
lands in, *lxxii*, 147, 172, 229, 230, 345, 347,
   378, 387, 429, 629, 635, 638, 650, 664,
   668, 735, 754, 766, 768, 827
manor of, 378
places in, 'Baggysholme havyddyn', 239, 239n
   'Baggysholmefeld', 239, 378
   Beck Row, 230n, 312
   'Bekke', 387
   Bell, sign of, 650
   'Berehylle', 'Berehyle', 239, 239n, 629,
      629n
   'Breche, le', 378
   'Corryesmedewe', 230
   'Fenhow Grene', 239
   'Fenhowcrose', 629
   'Fenhowyerd', 629
   fishery in 'Berewey', 629
   'Havydlonde', 629
   'Holmesey', 629
   Holywell Row, 312n
   'Lytyll Thremhowe', 239
   'Mundes', 629
   'Mundysfurlong', 230
   'Pollardes', 629
   'Sowteres Acre', 754
   'Swan, le' (messuage), 650
   'Tabbard' (messuage), 650
   'Thremhowehylle', 239
   'Thremowfeld', 378
   'Wamelfurlong', 230
   'Wedmerisholme', (*?*'Tedmerisholme'), 629
   'Welmere', 239
   West Row, 312n
   'Westyn dyche', 230, 629
   'William Penne' (tenement), 387
   'Wyesmedewe', 230
poor of, 107
testators of, *l*in, *li*in, *lx*n, *lxiii*, *lxviii**, *lxxiii*,
   **107, 147, 172, 177, 216, 229, 230, 239,
   260, 287, 312, 345, 347, 378, 387, 545,
   553, 611, 629, 635, 636, 638, 650, 664,
   668, 735, 754, 766, 768, 819, 827**
ways in, 'Grenewey', 230
   'Oxenhowepayth', 378
   'Westrowstret, le', 754, 754n
   Wilde Street, 'Wyldestre', 'Wyld stret',
      387, 387n, 735, 735n
wills proved at, 172, 215, 216, 302, 345, 377,
   378, 379, 399, 449, 633, 636, 650, 668,
   717, 719, 735

Millere, *see* Mellere
Milys, Robert, 737
Mody, Agnes, (née), 311
   Margaret, (née), 311
   Richard, of Newton, *lxx*, **311**
   Robert, of Polstead, 311
Molows, Almeric, of Wattisfield, 240n, 273n,
   542n, 741n
   John, of Rickinghall, 258; of Wattisfield, 542,
      542n, 561, 561n, 741
   Richard, 258
Mone, John, 110; the elder, 'meller', 110n
   Margaret, of Fornham St Genevieve, **110**
MONKS ELEIGH, church, 83, 122
   inhabitants of, 154, 247,
   lands in, 11
   peculiar of, *xlv*
Monnynge (Munnyng, Munynge(s)), Christian,
   362
   Henry, of Norton by Woolpit, *lix*, **362**
   John, rector of Felsham, 417, 417n; of
      Hadleigh, 362*; of Hunston, 362; the elder,
      of Norton, 362
   Richard, of Badwell Ash, 207n
   Robert, 362*
Monfortt, *see* Mumforte
Moone, Katherine, 110
Moor(e) (More), Ann, 451
   Joan, wife of William, 557
   John, 417, 729; of Felsham, 417; of Stanstead,
      22n, 541; of Whepstead, 801n
   Phyllis (*Felice*), 729
   Richard, 150
   Thomas, 332, 334, 451, 541, 729
   Walter, 417
   William, 490, 557, 801; of Great Cornard, **729**
Moordok, *see* Mordok
Mootte, William, of Wicken (Cambs), 513
Moour, William, chaplain, 405
Morall, Richard, friar, 22, 22n
   [*unnamed*], friar, 470
   see also Meryell, Morehall *and* Moryell
Morawnt, Adam, 290
   Amee, wife of Adam, 290
Mordok, Alice, wife of William, 546
   William, 546, 795
More, *see* Moore
Morehall, William, friar, of Sudbury, 166, 166n
   see also Meryell, Morall *and* Moryell
Morgan, John, of Earl Stonham, 774
Moriell (Muriell), *see* Moryell, Muryell
Morle(e), Alice, 378, 545, 545n
   Henry, 378; of Mildenhall, 664n
   John, 378; the elder, of Mildenhall, 378n, **545**
   Margaret, 545
   Richard, the elder, of Mildenhall, **378**, 545n
Morowhyll (Morwhyll), Alice, 554
   Joan, 554

John, 554
Robert, 554; of Mendlesham, **554**
Thomas, 554
William, 554
Mors *alias* Mos, Nicholas, *xlv*n
Morse, Nicholas, of Hengrave, 184
Morwhyll, *see* Morowhyll
Moryell (Moriell, Muriell), Clarissa, widow of
John, of Barrow, 152n
John, of Barrow, 152n
Stephen, of Weston, 268
William, of Barrow, 136, 761
[*unnamed*], friar, 38
see also Meryell, Morall, Morehall, Muryell
Morys, Robert, 387, 636
Motte, Joan, 286
John, 286
Katherine, 286
Margery, 286
Richard, 297
Robert, 286, 482
Thomas, of Wickhambrook, *lxviii*, **286**
MOTTENDEN (Kent), friars (canons) of order
of the Holy Trinity, *lxi*, *lxiii*n, 295n, 634, 636,
636n
fraternity of, *lxi*, 295, 295n
MOULTON, inhabitants of, 696
peculiar of, *xlv*
MOUNT BURES (Esx), church, 55, 729
rector of, 67
'MONYES', pilgrimage to, 146, 146n
Mows, Thomas, 154
Moyse, Isabel, 186, 661
John, of Hopton, **186**, 392n
William, 186
Mumforte (Monfortt), William, of Polstead, **248**
Mundeford, John, of Rishangles, 126n, 337n
Mundes, *see* Mundys
Mundson, Joan, of Kirtling (Cambs), **462**
Thomas, 462, 609
Mundys (Mundes), Adam, 680; of Stanton, 566
Munnyng, Munynges, *see* Monnynge
Muriell, *see* Moriell
Muryell, Alice, (née Walter), 294
Thomas, rector (*also as* Maryell) of All
Saints', Chelsworth, 154, 154n
see also Meryell, Moryell
Muskett, Alice, 324
Ed., 324,
Henry, of Haughley, **324**
John, 324
Thomas, 324
William, 324
Mychell, *see* Michell
Myggys, Agnes, (née Coldham), 338, 338n
Mylbourn, John, 206
Mylde, Thomas, of Clare, **148**
Myldenhale, [*unnamed*], friar, 488

Myles, *see* Mylys
Myller *alias* Vyell, John, 544
Myller(e), *see* Mellere
Mylon, Ann, (née), 687
Helen, 687
John, of Clare, **687**
Rose, 687
Mylys (Myles), Robert, 103, 109, 139, 325, 468,
669; of Stowmarket, 381
Mynnys, Alice, 415
Robert, of Great Ashfield, **415**
Mynton, Joan, of Stowmarket, *lxvii*, **648**
Myrton, John, the elder, 388
Myst(e), Joan, 698, 698n; of Melford, 698, 698n;
(née Flegge), 727, 727n
John, 727
Thomas, son of Joan, 727
William, 727

NAUGHTON, church, 50, 406, 483, 563
inhabitants of, 483
lands in, 483
testators of, **483**, **563**
NAYLAND, church, 48, 141, 439, 503, 549, 761,
783, 784
altar of BVM in, 141
image of St Nicholas in, 439
gilds in, 439, 439n, 783
inhabitants of, 141, 150, 439, 439n, 459, 556
lands in, 48, 150, 784
places in, 'Horswatryng, le', 783
testators of, *lin*, *lxxv*n, **48**, **86**, **141**, **439**, **503**,
549, **761**, **783**, **784**
ways in, highway to, 370
'Newlondelane', 784
Nedeham, Richard, 683
NEDGING, chapel of BVM, by Semer bridge,
50, 720, 721
church, 50, 720, 721
rector of, *see* John Hawkedon
inhabitants of, 284
places in, Semer bridge, 720n, 721
Nedham, Joan, 579
Nedom, John, 40
NEEDHAM (in Gazeley), *see* GAZELEY
NEEDHAM MARKET, lands in, 169, 501
Neel(e), Andrew, 602
John, 59
Margaret, 602
William, of Fordham (Cambs), **602**
Nek(e)ton, Robert, 592
Nell, Roger, 331
NETTLESTEAD, inhabitants of, 204n
Neve, Alexander, 18, 19, 388
John, 687
Marion, 275
Thomas, of Great Finborough, **275**
see also Catour *alias* Neve

173

Nevereys, Robert, 310
Nevman[sic], John, 681
Neweman (Newman), Joan, 529, 567
  John, 87, 371, 517, 517n; son of Richard,
    567; of Lavenham, 11, 681; the elder, of
    Lavenham, lxiiin, 87; of Sudbury, 166n; of
    Woolpit, 567
  Richard, 567
  Thomas, son of Richard, 567
Newhawe, Adam, 81
  Agnes, 81
  John, 81; of Great Horringer, 81
  Margery, 81*
  Thomas, 81*
Newman, see Neweman
NEWMARKET, chapels/churches of, 80n
  chapel/church of All Saints, 80n, 671
  chapel/church of St Mary, 80, 80n, 510
    pilgrimage to chapel of St Theobald in, lxiv,
      414, 414n
    tower of, 510
  inhabitants of, 510
  lands in, 160, 510, 671
  parish of All Saints, xlvn
  places in, 'Bocherye, le', lxxii, lxxiin, 80
    'Oolde Mersery', lxxii, lxxiin, 80
  shop in*, lxxii, 80
  testators of, 510, 671
  wills proved at, 12, 80, 426, 427, 428, 510,
    602, 630, 643, 656, 671, 762
Newres, Christine, (née), 354
  Denise, 354
  Joan, (née), 354
  John, 354; the elder, of Bures St Mary, 354
  Richard, 354
  Robert, 354
NEWTON by SUDBURY, inhabitants of, 398
NEWTON, church, 311, 516, 597, 669
    image of BVM in, 597
    lamp before image of St Saviour in, 597
  lands in, 83, 516
  places in, 'Cordewanerys', 311
    'Hervye' (messuage), 516
    'Pondfeld' (croft), 225
    'Wodyshed' (croft), 225
    'Wyottes' (messuage), 516
  poor of, 311
  testators of, lii, lxx, 311, 516, 597
  will proved at, 305
Newton, Robert, gentleman, 283
Nicol(l) (Nichole), Isabel, 642
  John, 642; rector of Fornham St Martin, 286,
    286n; of London, 398
  Peter, 642*
  Walter, of Great Bradley, lin, lxiii, 457n, 642
    (Al' Clerk in margin)
  William, 155
Noble (Nobyll), Adam, of Westley, 486n

Henry, 432; of Little Saxham, 486
Joan, 486
John, & family, of Bury St Edmunds, 432; of
  Great Horringer, 432n; of Nayland, lxxvn,
  141
Katherine, (née), 432
Ralph, 486
Richard, 486; of Westley, 432
Robert, of Great Horringer, 10
Stephen, 432
Thomas, 432
Walter, 320, 373, 486*, 486n; of Great
  Horringer, lxii, 432, 654n, 711n; of Little
  Saxham, 432
Noche, Margaret, widow, of Bildeston, 431
Nooke, Robert, of Kersey, lv, 153
Noote, Agnes, 265
  John, 265
  William, of Thurston, 265
Noreys (Nor(e)yce, Noris), Ed., of Palgrave, 618
  Ellen, 581
  Joan, of Brockford in Wetheringsett, 5
  John, 618, 721; of Brockford in Wetheringsett,
    581
  Margery, (née), 618
  Walter, 581
  William, 618; of Brockford in Wetheringsett, 5
Norfolke, Margaret, 42
Noris, see Noreys
Norman, Avice, daughter of Richard, 276
  Joan, 108*; wife of Richard, 276; widow, of
    Badlingham in Chippenham (Cambs), lxin,
    108n, 199n, 438
  John, 314, 438; the younger, 380; of
    Stansfield, 814
  Richard, 276, 456; of Clare, 46, 155, 276
  Thomas, of Badlingham in Chippenham
    (Cambs), 108, 108n, 438n,
  William, 108, 108n, 438
Nors, Geoffrey, of Downham, 777
Northaghe, Adam, of Thorndon, lxn, 146
  Julian, (née) & family, 146
Northfolk(e), Alice, servant, 72, 403
  John, the younger, 232, 232n
NORTON, church, 209, 295, 362, 743
    funeral cope for, lix, 362
    light before the crucifix, 743
    Our Lady's light in, 209, 362
  gilds in, 362, 362n, 661n, 743, 743n
  inhabitants of, 192, 321n, 362, 362n, 743,
    743n, 771
  lands in, 209, 295, 362, 743, 770
  manor of, 69n
    'Lytelhaughe', 'Litilaugh', 209, 362
    Norton Hall, 362
  places in, 'Brettysfeld', 743
    'Broomhylmedewe', 743
    'Clementes', 209

'Flemyng', 209
'Heth, le', 743
Little Haugh Hall, 209n
'Nortonbrigge', 362
'Pouncys', 209
'Reysthegge', 209
testators of, *lix*, **209, 362, 743**
ways in, 'Howstrete', 362
'Townestrete', 'Tunstret', 661n, 743n
'Upstrete', 661n, 743n
wills proved at, 192, 268n, 672, 795
NORWICH, archdeaconry of, *xlvi*
bishop of, *xlv, lxxiv*
consistory court of, *xlv, xlv*n
cathedral, 28, 193, 193n, 210, 502, 529, 688,
771
pilgrimage to image of Holy Trinity in, *lxiv*,
414, 414n
college of St Mary in the Fields, *xlviii*n
dean of, *xlviii*n
diocese of, *xliv* , 5, 30, 32, 74, 100, 102, 123,
125, 133, 153, 155, 166, 175, 188, 212,
220, 229, 242, 259, 265, 271, 276, 286,
290, 303, 311, 316, 335, 356, 362, 370,
385, 393, 407, 408, 412, 423, 425, 428,
429, 430, 431, 436, 437, 447, 451, 458,
459, 463, 465, 466, 482, 494, 502, 504,
505, 509, 510, 511, 518, 528, 531, 547,
564, 566, 574, 580, 581, 586, 589, 595,
596, 597, 598, 607, 608, 624, 626, 628,
651, 652, 655, 662, 666, 671, 683, 687,
691, 698, 701, 702, 713, 714, 720, 721,
724, 727, 731, 733, 734, 738, 742, 751,
767, 769, 774, 779, 780, 785, 788, 796,
803, 815, 816
house of Austin friars, 796n
Carmelite friars, *lx*, 269, 269n, 738, 755,
796n
Dominican friars, 796n
Franciscan friars, 796n
leper-hospitals, *lxiii*, 126
outside St Giles's Gate, 126n
master of, *xlviii*n
St Benedict, 126n
St Leonard, 126n
St Mary and St Clement, 126n
St Mary Magdalene, 126n
St Stephen, 126n
prior of, *see* John Bonewell
St Leonard's cell in, pilgrimage to image in,
lxiv, 414, 414n
Norwold, John, Sir, 109
Thomas, 697
Noryce, *see* Noreys
Notebeam, John, 38
Nott(e), Thomas, official of Boxford church, *lvi*n,
247; of Groton, *254*
NOWTON, church, 130, 291, 812

altar of St Peter in, 93
rector of, 291
lands in, 825
testators of, **291, 296, 812**
Nun(n)e, Agnes, (née), 613
Alice, (née), 613
George, 613
Henry, 613
Isabel, 634
John, 417, 613, 613n; servant, 634; the elder,
freeman, 417; of Felsham, 613, 613n, 634n,
647, 647n; the elder, of Rougham, *lxiv*,
240n, 613n, **634**
Marion, widow, of Thorpe Morieux, 131n, **613**
Nicholas of Hessett, 205n
Robert, 613; the elder, 588
Thomas, servant, 634
William, 613
Nycoll, *see* Nicoll
Nyghynghale, Andrew, 153

OAKLEY, church, 396
OCCOLD, church, 83, 443, 726
mortuary given to, *liv*n, 443
inhabitants of, 391n
lands in, 726
testators of, *liv*n, **443, 726**
Ocle, Thomas, 589
Odeham, Margaret, of Bury St Edmunds, *xlix*
Odelyn, *see* Odlyn
Ode, John, of Barway in Soham, 204n, 397n,
Odlyn (Odelyn), Agnes, widow, of Wortham, **34**
Ed., of Wortham, 269n
OFFTON, church, 406
Ofton, Agnes, 213
William, 213
Ofwade (Ofwode), Robert, 799
Thomas, 799
Okyre, William, 701
OLD NEWTON, chaplain of, 529, 529n
church, 180, 529, 576, 673
buttress on the north side of, 576
inhabitants of, 501n, 576n
lands in, 576
places in, 'Blakys' (tenement), 576
'Paynys' (tenement), 576
testators of, **529, 576**
will proved at, 201
Oldale (Oldhalle), Ann, wife of Walter, of
Sudbury, 702n
Christine, 702
Ed., 646
Joan, (née), 702
Walter, of Sudbury, *liii, lvii*, **702**
Oldman, John, of Chippenham (Cambs), *143*
Katherine, 143
Peter (Pers), Doctor, of Old House of
Thetford, 414, 414n, 797, 797n

Olyf(f)e (Olyve), Agnes, (née Cagge), wife of
    William, 574
  Joan, of Glemsford, widow, **317**, 508n
  John, 317
  William, & family, 574
Olyver(e), William, 365; of Wangford, **302**
ONEHOUSE, church, 665
  vestment for, 665
Onge, William, 452
Orderych, Alice, 587
  Isabel, (née), 587
  John, 587
  William, of Hitcham, *lxiii*, *lxiii*n, **587**
ORFORD, house of Augustinian friars, 6, 202,
    700, 726
  Friar John of, 726
  Friar Ralph of, 726
  Friar William of, 726
Osbern(e), John, 142; the elder, 365
  Margaret, of Cotton, 6
  Simon, of Cotton, 6
  William, of Cotton, **6**
  [*unnamed*], Master, 38
Osby, Joan, 248
Osmond(e), Alice, 459
  Joan, (née Salle *alias* Cooke, the elder), wife
    of Stephen, 484
  John, of Assington, husbandman, *li*n, **459**
  Margaret, (née), 459
  Stephen, 360; & family, 484
Otelee, *see* Otle
Othoo, Alice, 772
  Benedict, 772; the elder, of Bradfield St
    George, *lii*, **772**
  Isabel, 772
  Katherine, 772
  Margaret, 772
Otle (Otelee, Ottley), Margery, servant, 471
  Robert, 519
  William, 507, 507n; of Little Saxham, 506n
OUSDEN, church, 136, 286, 335, 696
  bells of, 696
  inhabitants of, 335, 696
  lands in, 335
  testators of, **335**, **696**
Overmede, Ellen, 823
Oversouth (Oversooth), Richard, 320, 373
OXBOROUGH (Nfk), inhabitant of, 650n
Oxford, earl of, 762, 762n
Oxne (Hoxne, Hoxon), Christian, (née Hervy),
    wife of Thomas, 800
  Marg', 89
  Thomas, 800

Paase, Agnes, 466
  John, 466
Pachet, *see* Paget
Padnale, William, 89

Padyll, John, 214
Page, Agnes, 709
  Alice, 22; of Ickworth, 695n, 708, **709**
  Anne, 77
  Cecily, 454
  Henry, 454
  Isabel, (née), 534
  Joan, (née), 534, 708, 709, 709n
  John, 22, 178; servant, 69; of Ickworth, 695,
    695n, **708**; of Stanstead, **22**; of Worlington,
    612
  Margaret, of Kirtling (Cambs), *lix*n, 281n,
    461n, 577n, **609**
  Robert, of Great Saxham, *lxviii*, **534**
  Roger, 534
  Rose, (née), 534
  Thomas, 612; of Ickworth, 708n, **695**; of
    Walsham, 175
  Walter, 695n, 708n, 709, 709n; of Eye, &
    family, **178**; of Lavenham, **454**
  William, of Barking, 454
Paget (Pachet), William, 827
PAKENHAM, church, 101, 295, 821
  inhabitants of, 101, 219, 417n
  lands in, 101, 219, 295
  places in, 'Browsters', 219
    'Pangyll, le' (meadow), 101
    Pakenham field, 219
  testators of, **101**, *167*, **295**
Pakenham, John, de, 69; of Preston, 190
PALGRAVE, chapel of St John the Baptist (now
    lost), 688, 688n
  church, 221, 251, 269, 323, 618, 688
    bells of, 618
    cross in the churchyard of, 618
    rector of, 221
    sepulchre light in, 688
    torches in, 251
    walls of, 618
  gilds in, 618, 688, 688n
  inhabitants of, 221, 251, 618n, 688, 688n
  lands in, 221, 269, 618, 688
  places in, 'Jamys Cranys' (tenement), 688
    Palgrave mill, 618, 688
    close at, 618
    'Payns', 618
    'Ponyscros', 251
    'Puntys' (tenement), 688
    'Westbrook', 688
  testators of, **217**, **221**, **251**, **618**, **688**
  ways in, 'castelweye, ly', 251, 251n
    'Lagmer wey', 688
  wills proved at, 269, 498
Palmer(e), Henry, of Elmswell, 519n
  John, 699, 763
  Robert, of Elmswell, 605
  William, of Wordwell, 657n
Panell, John, the younger, 508

Robert, 46
Pap', Walter, of Glemsford, 163n
Parker(e), John, clerk, 451
  Laurence, of Alpheton, 350, 350n
  Stephen, parson of Little Whelnetham, 191
  Thomas, of Thorpe Morieux, 350n
  William, the younger, 324
Parkyn, John, & family, of Ingham, 368
  Simon, the younger, 661
Parle, John, of Bildeston, 359n; of Hundon, 303n
  Robert, of Lavenham, 303
  Thomas, 532
Parman (Perman), Agnes, (née), 808
  Joan, (née), the elder, 808; (née), the younger, 808
  John, 808
  Katherine, 99, 808
  Margaret, (née), 808
  Robert, of Aldersfield in Wickhambrook, 99, **808**
  Thomas, 99, 808; of Wickhambrook, 1
Parmenter(e), Ada/Adam (*Ade*), 669, 669n
  Adam, & family, 1
  Agnes, 387
  Alice, of Great Finborough, 1; wife of John, 669n
  Joan, of Great Finborough, 1
  John, 669n; of Great Finborough, **1**
  Margaret, (née) & family, 1
  Peter, & family, 1
Parson, Agnes, 482
  Robert, 681
Partrich (Partrych(e)), Isabel, 661, 707
  Richard, of Lopham (Nfk), 661
  Robert, 661, 707
Parys, John, of Soham (Cambs), *lxi*n, **204**, 278n
  Katherine, 204
Parysche, Joan, 135
Passhbroke, William, chaplain, 301
Paston, John, 159n
Paternoster, Matilda, 765
Paton (Patown), Alice, 95
  George, 336, 716
  Joan, 336
  John, 205n, 336*, 336n; of Drinkstone, **95**
  Margaret, 336,
  Thomas, 336
Paxman, Alice, 643, 643n
  Edmund, 215, 215n, 234, 234n
  Ellen, 215
  Margaret, 215n, 643
  Robert, 643, 643n
  Thomas, 643; of Burwell (Cambs), 187n, **643**
  William, of Burwell (Cambs), 631, 631n, 643n
Payn, Geoffrey, of Wortham, 269n
  John, 580, 688
Pecas (Pegas, Pegays), Agnes, of Brandon, **466**, 792n

  Christian, 466, 466n
  Isabel, 466*, 466n, 792
  Joan, (née), 792
  John, 792
  Margery, 466, 466n, 792
  Robert, the elder, 792; the younger, 792
  William, 466, 466n, 792; the elder, of Brandon, **792**
Pec(c)he (Pechie, Petche), family, of Soham, 279n
  John, friar, 391
  Thomas, 279
  William, 659, 659n, 823, 823n
Pecok, John, 330
Peddere, Alice, 228; servant, 228; widow, of Ixworth, *lxvii*n, **228**
  John, 106
  Robert, 37, 228, 228n
  William, of Stoke by Clare, *106*
  see also Hamond *alias* Peddere
Peek, Margery, 541
  Thomas, the elder, of Lawshall, **541**
Peers, Emma, 271
  Joan, (née), 271
  Philip, of Sudbury, **271**
Pegas, Pegays, *see* Pecas
Pekerell, *see* Pykerell
Pellican (Pellycan), John, 225, 261
Pelter, Margaret, 298, 298n, 322, 322n
Peltyr, John, of Clare, **26**
Penteney *alias* Sporyere, Agnes & daughter Margery, 220
  Ralph, of Ixworth, *li*n, 69n, 219n, **220**
  Robert, 220
  William, 220
Pepyre, John, servant, 191
Percy, Robert, 788
Peretrych (Pertryche), Katherine, of Acton, 431n
  Thomas, 570
Perken (Perkyn), Edmund, of West Stow, 657
  John, 16; the elder, of Barningham, 36n, 555n
  Margaret, 36, 555
  Simon, of Hopton, **36**, **555**
  Thomas, of Coney Weston, 555
Perle, John, of Lavenham, 87n
Perman, *see* Parman
Person, Agnes, 515, 538
  Richard, of Ampton, *lxii*n, **515**, **538**
Persyvale, John, 199
Pertryche, *see* Peretrych
Perwe, William, 225
Pery(e), John, 767n; of Great Whelnetham, *lviii*n, **66**
  Mariota, 1
Peryn, John, of Nayland, 141
Petche, *see* Pecche
Pethyrton, Henry, 311n
Pette, Walter, 622

Petyt (Petyett, Petyte), Agnes, 377
   James, 377
   Joan, 377
   John, 377; of Brandon Ferry, **377**
   Margery, 377
   Richard, 377
   Robert, 377
   Thomas, 419
Petywate, Agnes, 504
   Joan, 504
   John, son of William, 504; the elder, 504; the
      younger, 504; of Glemsford, *lxix*, **504**
   Katherine, the elder, 504; the younger, 504
   Margery, 504
   William, 504
Peyine, John, 765
Peyntore (Peyntour), John, of Stowmarket, 592
   Richard, chaplain, 178
Peyte, Margaret, 456
Peyton, John, 232, 435
Phelipe, John, of Melford, 436n, **756**
   Rose, 756
Piers, [*unnamed*], of Stonham, 417
Place, John, of Lavenham, 190n
   Rose, widow of Walter, of Mildenhall, 378n
   Simon, 378
   Walter, 378
Plandon, John, of Melford, 779
Playford(e) (Playforth), Agnes, of Troston, **789**
   Alice, daughter of George, 754
   George, 312, 312n, 768, 768n; & family, 754
   Joan, wife of John, 754
   John, 312, 629, 754*, 789; son of George,
      754; son of Thomas, 754; of Mildenhall,
      230n, **312**; the elder, of Mildenhall, 312,
      312n, **754**, 768n
   Margaret, 754, (née), 789; wife of George, 754
   Robert, 312, 387, 789
   Thomas, 312, 312n, 754; friar, 187; son of
      George, 754
Plesauntes, John, 657
Podeney, John, 55
   Phyllis, 55
   Robert, 67; of Bures St Mary, **55**, 326n
Poleyn, Alice (née Pope), wife of John, 661
   John, 661
   Robert, of Ixworth Thorpe, 661
POLSTEAD, church, 97, 161, 247, 248, 331, 685
   image of BVM in, 97
   rector of, *see* Robert Lynkfeld
   inhabitants of, 248, 271, 311
   lands in, 33, 97, 104, 161
   testators of, **33**, **97**, **104**, **161**, **248**
Pond, Walter, 656
Pondere, Agnes, 192
   Ed., 192
   Henry, 192
   Isabel, 306

John, *lxx*, 192, 307; of Great Ashfield, **192**;
   fuller, of Sudbury, *li*n, 84n, **306**
Marion, 192
Ralph, 192
Roger, 363
Ponyard, John, 391
   Thomas, 391
Pope, Henry, of Mellis, 391n
   Joan, (née Baxtere), wife of Robert, 661
   John, of Eye, **222**
   Margery, 620
   Richard, of Knettishall, 661n
   Robert, 661
   Thomas, 620; of Redgrave, **620**; of Yaxley, 222
Poperyk, Richard, 171, 171n
Poperyle, Thomas, of Newmarket, 510
Port(e), Edmund, of Honington, **474**
   Margaret, 474
   Richard, chaplain, 134
Porter(e), Agnes, daughter of Ellis, 276
   Ellis, 276
   John, 96; of Castle Hedingham, 276
   Richard, 143
   William, 214
POSLINGFORD, manor of Wentford in, 148
Potager(e) (Poteger, Potenger), John, chaplain,
      271, 271n, 290, 290n, 306, 408, 425, 465,
      607, 651, 652
   William, chaplain, 175, 175n, 258, 496
Pottere (Poteer), Agnes, 400, 815
   Isabel, 400
   Joan, 400
   John, 400
   Nicholas, 400
   Robert, 400
   Roger, 400*
   Thomas, of Rede, **400**
Potyer, John, 55n, 326; the elder, of Bures St
      Mary, **326**
   Laurence, 326
Pouncy, Isabel, 213
   John, 213
   Thomas, of Wickhambrook, **213**
Powere, Alice, 584
   Henry, of [Great] Barton, 584, 584n
   Margery, of Great Barton, **584**
   Nicholas, 584
Powle, John, 632
   Thomas, 135
Powlyn, Christian, servant, 154
   John, clerk, 398
Prat(e) (Pratt), John, 331; of Barnardiston, 490
   Katherine, 677
   Margery, wife of William, 502
   Thomas, servant, 490
   Walter, 577
   William, 461, 502, 762
Prath, Richard, of Ashley, 80n

Pratt, *see* Prat(e)

Preen, William, of London ('Loondon'), 756

Prentys(e) (Prentis, Prenteys), Alice, (née At Lee *alias* Hurlebate), 370
George, 290, 408, 465, 652; of Sudbury, 189, 607
John, 251, 783
Thomas, 46, 722

PRESTON, church, 122, 190, 336, 716
sepulchre light of, 455
vicar of, *see* Robert Warnere
inhabitants of, 145, 162n, 190, 613
lands in, 11, 181, 716,
manor in, Mortimer's, 181n
places in, 'Damessell' (tenement), 716
'Hoodys' (tenement), 11
'Ingoldes' (tenement), 716
'Munkes' (tenement), 190
'Scottis' (tenement), 11
testators of, **145**, **190**, **716**
ways in, 'Cherchestrete', 190
'Cherchewey', 716
will dated at, 30
wills proved at, 309, 767

Preston, John, *lxiii*, 785, 785n
Thomas, 213

Profete, William, 761

Pryk(e), John, the elder, 531; the elder, of Barrow, 276n, 530n, **531**; the younger, 531
Margery, 531
Roger, chaplain and vicar of Graveney (*Kent*), 75
William, 531

Prynce, Laurence, of Fornham All Saints, 798

Prynchatt (Prynchett), Alice, (née Abbott), 267

Pryo(u)r, Agnes, of 'Cokkystrete', 247
John, 309
William, of Great Cornard, 212n

Pryst, Robert, 434

Pulsham, Joan, 529
Margaret, daughter of Richard, 529
Richard, 529
William, 529

Punder, Alice, wife of Thomas, 681
Thomas, 681; the elder, 681

Pundyr(e), Ralph, clerk, 644, 667

Punte, Thomas, of Occold, 391n

Purch, John, 334

Purdon, Cecily, 121

Purdy, Stephen, rector of Honington, 16, 489

Purpyll(e), John, 544; of Ixworth, 219n, 228
Marion, 402
William, 402

Purser(e), John, 207
Thomas, 207; chaplain, 247; clerk, 117, 117n, 247, 331
William, of Stoke, 150

Pury, Robert, *lv*, 153, 153n

Pusk(e), Alice, 92
James, 27; of Kersey, 92n
John, of Kersey, **92**
Margery, servant, 570

Puttok, Isabel & family, 147
Thomas, of Mildenhall, barker, *li*n, *lx*n, **147**

Pychese (Pykchese), Thomas, 281, 281n, 461, 461n, 577, 577n, 609, 609n; the younger, 609

Pydenale, Adam, of Ousden, **335**

Pye, Alice, of Assington, widow, **407**
Thomas, of Assington, 407, 407n
William, 531

Pykchese, *see* Pychese

Pykerell (Pekerell), John, of Thurston, **321**, 548n; the elder, of Thurston, 321n; (?*recte* Parker), rector of Beyton, 321, 321n; rector of Westhorpe, 321, 321n, 775
Robert, of Norton, 321n

Pynell, Eleanor, 511

Pyngyll, Robert, of Denston, *lxiii*, 785, 785n

Pynhorne, Robert, of Mildenhall, 260

Pynkeswall (Pynswale), John, rector of Redgrave, 546, 546n

Pypere, Agnes, 238
Alice, 238
Emma, 131; the younger, 238
John, 238*, 238n; of Thorpe Morieux, **131**
Thomas, 131, 131n; of Thorpe Morieux, 145n, **238**

Pyrty, Thomas, of Thorndon, 126n, 337n

Pytman, Richard, 568

Pytt, Alice, 542; wife of Robert, 542
John, the elder, of Wattisfield, 542n
Robert, 542
William, of Wattisfield, **542**, 561

Qwarry, Henry, of Hitcham, 154n

Qwedwelle, Alice, the younger, 310

Qweynt, William, 17
see also Qwynte

Qwhelmere, John, of Hundon, **78**

Qwhepsted, *see* Whepsted

Qwhytcherche, *see* Qwycherch

Qwhyttmowth, Thomas, 450

Qwhytyng, Olive, 568
see also Whytyng

Qwycherch (Qwhytcherche), Nicholas, of Wicken (Cambs), *lxi*n, **427**

Qwylter, Christine, 460
John, 510
Katherine, 510
Robert, of Bures St Mary, **460**
Thomas, of Newmarket, **510**

Qwynte, John, 741
see also Qweynt

Qwyntyn, Katherine, 43; wife of Roger, 745
Margaret, holy woman, 698, 698n

Peter, of Hitcham, **43**
Roger, 745
Walter, rector of Stoke Ash, 726
Qwytop, William, 799

Radclyf(e), Robert, of Eye, 457
Rose, daughter of Robert, 457
Ragge (Rage), John, chaplain, 18, 19
Ramsey, Isabel, wife of William, 533
John, official of archdeacon & rector of
    Thelnetham, *xlviii, xlviii*n
William, 417, 532, 533
Rande, John, 251
Rascald, Thomas, 738
Rastall, Margery, of Troston, 386
Rasure, Alice, 677
RATTLESDEN, church, 57, 231, 536, 615, 797
altar of BVM Mary in, 231
canopy over (high) altar in, 615
chapel of, 797
    image in, 797
font cover of, 369
glazing of window in, *lvii*, 797
image of BVM in, 57
light before cross in, 536
light before image of BVM in, 536
rectors of, *see* Robert Bernard, Henry
    Strother
gilds in, 536, 536n, 615, 615n
inhabitants of, 57, 173, 334, 369n, 398, 414n,
    536n, 797, 797n
lands in, 1, 90, 398, 536, 615, 797
manor of, 797, 797n
places in, 'Cowperis' (tenement), 57
    'Halydays' (tenement), 57
    'Stonhamys', 90
poor of, 90
testators of, *lii*n, *lvii*, **57, 90, 231, 536, 615,
    797**
wills proved at, 57, 369
Rawlyn, Isabel, of Chippenham (Cambs), *lxi*n,
    124, 124n, **199**
John, 93
Katherine, 73
Robert, of Chippenham (Cambs), *124*, 199n
Thomas, 199
William, 199; of Barnham St Gregory, *73*
Ray(e), Agnes, 630n
John, 580, 646, 646n; of Wickhambrook,
    586n; of Woodditton (Cambs), 646n
Rayson (Reyson), Anne, 355
Robert, 355
Thomas, 355
William, of Kedington, **355**
REACH (Cambs), inhabitants of, 747
Rechard, Agnes, 572
Joan, 572
John, 572; of Beyton, **572**

Marion, 572
William, & family, of Lawshall, 572
REDE, church, 53, 400, 682, 686
candlebeam in, 400
chalice for, 682
image of Holy Trinity in, 686
lights in, 686
rector of, *see* Richard Faryngton
lands in, 682, 686
places in, 'Millars Crofte', 682
    'Turnours House' (tenement), 682
testators of, *lii*n, **400, 682, 686**
Rede, *see* Sagor *alias* Rede
Redelysworth, Margery, 219
Redenale, Peter, 57
Reder(e), John, 295
Richard, of Redgrave, *811*
Thomas, 636, 773; of Bury St Edmunds, 10
William & wife, 226
REDGRAVE, BOTESDALE in, chapel of St
    Botolph, 15n, 327, 416n, 418, 467
inhabitants of, 308n, 365n, 391, 467n, 522
lands in, 327, 376, 467, 546
places in, 'Botysdale Felde', 327
    'Breggemedew', 327
testators of, **257, 327, 348, 376, 467, 546**
wills proved at, 15, 361, 416, 418, 437,
    546, 764
church, 195, 257, 308, 327, 348, 376, 416,
    418, 467, 522, 543, 546, 620
chapel in, 546
chapel of BVM in, 543
    window in, *lvii*, 543
rector of, *see* John Pynkeswall
sepulchre in, 416
gilds in, 416, 416n
inhabitants of, 543n
lands in, 170, 416, 620
places in, house called 'Aschman', 620
    'Menhaugh' (field), 170
    'Randolffes' (tenement), 348
testators of, *lvii*, **195, 308, 416, 418, 543, 620,
    811**
Redgrave, Richard, of Great Livermere, 241; of
    Livermere, 760
REDLINGFIELD, church, 83
priory of Benedictine nuns, *lx*n, 83, 83n, 89,
    126, 337, 726
nun of, 417
prioress of, 726
Rednale, Peter, 615
Redstone, Vincent Borough, Suffolk historian,
    xlvi
Redyk, William, 188
Reedehed, Margaret, servant, 259
Reefham, *see* Resam
Regnam, John, & family, of Hadleigh, 440
Katherine, 440

Robert, 440
Regnold, Agnes, (née), 570, 571
    Alice, (née), 570, 571
    Isabel, (née), 570, 571
    Joan, (née), 570, 571
    John, 570, 571; of Woolpit, **570**, 571, 571n, 579n
    Margaret, of Woolpit, 570, 570n, **571**, 579n
    Margery, (née), 570, 571
    Richard, 570, 571
    William, 570, 571
Rerey, Richard, & wife, 211
Resam (Reefham), John, 643, 643n
Reso(u)n, Thomas, 691
    William, 495
Resshey, John, 55, 67
Reve (Rewe), Christine, 490
    Isabel, 392
    Joan, wife of Richard, 808
    John, 186n, 247, 490; the younger, 117; of Hepworth, *lxviii*, **392**, 402n; of Whepstead, 39n
    Richard, 808
    Robert, 172
    William, 248; of Thelnetham, 186n, 392n
    see also Cake *alias* Reve
Revell, Annabel, wife of William, 698
    John, 541
    Robert, 14
    William, 698
Rewe, *see* Reve
Reyman, Robert, 503
Reynold, John, 371
Reynoldes, Thomas, 393
Reyson, *see* Rayson
RHODES, Knights of, house of, 449, 449n
Richere, Joan, wife of Walter, 276
    Walter, of Cavendish, 276,
RICKINGHALL (unspec.), inhabitants of, 258, 308
    wills proved at, 589, 590
RICKINGHALL INFERIOR, church, 194, 348, 365, 367, 376, 467, 500, 522, 700
    rector of, *see* Edmund Spark
    gilds in, 365, 365n, 376, 376n
    inhabitants of, 308, 365, 376, 820n
    lands in, 194, 365, 522
    places in, 'Costynys Clos', 522
        'Holm Medue', 522
        'Holme, le', 522
        'Horsmere', 327
        'Lothysted' (tenement), 500
        'Randolffe', 327
        'Redyng', 500
        'Runtynges and Berchere' (tenement), 194
    testators of, **194**, **365**, **367**, **500**, **522**
    ways in, way called 'Bussysscloth', 500
        'Pedderysweye', 365

RICKINGHALL SUPERIOR, church, 194, 253, 348, 365, 418, 467, 506
    gilds in, 365, 365n
    inhabitants of, 240n, 365n, 506n
    lands in, 253, 365
    places in, 'le Hevestech', 240n
    taxes of, 240n
    testators of, **253**, **506**
    will proved at, 475
RICKMANSWORTH (Herts), inhabitant of, *lxviin*
RIDDLESWORTH (Nfk), church, 522
RINGSHALL, lands in, 275
RISBY, inhabitants of, 624
Risby, John, chaplain, 290, 290n
RISHANGLES, church, 726
    rector of, *see* Robert Wade
    inhabitants of, 126n, 337n
Risshe, Thomas, 310
Roberd, John, of Lawshall, *616*
Robertson, Katherine, & sons, 640
    Nicholas, of Glemsford, *lxivn*, 508n, **640**
Robho(o)d, Elizabeth, 401
    Joan, of Walsham le Willows, widow, **401**, 495n, 502n, 737n
    John, of Walsham, 401, 495, 495n; the elder of, Walsham, 401, 401n
    Stephen, 401, 401n
    Thomas, 401, 522; of Walsham, 566
Robyn, Agnes, 535
    Richard, of Rushbrooke, **535**
Robynson, Robert, 628
ROCHESTER, bishop of, *xlv*, *xlvn*
Rod(e)land (Rudlonde), James, 271; of Sudbury, 212, 651
    John, 537, 537n; the elder, of Kersey, 92n
    Richard, 537
    Robert, of Great Waldingfield, **537**
    William, 434; of Great Waldingfield, 537n
Rodyng(e), Adam, of Great Horringer, *lxiin*, 81, 432, 432n, **654**, 773, 773n
    Joan, 654
    John, of Wetherden, 451
    Margaret, 654
    Margery, of Wetherden, **451**, 573n
    Robert, gentleman, 409
    Thomas, 654
    William, 654, 773
Rodys, Joan, 478
    Nicholas, of Combs, *lvin*, *lvii*, **478**
Rog(g)ere, Cecily, 619
    Geoffrey, of Great Finborough, **619**
    Isabel, 142
    Joan, maid, 275
    John, 619
    Thomas, 142, 619
Rogyll (Rogul), Agnes, 164
    Avice, 163

Meliore, 164
  Thomas, 164; of Glemsford, 163n, **164**
  William, 163, 163n, 164, 164n, 317, 504, 628
Rogyn, John, 615n; of Rattlesden, 369n, 536n
  Robert, 615
Rokell(e), Alice, 59
  John, of Borley (Esx), 59; of Melford Tye, **59**
  Nicholas, 756
  Robert, 207
Role, William, 732
Rolfe (Rolff), Joan, 126
  Margaret, (née Jay), 732
  Robert, 126
Rollecros(e) (Rollecrosse), Roger, 453, 453n,
  680, 711, 711n, 817, 817n
  Walter, of Stanton, 338n
Rolynham, Robert, 204n
ROME, *xlv–lxv*
  masses at, St Fabian and St Sebastian, *lxv*,
    *lxv*n, 579
    Scala Celi, *lxv*, *lxv*n, 495, 511, 579
  pilgrim to do, circle of, *lxv*, 490, 495
    stations and circles of, 544, 544n
    stations of, *lxv*, 89, 89n, 184, 251
  pilgrim to go, chaplain, 16
    priest, 89
  pilgrimage to, *lxiv-lxv*, 184, 323, 338, 348,
    348n, 401, 490, 522, 544, 579
    Basilica of St Peter in, 294, 454
    Scala Celi, *lxv*n, 294
    sepulchres of St Peter and St Paul, 467, 522
  places in, hospital of St Thomas the Martyr,
    319, 319n
    Scala Celi, 244, 244n, 490
    sepulchres of St Peter and St Paul, 401
ROMFORD (Esx), inhabitants of, 190
Roo, Agnes, (née Eryswell), wife of Robert, of
    Wangford, 342
  John, 302
  Margaret, 145
  Robert, of Wangford, 342
Roodese, John, glover, of Ixworth, *l*in, *l*xn, **37**,
    228n
  Katherine, 37, 228n
Rookbode, Roger, 544
Roole, Margaret, 514
  Richard, of Burwell (Cambs), **514**
Roos(e), John, of Nayland, 439n
  Richard, 47
Roote (Rote), Christine of Glemsford, 508n
  John, 508*; of Glemsford, 508n
  Margaret, 508
  Richard, 508, 508n
  Robert, 508, 508n
  Thomas, 317n; of Glemsford, *lxii*n, *lxiv*n,
    504n, **508**, 640n
Roper, *see* Lotkyn *alias* Roper
Ropkyn, Roger, of Thrandeston, 2n, 618n

Thomas, 765
Ros, Thomas, 784
Rose, Joan, 211, 211n
  John, the younger, of Thurston, 321n, 414n
Rosshey *alias* Barbour, John, 283
Rote, *see* Roote
ROUGHAM, church, 74, 184, 515, 538, 588,
    634, 679, 816
  light of BVM in, 634
  light of St Nicholas in, 634
  sepulchre of Our Lord, 184
  tower of, 74, 184, 588, 588n, 634, 634n,
    816, 816n
  gilds in, 184, 184n
  inhabitants of, *lxxiv*n, 240n, 535, 613n, 759,
    816, 825
  lands in, *lxiv*, *lxxii*, 184, 538, 634, 679, 816
  places in, 'Bakownis' (close), 634
    'Betryches', 634
    'Cherchefeld, le', 634
    'Collynes' (messuage), 184
    conventual land of monastery of Bury, 634
    'Cowperes', 634
    'Dokettesland' (close), 634
    'Flaxmere', 634
    'Margretes Lond', 184
    'Mellehill, le', 634
  poor of, 634
  taxes of, *lxiv*, 240n, 634
  testators of, *lxiv*, **184**, **588**, **634**, **679**, **816**
  ways in, 'le Netherstret(te)', 634
Roungtun, Matilda, of Troston, 789n
Rous (Rows), John, 602; of Pakenham, 417n
  William, of Long Melford, 436n
Rowe, William, of Tostock, 743
Rowgham, Alan de, 184
Rowhey, John, 23
  William, of Little Thurlow, **23**
Rowland, Joan, *xlv*n
Rownton, John, of Lawshall, **582**
  Margaret, 582
Rows, *see* Rous
Rowt(e), Christian, 231
  John, 231*; chaplain, 231; servant, 89;
    formerly of Kettlebaston, 455; of
    Rattlesden, **231**
  Mariota, 231
  Richard, 568
Rowyngton, Thomas, 54
ROYDON (Nfk), church, 323, 232n
  image of St Remigius in, pilgrimage to,
    769, 769n
  inhabitants of, 688
Rucwoode, Thomas, 755
Rudham, Thomas, 711
Rudlonde, *see* Rodeland
Rus, Agnes, 27
  Joan, 27

John, of Woolpit, **27**

RUSHBROOKE, church, 127, 191, 470, 535, 558, 816
    chapel of BVM in, *liii*, 191, 470n
    rector of, *see* William Barkere
    inhabitants of, 125n, 191, 413n, 558
    lands in, 535, 816, 825
    manor of 'Rushbrook', 191n
    places in, 'Geselislond', 191
        'Glovers' (tenement), 191
        'Longrowe, le' (close), 191
        'Rossebrok Hyll', 191
    poor of, 191
    testators of, *lin*, *liii*, **127**, **191**, **470**, **535**, **558**
RUSHWORTH (now RUSHFORD) (Nfk), church, 731, 731n
    gilds in, 731, 731n
Russell, Agnes, 424
    John, the elder, churchwarden, of Great Waldingfield, *lii*, **424**
    Robert, 424
    Thomas, 424
    William, 424
Russhebrook, John, 169
Russhford, John, of Sudbury, *lxii*, **189**, 290n
    Matilda, 189
    Richard, 189
    Thomas, 189
Rydere, John, 42
Rygge, Christian, 169
    Isabel, (née), 169
    John, of Combs, **169**
    Thomas, 169
Ryngbell, Andrew, 294
Rynggold, Henry, parish chaplain of Glemsford, 752
Ryngsted, Simon, monk of Bury St Edmunds, 88
Rys, Walter, 447
Rysby, Anne, 404
    Ed., of Buxhall, **404**
    John, 306; chaplain, 408, 698
Ryseng, Richard, the younger, 349

Saare, Thomas, 249
Sabbe, William, 226
Sabelotte, Isabel, servant, 819
Sadelere, John, of Cavendish, 276; monk, of Tilty (Esx), 276
Sadyngton, John, rector of Semer, 406, 406n
Sagor *alias* Rede, Helen, 529
    Joan, 529,
    Margaret, 529
    Thomas, 529
Saham, John, 593
    Robert, 64; of Wetheringsett, 581
    Thomas, chaplain, 788
ST EDMUNDSBURY & Ipswich, diocese of, *xlv*n

saints: for individual saints, *see* Subject Index, *sub* advower; church & chapel (dedication); church equipment (image; light; side-altar dedication; tabernacle); cross; feast-day; gild-patron (dedication); pilgrimage
Sake, John, the elder, of Great Waldingfield, 83
Salews, Robert, Sir, 222
Salle, John, 397
Salle *alias* Cook(e), Alice, 484
    Joan, the younger, 484
    John, 484; the elder, of Bildeston, *lin*, **484**
    Margaret, 484
    Simon, & family, 484
    William, 484
Salman, Lettice, 311
    Margery, (née Mody), 311
    Richard, 311
    Thomas, & family, 311
Salter(e), Alice, 404
    Edmund, 404, 591
    Edward, 591
    Henry, of Buxhall, **591**
    Isabel, daughter of John, 290
    John, 290, 591; the younger, 591; of Buxhall, 180
    Margaret, & family, of Buxhall, 180
    Marion, 591
    Roger, 398, 591
    Walter, 591
    William, 383
Salysbery, Marion, 748
    Richard, 748; of Soham (Cambs), 748n
    Thomas, of Soham (Cambs), **748**
Same, Roger, apprentice, 31
Sampson, Eleanor, (née), 795
    James, 184
    Joan, 795
    John, the elder, 738; the younger, 738; of Hinderclay, **795**
    Katherine, 38
    Margaret, 738, 795
    Robert, 738, 795
    Thomas, 738
    William, 738
Sampson *alias* Goore, Thomas, of Bardwell, **738**
SANTIAGO de COMPOSTELLA, *see* COMPOSTELLA (Spain)
SANTON DOWNHAM, church, 207, 777, 826
    gilds in, 777, 777n, 826
    inhabitants of, 777
    lands in, 777
    place in, 'Bolysyerd' (close), 777
    testators of, **777**, **826**
Santon, John, 47
    Robert, 319; of Wangford, **47**
    William, of Wangford, 47n
SAPISTON, church, 544, 544n
    inhabitants of, 16, 118, 544n

lands in, 544
place in, 'Davyes' (tenement), 544
testators of, *lxx*, *lxxv*, *288*, **544**
Sare, Alice, of Elmswell, widow, **318**
Isabel, 419, 496
Joan, 496; the younger, 496
John, 318, 419; of Withersfield, 419n
Marion, 496
Robert, of Walsham, **496**
Thomas, 496, 692
Saresson, *see* Wygenhale *alias* Saresson
Savage, John, of Winfarthing (Nfk), 4
Robert, 262
Saverey, Robert, 121
Sawere, *see* Sawyer
Sawndyr, Alice, (née), 623*
Edmund, 623
John, 623; the younger, of Cheveley (Cambs),
*lxi*n, **623**
Marg', (née), 623
Sawyer(e) (Sawere), George, *lxx*, 663
John, *lxx*, 663
Robert, of Lavenham, 223
Thomas, 66
William, *lxx*, 663
Sawyer *alias* Gylly, Isabel, *lxx*, 663
John, of Bradfield St George, *li*n, *lxx*, **663**
Saxcy (Saxci, Saxi, Saxsy, Saxy), John, 94, 405;
clerk, of Lavenham, 517; of Stanningfield,
517n
Robert, 2, 94, 178; of Eye, 405
SAXHAM (unspec.), church, 28
lands in, 468
SAXHAM, GREAT, church, 534
lands in, 534
places in, 'Mellers', 534
'Polyngdenfeld', 534
testator of, *lxviii*, **534**
SAXHAM, LITTLE, church, 320, 373, 486, 507
banner of St Nicholas, 507, 507n
lights before image of BVM, 507
rector of, *see* Ralph Holdernesse
(Holdirnesse)
gilds in, 507, 507n
inhabitants of, 320n, 432, 507n
lands in, 320, 373, 486, 507, 534
places in, 'le Hawe', 320
'Okys, le' (field), 507
'Westrycefeld', 320,
testators of, *li*n, **320**, **373**, **486**, **507**
SAXON (Cambs), lands in, 762
Saxsy, Saxy, *see* Saxcy
Say, Katherine, 747
Margaret, 427
William, of Wicken (Cambs), *lxi*n, 427n, 513n,
747
Sayyer, William, 681
Scaldere, William, of Sudbury, 259, 259n

Scalpy, Richard, 478
Scarlett, John, 237
Scarp(e) (Skarpp), Alice, daughter of William,
533; of Felsham, 398
Alison, (née), 532, 532n
Cecily, 532
John, of Felsham, 713
Thomas, 532
Walter, 532, 532n; son of William, 533
William, 532; of Felsham, **532**, 533, 533n
Scateron, John, of Elmswell, 519n
Schaftyng (Shaftyng), John, & sons, 745; of
Thorpe Morieux, 455
Margaret, (née), 745
Schalforth, John, servant, 669
Schapman (Shapman), John, 302, 420, 565; John,
of Withersfield, **565**
see also Chapman
Schedd(e), (Shedde), Agnes, daughter of John,
339
John, 339
Margery, 339, 432
William, of Lavenham, *lxiii*, *lxiii*n, 190n, **339**,
431n, 681n
Schelton (Shelton), Emme, 109
Richard, 109, 142, 669, 669n
William, of Stowmarket, *lxii*, 38n, **109**, 381n,
669n
Schepey, Thomas, 706
Scheppard, *see* Shepherd
Scherlynge, Ralph, 665
Schilderston, Schildyrston, *see* Childerston
Schorthose, Thomas, of Sudbury, weaver, 191n
Schucford, *see* Shukford
Scole (Scoule), John, rector of Hepworth, 392,
392n, 402
Scot(t) (Scotte), John, 209; of Mildenhall, 347
Nicholas, clerk, 393
William, of Glemsford, 125
see also Skott
Scowle, Thomas, chaplain, 68
Scoyle (Skoyle), John, of Brockley, 53n
William, 53; of Polstead, 248
Scrappe, Katherine, (née Walloure), 741
Screvener, John, the elder, 359, 359n, 360, 360n
Thomas, of Bildeston, 360,
See, Robert, 36
Seefrey, John, 738
Sefowle, John, of Rattlesden, 398
Segbrook, Joan, 521
John, of Stowmarket, **521**
Seger, John, of Tuddenham, **340**
Rose, 340
Segore, Alice, 272*
Isabel, 272
John, 272
Stephen, 272
William, of Stradishall, **272**

Segryn, John, 14
Selawys, Thomas, 285
Selot, John, archdeacon, *xlviii*, *xlviii*n, 381n
Seman, John, 205n; the elder, of Bury St
 Edmunds, 738; the elder, of Drinkstone, &
 family, **19**
 Robert, 555
 Thomas, 19; of Thelnetham, 820n
Semancroft, John, of Redgrave, **195**
 Robert, 195
 Rose, 195
SEMER, church, 50
 rector of, *see* John Sadyngton
 inhabitants of, 154n
 see also Semer bridge, NEDGING
Semere, Joan, 154
 John, servant, 154
Semper, Isabel, 803
Sendrell, John, Sir, 785
Sennow, John, of Thorpe Morieux, 322
Sergawnte (Sergeaunt, Sergeawnt), Nicholas, 74
 Robert, 480; of Stoke, 797
Serian, Edmund, 579
Sevepens, John, 266
Sewale, Alexander, 266
 Joan, 266
 John, the elder, 266; the younger, 266
 Matthew, 266
 Richard, 447
 Robert, 266; of Great Barton, **266**
 Thomas, 266
 William, 266
Shakyntyn?, William, 629
Shapman, *see* Schapman
Shedde, *see* Schedd
Sheldrak(e), John, 171; of Little Waldingfield,
 30n; of Stoke by Nayland, **480**
 Matilda, 480
 Simon, 171
 Stephen, 480
 Thomas, 480
SHELLAND, church, 40, 697, 786
 cope for, 697
 tapestry of 'Sarcenet' for, *lix*, 697
 inhabitants of, 109, 324n
 lands in, 109, 697, 786
 place in, 'Aylstonys' (tenement), 697
 testator of, *lix*, **697**
Shelton, *see* Schelton
Shene, Richard, 754
Shepherd (Cheppard, Scheppard, Sheppard,
 Shepperd), Alice, 722
 John, 779
 Margaret, 307; of Sudbury, widow, **652**
 Osbert, of Earls Colne, 779
 Richard, 779
 Thomas, of Long Melford, **722**
 William, 673

Sherecroft (Cherecrofte), Thomas, rector of All
 Saints', Icklingham, 471, 471n, 683
Sherewyn (Sherwyn), Katherine, 266
 Robert, 266
Sherlynge, Alice, 592
 Ralph, of Stowmarket, **592**
Sherman, John, of Yaxley, **244**
 Margaret, 244
 Richard, of Wattisham, 111n, **433**
 Robert, 244, 722
 William, chaplain, 244
Sherwyn, *see* Sherewyn
Sheryngton, Joan, 796
 William, of Wetheringsett, 778n, **796**
Sheve ... [*damaged*], Richard, of Stoke Ash, 16
SHIMPLING, church, 154, 494
 lands in, 494
 testator of, **494**
SHOTLEY, inhabitants of, 89, 417
SHOULDHAM (Nfk), Gilbertine priory of, 187,
 187n
 inhabitants of, 187
Shukford (Schucford, Shukforth), Joan, 207,
 (née), 561
 John, 207, 207n, 437n, 561; of Thelnetham,
  561, **769**
 Katherine, 561
 Marion, 769
 Richard, 561
 Robert, of Langham, *lxxv*n, **207**; of
  Thelnetham, 769n
 Thomas, 561
Shyllyng *alias* Bakere, Thomas, of Flempton, 539
Shyllyston, John, 548
SIBTON, Cistercian abbey of, 821
 abbot of, 435, 435n
Sillote, John
SILVERLEY (Cambs), church, 80
 vestment and cope for, 80
 will proved at, 124
Simond (Symonde), John, 144; of Barrow,
 507; of '?Berans', *144*; of Botesdale in
 Redgrave, 467n
 William, 144
Simpson (Sympson), Richard, rector of
 Barnardiston, 598, 598n, 655, 655n
Skarpp, *see* Scarp
Skeat (Skeet(e), Skete, Skett), Alice, of Great
 Livermere, widow, **241**
 Gregory, 826
 Robert, of Bardwell, 241
 William, chaplain, 409, 409n, 556, 556n
Skeith, *see* Sketh
Skelton, Thomas, vicar of Thurston, 295, 295n
Skennere, *see* Skynnere
Skeppere, Alice, 40
 Edmund, 40
 Joan, 40

John, 40; the elder, of Woolpit, **40**
Katherine, 40
Rose, 40
William, 40
Skete, *see* Skeat
Sketh (Skeith, Skeyth), Katherine, relict of
    Thomas, of Stanton, **453**, 711, 711n, 817,
    817n
    Margaret, of Stanton, daughter of Thomas, *lix*,
    lxii, 452, 453n, **711**, 817, 817n
    Richard, 817
    Thomas, of Stanton, 453, 711, 711n, **817**
Skett, *see* Skeat
Skeyth, *see* Sketh
Skonyng, Alice, wife of Richard, 819
    Richard, 819
Skott(e), Alice, widow, 708, 708n, 709, 709n
    John, 417
    William, 528
    see also Scot(t)
Skoyle, *see* Scoyle
Skreven (Skryvyn), Thomas, 461, 461n, 482,
    482n, 656, 656n
Skultoke, John, 558
Skulton, Nicholas, 251
    Thomas, 251
Skylman, Margaret, 148
    Richard, 148
Skynall, John, the younger, 9
    Margaret, 9
    Richard, of Snailwell (Cambs), **9**
Skynnere (Skennere), Christian, (née), 679
    Isabel, 679
    John, 679
    Margery, (née), 679
    Thomas, of Rougham, **679**
Skyte, Geoffrey, 777
Slaughter, John, 346
Slawe, John, 522
    see also Erlle *alias* Slaw
Slolee, [*unnamed*], Master, Augustinian friar, 790
Smal(le)bergh, Walter, 170, 323
Smalwode, Benedict, 583
    George, 583
    Isabel, of Bradfield St George, **583**
    Joan, (née), 583
Smert, Alice, 275
    Isabel, 142
Smeth(e), Geoffrey, of Bures St Mary, **781**
    Margaret, 781
Stephen, 105
Smith (Smyth), Adam, 618
    Agnes, 255, 487; (née Marham), 387
    Alice, 658; (née), 720; servant, 247
    Anne, (née), 566
    Beatrice, of Ixworth, 738
    Eleanor, of Nayland, **439**
    Geoffrey, of Melford Tye, 59

Henry, 271
Hugh, 641, 815; of Stoke by Nayland, 161
Isabel, & family, 655; of Great Finborough,
    lxvii, **141**
Joan, 156, 720, 721; (née Brett), 784; (née
    Garlyng), 358
Jankyn (John), of Bury St Edmunds, *xlix*
John, 45, 156, 327, 348, 720, 721, 733, 815;
    'cowpere', 166; Sir, 504, 508, 508n; the
    elder, 121; 'at Hyll', 204, 204n; 'at Waleys
    Hyll' (Soham), 278, 278n; of Barnardiston,
    655; the elder, of Barnardiston, 655n; the
    elder, of Botesdale in Redgrave, **327**, **348**;
    of Bury St Edmunds, *lxix*n, 68, 444n;
    gentleman, of Bury St Edmunds, 30; of
    Cavendish, 133; of Clare, *lvn*, **815**; of
    Kersey, 247; of Long Melford, 363, 436,
    779; of Norton, 771; of Soham (Cambs),
    *lxi*n, 204n, **397**; of Somerton, 463; of
    Stansfield, **255**; of Stanton, **566**
Katherine, (née), 815
Margaret, 348; (née Mody), 311; wife of John,
    327; widow, of Boxford, 247
Margery, (née), 487
Marion, 815
Matilda, 327, 348
Nicholas, of Walsham le Willows, 258n
Ralph, 196, 196n, 211n, 284; of Bildeston,
    720, **721**
Richard, 311; son of John of Somerton, 463;
    of Westley, **487**
Robert, 121, 156, 158, 358, 374, 424, 688; of
    Stoke, 142; of Stoke Ash, 374
Roger, 436, 779,
Seman, of Great Finborough, **156**
Thomas, 156, 167, 363, 387, 562, 720, 721;
    the younger, 78; of Long Melford, 449n; of
    Moulton, 696; of Stansfield, *lvn*, *lxi*, **121**; of
    Westley, 487n
William, 51n, 55n, 166, 326n, 527, 618, 688;
    & son, 570; of Bures St Mary, **658**; the
    elder, of Clare, 46n; rector of Combs, 621,
    621n; of Ixworth, 738; of Troston, 386
Smyth *alias* Barkere, Thomas, 601
Smyth *alias* Gardynere, Richard, of Somerton,
    125
SNAILWELL (Cambs), church, 24, 214, 551, 824
    image of BVM in, 24
    rector of, *see* John Lode
    inhabitants of, 24, 551n
    lands in, 24, 214, 551, 824
    places in, 'Foresleves' (toft), 24
    poor of, 214
    rectory (living) of, 24n
    testators of, **9**, **24**, **214**, **824**
Snell, John, the younger, 562
Snellyng, Alexander, of Elmsett, 483, 563
SOHAM (Cambs), BARWAY in, 397n

testator of, *794*
chapel of Our Lady by the highway, 744, 744n
church, 204, 232, 277, 278, 279, 382, 397,
  524, 525, 659, 744, 748, 758, 823
  common light of, 659, 748
  mortuary given to, *livn*, 204, 397
  pyx for sacrament, 823
  rood-loft light, 744
  sepulchre in, 279
  sepulchre light in, 524, 525, 758
  torches in, 278
  vicar of, 232
gilds in, *lxi, lxi*n, 204, 204n, 397
inhabitants of, 204, 232, 278, 382, 397n
lands in, *lxxii*, 204, 232, 277, 278, 279, 382,
  524, 659, 744, 748, 758, 823
places in, 'Berycroftes', 232, 232n
  'Brokestretesende', 232, 232n
  'Calow, le', 232
  'Downefeld, le', 382, 382n
  'dyche Furlong', 744
  'Estfeld', 204n, 232, 232n
  'Fenmedew', 232
  'Herpe' (close), 748
  'Horscroft', 232, 232n
  'Hyll', 204
  'Longmedew', 232
  mere, the, 232
  North Field, 232, 232n
  '?Obschortes Akyr', 232
  'Reedlond', 823, 823n
  'Toppe of the lake' (tenement), 758
  'Waleys Hyll', 278
poor of, 204
testators of, *liv*n, *8*, **204**, **232**, **277**, **278**, **279**,
  382, **397**, **524**, **525**, **659**, **744**, **748**, *749*,
  758, **823**
ways in, 'Cley Causy', 823
  Hall Street, 'Halle strete', 659, 823
  'Meere Strete', 758
  'Pratte strete', 748, 748n
wills proved at, 8, 232, 233, 234, 277, 278,
  279, 512, 513, 514, 524, 525, 659, 744,
  747, 748, 749, 758, 794
Solyard, John, Master, 788
SOMERTON, church, 125
  chapel of BVM in, 676, 676n
  rector of, *see* Gregory Cayle
  inhabitants of, 125, 463
  lands in, *lxxiii*, 125
  poor of, 125
  testator of, *lxxiii*, **125**
Sopere, Robert, of Barton Mills, 379
SOUTHAMPTON (Hants), inventory from, *lxxiv*n
Sowthgate, John, 745
Spaldynge, Thomas, 798
Sparham, John, of Eye, *176*

Spark(e), Edmund, rector of Rickinghall Inferior,
  194, 194n, 365, 376, 500, 522
  Peter, 711
  Simon, 152; of Barrow, 136, 136n
Spar(r)ow(e), Agnes, wife of Osbert, 779
  Marion, 779
  Osbert, 779; friar of Clare, 436, 779
  Robert, of Long Melford, *lvi, lvi*n, *lxvi*n, **436**,
    779
  William, of Chedburgh, 366
Sparue (Sparwe), Agnes, 89
  John, of Chedburgh, 53, 400
  Simon, 306, 652
  William, of Chedburgh, 53
Sped(e), James, 690
Spencer(e) (Spenser), Agnes, (née), 604
  Elizabeth, (née), 604
  Isabel, 604
  John, 604; of Edwardstone, 714; of
    Mildenhall, 717
  Richard, 335
  Thomas, of Bardwell, **604**
Sperlyng(e), Isabel, 641
  John, 641*; of Stoke By Nayland, 236n, **641**
  Julian, 641
  Katherine, of Combs, *200*
  Robert, 641
  Rose, 641
  Thomas, 641
Spetyllman, William, of Norton, 743n
SPINNEY (Cambs), *see* WICKEN
Sponer(e), Agnes, wife of John, 683
  Edmund, *lxx*, 307
  Isabel, of Sapiston, *288*
  Joan, 307
  John, 288, 288n; & family, of Icklingham, 683
  Peter, of Sapiston, 288n
  Thomas, son of John, 683
Spore, John, 236
  William, 784
Sporle, John, of Burgate, 218n, *715*
Sporyere, *see* Penteney *alias* Sporyere
Spragg (Spragy), John, 313
  Katherine, 511
  Laurence, of Haughley, **511**
Spring, *see* Spryng
Spront (Sprunte), Marion, 155
  Mariota, widow, of Clare, *lii*, 155n, **662**
  Richard, of Clare, **155**, 662, 662n
Spryng (Spring), Agnes, daughter of William,
  339
  John, 810
  Thomas, 237, 552; son of William, 339; the
    elder, 339; of Lavenham, 190, 339; ('I'), of
    Lavenham 11n, 190n; ('II'), of Lavenham,
    *lv*n, 190n, 339n
  William, 339

Spryng *alias* Wederdeyn, Joan, the younger, (née), 810
  Robert, of Brockford in Wetheringsett, *lin*, **810**
Spycere, Avice, & daughter Agnes, 175
  John, of Walsham le Willows, **175**
Spylman, Alice, 250
  John, of Finchingfield (Esx), 250
  Robert, official of archdeacon, *xlviii, xlviii*n
Stabelere (Stabilere, Stabyler), Richard, the elder, of Rattlesden, 173
  Valentine, clerk, 437, 437n, 589, 769
Stace, Matilda, of Sudbury, *lxx*, **307**
Stacy, Robert, of Barway in Soham (Cambs), **794**
Staley, Richard, of Thorndon, **791**
Stalham, Alice, 107
  Christian, 107, 107n
  Joan, 107
  John, tanner, of Haverhill, 107, 107n; of Mildenhall, 107; the elder, of Mildenhall, **107**
  Katherine, 107
  Margery, 107
  William, of the city of London, 107
Stalo(u)n, Alice, 46
  John, 46; the younger, of Mildenhall, 107n, 230n
Stannard, Anne, daughter of William, 547
  John, parish chaplain of Long Melford, 436, 436n, 446, 728, 756, 779
  William, 547
STANNINGFIELD, gilds in, 785, 785n
  inhabitants of, *lxiii*, 517n, 785
  lands in, 780, 785
STANSFIELD, church, 121
  cover for bier of, 121
  light of sepulchre in, 121
  painting of roodloft in, 121
  torches in, 121
  inhabitant of, 213n
  lands in, 255
  testators of, *lv*n, *lx*n, **121, 255**, *814*
STANSTEAD, church, 22, 463, 614
  rector of, *see* John Weste
  wardens of, 463
  inhabitants of, 463, 494, 541, 733
  lands in, 508
  place in, 'Cherche' (tenement), 22
  testators of, **22, 463, 614,**
STANTON, church (unspec.), 241, 241n
  church of All Saints, 183, 256, 333, 372, 453, 522, 566, 666, 680, 711, 739, 759, 759n, 817
    altar cloth for, *lix*, 711
    chapel of St Petronilla in, 111n, 759, 759n
    cope for, 711
    Easter sepulchre in, 566, 566n
    image of St Petronilla in, 111n
    rector of, *see* Edmund Bene

  church of St John the Baptist, 453, 522, 680, 711, 759, 759n, 817
    altar cloth for, 711
    vestments for, 175n
  gilds in, *lxii*, 338, 338n, 711, 711n
  inhabitants of, 338n, 372, 386, 415, 453, 566
  lands in, *lxxvi*n, 159, 241, 256, 333, 562, 566, 711, 739
  places in, 'Alecrofte', 372
    'Alyshege', 372
    'Amigeres' (tenement), 183
    'grendyll, le', 10, 10n
    'Honecrofte', 372
    'Oke', 256n
    'Persysben(e)' (tenement), 739
    'Prowdysroode', 372
    'Ryngolysmere', 372
    'Sowthhawe', 372
    'Stonys', 372
  testators of, *lv, lix, lxii, lxix*, **183, 256, 333, 372, 453, 566, 666, 680, 711, 739, 759, 817**
  ways in, 'Roschpath', 372
  will proved at, 666
Stanton, John, of Westley, 487
  Robert, of Bury, 114
  Roger, 588, 634, 679
Starlyng, Alice, 126
  John, 126
  William, clerk, 348, 348n
Stebbyng, William, of Cotton, 700
Stecheford, Katherine, 276
  Richard, 276
Steffe, John, of Rattlesden, 298
  Robert, 371
  William, 471, 471n, 479, 479n
Stephenes, Agnes, 232
Sterne, Joan, servant, 87
  Richard, 572
  Thomas, of Barton, 266
Sternrell, William, & wife, of Sudbury, 607
Sterre, Isabel, 611
  John, rector of Felsham, 417, 417n
  Katherine, daughter of William, of Worlington, 611
  William, of Worlington, 611
Stevynesson, John, 786n
Stobyn, John, 692
Stok, John, yeoman, 191
  Thomas, of Stradishall, 198
Stoke, Thomas, 46
STOKE (unspec.), inhabitants of, 142, 797
  lands in, 764
STOKE ASH, church, 726
  chancel of, 726
  rector of, *see* Walter Qwyntyn
  inhabitants of, 374
  lands in, 126
STOKE by CLARE, church, 637, 803, 803n

brass chrismatory for, 803, 803n
canopy for pyx in, 803, 803n
image of BVM in, 803
light before, 803
paving in, 803
'Rodlofte, le', in, 803, 803n
sepulchre light of, 803
vestment for, 803
viaticum for, 803, 803n
college of St John in, 637, 637n
gilds in, 637, 637n, 803, 803n
inhabitants of, 133n, 637n, 638, 638n
lands in, 803
places in, 'Babthernbregge', 803, 803n
'Dedwoman, le', 803
'Four Asshes, le', 803, 803n
'Stoke Grene', 803
'Wyndeowtes' (tenement), 803
poor of, 803
testators of, *lv*, *lxvi*, *lxvii*, *106*, **637**, **803**, *813*
timber cross on 'Stoke Grene', 803
ways in, highway from 'Babthernbregge' to 'le
    Four Asshes', 803
highway in 'Mooreende', 637
way from 'Babthernbregge' on riverbank,
    803, 803n
wills proved at, 601, 637
STOKE by NAYLAND, church, 38, 150, 161,
    197, 236, 409, 480, 491, 556, 641
tower of, 48
vicar of, *see* John Cranewyse
gilds in, 409, 409n
inhabitants of, 38, 104, 109, 150, 161, 197,
    236, 491n, 556
lands in, 197, 236, 409, 480, 491, 556, 641
places in, 'Boymans' (tenement), 556
    'Cokeres' (tenement), 491
    'Duffousfeld', 480
    'Grecys' (messuage), 503
    'Honeleys' (field), 641
    'Hydis' (tenement), 556
    'Jakes Crofte' (cottage), 236
    'Leveneys' (messuage), 641
    'Lokkes' (messuage), 503
    'Markellbrege', 480
    'Renteres, le', 491
poor of, 38
testators of, *lin*, *lxxiv*, **38**, **150**, **197**, **236**, **409**,
    480, **491**, **556**, **641**
ways in, highway from church to
    'Markellbrege', 480
wills proved at, 503
STONHAM (unspec.), inhabitant of, 417
STONHAM ASPAL, church, 809
testator of, **809**
STONHAM, EARL, church, 89, 451
    rector of, 89
inhabitant of, 774

place in, 'Ladyesbredge', 89
STONHAM PARVA, church, 374
inhabitants of, 374, 805
Stonham, Agnes, 764
    Katherine, (née), 764
    Margery, 76
    Matilda, (née), 764
    Peter, of Thorndon, **764**
    William, 764
Storur(e), Robert, rector of Felsham, 532, 532n,
    533, 647, 647n
Story, Henry, of Whatfield, **406**
STOW, deanery of, *xlivn*, *xlv*
STOW CUM QUY (Cambs), inhabitant of, 513
Stowe, Edmund, Sir, 723
STOWLANGTOFT, church, 445
inhabitants of, 101, 174, 295, 445, 672
testator of, **445**
STOWMARKET, Chilton hamlet in, 501, 501n
    chapel of St Margaret in, 501, 501n
    church of St Mary, 109, 205, 468, 381, 501,
        645, 665, 669, 737, 750, 750n
    vicar of, *see* Robert Ferore
    church of St Peter (and St Paul), *liin*, *liii*, 103,
        109, 139, 201, 325, 381, 501, 521, 592,
        627, 645, 648, 665, 669, 673, 689, 737, 750
    aisle beyond font in, *liii*, 750
    aisle called 'le Seynt Johannis heele' in,
        750, 750n
    aisle of St John the Baptist in, 109
        paving for, 109
    altar of the Holy Cross in, 669
    antiphoner for, 669
    basin for lamp for, 109
    books in, 521
    chapel of BVM in, 421, 592, 592n, 665
        beam in, 665
        image of BVM in, *lxvii*, 421
            beads to, *lxvii*, 421
        vestment for, 665
    chaplain of BVM in, 325
    copes for choirmaster in, 669
    cupboard for vestments in, 521
    image of St Paul in, 381
        painting of, 627
    marble paving in, 750
    mass of the Blessed Mary in, 103
    parclose in, 669
    paving of, work on, 750, 750n
    sepulchre light in, 592
    south door of, 750
    tabernacle of BVM in, 669
    tabernacle of Holy Trinity in, 669
    torches in, 750
    vestments and ornaments in, 592
    west door of, 750,
    will proved at, 669

gildhall, 'le Gyldehalle', *lxii*, 43n, 109, 109n, 669, 669n
  inhabitants of, 109, 109n, 361, 381, 381n, 421, 576, 592, 669n
  lands in, 103, 205, 325, 468, 501, 592, 665, 669, 750
    in parish of St Mary, 645
  places in, 'Bellys' (messuage), 381
    'Bernard(es)yerd' (pasture), 669, 669n
    'Bogays' (tenement), 665
    'Brostretys Pictyll', 665
    'Chylderhous' (tenement), 501
    'Coes' (tenement), 468
    'Cowper(e)s' (tenement), 468
    'Crosselaneland', 665
    'Dagworth Bregge', 103
    'Frostlond', 501
    'Newmannys', 103
    'Seynte Marie Rentere', 665
    shop, late John Byll's, 468
    shops near the church gate, *lxxii*n, 103
    'Sondyll' (meadow), 103
    'Spadeakere', 665
    'Stowemarye', 645, 645n
    'Stroneton', 501
    'Teyntor Clos, le' (pasture), 103
    'Thorneyschepecote', 381
    'Westmerheyth', 381
    'Whitecros', 665
  poor of, 521, 673
  testators of, *lin*, *liii*, *lxii**, *lxvii**, *lxxii*n, **103**, **109, 139, 201, 205, 325, 381, 421, 468, 501, 521, 592, 645, 648, 665, 669, 689, 750**
  THORNEY in, in parish of St Peter, 673
    inhabitants of, 89, 401n, 468
    lands in, 669, 673
    places in, highway, 645
      'Reves' (meadow), 673
      'Smethes' (messuage), 645
    poor of, 673
    testators of, **627, 673, 737**
  ways in, 'Breggestrett', 669, 669n, 750
    'Cowystrette', 'Crow(e)stret(e)', 501, 669, 669n
    'Haghlestrette', 665
    highway, 521
    from Stow to Haughley, 592
  wills proved at, 25, 103, 109, 139, 140, 142, 156, 180, 313, 325, 358, 421, 468, 472, 569, 573, 576, 592, 619, 645, 648, 665, 673, 689, 694, 706, 737,
STRADISHALL, church, 198, 264, 286, 640, 724, 787
  ornaments in, 724
  inhabitants of, *lxiii*, 198, 213n, 785
  lands in, 198, 272, 286, 787
  place in, 'Percy croft', 787

  testators of, *lxiv*n (*recte* Glemsford), **198, 264, 272, 787**
  will dated at, 640
  wills proved at, 91, 255, 301, 608, 640
Strange, Katherine, 470
Straunge, (L'Estrange), Henry, esquire, 417, 417n
Strewen, John, clerk, 251
Strother, Henry, rector of Rattlesden, 57n
Stroude, Joan, 637
  Richard, chaplain, 637
  Robert, 637
Stroude *alias* Taylour, Nicholas, of Stoke by Clare, *lin*, **637**, 803n
Strut(t) (Struth), Alice, widow, of Bildeston, **303**
  John, 473; of Wickham (Esx), 55
  Thomas, 55, 807n
Sturdy, Beatrice, 105
  John, of Kedington, *105*
STURMER (Esx), inhabitants of, 250
  place in, 'le Ovyrhell', 447
Sturnell, William, & family, 465; of Sudbury, 767
STUSTON, church, 167, 391
  inhabitants of, 165, 617
  lands in, 617
  testators of, *165*, **617**
Style, Joan, 107
Stysted, John, clerk, 574
Styward, Alice, 823
  William, of Dunwich, 765
Subborn, Edmund, 327, 376, 376n; of Botesdale, 391, 391n; of Rickinghall, 308, 308n
SUDBURY, almshouse in, *lxiiin*, 607
  archdeacon of, *passim* in Intro., *see also* Clement Denston, John Selot, John Wygenhale
  archdeaconry of, *passim* in Intro.
  church of All Saints, 166, 259, 727
    'arche' in, 259
    bell for, 727
    marble paving in, 727
    vicar of, *see* Robert Hynderwell, Thomas Tylere
  church of St Gregory, *xlviii*n, 31, 32, 189, 212, 290, 306, 311, 408, 425, 465, 505, 596, 607, 652, 698, 702, 782
    pair of censers for, 698
    pilgrimage to image of Our Lady in, *lxiv*, 414, 414n
    window in, *liii*, *lvii*, 702
  church/chapel of St Peter, 31, 32, 84, 150, 189, 212, 271, 290, 306, 307, 311, 408, 425, 465, 607, 652
  cloth-workers in, *lxiii*n
  college of St Gregory, 32, 505n
    library of, 782
    warden of, *xlviii*n*
  gilds in, *lxii*, 189, 189n, 290, 290n
  house of Dominican friars (Preachers) of, *lx*,

11, 11n, 38, 43, 50, 55, 67, 78, 79, 83, 87,
  96, 131, 133, 145, 154, 160, 184, 191, 205,
  212, 238, 247, 259, 271, 283, 290, 300,
  307, 309, 311, 317, 322, 339, 352, 357,
  404, 413, 424, 436, 454, 465, 494, 504,
  508, 528, 537, 570, 573, 579, 628, 681,
  682, 690, 698, 722, 729, 751, 767, 779,
  785n, 797, 816
  brick wall of, 290
  cemetery, 271
  church of, 181, 465, 505, 607, 613, 651
  confraternity of, 751
  friar of, 505
  inhabitants of, *lxxiv*n, 31, 32, 166, 189, 191n,
    212, 259, 311, 408n, 434, 440n, 505, 549,
    607, 608n, 651, 652, 698, 702, 714, 727n,
    767
  lands in, 31, 84, 166, 212, 259, 271, 290, 306,
    307, 408, 425, 434, 652, 698, 702, 727
  places in, 'Boromgate Ende', 271
    'Bromhyll', 307
    corner opposite wall of Friars Preachers,
      702
    'Cornereschope, le', 727
    market place, 607n
    'Melfordes' (tenement), 434
    shop opposite St Peter's, 607
  poor of, 465, 607
  testators of, *lin**, *lii**, *liii*, *lv*n, *lvii*, *lxii**, *lxiii*n,
    lxvii, *lxx*, **31**, **32**, **84**, *98*, **166**, **189**, **212**,
    259, **271**, **290**, **306**, **307**, **408**, **425**, **434**,
    465, **505**, **596**, **607**, **652**, **670**, **698**, **702**,
    727, **782**
  ways in, 'Croosse Strete', 259
    Friars Street, 11n
    lane to house of Friars Preachers, 702
  wills proved at, 20, 31, 51, 52, 67, 83, 84, 86,
    212, 225, 259, 271, 290, 306, 307, 326,
    331, 332, 354, 370, 407, 408, 423, 424,
    425, 434, 458, 459, 494, 505, 537, 574,
    596, 597, 651, 675, 702, 727, 728
Sudbury, William, of Kettlebaston, 455n
Suffeld, John, 290
SUFFOLK, archdeaconry of, *xliv, xliv*n
  county of, *xliv*
SUFFOLK, EAST, county (abolished 1974), *xliv*
SUFFOLK, WEST, county (formed 1889,
    abolished 1974) *xliv, xliv*n
Sutton (Suttun), Isabel, 650*
  John, 462, 609, 650; of Thetford, 338
  Richard, of Oxborough (Nfk), 650, 650n
  William, of Mildenhall, **650**
SWAFFHAM BULBECK (Cambs), priory of
    Benedictine nuns in, 646, 646n
  prioress of, 646, 646n
SWAFFHAM PRIOR (Cambs), church, 428
  Reach in, chapel in, 428, 428n
Swalwe, Joan, 154

John, the elder, & family, 154; the younger,
  154
Swan, Alice, widow, of Creeting St Peter, 89n,
  472n
  Joan, 555
  John, 661
Swanton, Henry, of Botesdale in Redgrave, 365n,
  376, 546n
  Isabel, of Botesdale in Redgrave, 376, 376n,
  546
  Joan, widow, of Depden, *lii*n, 366, 366n, **685**
  John, 366; of Rede, *lii*n, 685, 685n, **686**
  Walter, 366, 366n, 685, 685n, 686, 686n
  William, of Depden, **366**, 685, 685n
Swaston, Thomas, 776
Swastun, Alice, 466
Swayn, *see* Sweyn
Swetman, George, of Wattisham, 433
Swetto(c)k, Richard, rector of Bildeston, 284,
  284n, 303, 431, 720, 721n
Sweyn (Swayn), Agnes, 517
  Alice, 216, (née), 472
  Anne, (née), 472
  James, of Belchamp (Esx), 163; of Glemsford,
  163, 164n
  Joan, (née), 472
  John, 517; of Creeting St Peter, 472n;
    of Lavenham, 87n, 517n; the elder, of
    Lavenham, **517**
  Marion, 472
  Robert, 472, 517
  Thomas, of Creeting St Peter, **472**; of
    Mildenhall, **216**
  William, 517
Swyftt, John, of Walsham le Willows, *lvii*, **258**
  Katherine, 258
Swytbrede, John, 252
Sybly, Henry, Sir, 649
  John, of Cheveley (Cambs), 623n
Syday (Sydey), Alice, 225
  Elizabeth, 225
  Joan, (née), 225
  John, 225; of Chilton, 225; fuller, of Great
    Waldingfield, *lin*, **225**; weaver, of Great
    Waldingfield, 225n
  Margaret, 225
  Richard, 225
Sygo, Alice, (née), 429
  John, *lxxiii*, 664; of Worlington, **429**, 768n
  Margaret, (née Bowne), 768
Sylvester, (Sylvestre), Nicholas, incumbent of
    Haverhill, 341
Symes, John, the elder, 476
Symond(e) (Symondes), John, 342, 600, 820; of
    Mildenhall, 342
  Robert, 673, 754
  Thomas, 72, 403
  William, 437

Syngere, John, incumbent of Chippenham
(Cambs), 199, 199n
Syngewell, John, 642
Synton, Agnes, 31
Isabel, 31
Stephen, friar, 31
William, of Sudbury, **31**
Syre, Alice, of Ixworth, 738
Elizabeth, 639
Isabel, wife of Robert, 390
John, 639
Margaret, of Great Ashfield, **390**
Robert, 390; of Ashfield, **639**; bond tenant of
manor of Wattisham, 433
Thomas, 639
William, 390, 639, 667
Sythyng, Henry, official of archdeacon, *xlviii*,
*xlviii*n, *xlix*
Syward, William, of Stoke by Nayland, 104

Taberham, Elizabeth, of Great Waldingfield, **305**
John, 305
Talbon, Robert, 45
Talbot, Robert, 776
Talmage, John, of Finborough, 142
Talyfer, Agnes, 116
Talyour, *see* Taylor
Tame, Robert, the younger, 457
Taylor(e) (Talyour, Taylour) Agnes, 223
Alice, of Bradfield St George, **672**
Henry, of Brockford in Wetheringsett, 5n
Isabel, (née), daughter of Alice, 672
Joan, 126
John, 41, 160, 666, 711; the younger, 626;
rector of Brockley, 35; of Thorndon, *lv*,
lxiii, **126**, 337n; the younger, of Thorndon,
126n
Margaret, 126; servant, 611
Matilda, 681
Richard, 209, 546
Robert, of Lavenham, 431n
Rose, 126
Simon, 160
Thomas, of Beyton, 560; of Lavenham, **223**;
of Ousden, 696
see also Stroude *alias* Taylour
Taylyour (Teylyour), John, 372; Sir, 252
Tebald, Eleanor, 783
Tebaud (Tebawde), Agnes, 187
John, 60; the elder, 187; of Fordham (Cambs),
187
Margaret, 187
William, 187
Teele (Teell), Thomas, 646, 646n, 630, 630n
Terry, Robert, 549
[*unnamed*], of Burgate, 416
Teryton, Robert, 788,
Teylyour, *see* Taylyour

Teype, Thomas, 382
Thakere, Thomas, 588
Thebade, John, 602
Thedam, Margaret, 652
THELNETHAM, church, 437, 522, 561, 589,
703, 769, 820
book for, 820
ornament for, 820
rector of, *see* Thomas Bretown, John
Ramsey
gilds in, 186, 186n, 392n
inhabitants of, 186, 392n, 589, 769n, 802,
820n
lands in, 437, 561, 703, 769, 820
places in, 'Drurys' (tenement), 820
'Goodwyns' (tenement), 820
'Haweboschakyr', 769n
'Joys' (tenement), 561
'Mormanys' (tenement), 820
'Moyses' (tenement), 820
'Wodebotome, le', 561
testators of, *li*n, *132*, **437**, **561**, **589**, **703**, **769**,
820
ways in, 'Fenstret', 703
will proved at, 566
THETFORD (Nfk & Sfk), *xlvi*
house of Austin friars (the 'New House') in,
69, 72, 101, 157, 159, 191, 207, 219, 228,
239, 240, 246, 258, 266, 269, 294, 295,
323, 338, 348, 361, 365, 367, 379, 391,
392, 393, 453, 467, 475, 477, 485, 500,
507, 522, 544, 590, 600, 604, 624, 636,
657, 661, 668, 684, 700, 707, 723, 725,
731, 738, 754, 770, 789, 792, 795, 802, 820
house of Dominican friars (the 'Old House')
in, 68, 72, 74, 101, 116, 120, 134, 136, 152,
157, 209, 219, 228, 239, 240, 246, 258,
265, 266, 268, 294, 295, 321, 338, 348,
362, 365, 367, 379, 386, 393, 399, 414,
414n, 453, 467, 475, 477, 485, 489, 502,
507, 519, 522, 589, 590, 599, 600, 604,
606, 624, 636, 650, 657, 664, 684, 719,
723, 725, 732, 738, 754, 789, 792, 817,
820, 821
Doctor Oldman of, 797, 797n
inhabitants of, 338, 771
parish of St Mary the Less, *xlvi*
inhabitants of, *xlvi*, *xlvi*n
testator of, *xlvi*n
priory of Benedictine nuns in, *lx*n, 68, 107,
120, 157, 186, 294, 338, 453, 529, 590,
634, 792, 820
prioress of, 590
Thewytes, Agnes, 799
Alice, 799
Thomas, of Bildeston, **799**
William, 799
Thillott, *see* Tyllott

Thomas, John, & family, of Lawshall, 686
THORNDON, church, 126, 146, 337, 764
  chalice for, 126
  churchale in, 764
  image of crucifix in, 126
  mortuary given to, *liv*n, 146
  rector of, 126
  gild in, 126, 126n, 337, 337n
  inhabitants of, 126n, 337, 337n
  lands in, 218, 764
  places in, 'Cherchegrene', 126
    'Ebotes' (tenement), 126
    'Gyes' (tenement), 126
    'Horscroftes' (tenement), 126
    'Knollys' (tenement), 337,
    'Langemedewefeld', 764,
    'Lesser Bradhege' (close), 764,
  testators of, *liv*n, *lv*, *lix*n, *lx*n, *lxiii*, *64*, **126**,
    146, **337**, **764**, *791*
THORNEY, *see* STOWMARKET
THORNHAM (unspec.), inhabitants of, 498
  lands in, 498
THORNHAM MAGNA, church, 193
  gilds in, 193, 193n
    gildhall of, 193, 193n
  inhabitants of, 193, 374
  lands in, 193
  testator of, **193**
  will proved at, 165
THORPE (unspec.), church, 544
THORPE MORIEUX, church, 122, 131, 238,
    351, 613, 712, 713
  candlebeam in, 238
  chapel of BVM in churchyard of, 351
  image of BVM in, 351
    beads donated to, *lxviii*, 351
  mortuary given to, *liv*n, 131, 351
  paving of, 131
  rector of, *see* Robert Chapman
  whitening walls of, 131
  inhabitants of, 145n, 322, 350n, 455, 613, 713
  lands in, 131, 238, 712
  manor of Thorpe Morieux, 417n
  place in, 'Wedyrtonis', 131
  poor of, 238
  testators of, *liv*n, *lxviii*, **17**, **131**, **238**, **351**, **613**,
    712, **713**
Thorpp, Geoffrey, 170
  Richard, 149
THRANDESTON, church, 252, 765
  image of St Mary of Pity in, 252
  'throne of Eystrych boorde' for, 252
  inhabitants of, 165, 252, 618n, 765n
  lands in, 765
    bondland of Prior of Hoxne, 765
  places in, 'Langgesyk, le', 765
    'Mellefeld, le', 765
  testator of, **765**

will proved at, 244
THRIPLOW (Cambs), lands in, 187n
Throsshere, Joan (née Dyke), wife of Thomas,
    803
Thruston, Joan, 251
Thurberne (Thurburne), Richard, 700
Thurgor(e) (Thugor, Thurgur), Ann, & daughter
    Christian, 651
  James, 20; of Acton, 518n, **651**
  Joan, & family, 158
  John, of Waldingfield, 158n
  Robert, of Acton, **20**, 651n
  William, 20; of Great Waldingfield, **158**
Thurkeld, Agnes, wife of Richard, 436, 779
  Richard, 436, 779
THURLOW, GREAT, church, 23, 171, 601, 608
  chalice for, 601
  chancel of, *liii*, 608
  sepulchre light in, 601
  torches in, 601, 608
  vicar of, 601
  inhabitants of, 259n, 490
  lands in, 601
  poor of, 171, 601
  testators of, *lin*, *liii*, **601**, **608**
THURLOW, LITTLE, church, 23
  inhabitants of, 91
  lands in, 23
  testator of, **23**
Thurmod, Alice, wife of John of Great
    Finborough, 375
  Joan, daughter of, Richard, 351
  Richard, 351,
THURSTON, church, 74, 265, 295, 321, 364,
    414, 548, 560, 606, 821
  alabaster panel on altar of BVM in, 74
  alabaster panel of life of St Peter in, 74
  light of BVM in, 265, 321, 414, 560, 606
  vicar of, *see* Thomas Skelton
  inhabitants of, 74, 125n, 270, 321, 321n, 364,
    414n, 548, 606, 797n, 821
  lands in, 74, 265, 295, 364, 414
  places in, Thurston Field, 74
    'Whetecrofte', 74
  testators of, *lxiv*, **74**, **265**, **321**, **414**, **548**, **560**,
    606
Thurston, John, servant, 774
  Robert, 225
  Thomas, 374
THWAITE, church, 210, 218, 252, 374, 529, 745
  bell, 218
  image of St George, with tabernacle, 745
  torches for, 218
  inhabitants of, 764, 764n
  lands in, 126, 745, 764
  places in, 'Gar(y)pys' (tenement), 218
    'Margaretes' (tenement), 218
    'Thweytes Medwe', 218

rectory, 218
testators of, **218**, **745**
Thweyt(es), William, the elder, *xlix*; the younger,
   xlix; Master, *xlviii, xlviii*n, *xlix*, 799, 799n;
   of Bury St Edmunds, 69
Thyllott, *see* Tyllott
Thyrlyng John, A.M., 459n
Thystelden (Thystylden), Alice, of Stowmarket,
   lxvii, **421**
TIBENHAM (Nfk), church, pilgrimage to chapel
   of St Nicholas in, *lxiv*, 414, 414n
Tilbrook, *see* Tylbro(o)k
Tilere, *see* Tylere
Tillot, *see* Tyllott
TILTY (Esx), Cistercian Abbey at, 276, 276n
TIMWORTH, inhabitants of, 368
Toffay, Alice, 159
   Thomas, of Bardwell, **159**
Tofte(s) (Toftys), Joan, 304
   John, of West Stow, 185n, **304**
   Matilda, 185
   Reginald, 304; of Elveden, **185**, 304n
   William, 258, 304; of Bury St Edmunds, 134
Tollare (Tollere), Joan, 120
   Robert, of Wangford, **120**
   William, 246
Tolsent, Cassandra, 711
Torald, John, 193, 193n, 392
Tornore, *see* Turnore
Torold(e), Thomas, 396
Torp, Joan, 109
TOSTOCK, church, 40, 74, 205, 228, 435, 771,
      786, 821
   antiphoner for, 771
   cope and vestment for, 821
   light of St Mary in, 771
   rector of, 205, *see also* Henry Irby
   inhabitants of, 743, 821n
   lands in, *lxxii*, 771, 821
   places in, 'Baxster(y)s' (tenement), 821
      'Brook, le', 821
      'Carletones' (tenement), 821
      'Caschys' (tenement), 821
      close at the rectory gate, 821
      'Closmedwe', 821
      'Cokes' (tenement), 821
      'Wethereldes' (tenement), 821
   rectory, 821
   testators of, *li*n, *lx*n, **29**, **435**, **771**, **821**
Tought, John, chaplain, 5
Towne, William, 54
Tram, Margaret, 777
Trapet(t), Alice, 68
   Isaac, 68
   John, *lxix*n, 68, 268
   Katherine, 68
   Lettice, 68
   Margery, of ?Market Weston, **268**

Ralph, 68; of Hepworth, *lxix*n, **68**, 268, 268n
Robert, 68
Thomas, 68; of Hepworth, 68n, 268n
Walter, 68
William, 68; of Hepworth, 268, 268n
Traylys, Thomas, 708
   see also Treylys
Trekere, Ed., 680
Trewe, Alice, 681
   John, 681
   Laurence, 681
   Simon, 681
   Thomas, 681
Trew(e)peny, Joan, 735
   John, of Mildenhall, **735**
   Robert, 735
   Thomas, 387, 735
Treylys, Christian, 217
   John, 217
   William, of Palgrave, *217*
   see also Traylys
Tripp (Trypp), Joan, 210
   John, 210
   William, 210
Tropynell, Alice, wife of Thomas, of Sudbury,
   652
   Thomas, of Sudbury, 652
TROSTON, church, 386, 489, 544, 757, 789
   inhabitants of, 134, 386, 760
   testators of, **386**, **489**, **757**, **789**
Trowe, Beatrice (née Huske), 389
Tryll, Joan, servant, 80
Trypp, *see* Tripp
Tubby, William, of Wortham, 269n, 323n
TUDDENHAM ST MARY, church, 243, 340
   chancel of, image of BVM in, 340
   rector of, *see* John Legatt
   inhabitants of, 243, 340, 485
   lands in, 62, 243
   places in, 'Hoodes yerde', 243
   testators of, **243**, **340**
   wills proved at, 246, 387, 450, 638, 766, 768,
      776
Tuffeld, Alice, 76; of Whepstead, 179n
   Isodor, & daughter Margaret, 179
   John, 76; the elder, of Whepstead, 39n, **179**
   Thomas, 179
Tunman, Anne, 477
   James, of Westhorpe, **477**
Turfyge, John, 602
   William, 602
Turnour (Tornore, Turnewe, Turnore Turnowr),
      Agnes, 451, 594, (née), 405
   Alice, 94, 281, 745; of Sudbury, widow, *lxvii*,
      440n, **698**, 727n
   Beatrice, of Woolpit, 145n
   Ed., 621
   Elizabeth, 745

Henry, 698; esquire, 608, 608n; esquire, of
Haverhill, 259, 259n; gentleman, 213
Joan, *lxvii*, 698, (née), 405
John, 271, 281, 350, 698; the elder, 461n,
698; the younger, 698; of Brockley, 53; of
Chippenham (Cambs), *753*; of Depden, **53**;
gentleman, of Great Thurlow, *lin*, *liii*, 259n,
608; the elder, of Kirtling (Cambs), **281**
Katherine, 698
Margaret, 53*, 405, 745, (née), 745; of
Norton, 192
Marion, 53
Matilda, 53, 495
Richard, 281, 745; of Thwaite, 764
Robert, 2n, 94n, 405; of Bury, 826; of Eye,
405, 405n
Simon, 284, 344; of Combs, *lvii*, **594**
Thomas, 53, 281, 698
Thomasine, 608, 698
William, 495, 706; of Brockley, 53; of Bury,
826; of Walsham, **495**
Turnour *alias* Dyer, Henry, of Long Melford,
32n, 436n, 780n
Tweyth, John, 252*
Twychyn, John, rector of Barnham St Gregory,
292, 292n, 293
Tyd(de) (Tyde), Alice, 819
John, 239, 239n; of Mildenhall, 545n, 664n,
819n
Matilda, wife of Thomas, of Bury St
Edmunds, 629, 629n
Robert, of Mildenhall, 819n
Thomas, & family, 239, 239n; tanner, of Bury
St Edmunds, 629; of Mildenhall, 378n, **819**
Tye, Margaret, of Sudbury, **166**
William, 166
see also at the Tye
Tylbro(o)k (Tilbrook) Agnes, 610
Joan, 499
John, of Upend in Kirtling (Cambs), *lxin*, **499**,
610n
Peter, of Kirtling (Cambs), 499n, 610n
Thomas, of Upend in Kirtling (Cambs), 499n,
610
Tylere, Christian, (née Cowpere), 247
Hawise, 128, 128n
Isabel, 128
Joan, 128
John, 128, 154, 201, 729; the elder, of Monks
Eleigh, 154; of Westley, *lxxi*, **128**
Thomas, 89, 128, 128n; of Monks Eleigh, 247;
vicar of All Saints', Sudbury, 166, 166n,
727, 727n
Walter, 729; rector of Bradfield St George,
270, 270n
William, 729
Tylkys, Alice, 21
John, of Glemsford, **21**

Tylle, Agnes, 670; of Preston, **145**
John, 670, 670n; the elder, 145; of Sudbury,
670, 670n
Margaret, 670
Tyllot(t) (Thyllott, Thillott, Tillot, Tyllote)
Edmund, 634, 816, 816n
John, 634
Katherine, 634
Margaret, (née Nunne,), & family, 634
Robert, of Rougham, 759
Roger, 634*, 634n; of Rougham, *lxxiv*n, 816n
Thomas, 634; husbandman, 634
Tylney, Edmund, clerk, 130, 130n; parish
chaplain of Rougham, 184; rector of
Bradfield St Clare, 772
Tymbyrman, Joan, 668
John, 668; the elder, of Mildenhall, **668**
Tymton(e) (Tynton), Agnes, 383; (née Nunne) &
family, 634
Emme, 383
John, 142, 383, 383n; the younger, 383n;
of Finborough, 634; the elder, of Great
Finborough, 383, 383n
Margaret, (née Basse), 367
Stephen, 383
Tyrell, family, of Gipping, 89n
Margaret, 89
Tyso, Agnes, 205
Alice, 205
Elizabeth, 205
George, 205; Sir, *lxviii*n, 205
John, of Drinkstone, 205n; of ?Stowmarket,
*lxviii*n, **205**,
Thomas, of Drinkstone, 205n
Walter, 205

Ufford, Robert, of Hundon, 301
Umfrey, William, 171; of Withersfield, 740
Underwo(o)de (Undyrwo(o)d), Edward, 407
Emma, (née), 718
John, 718
Margaret, (née), 718
Roger, 718,
Thomas, 214
William, 718; of Burgate, **718**
see also Hundyrwod
Upchar, Thomas, 55
Ussheere, Ed., 773

Valentyn, John, 251, 601
Va(u)ncy, John, 762; canon, 220; of Woodditton
(Cambs), 630, 630n, 646, 646n
Venour, Selina, 729
Vipownd, *see* Vypownd
Vyell, Christian, 723, 723n, 804, 804n
Isabel, (née), 804
John, 220, 220n, 723*; of Ixworth, 219, 219n

Thomas, of Ixworth, *lxxv*n, 723, 723n, **804**;
   the elder, of Ixworth, 219n, **723**, 804n
see also Myller *alias* Vyell
Vyncent, John, 636
   Robert, Sir, 401, 737, 737n
Vyne, John, 434; of Sudbury, 698
Vypownd (Vipownd), Margaret, 188
   Stephen, of Lidgate, **188**
Vys, Robert, 762

Wade, Alice, of Woolpit, **375**
   John, 375
   Katherine, 375
   Robert, rector of Rishangles, 126, 126n
Wadsell, John, 198; of Stradishall, **198**
   Katherine, 198
   Margaret, 198
   Robert, 198
Wagard, Agnes, 789
Wagge, Alice, (née Cagge), wife of Thomas, 574
   Thomas, & family, 574
WALDEN (Esx), abbot of, 782n
   lands in, 782, 782n,
   testator's debtors of, 782
Walden, Dom John, monk, 782
WALDINGFIELD (unspec.), inhabitants of, 158
WALDINGFIELD, GREAT, church, 83, 122, 158,
   225, 305, 424, 537, 675, 689
   churchwarden of, 424
   inhabitants of, 83, 225
   lands in, 11, 30, 225
   places in, 'Abbottes' (tenement), 225
   'Herietes' (tenement), 225
   testators of, *li*n, **158**, **225**, **305**, **424**, **537**, **675**
   way in, 'Grenecroft Lane', 225
WALDINGFIELD, LITTLE, church, 83, 122, 349
   altar of St Mary in, 83
   doors of, 349
   font of, 349
   porch of, 349
   small bell for, 83
   tower of, 83
   vicar of, *see* John Dalton
   gilds in, 83, 83n, 349, 349n
   inhabitants of, 675
   lands in, 30
   place in, 'Holbrok', 83
   testators of, *li*n, *lii*, *lxix*, **30**, **83**, **349**
Waldyngfeld, Thomas, canon, 544
Wale, John, 153
Waleys, *see* Walleys
Walkfare, Agnes, 720, 721
Wall, John, 117n
Wallere, Joan, & family, 497
   John, 661
   Thomas, of Fornham St Martin, **497**
Walleworth, Matilda, 588
Walleys (Waleys), Elizabeth, 631

John, 631
Nicholas, 631
Thomas, of Burwell (Cambs), 551n, **631**
Walloure, John, 741
   Margaret, (née), 741
   Thomas, of Wattisfield, 240n, **741**
WALSHAM le WILLOWS, church, 175, 258,
   385, 401, 401n, 412, 475, 495, 496, 562
   aisle of St Katherine in, 475, 475n
   carpentry work of, 258
   chapel of St Katherine in, 175n
   lamp in, 401
   painting of image of BVM in, 562
   sepulchre in, 385
   vestments for, 175n
   window in 'le clerestory' of, *lvii*, 258
   gilds in, 258, 258n
   inhabitants of, *lxxiv*n, 16, 65, 175, 258, 294,
   385, 393, 401, 495, 566, 771
   lands in, 258, 401, 495, 496
   manor court roll, *lxxiv*n
   places in, great meadow, 401
   'Osbernis' (tenement), 258
   '?Prentys' (tenement), 401
   testators of, *lvii*, **175**, **258**, **385**, **401**, **412**, **475**,
   495, **496**, **562**
   ways in, 'Chyrchestret, le', 401
   'Westret', 401
   wills proved at, 390, 496, 526, 527
Walsham, John, 209; of Pakenham, *lxvii*, **295**
   Katherine, *lxvii*, 295
   Ralph de, 378, 378n
WALSINGHAM (Nfk), house of Franciscan
   friars (Minors) of, *lxi*, 45
   shrine of BVM of, beads & rings donated to,
   lxvii, 803
   pilgrimage to, *lxiv*, *lxiv*n, 166, 166n, 508,
   640
Walter(e), Edmund, 519n, 660
   Geoffrey, & family, 294, 294n
   Isabel, 590
   John, 294; of Hepworth, 16, 590; the elder, of
   Hopton, 294n, 393n
   Richard, 294, 294n, 590, 590n; of Coney
   Weston, **294**, 590n
   Robert, 294*, 294n, 590, 590n
   Thomas, 294, 294n, 590, 590n
   Walter, of Coney Weston, 294n, **590**
   William, 371
WANGFORD (by BRANDON), church, 47, 120,
   302, 319
   inhabitants of, 120
   lands in, 220, 319
   testators of, **47**, **120**, **302**, **319**
Ward(e), John, 508; of Icklingham All Saints,
   469; rector of Snailwell, 24n
   Margaret, of Haverhill, *lxxv*n, *341*
   Robert, of Elmswell, 318

William, chaplain, 471, 471n; priest, 469, 469n
WARE (Herts), inhabitants of, 530
Warewell (Warwell), Katherine, 480
Wareyn (Waryn), Alice, 547, 638, 651, 651n
    Amfritha, of Sudbury, & family, *lii**, *lxvi*, **32**
    Christian, 325
    Joan, 754
    John, *l*in, 15, 67, 139, 240, 325, 547, 592, 665, 738; at the sign of the Cock, 52; the elder, 92; of Bildeston, 431n; of Hartest, 640; of Long Melford, 32n; of Mildenhall, 635n, **638**; the elder, of Mildenhall, 638n; of Nayland, 439n; of Stowmarket, **325**; of Stuston, 617
    Richard, 32n, 547; the younger, of Halstead (Esx), 354; of Long Melford, 436n; of Whatfield, 406
    Robert, of Worlington, 638, 638n
    Rose, 259, 547, 767n
    Thomas, 436, 547, 779; of Haughley, *lvii*n, **547**; of Rushbrooke, 191
    William, 259; of Ely (Cambs), 638n
Wareyn *alias* Barkere, John, of Stoke by Clare, 611n, 638, 638n
Warner(e), Isabel, & family, 526
    John, of Barrow, 600n; of Great Livermere, 241, **599**, 760, 760n
    Katherine, of Great Livermere, 599, 599n, **760**
    Margery, 232
    Richard, 673
    Robert, vicar of Preston, 716, 716n
    Thomas, 152; of Bardwell, **526**
    William, of Bradfield St George, **61**; vicar of Bures St Mary, 55, 283; of Soham (Cambs), **232**
Warry, Thomas, 247
Waryn, *see* Wareyn
Warwell, *see* Warewell
Waspe, Ed., of Newton, 597
    Richard, 354, 729
Wasshpok, William, 14
Wasshscher, Alice, 440
    Joan, 440
    Robert, of Boxford, 331n, **440**, 698n
    William, 440
Wate, John, Sir, 782
Water, Thomas, 568
WATTISFIELD, church, 240, 273, 542, 741
    gilds in, 240, 240n, 741, 741n
    inhabitants of, 16, 240, 257, 273, 542, 542n, 561, 634n, 741, 741n
    lands in, *lxxvi*n, 10n, 240, 542, 741
    places in, 'Dawis-at-Grene', *lxiv*, 240
        'Dellond', 240
        'Derebowth', 240
        'Gardeyneshende', 273
        'Leparys' ('Leperys') (tenement), 240, 741n

'Metewynes' (tenement), 240
    taxes of, *lxiv*, 240
    testators of, *lv*, *lxiv*, *lxiv*n, *lxix**, **7**, **240**, **273**, **542**, **741**
    ways in, 'Upstrete', 240
    wills proved at, 7, 258, 268, 411, 667, 741
WATTISHAM, church, 50, 111, 433
    image for, 433
    image of crucifix in, 111
    image of St Petronilla in, 111, 111n
    sepulchre light of, 433
    inhabitants of, 433
    lands in, 433
    places in, 'Andrews' (toft), 111
        'Heyvardis' (messuage), 111
        'Shermans' (tenement), 433
        'Smethis' (land), 111
    testators of, **111**, **433**
Wattys, Isabel, 826
    Simon, of Santon Downham, 731n, 777n, **826**
Watyr(e), Alice, 442
    John, 442; of Eye, **442**
    Robert, 54
Watyrnas, John, of Norton, 362n
Waysborn, John, of Hinderclay, **802**
Wayte, Richard, 261; of Sudbury, 549
Webb(e), Alice, 603; of Palgrave, *lxvi*, **251**
    Edmund, of Risby, 624,
    John, of Elmswell, **603**; the elder of Palgrave, 251, 251n
    Phyllis, 251
    Robert, clerk, of Woolpit, *l*in, **624**
    Thomas, vicar of Acton, 518, 518n, 651, 651n
    William, clerk, incumbent of Wickhambrook, 286, 286n
    see also Clerk *alias* Webbe,
Webbere, John, 89, 731
Wedden, Joan, the younger, 778
    Robert, 778
Wederard, John, 205, 205n
Wederdeyn, *see* Spryng *alias* Wederdeyn
Wederton, Joan, 181
    Richard, of Hitcham, *lix*, **181**
Wedyr, John, of Elmswell, 519n; of Honington, 157
WEETING (Nfk), Bromehill in, Austin priory of 429, 429n
    church of St John, 776
    church of St Mary, 776
Welde, Ada, widow of John, of Woolpit, 519n, 660n, 786n
Welham, Isabel, wife of William, 10
    Joan, (née) & children, 10
    John, of Hitcham, 43n; the elder, 10, 773, 773n; the younger, 10
    Katherine, 10
    Margaret, 10; wife of William, 10
    Margery, wife of John, 10

William, 806; of Great Horringer, **10**, 773n
Well(e), Margaret, 1
   Robert, 16, 159
   Simon, & family, 1
   Thomas, 261
Wellys (Wellis, Welys), John, 9, 16, 152, 262,
   526
   Julian(a), 16
   Matilda, 16n
   Robert, 16, 526
   William, of Bardwell, **16**, 489n
WELNETHAM, *see* WHELNETHAM
Wenden (Wendon), Robert, 67, 283, 354
Went, John, 503
Wepsted, *see* Whepsted
Werden, Anne, 534
WEST STOW, church, 185, 227, 304
   mortuary given to, *liv*n, 304
   rector of, 304
   inhabitants of, 185n, 347, 445, 657
   lands in, 304
   testator of, *liv*n, **304**
Westbrom(e), Anne, 334
   Joan, 334
   John, 334*
   William, 334; of Wetherden, **334**
Westbroun, Agnes, 129
Weste, Hugh, 262
   John, rector of Stanstead, 262, 262n
WESTHORPE, church, 4, 102, 361, 477, 775
   altar of St James in, 4
   altar of St Mary in, 4
   rector of, *see* John Pykerell
   inhabitant of, 361n
   lands in, *lxxii*, 102, 361, 622, 775
   places in, '[*?the*] Welle', 775
   testators of, **4**, **102**, **361**, **477**, **775**
   way in, the street, 361
   wills proved at, 273, 337, 477, 715, 718, 726,
   774, 775, 818
WESTLEY, church, 128, 486, 487
   new bell for, 128
   inhabitants of, 432, 486n, 487, 487n
   lands in, 128, 487
   testators of, *lxxi*, **128**, **487**
WESTON, CONEY, *see* CONEY WESTON
WESTON, MARKET, *see* MARKET WESTON
Weston, Anne, 89
   John, 89
   Richard, 89
Wetewelle, John, servant, 819
Wether, Alice, 520,
   John, 520; of Honington, *520*
Wetherard, John, the elder, of Stowmarket, 669,
   669n
   Margaret, of Stowmarket, *li*n, *lxii*, 43n, 109n*,
   669
WETHERDEN, church, 149, 334, 451, 573, 706

   nave of, 451
   rector of, *see* Hugh Leigh
   gilds in, 451, 573
   inhabitants of, 149n, 315n, 451n, 573
   lands in, 149, 180, 334, 451, 573
   poor of, 573
   testators of, **149**, *315*, **334**, **451**, **573**
   wills proved at, 149, 344, 451
Wethere, Alice, (née), 256
   Katherine, *lxxii*, 256
   Margery, (née), 256
   William, *lxxii*, 256; of Stanton All Saints, *lxix*,
   lxxii, **256**
WETHERINGSETT, BROCKFORD in,
   inhabitants of, 5, 774
   lands in, 126, 581, 788,
   places in, 'Garneys and Lucas' (tenement),
   89
     'Pellynges Feld' (close), 5
     'Swanne, le', 818
   poor of, 5
   testators of, **5**, **581**, **763**, **810**,
   church, 5, 280, 374, 559, 581, 593, 763, 778,
   788, 796, 810
   altar cloth for, 593
   altar of BVM in, 788
   cloth with picture of BVM for, 788
   chalice for, 810
     of silver, 559
   chest for, 778
   image of St Thomas of Canterbury in, 778
   lead for south side of, 5
   light of BVM in, 559
   light of crucifix in, 559
   rector of, *see* William Heisham
   gilds in, 778, 778n
   inhabitants of, 64, 559n, 581, 778, 778n, 788n
   lands in, 126, 280, 593, 764, 778
   smith's shop in, 778
   testators of, *lxvi*, **280**, **559**, **593**, **778**, **796**
   ways in, 593
   wills proved at, 141, 280, 745, 763, 796, 809
Wever, Thomas, 106
Weykes, John, 584
Weyneyld, Christian, 154
   Katherine, (née), 154
   Simon, of Chelsworth, **154**
Weyng, Agnes, daughter of William, 635
   William, & family, 635
WHATFIELD, church, 406
   tower of, 406
   inhabitants of, 406
   testators of, **406**, 406n
   will proved at, 406
Whederarde, John & family, 1
Whelere, William, of Hundon, 78
WHELNETHAM (unspec.), inhabitants of, 572
WHELNETHAM, GREAT, church, 66, 130

altar of BVM in, 93
book of sacraments in, *lviii*n, 66
convent of Crutched Friars (Brethren of the
Holy Cross), 191n
inhabitants of, 66
lands in, 825
places in, 'Herrys Akere', 66
'Templeris Wodbrige', 66
testator of, *lviii*n, **66**
WHELNETHAM, LITTLE, church, 93, 130, 191,
413, 523, 825
parson of, *see* Stephen Parkere
inhabitants of, 93, 130, 413n, 825n
lands in, 93, 130, 413, 816, 825
testators of, **93**, **130**, **413**, **523**, **825**
WHEPSTEAD, church, 135, 179, 314
bells of, 135
light of BVM in, 135
parson of, *see* William Fege
inhabitants of, 179, 801n
lands in, 39
testators of, **135**, **179**, **314**
Whepsted (Qwhepsted), Hugh, 298, 298n, 322,
322n
John, the younger, 298, 298n, 322, 322n; of
Brettenham, *lxii*, **298**, **322**, 322n; the elder,
of Brettenham, 298
Margaret, 322, 322n; the elder, 298, 298n
Marion, 322
Nicholas, 322
Walter, 322
William, 322,
Whetle, John, clerk, 302
Wheyt, Thomas, 380
Whithed, Roger, 735
Whyte, Henry, 593
Joan, 25, 593
John, 585n
Thomas, of Haughley, **25**
William, of Wetheringsett, **593**
Whytfote, John, 376,
Whytterat, Henry, clerk, 48
Whytyng, John, 499
see also Qwhytyng
Wiburgh, Robert, 330
WICKEN (Cambs), church, 427, 513, 747
parish priest of, *see* Robert Wylton
gilds in, *lxi*, *lxi*n, 427, 427n, 747
inhabitants of, 747, 747n
poor of, 204
SPINNEY in, Augustinian priory church of,
657, 657n
testators of, **427**, **513**, **747**, *793*
WICKHAM MARKET, church, 83
WICKHAM SKEITH, church, 210, 498
vicar of, *see* Thomas Wylkeyns (Wylkyn)
gilds in, 193, 193n
lands in, 498

places in, 'Clynt, le', 498
'Holm Medew', 498
'Monsho[*damaged*]', 498
'Reves' (tenement), 210
testators of, *lxviii*, **210**, **498**
ways in, 'Copynslane', 498
WICKHAMBROOK, ALDERSFIELD in, 99,
99n
lands in, 213, 286
places in, 'Grenefe(e)ld', 286
'Pekchys ('Pekcheis') Medew', 286
testators of, **99**, **808**
ATTLETON in, 286, 410
lands in, 286, 410
testator of, **410**
church, 125, 263, 286, 410, 586, 808
new bell for, 286
incumbent of, *see* William Webbe
gilds in, 585, 585n
inhabitants of, 1, 345, 586n, 787n
lands in, 125, 286, 808
places in, Badmondisfield, 286
Boyden, 286
Farley, 286
testators of, *lxviii*, **213**, **263**, **286**, **586**
Wilke, John, 744
William, Master David, *xliv*
Willyngham, John, 317n, 508n
WINSTON, church, 559
inhabitants of, 559
Wiseman, Alice, 686
WISSINGTON, lands in, 370
WITHAM (Esx), inhabitants of, 148
WITHERSFIELD, church, 123, 171, 330, 356,
419, 420, 565, 692
alabaster panel for, 420
chapel in, 330
image of BVM in, 330
great cross in, 420
image of crucifix in, 692
candle for, 692
light before rood on rood solar in, 419
rector of, *see* William Chauncerell
sepulchre light in, *lix*n, 171, 330
'stokke, le' for, 330
torches of, 330
vestment for, *lviii*, 123, 171
wardens of, 171
Hanchet End in, 692, 692n
lands in, 692
testator of, **692**
inhabitants of, 123, 171, 356, 419n, 692, 693,
740
lands in, 330, 419, 420
places in, 'Capels medewe, le', 330
'Dowehows Crofte', 123
'Fermebetfeld', 330
'Gatesberyes' (tenement), 171

'Gaytesberyes Grove', 171
'Pollytes Croftt', 171
poor of, 171, 356, 420
testators of, *lviii, lix*n, **123**, **171**, **330**, **356**,
　419, **420**, **565**
ways in, causeway to church of, 420
Wode, Agnes, 737
Alexander, gentleman, 187n
John, 440; of Cowlinge, 787n
Richard, of Drinkstone, **388**
Woderes, Margaret, 172
Thomas, 172
Wolffe, Agnes, 628
John, 628
Wollerman, *see* Wolman
Wollet, Thomas, 38
Wolman (Wollerman), Robert, rector of Tostock,
　29, 205, 435, 435n
Wombe, John, of Great Cornard, 408n
Wood(e), John, of Elmswell, 116n
Thomas, Sir, 222
William, official of archdeacon & rector
　of Fornham All Saints, *xlviii, xlvii*in;
　commissary, 750, 795, 799, 800, 801, 802,
　809, 810
WOODBRIDGE, inhabitants of, 381
WOODDITTON (Cambs), church, 580, 630, 646,
　762
alabaster panel of high altar of, 580, 630
church cow for, 646
churchale in, 580
image of All Saints in, 762
panel of St Nicholas in, 646
torches of, 580, 630
vicar of, *see* Robert Drapere
gild in, *lxi, lxi*n, 630, 630n, 646, 762
gildhall of, 630n
inhabitants of, 630, 630n, 646n
lands in, 160, 646
　of Benedictine prioy of Swaffham Bulbeck,
　　646
manors in, 580, 580n, 762n
Ditton Camoys, 762n
Ditton Valence, 646, 646n, 762n
Saxton, or Saxton Hall, 762
places in, 'Taylours Crofte', 646,
testators of, **580**, **630**, **646**, **762**
wills proved at, 281, 646, 730
WOOLPIT, church, *lxv*, 27, 40, 375, 430, 567,
　570, 571, 579, 624, 704, 786
chapel of BVM in, 371, 371n
image of BVM in, *lxvii*, 142, 142n, 371,
　414, 519, 769
　jewellery donated to, *lxvii*, 142
pilgrimage to, *lxiv**, 166, 166n, 414, 414n,
　769
rector of, *see* Robert Lynton
repairs to north side of, 40

gilds in, 786
inhabitants of, 27, 145n, 375, 519n, 660n, 704,
　786
lands in, 90, 338, 375, 430, 567, 570, 579, 786
places in, 'Bekatys', 579
'brygge ledying to bury warde', 786
'Bromehyll' the, 579
'Colcyes' 'Colsys' (tenement), 371, 786
'Cooys' (tenement), 579
cross at the 'towyns ende', 786
'Eytheokes', 570
'Herte, the' (tenement), 786
'Inham', 579
'Jaksmethis', 570
'Pels, the' (tenement), 786
'Puskes' (tenement), 571
'Reycroft, le', 570
'Rychardys Place' (messuage), 371
'Skenners' (tenement), 786
'Wadys' (tenement), 786
'Watersslade' (close), 579
'Wente, le', 570
'Wolpet Grene', 371
'Wolpetbregge', 430
poor of, 27, 624
testators of, *lin, lxv*, **27**, **40**, **371**, **375**, **430**,
　567, **570**, **571**, **579**, **624**, **704**, **786**
ways in, common ways in, 430
'heywey' between cross and bridge, 786
highway, 579
way leading to Bury St Edmunds, 430
WORDWELL, church, 227, 539, 657
great cross in, *liii*, 657
light of BVM in, 539
inhabitants of, 539, 657
lands in, 657
ways in, 539
testators of, *liii*, **539**, **657**
Worliche *alias* Flecchere, Agnes, 345*
Isolde, 345
Margery, 345
Richard, of Mildenhall, *lin*, **345**
Simon, 345
see also Worlych *and* Wurliche
WORLINGTON, church, 426, 429, 481, 612
rector of, *see* Simon Bakhot
inhabitants of, 611, 638, 638n
lands in, 429, 481, 612
testators of, *l*, **481**, **426**, **429**, **612**
Worlych, Joan, of Ixworth, 723n
John, rector of Hopton, 36n
see also Wurliche *and* Worliche *alias*
　Flecchere
WORMINGFORD (Esx), church, 141
inhabitants of, 67
WORTHAM, church (unspec.), 269, 269n, 323,
　467
church of St Mary, 170, 269n

church of St Thomas (now lost), 269n
  rector of both churches, *xlviii*n
  gilds in, 323, 323n
  inhabitants of, 170, 269n, 323n
  lands in, 170, 269, 323
  medieties of, *xlviii*n
  poor of, 269
  testators of, **34**, **170**, **269**, **323**
  will proved at, 688
Worwold, Alice, daughter of Thomas, 631
  Thomas, 631*
WRATTING (unspec.), will proved at, 121
WRATTING, GREAT, inhabitant of, 677
  will proved at, 123
Wroo, Henry, of Rickinghall Superior, 365n
  Robert, 253
Wryght(e) (Writh, Wrygh, Wrygth, Wryht,
    Wryte, Wryth(e)), Agnes, & family, 524
  Alan, 96, 352
  Alice, *lxviii*, 67, 210, 239
  Beatrice, widow of John the elder, of
    Wortham, 323n
  Edward, 210
  Hugh, 284, 303, 799; of Bildeston, 613, 713,
    720, 721
  Isabel, 67, 210
  Joan, 67
  John, 67; Sir, 32; smith, 147; the younger, of
    Barway in Soham, 204n; rector of Bradfield
    St Clare, 11; of Soham (Cambs), **524**;
    parish chaplain of St Gregory's, Sudbury,
    434, 434n, 596, 596n; of Wickham Skeith,
    lxviii, **210**
  Richard, of Bures St Mary, *liii*, *lxix*, **67**
  Robert, 284, 524; of Brettenham, 298
  Roger, 765; of Thrandeston, 165
  Thomas, 192; of Groton, 309; of Stuston, *165*
  William, 210; of Polstead, 271
Wullette, [*unnamed*], wife of, 38
Wulward, Thomas, 43
Wurliche (Wurlyche), William, 46; of
    Wickhambrook, 345
  see also Worlych *and* Worliche *alias* Flecchere
Wyat (Wyott), Agnes, 190
  Alice, 190
  Isabel, 190
  Joan, 190, (née), in Romford (Esx), 190
  John, 190
  Katherine, 190
  Robert, 226, 450
  William, 190, 226; of Preston, **190**
Wyborowe, William, of Bury St Edmunds, *lxxvi*n
Wyborth, John, son of Elizabeth Hawe, 533
Wybour, Robert, 490
Wyburgh, John, 785
  Margaret, 785
  Robert, 785; of Withersfield, 692, 692n, 693,
    693n

William, of Denston, *lxii*n, *lxiii*, 724n, **785**
Wychham, John, of Sudbury, 714
Wyderelde, John, of Colchester, 67
Wygenale, John, 247
Wygenhale (*alias* Saresson), John, archdeacon,
    xlviii, *xlviii*n
Wyghteman, William, 715
Wykes, Peter, 456
Wykham, John, of Great Horringer, 81n
Wykyngham, Laurence, friar of Norwich, 68
Wylde, Alice, (née), 699
  Ed., 699
  Isabel, 699
  Robert, 699
Wylkyn (Wylkeyns), Alice, (née), 626
  John, 626; of Burwell (Cambs), 626, 626n
  Margaret, 626
  Nicholas, 551
  Thomas, 626; the elder, 626; the younger, 626;
    vicar of Wickham Skeith, 210, 218, 218n,
    374,715
  William, of Burwell (Cambs), *lvin*, **626**
Wylton, Robert, priest/curate of Wicken (Cambs),
    427n, 513, 513n, 747, 747n
Wylymot, Thomas, 681
Wymark, Alexander, 347
Wymbyll, Bartholomew, 207
Wymbyssh, Alice, 398
  Joan, wife of William, 398
  John, 398
  Stephen, of Buxhall, **398**
  William, 398
Wymere, John, 783
  Rose, 157n
Wynchestere, John, servant, 634
Wyneyeve (Wynyeve), Constance, of Troston, 386
  Edmund, 386
  Elizabeth, of Troston, **386**
  John, 386; smith, of Troston, 134
  Margaret, 386
  William, 386
Wynstede, William, 89
Wynter, Agnes, 525,
  Richard, of Soham (Cambs), **525**
  William, 525,
Wynyeve, *see* Wyneyeve
Wyott, *see* Wyat
Wysbeche, John, 693
  Margaret, 693
Wyse, Robert, of Barton Mills, 246, 650
Wys(e)man, Geoffrey, of Woolpit, 27
  John, 110; the elder, of Hengrave, 110n
  Simon, 372
  William, 686
Wyth, John, 395
WYVERSTONE, church, 700
  inhabitant of, 140n
  will proved at, 593

Yakesley (Yakysle), Henry, 232, 232n
   Richard, 232n
YAXLEY, church, 244, 790
     churchale in, 244
     vicar of, *see* Thomas Carman
   inhabitants of, 222, 790n
   lands in, 222, 244
   places in, 'Bukkesyerde', 244
     'Fyveacre', 244
     'herne, ly', 244
   testators of, **244**, **790**
   will proved at, 178
Yeppeswych (Yepisswich), family, of Burgate, 235n
   John, gentleman, of Burgate, 235, 235n
   Nicholas, 235n
Yermyn, John, 558
Yestas (Yystas), Alice, 251*
   John, 251; of Brockford, 774; of Thorndon, *64*
   Katherine, 774; servant, 774
   Robert, of Mendlesham, 568n, **774**
Yngham, Thomas, 334
Yonge (Yowng), Agnes, 333
   Isabel, 506
   John, of Rickinghall Superior, **506**
   Robert, 756; of Barton Mills, 379
   Simon, 506; of Rickinghall Superior, 506n
   Thomas, 333
Yowde, Agnes, 691
   John, 691; the elder, of Haverhill, **691**
   Thomas, 691
Yowng, *see* Yonge
Yystas, *see* Yestas

[*surname not given*], Agnes, servant, 50, 432
   Alexander, rector of Mount Bures, 55
   Alice, servant, 184, 232
   'Blaunche, le', servant, 220
   Denis, friar, 305
   Eleanor, servant, 709
   'Elyne, Lityll', 211
   George, Sir, parish chaplain of Exning, 450
   Helen, servant, *lxvi*n, 436, 779
   Hugh, Sir, sub-prior of Ixworth, 69
   Isabel, 682; servant, 399, 402
   John, 562; servant, 439; of Dyche, 417
   Katherine, servant, 1, 269, 368
   Laurence, 131
   Margaret, servant, 276, 320
   Margery, servant, 540
   Matilda, servant, 400
   Maurice, Sir, chaplain, 742
   Nicholas, Sir, parish priest of Stradishall, 787
   Philip, Sir, chaplain, 628
   Robert, servant, 60
   Rose, 38; servant, 559
   Seman, 432
   Thomas, chaplain, of Barrow, 530
   Urianus, Sir, priest, 243
   William, apprentice, 454; Master, chaplain, 196

Wills of the Archdeaconry of Suffolk
The Register 'Baldwyne' Part II
(Suffolk Records Society volume 53)

Index of Subjects

All references are to item numbers, not pages, except the italicised Roman numerals which refer to pages of the Introduction. An 'n' following a reference indicates that the subject is to be found in a footnote to that item; an asterisk * after a reference indicates that the subject occurs more than once in that item. **Bold** indicates that the reference is to a testator. Relationships mentioned are to the testator (their brother, daughter, father, son, wife, etc.); 'in-law' is used here in its modern sense. Where applicable, spellings have been modernised.

Abbreviations: BVM = the Blessed Virgin Mary; spec. = specified; unspec. = unspecified

access, *see* easement
accommodation, *see* dwelling
administration (admon), *lxxv, passim*
  granted by chaplain, 230
    by vicar, 55
  to be granted by named person, 503
    by vicar, 393
  to executrix, with supervision, 799
  see also executors: renouncing
advower, *lii*
  St Andrew, *lii*, 731
age, to earn living, 786
  full, 89*, 154, 621, 694, 723
  legal, 81*, 189, 225*, 266, 318, 461*, 501,
    519, 554*, 571, 579, 602, 648, 689, 763,
    805, 816, 819
  of marriage, 688, 692
  under, 113, 570, 571, 712, 786, 797, 816
agreement, consent, 89, 117, 136, 235, 247,
    286*, 306, 338, 353, 350, 626, 628, 650,
    661, 687, 729, 742, 803
  contract, 46, 118, 164*, 648
  covenant, 67, 338, 417, 661, 707
  by licence, of husband, 57
    of lord, 504*, 751
  peace and, between sons, 546
  recorded in probate register, *lxxii*, 353
  see also bargain; disagreement
agricultural equipment and tools, *lxviii*
  cart, *lxviii*, 1*, 22, 60, 172, 204, 209, 240,
    264, 374*, 392, 450*, 461, 474*, 482,
    490*, 525, 534*, 544*, 576, 633, 634*,
    635, 650, 734, 792

equipment for, 24, 204, 209, 262, 374, 461,
    482, 576, 634, 650, 792, 812
  iron-shod (-bound), 378, 561, 646, 683, 812
  unshod, 631
  fan, 354
  harness, 1, 172, 209, 374*, 392, 461*, 474,
    534, 544, 635, 734
  horse-collar, 240*
  saddle belonging to cart, 240
  traces, 240*, 374
  see also harness (non-agricultural)
  harrow, *lxviii*, 392*, 534*
  plough, *lxviii*, 24, 209, 210*, 240, 374*, 392,
    461, 474, 482, 490*, 534*, 544*, 576, 634,
    801
  beam, 240
  coulter, 210*, 240
  equipment for, 24, 204, 209, 210, 262, 374,
    461, 482, 490, 576, 634, 801
  shackles, 240
  share, 210*, 240
  tumbrel, 1
agricultural work, *lxviii*
  binding, 801
  carting grain, 322, 490
  cropping, 676
  harvest, harvesting, 229, 623, 659
  mowing, 801
  pasturing animals, 498, 590, 800
  ploughing, 192, 490
  reaping, 621, 801
  shredding, 676
  sowing, 22, 350, 621

barley, 192, 801
bullimong, 801
flax seed, 498
wheat, 192, 801
tilling, 22, 801
agriculture (gen.), *lxviii–lxix*
see also crops
aisle, *see* church building; church dedication
alabaster, 74*, 420, 469, 471
alias (in name), *li, lin*, 4, 37n, 119, 125, **172**,
172, **177**, **180**, 180n, **220**, 228n, 282, 283,
284, **345**, **347**, **370**, 370, **484**, 484, 528n,
529*, 539, 544, 601, **637**, 638, **642**, **646**,
663, **738**, **771**, **810**
alms, almsgiving, 11, 39, 55, 60, 61, 65, 89, 90,
92, 112, 121, 125, 154, 184, 210, 230, 266,
267, 300, 329, 368, 371, 376, 417, 420,
434, 436, 463, 471, 473, 479, 486, 487,
497, 555, 573, 579, 581, 594, 642, 647,
650, 661, 663, 664, 681, 687*, 699, 720,
728, 733, 738, 750, 759, 779, 785, 798, 816
see also charity
almshouse, *lxiii*, 11, 87, 339, 339n, 587, 587n,
607, 607n
altar, *see* church equipment
amber, *lxvii*, 129, 142, 701, 803
see also beads
ambry, *see* furniture
andiron, *see* household goods
animals, farm (stock, livestock) (unspec), 1, 21,
89, 125, 133, 154, 226, 230, 232, 240, 255,
256, 331, 338, 373, 405, 461, 474, 497,
498, 538, 599, 604, 631, 634, 765, 772,
773, 785
as mortuary, 204, 397, 443, 655
see also cattle; horse; pig; poultry; sheep
anniversary, *see* church services
annual, *see* church services
annuity (pension), 65, 89, 213, 218, 222, 244,
295, 327, 362, 450, 494, 576, 590*, 617,
626*, 628, 642, 661, 681, 703, 707, 720*,
733, 751, 764, 801, 809*, 815
antiphoner, *see* book; church equipment
antiquity, 504, 727
anvil, *see* tools and equipment
apprentice, *see* status
apprenticeship, completion of, *lxix*, 240, 247, 691
indenture of, 219
apron, *see* clothes
arable land, *see* land usage
arch, *see* church building
archdeacon (unspec.), *xliii*
of Norfolk, official of, *xlvi*
of Stafford, *xlviii*n
of Sudbury, *xlviii**
see Clement Denston, John Selot, John
Wygenhale

official of, *xlvi, xlviii*, *xlviii*n*, *lxix*n, *lxxiii*,
268, 293, 399
see John Crofftes, William Duffeld,
John Ramsey, Robert Spylman, Henry
Sythyng, William Woode
see also seal of official
of Suffolk, official of, 35n
archdeacon's visitation, *see* visitation
archdeaconry (unspec.), *xliii*
of Bury St Edmunds, *xlv*
of Norwich, *xlvi*
of Sudbury, *passim* in Introduction
of Suffolk, *xliv, xliv*n
archdeacon's court, *see* court
ark, *see* furniture
armour, *see* weapons and armour
arrows, *see* weapons and armour
attorney, appointed specially (not exec.), 130
letter of, 130, 417
to recover unpaid bequest, 69
auger, *see* tools and equipment
axe, *see* tools and equipment *and* weapons and
armour

bakehouse, bakery, *see* buildings
banker, *see* furniture: cushion
banner, banner-cloth, *see* gild
bargain, default in, 661, 707
of messuage, 818
of wood, 786
see also agreement
bark vat, *see* tools and equipment
barley, *see* crops
barn, *see* buildings
basilard, *see* weapons and armour
basin, *see* household goods *and* latten
beadle, *see* parish officers
beads, amber, *lxvii*, 129, 142, 803
with rings, 701
best, *lxvii*, 803
coral, *lxvii*, 579, 644
gauds ('gawdes'), painting of, 388
jet, 42, 228, 140, 436, 466, 523, 579, 667,
779, 803
with silver paternosters, *lxvii*, 421
with silver ring, 276
pair of, *lxvii*, 94, 252, 385
with gold ring, 94
with ring, 240
with silver ring, *lxviii*, 351, 613
rosary, *lxvii**
silver, 782
with gilt paternosters, *lxvii*, 698
see also jewellery
beam, iron, *see* iron
beans, *see* crops
beast, *see* cattle

bede-roll, *lx*

beds and bedding (unspec.), *lxvi*, 1, 19*, 41, 65, 87, 121, 174, 175, 181, 190, 191, 194, 225, 229, 240, 247, 255, 271, 290, 300, 306, 342, 342n, 363, 389, 407, 425, 465, 474, 485, 492, 494, 517, 552, 567, 587, 604, 607, 668, 676, 713, 733, 766, 772, 810, 818

    bed, 32, 320, 358, 392*, 436, 439, 445, 539, 544, 576*, 591, 683, 779

        accessories of, 401

        best, *lxvi*, 32

        black, 368

        death-bed, 292

        green, 470

        red, 470

        whole (complete), *lxvi*, 259, 333, 544, 731

        with curtains, 116

    bedclothes, 235, 392

    bedcover, *see* cover *below*

    bedding, set of, green, 354

        set of, red, 351*

        set of, white, 354

    bedstead, lack of, *lxvi*

    blanket, *lxvi*, *lxvi*n, 32*, 116, 142, 196, 228, 235*, 248, 259*, 276, 318, 330, 350*, 401, 436*, 466, 547, 579*, 613*, 667*, 685, 694*, 779*, 803*, 809*

        white, 240

        pair of, *lxvi*, 205, 228, 348*, 390*, 470, 621, 709, 782

        see also material

    bolster, *see* transom

    celure, *lxvi*, 32, 259, 348*, 368, 401, 697

    cover (bedcover, coverlet), *lxvi*, 32, 172, 205, 228*, 235*, 240, 248, 251, 259*, 305, 348*, 351, 358, 375, 377, 387, 390*, 417*, 572, 579*, 630, 613*, 667*, 694, 698*, 709, 716, 745, 782

        blue, *lxvi*n, 32, 436, 779

            and white and yellow, *lxvi*, 251

        felted, *lxvi*n, 436, 779

        green, 196, 228, 256, 466, 471, 711

            and blue, 421

            and white, 621

            with yellow birds, *lxvi*, 276

        red, 116, 240, 401*, 466, 685, 822

            and yellow, 318

            with roses, *lxvi*, 276

        ruby, 652

        sanguine-coloured, 32

            with white and blue roses interwoven, *lix*, 711

        say, of, 401

        white, *lxvi*, 32

        yellow, 741, 803*,

    curtains, 259*, 348*, 368, 698*

        blue, 401

        blue 'card', 32*

    donge, *lxvi*, 205, 228, 390*, 579, 613, 667*, 745

    featherbed, 38, 228, 259*, 348*, 381*, 421, 470, 505, 579, 667*, 698, 709, 803

    hangings, *lxvi*, 259*, 470

    mattress, *lxvi*, 32, 116*, 121, 311, 330, 350*, 354, 470, 652, 782, 803*

    pane (counterpane), of coney skins, *lxvi*, 259

    pillow, 38*, 259*, 439*

        pillow cover, 259*

    quilt, 205, 390

    sheet, 116, 235*, 248, 256*, 276*, 354, 377*, 421*, 439*, 445*, 547, 572, 613*, 630, 652, 709*, 711, 744, 745*, 803*

        for altar cloth, 57

        linen, *lxvi*n, 436*, 779*

        pair of, *lxvi*, 32*, 38*, 116, 142, 172, 205, 228*, 240*, 251*, 252, 259*, 276, 307, 311*, 318, 348*, 350*, 354, 387, 390*, 401*, 417*, 439, 466, 470*, 549, 579*, 611, 621, 667*, 698, 709, 741, 761, 782, 783, 803*

    tester, *lxvi*, 32*, 259, 348*, 401

    transom, *lxvi*, 579*, 698, 803

    underclothes (for bed), 235

bees, hive of, 251*, 672, 686*

behaviour (disposition, obedience), *lxxiii*, 65, 125*, 138, 189, 259, 371, 413, 501, 508, 604, 648, 650, 663, 664, 673, 687, 721, 727, 740, 785, 786, 803

bellows, *see* tools and equipment

bells, *see* church equipment

belt, *see* clothes

belt (axe), *see* tools and equipment

bench (dais), *see* buildings

bench, *see* church equipment *and* furniture

benefactors and malefactors, 434, 505

bequest(s) (legacies), *passim*

    to churches, *lvi-lix*

    due to testator, 69

    forfeited, 184

    legally made by a wife, 166

    made outside will, 282

    other, not recorded, 240

birthplace, 689

blanket, *see* beds and bedding

blind, relief of, 773

board, *see* furniture

boat, 354

bond land, *see* land tenure

book, antiphoner, 621, 642, 669, 771, 805

    Boccaccio's *Decameron*, *lxvi*

    chained, 247

    church (unspec.), 359*, 521*, 802, 820

    church records, *lxxvi*

    Domesday Book, 5n, 381n

    grammar, 782

    ?herbalist's, *lxxii*, 79*

lives of St Margaret and St Katherine, 779
missal, 69*, 314, 541, 626, 626n
primer, 174, 490
psalter, 247
of the sacraments, 66
boots, *see* clothes
borough (burgh), 2, 405, 442, 517, 552, 681
boundary, civil, *xliv–xlvi*
county, *xliv*
ecclesiastical, *xliv-xlvi,*
bovine animal, *see* cattle
bow, *see* weapons and armour
bower, *see* buildings
bowl, *see* household goods, pewter *and* silver
boy bishop, 247n, 507n
Braban cloth, *see* material
brass (unspec.), 191, 587
cauldron, 24, 235*, 558, 772
chafer, 276
chrismatory, 803
cooking pot, 276
ewer, 803
jug, 421
pan, 32*, 72, 83, 151*, 162, 163, 235*, 247*,
    256*, 276*, 311*, 324, 333, 387, 399, 403,
    417*, 439*, 466, 547, 558, 566, 579*,
    601*, 620, 621, 667, 725*, 734, 803, 806
    holding 1 gallon, 547
        2 gallons, 547
        3 gallons, 276, 613
        4 gallons, 142, 150, 421, 436, 511, 547,
        779
        8 gallons, 305, 456
        10 gallons, *lxv*, 571
        14 gallons, 779
        1 quart, 421
    'peynte panne', 256
    with a 'stele', 276
pitcher, 417
posnet, 803
pot, *lxii*, 10*,18*, 24, 32*, 40, 72, 83, 87, 129,
    135*, 151*, 228*, 231, 235*, 240, 247*,
    251, 259*, 284, 290, 311, 312*, 345*, 350,
    354*, 381*, 386*, 389, 390, 401*, 403,
    417*, 421, 433*, 439*, 450, 456, 466, 490,
    529, 539, 558*, 579*, 601*, 610, 611*,
    613*, 618*, 620, 667, 676, 683, 694, 699*,
    701, 734, 743*, 772, 777*, 779, 783, 792,
    806
    holding 1 gallon, 32, 116, 142, 256, 578
        2 gallons, 150, 290, 311, 318, 547, 803
        3 gallons, 205, 276*, 284, 319 , 436, 779
        4 gallons, *lxv*, 116, 803
vessel, 235*, 445*, 452*, 648*, 772*
see also household goods
brazen, candlestick, 620
laver, 779
brewing lead, *see* household goods

brick wall, 290
bridge (spec.), 2, 89, 219, 282, 343, 362, 389,
    430, 519, 740, 786, 803
of castle, 46
footbridge, 662
repairs to, *lxii*, 2n, 89, 94, 94n, 282, 362, 389,
    430, 519, 740, 803
bronze, ewer, 402*
brother, *see* relatives
bucket, *see* household goods
buckram, *see* material
building materials, 'calyon', *lvi*, 252
clay, *lxxii*, 457, 676
lead, *lviin*, 450
reeds, *lviin*, 450
stone, 350, 642
straw, *lxxii*, 676
tiles for room, 430
timber, 350, 354
trunk of oak, *lviin*, 457
from window in church, *lviin*, 543
buildings (unspec.), 22, 409
repair of, already done, 652
    to be kept up, 1, 51, 81, 91, 125, 180, 191,
        193, 205, 236, 240, 300, 318, 430, 480,
        482, 493, 517, 532, 534, 587, 601, 602*,
        659, 676, 681, 687, 699, 720, 721, 722,
        744, 748, 758, 786, 805, 822
    not to be kept up, 80
buildings (excluding churches and chapels) and
    rooms, *lxxii*
bakehouse (bakery), *lxxii*, 76, 178, 325, 348,
    417, 480, 676
barn, 12, 22, 46, 76, 221, 507, 519*, 544, 621,
    659, 683, 735, 799
    nether barn, 676
    newly-built, 46
bench (dais), 262
bower, 626
buttery, *lxxii*, 285
byre, 676
chamber, *lxxii*, 65, 68, 85, 178, 256*, 259,
    262, 277*, 285, 322, 333*, 348*, 417*,
    450, 480*, 519*, 620, 626*, 660, 661*,
    676*, 697, 707, 712, 756, 782, 799, 812
    at east end of hall, *lxxii*, 256
    lower, 74, 192
    over, 262
    with chimney, *lxxii*, 256
    with solar over, 322, 480*
chimney, 220, 256
cottage, *lxxii*, 142, 236*, 353, 409, 429, 442,
    481, 492, 687
gate, 142
division of, 76
fences, 30, 676, 697, 808
garret, 727
hall (main building), 68, 362, 417

common hall, community hall, *see* gildhall
hall (room), *lxxii**, 256, 285, 417, 494, 626,
    676, 697, 712
    door, 417
    east end, 256
    lower end, 712
    west end, 626
house (dwelling, place), *lxv*, 21, 46, 50, 76, 83,
    92, 97, 99*, 121, 125, 134, 158, 188*, 192,
    247, 277, 286*, 308, 319, 339, 377, 409,
    414, 417, 416, 449, 482, 485, 492, 494,
    530, 541, 587, 600*, 601, 618, 620*, 623,
    626, 633, 654, 682*, 690, 723*, 729, 756,
    768, 771, 776*, 784*, 786*, 803, 808*
    capital, 491, 688
    door, 579
    of earl of Essex, 67
    gate, 43, 78, 261, 417, 482, 615, 628, 784
    long, 333, 333n
    nether, 659
    new (newly built), 221, 587, 722, 755
    old, 480
    principal, *lxxii*, 676
    small, 587
kitchen, *lxxii*, 285, 348, 417
    door, 417
malting house, 417
maltkiln, 76
messuage, 11*, 27, 37*, 46*, 48, 50, 53, 72,
    74, 76*, 84, 85, 89, 93, 96*, 101, 108, 111,
    113, 133, 138, 146, 147, 152*, 153, 164,
    166, 181*, 182, 184*, 199, 205*, 212, 214,
    226, 232*, 241, 243, 255, 256, 266, 268,
    271, 272, 277, 278, 290, 304, 306, 313,
    318, 319, 322*, 327*, 338, 345, 346, 371,
    378, 380, 381, 383*, 399, 408*, 434, 437,
    450, 451*, 452, 456, 468, 482, 493, 498,
    503*, 508, 512, 515, 516*, 526, 538, 540,
    551, 566, 573, 585, 590, 592*, 604, 609,
    612, 629, 631, 635, 638*, 641, 645*, 650*,
    653, 661, 662, 664, 667, 668, 687, 699,
    703, 706, 711, 717, 719, 728, 731, 732,
    735*, 738*, 743, 750, 754*, 762, 765*,
    766, 768, 769, 782, 784, 801, 803, 810,
    818*, 823, 824, 827
    built-up, 480*, 617, 738
    capital, 31, 33, 247, 277, 290, 484, 576,
        579, 702, 727
    entrance, 521
    gate, 277
    newly built, 279, 508
    north end of, 85
mill-house ('melhows'), 350
    see also mill
moat, 417
neat-house, 76
pantry, *lxxii*, 285
parlour, 259, 417, 755, 779

renter, 247, 271, 300, 491*, 665*, 727*
room, next to door, 430
solar, 12, 166, 262, 322, 480*, 494
stable, 277, 417, 681
store-room, 348
tenement, *xlvn*, 10*, 12*, 14, 20, 22, 25, 26,
    41, 43, 46, 51, 52*, 53*, 54, 57*, 58, 60,
    65, 67, 70, 79, 80*, 81, 83, 87*, 89*, 92,
    103, 116, 117*, 119, 126*, 127, 139, 148,
    150, 151*, 153, 154, 160, 161, 164, 169,
    171, 178, 183*, 185, 186, 190, 191, 194,
    197, 198, 202, 203, 206, 207, 210, 211,
    213, 218*, 219, 220*, 221, 223, 224, 225*,
    227*, 230*, 240*, 244, 247*, 258, 259,
    268, 283, 284, 290*, 292, 300*, 314, 322*,
    323, 325, 329, 330, 332, 333, 336, 338,
    342, 348*, 350*, 361, 365*, 366, 371, 373,
    374*, 376, 389, 393, 395, 398*, 399, 401,
    404, 405, 407, 417, 430, 432, 433, 434,
    440*, 454, 455, 457, 461*, 468*, 471*,
    473, 482*, 486, 487, 490*, 491*, 495*,
    496, 497, 498, 500, 501*, 502*, 504, 507,
    510, 517, 519*, 522, 525, 534*, 536, 540,
    544*, 546, 552, 554, 556*, 561, 567, 568,
    570, 571*, 576*, 578, 579*, 581, 583*,
    590*, 591, 593, 594*, 595, 598*, 599, 602,
    619, 621*, 626, 628, 634*, 639, 642*, 643,
    646, 659, 660*, 665, 669*, 671, 681*,
    682, 684, 686, 687*, 688*, 694, 697, 702*,
    705, 710, 712, 716*, 720*, 721*, 724, 726,
    727*, 733*, 736, 739*, 743, 744, 748, 754,
    755, 758, 762, 763, 773, 774, 775, 777,
    778, 783, 786*, 787, 788, 797, 800, 801*,
    803, 805, 816, 820*, 821, 822, 826
    built-up, 337
    capital, 331, 440, 758
    copyhold, 272
    customary, 683
    door, 430
    gate, 10, 14, 378
    free, 683
    newly built, 681
    principal, 602
    well, 178, 409, 480
bull, bullock, *see* cattle
bullimong, *see* crops
burgh, *see* borough
burial (*inc.* funeral, obsequies), *liv–lvi*
    alms to poor present at burial, 1, 5, 42, 55, 79,
        89, 96, 142, 247, 286, 374, 436, 577, 772,
        779, 803, 815
    present at mass on day of burial, 42, 577,
        803
    bier at, *lv*, 121
    candles, burning about body, 665
    on bier, *lv*
    coffin, lack of, *lv*
    cope for, 362

207

cost (expense of, necessaries), *liv*, 10, 27, 46, 107, 125, 131, 267, 268, 369, 411, 420, 435, 450, 453, 456, 466, 490, 528, 531, 534, 595, 628, 645, 701, 712, 713, 724, 733, 742, 751, 767, 769, 772, 780, 785, 801
  customary expenses of, 450, 490
making (digging) grave, 436, 779
men carrying body to, 489
observed in convent (abbey), 821
office of, 592
payment (spec.) for, 316, 490, 628
  for breaking ground, 657
present at, *liv*
  all, 268
  beadle, 460, 658, 781
  boy (clerk), 11, 204, 283, 311, 374, 436, 490, 596, 779, 785
  canons, 228
  chaplain (priest), 1, 2, 5, 11, 14, 42, 46, 55, 70, 78, 79, 87, 89, 94, 96, 100, 133, 142, 161, 162, 171, 204, 247, 283, 310, 311, 326, 331, 348, 374, 397, 409, 420, 436, 440, 454, 460, 490, 491, 505, 577, 596, 640, 648, 658, 669, 687, 698, 740, 742, 772, 779, 781, 785, 799, 803, 815, 820*
    parish chaplain, 87
  clerk, 1, 5, 11, 42, 46, 55, 70, 78, 79, 87, 89, 94, 96, 100, 133, 142, 161, 162, 171, 204, 283, 309, 311, 331, 374, 397, 409, 420, 436, 440*, 454, 460, 490, 491, 505, 577, 596, 640, 648, 658, 669*, 687, 740, 742, 772, 779, 781, 785, 799, 803, 815
    holy-water clerk, 436*, 779*
    parish clerk, 46, 409
  neighbours, 399
  poor, 1, 5, 11, 42, 46, 55, 79, 89, 96, 142, 247, 286, 362, 374, 399, 436, 490, 577, 772, 779, 803, 815
    poor children, 362
  rector, 247
  sacrist, 436, 779,
  vicar, 46, 669
provision (food, refreshment) at, *liv*, 661, 665, 687, 707
  ale, *liv*, 268, 399, 681
  bread, *liv*, 399, 414
    white, 268
  cheese, *liv*, 268, 374, 399, 414
  drink, 414
  grain, 206, 206n
  malt, 770
  wheat, 770
ringing of bells at, 436, 779
sheet (shroud) for, *lv*
torch(es) for, *lv*, 388
  of gild, burning about body, 785
  men holding, *lv*, 353
  poor holding, 815

without pomp and vain glory, 107
burial, place of, *liii*
  in chapel, 351, 797
    in free-standing chapel, 501
    in Lady Chapel, *liii*, 191
  in church, *xlviii*n, *lv*, 67, 205, 228, 230, 366, 368, 398, 650
    in aisle, before altar, 96
    beyond font, 750
    in south aisle, 229
    before altar of St James, 723
    in chancel, *liii*, 608
    before great cross, 657
    by husband, 803
    before image of crucifix, 181
    in south porch, 247
    by wife, 785
  in church or churchyard, *liii*, 67, 522
  in churchyard, *liii*, *passim*
    by ancestors (elders, forefathers), 318, 417
    by children, 595
    by cross in, *xlviii*n
      by stone cross in, 46
    by father, 425
    by husband, 228, 238, 351, 401, 407, 451, 662, 698
      by first husband, 677
    near kin, 648
    by mother, 687
    by parents, 46, 229, 276, 528, 637, 764, 780
    by wall of Lady Chapel, 440, 440n
      by wall of south side, 639
    by wife, 189, 246, 290, 436, 779
  in friary church, 470
    burial ground of, 271, 295
  wherever God disposes (it occurs), 104, 258, 311
  see also grave; gravestone
burial-day, alms to poor on, 1, 5, 11, 136, 191, 238, 268, 356, 362, 490, 577, 665, 687, 691
  for alms to poor present at burial, *see* burial
burnet, *see* clothes *and* material
buttery, *see* buildings
byre, *see* buildings

calf, *see* cattle
candle, *see* church equipment: lights; household goods
candlebeam, *see* church equipment: rood-loft
candlestick, *see* household goods; latten; pewter
canon, *see* religious persons
canvas, *see* material
cap, *see* clothes
capon, *see* poultry
captives in the Holy Land, *lxiii*, *lxiii*n, 636, 636n
card, *see* material
cards (for carding), *see* cloth-making
cart, *see* agricultural equipment

cart-horse, *see* horse
carting, *see* agricultural work
cartload, *see* measurement
care during need, 268
cathedral, Ely, *lviii*n
cattle (unspec.), 21, 256, 331, 497, 498, 538, 599,
    705, 765, 773, 778, 805
  beast, 21*, 22*, 255*, 256
  bovine animal, 229*
  bull, 490*
  bullock, *lxviii*, 1*, 187, 190*, 298*, 319, 351,
    374*, 490*, 614, 631*, 654, 691, 725, 816*
    coloured, black, two-years old, 803
      red, 354
      red 'howyd', 22
    as mortuary, 474
    year-old, 570*,
  calf, 171, 172*, 322, 447*, 490*, 498, 519*,
    524, 622*, 653*, 659*, 729, 739, 754*,
    781*
    black, 387
    year-old, 402*
  cow (kine), *lxviii*, 1*, 9, 10*, 27, 43*, 60*, 66,
    67*, 68*, 76*, 85, 89*, 99, 111, 121*, 123,
    134*, 171, 172*, 178, 187*, 190*, 192*,
    196, 204*, 207, 209, 210*, 219*, 229*,
    239*, 240*, 243, 246*, 256, 257, 258*,
    266, 286, 312*, 319, 330, 338*, 343*,
    344*, 350*, 351, 354*, 356, 362*, 371*,
    374*, 389*, 390*, 399*, 400*, 402, 404*,
    405, 417, 419, 420, 421*, 437*, 440*,
    448*, 456*, 460, 461*, 462, 463*, 471*,
    482*, 490*, 507*, 511, 519*, 524*, 527*,
    528*, 534*, 536*, 540, 544*, 557*, 559*,
    576*, 596, 597, 599*, 600, 601*, 609, 614,
    620*, 622*, 628*, 633*, 634*, 635*, 636*,
    638, 646, 653*, 659*, 676*, 681*, 682,
    690, 697*, 699*, 700*, 713, 716, 722*,
    733*, 734, 738*, 754*, 761, 776, 778*,
    786*, 799, 800, 803, 808, 809, 816*, 818*,
    819
    bequeathed to/for, anniversary, 463*
      church, 511, 729*
      church cow, 646
      gild, 786
      high altar, 257
      light(s), *lix*, *lix*n, 111, 171, 171n, 207,
        330, 356, 417, 419, 420, 460, 462,
        507, 536*, 557*, 559*, 597, 609, 658,
        692, 781, 803
    coloured, black, 313, 717, 729*, 734, 803
      black 'howyd', 96
      dun, 470
      'howyd', 729
      red, 529, 717
    keeping of, 68
    as mortuary, 718
    named, 803
    as payment, 66
    profit(s) of, 357, 692
    with a calf, 754, 810
  heifer, 81*, 88*, 94, 126, 239, 246*, 286, 331,
    346*, 351, 385, 559*, 635, 716, 729, 738,
    754*, 776
    black, 699
    two-years old, 232*, 819
    with a calf, 382
  ox, *lxviii*, 89*, 229*, 343*
  stirk, 232
    'howyd', 524
    two-years old, 354
castle, 46,
  outer bridge of, 46
  way, 251, 251n
cathedral, Norwich, 414n
cauldron, *see* brass *and* household goods
causeway, 420
causey, 662
celure, *see* beds and bedding
censers, *see* church equipment
certain (sangred), *see* church services
chafer, chafing-dish, *see* household goods
chaff, *see* crops
chair, *see* furniture
chalice, *see* church equipment, household goods
  and silver
chamber, *see* buildings
chancel, *see* church building
chapel, in church, 46, 133, 142, 148, 180, 191,
    259, 259n 330, 352, 371, 414n, 421, 423,
    462, 499, 511, 519, 543, 546, 592, 609,
    665, 676, 676n, 699, 759, 759n, 797
  in churchyard, 351, 351n, 378n, 436, 436n,
    728, 733, 779
  separate building, 15, 31, 32, 50, 80, 80n*, 84,
    150, 189, 206, 206n, 212, 246, 271, 327,
    408, 416n, 418, 425, 436, 436n, 467, 508,
    510n, 607, 688, 688n, 721, 722, 750, 750n,
    779
  now lost, 428, 428n, 501, 501n, 720, 720n,
    740, 740n, 744, 744n
chapel dedication, *see* church dedication
chaplain, *see* parish clergy
charger, *see* household goods *and* pewter
charges due for property, 84, 540, 722, 805
charity (mercy, piety), deeds of, *lxii*, 5, 10, 11,
    16, 20, 27, 30, 31, 32, 38, 39, 43, 47, 55,
    60, 61, 65, 75, 76, 81, 85, 87, 88, 89, 90,
    92, 99, 100, 112, 121, 122, 125, 128, 134,
    147, 148, 154, 158, 171, 191, 205, 210,
    212, 215, 223, 225, 227, 230, 233, 238,
    247, 259, 266, 267, 268, 276, 283, 286,
    295, 300, 311, 314, 329, 339*, 345, 347,
    349, 362, 363, 368, 371, 373, 376, 380,
    383, 387, 389, 392, 398*, 400, 402, 417,
    420, 434, 456, 461, 463, 471, 473, 486,

487, 491, 494, 496, 497, 498*, 502, 522,
534, 535, 540, 555, 558, 571, 574, 576,
578, 581, 583, 587, 588, 589, 594, 595,
601, 602, 617, 621, 625, 626, 628, 629,
634*, 636, 642, 647, 650, 651, 661, 662,
663, 664, 677, 681, 692, 695, 704, 705,
709, 720*, 728, 731, 733, 741, 746, 750,
765, 769, 772, 773, 774, 780, 785, 788,
789, 799, 801, 803, 817, 818, 819
charnel, 378
cheese, *see* food
cheese-mould, *see* household goods
chest, *see* church equipment; furniture
chief lords, *see* fee
child, *see* relatives
chimney, *see* buildings
choir, *see* parish officers
chorus (of grain), *see* measurement
church, building, *lvi–lix*, 107, 234, 247, 575, 700,
   750, 784
  aisle, *liii*, *lvi*, 96, 331, 331n, 440, 440n, 507,
   750
   of St John the Baptist, 109, 519, 750
   of St Katherine, 475, 475n
   south, 229, 574
  arch, 259, 259n, 274, 274n, 352
  beam (of roof), 665
  buttress, 576
  ceiling, 519
  chancel, 21, 110, 327, 338, 340, 381, 417*,
   608, 627, 726
   entrance to, 417
  chantry chapel, 60n
  clerestory, 258, 779n
  door, 349*
   south, 750
   west, 750
  fabric, *passim*,
  gate, 103,
  Lady Chapel, *lviii*, 191, 46n, 351n, 421n,
   436n, 440n, 592, 592n
  nave, 214, 428, 428n, 451, 478n, 742
  roof, 428, 428n, 450, 450n
  paving, 131, 727, 750, 803
   for aisle, 109
   marble, 750
  pinnacle or lantern, 247
  porch, *lvi*, *lvi*n, 1, 88, 247, 247n, 331, 332,
   349, 350, 432, 440, 533, 557, 654
   window in, 557
  rood solar, 419
   stairs, *lvi*n, 478, 478n
  rood-loft, *see* church: equipment and
   furnishings
  roof, *lvi*, 700
   lead for, 5, 450
   leading of, 203
   reeds for, 450

truss, 547n
side, north, 40, 203, 247, 331, 607
  south, 247, 478, 594, 639
steeple, 222, 266, 579, 723
tower, *lvi*, 2, 28, 45, 48, 48n, 52, 74, 83, 178,
  184, 206, 230, 247, 252, 368, 395, 398,
  405, 406, 510, 575, 588, 634, 728, 770, 816
walls, whitening, 131
window, *liii*, *lvii*, 46, 46n, 258, 300, 478, 533,
  543, 594, 702
  'Babylwyndowe, le', *lvii–lviii*, 46, 46n
  east, *lvii*, 478, 594
  glazing/glass of, *lvii*, 12, 180, 219, 258,
   533, 557, 797
  of Lady Chapel, *lvii*, 543,
  story of the Assumption, *lvii–lviii*, 46, 46n
church, burial in, *see* burial
church, dedication of (including chapel, aisle), *liii*
  All Saints, 18, 58, 72, 80n, 152, 166, 183,
   186, 205, 211, 256, 259, 280, 286, 290,
   294, 308, 327, 333, 348, 354 (error), 372,
   393, 410, 416, 418, 428n, 429, 450n, 453,
   462, 467, 469, 471, 474, 479, 481, 492,
   499, 516, 522, 527, 543, 546, 555, 559,
   566, 580, 586, 593, 597, 598, 608, 609,
   610, 612, 617, 620, 646, 666, 667, 667n,
   670n, 671, 680, 682, 710, 711, 727, 739,
   759n, 762, 763, 777, 796, 798, 808, 810,
   817
   now lost, 89
  Blessed Mary of the Sea, 246
  Blessed Virgin Mary, 12, 14, 14n, 46, 51, 55,
   60, 66, 67, 74, 80, 88, 89, 93, 97, 101, 109,
   142, 148, 150, 153, 170, 174, 180, 191,
   193, 194, 205*, 215, 226, 229, 233, 239,
   269n, 283, 298, 310, 316, 317, 326, 330,
   334, 341n, 347, 351, 354, 356, 359, 361,
   378, 387, 390, 391, 399, 401, 409, 414n,
   415, 419, 420, 421, 427, 428, 430, 436,
   451, 455, 460, 462, 468, 475, 480, 483,
   484, 499, 500, 501, 506, 508, 510, 511*,
   513, 519, 522, 528, 529, 543, 545, 547,
   551, 563, 564, 565, 569, 592, 595, 598,
   602, 608, 613, 625, 626, 629, 631, 632,
   633, 635, 636, 641, 642, 645n, 658, 664,
   665*, 667n, 668, 669, 676, 676n, 678, 685,
   686, 691, 694, 699, 701, 713, 716, 722,
   728, 732, 733, 737, 740, 744, 747, 750,
   757, 766, 767, 768, 776*, 777, 779, 781,
   789, 804
   now lost, 381
  Holy Trinity, 162, 346, 464, 756
  St Andrew, 74, 209, 215, 232, 277, 278, 382,
   397, 452, 490, 524, 525, 544, 544n, 550,
   626, 643, 659, 700, 729, 743, 744, 748,
   758, 771
  St Augustine, 803
  St Botolph, 14n, 15, 327, 416n, 418, 467

St Clare, 66
St Denis, 47, 120, 213, 302*, 319
St Edmund, 291, 291n
St Ethelbert, 485n
St Etheldreda, now lost, 428, 428n
St Genevieve, now derelict, 110, 448
St George, 61, 270, 583, 663, 672, 745, 772, 776
St Gregory, 31, 32, 73, 189, 212, 282, 282n, 290, 292, 306, 311, 408, 414n, 425, 465, 493, 505, 578, 596, 607, 652, 684, 698, 699, 702, 745, 782
St James, 89, 72, 119, 206, 436, 439, 449, 450n, 471, 479, 492, 503, 545, 549, 683, 761, 783, 784
St John (unspec.), 74, 776
St John the Baptist, 109, 133, 423, 423n, 453, 519, 522, 588, 680, 711, 731, 750, 759n, 817
    now lost, 688
St John the Evangelist, 116
St Katherine, 475, 475n
St Laurence, 120, 342
St Leonard, 432n, 654
St Margaret, 199, 240, 309, 438, 477, 501, 501n, 542, 640, 741, 775
St Martin, 266, 286, 286n, 428, 497, 705
    now lost, 282, 282n, 299, 493, 578, 699
St Martin (wills proved at), 9, 10, 16, 17, 27, 30, 35, 38, 39, 48, 60, 61, 62, 63, 66, 73, 74, 75, 76, 78, 81, 82, 87, 88, 90, 93, 100, 101, 108, 110, 112, 113, 114, 115, 116, 118, 127, 128, 129, 130, 135, 136, 137, 138, 145, 147, 150, 151, 152, 157, 167, 173, 179, 184, 186, 189, 191, 204, 205, 208, 209, 211, 227, 228, 229, 230, 231, 241, 243, 245, 256, 260, 261, 265, 266, 270, 275, 286, 288, 293, 294, 295, 296, 297, 314, 318, 319, 320, 321, 327, 328, 333, 335, 340, 342, 347, 364, 365, 368, 371, 372, 373, 375, 376, 382, 386, 388, 389, 392, 397, 399, 400, 401, 402, 404, 410, 413, 414, 417, 430, 432, 435, 436, 454, 455, 466, 470, 471, 473, 474, 479, 480, 485, 486, 487, 489, 490, 493, 497, 499, 500, 502, 507, 519, 523, 528, 530, 531, 532, 533, 539, 548, 553, 557, 558, 560, 567, 570, 571, 575, 577, 578, 579, 581, 582, 583, 585, 586, 587, 588, 599, 600, 606, 626, 639, 653, 654, 663, 670, 679, 683, 684, 685, 686, 695, 696, 705, 710, 711, 714, 731, 732, 736, 743, 757, 771, 773, 785, 786, 789, 812, 819, 823, 825
St Mary (Our Lady), *see* Blessed Virgin Mary
St Michael, 443, 770
St Nicholas, *lii*n, 127, 414, 433n, 558, 697, 750, 750n, 769n, 776, 785n
St Olave, now lost, 89

St Peter, 31, 32, 68, 74, 84, 89, 93, 103, 109, 115n, 139, 189, 212, 251, 265, 271, 290, 306, 307, 311, 321, 325, 329, 335, 369, 381, 395, 405, 408, 417, 421, 425, 442, 447, 457, 465, 466, 472, 501, 521, 533, 557, 591, 599, 606, 607, 618, 645, 647, 652, 665, 669, 669, 673, 688, 737, 760, 792
St Peter and St Paul, *lii*n, 381n, 456, 592, 627, 689, 750, 776
St Petronilla, 759, 759n
St Thomas, now lost, 269n
see also altar; gild-patron
church, equipment and furnishings, *lviii–lix*
    altar, high, *liv, passim*
        canopy for, 615
        cloth for, *lviii, lix*, 57, 102, 276, 291, 593, 685, 711*
        painted cloth for, 479
        tapestry of sarcenet for, 697
    in new aisle, 96
    side-altar, dedication (unspec.), 46*
        BVM, 4, 11, 74, 83, 94, 112, 141, 148, 231, 438, 776, 788
            cloth for, 231*, 744, 788
            candlestick for, 94, 776*
        Holy Cross, 669
        Holy Trinity, 438
        St James, 4, 219, 723
        St John the Baptist, 750
        St Peter, 658
        St Peter and St Paul, 580n
        St Thomas the Martyr, 178
        see also panel
    bell(s), *lvi, lvi*n, 19, 54, 83, 97, 128, 135, 205, 218, 275, 286, 326, 350, 390, 401, 463, 541, 618, 619, 626*, 667, 696, 727, 728, 780
        great, 230
        small, *lvi*n, 626
        tenor, *lvi*n, 626
    benches, 276, 514
    book, *lviii, lviii*n, 359*, 521*, 802, 820
        antiphoner, *lviii*n, 621, 641, 669, 771, 805
        book of the sacraments, *lviii*n, 66
        missal, *lviii*n, 314, 541, 626
        psalter, *lviii*, 247
    candle, *see* lights
    candlebeam, *see* rood-loft
    carpentry work, 258
    censers, pair of, 698
    chalice, 110, 126, 137, 224, 309, 322, 459, 471, 582, 601, 603, 621, 694, 767, 810
        silver, 559, 682
    chest, 247, 778
    chrismatory, brass, 803
    church work, 197
    clock, or 'clokbelle', 247
    cloth, 728, 745*

for high altar, 57, 102, 276, 291, 479, 593, 685, 711*
for side altar, 4*
cover for bier, 121
cross (crucifix), 14, 163, 247, 331, 423, 536, 656, 736, 743
  banner-cloth for, 736
  canopy of, 14
  copper shaft for, 247
  see also image of cross
(Easter) sepulchre, 77, 88, 121, 171, 184, 279, 330, 385, 392, 397, 416, 433, 455, 462, 566, 566n, 658, 690
  candle for, 658
  wax for, 397, 416
font, 349, 750
  font cover, 369
housling towel, lix, 360
image of (unspec.), 433
  All Saints, 762
  BVM, 21, 24, 57, 97, 142, 142n, 148, 247, 252, 330, 331, 340, 350, 351, 371, 388, 417, 421, 440, 479, 507, 519, 536, 562, 597, 667, 699, 769, 803
    chained psalter before, 247
    cloth for, 479
    painting of, 57, 97, 562, 597
    painting of beads before, 388
    as the Pietà, 252, 460
  Corpus Christi, 557
  cross (crucifix), 352, 356, 692
    painting of, 352
  Holy Trinity, 686
  St Anne, 252
  St George, 745
  St James, 577
  St John (unspec.), 252
  St John the Baptist, 577
  St Katherine, 148, 557
  St Leonard, 432, 722
    painting of, 432, 722
  St Margaret, 428n
  St Mary (Our Lady), see BVM
  St Michael, 466
  St Nicholas, 439, 785
    painting of, 439
  St Paul, 381, 466, 627
    painting of, 381, 466, 627, 776
  St Peter, 148
  St Peter and St Paul, 580n
  St Petronilla, 111,111n
  St Remigius, 769, 769n
  St Saviour, 597, 597n, 781
  St Thomas of Judea, 621
    painting of, 621
lights (candle, lamp, torch), lix, lixn, 21*, 46*, 91*, 109, 111*, 121, 148*, 173*, 207, 218*, 251*, 252*, 278*, 316*, 330*, 353*,

359*, 385, 401, 462, 504, 512*, 580*, 601*, 608*, 623*, 630*, 676*, 678, 686*, 750*, 776*, 799*
  on altar, high, lix
  bachelors' tapers, lxii, 298
  basin for, 109
  before image, lix
    of BVM, lixn, 21, 24, 252, 330, 331, 350, 417, 507, 519, 536, 667, 699, 803
      as the Pietà, 252, 460
    of cross (crucifix), 111, 126, 331, 339, 356, 536, 692
    of Corpus Christi, lixn, 557
    of Holy Trinity, 686
    of St Anne, 252
    of St James, 577
    of St John the Baptist, 577
    of St John (unspec.), 252
    of St Katherine, lixn, 148, 557
    of St Peter, 148
    of St Petronilla, 111, 111n
    of St Saviour, 597, 781
  before rood, 419
    before great cross of, 420, 577
    on rood-loft, 207, 744
  chancel light, 109, 156
  common light, lix, 76, 659, 748
  dedicated to, BVM, 113, 135, 209, 219, 265, 321, 362, 414, 462*, 539, 559, 560, 606, 609*, 634, 672, 771
    crucifix, 559, 743
    Holy Trinity, 113
    St Nicholas, 634
  (Easter) sepulchre light, lix, 77, 88*, 121, 171, 184, 279, 330, 385, 392, 433, 455*, 462, 504, 519, 524, 525, 592, 601, 605, 688, 699, 738, 740, 758, 803
  funded by, cows, 111, 171, 171n, 207, 330, 356, 417, 419, 420, 460, 462, 507, 536*, 557*, 559*, 597, 609, 658, 692, 781, 803
    ewes, 539*, 634*
    wethers, 634*
  wax, 336, 605
    candle, 371
missal, see church equipment, book
mitre and crozier (for boy-bishop), 247
ornament (unspec.), 61, 112, 125, 368, 440, 592, 625, 683, 724, 748 (jewel), 754, 776, 799*, 820
painting, of cross, 352
  of 'gawdes' before Our Lady, 388
  of image, 57, 97, 352, 381, 432, 439, 466, 562, 597, 621, 627, 722, 776
  of rood, 262,
  of roodloft (candlebeam), 92, 121
panel (retable), 423
  of alabaster, 74*, 420, 469, 471

on altar of BVM, 74
  at/on high altar, 469, 471, 780
  of life of St Peter, 74
  for altar of St Peter, 658
  at/on high altar, 580, 630, 676
  of St Nicholas, 646
parclose, 96, 163, 669,
pulpit, 276
pyx, 803, 823
  canopy for, 803
rood, 262, 419, 676
  painting of, 262
rood-loft (candlebeam), *lvi*, 12, 12n, 207, 237,
    238, 276, 344, 400, 452, 478, 488, 718,
    744, 803
  painting of, 92, 121
  see also church building: rood solar, rood
    stairs
stool, 247, 803*
tabernacle (for image), *lviii*
  of BVM, 18, 338, 519, 669
  of Holy Trinity, 669
  of St George, 745
  of St Margaret, 309
  of St Peter, 18, 115, 488,
throne of 'Eystrych boorde', 252
thurible, 186, 303
towel, 178, 711*
vestment (unspec), *lviii*, 66, 123, 374, 461,
    482, 592, 706, 801, 803, 821
  for chaplain, 665*
    deacon, 681
      subdeacon, 681
    priest, 80
  complete, 171
  cope, *lviii*, 80, 298, 362, 697, 711, 821
    black, 681
    for choirmasters, 669*
    liturgical colours of, *lix*
    and matching vestment, 80
    silk, of 'sateyn cremesyn', 181
  cupboard for, 521
  gown, 101
  rochet, 767*
  surplice, 540*
    for choir, 484
viaticum, 803, 803n
church of friary, *see* friary church
church/chapel, now lost/derelict, 89*, 110, 269,
    269n, 282, 299, 381, 428, 448, 493, 501,
    578, 688, 699, 720, 721, 740, 744
church services and activities, anniversary (obit),
    lv, *lxiv*
  (duration unspec.), 67, 82, 83*, 92, 96, 111,
    184, 189, 205*, 232, 240, 243*, 307,
    330, 334, 401, 405, 425, 438, 547, 576*,
    605, 652, 659*, 667, 700, 768, 802, 824
  (duration spec.), *lv*

5, 6 or 7 years, 803
  7 years, 166
  10 years, 311, 431, 465, 607, 779
  12 years, 290, 408
  20 years, 153, 400, 440
  80 years, *lv*, 126
  for ever, *lv*, 463, 626, 646, 669, 678,
    758, 801, 823*
  alms given at, *lv*, 243, 290, 334, 465, 607,
    669
  celebration of mass at, 401, 463, 626, 669
    mass on morrow of, 240
  obsequies at, 240, 431, 626
  people present at, churchmen, 307
    clerk, 67, 189, 465, 607
    parish chaplain, 626
    priest, 67, 189, 465, 607
    sacrist, 626, 669
    vicar, 669*
  praying at, 646
  rector to perform, 240
  refreshment at, *lv*
  ringing of bells at, 401, 463, 626, 646, 669
  supported by meadow, 700
annual, 146, 270, 586
certain (sangred), *lx*, 37, 57, 110, 126, 126n,
    129, 146, 155, 221, 276, 276n, 291, 323,
    393, 435, 440, 532, 682, 686, 699, 700,
    718, 764, 772
  (duration spec.), 7 years, 533
    20 years, 400
    perpetual, 519, 821
  fee for, *lx*, 37, 110, 126, 129, 146, 400, 435,
    532, 533, 699, 718, 772
churchale (drinking), 244, 244n, 580, 764
dirige, *lv*, 21, 142, 162, 262, 436, 669, 779*
  celebrated by, friars, 142
  parson, 262
  people present at, clerk, 162*, 262*, 436*,
    779*
    parish clergy, 21
    priest, 162*, 222, 262, 436, 779*
divine prayers, said by curate, 290
elevation of the host, torches to burn at, 46
mass (divine service), *passim*
  celebrated at Rome, 16, 490
    Scala Celi, Rome, 244, 495, 511, 579*
    St Fabian and St Sebastian, Rome, 579*
  celebrated by, curate, 290
    friar(s), 111, 191, 300*, 504*, 602, 767,
      779
      30 said by friars, 291
    priest, 268, 579
  celebrated, for father and mother, 53
    for souls, 11, 38, 39, 48, 60, 61, 81, 87,
      90, 112, 128, 205, 210, 215, 225, 235,
      238, 266, 268*, 295, 297, 300, 338,
      368, 371, 373, 376, 401, 402, 417,

434, 471, 473, 479, 486, 487, 495,
497, 498, 522, 555, 558, 583, 588,
594, 602, 634, 636, 661, 686, 695,
699, 700, 709, 722, 732, 738, 741,
746, 759, 772, 780, 816,
    of wrongdoers, 434
    400 on one day, 11
mass of BVM, 103
    Jesu (Name of Jesus), *lx*, 45, 45n, 52,
        162, 206, 363, 722, 728
    requiem, *lv*, *lix*, 436, 669, 779*
    St Gregory, *see* trental
mass on burial day, *lv*, 42, 46, 100, 268,
    436, 697
    money offerings at, *lv*
    people present at, clerk, 100, 640, 785,
        803, 815
        priest, 100, 133, 436, 640, 697, 779,
            785, 803, 815
        vicar, 46,
mass, sung, 579
month-mind, *see* thirty-day
placebo, *liv*, 142, 162, 669
    celebrated by friars, 142
    parish priests and clerks present at, 162
requiem, *see* mass
sangred, *see* certain
seven-day, *liv*, *lv*, 46, 121, 267, 268, 290, 406,
    431, 450, 640
    ale for, 681
    expenses of, 490, 534
    mass on, 268
thirty-day (month-mind), *liv*, *lv*, 46, 121, 267,
    290, 406, 431, 450, 640
    ale for, 681
    cheese for, 374
    expenses of, 490, 534
    priests, clerks and boys present at, 596
trental, *lx*, 5, 21, 22, 38*, 39, 45, 48, 68, 81*,
    85, 96*, 101, 112, 115, 116, 119, 121, 127,
    145*, 146, 147, 149, 168, 170, 171, 175,
    179, 203*, 224, 238, 239*, 247*, 253, 260,
    261*, 264, 268*, 282, 284*, 286*, 291,
    299, 302, 305, 307, 313, 333, 334, 339,
    350, 352*, 353, 356, 364, 366, 374, 393,
    415, 424*, 437, 440, 452, 461*, 477, 481,
    482, 490*, 499, 516, 519, 537*, 559*, 567,
    568, 576, 588, 589, 595, 596*, 598, 599*,
    603, 604, 609, 618, 625, 640*, 647, 654,
    655, 661, 668*, 670, 672, 678, 682*, 686,
    699, 700*, 701*, 703, 707, 710, 712, 719,
    722, 723, 725*, 734, 741, 748, 755, 760,
    763, 768, 769, 770, 774, 775, 776, 786,
    790, 795, 796, 797, 807, 810, 816, 822
    celebrated by, canons, 776
        chaplain, 807
        friar(s), 21, 22, 38*, 39, 45, 48, 68, 81*,
            85, 96*, 101, 112, 115, 116, 119,

121, 127, 145*, 149, 168, 171, 179,
224, 238, 239*, 247*, 253, 260, 268*,
286*, 291, 302, 305, 307, 313, 333,
334, 339, 350, 352*, 356, 366, 374,
392*, 393, 415, 424*, 461*, 477, 482,
490*, 499, 519, 537*, 551, 567, 568,
576, 588, 589, 595, 598, 599*, 603,
604, 609, 625, 647, 654, 655, 661,
668*, 670, 672, 682*, 700*, 701*,
707, 712, 719, 722, 723, 725*, 734,
741, 755, 760, 763, 770, 775, 786,
789*, 790, 795, 797, 816, 822
    monk(s), 147
    priest, 768
    fee for, *lx*
    half a trental, 392*, 789*
trental of St Gregory, *lx*, 1, 88, 94, 95, 100,
    103, 125*, 128, 133, 134, 142, 148, 180,
    184, 205*, 221, 241, 244, 251, 271, 276,
    290*, 311*, 322*, 324, 343, 388, 398,
    404*, 414, 432, 433, 438, 454*, 466, 472,
    486, 488, 508, 523, 533, 536, 613*, 615,
    634, 665*, 688, 705, 709, 746, 772, 797,
    799, 803, 805, 812
    celebrated by, canons, 398
        friar(s), *lx*, 1*, 88, 94, 95, 125*, 128,
            133, 134, 180, 184, 205*, 241, 271,
            276, 290*, 311*, 322*, 324, 388,
            404*, 414, 432, 438, 454*, 486, 488,
            536, 613*, 615, 634, 665*, 705, 709,
            772, 797, 799, 803, 805, 812,
        rector, 221
churchale (drinking), 244, 244n, 580, 764
churchwarden, *see* parish officers
churchyard, 333, 728, 733
    burial in, *passim*
    cross in, *see* cross
    gate, 103, 587
    north side, 408
    walls, 294, 574, 618
clay, for road repairs, 457*
    see also building materials
clerk, in holy orders, *see* parish clergy
    registry, *l*
    singing, *see* parish officers
    'of the town', *see* parish officers
cloak, *see* clothes
clock, *lxvi*, 778
close, *see* land usage
cloth, *see* material
    see also church equipment; cloth-making;
        cloths, household
cloth-making, *lxix*
    cards, *lxix*, 256, 390
    cloth, *lxix*, 786
        russet, 2½ dozens of, 374
        woollen, 11 yards of, 430
        woollen, white, 2 yards of, 711*

woollen, white, 4 yards of, 456
cloth-workers, *lxiii*n
hanging of cloths, *lxix*, 504
loom, *lxix*, 67*
  equipment for, *lxix*, 67
  pair of, 572*
spinning-wheel, *lxix*, 256, 418
stoddles, pair of, 440*
tenter, *lxix*, 504
  tenter yard, 681
wool for '4 cloths of 30 cloths', 681
working of cloths, *lxix*, 504
yarn, clue of, 644*
  linen, 803
see also material
clothes (clothing) (unspec.), 18, 31, 452, 465,
  607, 648*
  bequests of, *lxvi*
    to poor, *lxvii*, 465, 607, 648
  for testator, 268
  for wife, 79, 389, 712, 735
  wife's own, of her body, *lxvii*, 295
apron, 276*
  'braboncloth', 662
belt (girdle etc), *lxvi*, 38*, 122, 677, 782*
  black, 'harnessed', 228
  black silk, ornamented with silver, 662, 698
  blue corse ('coarse' in error), 579
  blue, harnessed/ornamented with silver,
    246, 652
  crimson, 579
  green, 307
  green corse, 644
  green silver/silvered, 229, 311, 421
  harnessed, 247*, 350
  leather, harnessed with silver, 348*
  leather, silvered, 285
  ornamented with silver, 290, 698
  silk, harnessed with silver, 276
  silk, harnessed with silver and gilt, 417*
  silk, silvered, 115, 613
  silver, 229, 390, 445, 519, 701
  silvered, 32*
  studded (with) silver, 436, 490, 779
boots, riding, pair of, *lxviii*n, 205
cap, 350
  felt, 9
  red, 350
cloak, *lxvi*, 32*, 129, 251*, 364, 386, 711, 789
  black, 439
  furred, 38
  green and blue, 421
coat, 539*
  blue, 386
doublet, *lxvi*, *lxvii*, *lxxv*, 19*, 240, 312, 364,
  374, 471, 490*, 705
  black fustian, *lxvii*, 490
  fustian, 350, 351

green worsted, 1
dress, wedding, *lxvii*, 712
everyday clothes, 677
footwear, 79, 389
  for wife, 79, 389
  see also boots; shoes
frende, sanguine, 307
  violet, furred, 259
gown, *lxvi*, *lxvii*, 10*, 19, 24*, 38, 135, 161,
  191*, 196, 209, 226, 285, 309, 312, 314,
  330, 331, 348*, 350, 359, 374, 421*, 471,
  490*, 516*, 517, 525, 566, 570, 572, 586,
  630, 677, 686, 716, 743*, 745, 772, 777*,
  783, 799
  black, 38, 228, 259, 350, 589, 698
    furred with white lamb, 191
  blue, 32, 141, 214, 240, 240, 313, 330, 350,
    359, 512, 547, 569, 570, 589, 598, 642,
    686, 694, 706, 711, 737, 782*
    furred, *lxvi*, 259, 662, 803
    with fur lining, 351
  burnet, 247
  'dudde', 1
  furred, 32, 311*, 701
    with black, 38*
    with 'croppys', 38
  green, 1, 9, 228, 247, 324, 342, 350, 351,
    354, 512, 540, 570, 686, 716
    furred, 259
    lined, 259
  hooded, 247, 646
  lined, *lxvi*, 613
    with green, 38
  medley, lined with fur, 698
  musterdevillers, *lxvii*, 490, 598, 652, 662
    furred with grey, 38
  russet, *lxvii*, 1, 211, 313, 374, 398, 490,
    705, 738
  sanguine, 32, 333, 354, 597
    furred, 259
  short, 67*
  striped, 1, 116, 229, 240, 640
  two-coloured, 331
  violet, 40, 46, 313, 324, 374, 445, 466, 677,
    685, 804
    furred, 380
    lined, 803
    lined with grey fur, 698
hat, *lxxv*, 591
  red, 354
  straw, 471
  with liripipe ('typett'), 350
hood, *lxvi*, 1, 46, 67*, 135, 161, 209, 314,
  331, 375*, 701, 737
  black, 1*
  blue, *lxvii**, 135, 276
  burnet, *lxvii*, 276
  red, *lxvii*, 135, 390

sanguine and scarlet, *lxvii*, 276
hose (pair of), *lxvi*, *lxxv*, 226, 364, 471, 490, 646, 705
  black, 490
huke, *lxvi*, *lxvii*, 135, 228
kerchief, *lxvi*, 32*, 276*, 662*
  of 'pleyn clothe', 276
kirtle, *lxvi*, 32, 38, 129*, 539, 667, 737, 803
  black, 228
  blue, 672
  furred, 38,
  fustian, 38
  green, 228
  red, 466, 803
  sanguine, 32, 228, 677
  violet, *lxvii*, 276
  white, 27
leggings, leather, 456*
linen and woollen, *lxvii*, 79, 295, 362
pelisse, 1
petticoat, *lxvi*, 662
  white, 672
robe, sanguine, 549
shoes (pair of), *lxvi*, 79, 364, 705
  leather, 456*
smock (undergarment), *lxvi*, 226, 252, 276*, 662, 711
  pair of, 705*
tabard, *lxvi*, 339, 375*, 466*, 698, 745
  black, 9
  blue, *lxvii*, 276, 500
  blue and green, 662
  lined, 803
  russet, 705
  violet and green, 228
tunic, *lxvi*, 19*, 135, 251*, 252, 285, 375, 500*, 516, 570, 589*, 630, 667, 686, 789
  black, 466
  blue, furred with rabbit skin, *lxvii*, 276
  burnet, 677
  'dudde', 1
  green, 390
    furred, 803
  lined, 613, 698*, 737
  musterdevillers, 32
  red, 259
  russet, *lxvii*, 135
    russet-lined, 672
  sanguine, 652
  small, *lxvii*, 135
  violet, 129*, 259, 421, 466, 662, 711
  white, 591
veil, *lxvii*, 135
cloths (textiles), household, *lviii*
  (unspec.), 452*, 786
  boardcloth, 38, 259
  canvas, 256*
  cloth, for a housling towel, 360

hanging, 697
  painted, 439*, 782*
  'gansape', 228
  linen, 46, 74, 125, 456, 504, 628, 687, 751, 815
  tablecloth, 191*, 247*, 685, 741
    of diaper (work), 247, 276, 728
    of plain work, 711
    of 'pleynclothe holond', 276
  towel, 38*, 178, 228*, 247*
    board towel, 259
    of diaper, 711
    hand-towel, 390*
    of plain cloth, 247*
    of plain work, 711
  woollen (wool), 46, 74, 125, 456, 504, 628, 687, 751, 815
coat, *see* clothes
cock, *see* poultry
colander, *see* household goods
college (religious house), Bury, *xlix*
  London, St Anthony, 319, 319n
  London, St Thomas Acre, *lxiv*, 319, 319n
  Norwich, St Mary in the Fields, dean of, *xlviii*n
  Sudbury, St Gregory, 32, 32n
    library of, 782
    warden of, *xlviii*n*
commendation (of soul), *lii*, *passim*
  includes, St Andrew, *lii*, 544, 731
    St Denis, 302
    St John the Evangelist, 519
    St Katherine, *lii*, 32
    St Nicholas, *lii*n, 433
    St Peter and St Paul, *lii*n, 580, 630
  only to, the divine mercy, 438, 819
commissary, *lxxiv*
  admon granted by, 55, 393
  will proved before, 28, 790, 799, 804, 805
common hall, community hall, *see* gildhall
common rights, 30
  see also custom
consent, *see* agreement
contract, *see* agreement
convent (nunnery), repairs to, 590
  see also religious (persons); religious houses
conventual land, *see* land tenure
coomb (quantity), *see* measurement
cope, *see* church equipment: vestment
copper, pot, 333
  shaft for cross, 247
copse, *see* land usage
copyhold (copyland), *see* land tenure
coral, *lxvii*, 579, 644
  see also beads
corn, *see* crops
corporal deeds of mercy, *lxii*
  see also charity

corse ('coarse'), *see* material
cottage, *see* buildings
court of probate (gen.), Intro. *passim*
  archdeacon's, Intro. *passim*
  chosen by execs, *lxxiv*
  commissary's (Bury), *xlv*
  consistory (Norwich), *xlv, xlv*n
    (Rochester), *xlv*n
  deputy of, specially appointed, 444
  ecclesiastical, *lxxi*
  inventory exhibited in, *lxxiv*
  Prerogative (archbishop's), *xliv*
  sacrist's, *xlv*
  wills proved in more than one, *xlv, xlv*n
court roll, *see* manor
cousin, *see* relatives
covenant, *see* agreement
cover, coverlet, *see* beds and bedding
cow, *see* cattle
craft, subtleties of, 240
  see also tools and equipment
craftsman, to be hired, 240
creditors, 158, 229, 476, 548
  see also debts
croft, *see* land usage
cropping, *see* agricultural work
crops (unspec.), *lxviii, lxviii*n, 24, 700, 711
  barley, *lxviii*, 1, 10*, 20, 24, 54*, 60, 65, 68*,
    69*, 70, 80*, 93, 94*, 126, 130, 170*, 182,
    184, 199*, 209*, 210*, 214*, 215*, 224,
    227*, 232*, 234*, 239, 240*, 244*, 247,
    262, 265*, 266*, 309*, 312*, 320, 321,
    322*, 338*, 374*, 378, 382*, 387, 391*,
    402, 405*, 415, 420, 437, 438*, 448, 461,
    499, 507, 514*, 525, 534, 550*, 570*,
    579*, 580, 600, 602, 604*, 608*, 614,
    623*, 628, 629, 631, 634, 635*, 636*, 646,
    649*, 651, 659*, 664*, 683, 688*, 693,
    717*, 720*, 721*, 725*, 732*, 734, 737,
    741*, 743, 744*, 748*, 754*, 758, 765,
    790, 801, 803, 804, 823*, 824*
    growing, 220
  beans, *lxviii*, 240, 461
  bullimong, 801
  chaff, 240
  corn (unspec), 22, 210, 338, 373, 772
    growing, 210, 234, 322, 411, 634, 659
    profit of, 338
    seed-corn, 232
  flax, 498
  fodder, 240
  fruit, 417, 733
  grain (unspec.), 35, 89, 91, 115, 134, 206,
    210, 221, 226, 230, 266, 331, 338, 373,
    389, 440, 474, 498, 534, 610, 631, 634*,
    700, 733, 772, 773, 777, 778, 785, 804
    in barn, 221, 519, 544

    growing, 43, 131, 210, 218, 229, 354, 474,
      482, 490, 519, 544, 621,
    harvested, 474, 490
    profit of, 450
    for seed, 482
    sown and unsown, 125, 805,
  hay, 240, 354, 544
  maslin, 60, 214*, 232, 266
  mixtlin, 729*
  oats, *lxviii*, 1, 166, 240, 374, 461, 507, 614,
    646, 708, 725, 786
  peas, *lxviii*, 1, 374, 461, 507, 614, 725, 778,
    786
    green, 240
  rye, *lxviii*, 24, 60, 170, 240, 256, 266*, 365,
    387, 507, 653, 734, 786
  straw, 192, 240
  see also building materials
  timber, 171, 184, 240, 350, 354, 587, 764, 803
    see also wood
  wheat, *lxviii*, 1, 10, 31, 61, 68*, 69, 80*, 89*,
    97, 133, 138, 151*, 170, 184*, 190*, 192*,
    193, 196*, 209, 210*, 211*, 215, 226, 232,
    234*, 240, 244, 256, 259, 262, 266, 269,
    309*, 350, 362*, 374*, 391*, 392, 405,
    417, 455, 461, 482, 507, 512, 514*, 534,
    544, 587, 591, 609, 614, 620, 623, 625,
    628, 631, 634, 646*, 649*, 651, 653, 658*,
    681*, 687, 693*, 718*, 723, 725*, 729*,
    732*, 734, 737, 743, 764, 770, 785*, 786*,
    800, 801, 803, 804*, 823
    growing, 437
  see also agricultural work: sowing; trees and
    plants
cross, churchyard, *xlviii*n, 46, 314, 618
  of St Thomas, *xlviii*n
  stone, 203
  in field, 80
  roadside, 14, 591, 733, 786,
    timber, 803
cross (crucifix), *see* church equipment
cup, *see* household goods
cupboard, *see* furniture
curate, *see* parish clergy
curtains, *see* beds and bedding
curtilage, see land usage
cushion, *see* furniture
custom, of celebrating stations of Rome, 184,
  542
  of gild, 184
  goods bequeathed by, 166
  land held by due service and, 74, 101, 118,
    125, 159, 180, 188, 219, 220, 225, 344,
    370, 434, 461, 464, 661, 687, 740, 780
  of manor, 247, 362, 500
  of parish, 824
    for celebrating an anniversary, 824

for a certain, 764
customary, expenses of funeral, 450
  land, 209, 683
    croft, 683
    meadow, 209
    tenement, 683
  manner, candle burning in, 184
  right, land held by, 591, 601

dagger, *see* weapons and armour
date (of will, etc.), *l*
  regnal year in, *l, lxxi,*
  Roman calendar in, *li*
  probate grant, *lxxvi*
daughter, *see* relatives
day (working time), *see* measurement
deacon, *see* parish clergy
deanery, of Blackbourn, 393, 437, 589, 769
  of Bocking (Esx), *xlv, xlv*n
  of Dunwich, *lvii*n
  of Hartismere, *xliv*n, *xlv*
  of Stow, *xliv*n, *xlv*
death, nothing more certain than, 365, 755, 820
  sick unto (approaching, at point of, in fear of,
    etc), *lii,* 28, 33, 47, 93, 97, 104, 121, 123,
    127, 130, 145, 150, 161, 196, 257, 281,
    292, 293, 346, 362, 363, 365, 395, 406,
    419, 420, 447, 476, 488, 495, 510, 512,
    514, 541, 550, 551, 565, 582, 598, 608,
    633, 682, 685, 686, 687, 699*, 713, 714,
    795, 821
  see also sick in body
debts, due to testator (unspec), 46, 75, 125, 154,
    210, 411,
  (spec.), 1, 16, 18, 53, 55, 67, 69, 111, 115,
    118, 126, 171, 178, 228, 235, 268, 286,
    336, 374, 416, 450, 473, 517, 567, 661*,
    682, 707*, 782*, 798
  as appear in his papers, 174
  to be collected by execs, 242
  remitted, 754
  owed by testator (unspec.), *liii, passim,*
    (spec.), 153, 339, 555, 650, 822
  to father, 238
  for grain, 31
  known by supervisor, 628
  for prayers for parents' souls, 601
  owed by testator's son to others, 416
  see also creditors
deed (legal document), 117, 130, 154, 204*, 334,
    464*, 508, 661*
  of entail, 417
  of gift, 663
  indented, *lxxi,* 125, 508, 661*, 707*
degree (status), 687
diamond, 38
diaper (diaperwork), *see* material
diocese, of Ely, *xliv*n

of Norwich, *xliv,* 5, 30, 32, 74, 100, 102, 123,
    125, 133, 153, 155, 166, 175, 188, 212,
    220, 229, 242, 259, 265, 271, 276, 286,
    290, 303, 311, 316, 335, 356, 362, 370,
    385, 393, 407, 408, 412, 423, 425, 428,
    429, 430, 431, 436, 437, 447, 451, 458,
    459, 463, 465, 466, 482, 494, 502, 504,
    505, 509, 510, 511, 518, 528, 531, 547,
    564, 566, 574, 580, 581, 586, 589, 595,
    596, 597, 598, 607, 608, 624, 626, 628,
    651, 652, 655, 662, 666, 671, 683, 687,
    691, 698, 701, 702, 713, 714, 720, 721,
    724, 727, 731, 733, 734, 738, 742, 751,
    767, 769, 774, 779, 780, 785, 788, 796,
    803, 815, 816
  of St Edmundsbury & Ipswich, *xlv*n
dirige, see church services
disagreement (discord) (between beneficiaries),
    68, 235, 323, 604, 620
  see also agreement
dish, *see* household goods *and* pewter
disposition, *see* behaviour
distraint (including re-entry), 508
  right of, 89
ditch, 30*, 676*, 808*
Domesday Book, *see* book
donge, *see* beds and bedding
doublet, *see* clothes
dovehouse, 733
dower, *lxxii,* 41, 246, 256, 266, 417, 733, 764,
  bequest in recompense for, *lxxii,* 246, 256,
    266, 733
  'morngefte', 41
dozen (twelve), *see* measurement
dress, *see* clothes
dropping-pan, *see* household goods
'dudde', *see* material
dues (rents, services), owed by testator for
    property etc., *lxxii,* 1, 46, 74, 84, 101, 118,
    125, 159*, 170*, 180*, 188, 212, 218, 219,
    220, 225, 300, 306, 318, 344, 370, 434,
    435*, 461, 464, 480, 534, 587, 591, 595,
    601, 631, 634, 661, 687, 740, 751, 780*,
    785
  arrears of, 229, 497
  spiritual and temporal, 51
  received by testator from property, 11, 30,
    101, 148, 159, 170, 180, 184, 210, 229,
    268, 269, 275, 334, 339, 344, 370, 398,
    405, 411, 417, 503, 534, 555, 592, 673,
    712, 754, 772, 785
dwelling (accommodation)
  for mother, 139, 643
  for son, 65
    & family, 754
  for widow, 31, 68, 79, 139, 186, 206, 256,
    322, 416, 468, 485, 494, 541, 587, 592,
    626, 684, 731, 750, 756, 801, 818

earthenware, *see* household goods

easement (access, free entry), *lxxii*, 192, 256,
  417, 480*, 504, 626, 661, 707, 712, 754
  to 'Bachows, le', 76, 76n
  to bakehouse, bakery, 178, 325, 417
  to barn, 12, 735
  to chamber, 178
  to curtilage, 417
  to fire, 178, 262, 450
    fire and water, 192
  to gardens, 417
  for hens and fowl, 417
  to kitchen, 417
  to malting-house, 417
  to messuage, 498
  to 'Nethus, le', 76
  to parlour, 417
  for pigs, hogs-going, 417
  to solar, 12
  to stable, 417
  to tenter, 504
  to well, 178

Easter, celebration, 184, 187, 385, 519, 592, 602,
  658
  in date, 63, 219, 352n, 548
  payment time, 74, 235, 622, 733, 809
  sepulchre, *see* church equipment

education, reading and writing, 482
  see also school

enclosure, *see* land usage

English, testament/will in, 21, 22, 262, 414, 449,
  470, 515, 524, 525, 530, 532, 538, 579,
  600, 614, 622, 624, 639, 654, 659, 723,
  744, 748, 756, 758, 786
  partly in, 38, 208, 805,
  will 'proper' only in, 266, 417, 483, 623,
    720, 733
  words in, 1, 18, 32, 41, 83, 142, 166, 181,
    204, 207, 208, 228, 235, 240, 247, 255,
    256, 258, 259, 276, 311, 313, 324, 330,
    338, 348, 350, 354, 374, 386, 390, 401,
    418, 419, 421, 431, 445, 450, 459, 466,
    471, 475, 476, 490, 507, 511, 519, 539,
    540, 544, 545, 547, 557, 572, 576, 587,
    589, 593, 595, 613, 621, 629, 634, 635,
    644, 651, 652, 662, 667, 672, 677, 681,
    683, 685, 686, 697, 701, 705, 709, 711,
    718, 722, 725, 728, 729, 734, 737, 743,
    745, 755, 779, 782, 788, 803, 806, 809,
    815, 820, 821

entail, 417

entailed lands, *see* land tenure

estate (title to property), 46*, 53, 55, 67, 68*, 74,
  89, 130, 145, 166, 181, 182, 183, 184, 191,
  212, 213, 225, 238, 247, 259, 271, 286, 290,
  300, 307, 335, 338, 344, 348, 395, 414, 417*,
  426, 434, 467, 476, 498, 501, 507*, 532, 607,

650, 661, 662, 663, 702, 710, 714, 720, 727,
  736, 764, 772, 785, 801, 825

evidence (legal document), 51, 229, 374*, 577,
  659

ewer, *see* bronze, household goods *and* latten

executor(s), *lv, lxix-lxx, lxxv, passim*
  accounts of, *lxxv*, 141, 150, 207, 282, 391, 804
    received, 738
  acquitted, *lxxiv, lxxv*, 141, 207, 282, 328, 338,
    341, 391, 415, 789
  advice on wages of servant, 89
  agreement, to be in, 65, 136, 306, 338, 350,
    352
    with supervisor, 729
  appointment of, *lxix-lxx*
  charged for provision for son, 282
  competence of, *lxx*
  dismissed, by court, *lxxiv*, 282, 328, 338, 804
    by other execs (if contravene will), 350
  duties of, *lxxi, lxxiv*
  executors of execs, *lxxi*, 25, 164, 193, 225,
    697, 717, 721
    of mother, 405
    of named person, 239, 548
    of wife's former husband, 376
  expenses, *lxx*, 290, 452, 607, 687, 700, 729
  future challenge by beneficiaries, *lxx*, 184,
    259, 280, 350, 544, 663
  moral obligation of, *lxxv*
  not to be impeded, *lxx*, 374
  oath sworn by, 353
  obedience to, 89
  payment of, *lxx*
    as they deserve, 592
    augmented according to conscience, *lxx*,
      307, 700
    in animals, 636
    in barley, 636
    in clothing, 191, 276, 662*
    in household goods, 276
    in money (amount spec.), 1, 5, 10, 11, 16,
      19, 21, 30, 33, 35, 41, 43, 45, 46, 53, 65,
      74, 75, 78, 81, 88, 89, 93, 101, 109, 113,
      120, 121, 125, 130, 131, 134, 136, 137,
      141, 142, 148, 152, 155, 174, 179, 184,
      186, 189, 191, 196, 198, 202, 230, 204,
      205, 206, 207, 210, 212, 225, 227, 231,
      232, 238, 241, 251, 258, 266, 267, 268,
      273, 276, 285, 290, 291, 294, 299, 306,
      307, 311, 314, 319, 331, 337, 338, 339,
      342, 343, 362, 365, 374, 375, 376, 380,
      381, 382, 393, 399, 408, 418, 434, 436,
      451, 453, 456, 463, 464, 465, 471, 476,
      486, 487, 507, 517, 519, 530, 534, 544,
      545, 547, 554, 558, 559, 564, 570, 573,
      574, 576, 579, 581, 587, 590, 593, 596,
      602, 604, 607, 621, 622, 623, 628, 634,
      635, 651, 652, 653, 657, 661, 667, 676,

681, 687, 698, 700, 702, 704, 707, 716,
722, 726, 727, 728, 731, 733, 738, 741,
742, 744, 745, 754, 759, 764, 772, 773,
774, 776, 777, 778, 779, 782, 785, 786,
788, 802, 803, 805, 810, 815, 819, 823
in wheat, 61
whatever seems right, 340
'power reserved' to, *liv, lxix*n, *lxxv, passim*
property dealings, to let tenement, 571
purchase of land from, 239
put property up for public sale, 150
set purchase price, 540
renouncing administration, *lxx*, 175, 224, 225,
295*, 417, 504*
required to produce inventory, 150
status (relative etc.) (female as executrix), *lxix*
brother, 16, 81, 108, 108n, 109, 123, 144,
151, 208, 215, 215n, 219, 269, 312, 330,
346, 385, 421, 448, 452, 466, 508, 513,
519, 549, 551, 575, 586*, 591, 627,
638*, 648, 653*, 668, 693, 695, 713,
723, 729, 778, 786, 818, 818n
brother-in-law, 438, 438n, 493, 595
cleric, *lxix*, 2, 5, 11, 18, 19, 32, 35*, 39,
75, 92, 107, 109*, 123, 126, 127, 131,
154, 175, 178, 186, 191, 205, 218, 219,
231, 238, 242*, 244, 260, 282, 284, 291,
295*, 303, 311, 318, 321, 331, 338, 340,
341, 348, 395, 398, 401, 409, 429, 437,
442, 451, 457, 465, 469, 471, 489, 518,
527, 529, 573, 575, 589, 607, 611, 612,
635, 637, 638, 647, 650, 655, 715, 720,
721, 724, 726, 737, 777, 782, 790, 818,
820*, 822
'cousin', 291
daughter, sole, 73, 211, 411
with others, 94, 145, 278, 358, 407, 418,
453, 635, 718, 821
daughter-in-law, 370, 467, 597,
father, 144, 264, 524, 549, 614, 627, 771
female, not known relative, sole, 38*, 250
with others, 183, 527, 529, 640, 662
grandson, 244, 358
husband, 333, 644, 677, 689
kinsman, 375
mother, sole, 351
with others, 645, 804
nephew, 255, 312, 350, 754
principal (named man), 107, 518
sister, with others, 331, 782
son, 6, 8, 12, 20, 22, 24, 30, 32*, 35, 39*,
40, 53*, 54, 58, 65, 68, 69, 70, 77, 79,
80, 83, 87, 94, 96, 100*, 102*, 107,
114, 115, 116*, 118, 119, 121, 122, 127,
129, 131, 133, 139, 145, 156*, 160, 162,
168, 172, 173, 182, 186, 187, 190, 192,
194, 203, 205, 209*, 214, 217, 224, 229,
231, 235, 239*, 242*, 244, 246, 252,

256, 262, 263, 265, 267, 269, 270, 279,
280, 281*, 284, 286, 288, 305, 316*,
317, 320, 322, 323, 324, 326*, 334, 342,
352*, 353, 355, 357*, 361, 366, 368,
369, 370, 371, 372, 373, 374, 377, 379*,
385, 386, 389*, 390, 394, 401, 402*,
413, 414, 416, 417, 423, 424*, 429, 435,
438, 440, 450, 454, 458, 462, 467, 468,
469, 473, 479*, 480*, 481, 482*, 488,
492, 494, 502, 504*, 506, 523, 528, 534,
536, 543, 547, 558, 564*, 565, 569, 571,
577*, 580, 587, 590, 596*, 597, 600*,
608, 619, 620, 622, 625, 626, 631, 635,
637*, 639, 641, 642, 649, 656*, 659,
662, 663*, 668, 671, 675, 676, 682*,
685, 685n, 686, 686n, 698, 700, 701,
706, 712, 714, 718, 719, 725, 727, 734,
735, 739, 743, 746, 748, 750, 754, 758,
759, 762, 763, 765, 770, 776, 780*, 783,
784, 785, 787, 789*, 790, 792*, 803*,
807, 809, 815, 820*, 822, 824, 825
principal, 768
son-in-law, 247*, 268, 407, 495, 574, 800,
815
?step-son, 756
uncle, 508
wife, principal, 230, 245, 378, 387, 434,
629, 650, 653, 663, 682, 735, 766
sole, 13, 17, 29, 51, 56, 60, 84, 117, 124,
140, 143, 181, 185, 188, 210, 216,
274, 300, 301, 310, 315, 325, 329,
359, 410, 412, 425, 444, 446, 459,
460, 474, 477, 483, 484, 491, 496,
497, 512, 514, 521, 526, 535, 538,
550, 552, 553, 560, 563, 567, 594,
598, 603, 633, 670, 705, 730, 752,
757, 769, 781, 791, 796, 799, 812
sole but 'principal', 654
with others, 6, 10, 11, 12, 16, 20, 21, 22,
25, 28, 33, 35, 36, 39, 41, 42, 43, 46,
48, 50, 52, 54, 55, 58, 62, 65, 67, 69,
70, 72, 74, 76, 77, 79, 80, 81, 82, 90,
92, 93, 95, 99, 101, 103, 104, 105,
108, 111, 113, 120, 125, 130, 132,
133, 134, 137, 138, 147, 148, 149,
152, 155, 156, 158, 159, 161, 162,
164, 167, 169, 173, 180, 182, 183,
184, 187, 191, 192, 193, 194, 195,
198, 201, 202, 204, 207, 208, 212,
214, 215, 217, 223, 224, 225, 227,
229, 232, 236, 238, 242, 262, 263,
264, 265, 271, 272, 273, 275, 277,
279, 280, 281, 284, 286, 289, 290,
292n, 297, 304, 306, 313, 320, 322,
324, 331, 332, 337, 338, 340, 343,
344, 345, 348, 350, 355, 356, 365,
367, 371, 373, 379, 380, 383, 391,
392, 394, 396, 398, 399, 403, 404,

409, 413, 415, 416, 417, 419, 420,
424, 426, 427, 429, 440, 448, 449,
450, 455, 456, 464, 472, 473, 475,
476, 478, 480, 481, 487, 492, 493,
494, 495, 498, 499, 501, 503, 504,
506, 507, 510, 511, 513, 516, 517,
519, 520, 522, 524, 525, 531, 532,
536, 540, 541, 542, 543, 545, 545,
548, 551, 554, 555, 556, 561, 562,
568, 570, 573, 576, 578, 580, 582,
585, 595, 599, 601, 602, 604, 608,
610, 619, 620, 625, 628, 631, 632,
636, 637, 639, 641, 642, 643, 645,
646, 651, 655, 657, 658, 660, 661,
664, 665, 666, 668, 671, 673, 676,
678, 679, 684, 687, 691, 692, 697,
704, 706, 710, 717, 719, 720, 721,
722, 723, 724, 727, 731, 732, 738,
739, 740, 742, 744, 746, 747, 748,
750, 751, 755, 756, 758, 764, 765,
770, 771, 773, 774, 775, 777, 778,
780, 784, 787, 788, 795, 797, 800,
805, 807, 808, 809, 816, 817, 823,
824, 825, 826

expenses, for fulfilling vows, 508
of grammar school, 720
of repairs, 1, 430
see also burial: cost
eye, of executors, 184
eyes, having God before, lxx, 54, 80, 90, 104, 109,
111, 150, 205, 238, 247, 317, 331, 372, 375,
404, 454, 478, 483, 484, 516, 563, 591, 681,
712, 731*, 775

fan, see agricultural equipment
farm (rent), 10, 53, 80, 82, 92, 131, 212, 218, 222,
259, 392, 405, 411*, 417*, 461, 490, 669*,
673*, 699, 733
cow put out to, 171, 456
farmer (lessee), 89
father, see relatives
feast-days and festivals (used in dating),
xvi–xvii, l
All Saints, 89, 818
All Souls, 521, 649
BVM, annunciation of, 174, 698
assumption of, 613
nativity of, 41
purification of, 190
Corpus Christi, 115
Easter, 63, 219, 548
Epiphany, 388, 725, 821
Feast of Relics (Relic Sunday), 359, 410
Holy Cross, exaltation of, 233, 689
Holy Trinity, 28, 28n
Lent, first day of, 153
mid Sunday of, 472, 750
Nativity of Our Lord, 605

Passion Sunday, 527
Pentecost, 757
St Agatha, 163
St Andrew, 67
St Augustine, 186
St Barnabas, 344, 657
St Bartholomew, 752
St Brice, 351
St Dunstan, 1
St Ed', 741
St Faith, 209
St Francis, 452, 584, 627
St Gregory, 763
St Hilary, 673
St James, 119, 743
St Jerome, 96
St John before the Latin Gate, 777
St John the Baptist, 579
nativity of, 37, 294, 369, 430
St Katherine, 20, 211
St Lawrence, 713
St Leonard, 54
St Luke, 602, 645
St Margaret, 336
St Martin, 27, 65
St Matthew, 142, 150, 207, 235, 268, 808
St Michael, 661
St Nicholas, 512
St Paul, conversion of, 489, 544, 679
St Peter ad vincula, 539
in cathedra, 640
St Peter and St Paul, 187, 268, 739
St Silvester, 69
St Simon and St Jude, 141, 506, 699
St Stephen, 188
St Thomas the Martyr, 160, 498
St Thomas, translation of, 223, 371, 537
St Valentine, 484
St Wulfstan, 552
feasts, liturgical, xlviii, lix
celebration of, Apostles, lix
double festivals, 678, 692
Easter, 187, 592, 602, 658
Easter day, 385
male martyrs, lix
Nativity of Our Lord, 187, 602
Our Lady, 24
Pentecost, lix, 187, 602
St Ed'[sic], 229,
St Nicholas, 229, 247, 247n
greater, and principal days, 171
lights to burn on, 339
used in specifying time of year (for payments,
etc.), liv
All Saints, 235
BVM, assumption of, 801
purification of, 74, 334
Easter, 74, 235, 519, 622, 733, 809

Hallowmass, 622
Holy Cross, invention of, 490
Lent, 544
Nativity of Our Lord, 74
St Etheldreda, 322
St John the Baptist, 653
St Michael (Michaelmas), 1*, 46, 74, 89,
  226, 229, 240, 322*, 405, 411, 455, 495,
  540, 621, 634*, 676, 699, 733*, 734,
  809, 818
featherbed, see beds and bedding
fee, chief lord(s) of, lxxii, 46, 74, 101, 118, 125,
  159, 170, 180, 188, 191, 219, 220*, 225*,
  235, 265, 269, 271, 318, 344, 370, 434,
  461, 464*, 534, 591, 595, 601, 604, 661,
  687, 691, 738, 740, 751, 773, 780*, 785
  land held in, 733
fee (?monetary), granted by knight, 398
fee simple, 664, 668, 754*
feedings, see land usage
felt, see material
fences, see buildings
feoffee(s) (including enfeoff), xlix*, lxxi*, 29, 31,
  46, 51, 53, 55, 67, 68, 70, 74, 80, 82, 89, 101,
  127, 138, 145, 150, 166, 171, 181, 182, 183,
  184, 191, 205, 210, 212, 213, 225, 233, 238,
  247, 259, 271, 286, 290, 295, 300, 307, 332,
  335, 338, 344, 347, 348, 391, 395, 405, 414,
  417*, 426, 434, 456, 464, 467, 476, 498, 501,
  503, 507, 532, 555, 571, 587, 592, 595, 607,
  625, 634, 650*, 661, 663, 669, 678, 682, 697,
  699, 702, 707, 710, 712, 714, 720, 727, 733,
  736, 764, 765, 772, 773, 785, 801, 805, 816,
  825
feoffment, 51, 82, 89, 286, 335, 417, 464
  Guildhall Feoffment, xlixn
festivals, see feast-days
field, see land usage
fifteenths, see taxes
finding (payment, provision, support), of/for
  animals 622*
  brother, 50
  children, 417
  fuel, 801
  lights, 577, 678, 699, 738, 743
  priest(s), 240, 450, 503, 583, 733, 788
  son, lxxv, 282, 694
  widow, 262, 480, 622
  see also maintenance
fire (domestic), lxxii, 256, 450
  fire and flet, 262
  plate (fireback) for, 375, 490
    iron plate, 83, 374, 818
  see also easement; fuel
firewood, see wood
fishery, 354, 629
  leaps of, 354
fishings, 417

fishpond, 706
flax, see crops
foal, see horse
fodder, see crops
foldage, liberty of fold, 16, 820
font, see church equipment
food (refreshment, victuals), at burial, l, 661,
  665, 687, 707
  and seven-day, 268
  see also burial: provision
  for testator, 268
  for widow, 69, 79, 243, 325, 350, 362, 389,
    429, 450, 461, 620, 712, 735
    for her household, 350
food and drink (unspec.), for father, 603
  for mother, 219
  for testator, 414
  for widow, 74, 175, 362, 450, 468, 480, 622
  ale, 268, 327, 399, 681
    malt in (?for), 97
    small, 327
  bacon, 354,
    flitch of, 587*
  beef, 354
  bread, 399, 414
    wheat in (?for), 97
    white, 268
  cheese, 196*, 240, 268, 374, 399, 414, 587
  drink, 414
  fowl, roasted, 276
  meat, 414
  salt, 247
  see also crops; malt
foot (linear), see measurement
footbridge, see bridge
footway (footpath), to church, 78, 352
footwear, see clothes
forcer, see furniture: chest
forge, 247
  equipment for, 247
fother (of lead), see measurement
fowl, see poultry
fraternity (confraternity), of Knights of St John
  (London), 319, 319n
  of religious house, lxi, 80, 121, 295, 295n,
    751*
  see also gild
free entry, see easement
freehold (free land), see land tenure
frende, see clothes
friar, see religious persons
friary, church, repairs to, 181, 465, 505, 607,
  651*
  common profit of, 311
  repairs to, 271
  wall of, 702
    repairs to brick wall, 290

see also burial: place of; fraternity; religious
  (persons); religious houses
friends, obstruction by, 218
fruit, *see* crops; trees and plants
frying pan, *see* household goods
fuel, 803
  faggots, 801, 803, 815
  provision of, 68, 681, 801
  taleshides, 803
funeral, *see* burial
fur, *see* material
furlong, *see* land usage
furniture and furnishings, ambry, 374
  ark, 259, 389
  bench, 191*, 779
  board, 228*, 240*
  chair, *lxv*, 83
    best, *lxv*, 259
    turned, 354
  chest (forcer, hutch), *lxv*, 24, 32, 83, 180, 237,
    252, 276, 354, 374, 385, 390*, 401, 418,
    431, 549, 613, 621, 652, 803
    fir, 822
    painted, *lxv*, 456
    red-painted, 271
    spruce, *lxv*, 697
    with lock and key, 32, 456
    with 'middilwarde', 276
  cupboard, 24*, 259, 374, 611, 697
  cushion, 38, 259*, 779
    banker, 259
  'flat', 259
  forcer, *see* chest
  form, *lxv*, 191*
  hutch, *see* chest
  plank, 240*
  screen, 697
  stool, 648*
  table, *lxv*, 191*, 228, 354, 431, 611, 648*
    closing, 779
    'falt-table', 228, 579
    folding, *lxv*, 374, 402, 523
    meal-table, 83*
      with 2 leaves, 259
    trestle, *lxv*, 354
      pair of, 431
fustian, *see* material

gallon (liquid), *see* measurement
garden, *see* land usage
garnish, *see* pewter
garret, *see* buildings
gate, of house (cottage etc), 10, 14, 43, 78, 142,
  261, 277, 378, 417, 450, 482, 615, 628, 665,
  784
gauds (paternosters), *see* beads
general acquittance, sealed, 246
gift (and feoffment), 51

gild, *lxi–lxii*, 2*, 19, 32, 32n, 43, 51, 55, 69, 77*,
  79*, 83, 88, 94*, 95*, 107*, 126, 184, 186,
  189, 193*, 199*, 204*, 205, 207, 219, 220,
  228*, 230, 240, 247, 258*, 283, 290, 290n*,
  317, 323, 326, 331, 337, 338, 339, 343, 349,
  362, 365*, 376, 378, 380, 391, 392, 395, 397,
  399*, 404*, 405*, 409, 416, 427*, 428, 431,
  431n, 432*, 436, 438, 439, 451*, 457*, 466*,
  476, 485, 499, 507, 508, 515, 536*, 538, 540,
  540n, 568*, 573, 585*, 615*, 618, 623, 630,
  637, 646, 649*, 654*, 658*, 661, 681, 688,
  707, 711, 717*, 723, 724, 731*, 741, 743, 747,
  754, 762, 767, 774*, 777, 778, 779, 780, 783*,
  785*, 786, 788*, 800, 803, 819, 826*
  alms of, 184
  annual dinner of, *lxii*
    equipment for, *lxii*, 189, 290, 432, 711
  banner for, 507
  banner-cloth for, 392n
  brothers and sisters of, 362, 508, 780, 785*
  cattle (?chattels) of, 431
  chaplain of, 499, 499n, 681
  cow to, 786
  customs of, 184
  debts owed to, 416
  fines of, *lxii*
  fraternity of, *lxii*, 32, 94*, 193, 247, 326, 331,
    339, 681, 731, 767
  lights (candles) of, *lxii*, 404*
  mass-pence of, *lxi*, *lxiin*, 43, 75n, 207n, 258*,
    338n, 362n, 427n, 432*, 508, 515, 538,
    540, 586, 654*, 724, 747, 770, 780, 785
    to cleric, 785*
    to friars, 43, 75n, 207n, 258*, 432, 508,
      770, 785
    to poor, 540, 724
    to priest, 586, 724*, 747
    to rector, 432, 780
  membership dues, *lxii*
  minor, or 'light', *lxii*
  missal of, 69*
  officers of (unspec.), 184
    alderman, 339
  procession of, *lxii*,
  torches of, 785
gildhall (common hall, community hall), *lxii*,
  43n*, 75, 75n, 109, 109n, 199n, 229n, 317n,
  432, 585n, 654, 669
  new, 193
  survival of, *lxiin*
  vessels of, 432
gild-patron (dedication), All Saints, *lxii*, 43, 75n,
  427, 711, 747
  BVM, 2, 32, 51, 77n, 94, 193, 204, 204n,
    290n, 365, 378, 395, 399n, 405, 427, 431,
    457, 466, 499, 499n, 568, 568n, 649, 767,
    767n, 774, 785, 788, 819, 826,
    assumption of, 658

Corpus Christi, 199, 199n, 204, 204n, 229,
  229n, 230, 362n, 404, 404n, 431n, 717, 754
Holy Ghost, 290n
Holy Trinity, *lxii*n, *lxiii*, 19, 19n, 77n, 79, 79n,
  95, 95n, 126, 126n, 199, 199n, 205, 229,
  229n, 247, 247n, 258, 258n, 323, 323n,
  331, 337, 339, 339n, 391, 391n, 404, 404n,
  431n, 432, 439, 439n, 466, 536n, 540, 568,
  568n, 585, 585n, 615, 615n, 630, 630n,
  637, 637n, 646, 654, 681, 762, 774, 777,
  777n, 780, 780n, 783, 786, 788, 803, 826
Jesus, 32, 204n, 436, 451, 451n, 779
  Holy Name of, 88, 88n, 338, 338n
St Andrew, 77n, 362, 731, 826
St Botolph, 416, 416n
St Christopher, 283, 283n, 331n
St Ethelbert, 485, 485n
St George, *lxii*, 107, 107n, 189, 290, 290n
St Gregory, 466
St James, *lxi*n, 290n
St John the Baptist, *lxii*n, 55, 69, 77, 79, 79n,
  107, 107n, 184, 186, 186n, 193, 207, 220,
  229n, 258, 258n, 326, 343, 365, 380, 397,
  399n, 409, 409n, 432, 451, 476, 536, 536n,
  623, 649, 654, 658, 717, 724, 731n, 743,
  743n, 785, 800
St John the Evangelist, 731, 731n
St John (unspec.), 19n, 95, 95n, 199, 199n,
  229, 331n, 362n, 451n, 573, 585, 585n
St Katherine, 107, 107n, 258, 258n
St Lawrence, 83, 349
St Margaret, 199, 199n, 240, 240n, 428, 428n,
  438, 536, 536n, 615, 741
St Nicholas, 186n, 392n, 507, 507n
St Peter, *lxii*n, 2, 94, 204, 204n, 331n, 365,
  376, 391n, 392, 392n, 405, 457, 466, 485n,
  515, 538, 538n, 540n, 618, 618n, 661,
  661n, 688, 707
St Peter and St Paul, 2n, 391n, 431n
St Thomas, *lxii*n, 317, 508, 723, 783, 783n
St Thomas of Canterbury, 219, 778, 778n
gilt, gilded, 229, 309, 417*, 698
  see also gold
girdle, *see* clothes: belt
goblet, *see* household goods; silver
God, guidance of, 189
godchild, 5, 6, 10, 27, 40*, 42*, 50*, 62, 66*, 72*,
  80*, 87*, 89*, 93*, 94*, 96, 107*, 121, 126*,
  142*, 151*, 152*, 154*, 175, 184*, 187*,
  205*, 214*, 218*, 229*, 230*, 235, 239*,
  247*, 255, 266, 275, 276, 282*, 284*, 295*,
  310, 311*, 318, 319*, 323*, 331*, 334*, 336*,
  342*, 343*, 352, 359, 361*, 362*, 367*, 374*,
  378*, 380*, 391, 399*, 400*, 403*, 405*, 417,
  420*, 436, 438*, 440, 463, 466, 482*, 488*,
  490*, 504, 512*, 514*, 519*, 529*, 555*,
  558*, 573, 579*, 581*, 604*, 623*, 628*,
  634*, 638*, 641*, 642*, 644*, 646*, 649*,
  661*, 669*, 676*, 688*, 695, 706*, 707*, 719,
  722*, 728*, 731, 733, 738*, 744*, 745*, 754*,
  764*, 772, 779*, 785, 786*, 799*, 803*, 824*,
  826*
godmother, 591
gold (unspec.), 405
  annulet, 38*
  cross (jewellery), 38
  decorated with (spoon), 803*
  ring, 94
    ring on beads, 94
  see also gilt
good (real estate, property), 579, 592, 763, 786
goods, insufficiency/deficiency of, *lxxv*, 141, 207,
  282, 327, 341, 391, 804
  residue of, *lxx*, *passim*
  time allowed for removal of, 322
  value of, *lxxiv*
  wife's own, *lxvii*n, 623, 776
goose, *see* poultry
gown, *see* clothes
grain, *see* crops
grammar, *see* book; school
grandchild, -parent (etc), *see* relatives
grave, *lv*
  same style as another, 181
  see also burial, place of
gravestone, *lv*, 266,
  of marble, *lv*, 89*, 153, 339, 381, 803
  engraved with image, 339
green, *see* land usage
gridiron (griddle), *see* household goods
groundfast and nailfast, 374
grove, *see* land usage

hale, *see* household goods
hall, *see* buildings
hamlet, *xlvi**, 245, 246, 380, 610, 627, 737
hammer, *see* tools and equipment
hangings, *see* beds and bedding
harness (non-agricultural), bridle, 205, 219
  collar, 1*, 635*
  complete set, 354
  pack-cloth, 544*
  saddle, 1*, 205, 219, 697
    pack-saddle, 1*, 219, 544*
  spurs, pair of, *lxvii*n, 205
  traces, 210
    hand-traces, pair of, 1*
  trappings, pair of, 635
  'wan(g)tayll', 544*
  see also agricultural equipment
harrow, *see* agricultural equipment
harvest, *see* agricultural work
hat, *see* clothes
hatchet, *see* tools and equipment
hay, *see* crops
hearth equipment, *see* household goods

heath, 370
hedge, *see* land usage
heifer, *see* cattle
heir, *passim*
　brother to be, of sister, 251
　daughter and, 661*
　eldest son and, 156
　heirs male, 89, 170, 370, 625, 639*
　legal (right, next), 570*, 571, 612, 661, 768
　by right as, 130
　qualifier for surname, 673
　word 'heir' inserted, 417
helmet, *see* weapons and armour
hen, *see* poultry
hive, *see* bees
hogs-going, 417
holy orders, son to take, 636
holy woman, 698, 698n
holy-water clerk, *see* parish officers
horn (instrument), harnessed with silver, 505
　silver belt for, 505
horn, goblet of, bound with silver, 445
hood, *see* clothes
horse, 1, 10*, 22, 24*, 60*, 89*, 131, 172, 209,
　210*, 213, 219*, 229*, 240, 264*, 324, 350*,
　354, 374*, 450*, 461*, 482*, 485*, 490*, 495,
　507*, 534*, 544*, 561*, 576*, 600, 621*,
　633*, 634*, 635*, 636*, 646*, 650*, 676*,
　683, 699, 700*, 725*, 734*, 738, 792*, 801*,
　812*, 816*
　ambling, 1
　bay, *lxviii*, 629, 738
　black, 56, 623, 659
　cart-horse, 389*
　foal, *lxviii*, 382, 629, 659*, 754
　grey, *lxviii*, 629, 683
　mare, 319, 440*, 525*, 631*, 754*
　　bay, 382, 659
　　dun 'sterryd', 659
　　grey, 279, 387, 659
　　red, 279
　　sorrel 'sterryd', 659
　as mortuary, 351
　named, *lxviii*, 210*
　plough-horse, 389*
　red, *lxviii*, 629
　white, 351
　young, 635
hose, *see* clothes
hospital (non-specific), Battisford, St John of
　Jerusalem, 449n
　Bury, St John, 558n
　　St Nicholas, *xlviii*n
　　St Saviour, 128
　London, St Thomas of Acre (or Acon), *lxiv*
　　see also under college
　Rome, St Thomas, 319, 319n,
　leper-hospital, bequest to, *lxiii*

Bury, *lxiii*, 126
　by Risby gate, 126n
Eye, St Mary Magdalene, *lxiii*, 2, 2n, 94,
　94n, 126, 126n, 222, 457n
Ipswich, *lxiii*, 126
　St James, 126n
　St Leonard, 126n
　St Mary Magdalene, 126n
Norwich, *lxiii*, 126
　St Benedict, 126n
　St Clement, 126n
　St Giles, 126n
　St Leonard, 126n
　St Mary Magdalen, 126n
　St Stephen, 126n
house, *see* buildings
household goods (stuff, utensils, ostilments)
　(unspec.), *lxv*, *passim*
　belonging to mother, 470
　wife to retain her own, 490
　see also brass; pewter; silver
　andiron, *lxv*, 32, 142, 228, 240, 431, 579, 613,
　　803*
　basin, *lxv*, 4, 32*, 204, 205, 228*, 140, 247,
　　256, 259*, 311, 390, 401, 402*, 431, 436,
　　529, 558, 579, 613*, 665, 698, 779, 803
　bowl, 228*, 374*
　　with gilt rim, 229
　brewing lead, 587
　bucket, 256
　candle, 247
　candlestick, *lxv*, 32*, 94, 228*, 252, 259*,
　　284, 381*, 549*, 579*, 613*, 698*, 745,
　　783*
　cauldron, 172, 228, 247, 259*, 390, 401, 418*,
　　433, 476, 697, 701, 703
　chafing-dish (chafer), 32, 228, 401, 703
　chalice, 470
　charger, 204*, 205, 290*, 311*
　cheese-mould, 354*
　colander, 782
　cup, 46*, 125*, 456*, 504*, 628*, 751*, 815*
　dish, 204*, 228, 311*, 572*, 618
　　wooden, 711*
　dropping-pan, 401, 579
　earthenware, 74
　ewer, *lxv*, 4, 32*, 204, 205, 247, 259*, 390,
　　401, 431, 529, 558, 579, 613, 665, 698
　　hanging, *lxv*, 374, 579
　frying pan, 142, 259, 418
　goblet, *lxii*, 711*
　　horn, bound with silver, 445
　gridiron (griddle), 142, 259, 579*
　'gromy', 259*
　hale, 374
　hearth equipment, *lxv*
　　see andiron, gridiron, plate, trivet, spit
　jug, 228, 333, 431

kettle, 205, 350, 390, 579*, 745
    holding 1 gallon, 350
kneading-trough, 803
laver, 228*, 234, 311
    brazen, 436, 779
    hanging, 228, 311
lead (vessel), 240, 382, 803
mashing-vat, 390*, 723
mazer, *lxvi*, 32, 205, 237, 245, 259, 276, 316,
    456*, 470*, 579, 662, 698
    bound with silver, 779
    bound with silver-gilt, 83
    ornamented with silver and gilt, 698
mill (hand), 803
mortar, 259*
    stone, 806
ornament, 810*
pan, *lxv*, 46*, 125*, 135*, 220, 237, 259, 311,
    314, 354, 386*, 390, 439, 450, 456*, 504*,
    628*, 688, 694, 699, 701*, 745, 751*,
    815*, 824
    holding ½ gallon, 672
        1 gallon, 539, 703
        2 gallons, 40, 259
        3 gallons, 311
        4 gallons, 401*, 571
    'stelyd', 205, 579*, 672
    'stertepane', 745
    see also under brass
pewter ware, *see* pewter
pitcher, 701*
plate (fireback), 375, 490
    iron plate, 83, 374, 818
platter, 311*, 803
    wooden, 711*
posnet, 18*, 40, 205, 375, 545, 547, 635, 672*
pot, *lxv*, 19, 46*, 125*, 220, 314, 390, 456*,
    504*, 621, 628*, 725, 751*, 815*
    cooking, 251*, 359, 529
    holding 1½ gallons, 476
    see also under brass
quern, 118, 579
rack, *see* iron
salt-cellar, 228, 252, 579*
saucer, 311*
    wooden, *lxii*, 711*
scales, 118*
silverware, *see* silver
smaller necessaries, 392
soap, 247
spit, *lxv*, 32, 142, 228, 237, 240, 259, 290n,
    401, 418, 431, 433, 529, 579, 613, 803
    small, for roasting fowl, 276
    see also iron
spoon, 46*, 125*, 504*, 628*, 751*, 815*
stock (goods), 354
trammel, 375
trencher, *lxii*, 711*

trivet, *lxv*, 256, 354, 579*
vat, 118*, 417
vessels (unspec.), 65, 74, 810
    brewing, 354
woodenware (treen), *lxv*, 74
    'bolle', holding 4 gallons, 256
    dish, *lxii*, 711*
    platter, *lxii*, 711*
    saucer, *lxii*, 711*
    vessel, 452*
        called a 'stonde', 256*
household work, baking, 76, 417
    brewing, 76, 327, 417
    drying malt, 417
    wetting barley, 417
housling towel, *see* church equipment
huke, *see* clothes
hundred (quantity), *see* measurement
hundredweight, *see* measurement
husband, *see* relatives
hutch, *see* furniture: chest

image, *see* church equipment
indented bill, 118, 451
indented deed, *see* deed
indenture (legal document), 67, 417, 492, 662,
    703
    listing goods & livestock, 154
indulgence, *lxix*, 558
inheritance (land passed down as), 532, 661
inn, 53, 650*, 818
    inn-sign, 52, 650
insufficiency of goods, *see* goods
intestate, not wishing to die, 54
inventory (probate), 150
iron, andiron, 32
    beam, 779
    goods, 191
    'heke', 256
    plate (fireback), 83, 374, 818
    rack, 779*
    spit, *lxii*, 32, 189, 276, 433, 529
iron-bound, cart, 378, 561, 646, 683, 812
    vessel, 276

jack, *see* weapons and armour
javelin, *see* weapons and armour
jet, *lxvii*, 42, 228, 140, 276, 421, 436, 466, 523,
    579, 667, 779, 803
    see also beads
jewel(s) (unspec.), 10, 11, 31, 125, 225, 408, 456,
    465, 505, 517, 607, 681, 687
jewellery, *lxvii*
        donated to images and shrines, *lxvii*, *lxvii*n
    annulet, gold, 38*
    brooch, silver, *lxvii*, 142
    cross, gold, 38
    ring, *lxvii*, 142*

gold, 94
  wedding, *lxvii*, 803
  with diamond, 38
  see also beads
jubilee year, 280, 280n
Judgement, day of (Last Day, before High Judge),
  lxx, 31, 46, 66, 83, 93, 101, 130, 148, 184, 223,
  276, 304, 342, 433, 451, 465, 483, 495, 501,
  537, 607, 628, 764, 765, 767
jug, *see* household goods
juger (of grain), *see* measurement

Kalends (celebrating anniversary), 669
  (dating will), 326, 612, 789
Kendal (cloth), *see* material
kerchief, *see* clothes
kettle, *see* household goods
kin, *see* relatives
kirtle, *see* clothes
kitchen, *see* buildings
kneading-trough, *see* household goods
knife, *see* silver

ladle, *see* latten
Lady Chapel, *see* church building
lame, relief of, 773
lamp, *see* church equipment: lights
land (general), *lxxii*
  alienation of, 89, 661
  commodities and 'fredoms' of, 209
  in part-ownership, 66
  to pay for a perpetual certain, 519
  to pay for lights, 519, 776
  profits of, 79, 126, 198, 362, 450, 482, 576,
    604, 634, 669, 786, 787
  public sale of, 150
  received by right of marriage, 544
  recovery of, 62, 417
  sale of, to pay bequests, etc, *passim*
  surrender of, 433
  tenant of (named), 151, 638, 650, 683
  unjust claim to, 700
land (and property) (spec.), 60*, 66, 68, 74, 112,
  191, 205, 220, 222, 227, 230*, 239*, 240*,
  244, 251, 268, 273, 290, 320, 322, 327*,
  338*, 342, 354, 372*, 373, 378*, 381, 383,
  392, 401*, 417*, 450, 452*, 459, 464, 468,
  480, 482*, 492*, 498, 501, 502, 507, 512,
  519*, 544, 551, 554, 561, 570*, 576*, 579,
  581, 583, 590, 602*, 604*, 612, 626, 629*,
  634*, 642*, 653, 654, 660, 661*, 665*,
  678, 688*, 720, 727, 732*, 738, 745, 754*,
  755*, 758*, 764, 765, 768, 773, 776, 801,
  803, 820
  lands and tenements (unspec.), *lxxii, lxxvi*n, 1,
    2, 6, 23, 29, 30, 31, 33, 39, 42, 53, 55, 58,
    59, 61, 62, 67, 68, 72, 76, 82, 89, 90, 91,
    93, 99, 101, 102, 118, 125*, 128, 130, 131,

134, 145, 149, 159, 160, 169, 170, 175,
    180, 181, 188, 193, 196, 209, 210, 212,
    215, 220, 233, 235, 238, 243, 256, 259,
    265, 266, 269, 275, 276, 280, 281, 286,
    294, 295, 320, 323, 334, 335, 339, 343,
    344, 346, 347, 357, 362, 365, 370, 372,
    375, 387, 391, 392, 398, 410, 413, 420,
    422, 426, 447, 455, 461, 467, 468, 472,
    476, 479, 494, 504, 508, 532, 534, 542,
    555, 557, 601, 604, 607, 615, 622, 625,
    626, 640, 651, 657, 663, 665, 673, 679,
    690, 691, 692, 695, 700, 714, 733, 738,
    740, 751, 752, 754, 765, 770, 772, 779,
    780, 785, 799, 808, 809, 816, 825
land tenure, form of (unspec.), *lxxiii, passim*
  bond land, *lxxii*, 11*, 58, 169, 194, 318, 365,
    374, 405, 449, 498, 500, 561, 602*, 620,
    621, 622, 673, 683, 700, 738*, 765, 774,
    788
  conventual land, 634
  copyhold (copyland), *lxxiii*, 21, 212, 272, 504,
    646, 720
  customary land, 209, 683*
    customary meadow, 209
  entailed lands, 30, 661
  freehold (free land), *lxxii, lxxiii*, 11*, 21, 22,
    58, 104, 126, 169, 194, 220, 232, 318, 365,
    374, 449, 498, 504, 514, 561, 620, 621,
    622, 673, 683, 700, 720, 738, 751, 769,
    774, 788, 799
    freehold arable, 232, 632
  held by charter, 799
    by the rod, at the will of the lord, 799
  leased, 365
  part by copy, part in free tenure, 24
land usage (unspec.), 16, 172, 203, 207, 268,
  308, 322, 361, 382, 414, 440, 474, 483,
  485, 566, 585, 633, 655, 711, 729, 756,
  763, 800, 823
  arable, 16, 46, 80, 81, 118, 156, 159, 182, 186,
    204*, 232*, 247, 253, 278, 279, 307, 318,
    330, 331, 350, 378, 382, 429, 450*, 502,
    519, 534, 550, 579, 629, 631, 643, 768,
    771, 780, 820, 823*, 824
  close, *lxxii*, 2, 5, 37, 68*, 116*, 138, 184*,
    191, 205, 209*, 220, 243, 300, 318, 320*,
    374, 381*, 395, 452, 519*, 522*, 534*,
    570*, 576, 579, 601, 634, 644, 660, 700*,
    721, 748, 764, 777, 818, 821
  copse, 171
    crop of a copse, 171
  croft, 1, 10*, 50, 53*, 55, 56*, 80, 91, 92,
    108, 123, 138*, 154, 171, 225*, 232, 240*,
    272*, 330, 338, 373, 452, 455, 482*, 484,
    498*, 508, 519*, 532, 536, 561, 604*, 628,
    631, 634, 646*, 676*, 678, 681*, 682*,
    690, 692, 720, 721*, 722, 733, 738*, 742,
    743, 769, 773*, 787, 801, 824

arable croft, 46
customary croft, 683
enclosed croft, 687
curtilage, 235*, 417
enclosure (enclosed), 156, 240, 327, 338, 372, 498
extended, 374
feedings, 6, 11, 30, 57, 80, 111, 159, 184, 209, 210, 235, 268, 318, 334, 335, 375, 417*, 456, 467, 472, 498, 522, 604, 682, 700, 754, 772, 801, 820
field, *lxxii*, 14, 39, 60, 74, 76, 80, 154, 159, 170, 182, 188, 196, 204, 219, 220, 232, 233, 235, 247, 265, 268, 273, 286, 320, 327, 331, 335, 338, 342, 347, 374, 389, 401, 429, 474, 480, 491*, 498, 507, 512, 519, 534, 544, 551, 562, 570, 591, 602*, 612, 614, 626*, 631, 632, 641, 643, 661, 678, 679, 682*, 727, 732*, 743, 764, 765*, 773*, 801, 825
furlong, 16, 60, 68*, 230*, 602, 604, 632, 661, 744
garden, 2, 10*, 26, 50, 72, 84, 194, 227, 232, 244, 306, 325, 353, 395, 409, 417, 471, 480*, 491*, 498, 503, 517, 638, 676*, 682*, 687*, 717, 720, 727, 733, 784*
enclosed garden, 504
green, 25, 68, 89, 126, 206n, 239, 240, 350, 371, 432, 502, 583n, 600, 623*, 649*, 803
'grendyll, le', 10, 10n
grove (grovet), 89, 300, 419*, 482*, 490, 491, 519, 634, 720
ground of messuage, 279
hedgerows (hedges), 209, 335, 417
leasows, 361
meadow, 1*, 6*, 30*, 53, 55, 68, 90, 92, 101, 103, 126, 138*, 156, 159, 184*, 204*, 210*, 218, 230*, 232*, 235*, 262, 286, 300, 327, 334, 335*, 350*, 375, 378, 387, 399, 401*, 417*, 440*, 456, 467, 468, 472, 474, 482*, 498, 508, 519, 522*, 604*, 612, 629*, 673, 676, 678, 688, 698, 700*, 706*, 720, 721, 735, 738, 743*, 751, 754, 764, 772, 780, 799, 801, 808, 821, 823
enclosed meadow, 456
to support obit, 700
non-arable, 771
pasture, 6, 11, 30, 57, 80, 81, 103, 109, 111, 126, 159, 182, 209, 210, 225, 235*, 240, 268, 286, 318, 334, 335*, 350*, 361*, 375, 387, 395, 417*, 440*, 457, 467, 472, 498, 522, 562, 576*, 604, 634*, 669*, 676, 682*, 688, 697*, 700, 706*, 729, 733, 743, 754, 764, 772, 801, 808, 820
enclosed pasture, 464, 504
pightle, 68, 76, 219*, 225, 239, 323, 338, 519*, 634, 665, 688, 738, 773*
enclosed pightle, 504

tenement, *see* buildings
toft, 24, 182
wood(s), 1, 10, 11, 148, 184, 335, 519, 634, 697, 721*, 772, 780, 786
underwood, 184
yard, 240, 262, 494, 676
latten, basin, 32*, 276*, 399
round, 162
candlestick, 32*, 276*, 381, 558*, 652, 776*
ewer, 276*, 399,
goods (pieces, vessels), 191, 256*, 772*
ladle, 205, 401
pot, 381
holding 3 gallons, 476
laver, *see* household goods
law, estate (sufficient) in, 348, 498, 507*
feudal, *xlix*
form of, 276
regarding widow's inheritance, 35
title in, 184
lead, for roofing, 450
vessel made of, 382, 445*
weights, 779
see also household goods: lead
lease (farm), 89
leasows, *see* land usage
leather, clothing, belt, 285, 348*
leggings, 456*
shoes, 456*
raw material
dressed and undressed, 456
legacies, *passim*
see also bequest
legal evidence, *see* evidence
leggings, *see* clothes
Lent, 153, 472, 544, 544n, 750
leper-hospital, *see* hospital
let, *see* rent
lights, *see* church equipment
linen, *see* cloth-making, cloths (household) *and* material
lives of St Margaret and St Katherine, *see* book
livestock, *see* animals
loom, *see* cloth-making

maintenance (upkeep), of children, 99, 113, 125, 126, 147, 158, 183, 266, 274, 448, 535, 555, 586, 691, 752, 786, 819
of cow, 818*
of father, 508
by widow, 603
of mother, 139
of sister, 708*
of widow, 139, 400, 434, 683, 704, 707, 725, 752, 767, 810
see also finding
malefactors, *see* benefactors

malt, *liii*, 31, 67*, 69, 76, 77*, 85, 95, 97, 126,
    133, 151*, 152, 170, 187, 190, 210*, 226,
    247*, 256, 266, 286, 290*, 295*, 300, 309*,
    323*, 337*, 338, 350*, 361, 365, 374, 382*,
    383, 387, 392, 405*, 425, 461, 482*, 519, 540,
    544*, 560, 570, 587, 620, 625, 634, 653, 681,
    687, 693*, 723, 732*, 744, 763, 764, 770,
    785*, 786*, 800*, 803, 809
  malt-house, 417
  malt-kiln, 76
  malt-making, 76, 800
  malt-mill, 587
manor, 11, 35, 148, 209, 213, 362*, 378, 411,
    433, 587, 646, 740n, 762n, 797
  court rolls of, *lxxiv*n, 517
    copy of, 212, 748, 751
    inventory recorded in, *lxxiv*n
  custom of, 74, 247, 362, 500
  lady of, 342
  lord of, 417n, 457n, 517, 661, 716, 799
    licence of, 504, 751
  reversion of, 148
  tenants of, 11
    bond tenant of, 433
marble, paving in church, 727, 750
  see also gravestone
mare, *see* horse
market place, 26, 46, 122, 359, 405, 607n, 669,
    687, 706
market stall, *lxxii*, 80*, 818
marriage, according to wishes of parents, 53
  advice by execs, 803
  bequest at/for, 1*, 11, 12, 22, 84, 89, 90, 125,
    154, 225*, 247, 251, 286*, 365, 374, 393,
    412, 456, 501, 504*, 519, 532, 587*, 598*,
    634, 655*, 662, 677, 683, 712, 713, 721,
    763, 788, 795*, 799
  with consent of mother and/or execs, 286*,
    803
  land given to testator at, 118
    received from wife at, 661
    received by right of, 544
  portion, 363
  proposed, of daughter, 587
  remarriage, of daughter-in-law, 542
    of widow, *lxxii*, 2, 6, 21, 41, 48, 68, 70, 90,
    91, 195, 225, 238, 240, 292, 293, 313, 343,
    393, 398, 417, 485, 508, 522, 570, 634,
    659, 690, 700, 722, 744, 774, 777, 778,
    787, 788, 809
  utensils had with wife in, 220
mashing-vat, *see* household goods
maslin, *see* crops
mass, *see* church services
mass-pence, *lv*
  see also gild: mass-pence
material (fabric, textiles, etc), 'bankes', 572,
    572n

blanket, 374, 589*, 706
buckram, 'bokeram', 32
Braban cloth, 662
burnet, 247, 276, 677
canvas, 256*
card, blue, 32
cloth, 83, 240, 374
  brown, 276
  old, 276
  painted, 479*
  of plain work, 711
  sanguine-coloured, 669
  'steyned', 788
  white, 240
corse ('coarse'), 579, 644
diaper (diaperwork), 4*, 247, 276, 711, 728
'dudde', 1*
felt (felted), 9, 436
fur (furred) (unspec.) 32, 38*, 259*, 311*,
    351, 380, 662, 698, 701, 803
  black, 38*
  coney skins, 259
  'croppys', 38
  grey, 38, 698
  rabbit skin, 276
  white lamb(skin), 191
fustian, 38, 350, 351
  black, 490
leather, 285, 348*, 456*, 517
  dressed and undressed, 456
linen, 46, 74, 79, 125, 295, 362, 436*, 456,
    504, 628, 687, 751, 767, 779*, 803, 815
medley, 698
musterdevillers, 32, 38, 490, 598, 652, 662
plaincloth, 247*, 276
  plaincloth holland, 276
russet, 1, 135, 211, 313, 374*, 398, 490, 672,
    705, 738
sarcenet, tapestry of, *lix*, 697
satin, 'sateyn cremesyn', 181
say, 259, 401
  red, 240
silk, 115, 181, 276, 417*, 613
  black, 662, 698
velvet, 276
woollen, *see* woollen cloth
worsted, 1
mattress, *see* beds and bedding
mazer, *see* household goods; silver
meadow, *see* land usage
measure, *see* measurement
measurement, unit of, *xi-xii*
  acre, *passim*
  bushel, *passim*
    of the great measure, 322
  cartload (clay), *lxiii*, 457*
    (stone), *lxiii*, 80, 182, 252, 642, 649
    (timber), 764

chorus (grain), 664
coomb (grain & malt), 60*, 61, 89*, 95, 151*,
 187, 199*, 214, 232*, 240*, 266*, 320,
 365, 382, 415, 438, 519, 544*, 579*, 604*,
 620*, 623*, 634*, 649*, 659*, 664*, 723,
 725*, 744, 763, 786*, 800*, 823
day (working time), 2 days-worth of arable,
 192
 4 days' work, 785
dozen (cloth), 374*
foot (linear), 480*
fother (lead), 450
gallon (liquid) 32, 40, 116*, 142*, 150, 205,
 256, 259, 276*, 284, 290, 305, 311*, 318,
 319, 327*, 350, 401*, 421, 436*, 456,
 476*, 511, 539, 547*, 571*, 578, 613, 672,
 703, 779*, 803*
hive (bees), 672, 686
hundred (faggots), 815
 (long, of sheep), lxviii*, lxviiin*, 230, 230n,
 286
 (reeds), 450
 (wood), 262
hundredweight, 779
juger (grain), 372
measure (grain), 580
noble (money), 224*, 229*
pack (wool), 309*
peck (grain), 211*
 (flax seed), 498
perch (area), 232*, 253, 480*
perch (distance), 785
pottle (liquid), 276, 421
pound (wax, candle), 46, 359, 371, 397, 519,
 605, 658
 (wool), 83, 374, 587
quart (liquid), 421
quarter (firewood), 256, 472
 (grain), liii, 1, 10*, 54*, 67*, 68*, 70, 85,
 126, 130, 151, 184*, 190*, 214*, 226,
 240, 247*, 259, 286, 295*, 309*, 323,
 338, 350*, 374*, 382*, 392, 405*, 417,
 420, 437, 448, 499, 534, 540, 587*, 608,
 636*, 646, 664, 681, 693*, 717*, 720*,
 721*, 725*, 729*, 732*, 737*, 741, 765,
 770, 790, 803, 823, 824
 of the great measure, 322*
rood (land), 24*, 156, 170*, 209*, 221*, 225*,
 227, 232, 239*, 240*, 262, 268, 273, 278,
 312*, 323, 372*, 382*, 401, 437, 452*,
 498*, 508, 512*, 514, 519, 522, 561, 602*,
 614, 626*, 629, 632, 688, 732*, 736, 743,
 768, 809,
 (wheat), 609
score (twenty) (lbs) 83
 (sheep), 60, 636, 816
seam (grain), 290, 651*
sleeve (grain), 166, 166n

yard (cloth), 276*, 430, 456, 572, 589*, 705,
 706, 711*, 803*
medicines, lxxii, 79
medley, see material
merchandise, in an inn, 650
mercy, deeds of, see charity
 of God, 477
mere (water), 232
messuage, see buildings
metal, see brass, bronze, copper, gold, iron, latten,
 lead, pewter, silver
metes, divided by, 508
mill, 618, 688, 778
mill-house, 350
mill-mound, 159*, 159n
mill-stones, pair of, 618
 see also household goods
missal, see book; church equipment: book
mixtlin, see crops
moat, see buildings
monastery (abbey), 46, 88, 128, 147, 178, 295,
 432, 519, 634, 772, 826
 refectory, glazing of, 519
 tower, 88
money, see silver
monk, see religious persons
mortar, see household goods
mortuary (principal), liv, livn, 131, 146, 157, 204,
 304, 351, 397, 443, 474, 598, 655, 718
 see also animals; cattle: bullock; cattle: cow;
 sheep
mortuary-roll, lxi
mother, see relatives
mother church, of Norwich, 193, 210, 502, 518,
 529, 688, 771
mowing, see agricultural work
musterdevillers, see material

name, given to animals, lxviii, 210*, 803
 occupation used as surname, 166
 relatives with same Christian name, see under
 relatives: brother, daughter, son
 see also alias
nave, see church building
neat-house, see buildings
need (poverty, etc.), of testator, 268
 of widow, 22, 48, 117, 175, 198, 218, 224,
 258, 262, 279, 300, 320, 325, 380, 399,
 420, 429, 440, 442, 449, 487, 592, 617,
 626, 641, 687, 690, 712, 722, 733, 735,
 740, 805
nephew, see relatives
next of kin, see relatives
niece, see relatives
noble (money), see measurement
Nones (dating will), 282
notary, see occupation
notarial instrument, lxxi

notarial sign, *xlviii*, *xlix*
nun, *see* religious persons

oats, *see* crops
obedience, *see* behaviour
obligation (bond) (legal), 417, 470*, 687, 741
  sealed, 693
  written, 171, 772
occupation, *li*, *lxxii*
  as aid to identification, *li*
  as an *alias*, *li*
  barber, 224, 266, 650
  barker, *li*, *lin*, *lxix*, **147**, **771**
  'bocher', *li*, **71**, **349**, **403**
  butcher, 607
  carpenter, 31n, 151*
  carver and painter, 338
  clothier, *lvn**, 190n
  cooper, 166
  cordwainer (implied), **456**
  craftsman, 240
  cutler, 31n
  draper, 381
  dyer (implied), *lxix*, **83**
  fuller, *li*, *lin*, 84n, **225**, **306**, 504n, 614, **727**
  glover, *li*, **37**, 228n, 376
  grocer, 505
  herbalist (implied), **79**
  'kerver', 347
  mercer, 229n, 408n, 788, 788n
  notary, *xlviii*, *lxxvin*, 459, 799, 799n
  painter, 331n
  salter, *lxxvin*
  scrivener, *lxxi*
  smith, *li*, 20n, 134, 147, **300**, 743
    (implied), **778**, **815**
  stainer, 374
  tailor, 163, 275n
  tanner, 107, 239n, 517n, 629
  turner, *li*, **703**
  weaver, *lxix**, 225n
  wheelwright (implied), *lxix*, **240**, 240n
  workman ('menys'), 350*
offerings (to church), *liv*, *passim*
official, of archdeacon, *see* archdeacon
  of parish, *see* parish officers
ordinary, of bishop, 276
ornament, *see* church equipment *and* household
  goods
ox, *see* cattle

pack (of wool etc), *see* measurement
pack-saddle, *see* harness: saddle
pagans, 636
painting (of images), *see* church equipment
pan, *see* brass *and* household goods
pantry, *see* buildings
pane (counterpane), *see* beds and bedding

panel (retable), *see* church equipment
parclose, *see* church equipment
parent (living), 2, 5, 123, 139, 144, 187, 208,
  210, 219, 226, 264, 309, 343, 351, 430,
  437, 508, 519, 524, 525, 549, 572*, 588*,
  591, 603, 614*, 623, 627, 643, 645, 680,
  681, 705, 716, 763, 771, 804
  (named), 11, 60, 89, 92n, 123, 144, 166, 219,
    226, 264, 343, 351, 425, 430, 437, 447,
    452n*, 470, 471, 489, 490*, 508, 519, 524,
    549, 550, 572, 581, 591, 626, 627, 643,
    645, 670, 673, 681, 689, 705, 709*, 711,
    763, 771, 779*, 804, 824*
  grandparent(s) (named), 60, 550
parish clergy (general), bequests to, for prayers, *liv*
  as execs and supervisors, *lxix*
  see also executor: status; supervisor: status
  chaplain, *lix*, *passim*
    (named), 5, 5n, 11, 11n, 18, 19, 23*, 39,
      39n, 46, 60*, 60n, 68, 75, 107, 127, 133,
      134, 152, 152n, 175, 178, 187, 189, 194,
      194n, 196, 205, 231, 241, 241n, 247,
      271, 271n, 276, 276n, 282, 290*, 290n*,
      301, 306, 311, 338, 338n, 342, 405,
      408*, 408n, 409, 437, 437n, 440, 440n,
      452, 452n, 471, 471n, 479, 504, 504n,
      529, 529n, 531, 551, 551n*, 552, 552n,
      556, 559, 559n, 596, 597, 602, 611,
      628*, 631, 635, 638, 651, 698*, 727,
      742*, 765, 779, 785, 788, 798, 807, 820
    of BVM, 325, 669
    celebrating Mass of Jesu, 363
    as pilgrim to Rome, 16
  clerk (in holy orders) (named), 1, 11, 11n, 16,
    32, 35, 35n, 36, 38*, 38n, 46, 48, 69, 92,
    102, 109*, 112, 112n, 117, 117n, 118, 127,
    130, 135, 135n, 136, 152, 152n, 154, 154n,
    171, 191*, 199, 199n, 210, 213, 219, 219n,
    222*, 242, 244, 247, 251, 252, 258, 259,
    284*, 286, 286n, 302, 303, 303n, 320, 331,
    338, 340, 341, 341n, 348, 348n, 365, 376,
    392, 393*, 395, 398, 401, 425, 442, 451,
    451n, 457, 465, 471, 471n, 476, 476n, 496,
    508, 508n, 517, 517n, 530, 533, 555, 574,
    575, 589, 607, **624**, 644, 649, 650, 652,
    666, 667, 670, 670n, 673, 680, 683, 723,
    724, 737, 756, 759, 769, 775, 777, 778,
    782, 785, 788, 796, 810, 818
  curate, 290, 400, 408
    (named), 513, 747
  deacon, 681
    subdeacon, 681
      (named), 342
  parish chaplain, *lvi*, 37, 87, 107n, 213, 338,
    390, 452, 626, 634, 672, 807
    (named), 170, 184, 213, 260, 434, 434n,
      436, 436n, 446, 450, 471, 490, 596, 681,
      698, 728, 752, 776, 779

parish clerk, *see* parish officer: parish clerk
parson, 21, 171, 262*, 538, 654
    (named), 191, 262, 295, 624, 720
priest, *lix, passim*
    (named), 136, 136n, 240, 240n, 243, 417,
       469, 469n, 622, 733, 747, 787
    as pilgrim to Rome, 89
    parish priest, *lvi*, 262, 290, 411, 742, 763
    to sing, 38, 222, 470
rector, 24, 24n, 35, 65, 67, 89*, 126, 129, 157,
    221, 240, 247, 291, 299, 304, 350, 432,
    628, 655, 682, 708, 721, 729, 755, 772, 821
    (named), *xlvn, xlviiin*, 11n, 16n, 29, 29n,
       35*, 35n, 36, 36n, 39n, 55, 57, 57n, 123,
       126, 126n, 130n, 131, 131n, 154n, 186n,
       191, 194n, 205, 238, 238n, 243, 243n,
       248, 248n, 262n, 270, 270n, 281, 281n,
       284, 284n*, 286, 286n, 292, 292n, 293,
       295, 295n, 303, 303n, 318, 318n, 320n,
       321*, 321n*, 333, 333n, 338n, 340n,
       342, 342n, 350, 350n, 368, 368n, 392n,
       393, 393n, 401, 401n, 402, 406*, 406n*,
       417*, 417n*, 431*, 435, 451, 451n,
       471n, 472, 472n, 489, 502, 507, 507n,
       522, 532, 532n, 533, 546, 546n, 555*,
       555n, 566, 573, 573n, 598, 598n, 610,
       610n, 612, 612n, 613, 621, 621n, 624n,
       647, 655, 701n, 714, 714n, 720*, 721,
       726, 726n, 729, 729n, 743, 772, 775n,
       778, 778n, 780, 780n, 796, 820*, 820n*,
       822, 822n, 824
vicar, 38, 155, 232, 301, 438, 526, 601, 630,
    669
    (named), 2, 2n, 46, 46n, 55, 55n, 75, 75n,
       109, 109n, 150, 150n, 166, 166n, 178,
       187, 218, 218n, 222, 236, 276, 283, 295,
       295n, 349, 349n, 374, 380, 380n, 407,
       407n, 409, 442n, 456, 457n, 500, 518,
       518n, 556, 646, 646n, 651, 669, 669n,
       687, 715, 716, 716n, 727, 727n, 790,
       790n
parish (church) officers, *lvi*
    beadle, *lvi*, 310, 326, 460, 658, 781
    bedesman, *lvin*
    choir, *lvi*, 484
    choirmaster, 669*
    churchwarden (guardian), *liin*, 171, 229*,
       240*, 317*, **424**, 463*, 626*, 742*
    clerk (singing) (boys, greater, lesser), *liv*, 1,
       2, 5, 21*, 42*, 46*, 67, 70, 78, 79, 89, 94,
       96*, 100, 125, 133, 161, 171, 204*, 222,
       238, 247*, 262*, 309*, 311*, 326*, 331*,
       409*, 420, 436*, 440*, 460, 490*, 491,
       505, 577, 658, 665, 669, 742, 779*, 781,
       799*
    clerk 'of the town', 11, 87
    holy-water clerk, *lvi*, 436*, 779*
    official (named), 247*, 247n

parish clerk, *lvi*, 14, 46*, 180, 205, 229*, 240,
    251, 273, 319, 338, 391, 404, 409, 411,
    452, 453, 506, 542, 634, 741, 763
    (named), 184
sacrist (sacristan), *lvi*, 205, 436, 626, 669, 746,
    779
sexton, *lvi*
parish, custom of, 824
parishioner(s), *liii*, 67, 290, **342**, 350, 626, 692,
    727, 824
    agreement over bell, 626
    burial, *liii*, 67
    great of the parish, 424
park, 681
parlour, *see* buildings
parson, *see* parish clergy
pasture, *see* land usage
pasturing, *see* agricultural work
pasturage, 240
paternosters, *see* beads
patron saints, *see* advower, church dedication
paving, *see* church building
payment, for or out of property, allowance
    (reduction, remission) of, 31, 432
    distribution of, *passim*,
    fraud and deceit apart, 803
    owed by testator, 84, 555
    owed to testator, 268, 399, 517, 703, 719
    see also finding
peas, *see* crops
peck (of grain), *see* measurement
peculiar (ecclesiastical), *xlv*
pelisse, *see* clothes
pension, *see* annuity
perch (length), *see* measurement
petticoat, *see* clothes
pewterware (unspec.), *lxvi*, 32, 74, 196*, 211*,
    381*, 587, 613*
    bowl, 228*
    candlestick, 256
    charger, 32*
    dish, 32*, 205*, 220*, 228*, 276, 290*, 401*,
       402*, 436*, 579*, 618, 779*, 803*
    garnish of, 259
    half, 271, 401, 697
    goods, 191
    piece, 354*, 676*, 803*
    plate, 220*
    platter, 32*, 205*, 228*, 276*, 290*, 312*,
       401*, 402*, 436*, 579*, 652*, 779*
    pot, 228
    salt(-cellar), *lxii*, 228, 276*, 389, 436*, 711,
       776*
    saucer, 32*, 205*, 220*, 228*, 290*, 401*,
       402*, 579*
    vessel, 247*, 421*, 648*, 772*
piety, deeds of, *see* charity

pig, *lxviii*, 192, 210*, 240*, 343*, 374*, 490*, 498, 628*, 653*, 676*, 690, 734
  'le barwe', 354
  piglet, 240*, 346*, 354*, 437, 490*
  sow, 354*
  young, 178
pigeon, 733*
pightle, *see* land usage
pilgrimage, *lxiv*, 16, 89, 146, 166*, 184, 280, 294*, 323, 338, 348, 401, 401n, 414*, 414n*, 437, 454, 467, 490*, 495*, 508, 522*, 544*, 579*, 640*, 769
  pilgrim to go on (unspec.), *lxiv*, 89, 146, 280, 294*, 437, 490, 640, 769
    chaplain, 184, 348, 454
    named person, 166
    priest, *lxv*, 89, 522, 544, 579
    son, 414
  pilgrim to do/go to, Canterbury, St Thomas, *lxiv*, 437, 508, 640*
    Compostella, St James, *lxiv*, *lxv*, 89, 280, 294
    Manston (Dorset), Maid of, 166
    'Moynes', 146
    Newmarket, St Theobald, *lxiv*, 414, 414n
    Norwich, Holy Trinity, *lxiv*, 414, 414n
      St Lawrence, *lxiv*, 414, 414n
    Rome, *lxiv*, *lxv*, *lxv*n, 16, 89, 184, 323, 338, 490, 579
      circle of, *lxv*, 490, 495, 544
      Court of, 348, 522, 544
      Scala Celi, *lxv*, *lxv*n, 294, 490, 495, 579
      St Fabian and St Sebastian, *lxv*, 579
      St Peter, 294, 454
      St Peter and St Paul, sepulchres of, 401, 401n, 467, 522
      stations of, *lxv*, *lxv*n, 544
    Roydon (Nfk), St Remigius, 769
    Sudbury, Our Lady, *lxiv*, 414, 414n
    Tibenham (Nfk), St Nicholas, *lxiv*, 414, 414n
    Walsingham (Nfk), Our Lady, *lxiv*, 166*, 508, 640*
    Woolpit, Our Lady, *lxiv*, 166, 414, 769
  vows for, 508
pillow, *see* beds and bedding
pinfold, 700
pitcher, *see* household goods
placebo, *see* church services
plaincloth, *see* material
plate, *see* iron *and* pewter
platter, *see* household goods *and* pewter
plough, *see* agricultural equipment
ploughing, *see* agricultural work
poor, bequests to (of goods etc), of bedcover, 251
  of beds in a house, 342
  of clothing, *lxvii*, 465, 607, 648
  of food and drink, bacon, 354

    beef, 354
    cheese, 196
    grain, *lxiii*, 171
    malt, 151, 152, 171, 634, 785*
    maslin, 214
    rye, 170
    wheat, 151, 196, 269, 785*
  of fuel, 803
  of linen, 803
  of mass-pence, 540
  of money (unspec. & unconditional), 19, 21, 55, 60, 61, 78, 90, 116, 154, 191, 204, 232, 297, 300, 311*, 327, 338, 353, 369, 388, 408, 420, 421, 432, 434, 481, 482, 498, 521, 525, 573, 600, 624, 625, 673, 706, 733, 748, 797
  bequests to, payable on, anniversary, 243, 290, 334, 465, 607, 669
    on burial day, 1, 5, 11, 136, 191, 238, 268, 356, 362, 490, 577, 665, 687, 691
    on day of death, 290
    at seven-day, 290, 431
    at thirty-day, 290, 431
    for 12 years, 171
    weekly (duration spec.), 50, 87, 122, 223, 228, 339, 454, 517, 681, 786
      on Sunday, 92, 246
      on Thursday, 11
      on Friday, 46, 436, 779
  bequests to (purpose), for prayers, *lxiii*, 601, 610
    for taxes, *lxiv*, 240, 383, 634
  bequests to (situation, status), beggars, 142
    blind, *lxiii*, 773
    children, 362
    clerks, 125
    deserving, *lxiii*, *lxiii*n
    in hospital, 2, 2n, 94, 94n, 222
    indigent, 133
    lame, *lxiii*, 773
    most in need, 38, 107, 189, 408
    needy, *lxii*, 20, 46, 60, 125*, 709, 803
    neighbours, 171, 648
    parishioners, 214
    present at burial, 1, 5, 42, 55, 79, 89, 96, 142, 247, 286, 374, 436, 577, 772, 779, 803
      holding torches, 815
      at mass on day of burial, 42, 577, 803
    priests, 125, 148
    prisoners, *lxii*, *lxiii*, 773
    townsfolk, 27
    vagrant, *lxiii*, 342
  dwelling for, *see* almshouse
porch, *see* church building
posnet, *see* household goods
possession (seisin), 68*, 70, 74, 80, 89, 101, 130, 145, 150, 171, 182, 184, 213, 238, 343, 391,

426, 440, 467, 476, 503, 555, 634, 650, 661, 662, 663, 697, 699, 712, 736, 765, 785, 801, 824, 825

pot, *see* brass, household goods, latten *and* pewter

pottle (volume), *see* measurement

'pouder boxe', *see* silver: container

poultry, *lxviii*
  capon, 354*
  cock, 178, 354*, 490*, 690
  fowl 'clovefotyd', 417*
  goose, 354*, 490*
  hen, 178*, 192*, 262*, 354*, 417*, 490*, 690*

pound (weight), *see* measurement

prayers for souls, *liv, lix, passim*
  chaplain to pray, *lix*, 39, 133, 184, 471*, 785
  clerk (in holy orders) to pray, 109, 222, 238, 246, 259, 778, 785
  daughter to pray, 803*
  executors to pray, 24
  former servant to pray, 46*
  friars to pray, *lix*, 46*, 90*, 109*, 111*, 145, 189, 259, 281, 413, 436, 448, 461*, 505*, 507*, 508*, 515, 528*, 538, 565, 570, 579*, 594*, 602, 636*, 651*, 654, 665, 714, 733, 751, 779*, 785*
  gild to pray, *lxi*, 826
  goddaughter to pray, 785, 803*, 826*
  godson to pray, 803*, 826*
  grandchild to pray, 574*, 803*
  inhabitants of almshouse to pray, *lxiii*, 11, 87, 339, 587, 607
  monks to pray, 46, 276
  named female to pray, 148, 276, 436*, 662*, 779*, 803*, 815
  named male to pray, 574*, 601, 779*
  neighbours to pray, 399
  nephew to pray, 125
  nuns to pray, 634
  parishioners to pray, 290
  poor to pray, 79, 87, 122, 133, 399, 600, 610, 785
    in almshouse, 11, 87, 238, 587
    at burial mass, 46, 436, 779, 803
    in hospital, 222
  priest(s) to pray, 238, 246, 259, 697, 780
    in Rome, 89
  priest(s) to sing, 38, 222, 470, 579, 733, 786, 805
  rector to pray, 500, 682
  servant to pray, 803
  son to pray, 803*
    and daughter-in-law, 597

price (spec.) of, beads, pair of, 252
  cope, 298
  coverlet, 32
  cow, 419, 587, 819

firewood, 256

house (place), 158, 195

land, 89, 633

sheets, pair of, 318

torch, 388

wax, 359

woollen cloth, 430
  see also purchase

priest, *see* parish clergy

primer, *see* book *and* church equipment: book

principal, *see* mortuary

priory church, 228, 657
  see also religious (persons); religious houses

prisoners, Christian captives, 636
  relief of, 300, 773

probate, *passim*
  bona notabilia, xliv
  date of, *lxxvi*
  inventory, *lxv, lxv*n, *lxviii*n, *lxxiv–lxxv*, 150
    from Cornwall, *lxxiv*
      Exeter, *lxxiv*
      Southampton, *lxxiv*n
    mentioned in Part I, *lxxiv, lxxiv*n
    survival of, *lxxiv*
  jurisdiction, *xliii–xlvi*
  obtained by execs, *lxxiv*
  peculiars, *xlv*
  Principal Probate Registry, *xliii*
  Probate Act (1857), *xliv*
  sede vacante, xliv
  sentence, *xlv*n, *l, lxxiii, lxxv*
  see also court of probate

procession, of boy bishop, 507n

profit(s) of, corn, 338
  cow, 357, 692
  grain, 450
  land, 79, 126, 198, 362, 450, 482, 576, 604, 634, 669, 786, 787

prosecution (accusation), unjust, 221

provision, *see* finding

psalter, *see* book *and* church equipment: book

pulpit, *see* church equipment

purchase (sale), of property, *passim*
  best price, 90, 127, 148, 184, 230, 313, 338, 373, 384, 454, 456, 507, 508, 581, 585, 615, 634, 650, 665, 682, 697, 700, 706, 712, 731, 736, 748, 769, 779, 797, 826
  fair price, 318
  price spec., 16, 31, 68, 82, 85, 126, 153, 222, 184, 279, 294, 327, 440, 470, 481, 482, 490*, 532, 541, 570, 587, 599, 626, 631, 633, 650, 664, 673, 699, 700, 706, 732, 735, 738, 743, 744, 776, 788, 803*, 818, 820, 827
  purchaser spec. or preferred, 16, 31, 68, 82, 85, 89, 126, 153, 172, 182, 184, 209, 218, 224, 230, 258, 279, 294, 322, 327, 374, 391, 392, 408, 440, 451, 470, 481, 482,

490, 507, 532, 540, 541, 546, 570, 587, 594, 600, 604*, 617, 620, 626*, 631, 633, 641, 642, 644, 650, 652, 659, 663, 664, 673, 682, 683, 699, 700, 706, 732, 735, 738, 740, 743, 744, 748, 756, 758, 776, 788, 803*, 820*, 824, 826, 827
purgatory, *liii, lix, lxiv*
  souls in, 337
purse, velvet, 276
  with silver ring, 490
pyx, *see* church equipment

quart (volume), *see* measurement
quarter (of grain etc), *see* measurement
quern, *see* household goods
quilt, *see* beds and bedding

readeption of Henry VI, *li*, 426, 426n
real estate, *xlix, lxv, lxxi*
reaping, *see* agricultural work
rector, *see* parish clergy
rectory (benefice), 24n, 527n, 657
  (building), 80, 218, 350, 519
    gate, 821
  (manor), 581
reeds, for roofing, 450
re-entry, *see* distraint
register, of archdeaconry of Sudbury, Intro.
    passim
  'Baldwyne', *xlvi, xlvin, xlviii,*
    agreement recorded in, *lxxii*, 353
    assembling of, *lxxvi-lxxvii*
    binding errors in, *xlvi-xlviii, lxxvi*
    description of, *xlix, lxxv*
    probable lost folios of, *lxxvi-lxxvii*
    writing in, *lxxv,*
  'Fuller', *xlvin, xlviii, lxxvi, lxxvin*
    wills now in, included here, *lxxvin,*
      811–827
  'Hervye', *xlvin, xlviiin, lxxvi, lxxvin*
  'Holland', *lxxvin*
  'Sunday', *xlvn*
  of consistory court of Rochester, *xlvn*
  of sacrist of Bury, *xlv, xlvn*
relatives, *see also* executor (executrix): status;
    supervisor: status
  brother (deceased), 107, 168, 189, 210, 294, 754n, 824
    (living), 16, 38*, 50, 81, 89, 144, 151, 208, 247, 259, 285, 290, 312*, 312n, 330, 338, 345, 346, 367, 376, 385, 421, 431, 436, 447, 448, 452, 452n, 461, 461n, 466, 471, 508, 519, 525, 540*, 549*, 550*, 551, 572, 586*, 591*, 608*, 623, 626, 627, 629, 638*, 643, 646, 648, 656n, 668, 692, 695, 705*, 713, 723, 754, 778, 779, 818, 818n
      friar, 436, 779

with same Christian name (as testator), 247, 638, 812
brother-in-law, 359, 420, 420n, 493, 572, 595
child (deceased), 491*, 700*
  (living) *passim*
  step-child, 69*
cousin, 291, 530, 754, 754n
daughter (deceased), 646
  (living), *passim*
  with same Christian name, 53*, 237, 238, 247, 455, 484, 496, 504, 682, 808, 810
  daughter-in-law, 10, 32, 128, 138, 316*, 370, 542, 569, 597, 662, 698, 790, 803
  step-daughter, 112, 175, 179, 220, 527*, 630, 651, 786
father (deceased), 11, 24, 41, 46, 60, 79, 92, 125, 148, 278, 322, 408, 425, 447, 452, 470, 471, 489, 490, 519, 527, 559, 581, 601, 612, 621, 623, 626, 643n, 650, 651, 651n, 662, 670, 673, 687, 689, 709, 711, 772, 775, 779, 780, 785, 815, 823, 824
  (living), 5, 123, 144, 226, 264, 430, 508, 508n, 524, 549, 572, 588, 591, 603, 614, 627, 681, 705, 716, 771
  father-in-law (deceased), 661
  step-father, 166
grandchild, 10, 72, 76*, 209, 229*, 239*, 316*, 403*, 403n, 484*, 507*, 528*, 574*, 577*, 596*, 635*, 661*, 701*, 706*, 707*, 754*, 776*, 803*, 815*, 821*
granddaughter, 32*, 80, 94*, 94n, 128*, 239, 379, 401, 401n, 440, 498, 523n, 547, 634*, 662, 698, 701, 703*, 732*, 803*
grandfather (deceased), 60, 550
grandmother (deceased), 60
grandson, 1*, 32*, 60, 69*, 80*, 94, 97*, 116*, 128, 131*, 146, 180*, 244, 336*, 358, 379*, 401*, 401n, 431*, 523n, 533, 547*, 634*, 635, 642, 662, 725, 727*, 733, 790, 803,
  cleric, 244
  with same Christian name, 698*
husband (deceased), 32*, 32n, 57, 57n, 94, 100, 150*, 171*, 196, 211, 228, 241, 259, 268, 276, 333, 336, 352, 360, 368, 401, 407, 421, 438, 445, 451*, 453, 469, 470, 479n, 505, 546n*, 571, 584, 596, 605, 613, 647, 652*, 662*, 667, 669, 677, 685, 698, 699, 728*, 745, 760, 762, 768, 789, 803, 822
  former, of testator's wife, 205, 376
  (living), 57, 166, 233, 305, 333, 336, 435, 469, 583, 644, 677, 689, 728
kinsman, 574
kinswoman, 229, 436, 698*, 779
mother (deceased), 11, 16n, 24, 41, 46, 60, 66, 79, 125, 148, 166, 278, 405, 408, 425, 452,

452n, 470, 490, 503, 527, 550, 559, 601,
    621, 650, 651, 651n, 656, 662, 687, 688,
    709, 711, 768, 772, 775, 779, 780, 785,
    815, 823, 824
    (living), 2, 139, 187, 208, 210, 219, 309,
        343, 351, 382, 437, 519, 525, 572, 588,
        614, 623, 643, 645, 680, 763, 804
        husband of, 405n
    mother-in-law (deceased), 90n, 621
    step-mother, 716
nephew, 38, 125, 131, 151*, 168, 189, 210,
    229, 255, 294*, 350*, 402, 461*, 463*,
    495, 523, 629, 648*, 738, 754, 786*
next of kin, 360
niece, 12, 50, 69, 107, 151*, 294, 500, 523,
    648*, 682, 720, 782*, 786*
sister (living), 50, 154, 225, 251, 331*, 338,
    351, 359, 365, 417, 420, 428, 447*, 463,
    466, 519, 549, 550, 566, 572*, 591, 608*,
    623*, 648, 651, 662, 680, 688*, 708*, 772,
    782, 804
    sister-in-law (deceased), 824
        (living), 11, 38, 107, 466n, 661
son (deceased), 128, 596, 596n, 646
    (living), *passim*
    canon, 242, 429
    cleric, *lix*n, 32, 32n, 127, 205, 231, 242,
        252, 469, 519, 596, 650, 733, 820
    friar, 31, 374, 428, 436, 726*
    marriage of, 65
    with same Christian name, 10, 35, 39, 60,
        70, 71, 77, 121, 125, 145, 187, 194*,
        214, 224, 233, 266, 320, 389, 422, 464,
        504, 531, 536, 544, 596, 626, 628, 661,
        673*, 676, 707, 738, 761, 777, 792, 809
    son-in-law (deceased), 259
        (living), 148, 180, 247n*, 268, 311, 417,
            476*, 484, 502, 507, 522, 574*, 634,
            635, 733, 821
        ?step-son, 756
    step-son, 562, 630, 640*
uncle, 11, 53, 508, 508n, 598
wife (deceased), 10, 24*, 83*, 101, 107*, 109,
    111*, 154, 189, 203, 204*, 205, 221, 246*,
    278, 312, 313*, 342, 345*, 354, 381, 428,
    436, 454, 472n, 490, 586, 621, 626*, 630,
    646, 678, 687, 694, 700, 714*, 763, 772,
    779, 785, 819, 820
    (living), *passim*
    pregnant, 193, 226, 240, 350, 405, 581,
        601, 688, 744
religious (persons), abbess, 212, 782
    abbot, *lxxvi*n, 435, 492, 555
    canon(s) (Austin), 69, 126n, 220, 228, 362,
        398, 723, 738, 776, 777, 799
        (named), 125, 220, 240, 429, 527, 544
        and nuns (Gilbertines), 187
    cellarer, 821

friar(s) (unspec.), 206, 438, 552, 603
    chaplain, 602
    (named), 22, 22n, 31, 32, 32n, 34, 38, 46,
        57n, 68, 109*, 109n, 133, 133n, 145,
        145n, 160, 166, 171, 187, 191, 238,
        238n, 240, 240n, 276, 305, 372, 372n,
        374, 381, 381n, 391, 414, 414n, 436,
        470, 488*, 505, 574, 659, 665, 670*,
        726*, 741, 760, 779*, 790, 797, 799,
        803*
    Augustinian (Austin), *lx*, 1, 1n, 6, 6n, 11,
        21, 38, 42, 46, 50, 96, 69n, 72, 78, 79,
        83, 87, 90, 96, 101, 121, 125, 126, 131,
        133, 152, 154, 157, 159, 160, 173, 184,
        189, 191, 202, 207, 219, 224, 228, 238,
        239, 240, 246, 247, 258, 266, 269, 290,
        294, 295, 300, 311, 317, 323, 338, 339,
        348, 361, 365, 367, 379, 391, 392, 393,
        404, 410, 420, 424, 427, 436, 453, 454,
        461, 467, 475, 477, 482, 485, 500, 504,
        507, 508, 522, 528, 537, 544, 565, 570,
        590, 598, 600, 604, 624, 628, 634, 636,
        657, 661, 668, 673, 682, 684, 700*, 714,
        722, 723, 725, 729, 731, 738, 754, 770,
        779*, 785, 789, 792, 795, 802, 820, 821
    Carmelite, *lx*, 1, 1n, 42, 42n, 50, 78, 79, 80,
        83, 87*, 89, 90, 94n, 111, 126, 133, 136,
        136n, 152, 157, 160, 191, 205, 246, 247,
        269, 381, 382, 436, 449, 461, 467, 482,
        484, 508, 528, 576, 594, 628, 659, 665,
        669, 673, 700, 706, 733, 738, 751, 754,
        755, 779, 785, 805
    Crutched, 191
    Dominican (Preachers), *lx*, 11, 11n, 38, 43,
        46, 50, 50n, 55, 65, 67, 68, 68n, 72, 74,
        78, 79, 80n, 83, 87*, 89, 94n, 96, 101,
        107, 109, 116, 120, 126, 131, 133, 134,
        136, 145, 152, 154, 157, 160, 180, 184,
        191, 205, 209, 212, 219, 228, 238, 239,
        240, 246, 247, 258, 259, 265, 266, 268,
        271, 281, 283, 290, 294, 295, 300, 307,
        309, 311, 317, 321, 322, 338, 339, 348,
        352, 356, 362, 365, 367*, 367n, 379,
        381, 382, 386, 393, 399, 404, 413, 414,
        424, 427, 436, 453, 454, 461, 465, 467,
        475, 477, 482, 484, 485, 489, 494, 499,
        502, 504, 505, 507, 508, 519, 522, 528,
        537, 570, 573, 579, 589, 590, 594, 599,
        600, 604, 606, 607, 613, 624, 628, 636,
        650, 651, 657, 664, 669, 673, 681, 682,
        684, 690, 698, 700, 702, 719, 722, 723,
        725, 729, 731, 732, 738, 744, 751, 754,
        767, 779, 785, 789, 792, 797, 805, 816,
        817, 820, 821
    Franciscan (Minors), *lx*, 1, 1n, 10, 11*,
        35, 37, 38*, 39, 45, 45n, 48, 50*, 54,
        55, 65*, 67, 68, 72, 74, 78, 79, 80, 81,
        83, 85, 87*, 88, 89*, 93, 94n, 95, 101,

107, 109, 111, 112, 115, 119, 120, 121,
125, 126, 127, 128, 131, 133, 134, 135,
136, 138, 145, 149, 150, 152, 154, 157,
159, 160, 168, 179, 180, 184, 191, 202,
205, 207, 207n, 209, 210, 219, 224, 227,
228, 238, 239, 240, 241, 243, 246, 247,
253, 258, 260, 265, 266, 268, 281*, 291,
294, 295, 300, 302, 313, 317, 321, 322,
323, 324, 333, 334, 337, 339, 348, 350,
352, 361, 362, 365, 366, 367, 378, 379,
381*, 388, 391, 392, 399, 404, 410, 415,
424, 427, 432, 436, 448, 451, 453, 454,
461, 467, 470*, 477, 482, 484, 485, 486,
490*, 494, 502, 507, 508, 515, 519, 528,
529, 536, 537, 538, 540, 567, 568, 569,
570, 573, 579, 588, 590, 591, 594, 595,
599, 604*, 606, 609, 613*, 615, 624,
625, 628, 634, 636, 647, 651, 654*, 655,
657, 665*, 666, 668, 669, 672, 673, 681,
682, 697, 700, 701, 705, 706, 709, 712,
719, 723, 725, 729, 732, 733, 734, 738,
751, 754, 760, 770, 772, 773, 775, 779,
785, 786, 789, 792, 797, 805, 812, 816,
817, 820, 821, 822
  of all four orders, lx, lxn, 22, 78, 79, 83,
    126, 133, 133n, 142, 152, 157, 160, 187,
    191, 204, 244, 246, 247, 286, 436, 461,
    467, 482, 508, 528, 628, 673, 700, 738,
    754, 763, 779, 785, 796
  Trinitarian, lxi, lxiiin, 295, 634, 636
hospitaller, of Bury St Edmunds, 128, 128n
  of St John of Jerusalem, 449n
monk(s), lx, lxn, 46, 88, 159, 276, 636, 821
  (named), 88, 147, 276, 282, 782, 790n
  novice, 723*
nun(s), lx, 68, 68n, 83, 83n, 89*, 107, 120,
  126, 157, 186, 294, 337, 338, 453, 529,
  590, 634, 646, 698, 726, 792, 820
  (named), 89, 187, 417
prior, 69, 220, 362, 723, 723n, 726, 765, 777,
  790n, 797n
  sub-prior, 69, 723
prioress, 83, 590, 646, 726
sacrist (monastic), xlv, xlvn, 826
vicar of college (named), 637
religious houses, xlviii, lx
  for individual houses see Index of People and
    Places, sub:
  BABWELL, house of Franciscan friars
  BATTISFORD, preceptory/hospital of Knights
    Hospitallers
  BROMEHILL (Nfk), priory of Augustinian
    canons
  BROMHOLME (Nfk), priory of Cluniac
    monks
  BRUISYARD, abbey of Franciscan nuns
  BURY ST EDMUNDS, abbey of Benedictine
    monks
    hospital by Risby gate (St Peter)
    hospital of St Saviour
  CAMBRIDGE, house of Augustinian friars
    house of Carmelite friars
    house of Dominican friars
    house of Franciscan friars
  (CASTLE) HEDINGHAM (Esx), priory of
    Benedictine nuns
  CLARE, house of Augustinian friars
  COLCHESTER, house of Franciscan friars
  DUNWICH, house of Dominican friars
    house of Franciscan friars
  EYE, hospital of St Mary Magdalene
    priory of Benedictine monks
  FORDHAM (Cambs), priory of Gilbertine
    canons
  HOXNE, priory of Benedictine monks
  IPSWICH, hospital of St Leonard
    hospital of St Mary Magdalene and St
      James
    house of Carmelite friars
    house of Dominican friars
    house of Franciscan friars
    priory of Austin canons
  IXWORTH, priory of Austin canons
  LANGLEY (Nfk), house of Premonstratensian
    canons
  LONDON, college of St Anthony
    college of St Thomas of Acre
    house of Dominican friars (unspec.)
    priory of Knights Hospitallers, Clerkenwell
  MALLING (Kent), abbey of Benedictine nuns
  MOTTENDEN (Kent), priory of Trinitarian
    friars
  NORWICH, hospital of St Benedict
    hospital of St Giles
    hospital of St Leonard
    hospital of St Mary and St Clement
    hospital of St Mary Magdalene
    hospital of St Stephen
    house of Austin friars
    house of Carmelite friars
    house of Dominicans
    house of Franciscans
  ORFORD, house of Augustinian friars
  REDLINGFIELD, priory of Benedictine nuns
  SHOULDHAM (Nfk), priory of Gilbertine
    canons
  SIBTON, abbey of Cistercian monks
  SPINNEY (in WICKEN, Cambs), priory of
    Augustinian canons
  STOKE by CLARE, college of St John the
    Baptist
  SUDBURY, college of St Gregory
    house of Dominican friars
  SWAFFHAM BULBECK (Cambs), priory of
    Benedictine nuns
  THETFORD, house of Austin friars

237

house of Dominican friars
priory of Benedictine nuns
WALSINGHAM (Nfk), house of Franciscan
   friars
WHELNETHAM, GREAT, house of Crutched
   friars
see also convent; friary; priory
remuneration, *see* wages
rent (income), yearly (spec.), 417
   rent-rolls, 229
rent (let), property, 483, 571
renter, *see* buildings
repairs to (house, etc.), *see* buildings
   (road, etc.,) *see* road
requiem, *see* church services: mass
retable, *see* church equipment: panel
reversion (of right to property), 89, 148*, 268,
   276, 550, 626, 650
ring, *see* gold *and* silver
river, *xlvi*
   bank, 803
road (path, lane, street, way, etc) (spec.), 2, 11,
   11n, 12, 12n, 30*, 43, 52, 56, 60*, 67, 78, 80,
   83, 89, 90, 102, 117, 122, 125, 133, 142, 180,
   181, 182, 190, 203, 206, 209*, 220, 225, 228,
   232*, 247*, 251, 261, 268*, 282, 285, 311,
   314, 332, 338, 339, 343*, 350, 352, 355, 361,
   362, 365, 370, 371, 383, 388, 401*, 402, 404,
   423, 430, 432, 436, 440*, 454, 457*, 459, 480,
   482, 500, 501, 502, 504*, 512, 517, 519*, 521,
   552, 559, 579, 590, 591*, 592, 615, 621, 628,
   634, 637, 642, 643, 645, 649, 659*, 661, 662,
   665, 669*, 681*, 683*, 684, 687*, 688, 700*,
   702, 703, 707, 716, 720, 722, 735, 738*, 748,
   750, 754, 758, 762, 770, 773, 779, 784, 785,
   786, 803*, 823*
   'caste and graveled', 350
   repairs to, *lxii, lxiii*, 2n, 19, 21, 43, 55, 60, 76,
      78, 80, 83, 87, 89, 90, 102, 122, 125*, 142,
      148, 152, 180, 182, 212, 228, 251, 261,
      268*, 282, 285, 295, 300*, 311, 314, 335,
      338, 339, 343*, 350*, 352, 355, 361, 362,
      365, 370, 388, 402, 404, 420, 423, 430,
      432, 452, 454, 457*, 482, 498, 500, 518*,
      521, 525, 539, 559, 579, 590, 591*, 592,
      593, 615, 618, 621, 625, 628, 634, 637,
      642, 645, 649, 662, 665, 669, 681, 700*,
      706, 716, 733*, 735, 744, 748, 770, 773,
      785, 786*, 798, 803*
      materials for, *lxiii*, 457, 642, 785
         clay, *lxiii*, 457
         sand, 785
         stone, *lxiii*, 642
   sloughs in, 361
robe, *see* clothes
rochet, *see* church equipment: vestment
rood, rood-loft, *see* church equipment
rood (of land), *see* measurement

roof, *see* church building
room (bakehouse, chamber, hall, solar etc,) *see*
   buildings
rosary, *see* beads
russet, *see* material
rye, *see* crops

sacrist, *see* parish officers
saddle, *see* harness
saints, *see* advower, church dedication, feast-
   days, feasts, gild-patron, image, pilgrimage,
   tabernacle
salary/stipend, of canon, 799
   of chaplain/priest, 11, 43, 51, 55, 66, 75, 79,
      80, 83, 87, 93, 100, 101, 107, 148, 184,
      187, 189, 225, 230, 238, 239, 240, 259,
      276, 290, 311, 339, 350, 374, 401, 421,
      451, 456, 469, 490*, 507, 537, 546, 555,
      571, 607, 642, 648, 661, 662, 669, 681*,
      682, 687, 707, 710, 724, 750, 754, 769,
      773, 774, 779, 801, 803, 805, 818*, 819
   of clerk, 517
   of friar, 46, 240, 438, 552
   of pilgrim, 508, 640,
      half a salary, 294*
   of servant, 634*
salet, *see* weapons and armour
salt-cellar, *see* household goods, pewter *and* silver
sand, for road repairs, 785
sangred, *see* church services: certain
sarcenet, *see* material
satin, *see* material
saucer, *see* household goods *and* pewter
saw, *see* tools and equipment
say, *see* material
scales, *see* household goods
school, 579, 733
   grammar, *xlviiin*, 482, 720, 721
score (twenty), *see* measurement
screen, *see* furniture
seal, of official, 13, 14, 15, 55, 68, 72, 73, 81, 82,
      89, 101, 118, 119, 120, 124, 145, 147, 148,
      151, 152, 159, 162, 167, 171, 187, 188,
      193, 194, 197, 204, 205, 209, 210, 211,
      232, 240, 251, 252, 255, 279, 281, 290,
      293, 302, 365, 375, 404, 405, 406, 431,
      474, 476, 484, 490, 507, 549, 593, 629,
      634, 650, 661, 668, 682, 683, 684, 685,
      686, 697, 700, 708, 709, 714, 733, 756,
      763, 797, 799, 819
   of testator, 1, 2, 11, 14, 21, 22, 25, 27, 28, 31,
      32, 36, 46, 47, 50, 54, 56, 58, 67, 70, 72,
      81, 82, 83, 85, 87, 88, 89, 101, 104, 107,
      113, 117, 118, 120, 121, 122, 123, 125,
      127, 134, 138, 147, 148, 150, 153, 154,
      155, 157, 158, 160, 171, 174, 175, 180,
      181, 183, 189, 191, 194, 197, 198, 203,
      204, 205*, 209, 212, 216, 220, 225, 229,

230, 232, 235, 240*, 242, 243, 245, 246,
247, 251, 255, 259, 260, 262, 270, 271,
272, 276, 279, 286, 294, 295, 297, 298,
300, 302, 311, 331, 337, 338, 350, 352,
355, 362, 368, 369, 371, 372, 373, 374,
375, 376, 378, 379, 381, 382, 383, 385,
387, 388, 389, 391, 393, 395, 397, 398,
399, 400, 401, 402, 403, 404, 405*, 406,
407, 409, 410, 412, 413, 417*, 419, 420,
423, 426, 428, 430, 431, 434, 436, 437,
440, 442, 450, 452, 453, 454, 455, 456,
457, 461, 462, 463, 464, 465, 466, 467,
468, 471, 473, 475, 476, 478, 479, 483,
486, 487, 489, 490, 491, 493, 497, 499,
503, 506, 508, 511, 512, 514, 516, 517,
521, 522, 527, 528, 532, 535, 538, 540,
544, 545, 547, 549, 550, 551, 552, 555,
556, 557, 558, 559, 561, 563, 564, 565,
566, 567, 569, 570, 573, 574, 576, 579,
580, 581, 583, 594, 595, 596, 598, 601,
603, 606, 607, 608, 609, 610, 611, 613,
615, 617, 619, 621, 622, 625, 628, 629,
630, 632, 634, 635, 636, 637, 638, 640,
642, 643, 646, 647, 650, 657, 660, 661*,
662, 663, 664, 665, 666, 667, 668, 669,
671, 673, 675, 678, 679, 680, 682, 683,
684, 687, 688, 693, 694, 695, 696, 697,
700, 701, 702, 704, 706, 709, 710, 711,
712, 713, 716, 717, 719, 720, 723, 724,
726, 727*, 728, 731, 733*, 734, 738, 739,
740, 741, 746, 750, 751, 754, 755, 759,
761, 762, 763, 765, 766, 767, 769, 772,
773, 776, 777, 778, 779*, 780, 782, 783,
784, 785, 787, 789, 792, 795, 797, 801,
803, 804, 806, 810, 812, 815, 816, 820
sealed, not (specifically stated), 392
  with own hand, 262, 272, 276, 434
seam, *see* measurement
security (surety) (for payment), 46, 74, 89, 417,
  784
seisin, delivery of, 31
  see also possession
sepulchre, *see* church equipment
servant, *see* status
seven-day, *see* church services
sexton, *see* parish officers
sheep, *lxviii**, 22*, 28*, 80*, 81*, 116*, 152*,
  157*, 185, 187*, 190*, 215, 226*, 232*,
  272*, 286*, 298*, 304*, 343*, 350*, 351,
  355, 362, 368, 379*, 417*, 461*, 466*,
  490*, 507*, 544*, 599*, 622*, 623*, 630*,
  636*, 654*, 700*, 729*, 742, 754*, 773*,
  790*, 800, 823*
  as mortuary, 304
  ewe (mother sheep), *lxviii*, 1*, 10*, 60*, 72*,
    76*, 80*, 93*, 129*, 142*, 187*, 204*,
    208*, 219*, 226*, 229*, 230*, 232, 234,
    239*, 243*, 246*, 258*, 265, 282*, 286*,

298, 319*, 321*, 324, 338*, 362, 374*,
    399*, 403*, 414, 461*, 471*, 483*, 534*,
    539*, 563*, 622*, 634*, 636*, 731*, 733*,
    754*, 777*, 790, 809*, 816*
  and/with lamb, 142, 234, 282*, 291, 370,
    402*, 472, 544*, 588*, 623, 731*, 757*,
    826
    with their wool, 653*
  to provide for light(s), 539*, 634*
  ewe-hogge, 60*, 208*
  flock, 229*
  hog (hogget, sheephog), *lxviii*, 229*, 319*,
    414, 461*, 636*, 826*, 826n
  lamb, *lxviii*, 60*, 97*, 142, 204*, 219, 232,
    234*, 282*, 298*, 304*, 319*, 324, 331*,
    342*, 417, 461*, 485*, 630*, 636*, 654,
    733*, 823*
  wether, 219*, 226*, 229*, 258*, 319, 342*,
    471*, 485*, 590*, 626*, 634*, 754*, 816*,
    826*
  to provide for light(s), 634*
  wether hog, *lxviii*, 636*
sheet, *see* beds and bedding
shield, *see* weapons and armour
shoes, *see* clothes
shop, *lxxii*, *lxxii*n, 103*, 468
  'Cornereschope, le', 727
  in High Street, 87
  in town/market, *lxxii*, *lxxii*n, 80*, 359, 607,
    607n
  stuff, 456
  workshop, *lxix*, *lxxii*, 668, 740
    ?herbalist's, 79
    smith's, 778
  see also market stall
sick in body (etc), *lii*, 35, 50, 53, 55, 67, 120,
    121, 133, 150, 154, 155, 160, 166, 189,
    285, 303, 318, 321, 370, 379, 408, 423,
    425, 427, 431, 433, 458, 498, 518, 596,
    597, 628, 682, 685, 686, 713, 742
  see also death (sick unto)
silk, *see* material
silver (unspec.), 405
  beads, 698, 782
  belt (girdle), 229, 390, 445, 519, 701
    for horn, 505
    bound with, 445, 779
  bowl, 247, 259, 698*
    with cover, 191
  brooch, 142
  chalice, 559, 682
  container, called a 'pouder boxe', 191
  goblet, 38, 470
    and gilt, 309
  horn goblet bound with, 445
  knife, 42*
  mazer, bound with, *lxvi*, 779
    bound with silver-gilt, 83

ornamented with, and gilt, 698
money, 797
paternosters (on beads), 421
piece, 32
ring (on beads), 276, 351, 613
  (on purse), 490
salt(-cellar), 191
  with cover, 191, 259
spoon, *lxvi*, 32*, 83*, 191*, 205*, 245*, 247*,
  259*, 276*, 316*, 446*, 456*, 579*, 601*,
  662*, 669*, 698*, 728*, 779*, 782*
  of one pattern, 803*
  with lions & crowns, decorated with gold,
    lxvi, 803*
  with the round 'Acres', 436*, 779*
  studded with, 436, 490, 779
silvered (harnessed, ornamented etc), 1, 32*, 115,
  228, 229, 246, 247*, 276, 285, 290, 311, 348*,
  350, 390, 417*, 421, 505 , 613, 652, 662, 698
  and gilt, 417
silver-gilt, 83, 191*
sister, *see* relatives
sleeve, *see* measurement
smock, *see* clothes
soap, *see* household goods
solar, *see* buildings
son, son-in-law, step-son, *see* relatives
sowing, *see* agricultural work
spinning-wheel, *see* cloth-making
spit, *see* household goods
spoon, *see* household goods *and* silver
stable, *see* buildings
stall, *see* market
stations, of Rome, 89, 184, 251
status, *li*, *liv*
  abbess, *see* religious persons
  abbot, *see* religious persons
  apprentice, 31, 219, 247, 454, 803
    see also apprenticeship
  archbishop, *xlivn*, *xlv*
  beadle, *see* parish officers
  better sort, *lxiii*
  bishop, *xlv*
  canon, *see* religious persons
  cellarer, *see* religious persons
  chaplain, *see* parish clergy
  chief inhabitants, 342n
  choirmaster, *see* parish officers
  churchwarden, *lii*, **424**
    see also parish officers
  citizen of London, 505n
  clerk, *li*, **624**
    see also parish clergy; parish officers
  confessor, 213
  curate, *see* parish clergy
  daughter, **711**
    see also relatives
  deacon, *see* parish clergy

dean, of college, *xlviiin*
dearest friends, 405
discreet man, 17*
Doctor, 797
Dom., 519, 782
earl, 67, 762
esquire, *li*, 51, 69, 125*, 154, 174, 181*, 187,
  191*, 213, 243, 259, 297, 409, 417, 436,
  457, 650, 733, 785, 789
executor, **153**
executrix, **268**, 276, **360**
faithful friend, 406
freeman, 417*
friar, *see* religious persons
gentleman, *li*, *lxxvin*, 30, 67, 148, 213, 235,
  283, 295*, 297, **402**, 409, **417**, 480, 508,
  608, 789
great of the parish, 342
hospitaller, *see* religious persons
holy-water clerk, *see* parish officers
husbandman, *li*, **373**, **459**, **595**, 634
knight (Sir), 38, 372, 398
labourer, 595
lady (Dame), 38, 398, 709*
  see also manor: lady of
maid (servant), 275
master (superior, lord), *lxiii*, 1, 38, 187, 213,
  398, 785
  see also manor: lord of
Master (title), *xlivn*, *xlvn*, *xlviii*, *lxxvin*, 29,
  38, 46, 69, 89, 109, 127, 150, 154, 196,
  205, 236, 248, 276, 286, 318, 341, 348,
  409, 414, 435, 444, 459, 503, 546, 556,
  573, 621, 624, 646, 650, 673, 687, 778,
  785, 786, 788, 799, 820, 822*
  venerable, 790
Master of Arts, 459
mistress (lady), 779
monk, *see* religious persons
needy poor man, 785,
neighbours, 399, 665, **714**
  poor, 171, 648
nun, *see* religious persons
of the 'botery', 38
official, archdeacon's, *see* archdeacon
  of parish, *see* parish officers
parish clerk, *see* parish officers
parishioner, **342**
parson, *see* parish clergy
poet laureate, *lxxvin*
priest, *see* parish clergy
prior, *see* religious persons
prioress, *see* religious persons
rector, *see* parish clergy
sacrist (monastic), *see* religious persons
  (parochial), *see* parish officers
servant, 31, 32, 46*, 50*, 60, 69, 72, 80, 87,
  89*, 150, 154*, 181*, 184*, 191*, 209,

220, 228, 232, 233, 240, 247*, 259, 269,
276, 320, 374*, 381*, 399, 400, 402*, 403,
432, 436, 439, 440, 457, 470*, 470n, 471,
490, 517, 519, 540*, 559, 570, 586, 608,
611, 634*, 636, 652, 665, 669*, 677, 698*,
709, 774*, 779, 803*, 819*, 823
sexton, *see* parish officers
sub-prior, *see* religious persons
townsman, 392*
trustworthy person, 17*, 65*, 502*, 546*
vicar of college, *see* religious persons
  of parish, *see* parish clergy
virginity, pure, **709**
widow (relict, late the wife), *li*, **34**, **150**, **196**,
  228, **239**, **241**, 258, **259**, **276**, 276, **317**,
  318, **352**, **368**, **401**, **407**, **431**, **438**, **445**n,
  453, **458**, **479**, **500**, **505**, **528**, **533**, **584**,
  596, **613**, **647**, **652**, **656**, **662**, **685**, **698**,
  699, **701**, 709*, **759**, **762**, **768**, **803**, **822**
  remarried, **469**
widowhood, pure, 168, 170, 240, 246, 276,
  318, 620, 652
wife, *passim, but also*, *li*, **305**, **333**, **336**, **644**,
  677, **689**, **728**
yeoman, 191*, 470n
steeple, *see* church building
stile, near church, 203
stirk, *see* cattle
stock (goods of all kinds), 11, 247, 354
  children, 102
  of cows, to maintain light in church, 330
  valuation, 11
  see animals: farm, *for* livestock
stoddles, *see* cloth-making
stone, for building, 350
  cartloads of, *lvi*, 80, 182, 252, 642, 649
  for grave, 266
  mortar, 806
  precious, diamond, 38
  semi-precious, amber, 129, 142, 701, 803
  walls, of churchyard, 574
stool, *see* church equipment *and* furniture
store-room, *see* buildings
straw, *see* building repairs *and* crops
straw hat, *see* clothes
suit (legal), 417
supervisor, *lxix*, *lxxiv*
  admon. granted to, 476
  appointed by probate court, *lxix*, 68, 399*
  appointed by testator, *lxix*, 1, 10, 16, 29, 36,
    50, 51, 53, 57*, 61*, 65, 66, 68, 80, 89, 92,
    112, 126, 134, 135, 139*, 152, 154, 171,
    174, 180, 181, 188, 190, 194, 196, 205,
    210, 214, 220, 237, 241, 243, 247, 250*,
    258, 262, 270, 285, 286, 294, 295, 297*,
    303, 314, 320, 321, 324, 325, 334*, 338,
    339, 342, 345, 349, 350, 359, 365, 371*,
    376, 380, 382, 393, 417*, 425, 432*, 435,

436, 438, 446, 457, 459*, 461*, 468, 471,
472, 476, 482*, 483, 490, 500, 502, 504*,
516, 522, 524, 532, 533, 544, 546, 555,
560, 561, 562, 563, 573, 574, 580, 585,
602, 621, 626, 628, 631, 650, 651, 654*,
673, 677, 692, 704, 713, 716, 720*, 721*,
729, 731, 737, 738, 742, 743, 744, 764,
765, 769, 772, 775, 779, 785, 788, 799,
815, 822, 825
  payment of, 1, 80, 180, 205, 210, 243, 258,
    262, 294, 334*, 339, 342, 365, 376, 380,
    432, 436, 471, 476, 544, 574, 628, 654*,
    738, 744, 772, 779, 788, 815
  status of, brother, 247, 345, 626, 692
    brother-in-law, 482
    cleric, *lxix*, 16, 29, 36, 65, 112, 118, 134,
      135, 152, 187, 194, 196, 205, 241, 258,
      262, 270, 286, 303, 320, 321, 338, 342,
      365, 376, 392, 393, 425, 435, 438, 446,
      472, 476, 500, 502, 522, 532, 533, 546,
      555, 574, 602, 621, 628, 631, 673, 716,
      720, 721, 729, 742, 769, 775, 788, 822
    daughter, 432
    husband, 57
    notary, 799
    son, 152
    wife, 53, 285, 461, 482
support, *see* finding
surety, *see* security
surplice, *see* church equipment: vestment
surrender (of copyhold), 45n, 238, 433, 661, 707
sword, *see* weapons and armour

tabard, *see* clothes
tabernacle, *see* church equipment
table, *see* furniture
tablecloth, *see* cloths (household)
tallow, 456
taxes, bequest for paying, *lxiv*, 383, 634
  fifteenth, *lxiv*, 240
    bequest for paying, *lxiv*, 240, 240n, 634
    subsidy to pay archers' wages (1472), *lxiv*n
  taxation 'quota', *lxiv*
tenant, *see* manor
tenement, *see* buildings
tenter, *see* cloth-making
tester, *see* beds and bedding
thirty-day, *see* church services
throne, *see* church equipment
tiles, to repair room, 430
tilling, *see* agricultural work
timber, *see* crops
tithe(s), *liii–liv*
  of woods, 35
title, right and (to lands), 474
  see also estate
toft, *see* land usage
tools and equipment (necessaries), of craft

(trade), *lxix*, 160, 240, 413, 456, 490, 508, 668, 704, 771, 818
anvil, 815
auger, 240*
axe (belt), 240, 490
  'brod', 723
  chipaxe, 490
  felling, 490, 723
  'luggyng', 723
bark vat, 517
bellows, pair of, 815
hammer, 815*
hatchet, 490
ostilments, 325
saw, compass, 723
  hand, 723
  'kyttyng', 723
  splitting, 723
  wimble, 723*
shears, pair of, 354
'sqwyer', 723
tongs, pairs of, 815*
'tovere', 815
twbyll, 490, 723
wheel, 815
wood-knife, 205
of craftsman, smith's, 778, 815
  to make door & plank nails, 815
  tanner's, 517
  wheelwright's, 240
torch, *see* church equipment: lights
towel, *see* church equipment *and* cloths
  (household)
tower, *see* church building
town, clerk of, 11, 87
  men of, 450
  precincts of, 102
trammel, *see* household goods
transom, *see* beds and bedding
treen, *see* woodenware
trees and plants, fruit, 417, 733
  herbages, 417
  quick hedge, 417
  trees, apple, 262, 417
    not to be cut down, 417, 472
    for repairing bridge, 362
    pear, 417
trencher, *see* household goods
trental, *see* church services
trestle, *see* furniture
Trinity, invocation to, 229
trivet, *see* household goods
trustworthy, *see* status
tumbrel, *see* agricultural equipment
tunic, *see* clothes

uncle, *see* relatives
underclothes, *see* beds and bedding

undergarment, *see* clothes: smock
university of Cambridge, 24, 24n
  scholar of, 187
unjust claim, *see* land
upkeep, *see* maintenance
usufruct, 824

vacancy of episcopal see, *xliv*, 790
vagrant poor, hospitality for, 342
valuables (general), 306
vat, *see* household goods
veil, *see* clothes
velvet, *see* material
vessels, *see* brass, household goods *and* pewter
vestment, *see* church equipment
viaticum, *see* church equipment
vicar, *see* parish clergy
visitation, of archdeacon, *lxxiii*
visitor for chapter of Norwich Cathedral, 790

wages, of servant, 50*, 89
waste (or strip), impeachment of, 76, 405
  not to be committed, 91, 125, 126, 182, 193, 205, 472, 532, 576, 634, 692, 780
water way, private, 717
wax, 397
  at burial, *liv*, 46
  candle(s), 24, 330, 371, 692, 699
  for church, 336
  for Easter sepulchre, 416, 519, 605
  as gild membership dues or fines, *lxii*
  seal, of will, *lxxi*
  for torches, 359
wealth, tithes as a guide to, *liv*
weapons and armour, *lxvii*
  archer's bracer, 697
  arrows, *lxvii*, 240, 266, 572
  axe, *lxvii*, 697
  basilard, 350
    ornamented with silver, 290
  body armour, complete suit of, 181
  buckler ('bokelere'), *lxvii*, 697
  bow, *lxvii**, 240, 266, 572, 697
  dagger, 572
    silvered, 1
  helm (helmet), 697
  jack, 'jakke', *lxvii*, 240, 456, 540, 547
  javelin, 697
  salet, *lxvii*, 240, 266, 456, 547
  shield, *lxvii*, 240
  sword, *lxvii**, 240, 697
  tapet, 697
  tunic, defensive, *lxvii*, 697
weights, *see* lead
well, *see* buildings
wheat, *see* crops
wheel, parts of, 240
  felloes, 240

naves, 240
spokes, 240
widow, *passim*
  companion for, 218
  contesting will, 778
  death of, goods distributed after, 162
    goods kept safe after, 74
  legal inheritance of, 35, 35n
  making unjust accusation, 221
  marriage of, *see* marriage: remarriage
  not to cause trouble, 374
  obstructing inheritance, 91
  see also maintenance; need; status
wife, *see* relatives
will, *passim*
  bipartite, 125
  closed and sealed, 204
  codicil to, 292, 293
  deletions and insertions in, 417
  doubts, difficulties (etc.) in, 229
  in English, *see* English
  entered twice (with/without variations), 44 &
    89, 48 & 86, 72 & 403, 74 & Vol I: 1440,
    99 & 808, 172 & 177, 196 & 211, 210 &
    Vol I: 1200, 229 & 287, 291 & 296, 292 &
    293, 384 & 399, 436 & 779, 463 & 563,
    465 & 607, 515 & 538, 621 & 694, 661 &
    707, 669 & Vol I: 943, 720 & 721, 792 &
    Hervye, fol. 357
  form of, *xlix–l*
  of husband and wife proved together, 233 &
    234, 359 & 360, 570 & 571
  invocation in, *l*
  made by licence and will of husband, 57
  made in testator's dwelling, 46, 125
  memorandum/note added, 1, 53, 353
  original, *lxxi*, 89, 211, 261, 299, 459, 523,
    783
  previous, revoked (renounced), 209, 408, 634
  'proper', form of, *lxxi*
    as indented deed, *lxxi*, 125
    proved separately from testament, *lxxi*, 327
     & 348
  referred to, of father, 447, 489, 626, 670, 673,
    689, 769
    of grandfather, 550
    of husband, 57, 94, 259, 268, 276, 305,
     360, 445, 505, 571, 613, 677
    of mother, 405
    of wife's former husband, 89
  seal, *xlvin*, *lxxi*
    sealing, *lxxi*
    seal-tag, *xlvin*, *lxxi*
  testament and, *xlix–l*
  written, 'by my hand', 22
    in parish missal, 626, 626n
    remembered and (not nuncupative), 166,
     225

    in third person (not nuncupative), 345
  see also probate
will, nuncupative, *lii*, 17, 23, 30, 59, 79, 117, 119,
  129, 145, 213, 248, 281, 283, 299, 301, 333,
  360, 363, 392, 415, 435, 446, 447, 490, 496,
  526, 548, 566, 572, 584, 605, 627, 648, 656,
  670, 708, 714, 725, 752, 798, 807
will 'proper' (with separate testament), *xlix*, *lxxi*,
  10, 27, 46, 55, 74, 79, 80, 89, 107, 113, 118,
  125, 126, 154, 160, 182, 188, 191, 204, 205,
  225, 240, 244, 266, 319, 327 (testament is
  348), 335, 344, 377, 399, 405, 417, 433, 461,
  482, 483, 490, 501, 544, 623, 629, 661, 669,
  682, 687, 720, 727, 733, 776, 779, 809, 818
  (only), *lxxiii*, 28, 153, 290, 336, 345, 434, 801
  partial, 292, 293
will, testament and last (composite), *l*, *lxxiii*, 53,
  181, 229, 359 (see 360), 381, 459, 467, 492,
  500, 521, 545, 554, 581, 591, 595, 597, 604,
  611, 624, 635, 638, 644, 648, 650, 663, 664,
  668, 673, 689, 694, 701, 717, 719, 721, 735,
  737, 754, 764, 766, 767, 773, 788, 796, 797,
  801, 819, 827
  'last will' but composite, 765
window, *see* church building
witnesses, to testament, *lxxi*, *lxxiii*
  (named), 9, 17, 23, 30, 46, 48, 54, 55, 59, 96,
    119, 125, 145, 151, 152, 154, 155, 160,
    166, 175, 184, 191, 210, 211, 213, 214,
    222, 225, 236, 243, 246, 247, 248, 251,
    260, 261, 262, 271, 276, 281, 283, 284,
    286, 290, 292, 293, 295, 297, 299, 301,
    302, 303, 306, 313, 318, 320, 327, 331,
    332, 333, 340, 342, 347, 349, 350, 352,
    354, 360, 363, 371, 373, 374, 376, 380,
    385, 386, 392, 406, 407, 409, 413, 417,
    431, 434, 436, 440, 446, 447, 450, 451,
    452, 455, 456, 462, 463, 467, 471, 473,
    479, 483, 484, 490, 496, 503, 504, 505,
    507, 508, 513, 517, 526, 528, 529, 531,
    532, 535, 538, 541, 548, 549, 551, 552,
    554, 555, 556, 557, 558, 559, 566, 568,
    572, 574, 576, 580, 581, 583, 584, 587,
    588, 597, 598, 600, 609, 613, 614, 622,
    624, 628, 630, 634, 636, 637, 640, 641,
    643, 644, 646, 651, 652, 654, 656, 657,
    662, 663, 666, 669, 670, 673, 680, 681,
    683, 687, 688, 695, 700, 701, 704, 706,
    708, 709, 711, 713, 714, 720, 721, 725,
    727, 728, 729, 733, 739, 742, 743, 747,
    751, 752, 756, 759, 761, 762, 765, 771,
    772, 772, 776, 778, 779, 780, 783, 784,
    785, 788, 789, 796, 798, 799, 803, 807,
    808, 810, 820, 822, 824
  examined, 99, 293, 417, 808
  present but none named, 158, 305, 424, 537,
    675, 682, 685, 686
  to will 'proper' (named), 46, 191, 417, 733

wood, boards, 587
  fir, 822
  firewood, 256, 472, 587, 818
  oak, 547, 778
  spruce, 697,
  'stodes' and 'sparrys', 1
  timber, *see* crops
  for widow's use, 262
  see also land usage
wool (unwoven), 1, 374, 681, 786
  blue, 587
  blue and madder-red, *lxix*, 83
  pack of, 309*
  on sheep, 653
  white, *lxix*, 83
woollen cloth, 46, 74, 79, 83, 125, 295, 362, 430,
      456, 504, 628, 681, 687, 751, 815
  blue, 83

coloured, 83
  for kirtle, 803
  medley, 83
  musterdeviller, 83
  sanguine-coloured, 669
  violet, 705
  white, 456, 711*
  see also cloth-making
worsted, *see* material

yard (ground), *see* land usage
  (linear), *see* measurement
yarn, *see* cloth-making
year, dominical letter of, 351